T
GENE_____
of the
FIRST METIS NATION
The Development and Dispersal
of the
Red River Settlement
1820 - 1900

Compiled by
D. N. SPRAGUE AND R. P. FRYE

Introduction by
D. N. SPRAGUE

Maps by
Victor Lytwyn

0-919143-34-2

Pemmican Publications gratefully acknowledges the assistance accorded to its
publishing program by the Manitoba Arts Council, the Province of Manitoba
– Department of Culture, Heritage and Tourism, Canada Council for the Arts
and Canadian Heritage – Canada Book Fund.

Printed and Bound in Canada.

First printing: 1983
Second printing: 1988
Third printing: 1993
Fourth printing: 2000
Fifth printing: 2012

**PEMMICAN
PUBLICATIONS
INC.**
Committed to the promotion of Metis culture and heritage

150 Henry Ave., Winnipeg, Manitoba,
R3B 0J7 Canada

www.pemmicanpublications.ca

 Canadian Patrimoine
Heritage canadien

 **Canada Council Conseil des Arts
for the Arts du Canada**

 MANITOBA ARTS COUNCIL
CONSEIL DES ARTS DU MANITOBA

 **Manitoba**

Contents

Preface

FEW POPULATIONS are more thoroughly documented in the pattern of their marriages and geographical distribution than the people who developed the Red River Settlement between 1820 and 1870. This volume is the product of an attempt to record such information, to file the data by individual household, and to link the files of households across generations. An historical introduction is offered for general background to the growth of the community from its earliest beginnings to dispersal after 1870. But the bulk of the work consists of tabular material from which family histories are easily constructed.

Although pains have been taken to provide an accurate guide, it must be added that the compilers of the volume are well aware that their sources of information are far from perfect. None of the sources are without gaps or omissions, and none are error free in the information that they do contain. In some instances it has been possible to make up for deficiencies in a census by reference to a parish register, or to amend an incomplete census with land surveyor's reports. But in many other cases the limitations of the sources (or our own mistakes) have prevailed even after careful editing and running a number of computer tests to identify nonsense linkages or values. The point that needs to be stressed is that the information in the tables must be used cautiously and critically.

A word of acknowledgement of assistance in the preparation of the volume is also in order. Financial support was provided by the Social Sciences and Humanities Research Council of Canada, the Manitoba Métis Federation, and the University of Manitoba Research Board. Help in locating and using documents was provided by archivists and staff at the Public Archives of Canada, Provincial Archives of Manitoba, Hudson's Bay Company Archives, and Winnipeg Land Titles Office—the principal depositories of the information on which the tables are based. Special acknowledgement must be given to the Hudson's Bay Company Archives, Provincial Archives of Manitoba, for permission to reproduce a sample page from the Red River Census and to quote at length from other documents cited in the introduction.

Historical Introduction

Origins

A NATIVE population unlike any of the others began to emerge in the context of the fur trade launched in the 1600s separately by Britain and France. The English found their access to the continent via Hudson Bay, the French found theirs' by following the St. Lawrence River to the Great Lakes and beyond.[1]

In both cases, they established long lasting business relationships with the Indians that extended to the sharing of gifts and other courtesies including women. The taking of an Indian wife was not a casual encounter, however. Normally the traders remained with such "country wives" for years, perhaps extending to the entire length of a trader's stay in Indian country because it was good for business. "While I had the Daughter I should not only have the Father's hunts but those of his relations also," one trader explained.[2] What emerged, then, was a form of marriage inspired by the profit motive, rather than casual relations for brief or promiscuous sexual gratification.[3] And since such marriages tended to be as durable as a trader's stay in North America, family units (including children) emerged.

But nearly all Hudson's Bay Company newcomers saw their posting to the wilderness as temporary (profitable) excursions to be followed by a return home and a rise in British society. More than 80 percent of the personnel recruited by the HBC before 1800 were taken from the impoverished Orkney Islands northeast of Scotland. Most of the Fletts, Taits, Spences, and Sutherlands recruited there were hired young (before age 21) and worked as contract labourers for periods as short as three or four years at 6 pounds per year. Some, remaining ten, fifteen, or more than twenty years had stayed long enough to father large families before leaving their native wives and children to return home with their savings for a comfortable retirement. In some cases, departure was preceded by provision of annuities or substitute fathers. But whether the returning fur trader made provision for his wife and children or simply abandoned them without support, the people left

---

[1] The differences attributable to the two native populations' attachments to the different companies are discussed briefly by John Foster, "Origins of the Mixed Bloods in the Canadian West," in Lewis H. Thomas, ed., *Essays in Western History in Honour of Lewis Gwynne Thomas* (Edmonton, 1975).

[2] Jennifer Brown, *Strangers in Blood: Fur Trade Company Families in Indian Country* (Vancouver, 1980), p. 105.

[3] Sylvia Van Kirk, *"Many Tender Ties": Women in Fur-Trade Society in Western Canada, 1670-1870* (Winnipeg, n.d.), p. 4.

behind were "a breed of People easily distinguished from the real Indians . . ."[4] Moreover, it was they who were most likely to provide the "country wives" for later newcomers who regarded such women as no less native than other aboriginal people as one James Spence made clear in referring to his "Indian wife Nostishio". But he identified her also as the "daughter of Isaac Batt"—another fur trader.[5] The comment is significant not only for the way the people were regarded as native but also because it shows a possible fondness of Batt for his daughter by what may have been an arranged marriage for her with the junior trader Spence. In return, Spence may have gained career advantages by accepting the patronage of Batt.[6]

A similar pattern of intermarriage first with leaders of Indian bands to secure their trade, then marriage of the daughters of older employees to junior colleagues was evident in the history of the Montreal-based company as well. The only important deviation from the pattern was a stronger tendency for the lower ranking employees to remain with their native families once their term of service was completed because the French *voyageur* seems to have regarded his familial responsibilities more seriously than did the upwardly mobile Orkney Scot who married and saved. The French Canadian servant of the North West Company more frequently married and stayed.

Another important difference was that the officers of the Montreal based company recognized that a population of retired employees and their families did not pose a serious threat of competition in the fur trade. Given the long lines of supply, the Bonneaus, Brelands, Ducharmes, Larocques and the others performed indispensable work as provisioners making it unnecessary to transport all the fur trader's food west or to divert Indians from their trapping activities to hunting roles. Consequently, in sharp contrast to the region under the control of the Hudson's Bay Company, the Montreal based firm gave rise to literally dozens of small villages inhabited by people of mixed ancestry—the Métis.[7] But with the advance of white settlers many Métis retreated west and north, and gathered in largest concentration at Pembina on the Red River in the early 1800s. Large herds of buffalo were readily accessible in the area, and dried buffalo meat (pounded into bits and mixed with buffalo fat and berries) made a wholesome nonperishable food-concentrate called "pemmican" that was highly marketable to the North West Company once it began to operate west of Lake Winnipeg. The Nor'westers' Fort Gibraltar at the forks of the Red and Assiniboine rivers thus emerged as an important provisioning point. But just as the new Métis

[4] William Falconer's "Remarks on the Natives" quoted in Brown, *Strangers*, p. 69.

[5] Spence's "Last Will and Testament" quoted in Brown, *Strangers*, p. 70.

[6] The issue of marriage for career advantage is discussed by Brown, *Strangers*, p. 74.

[7] Jacqueline Peterson, "Prelude to Red River: A Social Portrait of the Great Lakes Métis," *Ethnohistory* 25(1978), pp. 41-67.

economy was becoming established, the Hudson's Bay Company decided to break the competition of its Montreal rivals.

Red River Colony versus the "New Nation"

The HBC pursued two strategies to defeat its competition. One was to establish new posts wherever the North West Company was also in operation. The other was to plant a settlement astride the Nor'westers' pemmican supply line. Incidentally, the settlement would also serve philanthropic purposes since the settlers were to be recruited from the growing ranks of impoverished Scots. Another source of potential settlers was the HBC itself to accommodate that minority who might find it preferable to retire on their savings with their native families to a Company colony rather than abandoning them and returning home in the usual manner.

The officer who took charge of the settlement scheme was Thomas Douglas, the Earl of Selkirk. But his efforts were frustrated from the start by North West Company directors who knew that the success of Selkirk's venture threatened their own. On this account, Simon McGillivray, one of the leading directors, launched a propaganda campaign in Scotland to convince prospective settlers that the promised farmland along the Red River was anything but the Garden of Eden described by Selkirk's agents. In McGillivray's version, the land was an arctic waste, sparsely treed, and filled with dangerous beasts and hostile Indians.[8] Perhaps because of the impact of the Nor'westers' negative advertisements, only 105 recruits had signed on by the date of the departure of the first contingent in 1811. Arriving on Hudson Bay too late to reach Lake Winnipeg before freeze-up, they spent their first winter on the shore of the Bay in total misery. Then, in the spring of 1812 they fought their way through clouds of black flies and mosquitoes on their trek south to proclaim possession of a stretch of river front near the Nor'westers' Fort Gibraltar.[9] In 1813 a second group arrived on the scene and, looking to the future agricultural development of the colony, the company surveyor, Peter Fidler, laid out seven lots for farming. No crop had been planted in 1812; that of 1813 failed. But the colonists did not starve because of the generosity of the Métis who fed them over both winters.[10]

In January of 1814, the company-appointed leader of the settlers, Miles Macdonnell, rewarded their generosity by forbidding the natives from trad-

[8] Article in *Inverness Journal* quoted by E.E. Rich, *The Fur Trade and the Northwest to 1857* (Toronto, 1967), p. 210.

[9] A brief account of the Selkirk venture is found in Rich, *The Fur Trade*, pp. 209-235.

[10] Alexander Ross described their hospitality as "extreme kindness," in his mid-nineteenth century history of *The Red River Settlement: Its Rise, Progress, and Present State*, recently reprinted (Edmonton, 1972), p. 24.

ing pemmican with anyone but the HBC. The Métis, for their part, ignored Macdonnell's bad manners and traded as usual but began to regard the Scot "gardeners" with increasing suspicion.[11]

Once the Nor'westers' learned of developments since 1813, they sent their own man, Duncan Cameran, to build on Métis suspicion by telling them that the HBC intended to take over the whole territory. At the same time, the Scot settlers were told that better land and a more hospitable climate awaited them in Canada. About three quarters (more than 140 persons) took advantage of the Nor'wester's offer of transportation to the alternate promised land in June.[12] The remaining part were harrassed by the Métis who trampled their crops on horseback.

The stubbornly persistent group of about sixty remaining settlers were reinforced in November of 1815 with what proved to be the last contingent of Selkirk colonists. With a new leader, Robert Semple, and a fortified stronghold they called Fort Douglas (named after Selkirk), the Scots prepared to remain and to fight if necessary.

But the Métis had become equally determined to protect their prior claim that was apparently undisputed by the Indians of the area (perhaps because the Métis were allies in the continuing struggle against the Sioux).[13] The result of the Métis hostility to the Scots' invasion was intensified conflict in 1816. On June 19 a group of about 35 led by Cuthbert Grant approached Semple's fortress. Semple responded by riding out to meet them with twenty-six of his own men and attempted to address the natives like a schoolmaster shouting at a gang of unruly children. In the course of his speaking, he reached for someone's gun, a shot was fired, and the shooting became general. In the melee that followed, Semple himself and 21 of his fellows were struck dead, mutilated, and stripped naked.[14] Thus, the first manifestation of the political consciousness of the Métis resulted in bloodshed. They served notice to intruders that they were the people who owned the land and were prepared to back that claim by force if necessary. To the Métis, the "Battle of Seven Oaks" was an heroic moment of self-defence and self-affirmation. To the HBC, however, the action was an episode of brutal mass murder—a massacre.

Selkirk retaliated by raising a private army of Swiss mercenaries and taking his case to court in Canada. Eventually, in 1821, the two companies agreed to settle their dispute by a merger rather than by a continuation of the legal and military action. Since no fresh waves of farmers poured into

---

[11]The "gardener" label is found in James Jackson, *The Centennial History of Manitoba* (Toronto, 1970), p. 49.

[12]Rich, *Fur Trade*, p. 220.

[13]M.A. Macleod and W.L. Morton, *Cuthbert Grant of Grantown: Warden of the Plains of Red River* (Toronto, 1963), p. ix, 112.

[14]Macleod and Morton, *Cuthbert Grant*, pp. 48-51.

the territory from Scotland, and since one buyer of pemmican was as good as another, the Métis also gave up the fight, eventually agreeing to settle in the vicinity of the old Selkirk colony, led by none other than Cuthbert Grant.

A New Colony

The settlement that developed on the site of Selkirk's old colony continued to serve the purposes of the Hudson's Bay Company but without becoming the haven of Scot farmers that Selkirk had envisioned. In 1818, fewer than fifty of the families he had brought over still remained in the area.[15] A handful of his private army had also been persuaded to stay but increasingly through the 1820s, the colony emerged as a gathering-place for the two groups of native people that had developed along with the two companies before 1821.

After the merger, almost 1,300 employees lost their jobs since the single organization that emerged had no need for most of the *voyageurs* and many of the old HBC staff.[16] About 15 percent of the "retired" employees made their way to Red River in the 1820s.[17] Those headed by Orkney Scots tended to find river frontage just to the north of the tiny remnant of the Selkirk settlement. Those whose attachment was to the other company located south of the Scots, and below the mercenaries at the other end of the colony. To the west, yet another group appeared after 1824 because the HBC was afraid of Cuthbert Grant's Métis remaining at Pembina. Grant was given a title ("Warden of the Plains"), a salary, and orders to bring his people to a tract of river frontage west of the Red on the Assiniboine. Before the end of 1824, he had persuaded about 100 families to abandon Pembina and join him at Grant Town, also known as White Horse Plain.[18]

The colony that started afresh in the 1820s was thus overwhelmingly native in origin. That tendency became even more pronounced after a disastrous flood in the spring of 1826 so discouraged the Swiss that they abandoned the region for a less challenging climate and drier ground, but the

---

[15] A list of "Settlers at Red River" dated August, 1818 enumerates 45 "Scotch" families and 46 de Meurons, Swiss mercenaries (Public Archives of Canada [hereinafter abbreviated as PAC], Selkirk Papers, pp. 5237-5238.

[16] Figures established by Philip Goldring indicate that the HBC's labour force fell from 1,927 in 1821 to 694 by 1826, "Papers on the Labour System of the Hudson's Bay Company," in Parks Canada, *Manuscript Report Series*, No. 362, p. 32-33.

[17] The 15 percent value is derived from the genealogies of the native people in the Archibald Census of 1870. In the "French Métis" line, 107 white forebears appear to have settled at Red River. In the "English Métis" line, the number is 74, for a total of 181—roughly one seventh of the European labour force discharged between 1821 and 1826.

[18] Macleod and Morton, *Cuthbert Grant*, p. 94.

colony continued to receive new infusions of native families—sometimes headed by a former servant of one of the two companies.

Maintaining the geographical and social separation of the several populations that was evident even before the flood were missionaries who indoctrinated the people in different versions of Christianity. At the same time, the Company granted land to the two groups of Christian natives favouring Protestants over Catholics. The Scots and the "natives of Hudson Bay" were supposed to become Anglicans and good farmers. They received grants of 50 to 100 acres each. The others were granted 25 acres or less.[19] In this way, although the two populations born of the fur trade came into geographical proximity in the 1820s, they were kept separate in religion and expected social position.

The tiny remnant of the Selkirk colony was held up as the community of model colonists; they were Protestant and the most stubborn farmers despite agricultural practices that lead usually to failure or barest subsistence.[20] But they were the best colonists from the Company's standpoint. They had no influence with the Indians. They were orderly. They were no competition. Below the Selkirk Settlers were the natives descended from HBC paternal ancestors. Although not properly British, they were at least Protestant and believed to be more stable than the other native population because of their Scottish paternal ancestry. The last place group were the Métis: Catholic, inclined to speak a native language as commonly as French, and believed to be totally uninterested in agriculture. Notwithstanding the HBC's low estimate of their worth, however, they were the most important group in the colony. They were the most numerous; and thanks to their work in the hunt, the colony did not starve. Normally, it was the produce of the plains that fed the Red River Settlement and provisioned the fur trade.[21]

---

[19] Hudson's Bay Company Archives, Provincial Archives of Manitoba, Memoranda Respecting Grants of Land No. 1 and 2, E.6/7-8.

[20] A brilliant work by G.H. Sprenger develops the idea that insistence upon farming at Red River before the 1870s indicated more of stubbornness than rational development. His content analysis of the settlers' own evaluations of their efforts in farming shows that crops were either "short" or outright "failures" in 31 of the 50 years between 1820 and 1870. See Sprenger, "An Analysis of Selective Aspects of Métis Society, 1810-1870" (unpublished MA Thesis, University of Manitoba, 1972), pp. 79-86.

[21] W.L. Morton has described the attempts at farming in the colony as "slovenly, squatter agriculture, ancillary to the hunt" in "Agriculture in the Red River Colony" reprinted in A.B. McKillop, ed., Contexts of Canada's Past (Toronto, 1980), p. 81. Morton also suggests that "most of the meat eaten in the Settlement [not to mention the fur trade] was 'plains provisions'" in his Manitoba: History of a Province (Toronto, 1957), p. 87.

The Pemmican Industry

By 1830 the Hudson's Bay Company stabilized at about 1,000 employees and remained at that level for the next several decades.[22] To operate the trading system from its streamlined network of posts, the Company needed more than 60 tons of pemmican per year.[23] With perhaps 40 million buffalo on the prairies, there was a seemingly unlimited supply of the raw material. The problem was processing and distributing the finished product. Consequently, the main line of the economic development of the native community at the forks of the Red and Assiniboine rivers from about 1830 to 1840 was in responding to that need.

From the mid 1820s, expeditions involving nearly the entire community left in mid-June to exploit the largest of the herds in the valley of the Missouri River.[24] Having located their quarry and slaughtered what could be processed and hauled home, the meat was transformed on the spot into pemmican and the produce of the hunt was loaded onto two-wheeled horse-drawn carts and the "wagon people" (as the Indians called them) made their way the hundreds of miles back to Red River.

The amount of pemmican that might be traded with the Company depended upon the labour supply for hunting and processing, and the supply of carts available for transport. Since it was not until about 1835 that the community had enough hunters, pemmican makers, and transportation to

---

[22] Goldring, "Papers on the Labour System," p. 33, 84.

[23] See Arthur Ray's "Table 9: Hudson's Bay Company Provision Orders for the Northern Department," in *Indians in the Fur Trade: Their Role as Hunters, Trappers, and Middlemen in the Lands Southwest of Hudson Bay, 1660-1870* (Toronto, 1974), pp. 208-209.

[24] The classic description of the hunt is that of Alexander Ross, *Red River Settlement*, pp. 243-300. But Ross emphasized waste more than productivity. More recent historians have a keener appreciation of the hunt as a light manufacturing process. In this regard, Irene Spry has denied that the hunt was wasteful until American skinners armed with repeating rifles went after the southern herd for hides alone. Buffalo hide drive belts in factories were good for American industrial development but the southern herd was totally decimated between 1871 and 1875. What followed were repercussions on the northern herd as more people began to hunt northward. See Spry, "The Great Transformation: The disappearance of the Commons of Western Canada," in Richard Allen, ed., *Man and Nature on the Prairies* (Regina, 1976), pp. 21-45. For more precise measures of native productivity see Sprenger, "Aspects of native Society," p. 68 and Robert Gosman, "The Riel and Lagimodière Families in Métis Society" (unpublished report to Parks Canada, 1977). Gosman has found evidence that a group of about 50 families in 1849 slaughtered roughly 1,700 buffalo in the autumn of 1849. From that kill they obtained:

1,213 bales of dried meat

166 sacks of fat

556 bladders of bone marrow with a market value of about 2,000 pounds sterling. Clearly, hunters did not chase buffalo simply for the thrill of the shoot, nor did they slaughter animals only for a few "choice bits" leaving the rest for the wolves (as Morton alleges in *Manitoba*, p. 81).

meet the colony's and the Company's needs, the production of plains provisions was a growth industry through the 1830s. By 1835, approximately 500 families with as many carts were available to rendezvous at Pembina for the spring hunt. If all went well, each cart would return by August with its full load of six ninety-pound bags of pemmican–more than 130 tons of cured meat in total. Such a return would be enough to feed the settlement through the winter, and to satisfy the demand of the Company as well. That level of population assured security to the Company and prosperity for the producers. The Métis had their independence and also the wares of the HBC (since each family's summer haul of pemmican was worth about as much as the same season's wage to the Company's salaried employees who laboured the year round for 20 pounds per annum).[25] But the native population of the Red River settlement continued to grow at a rapid rate (doubling every fifteen to twenty years).[26] As a result, the much larger population of the 1840s had to find alternate lines of work or suffer a drop in its standard of living.

Native People and the HBC

The first alternative to pemmican production was wage labour for the Hudson's Bay Company. Since the HBC considered native people in general to be inferior to Europeans, and the natives with French Canadian backgrounds to be worse than those who were partly British, George Simpson, the on-site manager of operations after 1821 ("Governor of Rupert's Land"), decided that the "indolent and unsteady" Métis could become suitable replacements for the increasingly expensive Orkney Scots only with careful management.[27] Their qualities were that they knew the country, the languages, could be hired on a merely seasonal basis, and could be worked for wages that were about 25 percent less than what was needed to attract European labour.[28] Consequently, more and more natives became part of the

---

[25] According to Goldring, 20 pounds was an average wage for a low-ranking salaried employee from the 1830s to the 1850s ("Papers on the Labour System," p. 60). In the same period, top quality pemmican sold for 2 or 3 pence per pound according to Ross and Morton (Ross, *Red River Settlement*, p. 273; and Morton, "Agriculture in the Red River Colony," p. 81). At the higher price, a full cart load of six, 90 pound bags was worth 6.75 pounds sterling.

[26]

YEARS	1827	1840	1856	1870
PERSONS	1,100	4,700	7,000	12,000

Data for 1827-56 are from the HBC Censuses, the 1870 total is from the enumeration of population under Governor Archibald's auspices after the transfer to Canada. To convert PERSONS to FAMILIES, divide by 5.

[27] Quoted in Carol M. Judd, "Native Labour and Social Stratification in the Hudson's Bay Northern Department, 1770-1870," *Canadian Review of Sociology and Anthropology* 17(1980), p. 310.

[28] 15 versus 20 pounds. Compare the wage scales in Goldring, "Papers on the Labour System," p. 60 and 103.

York Boat and Crew, c. 1910 (Provincial Archives of Manitoba)

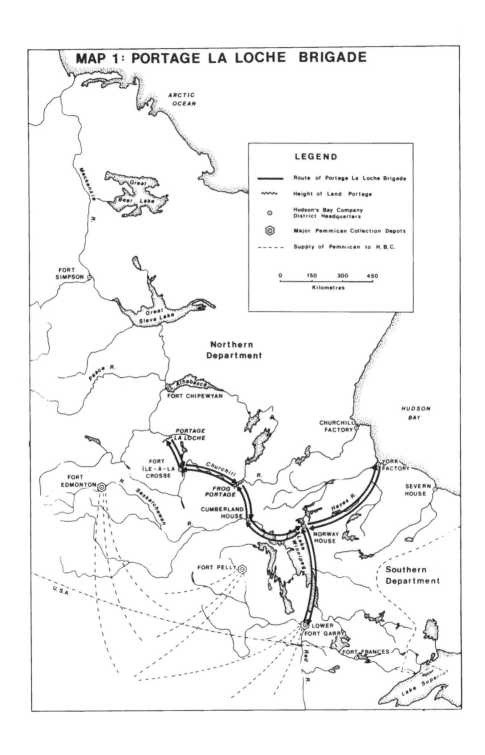

MAP 1: PORTAGE LA LOCHE BRIGADE

LEGEND

Route of Portage La Loche Brigade

Height of Land Portage

Hudson's Bay Company
District Headquarters

Major Pemmican Collection Depots

Supply of Pemmican to H.B.C.

0   150   300   450
Kilometres

ARCTIC
OCEAN

Great
Bear Lake

Mackenzie R.

FORT
SIMPSON

Great
Slave Lake

Northern
Department

Peace R.

Athabasca
FORT CHIPEWYAN

HUDSON
BAY

PORTAGE
LA LOCHE

CHURCHILL
FACTORY

FORT
ÎLE-À-LA
CROSSE

Churchill R.

YORK
FACTORY

FORT
EDMONTON

N.
Saskatchewan

FROG
PORTAGE

CUMBERLAND
HOUSE

SEVERN
HOUSE

Hayes R.

R.

NORWAY
HOUSE

Lake Winnipeg

FORT PELLY

Southern
Department

U.S.A.

LOWER
FORT GARRY

FORT FRANCES

Red R.

Lake Superior

seasonal and even the permanent labour force, accounting for about one third of the manpower by the end of the 1830s and roughly one half by 1850.[29]

The work for which native labour became most important was "voyaging" to Portage La Loche.[30] Beginning in June of 1831 (and continuing every June thereafter until 1870), a force of about 30 to 60 men, 8 men to a craft called York boats (each capable of carrying three or four tons freight) departed from Lower Fort Garry laden with "plains provisions" and headed for Norway House. There they collected "pieces" of trade goods (parcels weighing about 100 pounds each). Then, they proceeded out the Saskatchewan system travelling as far as Portage La Loche (see map 1). Thus, it was they who provisioned the Mackenzie River district, and after reaching their ultimate northwestern destination, they of course retraced their route taking fur back to Norway House. (Sometimes another brigade linked that port with the HBC's main warehousing point on the Bay–York Factory). But the Portage La Loche brigade was the main link in the overall system. They covered the most territory and were the most vital carriers of plains provisions, trade goods, and bales of fur, on their last leg transporting whatever was imported from Europe to Lower Fort Garry. Since the work of the "tripmen" was as hazardous as it was arduous, the job was distinctly second choice relative to pemmican production. But the Company was able to entice workers with advance payments of one third of their wages in December, another third before departure in May, and the final installment of 6 or 7 pounds after returning to Red River.[31] Thus, the men engaged in voyaging earned more than pemmican producers but after returning home in the Autumn they still had to hunt for their winter subsistence on fish, fowl, and buffalo.

Somewhat more attractive than lake freighting was land cartage because a man and a cart could be more independent than a lake freighter, and still earn the same wage.[32] But work by the job was somewhat unpredictable. Consequently, a growing number of natives became traders in their own right in the 1840s by re-establishing links with the Métis of the United States and exchanging fur or pemmican for imports as far away as St. Paul Minnesota.[33]

---

[29] Judd, "Native Labour," pp. 310, 311 and John Nicks, "Orkneymen in the HBC, 1780-1821," in C.M. Judd and A.J. Ray, eds., *Old Trails and New Directions: Papers of the Third North American Fur Trade Conference* (Toronto, 1980), p. 123.

[30] See Goldring, "Papers on the Labour System," pp. 98-107 and John Gunn, *Echoes of the Red* (Toronto, 1930), pp. 24-58.

[31] Gunn, *Echoes*, p. 36; Goldring, "Papers on the Labour System," p. 103.

[32] Tripmen worked about 5 months for as little as 15 pounds or 300 shillings—2 shillings per day (the same wage as day labourers). Goldring, "Papers on the Labour System," p. 112.

[33] Gosman, "Riel and Lagimodière Families," p. 16.

A select few of the native people had the option of rising above voyaging roles and filled a special officer candidate position that was created by 1840 to suit the heirs of former "gentlemen" of the HBC.[34] Eventually, a group of about twenty native sons of former Chief Factors and Chief Traders were appointed "Apprentice Postmasters" in the 1840s and 50s and subsequently a few rose to higher levels in the Company's service. But since such clerks in training were natives in every respect but paternal ancestry, their starting pay was set almost as low as a tripman's wage, and their apprenticeship was longer than that demanded of Europeans. On this account, one of their fathers complained that they suffered a "glaring injustice".[35] But those who did complete their eleven-year apprenticeship gained a large reward for suffering the Company's racism so long: their pay rose from less than 20 pounds per annum to more than 75 pounds.[36]

The discrimination inherent in the rank of Apprentice Post Master thus cut two ways. It showed the Company's bias toward Europeans for clerical-managerial positions; and the rank also showed that the Company believed that one segment of the native population was capable of such duties with special training. By preferring one native group over another, however, they further divided natives who were already separated by religious training. Consequently, the theoretical possibility of the emergence of one Métis nation continued to be an abstraction that was lost in day to day living. The first special favour accorded to the natives of Hudson Bay (the larger grants of land) and the later patronage (superior employment) set them further apart from the "inferior" Catholic Métis. Of course, the continuing discrimination of the HBC served further to sour relations between the Métis and the Company, a matter that reached crisis proportions in the 1840s when the HBC decided to restrict the independent trading activities of the more enterprising free traders.

The Disintegration of Company Rule

In 1844 the Hudson's Bay Company decided that the native people who traded independently posed a threat to their own profits. Theoretically, the Company enjoyed a complete monopoly of the fur trade by Royal Charter. The problem was enforcement. In the 1840s the only police or military force of any consequence in the area were the Métis horsemen, and they paid more allegiance to the free traders than to the HBC. Consequently, the Company did not take any serious steps to limit their activities until they had successfully persuaded the British to garrison the colony by telling them the Amer-

---

[34] Judd, "Native Labour," p. 312.

[35] James Anderson, quoted in Judd, "Native Labour," p. 312.

[36] Goldring, "Papers on the Labour System," p. 61;
Judd, "Native Labour," p. 312.

icans planned to take over the region south of Lake Winnipeg just as they had recently grabbed the southern half of British Columbia (renaming it "Oregon").[37] But the troops provided by Britain were no match for the Métis cavalry. As a result, when Guillaume Sayer was charged in 1849 with illegal trading a committee of other native smugglers called out the hunters and tripmen and together they broke the Company's authority. The Judge, Adam Thom, defied what he called a half-breed rabble, tried Sayer in his absence, and an all-white jury brought in a verdict of guilty but the Company wisely decided not to proceed further. Once it became known that all charges were to be dropped, the Métis left the scene shouting that "the trade is free."[38]

The Sayer trail was thus a milestone in the history of the native people in the area—for two reasons. First, the committee included leaders from both groups, the Protestant as well as the Catholic. Second, they had shown that with the whole community united they could force outsiders to back down. Of course, the HBC continued to claim authority and also to pretend that they ruled Red River through their appointed Council of Assiniboia but that structure by-passed the real leaders of native society. The Council of Assiniboia consisted almost exclusively of retired fur traders and the clergy.[39] The persons who probably commanded more respect were the Métis entrepreneurial elite on whom the Company heaped nothing but scorn.

The HBC's failure to defer to the natural leaders of native society showed that the colony was forced into a dual existence between ideal and actual reality. On the level of fantasy, the Company's ideal was a "Little Britain" in the wilderness, a community of Christian farmers owing allegiance to none but the "Honourable Company" (and through them to the English Crown). On this account, the persons supposed to become the best farmers were pampered with a wide assortment of special favours and throughout the 1830s a number of weird and wonderful experiments were launched to nurture the agricultural development of the colony.[40] Since the agricultural experiments all failed, it was clear that the more rational lines of development ran toward pemmican and trade. But those who prospered outside the approved spheres of economic activity were never rewarded with political power. Consisting mainly of the relics of the Church and the HBC, the Council of Assiniboia never included the personnel who led in the real energy and growth of the colony.[41]

---

[37] An excellent account of Simpson's use of imperial crises to further Company interests is found in J.S. Galbraith, *The Little Emperor: Governor Simpson of the Hudson's Bay Company* (Toronto, 1976).

[38] A brief but lucid account of the Sayer trial is found in Morton, *Manitoba*, p. 76-79.

[39] See Lionel Dorge, "The Métis and *Canadien* Councillors of Assiniboia," *Beaver* 305(1974), 1:12-19, 2:39-45, 3:51-58.

[40] See Ross, *Red River Settlement*.

[41] Interestingly, in the first elections in the history of the colony–the process for choos-

Naturally, the conflict between the two realities led to difficulty. Curiously, the group that was most outspokenly opposed to the HBC's petty tyranny was the population most favoured in the past because a new group of Protestant missionaries arriving in the colony in the 1850s persuaded the native English that the Company had erred in placing Romish priests on the Council.[42] The denunciation of the HBC in the form of complaints against "Popery" thus led to a controversy that drove Protestant further from Catholic. Already trained to seek their marriage partners exclusively from the population of their coreligionists,[43] a new element of animosity was added to their already wide separation. As a result, the remarkable cooperation of the two native groups in 1849 emerged as a passing phenomenon, an event that did not lead to a firmer alliance or assimilation before 1869. But at the end of the 1850s, the two communities faced a threat that was much greater than gratuitous discrimination or the supposed advancement of one branch of Christianity over another. In the 1850s, the native people of Red River witnessed the vanguard arrival of those who would displace them almost entirely.

Canada Discovers a Western Destiny

Separated from the old fur trade hinterland since 1821, Canadians looked westward with new interest in the late 1850s as hard times made them anxious to find "new lands to conquer".[44]

As with other episodes of expansion, exploration was to precede colonization. Henry Youle Hind, a Toronto geology professor, was hired in 1857 to tour the west and to report on its potential for agriculture. Reporting in 1860, Hind described the prairies around Red River as a "vast

---

ing delegates to the national convention late in 1869–every Councilor but one was rejected (Dorge, "Councillors," Part 3, p. 56).

[42]The fullest account of the new religious division is found in F. Pannekoek, "The Churches and the Social Structure in the Red River Area, 1818-1870" (unpublished PhD Thesis, Queen's University, 1973).

[43]Marriages between Protestants and Roman Catholics did occur. Comparing the religions of the householders in Table 1 of this volume with the religions of their parents the following pattern emerges:

	PARENTS PROTESTANT		PARENTS CATHOLIC	
	Prot.	Cath.	Cath.	Prot.
CHILDREN AS HOUSEHOLDERS	510	54	1,132	35

[44]See Doug Owram, *Promise of Eden: The Canadian Expansionist Movement and the Idea of the West, 1856-1900* (Toronto, 1980).

ocean [that] must be seen in its extraordinary aspects before it can be rightly valued . . ."[45] Such unqualified praise was the kind of advertisement that discoverers had been making since the days of Christopher Columbus. So also was another of Hind's themes—the notion that the natives had not the slightest idea of the region's true value.

Everything Henry Hind wrote in description of the Red River colony was to suggest that no true settlement had yet occurred. He pointed out that the 7,000 inhabitants reported to be living in the area according to the HBC census of 1856 were almost all native and the colony was becoming less and less European each decade. He cited the same statistics to show that between 1843 and 1856 "the increase of native or half-breed families was 132," but the white population had actually declined by 102 families.[46] What remained were the Métis like Pierre Gladu whose house fronted on the Red River in St. Vital. Nearby, was a cattle yard that Hind said also held pigs, horses, and poultry. In the stable in which the horses should have been kept Hind found a "neat, light, four wheeled carriage". But the most peculiar aspect of the Gladu farm (from Hind's point of view) was that Pierre was preparing to go off on an autumn buffalo hunt instead of looking after his numerous stacks of peas, wheat, and hay or splitting wood for the winter. In Hind's judgement, Gladu and the others were "improvident and . . . indolent, they prefer the wild life of the prairies to the tamer duties of a settled home."[47] Consequently, Canada's explorer of Red River looked forward to the day when Gladu and his neighbors would be succeeded by "an energetic and civilized race, able to improve its [the land's] vast [agricultural] capabilities and appreciate its marvellous beauties."[48]

Hind did not have long to wait. Encouraged by Hind's glowing report (but ready to move westward in any event) a vanguard of white newcomers from Ontario began arriving in the Red River region at the end of the 1850s.[49] At the same time, the Hudson's Bay Company started a steamer service on the Red River to bring trade goods into Rupert's Land by way of the United States, thus eliminating some of the growing labour cost associated with land freighting by cart or the utilization of the water route from York Factory.[50] Thus, native people along the Red faced the prospect of declining employment just as they also observed the first arrival of what was likely

---

[45] Henry Youle Hind, *Narrative of the Canadian Red River Exploring Expedition of 1857 and of the Assiniboine and Saskatchewan Exploring Expeditions of 1858* (London, 1860), I, p. 134-135.

[46] Hind, *Narrative*, I, p. 177.

[47] *Ibid.*, I, pp. 164-165, 179.

[48] *Ibid.*, I, p. 134.

[49] W.L. Morton, ed., *Alexander Begg's Red River Journal and Other Papers Relative to the Red River Resistance* (Toronto, 1956), "Introduction," p. 13.

[50] Morton, *Manitoba*, p. 101; see also Galbraith, *Little Emperor*, p. 188.

to be a future invasion. One other disturbing development was a realization that the vast—seemingly inexhaustible—herds of buffalo were in fact "dwindling".[51] No prospect of extinction was evident in 1860 but there was some sign that the population dependent upon buffalo might not continue to double every generation and still expect a comfortable subsistence. The result was a land rush in the 1860s—a definite, perceptible recognition that the economy was on the verge of major changes, and the realization that land was going to be critically important in establishing one's security in society.

The Council of Assiniboia responded by adopting an ordinance to legitimize what had already occurred since 1835 and was proceeding with new emphasis since the late 1850s. In 1860, the nominal government of the community adopted a rule to the effect that anyone could occupy vacant riverfront of up to twelve chains (about 800 feet) in width. Since the normal depth of a river front claim was two miles, the area of vacant land that might be occupied by such squatter's rights was thus established at about 200 acres.[52] The new rule accommodated the first newcomers from Ontario (a group of more than forty families arriving in the 1860s).[53] At the same time, the ordinance also secured the occupancy of about 2,000 native families— passed over in the general distribution of 1835, or officially landless from the time of their appearance after that date. The land ordinance of 1860 was thus one of the few (perhaps the only) significant achievement of the Company's puppet government. But at the end of the 1860s, in the face of a horrible drought in which the produce of the hunt and the river front farms and gardens both failed,[54] the people of the colony learned that the Hudson's Bay Company had just completed an arrangement with the new federation of Canada that was to transfer the west to the Canadians with compensation to be paid only to the HBC and to the Indians. There was no indication in 1869 that anyone intended to consult or to recognize the rights of the "wagon people".

---

[51] Contemporary observers warned that the numbers of buffalo were "falling off" as early as the 1850s. See Ross, *Red River Settlement*, p. 267; and Hind, *Narrative*, I, p. 180.

[52] For the background to the regulation's adoption see Dorge, "Councilors," Part 2, p. 43. For the Government of Canada's careful study of the same see PAC, RG15, Volume 235, File 5537.

[53] The Archibald Census of 1870 enumerated 38 white, male householders who were born in Ontario. Since a number of persons born in the United Kingdom emigrated to Manitoba in the 1860s (after having lived in Ontario for a number of years), it is safe to assume that the "Canadian Party" included considerably more than the 38 persons who are positively in that category.

[54] B. Kaye, "Some Aspects of the Historical Geography of the Red River Settlement" (unpublished MA Thesis, University of Manitoba, 1966), p. 251.

Resistance

In preparation for Canada's taking possession of Rupert's Land, a statute was passed by Parliament in June of 1869 "to make some temporary provision for the Civil Government" of the territory with an appointed council to be sent from Ottawa.[55] As soon as enough Ontario farmers came into the territory, the period of "tutelage" was supposed to end and a more democratic form of government was to replace the Ottawa oligarchy. But since vast migration was expected immediately, surveyors were sent to Red River in July of 1869 to prepare for the land rush by devising a system for distributing vacant lots to newcomers.[56] Unfortunately, the official in charge, J.S. Dennis, did not clarify what was meant by vacancy or the kind of occupancy that the Government of Canada intended to recognize and thus to withhold from incoming settlers. Moreover, nothing Dennis and his men did by word or by deed diminished the suspicion of the natives that they were about to be "driven back from the River & their lands given to others."[57]

To defend their holdings from the strangers, the Métis organized patrols and monitored the activities of the surveyors in the summer of 1869. Whenever the Canadians came too close to occupied land, they were warned off by the natives' spokesman, a bilingual son of the leader of the committee that confronted the HBC in 1849 over the Sayer matter. Only twenty-five years old in 1869, Louis Riel emerged as the pivotal figure in the natives' struggle for recognition because of a superior education and family connections. It was he who warned the surveyors in August that they needed "the express permission of the people of the settlement" to continue. Once such authorization was neither sought nor given, it was Riel again who stood at the head of a group of Métis and placed his foot on the surveyors' chain to tell them that their work was finished on October 11.[58]

A few days later, rumours circulated that the made-in-Ottawa council was approaching via St. Paul and the resistors decided to give that party the same treatment they had dealt the surveyors: no proceedings without permission. More people—especially the tripmen and the pemmican producers—rallied to the support of the leaders who started calling themselves the National Committee once they were denounced as "rioters" by the Council of Assiniboia. In the committee's view, the people of Red River had

---

[55] 1869 Statutes of Canada, Chapter 3: An Act for the Temporary Government of Rupert's Land and the North-Western Territory when united with Canada.

[56] See A.C. Roberts, "The Surveys in the Red River Settlement in 1869," *The Canadian Surveyor* (1970), p. 238-248.

[57] PAC, Macdonald Papers, William McDougall to J.A. Macdonald, 31 October 1869; and J.A. Macdonald to William McDougall, 23 November 1869.

[58] Roberts, "Surveys," p. 243.

been abandoned by the HBC and they "objected to any Governor coming from Canada without their being consulted. . ."[59] As in 1849, the issue was a grievance on which Protestants and Catholics could unite in common cause agreeing that "we own the country and don't want to part with it."[60]

To create a platform for defining their mutual interests, Riel urged each district to elect two delegates to a convention set for November 16 at Fort Garry. On the appointed day, after opening preliminaries, Riel suggested that they should form their own government because the Council of Assiniboia represented no interest but the Company's and the HBC had sold out to Canada. The Protestant delegates agreed that transfer without consultation was potentially dangerous but they hesitated to join in the proclamation of a provisional government without a clearer idea of its goals–the guarantees that were to be sought from Canada. That was completed in the next several weeks and the Red River republic was proclaimed on December 8.[61]

In the meantime, Canada's Prime Minister was devising a strategy for defeating the "half-breeds". The time of year and the lack of any kind of road between Canada and Red River prevented sudden and decisive military action. Consequently, John A. Macdonald decided that Canada would have to appear to take their demands seriously and to seek British assistance for the military action that would follow the apparent concession of the insurgents' demands. "The impulsive Half-breeds have got spoilt by their emeute [riot], and will have to be ruled by a strong hand until they are swamped by the influx of settlers," he confided to a political crony.[62]

Macdonald's strategy succeeded. Convinced that Canada did wish to negotiate in good faith, the natives sent a delegation to Ottawa in the spring of 1870 and their principal demands did appear to be met in a series of amendments to the law concerning the territories that had been enacted the previous June. Then, having given the delegates "the impression that justice had been done,"[63] a military force of 1,200 troops sanctioned by the British set out for the colony and arrived at Red River in August after the Portage La Loche Brigade had departed for the Mackenzie River District and the pemmican producers set off on the hunt. The troops arrived unopposed and consolidated their positon at Fort Garry without a single shot being fired. Thus, the stage was prepared for undoing that which had been

---

[59] Riel quoted in G.F.G. Stanley, *The Birth of Western Canada: A History of the Riel Rebellions* (Toronto, 1961), p. 70.

[60] PAC, Macdonald Papers, George Keyne to Allen Macdonald, n.d., 1869.

[61] See Thomas Flanagan, "Political Theory of the Red River Resistance: The Declaration of December 8, 1969," *Canadian Journal of Political Science* 11(1978), p. 69; and Morton, *Begg's Journal*, p. 69.

[62] PAC, Macdonald Papers, J.A. Macdonald to J. Rose, 23 February 1870.

[63] Francis Hincks in House of Commons *Debates*, 9 May 1870.

Metis encampment on the Prairies, 1874 (Public Archives of Canada)

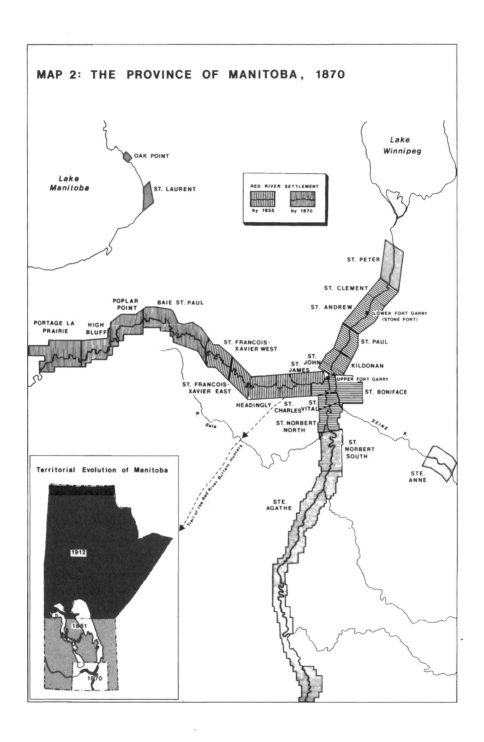

MAP 2: THE PROVINCE OF MANITOBA, 1870

Lake Winnipeg

Lake Manitoba

OAK POINT

ST. LAURENT

RED RIVER SETTLEMENT

by 1835   by 1870

ST. PETER

ST. CLEMENT

ST. ANDREW

POPLAR POINT   BAIE ST. PAUL

LOWER FORT GARRY (STONE FORT)

PORTAGE LA PRAIRIE   HIGH BLUFF

ST. PAUL

ST. FRANCOIS-XAVIER WEST

KILDONAN

ST. JOHN

ST. JAMES

UPPER FORT GARRY

ST. FRANCOIS-XAVIER EAST

ST. BONIFACE

HEADINGLY   ST. CHARLES   ST. VITAL

R. Sale

ST. NORBERT NORTH

SEINE R.

Trail of the Red River Buffalo Hunters

ST. NORBERT SOUTH

STE. ANNE

Territorial Evolution of Manitoba

STE. AGATHE

1912

1881

1870

conceded in the "Act to amend and continue" the law "for the temporary Government of Rupert's Land and the North-Western Territory when united with Canada".

Dispersal

An unexpected complication delayed the repudiation of the promises that were embodied in the apparent settlement of the Red River resistance in 1870, the law that soon came to be known as the *Manitoba Act* for its creating a small, largely native province with the same name in the extreme southeast corner of Rupert's Land (see map 2). The difficulty was that in order to clear the way for changing the *Manitoba Act's* provisions (especially the two sections[64] making generous allowances for land claims), the Government of Canada sought clarification of its power in such matters and gained more than John A. Macdonald bargained for. In December of 1870, Macdonald sought a constitutional amendment giving Ottawa undoubted power to enact such laws as the statute that created Manitoba.[65] The British were quite willing to clarify Ottawa's power to create provinces in the territories, but they wished to avoid granting a license for making a tier of second class provinces by their being uniquely vulnerable to continual tampering by Ottawa. Consequently, the clarification Macdonald originally sought was conceded in 1871, but the same measure also declared that the Parliament of Canada "shall not be competent . . . to alter the provisions" of laws creating new provinces later.[66]

Since the Government of Canada apparently had to defy the Constitution to tamper with the land promises in the *Manitoba Act,* Macdonald's government moved slowly and cautiously before adopting the first of its amendments in 1873. But at the end of the year, the party that had opposed the *Manitoba Act* most outspokenly came to power and within months of their taking charge, the most important in a long series of amendments came before Parliament to alter the unconditional pre-emptive right to occupied land along the rivers that was found in section 32 by conceding only the qualified assurance that "persons satisfactorily establishing undisturbed occupancy" would be "entitled to receive letters patent" confirming their ownership.[67] The problem, of course, was in establishing what level of occupancy was "satisfactory".

[64] 1870 Statutes of Canada, Chapter 3: An Act to Amend and continue the Act 32 and 33 Victoria, chapter 3; and to establish and provide for the Government of the Province of Manitoba, Sections 31 and 32.

[65] PAC, RG13 A3, Volume 559, J.A. Macdonald to the Earl of Kimberly, 29 December 1870, pp. 225-230.

[66] 1871 Statutes of Great Britain, Chapter 28: An Act respecting the establishment of Provinces in the Dominion of Canada.

[67] 1874 Statutes of Canada, Chapter 20: An Act Respecting the appropriation of certain

Two years passed before the Government of Canada decided that the normal proof of "undisturbed occupancy" would be papers establishing a grant from the Hudson's Bay Company or recognition of agricultural improvements by Dominion Land Surveyors operating in the old settled areas between 1871 and 1874.[68] Since most native people were neither listed in the HBC's Land Register nor named as "occupants" by the personnel making the surveys, the original population of Manitoba had no basis for retaining its homeland and dispersed west and north under the watchful eye of the national police.[69]

Eventually frustration with the Canadian government led to a second resistance in the part of the territories to which most people had gathered having been displaced from Manitoba. Emboldened and embittered by the false promises of the past, the participants in the North West Rebellion of 1885[70] sought a complete break with Canada. Having, in a sense, prepared for such a development since 1870, the Government of Canada moved swiftly and brutally to supress the rebellion. What followed was a second dispersal, a further scattering of that population whose genealogies spanned about three generations earlier in the vicinity of Red River. In their first and second dispersal they scattered as the seed population not only for the Métis communities that emerged in isolated parts of what are now the three prairie provinces, but also as far west and north as the territories that are still held in the "tutelage" that was originally intended for Manitoba.

Dominion Lands in Manitoba, Section 3.

[68]See D.N. Sprague, "Government Lawlessness in the Administration of Manitoba Land Claims, 1870-1887," *Manitoba Law Journal* 10(1980), pp. 415-442.

[69]Customarily, the dispersal of the Métis is attributed to their alleged "improvidence" and "semi-nomadism"–they left of their own free will. According to the myth of *voluntary* withdrawal, the Métis people were inveterate wanderers who were simply uninterested in taking advantage of the splendid accommodation of their more settled leaders' land claims (see Morton, *Manitoba*, pp. 142-155; and H.D. Kemp, "Land Grants Under the Manitoba Act," *Historical and Scientific Society of Manitoba Transactions*, Series 3, No. 9 (1952-53), pp. 33-52). The principal difficulty with the myth is its failure to account for the amendments that transformed sections 31 and 32 of the *Manitoba Act*. Another of the myth's inadequacies is that the Métis were in no sense "nomadic" before 1870. Consider the following table based on the persistence of the families covered by this volume:

GROUPS*	Before 1849	Also 1870	Persistence Rate
Catholic Métis	374	202	54%
Protestant Métis	195	116	59%
Selkirk Scotts	45	23	51%

*The unit within groups is the household.

[70]See Desmond Morton, *The Last War Drum: The North West Campaign of 1885* (Toronto, 1972).

Using the Tables

THE DEVELOPMENT and dispersal of the Red River colony, described in general historical terms in the preceding pages, is documented individivually in the six tables that follow. They catalogue a vast amount of information on the development of particular families, their relation to the Hudson's Bay Company, their geographical location, and their persistence after 1870. Linking the information in one table with the others, it is possible to draw portraits of individual families longitudinally across generations, or horizontally across broad kinship networks. Using the tables for either task is neither technical nor complicated, as two illustrations will shortly make apparent. But before illustrating the use of the tables with particular cases, it is necessary to give some fuller description of their compilation and what they contain.

Notes on the Tables
Table 1: Genealogies of Red River Households
General vital statistics on persons known to have been heads of families before 1870 are found in Table 1. The sources are census returns, parish registers, and genealogical affidavits collected by the Government of Canada in 1875.

Before 1824, the enumeration of inhabitants in the Red River Colony was done by agents of Lord Selkirk.[71] In 1824, however, the Hudson's Bay Company began periodic enumerations of its own at the end of the fiscal year in May. In the early 1830s such inventories of population were almost annual. But after 1856 the Company appears to have abandoned the practice

---

[71] About thirty such inventories are found in the Selkirk Papers, Public Archives of Canada (hereinafter abbreviated as PAC), and on microfilm in various other archives elsewhere including the Provincial Archives of Manitoba (hereinafter cited as PAM).

altogether. The years that are covered by at least one complete surviving copy of a census are 1824, 27, 28, 29, 30, 31, 32, 33, 35, 38, 40, 43, 46, 47, and 1849.[72]

A sample of a typical return, a page from the 1843 census, appears opposite this page and illustrates a number of the imperfections of the HBC Census. The most obvious defect is that the reporting was of the household aggregate rather than of the group as individuals. The only named person in each household is the male head of family. He too is the only person whose age is reported. Female heads of household are anonymous–even as single parents. Moreover, natural children are not distinguished from adopted dependents–a serious flaw in the early years because of the custom of "turning off" (that process by which a relatively low-status Company servant was paid to takeover responsibility for the "country" wife and children of an officer who wanted to abandon his native family). Thus, Amable Hogue took charge of one of George Simpsons's country families,[73] but nothing in the Red River Census would distinguish Hogue's natural children from his adopted family). Similarly, the census does not record the names of the natural parents of other adopted children, even though other sources make it plain that in the event of the death of a female head of family before children had reached the age of puberty, they normally left the household of their natural father to be raised by maternal aunts or grandparents. Consequently, men appear to have fathered children late in life, as indeed may have been the case, but since women's ages are not recorded it is impossible to assess probabilities of adoptions.

Some of the problems raised by the inadequacies of the census are solved by parish registers. There are thirteen such records of baptisms, marriages, and burials dating from various beginnings–from the 1830s to the 1860s.[74] Only three date from periods of early settlement. But if the event was recorded, recorded fully, and the record has survived, the parish register is helpful in identifying the names of female heads of family–one of the most glaring deficiencies of the HBC censuses.

Unfortunately, in the Protestant parishes the clergy tended to record a marriage as a milestone in the life of isolated individuals, frequently recording only the names of the bride and groom and the date of the wedding.

---

[72]The 1824 census is not catalogued as a "Census Return". Instead, it is a roll of papers called "Red River Settlement-Index to Plan by William Kempt" [one of the first surveyors of the colony] (Hudson's Bay Company Archives [hereinafter abbreviated as HBCA], PAM, E.6/11). Other years are available in the Hudsons's Bay Company Archives, E.5/1-11; Provincial Archives of Manitoba, MG-2, B3; or from the Public Archives of Canada with the Census of the Province that was done in 1870, microfilm C-2170.

[73]See J.S. Galbraith's biography of Governor Simpson, *The Little Emperor* (Toronto, 1976).

[74]The registers are found in the Provincial Archives of Manitoba (PAM, MG-7) and include: St. Marys (Portage La Prairie), 1855-1883; St. Andrews, 1835-1910; St. Peters Dynevor,

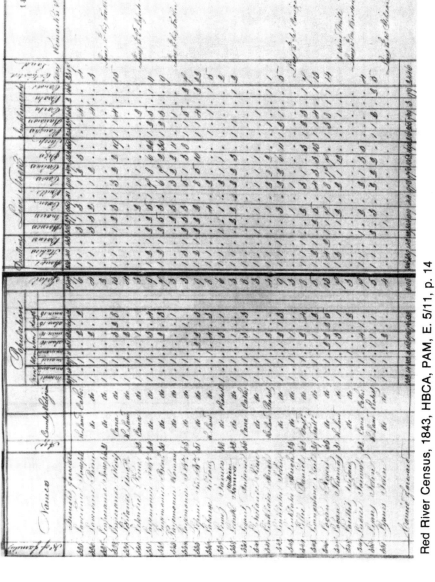

Red River Census, 1843, HBCA, PAM, E. 5/11, p. 14

Claimant	Scrip Record	Parish	Affidavit	Form
Riel, Francis	Born: Aug. 15, 1833 Father: Baptiste Riel (French Cdn.) Mother: Marguerite Boucher (Halfbreed) Claim No: 2559 Scrip No: 12137 Date of Issue: Apr. 17, 1877 Amount: $160	St. Boniface	858	C
Riel, Julie	Born: July 23, 1822 Father: Jean Baptiste Lagemodiere (French Cdn.) Original white settler from Muskinangi, Quebec, entered Red River Country between 1813 & 1835 Mother: Marianne Gaboury (French Cdn.) Husband: Louis Riel (Deceased)	St. Vitals	366	D.2
Ritchot, Alexandre	Edouard Ritchot Eleanore Magdeleine Ritchot AFFIDAVIT MISSING!	St. Vitals	5404 to 5406	
Ritchot, Andre	Born: Oct. 1, 1828 Father: Joseph Ritchot (French Cdn.) Mother: Josephte Maillot (Half- breed) Claim No: 2560 Scrip No: 12138 Date of Issue: Apr. 17, 1877 Amount: $160	St. Boniface	857	C
Ritchot, Antoine	Father: Jean Baptiste Ritchot (Halfbreed) Mother: Louise Henault (Halfbreed) Born: Feb. 10, 1870 Wishes to partake in allotment & distribution of land set apart for Halfbreed children.	St. Vitals	5403	B
Ritchot, Baptiste	Born: Jan. 1, 1823 Father: Joseph Ritchot (French Cdn.) Mother: Josephte Guilmot (Half- breed) Claim No: 2492 Scrip No: 11345 Date of Issue: Oct. 2, 1876 Amount: $160	St. Vitals	2722	C

Abstract of Half-Breed Affidavits, Public Archives of Canada, RG 15 finding aid

Such sparse reporting poses severe linkage problems with enormous clans such as the Andersons, Favels, and McKays.

The Catholic parish records are more complete in the sense that a marriage entry was normally recorded in a full family context. For the Parish of St. Francois Xavier, for instance, the register reports that Jean Baptiste Malaterre (son of Jean Baptiste Malaterre and Angelique Adam) married Therese Courtois (daughter of Jean Baptiste Courtois and Angelique Paille) on 26 November 1839. After Therese died in "early January 1846" the funeral was for "Therese Comtois wife of Jean Baptiste Malaterre" (notice the small variation in the spelling of her maiden name). Four years later, Jean Baptiste remarried, with the marriage entry identifying the bride in the usual manner (naming her father and mother) but since Jean Baptiste had the family status of husband more recently than that of son, he was identified as the "widower of Therese Comtois".

Although the parish registers such as the one for St. Francois Xavier can be valuable supplements to the Red River Census, more useful still are genealogical affidavits collected by the Government of Canada in 1875. Commissioners collected family histories to decide who would be eligible to receive scrip once it was decided to bonus the "original white settlers" and "half-breed heads of families" (having dealt the later category out of some of the land they had been promised by the *Manitoba Act*). Accepting applications from all descendants of Selkirk settlers, Canadian settlers entering the territory between 1818 and 1835, and all married Métis, Commissioners took concise genealogies from about 9,000 persons in all.

Reference to a sample page from the typewritten abstract of the affidavits in the Public Archives of Canada[75] shows the importance of the source at a glance. Each entry provides information on parentage, age, spouse, and ethnicity–all in one place and for virtually every case. Once the data are transcribed into machine readable form, each affidavit maker can be identified as a sibling, as well as a mate, or child. By this means, it is possible to link families across two, three, and sometimes four generations.

Government of Canada genealogical affidavits and the less complete parish registers identify many of the otherwise anonymous persons in the households covered by the Red River Census. Moreover, the same sources also identify households that formed after 1849. Together with the Archi-

1839-1913; St. Pauls, 1850-1911; St. Johns, 1813-1901; St. James, 1853-1908; St. Clements, 1862-1928; Headingly, 1857-1928; Kildonan, 1851-1932; Sisters of Charity (Grey Nuns), 1741-1841; St. Francois Xavier, 1834-1900; St. Bonfiace (fragments from pre-1860), 1860-1974; and St. Norbert, 1857-1934. The Hudson's Bay Company also maintained its own Register of Marriages and Burials, 1841-1851 (HBCA, PAM, E.4/1b,2), but its entries are almost always duplicated in one of the church records.

[75] The affidavits are also found in the same archive, RG 15, Volumes 1319-1324.

bald census (described in connection with Table 4 because of its importance in establishing geographical location and the names of children in the last year of Company rule) it is possible to compile a nearly complete tabulation of all marriage units that were found in—or related to—persons in the Red River colony for the period between 1818 and 1870.

Since Table 1 is a synthesis of several different documents, and since more than 60 percent[76] of the inhabitants could neither read nor write even to the extent of making a signature, spelling variations proliferated without check. As a result, the spelling in Table 1 represents a somewhat arbitrary selection from a broad range encountered in the records. By today's standards many of the names in the table are spelled "incorrectly". Moreover, a spelling of a name in Table 1 does not always correspond to that in Tables 2 through 6—based on different documents, therefore, additional variants.

Persons are not identified by a uniformly spelled family name so much as by a broader pattern of vital information. But having ascertained that a pair of householders were distinct in that sense, a unique identity number (labelled ID in the table) identifies them in Table 1 and is carried through wherever possible on the tables following. DADS ID in Table 1 is of course the ID of a subject's father. DATES are approximate years of birth and death; RACE, FAITH, and BIRTH PLACE are abbreviated as follows:

MET=Métis
EUR=European
IND=Indian
OTH=Other
RC=Roman Catholic
P=Protestant
O=Other
ORK=Orkney Islands
SCT=Scotland
ENG=England and Wales
IRE=Ireland
CAN=British North America east of Lake Superior
NWT=British North America west of Lake Superior
LC=Lower Canada, the colony that became Quebec
UC=Upper Canada, the colony that became Ontario
RRS=Red River Colony
USA=United States
OTH=Other

---

[76]The measure is observed in the percentage of "X" marks rather than signatures in the Powers of Attorney by which land speculators acquired the land rights of the Métis (PAC, RG15, Volumes 1421-1423).

Table 2: Family Size and Location, 1835

Families who were awarded land between 1814 and 1835 appear in Table 2. The first such recipients received their land from Selkirk's agents or directly from Selkirk himself when he appeared in the colony in 1817. But after the amalgamation of the two fur trading companies and the reduction in staff, some of the persons who "retired" arrived in the Red River Colony in the late 1820s. The appearance of hundreds of such newcomers led the Company to make a general survey of land fronting along both rivers and to divide it into more than 1,400 one-hundred acre lots, each about 400 feet wide and two miles deep (see map 2). Old grants by Selkirk, and the land then awarded to approved new arrivals were subsequently recorded in land grant "memoranda".[77] Such notes on land grants are the source for the information on geographical location in Table 2. Since the same lots were resurveyed (but only renumbered) by the Government of Canada in the early 1870s, the later lot and parish designations are what appear in the table in order to facilitate comparisons with the data in Tables 4 and 5.

The other information in Table 2 (the columns on family size and property) are taken from the HBC census of 1835, the year most of the land grants were made. But the data are not merely transcribed from the census return. Some of the information, such as that pertaining to family size is a computed variable. PERSONS is the sum of the eight categories of men, women, sons, and daughters reported in the census for a measure of overall family size. In some cases the value is nil because some households appeared in a preceding or succeeding census, received land in 1835, but were not included in the 1835 census return.

Other computed values in the table are HORSES, CATTLE, and FARM IMPLEMENTS. The variable HORSES is the sum of horses and mares; CATTLE is oxen, bulls, cows, and calves; FARM IMPLEMENTS is plows and harrows. FARMED ACREAGE (though not computed) is an estimate representing the portion of the lot reported to have been under cultivation, rounding up to the nearest whole acre. Thus, a number of 2 1/2 reported in the census, is printed in Table 2 as 3.

Table 3: Contract Employees of the HBC

The exploitation of the Red River Colony as a labour pool and the kinds of positions that native people occupied are illustrated by the data in Table 3. The information is only illustrative, however, because the data are drawn from the Company's records of persons under formal contract, whereas most people who worked for the HBC at Red River were probably employed casually, on a seasonal basis, and without formal contract. Still, the selection presented in Table 3 does cover all servant-level[78] contract labour that was

---

[77]HBCA, PAM, Memoranda Respecting Grants of Land No. 1 and 2, E.6/7-8.

[78]The basic division in the Company was between "Officers" and "Servants". Servant

hired from–or retired to–the colony between 1821 and 1870.

Since the data are neither abbreviated nor otherwise modified the table is self-explanatory except some job classifications are not what they seem. A BOWSMAN, for example, is not an archer but a lookout in the bow of a York boat watching for reefs and shoals–a kind of pilot. Similarly, a MIDDLEMAN is not a go-between or retailer but a labourer in the middle of a boat bending his back to the work of rowing, towing, and portaging. The STEERSMAN was the man in the stern on the tiller but unlike a mere helmsman, he was the person in charge of the crew of eight or nine; in effect, the steersman was the York boat captain.

Table 4: Geographical Location and Children, 1870

The children and 1870 location of households are listed in Table 4, drawing primarily from the 1870 census. A sample page from the original[79] shows that the unit of record was individual persons rather than whole families (as was the practice in the earlier inventories of persons done by the HBC). But since each individual in the 1870 census is listed with his or her parentage, it is possible to distinguish householders from children, and to draw boundaries between one set of family members and the next. Moreover, comparison of the order in which families are listed with the reports of land surveyors[80] working through the parishes in the early 1870s confirms that the order of their appearance in the census was not random but a regular pattern of geographical distribution that can be traced through maps of the parishes drawn by the Dominion Land Surveyors. Thus, it is possible to identify households AT a particular lot. But since the surveyors did not name everyone, the others fall BETWEEN those who are identified on specific land. In a few instances, persons were passed over by the surveyors but still managed to secure a patent to the lot that the family occupied in 1870. Such cases are flagged with an asterisk (*) in the AT column of Table 4.[81]

Turning to the variable PARISH, it should be noted that names are sometimes printed in rather abbreviated form:

> ST. LAURENT=St. Laurent and Oak Point
> SFX=St. Francois Xavier (east and west)
> ST. NORBERT=St. Norbert (north and south)

---

ranks are as indicated by the wage-levels in Table 3. Officer ranks were as follows: chief factors, chief traders, clerks, and surgeons. In-between Officers and Servants were various classes of apprentices that included the position of postmaster, registered with other servants. See C. Judd, "Native labour and Social Stratification in the Hudson's Bay Company's Northern Department, 1770-1870," *Canadian Review of Sociology and Anthropology* 17(1980), p. 306.

[79] Available on microfilm from the Public Archives of Canada, C-2170.

[80] Surveyors' field notes are found in the Provincial Archives of Manitoba.

[81] Both procedures failed in a few other cases. They do not appear as patentees and do not fall between others whose location is known. In these instances both columns are blank.

Census of Manitoba, 1870, PAM, MG2 B3

PORTAGE=Portage la Prairie
ST. BONIFACE=St. Boniface (north and south)
ST. ANDREW=St. Andrew (north and south)

Another foible of the parish variable is that the census enumerators did not always agree with the land surveyors on the location of parish boundaries. The census takers were rather confused in finding the northern limit of St. Clements and the southern boundary of St. Peters and also the lines between St. Johns and Kildonan, for example. Since the surveyors were the better authority on metes and bounds, geographical location follows surveyors' field notes but the cases in which a discrepancy has been found are flagged with an asterisk.

The last variables in Table 4 indicate children living with parents listing them from oldest to youngest. The variable AGE, refers to reported age at next birthday.

Table 5: Recognition of Occupancy by Canada
The 1870 population's status as landowners is found in Table 5. The first few variables (names of occupants, lot, parish, and area in acres) are drawn from the field notes of the Dominion Land Surveyors cited above. The acreage patented, name of patentee, and year of patent are drawn from the Abstract Books in the Winnipeg Land Title Office. In many cases, however, land patents were not registered. Non-registered patents issued before 1883 are found in the register of the Canadian department charged with the issuing of patents until 1883, the Secretary of State.[82] The non-registered patents that cover riverlots patented after 1883 must be searched in the more cumbersome records of the Department of the Interior divided between Parish Files recently deposited in the Provincial Archives of Manitoba and the balance of such lot by lot records in the Public Archives of Canada.[83] Thus, the data on land patents are drawn from three different sources.

Table 6: Dispersal and Relocation of the Manitoba Métis
The 1870 population's dispersal is illustrated by Table 6. The source is the record of various "Half-Breed Commissions" struck by the Government of Canada between 1885 and 1900[84] to extinguish the aboriginal title of the

---

[82] "Alphabetical Index, Parish Land, Manitoba, from 16 February 1875 to 13 July 1883," Public Archives of Canada, microfilm M-1640.

[83] "Manitoba Act Files," RG15, Volumes 140-169.

[84] One rush came in 1885, 86, 87 and 88. The persons whose claims were allowed are recorded in three registers, Public Archives of Canada, RG15, Volumes 1501-1503. Two end of the century surveys led to two more registers of scrip issues covering Saskatchewan, RG15, Volumes 1488 and 1489 and three more volumes of recognized claimants identified in Alberta, RG15, Volumes 1491-1493. In the late 1970s, researchers for the Association of Métis and Non-status Indians of Saskatchewan transcribed the contents of all seven registers for machine processing and kindly provided the compilers of the present volume with a magnetic tape of the data.

Métis who were not dealt with in Manitoba in the 1870s with issues of land or money scrip.[85] At each scrip commission hearing, a number of claims were allowed from persons born in the territories after 1870 but whose parents are found in the Manitoba census of that year. It follows that they left their homeland sometime after the Red River Colony was transferred to Canada. The claims of their children say nothing about the reasons for the parents' exodus, but they do document the scope of the general pattern of dispersal.

Reconstituting One Family

The data from which the six tables are printed is a set of integrated machine-readable files enabling social historians with access to a computer to test a vast array of hypotheses concerning the development of the Red River Colony. In tabular form the same data can be used by investigators to trace individual families or kinship networks using the more portable and versatile device of the printed book.

Suppose for example, that one wished to learn more about "Michael Lambert", a tripman described as the "champion" of his brigade of York boats by John Gunn in his reminiscences about life in the old Red River Colony.[86] Gunn's account suggests that Lambert was one of the leaders of his society, a person who commanded the respect of his peers, if not power with the Hudson's Bay Company or position on the Council of Assiniboia.

Table 1 indicates that Lambert was native, born about 1792 but almost nothing is known of his parents. His father, apparently, is only an unattached name, not linked to a spouse and consequently does not appear in the table. The same tabulation indicates that Lambert appears to have married only once, to Marguerite Favel who was born about 1803. Even less is known of her parentage. But much is known of their children. Michael Lambert and Marguerite Favel appear to have brought no fewer than three sons and four daughters through childhood to become householders in their own turn: Thomas, James, and John; and Catherine, Charlotte, Maria and Mary.

The size and location of the Lambert household is documented by Table 2 as well. In the census of 1835, a total of eight persons were counted in Lambert's family. The same table also shows that Michel Lambert was the Company's recognized owner of two riverlots in what was emerging as St. Andrew's Parish. There, the Lamberts raised their family, kept a horse, some cattle, and in 1835 looked after a four-acre garden.

In the same period, according to Gunn, the middle-age Lambert was emerging as the leader of his brigade. Scanning Table 3 for some confirmation of that occupational status it is found that a Michel Lambert was given a contract to work as a "steersman" but only in 1832. In the other years, Lambert must have been employed casually, without contract.

---

[85]The story of scrip is presented in Joe Sawchuk, *et al., Métis Land Rights in Alberta: A Political History* (Edmonton, 1981), pp. 87-146. See also his article in *The Pemmican Journal* (1983), pp. 30-32.

[86]*Echoes of the Red* (Toronto, 1930), p. 55.

Table 3 does not indicate when Lambert retired from lake freighting, but Table 1 suggests that Lambert was still alive in 1870 and Table 4 shows that the Lambert family was still on lot 33 in St. Andrews. At home were two unmarried daughters, Elizabeth and Françoise ages 20 and 17 respectively (suggesting that when the Lambert's last child was born—if Françoise was their own, not an adopted daughter—Marguerite Favel was nearly fifty and Michel Lambert was over sixty). Regardless of their true parentage, the two children at home were probably an important aid and comfort to their parents who were both well beyond their mid sixties by 1870. Similar support may have been provided by the Lamberts' married sons and daughters who lived nearby. Table 4 shows John and Thomas lived on lots 32 and 31, just south of their father. James was just across the river on lot 248; Charlotte (married to William Philips) lived on the same side of the river just a bit further north on lot 234. But Maria (married to George Sinclair) and Mary (wife of James Tait) were almost as close as John and Thomas on lots 25 and 34 respectively. Thus, altogether, the Lamberts were a sizeable clan in St. Andrews. Moreover, they were one family who persisted in their homeland long after its transfer to Canada.

In the 1870s and 80s, the children of Michael Lambert, unlike most of the native people of Manitoba, won their claims for recognition of the river frontage they had developed since the 1830s. Table 5 shows that James received the patent to his father's lot 33 and his own lot 248 in 1885. John secured lot 32 in 1878. The Taits and Sinclairs were recognized as the owners of their land in 1875 and 1884. Table 5 shows that the land of the others passed to speculators such as John Schultz, but the Lamberts—as a family— still persisted to a remarkable extent. Perhaps for that reason, no Lamberts linked to Michel and Marguerite were identified by the various commissions that operated in the Northwest Territories after 1885. No Lamberts are found in Table 6. They were one family on whom the transfer does not appear to have fallen as a break in continuity. The Lambert case illustrates how the tables can be used to document a pattern of persistent development before and after 1870. In a thousand other cases, the same tables would document the more typical pattern of broken continuity and dispersal.

Reconstitution of an Entire Kinship Network

Another use of the tables will be found in mapping relationships within a larger network joined by inheritance or marriage. To illustrate that task, suppose one wished to reconstruct the relation of Louis Riel to the larger community starting from the knowledge that his mother was Julie Lagimodière and his father's given name was also Louis. Entering Table 1 looking for that pair of householders, the identity number 4155 is found for entry to the other tables. Going to Table 4 it is discovered that Louis the younger lived at home with his widowed mother on lot 50 in St. Vital along with seven brothers and sisters ranging in age from eight to twenty years.

Here, then, is the immediate family of the 26 year old bachelor who played such an important role in securing legal recognition for his countrymen in 1870. Who were his grand parents, aunts, uncles and cousins? And where did the family fit in the Red River social hierarchy? Starting with the Riel side, Table 1 does not at first seem to be very helpful. There is no link between Louis Riel the elder and any of the other Riels who are included. Further investigation, in Table 2, is another fruitless search since it appears that no Riels were among the group upon whom the Hudson's Bay Company bestowed land in the 1830s. Moreover, Table 3 shows that no Riel was a contract employee of the HBC between 1820 and 1870. The conclusion that follows from the very lack of information on the Riel side of the family is that they were obscure Métis, not among the economic elite of the colony.

Louis Riel the elder did very well by marriage, however. Table 1 shows that Julie Lagemonier (notice the spelling) was the daughter of Baptiste Lagemonier and Marie Gaboury, a family that was awarded lot 76 in St. Boniface and ranked among the leading owners of personal property judging by what they possessed in 1835. Through Riel's four uncles (Benjamin, Jean Baptiste, Joseph, and Roman) he was linked by marriage to a broad network of other leading landowners, including Andrew McDermot, perhaps the wealthiest person in the colony.[87] On the basis of kinship, Louis Riel the younger was well placed to operate as a kind of broker between the economically obscure and the socially prominent. He could talk about the rights of the plain people without speaking as a stranger to society's mighty. At the same time, he could identify with ordinary folk and speak to them with a familiarity that would ring true because a humble position was indeed that of his father's family.

Some of this is speculative and to the extent that the analysis is based on the assumption that a kinship network is a group of allies, the argument is also possibly misleading because it is as likely that family relationships can lead to conflict as much as to cooperation and trust. The fact remains, however, that mapping the kinship pattern can be a useful starting point in the study of the politics of small communities such as the Red River Colony. If it is found on closer examination of other sources that some persons are curiously supportive or inexplicably—and excessively—hostile, the family connection becomes an additonal item of significant information. In this way, the tables offer investigators assistance in plotting the broader patterns of kinship, as well as providing general readers with a few items of information about individuals who are unknown or obscure branches on a family tree.

---

[87]The McDermot connection was as follows: McDermot's son Miles was married to the sister of the wife of Riel's cousin Elzear Lagemonier. By similar connections Riel was related to Bruneaus, Dumonts, Naults, Grants, and Ducharmes—the Métis elite.

Table 1:

Genealogy of Red River
Households, 1818-1870

TABLE 1: GENEALOGIES OF RED RIVER HOUSEHOLDS, 1818-1870

ID	MALE HEAD OF FAMILY	RACE	FAITH	BIRTH PLACE	DATES	DADS ID	FEMALE HEAD OF FAMILY	RACE	FAITH	BIRTH PLACE	DATES	DADS ID
13	ABLES EDMOND	EUR	P	ENG	1825	14	NAULT NANCY	EUR	·	USA	1836	·
14	ABLES RICHARD	EUR	P	USA	1795	·	COPER ANNE	EUR	P	ENG	1793	3754
3490	ADAM CHARLES	MET	P	RRS	·	·	NORQUAY ANNE	·	·	·	·	·
20	ADAM GEORGE	·	P	RRS	1837	19	HAYWOOD MARY	MET	P	NWT	1839	·
3339	ADAM GEORGE	MET	P	RRS	1837	·	HAYWOOD ANN	·	·	·	1818	3339
4551	ADAM GEORGE	MET	P	RRS	1845	3339	·	·	·	·	·	·
21	ADAM JAMES	MET	RC	RRS	1820	19	BRUCE ELIZABETH	MET	P	RRS	1847	559
15	ADAM JEAN BTE	MET	RC	RRS	1820	·	BRUCE NANCY	IND	RC	RRS	1825	·
18	ADAM JEAN BTE	MET	RC	RRS	1800	·	BOYER MARIE	MET	RC	RRS	1825	3
27	ADAM JEAN BTE	·	·	RRS	·	·	LAMIRE MAGDELEINE	·	·	·	1802	2948
23	ADAM JOSEPH	MET	P	RRS	1842	19	BIRD ANN	MET	P	RRS	1844	·
24	ADAM JOSEPH	MET	RC	RRS	1785	·	RACETTE ANGELIQUE	MET	RC	RRS	1785	·
24	ADAM JOSEPH	MET	RC	RRS	1785	·	RIVARD ISABELLE	MET	RC	RRS	1805	·
25	ADAM JOSEPH	MET	RC	RRS	1825	24	ARCAND PIERRETTE	MET	RC	RRS	1826	4193
26	ADAM ROBERT	MET	P	RRS	1847	19	POCHA ANN	MET	P	RRS	1849	·
3343	ADAM THOMAS	·	·	RRS	·	·	·	·	·	·	·	·
16	ADAMA WILLIAM	MET	P	RRS	1844	·	FIDLER ELIZABETH	MET	P	RRS	1846	1550
28	ADEMAR AUGUSTIN	EUR	P	RRS	1846	29	LYONS CATHERINE	MET	P	RRS	1852	3013
30	ADSHEAD JOHN	IND	P	CAN	1830	·	MCDONALD RACHEL	EUR	P	CAN	1848	·
31	AISQUASS MICHEL	EUR	·	NWT	1842	·	MESSIAPET JOSEPH	IND	P	NWT	1822	·
32	AITKIN ALEXENDER	MET	RC	ORK	1805	47	STRANGER ELIZABETH	EUR	·	ORK	1835	·
48	ALLARD AMBROISE	·	·	NWT	1757	·	CHALIFOUX MARGUERITE	·	·	·	1811 66	·
58	ALLARD AMBROISE	·	·	·	1757	·	CREE LISETTE	·	·	·	·	·
58	ALLARD AMBROISE	·	·	·	1817	·	LONTEUSE MARGUERITE	·	·	·	1763	·
8077	ALLARD AMBROISE	·	·	·	1817	·	CHALIFOUX MARGUERITE	·	·	·	1811 66	·
8077	ALLARD AMBROISE	MET	RC	RRS	1836	48	ST DENIS FRANCOISE	·	·	·	·	·
50	ALLARD JEAN BTE	MET	RC	RRS	1836	48	ST GERMAIN MARIE	MET	RC	RRS	1834 65	4246
50	ALLARD JEAN BTE	MET	RC	RRS	1843	48	ROSS CATHERINE	MET	RC	RRS	1848	4246
52	ALLARD MICHEL	MET	RC	LC	1836	·	ROSS ELIZABETH	MET	RC	RRS	1846	1923
55	ALLARD OCTAVE	EUR	RC	LC	1836	·	GAUDRY MARIE ROSE	EUR	RC	·	1841 64	·
55	ALLARD OCTAVE	EUR	RC	RRS	1840	·	LAGEMONIER CELESTE	·	·	·	·	·
33	ALLARY ANTOINE	MET	RC	NWT	1819	41	LAROCQUE JULIE	MET	RC	RRS	1838	4574
34	ALLARY ANTOINE	MET	RC	NWT	1799	35	SWAIN MARY	MET	RC	NWT	1823	677
35	ALLARY ANTOINE	MET	RC	RRS	1797	·	CAPLETTE SUZETTE	MET	·	RRS	1805	3378
38	ALLARY JEAN BTE	MET	RC	NWT	1829	41	MCKAY MAGDELEINE	MET	RC	RRS	1846	·
39	ALLARY JOSEPH	·	·	·	·	·	SAYER MARGUERITE	MET	·	RRS	·	·
40	ALLARY LOUIS	MET	RC	NWT	1832	35	DESJARLAIS MARIE	MET	RC	NWT	1830	·
41	ALLARY LOUISON	MET	RC	RRS	1847	·	MARIE	MET	RC	·	·	·
42	ALLARY MICHEL	MET	RC	RRS	1846	·	POCHA MARIE	IND	·	·	·	·
43	ALLARY MICHEL	MET	RC	RRS	1800	42	ZASTRE GENEVIEVE	MET	RC	RRS	1829	·
44	ALLARY PIERRE	MET	RC	RRS	1840	42	PARISIEN ANGELIQUE	MET	RC	RRS	1839	5210
45	ALLARY PIERRE	MET	RC	RRS	1841	35	BERIAULT CELINA	MET	RC	RRS	1837	3841
66	ALLARY. FRANCOIS	MET	RC	RRS	1800	68	DUPUIS MARIE	MET	RC	RRS	1840	·
67	AMIOTTE JEAN BTE	MET	RC	SCT	1840	68	GAUDRY CATHERINE	MET	RC	NWT	1842	1407
145	AMIOTTE JOSEPH	·	·	·	·	·	HAMELIN MADELEIN	MET	RC	·	1809	1917
8075	AMIOTTE JOSEPHH	·	·	RRS	·	·	MCLEAN MARY	·	·	·	1840	·
69	ANDERSON ALEXANDER	EUR	·	RRS	1841	·	MARY	EUR	·	UC	1851	·
72	ANDERSON CALEB	MET	RC	RRS	1833	78	DENNET ISABELLA	MET	·	RRS	1838	1223
70	ANDERSON CHARLES	MET	RC	RRS	1826	78	BIRSTON ANN	MET	·	RRS	1830	·
71	ANDERSON CHARLES	MET	·	RRS	1835	88	COOK MARIA	MET	·	RRS	1841	3616

ID	MALE HEAD OF FAMILY	RACE	FAITH	BIRTH PLACE	DATES	DADS ID	FEMALE HEAD OF FAMILY	RACE	FAITH	BIRTH PLACE	DATES	DADS ID
73	ANDERSON DAVID	MET	.	RRS	1828	88	BADGER NANCY	MET	.	NWT	1836	.
74	ANDERSON DAVID	IND	.	NWT	1822	.	MARY	MET	.	RRS	1826	.
3602	ANDERSON DAVID	.	.	.	.	.	MATILDA	.	.	.	.	.
3603	ANDERSON DAVID	.	.	.	.	.	NANCY	.	.	.	.	.
75	ANDERSON FRANCOIS	IND	P	RRS	1835	95	SMITH ANNE	IND	P	RRS	1840	.
76	ANDERSON HENRY	MET	P	RRS	1829	94	COOK SOPHIA	MET	.	NWT	1820	.
78	ANDERSON JAMES	MET	P	NWT	1808	79	HARPER HARIET	MET	P	RRS	1815	4409
78	ANDERSON JAMES	MET	P	NWT	1808	79	SMITH JANE	IND	.	.	1816 43	.
79	ANDERSON JAMES	EUR	P	ORK	1775	78	TRUTHWAITE JANE	MET	.	.	1780	.
80	ANDERSON JAMES	MET	.	RRS	1832	88	DEMORAN MARY	EUR	P	SCT	1837	1961
81	ANDERSON JAMES	EUR	P	ORK	1833	.	GILL FANNY	IND	.	.	1838	.
82	ANDERSON JAMES	EUR	.	.	.	.	MCKENZIE ANN	MET	.	.	.	.
83	ANDERSON JOHN	MET	.	RRS	1850	94	HALCROW ANNA	MET	P	RRS	1852	2088
84	ANDERSON JOHN	MET	P	RRS	1827	88	WHITFORD CHRISTIANA	MET	.	RRS	1833	5180
85	ANDERSON JOHN	EUR	.	OTH	1838	79	COOK LYDIA	MET	P	RRS	1845	945
88	ANDERSON JOHN	MET	P	RRS	1803	78	DESMARAIS MARY	MET	.	RRS	1804	.
90	ANDERSON PETER	MET	.	RRS	1827	88	MCKAY LATITIA	MET	.	NWT	1837	3412
91	ANDERSON ROBERT	MET	.	RRS	1842	94	KIP ELIZABETH	MET	.	RRS	1843	.
92	ANDERSON THOMAS	MET	.	RRS	1833	78	POCHA FANNY	MET	.	.	1840	3943
93	ANDERSON THOMAS	MET	P	RRS	1835	79	DESMARAIS ELIZABETH	MET	.	NWT	1838 58	.
94	ANDERSON THOMAS	MET	.	NWT	1806	.	COOPER LOUISE	MET	P	NWT	1837	951
3604	ANDERSON THOMAS	.	.	.	.	.	LANDRY CATHERINE	MET	.	.	1809	.
3605	ANDERSON THOMAS	.	.	.	.	.	MARY	.	.	.	.	.
95	ANDERSON WILLIAM	MET	P	NWT	1820	99	ELIZABETH	IND	.	NWT	.	4308
98	ANNAL JOHN	MET	P	.	1823	.	SAUNDERS NANCY	MET	P	.	1825	.
99	ANNAL PETER	MET	.	.	.	.	MAGNUS MARY	MET	.	.	1830	.
100	ANTILL GEORGE	MET	P	RRS	1813	.	SAUNDERS MARGARET	MET	P	.	.	.
101	ARCAND ALEXANDRE	MET	.	RRS	1843	105	JEFFERSON JULIA	MET	P	RRS	1815	.
101	ARCAND ALEXANDRE	MET	.	RRS	1843	105	MARGUERITE	.	P	.	1844	.
102	ARCAND FRANCOIS	MET	RC	RRS	1843	105	MCKAY FRANCOISE	MET	.	RRS	1844	301
103	ARCAND JEAN	MET	RC	RRS	1840	105	ARCAND PHILOMENE	MET	RC	RRS	1843	3393
104	ARCAND JOSEPH	MET	RC	CAN	1834	105	BERARD ANNIE	MET	.	RRS	1843	3393
105	ARCAND JOSEPH	EUR	RC	.	1780	.	MCKAY JOSEPHTE	MET	RC	.	1848	.
112	ARCUS DAVID	EUR	P	ORK	1826	114	VESTREAU MARIE	EUR	.	RRS	1785	.
114	ARCUS DAVID	MET	P	NWT	1798 45	114	TAYLOR JANE	MET	P	NWT	1838	.
115	ARCUS GEORGE	EUR	P	ORK	1831	.	WIDOW	.	.	.	1796	2959
2122	ARCUS GEORGE	EUR	P	ORK	1799	.	LILLIE ANNE	MET	P	RRS	1833 59	.
2124	ARKNEYS ANDREW	.	.	.	.	.	PARK ISABELLA	EUR	P	.	1807	.
121	ARMSTRONG ELLIOT	EUR	P	IRE	1843	122	FIDLER ANN	IND	.	RRS	1845	1532
122	ARMSTRONG JAMES	EUR	P	IRE	1780	.	MCKAY JANE	MET	P	IRE	1803	.
123	ARMSTRONG JOSEPH	EUR	P	ENG	1840	122	SHARP SARAH	EUR	P	ENG	1846	4798
129	ASHAM CHARLES	.	.	.	1781 41	.	HENDERSON NANCY	IND	P	RRS	1790	.
130	ASHAM CHARLES	.	.	.	1810 43	.	ANN	MET	.	.	1816	.
128	ASHAM ISAAC	MET	P	RRS	1845	127	THOMAS MATHILDA	IND	.	RRS	1846	4887
126	ASHAM JAMES	MET	.	RRS	1848	127	KENNEDY CHRISTINE	IND	.	RRS	1849	1741
131	ASHAM JAMES	.	RC	.	1840	130	CORRIGAL CAROLINE	.	RC	.	1842	.
835	ASHAM JOHN	.	.	.	1819	.	JANE	.	.	.	1819	.
2382	ASHAM PRICE	.	P	NWT	1789	.	SMITH HANNAH	IND	.	NWT	1816	.
125	ASHAM THOMAS	.	.	.	1792 62	.	NANCY	.	P	.	1790	.

TABLE 1: GENEALOGIES OF RED RIVER HOUSEHOLDS, 1818-1870

ID	MALE HEAD OF FAMILY		RACE	FAITH	BIRTH PLACE	DATES	DADS ID	FEMALE HEAD OF FAMILY		RACE	FAITH	BIRTH PLACE	DATES	DADS ID
2370	ASHAM	THOMAS	MET	P	NWT	1810			NANCY	IND			1812	
133	ATKINS	JOHN		P		1808 68		SWAIN	MARGARET				1827 69	
134	ATKINSON	GEORGE		P	NWT	1770 30			MARGARET				1780	
135	ATKINSON	GEORGE	MET		NWT	1820		STEAD	ANN	MET			1830	4465
136	ATKINSON	GEORGE	MET	P	NWT	1815		KIPPLING	NANCY	MET			1815	2298
142	ATKINSON	HENRY	MET		NWT	1824	134	VILLENEUVE	SCHOLASTIQUE	MET		RRS	1834	5127
139	ATKINSON	JOHN	MET		RRS	1825	134	GUNN	MATILDA	MET		RRS	1831	2064
141	ATKINSON	THOMAS	MET		RRS	1825		MORRISETTE	SUSETTE	MET		RRS	1827	3206
143	AUBUCHON	PIERRE						DAZE	MARIE	MET				
96	AUGER	ANTOINE						KLYNE	MARIE	EUR				
97	AUGER	BAPTISTE	MET	RC	NWT	1824		MCNAB	SARAH	MET	RC	RRS	1829	3468
155	AZURE								WIDOW					
147	AZURE	ANTOINE	MET	RC	RRS	1825	149	LARIVIERE	VICTOIRE	MET	P		1830	2656
149	AZURE	ANTOINE	MET	RC	RRS	1810		PELLETIER	CHARLOTTE		P		1815	
150	AZURE	CHARLES	MET	RC	RRS	1821	149	GRANT	NANCY	MET	P		1832	2030
150	AZURE	CHARLES	MET	RC	RRS	1821	149	ALLARD	CHARLOTTE		P		1814 44	47
152	AZURE	JOSEPH				1810		BEAUCHEMIN	MARIE	MET			1815	
153	AZURE	JOSEPH	MET	RC	NWT	1829		MONGENI	JOSEPHTE				1830	
154	AZURE	JOSEPH	MET	RC	NWT	1770			LISETTE				1775	
837	BADGER	JAMES				1814			MARGARET				1816	4378
157	BADGER	JOHN	IND	P	RRS	1830	159	MCKEE	CATHERINE	MET	P	RRS	1830	
158	BADGER	PIERRE	IND	P	RRS	1839	159	SINCLAIR	THERESE	IND	P	RRS	1845	
159	BADGER	THOMAS				1810			MARY	IND	P	RRS	1810	
160	BADGER	WILLIAM	IND	P	RRS	1820		COOK	ELISE	IND	P	RRS	1822	
6051	BAGLEY	JOHN				1850		VILLEBRUNE	PHILOMENE				1850	
162	BAILLIE	ALEXANDRE				1800			NANCY	MET			1802	
6050	BAILLIE	ROBERT				1830		SINCLAIR	ELIZABETH				1830	
163	BAILLIE	WILLIAM	MET		RRS	1822	162	MORRIS	M				1824	961
167	BALLENDINE	ADOLPH	MET	P	RRS	1842		CORRIGAL	MARGUERITE	MET	P	RRS	1844	
168	BALLENDINE	GEORGE	MET	P	NWT	1808		BLACK	JANE	MET	P	NWT	1812	
172	BALLENDINE	JAMES			RRS	1807 64	171	STEVENS	MARY		P	NWT	1808	
172	BALLENDINE	JAMES			RRS	1807 64		LEWIS	FRANCOISE	MET	P	RRS	1812	2951
173	BALLENDINE	JAMES	MET		RRS	1837	172	NORQUAY	MARIANNE	MET	P	RRS	1837	3752
171	BALLENDINE	JOHN	EUR			1780			ANN	MET	P	RRS	1781	
175	BALLENDINE	JOHN	MET	P	RRS	1835	172	HAYWOOD	ELIZABETH	MET	P	RRS	1837	4417
176	BALLENDINE	SAMUEL		P	RRS	1839	168	SMITH	MARY	MET	P	RRS	1829	
177	BALLENDINE	WILLIAM		P	NWT	1790 69		STEVENS	CHARLOTTE	MET	P	NWT	1808 43	
177	BALLENDINE	WILLIAM		P	NWT	1790 69		BICKERSTETH		MET	RC	NWT	1820	
180	BALLSOLIE	JOHN	EUR	P	SCT	1849		ROWAND	ADELAIDE	MET	P	NWT	1852	
179	BANNATYNE	A G B	EUR	P	SCT	1830		MCDERMOT	ANNIE	EUR	RC	NWT	1832	4256
182	BANNERMAN	ALEXANDER	EUR	P	SCT	1800	204	MCKAY	JANNET	EUR	P	SCT	1845	3304
184	BANNERMAN	DAVID	EUR	P	RRS	1838	182	MATHESON	JANE	EUR	P	SCT	1813	3655
189	BANNERMAN	DONALD	EUR	P	SCT	1805	204	MATHESON	JANET	EUR	P	SCT	1808	3090
192	BANNERMAN	GEORGE	EUR	P	SCT	1838	182	TAYLOR	MARY	MET	P	RRS	1837	4639
198	BANNERMAN	SAMUEL	EUR	P	RRS	1838	204	OMAND	MARGARET	EUR	P	ORK	1844	3719
204	BANNERMAN	WILLIAM	EUR	P	SCT	1757			BARBARA	EUR			1759	
205	BARBEAU	PIERRE				1825		DANIEL	MARGUERITE	MET	P	RRS	1834	1014
206	BARBER	EDWARD	EUR	P	USA	1834		LOGAN	BARBARA	MET	P	RRS	1835	2988
217	BARNARD	REVEREND							MARY	EUR				
213	BARRON	CHARLE						BRUNET	MARIE	EUR				

TABLE 1: GENEALOGIES OF RED RIVER HOUSEHOLDS, 1818-1870

ID	MALE HEAD OF FAMILY		RACE	FAITH	BIRTH PLACE	DATES	DADS ID	FEMALE HEAD OF FAMILY		RACE	FAITH	BIRTH PLACE	DATES	DADS ID
211	BARRON	CHARLES	MET	RC	NWT	1851	212	COMTOIS	MARIE	MET	RC	USA	1855	923
212	BARRON	CHARLES	EUR	RC	LC	1799	.	BRACONNIER	LOUISE	MET	RC	RRS	1820	489
836	BASHE	CHARLES	.	.	.	1800	.	BANOU	PHILLIPHINE	.	.	.	1800	.
224	BAUVEN	EMILE	MET	RC	RRS	1838 40	.	VANDRY	SUSANNE	.	RC	.	1838	5078
227	BAUVIER	ALEXIS	.	.	.	1768	229	SAULTEAUX	JOSEPHE	.	.	.	1770	.
479	BAUVIER	ANTOINE	.	.	.	1810	.	BRELAND	GENEVIEVE	MET	.	.	1812	4616
229	BAUVIER	JEAN BTE	.	.	.	1790	.	LAURENT	MARGUERITE	.	.	.	1791 61	3874
229	BAUVIER	JEAN BTE	.	.	.	1790	.	.	MARGUERITE	.	.	.	1812 45	.
230	BAUVIER	JEAN BTE	.	.	.	.	.	ST PIERRE	MARIE	MET	.	NWT	1798 68	.
480	BAUVIER	JEAN BTE	MET	.	RRS	1813	229	PAUL	MARGUERITE	.	.	.	1835	.
238	BEADS	JACOB	.	P	RRS	1830	242	LADHIMAR	CHARLOTTE	.	P	NWT	1830 53	.
240	BEADS	JOHN	.	P	NWT	1820	239	ROBILLARD	CATHERINE	.	P	.	1852	.
1185	BEADS	JOHN	.	.	.	1847 69	240	BREMNER	ELIZA	.	.	.	1810	.
138	BEAR	JOHN	MET	.	NWT	1804 64	.	ERASMUS	CATHERINE	.	.	.	1820	.
195	BEAR	THOMAS	IND	P	NWT	1810	.	.	ISABEL	.	.	.	1815	.
195	BEAR	THOMAS	IND	P	NWT	1810	.	TATE	NELLY	.	.	.	1820	.
183	BEAR	WILLIAM	MET	P	NWT	1813	241	.	MARGARET	.	.	.	1836	.
201	BEAR	WILLIAM	IND	P	RRS	1836	241	.	SOPHIE	.	.	RRS	1832	.
201	BEAR	WILLIAM	IND	P	RRS	1836	.	.	MARY	.	.	RRS	.	.
840	BEARDY	JAMES	IND	.	.	.	.	.	ELIZABETH	.	.	.	.	.
120	BEAUCHAMP	CHARLES	MET	RC	NWT	1795	.	FALARDEAU	CATHERINE	MET	RC	RRS	1820	2496
181	BEAUCHAMP	CHARLES	.	.	.	1829 61	.	LADEROUTE	SOPHIE	MET	RC	RRS	1800	.
185	BEAUCHAMP	JEAN	MET	RC	.	1800	185	PANGMAN	ANGELIQUE	MET	RC	RRS	1834	.
196	BEAUCHAMP	JEROME	MET	RC	RRS	1829	.	JANEVILLE	MARIE ANNE	MET	RC	RRS	1834	2361
188	BEAUCHAMP	JOSEPH	.	.	.	1830	.	PARISIEN	GENEVIEVE	MET	RC	.	1818	3841
838	BEAUCHAMP	PIERRE	.	.	CAN	1816	.	LAPOINTE	MARIE	.	.	.	1805	.
169	BEAUCHAMP	PIERRE	MET	RC	.	1800 65	.	VERSAILLES	SCHOLASTIQUE	.	.	.	1810 62	.
190	BEAUCHAMP	ANDRE	MET	RC	.	1812	.	MORIN	MARIE	MET	RC	RRS	1827	.
174	BEAUCHEMIN	ANDRE	EUR	RC	RRS	1824	202	DELORME	GENEVIEVE	MET	RC	RRS	1827	3122
202	BEAUCHEMIN	ANDRE	EUR	RC	RRS	1824	202	MILLET	MARIE	EUR	.	.	1785	.
202	BEAUCHEMIN	ANDRE	EUR	RC	.	1778	.	PELLETIER	CHARLOTTE	MET	RC	RRS	1801	.
197	BEAUCHEMIN	BAPTISTE	MET	RC	RRS	1778	194	DUCHARME	MADELEINE	MET	RC	RRS	1839	1362
194	BEAUCHEMIN	BENJAMIN	MET	RC	.	1838	.	MCMILLAN	MARGUERITE	MET	RC	.	1815	3120
186	BEAUCHENE	JOSEPH	EUR	RC	LC	1810	.	PARENTEAU	MARIE	MET	RC	.	1840	3801
166	BEAUCHENE	PIERRE	EUR	RC	.	1820	166	FLETT	JOSEPHTE	EUR	RC	.	1787	2454
232	BEAUDRY	JEAN BTE	.	RC	.	1785	.	ST GEORGE	GENEVIEVE	EUR	RC	NWT	1825	.
233	BEAUDRY	LOUIS	MET	RC	NWT	1820	232	LADOUCEUR	LOUISE	MET	RC	RRS	1848	.
253	BEAUDRY	NARCIS	.	RC	.	1845	256	BRABANT	CHARLOTTE	MET	RC	.	1799	508
257	BEAULIEU	FRANCOIS	.	.	.	1825	.	BRELAND	LUCIE	MET	RC	.	1825	.
258	BEAULIEU	FRANCOIS	.	.	.	1798	.	SAULTEAUX	ANGELIQUE	MET	RC	.	1848	.
259	BEAULIEU	JEAN	.	RC	.	1819	260	GARIEPY	MARIE	.	.	.	1799	1898
256	BEAULIEU	JEAN BTE	.	.	.	1805	.	RICHARD	JOSETTE	MET	RC	NWT	1825	.
260	BEAULIEU	JEAN BTE	.	.	.	1799 59	.	SAULTEAUX	MARGARITE	.	.	.	1844 63	.
8070	BEAULIEU	NOEL	.	RC	.	1844	.	LAPLANTE	LINA	.	.	.	1805	.
263	BEAUPRE	JOSEPH	EUR	RC	CAN	1778	.	CADOTTE	JOSEPHTE	MET	.	RRS	1807	3759
264	BEDDOME	HENRY	EUR	P	ENG	1828	.	OMAND	FRANCOISE	EUR	P	SCT	1780	.
265	BEGG	ALEXANDER	EUR	P	LC	1840	.	HAMILTON	CATHERINE	EUR	P	RRS	1840	.
266	BEGG	CHARLES	EUR	P	SCT	1824	.	SPENCE	CATHERINE	MET	P	NWT	1848	4435
267	BEGG	DUNCAN	MET	P	NWT	1845	266	BOULTON	JANE	MET	P	.	1847	454

TABLE 1: GENEALOGIES OF RED RIVER HOUSEHOLDS, 1818-1870

ID	MALE HEAD OF FAMILY	RACE	FAITH	BIRTH PLACE	DATES	DADS ID	FEMALE HEAD OF FAMILY	RACE	FAITH	BIRTH PLACE	DATES	DADS ID
210	BELANGER ABRAHAM	MET	RC	RRS	1849	245	DELORME PHILOMENE	MET	RC	RRS	1847	1102
245	BELANGER ABRAHAM	MET	RC	RRS	1818	249	VERSAILLES MARIE ANNE	MET	RC	RRS	1821	5111
248	BELANGER HORACE			CAN	1840		MARION ROSALIE		RC		1845	3045
249	BELANGER LOUISON	EUR	RC		1770		DAZE JOSEPHTE	MET	RC		1775	
13276	BELIVEAU JEAN BAPTIST	EUR			1835		COULOMBRE APPOLLINE	MET				
276	BELLE JOHN	MET	P	NWT	1825	276	ANNE	MET	P	NWT	1830	
303	BELLE WILLIAM	EUR	RC	LC	1837		MORRIS MARY	MET	RC	RRS	1851	1105
278	BELLEFEUILLE RAPHAEL	EUR	RC		1820	279	DELORME PHILOMENE	MET	RC		1820	
280	BELLEHUMEUR JEAN		RC	CAN	1772		WITIMASE MADELEINE	EUR	RC		1792	
279	BELLEHUMEUR MICHEL		RC	CAN	1772		LAGEMONIER LAREME	MET	RC		1775	
279	BELLEHUMEUR MICHEL	MET	RC	RRS	1820		GRANT MARGUERITE	MET	RC	RRS	1824	1987
281	BELLEHUMEUR MICHEL	EUR					GONEVILLE LOUISE	MET	RC			
277	BELLISLE						JOSEPHTE	MET	RC			
236	BENDER JACOB	MET	RC	NWT	1845		ROSETTE	MET	RC	RRS	1834	
291	BERARD DANIEL	MET	RC	NWT	1835	297	MONETTE MATHILDA	MET	RC	RRS	1840	1449
293	BERARD EUSTACHE	MET	RC	NWT	1837	297	IRVINE MARGUERITE	MET	RC	RRS	1825	3984
292	BERARD FRANCOIS	MET	RC	NWT	1825	297	PRIMEAU MARGUERITE	MET	RC	NWT	1843	4254
290	BERARD JEAN BTE	MET	RC	RRS	1840	297	ROUSSIN HELENE	MET	RC	RRS	1810	2814
294	BERARD JEREMIE	EUR	RC	RRS	1796		LAVALLEE PHILOMENE	MET	RC	RRS	1820	1002
297	BERARD LOUIS	MET	RC		1792		HUPPE CATHERINE	MET	RC	RRS	1815	
300	BERARD PIERRE	MET	RC	NWT	1800		HUGHES MARIE	MET	RC	NWT	1817	3175
301	BERARD PIERRE	MET	RC	NWT	1800	300	FORTIN LOUISE	MET	RC		1850	
301	BERARD PIERRE	MET	RC	RRS	1838	300	MOREAU JOSEPHTE	MET	RC		1848	
302	BERARD SIMON	MET	RC		1836	300	MEUNIER JOSEPHINE	MET	RC	NWT		1002
285	BERCIER ALEX		RC	CAN	1771		HUPPE MARGUERITE	MET	RC		1850	
282	BERCIER ALEXIS		RC	CAN	1771		SINCLAIR JOSEPHTE	MET	RC		1848	
282	BERCIER ALEXIS	MET	RC		1834		SAULTEAUX MARGARET	IND	RC		1779 53	
284	BERCIER ALEXIS	MET	RC		1848	287	ROSALIE	MET	RC		1835	
286	BERCIER ANTOINE	MET	RC	RRS	1808	282	FOURNIER JUSTINE	MET	RC		1848	1644
287	BERCIER BAPTISTE	MET	RC	RRS	1832	287	BOYER MARIE	MET	RC	RRS	1815	7
288	BERCIER JEAN BTE	MET	RC	RRS	1839	287	ST PIERRE MARGUERITE	MET	RC	NWT	1837	4661
289	BERCIER JOSEPH	MET	RC		1814		THIBERT FLAVIE	MET	RC	RRS	1841	1481
306	BEREVIN FILBERT		RC		1814		FALCON REMI		RC		1830	
306	BEREVIN FILBERT		RC		1780		BERNARD ELISE	MET	RC		1838	1346
308	BERGIS JACQUE	MET	RC	RRS	1836 12		DUCHARME CECILE	MET	RC		1785	
309	BERIAULT FRANCOIS		RC	RRS	1802 64	310	DEMOND SUZANNE	MET	RC	RRS	1841	4543
310	BERIAULT GILBERT	MET	RC		1803	313	SUTHERLAND SUZANNE	MET	RC	LC	1816	401
312	BERIAULT JOSEPH	MET	RC	RRS	1775	313	BLONDEAU ISABELLE	MET	RC	RRS	1820	1415
313	BERIAULT JOSEPH	MET			1841		DUVAL MARIANNE	EUR	RC		1777	
314	BERIAULT LOUIS		RC	RRS	1839	310	BEAUPRE MARGUERITE	MET	RC	RRS	1843	
315	BERIAULT MAXIME	MET	RC	RRS	1808	310	NOLIN ELISE	MET	RC	RRS	1845	4543
316	BERIAULT PIERRE	MET	RC		1848		SUTHERLAND MARIE		RC		1805	
8068	BERNIER THOMAS	MET	RC		1851		FORTIN MALVINA	MET	RC	RRS	1848	
320	BERTHELET ANTOINE	MET	RC	RRS	1810	327	DEMERS CATHERINE	MET	RC	RRS	1853	2508
321	BERTHELET JOSEPH	MET	RC	RRS	1834	327	LAFERTE ANGELIQUE	MET	RC	LC	1839	2504
321	BERTHELET JOSEPH	MET	RC	RRS	1832		LAFERTE MARGUERITE		RC		1780 68	
322	BERTHELET JOSEPH		RC	RRS	1800	321	DUBOIS FRANCOISE	MET	RC	RRS	1838	687
324	BERTHELET PIERRE	MET	RC	RRS	1780	326	CARRON LOUISE	MET	RC	RRS	1842	
326	BERTHELET PIERRE	MET	RC	RRS			BRACER ELISE	MET	RC	RRS	1800	
327	BERTHELET TOUSSANT	EUR	RC				DUBOIS MARGUERITE	IND	RC	RRS	1776	

TABLE 1: GENEALOGIES OF RED RIVER HOUSEHOLDS, 1818-1870

ID	MALE HEAD OF FAMILY		RACE	FAITH	BIRTH PLACE	DATES	DADS ID	FEMALE HEAD OF FAMILY		RACE	FAITH	BIRTH PLACE	DATES	DADS ID
358	BERTRAND	ALEXANDRE				1810		WILLS	EMILIE				1813	
8064	BETOURNAY	LOUIS	EUR			1838		MARCILLE	MARIE				1838	
362	BEUTON	ANGUS	EUR			1785		ASSINIBOINE	LOUISE	IND		RRS	1787	
364	BEYAIS	JOHN			ORK	1823		BROWN	JANE	MET		RRS	1844	
8057	BIBEAU	JOSEPH	MET			1845		COURCHENE	SOPHIE	MET			1845	
367	BIRD	CHARLES	EUR	P	RRS	1840	387	HALCROW	ANN	MET			1843	2086
370	BIRD	CURTIS				1837	379	ROSS	ANNABELLA	EUR	P	NWT	1833	4232
371	BIRD	DAVID	MET	P		1800 48		CALDER	HARRIET	MET			1815	628
372	BIRD	FREDERICK	MET			1823		GARRIOCH	ANN	MET			1826	628
373	BIRD	GEORGE	MET			1798		THOMAS	ANN				1800	
377	BIRD	HENRY	EUR			1805	378	CALDER	HARRIET	EUR			1815	628
3611	BIRD	HENRY	EUR			1841		LOUIS	CHLOE	EUR			1845	
378	BIRD	JAMES	MET	P	NWT	1798	379		ELIZABETH	IND	P		1808 46	
378	BIRD	JAMES	MET	P	NWT		379	BUTTS	ELIZABETH	IND	P	NWT	1809	
379	BIRD	JAMES	EUR		ENG	1775			SARAH	IND			1789 34	
379	BIRD	JAMES	EUR		ENG	1775			ELIZABETH	IND			1777	
380	BIRD	JAMES	MET	P	RRS	1824	399	KELLY	MARY	MET	P		1829	1954
384	BIRD	JAMES	MET	P	RRS	1848	382	GIBSON	ISABEL	MET	P	RRS	1848	1562
3608	BIRD	JAMES	EUR			1783		FINLAYSON	ELIZA	MET			1838	1407
3609	BIRD	JAMES	MET			1838			MARY	IND			1838	
3610	BIRD	JAMES	MET			1810 40			SALLY				1806	
376	BIRD	JOHN				1801	369		MARY	EUR				
3615	BIRD	JOHN				1848 71		LINKLATER	MARY					
387	BIRD	JOSEPH	MET			1815		MCKAY	MARY ANN				1808 46	2948
3617	BIRD	JOSEPH	MET	P		1848	399		MARY	MET	P		1848	
388	BIRD	LEVY	MET			1850		THOMAS	ELIZABETH	MET	P		1816 41	2295
390	BIRD	NICOLAS	MET			1819		LOUIS	SARAH	MET	P		1850	
391	BIRD	PHILIP	MET	RC	RRS	1850	379	THOMAS	JANE	MET	P		1848	
392	BIRD	PHILIP	MET	P		1815	394	SHARP	MARGARET	MET	P			
393	BIRD	ROBERT	MET	P	RRS	1832		KIPPLING	MARY	MET	P	RRS	1852	3204
394	BIRD	THOMAS				1838 60	373	FIDLER	MARY	MET	P	RRS	1819	3304
395	BIRD	THOMAS	MET		RRS	1841		MORRISETTE	ADELAIDE	MET	P	RRS	1842	1646
3150	BIRD	THOMAS				1847		MCDERMOT	ELLEN	MET	P		1846	2948
3612	BIRD	THOMAS				1840		FOX	NANCY				1843	
3613	BIRD	THOMAS				1802		LOUIS	SARAH					
397	BIRD	WILLIAM	MET	P	RRS	1826	372	BROWN	ELIZABETH	MET	P	RRS	1853	991
398	BIRD	WILLIAM	MET	P	RRS	1804 69	373	MONTRE	ROSALINE	MET	P	RRS	1846	4516
399	BIRD	WILLIAM	MET	P	RRS	1804 69	379	CUMMINGS	HARRIET	MET	P		1801 64	915
400	BIRD	WILLIAM	MET	P	NWT	1811		SUTHERLAND	MARY	MET	P		1825	
329	BIRSTON	ALEXANDER	MET	P	NWT	1809		HAY	SOPHIA	IND	P		1806 33	
329	BIRSTON	ALEXANDER	MET	P	NWT			COCHRANE	SARAH	MET	P			
330	BIRSTON	ALEXANDER	MET	P			328	BUDD	BETSY	MET	P	NWT	1813	
505	BIRSTON	BERNARD	MET	P				ATKINSON	JANET	MET	P	RRS		3862
332	BIRSTON	JAMES	MET	P	ORK	1769 37	336	TAIT	MAGDELEINE	MET	P	NWT	1775	
333	BIRSTON	MAGNUS	MET	P	RRS	1815		ROSSELIN	GRIZEL	MET	P	RRS	1815	
334	BIRSTON	MAGNUS	MET	RC	RRS	1828	336	LYONS	NANCY	MET	RC	NWT	1828	3008
335	BIRSTON	MAGNUS			NWT	1802 35	328	PAUL	NANCY	MET	RC	NWT		
336	BIRSTON	WILLIAM	MET	P	RRS	1827		BERCIER	ANGELIQUE	MET	RC		1810	
338	BIRSTON	WILLIAM	MET	RC	RRS	1808		GONEVILLE	MADELEINE	MET	RC	RRS	1829	
529	BIRSTON	WILLIAM	MET	P	NWT		328	KIRKNESS	MARY	MET	P	NWT	1818	2289

TABLE 1: GENEALOGIES OF RED RIVER HOUSEHOLDS, 1818-1870

ID	MALE HEAD OF FAMILY	FAMILY	RACE	FAITH	BIRTH PLACE	DATES	DADS ID	FEMALE HEAD OF FAMILY	FAMILY	RACE	FAITH	BIRTH PLACE	DATES	DADS ID
341	BLACK	ALEXANDER	MET	P	NWT	1832	346	MILLER	NANCY	MET	RC	RRS	1841	3118
343	BLACK	JOHN	MET	P		1780		ROSS	MARGARET	IND	P		1785	
344	BLACK	JOHN	EUR	P	SCT	1817		MARCOTTE	MARGUERITE	MET	P	RRS	1830	4228
345	BLANCHETTE	ATHANASE						DESJARLAIS	HENRIETTE	MET			1842	
8072	BLAYONNE	ANTOINE	MET	RC	NWT	1850		DESMARAIS	ANNA	MET	RC	NWT	1848	
347	BLAYONNE	JOSEPH	MET			1829	347	ALLARY	MARIE	MET	RC		1831	1242
348	BLAYONNE	LOUIS	EUR	RC				RIEL	VIRGINIE	MET	RC			35
350	BLAYONNE	ROCH	MET	RC	NWT	1811		DEFOND	CATHERINE	MET	RC			
353	BLEUVE	LOUIS	EUR		RRS			LAFRAMBOISE	MARGUERITE	MET	RC	RRS	1824	1198
351	BLONDEAU	LOUIS	MET		RRS	1827	401	DESJARLAIS	JOSETTE	MET			1826	
401	BLONDEAU	SIMON			RRS	1827		ROBILLARD	MARIE				1829	
402	BLONDEAU	PAUL				1827		GRAY	FRANCOISE	MET			1830	
356	BLONDIN	PAUL	EUR	RC	LC	1792 68	357	LIMOGES	MARIE				1795	
357	BLONDIN	PIERRE			CAN	1848 26	357	DUVAL	ESTHER	MET	RC			
405	BLONDIN	BENJAMIN		RC		1800		LAVOIE	MARIE	MET	RC	LC	1810	1425
407	BOHEMIER	JOSEPH	EUR	RC	LC	1845 5		FIDLER	MARIE LOUISE	MET			1855	4711
409	BOISCLAIR	ONESIME						TROTTIER	ISABEL	MET	RC	LC	1848	
411	BOIVUN	PHILIUS	EUR	RC		1837	414		ANNE	MET				
412	BONE	LOUISON			RRS	1803			CAROLINE	MET			1847	
413	BONER	JEAN BTE	MET			1849		GARIEPY	MADELEINE	MET	RC		1815	1898
414	BONHOMME	PETER	MET	RC		1794	418	GARIEPY	LAROSE	MET	RC		1800	1099
415	BONHOMME	ANTOINE	MET	RC	RRS	1752 42	422	DELORME	LOUISA	MET	RC	RRS	1852	3951
416	BONNEAU	CHARLES	MET	RC		1827		POITRAS	ANGELIQUE	MET	RC		1795	1510
417	BONNEAU	FRANCOIS		RC		1780		FAVEL	ROSALIE	MET	RC		1845 68	
8078	BONNEAU	JEAN BAPT				1816	415	MORIN	MARIE	IND	RC		1760	
418	BONNEAU	JEAN BTE	MET	RC	RRS	1798		MORIN	APPOLINE	MET	RC	RRS	1832	3198
419	BONNEAU	JOSEPH	MET	RC	RRS	1836		MORIN	LOUISE				1780	
420	BONNEAU	JOSEPH	MET		RRS	1816		GOURNEAU	MADELEINE	MET	RC	RRS	1825	
421	BONNEAU	LOUIS	MET		NWT	1807		GARIEPY	LISETTE	MET	RC	RRS	1800	2019
422	BONNEAU	PIERRE	MET			1765		PEPIN	MARY ANNE	MET		NWT	1846	
425	BONNEAU	ALEXIS	EUR	RC	CAN	1807		TROTTIER	LOUISE	MET		RRS	1824	
426	BONNEVILLE	ALEXIS	EUR	RC	NWT	1818		PARENTEAU	MARY	MET		RRS	1836	3897
428	BONNEVILLE	CHARLES	EUR	RC	RRS	1838		CARDINAL	SUZETTE	MET		RRS	1816	3811
429	BOTTINEAU	JOSEPH	MET	RC	RRS	1838		PARENTEAU	FRANCOISE L	MET			1807	683
433	BOTTINEAU	FRANCO		RC	CAN	1801		CARDINAL	ANGELIQUE	IND			1765	
434	BOUCHER	FRANCOIS		RC	NWT	1801	439	AZURE	JOSSETTE				1817	
435	BOUCHER	ISADORE	MET	RC	RRS	1846		BROWNSEL	JOSEPHTE	MET			1828	
436	BOUCHER	JEAN	MET	RC	RRS	1835	439	LAPLANTE	JOSEPHTE	MET	RC	NWT	1834	
437	BOUCHER	JEAN	EUR	RC	RRS	1817		LESPERANCE	CHARLOTTE	MET	RC	RRS	1840	2930
439	BOUCHER	JOSEPH	EUR	RC	LC	1801	439	MINSEY	CAROLINE	MET			1814 69	
441	BOUCHER	JOSEPH	EUR	RC	LC		445	ROBINSON	CHRISTINE	MET	RC	RRS	1804 68	4200
442	BOUCHER	JOSEPH	MET	RC	RRS			BOUSQUET	MARGUERITE				1850	
8071	BOUCHER	LOUIS			RRS			MCGILLIS	CATHERINE				1840 65	
443	BOUCHER	PAUL	MET	RC		1841	439	NABASE	JULIENNE	MET	RC	RRS	1817	3559
445	BOUCHER	PAUL	MET	RC		1779	445	ST GERMAIN	N	MET	RC	OTH	1843	
446	BOUDREAU	ALEXANDRE	MET	RC	RRS	1821		MARCELLAIS	FRANCOISE	MET		RRS	1770	3356
448	BOUDREAU	FRANCOIS	MET		NWT	1834		MCGILLIS	LOUISA	MET	RC		1830	
450	BOUDREAU	FRANCOIS						LEABRECHE	MARGRET	EUR		RRS	1834	

TABLE 1: GENEALOGIES OF RED RIVER HOUSEHOLDS, 1818-1870

ID	MALE HEAD OF FAMILY	RACE	FAITH	BIRTH PLACE	DATES	DADS ID	FEMALE HEAD OF FAMILY	RACE	FAITH	BIRTH PLACE	DATES	DADS ID
451	BOUDREAU FRANCOIS	EUR	RC	LC	1811	450	AUBUCHON AMELIA	MET	RC	RRS	1827	143
453	BOUER BAPTISTE						MCMULLEN HELENE	MET		RRS	1845	
454	BOULTON JOSEPH					458	MARY					
455	BOURASSA AMBROISE			RRS	1841		OUELLETTE GENEVIEVE			RRS		3765
456	BOURASSA JEAN BTE					456	TALLIE MARIE					
456	BOURASSA JOSEPH	MET	RC	RRS	1845		PELLETIER MAGDELEINE					
457	BOURASSA LOUIS						LADOUCEUR PHILOMENE	MET	RC	RRS	1853	2503
458	BOURASSA MICHEL	MET					GRANDBOIS GENEVIEVE	MET		RRS	1810	2026
459	BOURASSA AUGUST						BEAULIEU GENEVIEVE	MET				259
460	BOURBON	MET	RC		1800		MARGUERITE	MET				
463	BOURIER ANTOINE	MET	RC	RRS	1825		JANNOT MAGDELEINE	MET	RC	RRS	1840	2356
465	BOURKE ANDREW	MET	P	RRS	1834	466	WELSH MADELEINE	MET	P	RRS	1837	5155
466	BOURKE EDWIN	MET	P	RRS	1835	466	HALLET ISABELLA	MET	P	RRS	1841	2101
467	BOURKE JOHN	MET	P	RRS	1822	467	FIDLER ELIZABETH	MET	P	RRS	1830	1531
601	BOURKE JOHN	EUR	RC	IRE	1792		CAMPBELL NANCY	MET	P	USA	1794	662
468	BOURKE WALTER	EUR	RC	RRS	1800		CAMPBELL MARY	EUR	P	RRS	1805	
469	BOUSQUET HENRI	MET	RC	RRS	1825	467	HALLET FLORA	MET	P	RRS	1834	2100
470	BOUSQUET LOUIS	MET	RC	RRS	1845	471	WILKEY MARGUERITE	MET	RC	RRS	1846	5187
471	BOUSQUET LOUIS	MET	RC	RRS	1849	473	ST DENIS ELISE	MET	RC	RRS	1847	
472	BOUSQUET LOUIS				1823	472	FISHER BETSEY	MET	RC	RRS	1823	1568
473	BOUSQUET MICHEL	MET		RRS	1800		MARIE	MET			1800	
474	BOUSQUET WILLIAM	MET			1810	473	VENDETTE LOUISA	MET		RRS	1825	
475	BOUVET CHARLES	EUR		RRS	1835	476	LECLAIR MARGUERITE	MET	RC	RRS	1835	2857
476	BOUVET FRANCOIS	EUR	P	CAN	1797 62		VANDRY SUSAN	MET		RRS	1839	5078
481	BOYD ALFRED	EUR	P	ENG	1825		MARCHAND MARGARET				1800	
482	BOYD ANDREW	EUR	P	UC	1846		WARNER SARA	EUR	P	ENG	1843	
483	BOYDEN GEORGE	MET	P	USA	1840		GOWLAR JANE	EUR		RRS	1851	2020
9	BOYER BAPTISTE	MET	RC	RRS	1845	3	CORRIGAL ELISE	MET	RC	RRS	1810	962
9	BOYER BAPTISTE	MET	RC	RRS	1845	3	MCMILLAN HELENE	MET	RC	RRS	1849	3459
8	BOYER ISADOR	MET	RC	RRS	1829	3	BOUSQUET ELIZABETH	MET	RC	RRS	1843	471
4	BOYER JEAN BTE	EUR	RC	RRS	1807	1	BOUDREAU MARIE	MET	RC	NWT	1835	451
12	BOYER JOSEPH	EUR	RC	RRS	1807	5	ALLARY MARGUERITE	MET	RC	RRS	1824	42
1	BOYER LOUIS	EUR	RC		1830	3	ALLARD ELISE	EUR	RC	RRS	1835	58
6	BOYER LOUIS	EUR					PATENAUDE FELICITE	EUR				
3	BOYER PIERRE	MET			1828 58	2	LECUYER LOISETTE	EUR				4711
7	BOYER PIERRE	MET	RC	NWT	1786		TROTTIER MADELEINE	MET	RC	RRS	1822	
11	BOYER WILLIAM	MET		RRS	1825		BONNEAU MARGUERITE	MET	RC	RRS	1810	3064
484	BRABANT AUGUST	MET		RRS	1840	484	MARTIN GENEVIEVE	MET		RRS	1826	471
485	BRABANT AUGUSTIN	MET					BOUSQUET GENEVIEVE	MET		RRS	1847	
486	BRACONNIER AMABLE	MET	RC	RRS	1830	489	PHILIPS JULIE	MET	RC	RRS	1832	4480
487	BRACONNIER ANTOINE	MET	RC	RRS	1838	486	STEVENSON BETSY	MET	RC	RRS	1830	
488	BRACONNIER DANIEL	EUR	RC	RRS	1847	489	BIRD SARAH	EUR	RC	RRS	1841	1363
490	BRACONNIER JEAN	MET	RC	RRS	1828		DUCHARME SARAH	MET	RC	NWT	1850	5118
489	BRACONNIER JEAN BTE		RC	CAN	1791		VILLEBRUNE JULIE	MET	RC	USA	1831	202
496	BRAMNER PETER		RC		1830		BEAUCHEMIN ELISE		RC	NWT	1790	
519	BRASSEAU LOUIS	EUR	RC	USA	1774		DUBOIS JOSEPHTE	MET			1835	
519	BRASSEAU LOUIS	EUR	RC	USA	1774		MINVILLE MARGUERITE				1780 10	
520	BRASSEAU LOUIS	MET	RC	RRS	1807	519	LAGARDE ISABELLE				1800 69	
520	BRASSEAU LOUIS						RICHARD MARIE	MET	RC	RRS	1820	4170

TABLE 1: GENEALOGIES OF RED RIVER HOUSEHOLDS, 1818-1870

ID	MALE HEAD OF FAMILY		RACE	FAITH	BIRTH PLACE	DATES	DADS ID	FEMALE HEAD OF FAMILY		RACE	FAITH	BIRTH PLACE	DATES	DADS ID
491	BRAYANT	ANTOINE			RRS	1825		AZURE	JOSEPHTE			RRS	1826	149
1674	BRAYANT	ANTOINE				1800	1674		GENEVIEVE			RRS	1800	
507	BRELAND	ALEXANDER	MET	RC	RRS	1803 59	507	WELLS	EMILIE	MET	RC	RRS	1810	5152
513	BRELAND	ALEXANDER	MET			1842	508	JANNOT	CATHERINE	MET	RC		1851	2356
516	BRELAND	CLEMENT		RC	RRS	1850		HAMELIN	F	MET			1855	
509	BRELAND	FRANCOIS	MET	RC	RRS	1839	507	MONTOUR	MARIE	MET	RC	RRS	1843	3159
512	BRELAND	GILBERT	MET	RC	NWT	1832	507	BOYER	FILICITE	MET	RC	RRS	1846	3776
510	BRELAND	MOISE	MET	RC	RRS	1811	506	PAGE	PHILOMENE	MET	RC	NWT	1820	2030
508	BRELAND	PASCAL	MET	RC		1837	508	GRANT	MARIE	MET	RC	RRS	1841	1056
511	BRELAND	PATRICK	MET	RC	RRS		508	DEASE	HELENE	MET	RC			
506	BRELAND	PIERRE							JOSEPHTE	MET	RC	RRS	1846	3780
514	BRELAND	THOMAS	MET	RC	RRS	1842	508	PAGE	PHILOMENE	MET	RC	NWT	1800	4729
492	BREMNER	ALEXANDER	MET	P	RRS	1793	492	TWAT	ELIZABETH	MET	P	RRS	1844	1531
494	BREMNER	ALEXANDER	MET	RC	NWT	1832	492	FIDLER	VICTORIA	MET	P	NWT	1842	5151
500	BREMNER	CHARLES	MET	RC		1835	492	WELLS	EMILY	MET	P	RRS	1834	1535
499	BREMNER	JAMES	MET	RC		1830		FIDLER	LETITIA	MET	RC	RRS	1811 34	
493	BREMNER	JOSEPH	EUR	P	IRE	1803		MCKAY	DOROTHEA	EUR	RC	OTH	1844	1754
521	BREMNER	MICHEL	EUR	RC		1821	497	KENNEDY	ELLEN	MET	P	RRS	1853	4725
503	BREMNER	PETER	MET	P	NWT	1845 53		TURCOTTE	MARGUERITE	MET	P	NWT	1827	
498	BREMNER	THOMAS		P	RRS		492	SUTHERLAND	LOUISA	MET	P		1822	2211
497	BREMNER	WILLIAM	MET	P		1824		HOGUE	MARY	MET	P		1837	4574
530	BROOKS	DAVID	EUR	P	CAN	1833		SWAIN	ELIZABETH	MET	P		1806	4391
532	BROWN	HENRY	EUR	P	ORK	1799	533	SLATER	ISABELLA	MET	P		1851	
536	BROWN	JAMES	MET	P		1846	532	ALLARY	MARY	MET	P		1840	4516
547	BROWN	JAMES	MET	P		1837	541	SUTHERLAND	ELIZABETH	MET	P		1825	4169
540	BROWN	JOHN	MET	P		1820		RICHARD	NANCY	MET	P		1780	
542	BROWN	JOHN	EUR	P		1778			ELIZABETH	EUR	P		1789	
541	BROWN	JOSEPH	EUR	P		1787		OLIVER	ELIZABETH	MET	P	ENG	1811	492
543	BROWN	MAGNUS	EUR	P	SCT	1813		BREMNER	ANN	EUR	P		1818	
533	BROWN	PETER	EUR	P	ORK	1806 58	532	BIRD	SARAH	MET	P		1844	
546	BROWN	PETER	EUR	P		1843	532	BIRD	ANNIE	MET	P		1842	377
534	BROWN	PIERRE	MET	P	NWT	1839		MOWAT	MARY ANNE	MET	P	NWT		
538	BROWN	THOMAS	MET	P	ORK	1827	541	SCOTT	JANE	MET	P		1844	4352
539	BROWN	THOMAS	EUR	P	SCT	1839		SPENCE	JANE	MET	P			
544	BROWN	WILLIAM	EUR	P	ORK	1809		OMAND	CRAWFORD	MET	P	NWT	1829	3759
548	BROWN	WILLIAM	MET	P		1819			CHARLOTTE	IND				
1682	BROWN	WILLIAM	EUR	P	OTH	1836		DANIEL	INDIAN	MET	P		1838	1014
549	BROWNSEL	ANGUS	EUR	P	NWT	1810	553	MONTOUR	ELIZABETH	MET	P	RRS	1819	3116
556	BRUCE	ANTOINE	MET	RC	RRS	1809	553	PERREAULT	JOSETTE	MET	RC	RRS	1820	3906
555	BRUCE	BAPTISTE	MET	RC	RRS	1809	553	BEAUCHEMIN	CATHERINE	MET	RC	RRS	1820	202
555	BRUCE	BAPTISTE	MET	RC					CATHERINE	MET	RC		1820	
552	BRUCE	BENJAMIN	MET		OTH	1775	558		MATHILDA	MET			1778	
575	BRUCE	BENJAMIN	MET			1844	558	COOK	ELIZABETH	MET			1842	945
573	BRUCE	GAVIN	MET			1837	564	BROWN	LAETIT	MET			1848	532
565	BRUCE	GEORGE	MET			1846	552	MURRAY	CHRISTINE	MET			1850	3255
571	BRUCE	HERMENGILDE	MET	RC	RRS	1801	554	LACERTE	ADELE	MET	RC	RRS	1801	2469
558	BRUCE	JAMES	MET	P	NWT	1815	558	MCNAB	MARY	MET		NWT	1825	3463
560	BRUCE	JAMES	MET	P	NWT	1848	558	GARRIOCH	ELIZABETH	MET	P	RRS		
566	BRUCE	JAMES	MET	P	RRS	1834		GARRIOCH	ELIZABETH	MET	P	RRS	1853	1827
568	BRUCE	JAMES	MET	P	RRS			LIVINGSTON	ANN	EUR	P	RRS	1840	2972

TABLE 1: GENEALOGIES OF RED RIVER HOUSEHOLDS, 1818-1870

ID	MALE HEAD OF FAMILY	RACE	FAITH	BIRTH PLACE	DATES	DADS ID	FEMALE HEAD OF FAMILY	RACE	FAITH	BIRTH PLACE	DATES	DADS ID
551	BRUCE JOHN	MET	P	RRS	1822	558	GROAT JANE	MET	P	RRS	1836	
570	BRUCE JOHN	MET	RC	NWT	1830	553	GAUDRY ANGELIQUE	MET	RC	NWT	1830	1918
13400	BRUCE JOHN						HICKENBURG JANE					
574	BRUCE JOSEPH	MET	RC	RRS	1846	561	LADOUCEUR ISABEL	MET	RC	RRS	1852	2501
561	BRUCE LOUISON	MET	RC	NWT	1821 61		DELORME ROSALIE	MET	RC	RRS	1822	1114
13390	BRUCE PATRICK	MET	P		1848		GARRIOCH ELIZABETH	MET	P		1853	1827
567	BRUCE PETER	MET	P	RRS	1835	558	HALLET CATHERINE	MET	RC	RRS	1845	2101
553	BRUCE PIERRE	MET	RC	NWT	1785 64	577	DESROSIERS MARGUERITE				1785	
563	BRUCE PIERRE		P	NWT	1824 61		LAVALLEE MARIE				1826	
554	BRUCE WILLIAM	MET	P	NWT	1795 56	577	ALLARY FRANCE	MET	P	NWT	1797	
839	BRUHLER ANTOINE				1800		RENDISBERGER ELIZABETH			NWT	1800	
578	BRUNEAU FRANCOIS	MET	RC	NWT	1810 65	578	HARRISON MARGUERITE	MET	RC		1809 65	2592
579	BRUNEAU THOMAS	MET	RC	RRS	1833		LANDRY ADELAIDE	MET	RC		1839	
583	BRUNET JEAN BTE				1810		BRUYERE MARGUERITE				1812	
582	BRUNNER PETER	MET	RC		1843		TURCOTTE MARGARET	MET	RC		1852	4725
586	BRUYERE JEAN BTE	MET	RC	CAN	1772 41	586	SERPENT FRANCOISE	IND			1791 52	
587	BRUYERE JEAN BTE	MET	RC	NWT	1811	587	GUILBEAULT ANGELIQUE	MET	RC		1815	2055
588	BRUYERE JOSEPH	MET	RC		1826		MAINVILLE FRANCOISE	MET	RC		1827	
523	BRUYERE LOUIS	MET		RRS	1845		SUZETTE	MET			1850	
590	BRYANT WILLIAM	EUR	P	ENG	1821		MILLHAM CAROLINE	EUR	P	RRS	1823	
593	BUBIE JEAN BTE	MET		RRS	1805		COURCHENE MARY	MET		ENG	1810	967
594	BUDD HENRY	MET	P		1814		WORK BETSY	MET		RRS	1820	
596	BUNN JOHN	MET	P	ENG	1803 61		THOMAS CATHERINE	MET	P		1810 34	
597	BUNN THOMAS	EUR	P	ENG	1765		SINCLAIR PHOEBE	MET	P		1792 48	
598	BUNN THOMAS	MET	P	RRS	1830		HARRIOT RACHEL	MET	P	RRS	1840	
599	BUNN WILLIAM	MET	P	NWT	1817		CAMPBELL MAGDELEINE	MET	P	NWT	1822	
602	BURNARD ONES	EUR			1780		MCLEOD SUZETT	MET			1785	2137
603	BURR FREDERICK				1835		HENRY SARAH	MET			1840	658
604	BUSHEN JEAN BTE	MET			1818		BONNEVILLE MARY	MET			1830	
608	BUTLER JOHN	EUR	RC	IRE	1820		CRAMER ANN	MET			1815	
609	BUTTS JOHN	EUR	RC	IRE	1808 68		PURCELL JULIE	EUR	RC	IRE	1810 60	425
609	BUTTS JOHN	EUR	P	IRE	1808 68		WATTS ELEONOR	EUR	RC	IRE	1809	977
611	BUXTON HENRY	EUR	RC	ENG	1792		THOMAS FRANCISE				1795	
622	CADOTTE AUGUSTIN	MET			1837 62	616	LAFERTE ANGELIQUE	MET	RC		1840	2504
617	CADOTTE BAPTISTE	MET	RC	RRS	1830	616	PILON ELISE	MET	RC	RRS	1839	3935
613	CADOTTE JOSEPH	MET	RC	RRS	1813	612	CHARTRAND CHRISTINE	MET	RC	RRS	1843	
618	CADOTTE JOSEPH	MET	RC	CAN	1832	616	CARRON SUSAN	IND			1760	687
612	CADOTTE LAURENT	MET	RC	NWT	1758	616	WILLIAM BETSY	MET			1786	
616	CADOTTE LAURENT		RC	RRS	1786	613	COCHRANE NANCY	MET	RC	RRS	1820	
619	CADOTTE MICHEL	MET	RC	RRS	1811	631	BLONDIN JULIE	MET	P	RRS	1820	
620	CADOTTE PIERRE	MET	P	RRS	1829	628	DESMARAIS CATHERINE	MET	RC	RRS	1835	1236
621	CADOTTE PIERRE	MET		RRS	1843	626	LYONS CHARLOTTE	MET	RC	RRS	1849	3008
626	CALDER GEORGE	MET		NWT	1823		REIN NANCY	MET		NWT	1827	
624	CALDER HORATIO	MET	P		1806		GIBSON MARIA	MET			1810	
627	CALDER JAMES	MET	P		1826		NANCY	MET	P		1834	1955
631	CALDER JAMES	MET			1785		NANCY	MET			1786	
628	CALDER JOHN	EUR			1790		HUMPHREY SARAH	MET	P		1786	
629	CALDER MARCUS	EUR					MARGARET	IND			1795	
632	CALDER PETER	MET			1810		BOUSQUET LOUISE	MET		RRS	1815	1490
623	CALDER THOMAS	MET	P	RRS	1844		FOLSTER ANNIE	MET	P		1847	

TABLE 1: GENEALOGIES OF RED RIVER HOUSEHOLDS, 1818-1870

ID	MALE HEAD OF FAMILY	RACE	FAITH	BIRTH PLACE	DATES	DADS ID	FEMALE HEAD OF FAMILY	RACE	FAITH	BIRTH PLACE	DATES	DADS ID
630	CALDER WILLIAM	MET	P		1840		SINCLAIR MARIA	MET	P	NWT	1833	4390
633	CALDER WILLIAM		P		1785		PAMAREAU SARAH	MET	P		1788	4340
636	CALDWELL LUKE	MET	P		1838		SABISTON SARAH	MET	P		1843	
638	CAMERON ALEXANDER	EUR	P		1831	644	WALKER CATHERINE	EUR	P		1841	
639	CAMERON ALLAN	EUR	P		1820		LEWIS EMMA	IND			1824	
640	CAMERON DOUGAL		P		1770		LESPERANCE MARIE	IND			1770	
644	CAMERON EWEN	EUR	P	SCT	1793 66		MCLEAN MARY	EUR	P	SCT	1797	
645	CAMERON HUGH	EUR	P		1792		JORDAN MARY		P		1795	
650	CAMERON JAMES	IND	P		1828		BALLENDINE JANE		P		1834	
649	CAMERON JOSEPH	MET	P	RRS	1842	652	ADAM MARIE	MET	RC	RRS	1844	177
3517	CAMERON PETER			NWT			JOKAN ELIZABETH					27
648	CAMERON THOMAS				1827 63		BADGER SOPHIA	MET		RRS	1832	
648	CAMERON THOMAS				1827 63		RICHARD ELIZABETH	MET			1817	
655	CAMPBELL ALEXANDER				1815	655	THORNE LOUISE				1825	4689
672	CAMPBELL ALEXANDER	EUR	P		1820		JORDAN ANGELIQUE	EUR		RRS	1847	532
656	CAMPBELL ANGUS				1845		BROWN CATHERINE	MET		RRS	1801 62	
665	CAMPBELL ARCHIBALD	MET	P	NWT	1850	658	MCGILLIVRAY ELIZABETH	MET	P	RRS	1844	4685
658	CAMPBELL COLIN	EUR	P		1790		THOMAS FRANCIS				1798	
657	CAMPBELL DUNCAN	MET	P	NWT	1842	658	SUTHERLAND CATHERINE	MET	P	RRS	1820	
660	CAMPBELL DUNCAN	MET	P	NWT	1810	661	HENRY NANCY	MET	P	NWT	1785	
660	CAMPBELL DUNCAN	MET	P	NWT	1810	661	CATHERINE				1827	
661	CAMPBELL DUNCAN				1780		PRUDEN ANN				1848	
842	CAMPBELL DUNCAN				1820	658	SCOTT ELIZA	MET	P	RRS	1778	4035
666	CAMPBELL JAMES	MET	P	NWT	1840		DEMONTIGNY CATHERINE	IND			1848	4352
662	CAMPBELL JOHN	EUR	P		1775	671	FRASER BARBARA	EUR	P		1833	
663	CAMPBELL NEIL	EUR	P	RRS	1847		ANNE				1836	
671	CAMPBELL NEIL				1830 55		MCDONALD MARGARET	MET	RC	RRS	1840	
664	CAMPBELL PAUL	MET	RC	USA	1833		BOUSQUET JESSIE	IND	P	USA	1825	3324
667	CAMPBELL RODRICK	EUR	RC	SCT	1842	677	BREMNER ISABELLE	MET	P	RRS	1780	473
670	CAPISISET JOSEPH	IND	RC	NWT	1834		GUIBOCHE ELIZABETH	MET	RC	NWT	1829	492
675	CAPLETTE DENIS	MET	RC	RRS	1823	677	WARD ANGELIQUE	MET	RC	RRS	1828	
677	CAPLETTE JOSEPH		RC	CAN	1770 62	677	DAIGNEAULT MARIEANNE				1816	5146
1600	CAPLETTE JOSEPH	MET	RC	RRS	1827		GENEVIEVE	MET	RC	RRS	1849	1007
1600	CAPLETTE JOSEPH	MET	RC	RRS	1827		ROCHON ISABEL	MET	RC		1802	
681	CAPLETTE LOUIS	MET	RC		1814		MOREAU ELISE				1843	3162
693	CARDINAL ALEXANDER				1845		MARIE				1802	
691	CARDINAL ANTOINE		RC	RRS	1800		COMTOIS JOSEPHTE	MET	RC	RRS	1843	
695	CARDINAL CHARLES	MET	RC		1834		DESMARAIS JOSEPHTE	IND			1792	
683	CARDINAL JACQUE				1790	689	LOUISE				1813	
689	CARDINAL JEREMIE		RC		1797	691	ADAM FRANCOISE	MET	RC	RRS	1833 70	24
688	CARDINAL JEREMY	MET	RC	RRS	1842	700	SAYER MADELEINE	MET	RC	RRS	1833	4269
692	CARDINAL NARCISSE				1831		GARIEPY MADELEINE		RC	CAN	1842	1898
765	CARRIBOU FRANCOIS	MET	RC		1841		RACETTE JOSEPHETTE	MET	RC		1822	
705	CARRIERE JEAN	MET	RC	RRS	1821	712	BEAUCHEMIN PHILOMENE	MET	RC	RRS	1843	
702	CARRIERE ADRIEN	MET	RC	NWT	1839		DUCHARME SUZANNE	MET	RC	RRS	1803	202
707	CARRIERE ALEXIS	EUR	RC	CAN	1810	712	LYONS ANGELIQUE	EUR	RC		1791 61	
709	CARRIERE ANDRE	MET	RC	RRS	1782	707	MCIVER CATHERINE	MET	RC	RRS	1839	3375
712	CARRIERE ANDRE	MET	RC	RRS	1830		RIVARD MARIE ANNE	MET	RC	RRS	1809	4192
716	CARRIERE ANDRE	MET	RC	RRS	1808		GLADU MARIE	MET	RC	RRS	1849	717

TABLE 1: GENEALOGIES OF RED RIVER HOUSEHOLDS, 1818-1870

ID	MALE HEAD OF FAMILY	RACE	FAITH	BIRTH PLACE	DATES	DADS ID	FEMALE HEAD OF FAMILY	RACE	FAITH	BIRTH PLACE	DATES	DADS ID
711	CARRIERE AUGUST	MET	RC	RRS	1840	712	DENNING SARAH	MET	RC	RRS	1845	1227
710	CARRIERE CHARLES	MET	RC	RRS	1821	712	BEAUCHEMIN CECILE	MET	RC	RRS	1842	194
714	CARRIERE DANIEL	MET	RC	RRS	1823	707	LANDRY DOROTHEE	MET			1824	2592
704	CARRIERE ELIE	MET	RC	RRS	1842	702	HOGUE FLAVIE	MET	RC	RRS	1852	2205
717	CARRIERE ELIE	MET	RC	RRS	1821	707	LANDRY ELMIRE	MET	RC	RRS	1824	2592
708	CARRIERE FRANCOIS	MET	RC	RRS	1830	707	MORIN THERESE	MET	RC	NWT	1832 70	4465
135	CARRIERE J	MET	RC		1843		STEAD ANN				1830	3032
719	CARRIERE LOUIS	MET	RC	RRS	1814	707	MARCHAND JULIE	MET	RC		1815	739
720	CARRIERE MOISE	MET	RC		1819	707	CHAMPAGNE JOSEPHTE	MET	RC	NWT	1828	3457
703	CARRIERE SOLOMON	MET	RC		1839	702	MCMILLAN MARIE	MET	RC		1842	
877	CARRON ALFRED		RC		1849		JOSEPHINE	MET	RC		1850	
687	CARRON ANTOINE	MET	RC	CAN	1784		ST GERMAIN ANGELIQUE	MET	RC		1788	1387
697	CARRON JEAN	MET	RC	RRS	1833	687	DUMAS MARGUERITE	MET	RC	RRS	1844	4457
778	CARTWRIGHT DAVID	EUR		ORK	1827		SPENCER SARAH	EUR			1840	
767	CASITAR ALEXANDRE	EUR	RC	ORK	1835		WHITFORD MARGARET				1837	3356
777	CAYEN EUSTACHE				1830	727	MCGILLIS MARIE				1833	
770	CAYEN LOUISON				1810		BEAULIEU EUPHROSINE				1815	
724	CAYEN CHARLE				1843		INDIAN INDIAN	IND			1845	
726	CHABOYER CHARLE	MET	RC		1843		C FRANCOISE	MET			1839	
731	CHABOYER JOSEPH	MET	RC		1834		BONNEAU NANCY	MET			1842	417
774	CHABOYER JOSEPH	MET	RC		1803		BONNEAU LOUISE	MET			1820	759
728	CHABOYER LOUIS	MET	RC	NWT	1844	727	CHARTRAND BETSY	MET			1842	3789
727	CHABOYER NORBERT	MET	RC	NWT	1840	727	PANGMAN PHILOMENE	MET			1842	1219
730	CHABOYER PIERRE	MET	RC		1839		DEMONTIGNY JULIA	MET		RRS	1839	
781	CHALE JEAN BTE	EUR	P	ENG	1853		BRAULT JOSEPHTE	MET			1853	5043
733	CHALIFOUX LOUIS	MET	RC	RRS	1849	736	LAVALLEE MARGUERITE	MET	RC	RRS	1853	4805
734	CHALIFOUX MICHEL	MET	RC	CAN	1757	736	SHORT ELIZABETH	MET	RC		1760	
735	CHALIFOUX MICHEL	MET	RC	NWT	1805	735	COLLIN FRANCOISE	MET	RC	RRS	1815	3926
736	CHALIFOUX MICHEL	MET	RC	NWT	1805	735	PICHE MARGUERITE	MET	RC		1820	735
779	CHAMBERLAIN JOHN	EUR	P	ENG	1841		BRELAND NANCY	MET	P	RRS	1834	1535
729	CHAMPAGNE AMBROISE	EUR	RC		1848		FIDLER JUDITH	MET			1850	
739	CHAMPAGNE EMMANUEL	MET	RC	CAN	1801		PARISIEN MAGDELEINE	MET	RC	RRS	1846	2496
738	CHAMPAGNE MAXIME	MET	RC	RRS	1846		LADEROUTE MARIE	MET	RC	NWT	1834	973
737	CHAMPAGNE PIERRE	EUR	RC	CAN	1839	750	COUTETOIS MARGUERITE	MET			1800	120
749	CHARBONNEAU JEAN BTE	EUR	RC	CAN	1797		BEAUCHAMP LOUISE	MET	RC		1780	
750	CHARBONNEAU JOSEPH	EUR			1777		BOUCHER MARGARET	MET			1839	
741	CHARETTE ALEXANDRE	MET	RC	RRS	1841	742	LAMOUREAUX BRIDGET	MET		RRS	1820	686
742	CHARETTE BAPTISTE	MET	RC	NWT	1814		CARDINAL ANGELIQUE	MET			1785	
743	CHARETTE BAPTISTE	MET	RC		1784		PETIT CHARLOTTE	MET			1843 69	
746	CHARETTE BAPTISTE	MET	RC	RRS	1842	747	SANSREGRET MARIE	MET	RC		1841	
745	CHARETTE DANIEL	MET	RC	RRS	1841	747	PARENTEAU MARIE ANN	MET	RC	RRS	1842	245
744	CHARETTE JOSEPH	MET	RC	RRS	1816	743	BELANGER ROSALIE	MET	RC	RRS	1820	921
747	CHARETTE JOSEPH	MET	RC		1800		COLLIN MARIE	MET		RRS	1801 42	2001
845	CHARLES JOHN				1818		GOSSELIN JANE				1816	
876	CHARON AMABLE	MET	RC		1800	752	AULD GENEVIEVE	MET			1802	1969
752	CHARON FRANCOIS			RRS	1822		GLADU LOUISA				1828	
751	CHARON PROSPER			NWT	1840	752	RIVEL MARIE ANNE				1800	
783	CHARTIER ANTOINE	MET	RC	NWT	1840	785	MONETTE JOSEPHTE	MET		RRS	1840	
784	CHARTIER JOSEPH	MET	RC	NWT	1847	785	DORION FANNY	MET		NWT	1842	3143

TABLE 1: GENEALOGIES OF RED RIVER HOUSEHOLDS, 1818-1870

ID	MALE HEAD OF FAMILY		RACE	FAITH	BIRTH PLACE	DATES	DADS ID	FEMALE HEAD OF FAMILY		RACE	FAITH	BIRTH PLACE	DATES	DADS ID
785	CHARTIER	JOSEPH				1813 63		LAVIOLETTE	ANGELIQUE	MET	RC	NWT	1820 55	2848
785	CHARTIER	JOSEPH				1813 63		LAVIOLETTE	MARIE	MET	RC	NWT	1835	2582
799	CHARTRAND	AMBROISE				1820		LAMBERT	JANE	IND			1825	5174
798	CHARTRAND	ANTOINE	MET		RRS	1834		WHITFORD	GENEVIEVE			NWT	1839	
754	CHARTRAND	BAPTISTE	MET		RRS	1837	759		FRANCES	IND			1835	
757	CHARTRAND	BAPTISTE	MET		RRS	1842	759	ROBERT	GENEVIEVE			NWT	1845	
757	CHARTRAND	J BAPTISTE				1842	759	MESSIAPET	MARY	MET			1835	
800	CHARTRAND	LOUIS	MET		NWT	1830	758	MASKEGON	LOUISE	MET			1830	
755	CHARTRAND	MICHEL	MET		RRS	1839	759	DELORME	MONIQUE	MET		RRS	1843	1097
797	CHARTRAND	PAUL	MET		RRS	1829	758	PANGMAN	MARGUERITE	MET		USA	1832	
756	CHARTRAND	PAUL	MET		NWT	1839	759	PANGMAN	MADELIENE	MET		RRS	1842	3123
758	CHARTRAND	PAUL	MET		NWT	1812		MILLET	JOSEPHTE	MET		NWT	1813	616
759	CHARTRAND	PAUL		RC		1800		CADOTTE	LOUISE	IND			1803	
761	CHARTRAND	PIERRE	MET		RRS	1825	762		MARIE	MET	RC	RRS	1829	
762	CHARTRAND	PIERRE				1805	764	VERSAILLES	MARIE	MET			1825	
763	CHARTRAND	PIERRE	MET	P	RRS	1827	759	BERTHELET	M	MET			1805	
764	CHARTRAND	PIERRE	MET		RRS	1850			MARGARET	MET	P		1843	
788	CHATELAIN	LOUIS	MET	P	RRS	1847	789	PANGMAN	MARY	MET		RRS	1855	
786	CHATELAIN	NARCISSE	MET	RC	RRS	1844	787		SARA			RRS	1830	
787	CHATELAIN	NARCISSE	MET	RC	RRS	1821	789	SPENCE	NANCY	MET	P	RRS	1843	4432
787	CHATELAIN	NARCISSE			RRS	1821	789	FINLAYSON	FANNY	MET			1815 69	1563
789	CHENIER	NICHOLAS				1820		HOURIE	NANETTE			RRS	1842	
8061	CHEVALIER	FELIX				1846		CHARTIER	LEVINA				1824	
791	CHEVALIER	SIMON	EUR	P	OTH	1810		POITRAS	LOUISE				1846	
794	CHRISTIANSON	ALPHONSE	EUR			1825		DAOUST	ELISSE	EUR	P	OTH	1815	
844	CHRISTIE	ALEXANDER				1810		GILLIAMSON	ANNE	MET			1839	4384
843	CHRISTIE	ANDREW				1810		THOMAS	MARY	MET			1815	3389
795	CLARK	JAMES	MET			1840		DONALD	MARGARET	MET			1818	138
790	CLARK	WILLIAM		P		1809 56		SINCLAIR	MARY	MET		RRS	1842	4480
803	CLEMENS	JOHN	EUR	P	USA	1846		MCKAY	MARGARET	MET	P		1809	866
803	CLEMENS	JOHN	EUR	P	USA	1843		BEAR	HELEN	MET	P	RRS	1849	
903	CLOUSTON	ALEXANDER	MET	P	NWT	1829		STEVENSON	HENRIETTA	MET	P	RRS	1848	
905	CLOUSTON	JAMES	MET	P	RRS		902	CUNNINGHAM	ELIZA	MET	P	RRS	1849	
3524	CLOUSTON	JAMES				1824			MARGARET				1846	
806	CLOUSTON	JOHN	EUR	P	SCT	1844		MCLEOD	ANN	MET	P	RRS	1840	3439
807	CLOUSTON	JOHN	IND	P	RRS	1793 50	806	COMTOIS	ADELAIDE	MET	RC	RRS	1849	926
902	CLOUSTON	ROBERT	EUR	P	ORK	1823			NANCY	MET			1804 48	
904	CLOUSTON	WILLIAM	EUR	P				CAMPBELL	CATHERINE	MET	P	NWT	1815	658
3523	CLOUSTON	WILLIAM	IND	P	RRS	1845			INDIAN	IND				
810	COCHRANE	ALEXANDER	IND	P		1825	811		NANCY	MET	P	RRS	1843	
909	COCHRANE	G				1835		HARPER	NANCY	IND			1828	3143
812	COCHRANE	HENRY	MET	P	RRS	1835	918	MONETTE	MARIA	MET	P		1840	917
814	COCHRANE	HENRY	MET	P	RRS	1790	918		MARIA	IND		RRS	1844	594
914	COCHRANE	HENRY				1832		BUDD	ELIZABETH	MET	P	RRS		
809	COCHRANE	JAMES	MET		RRS	1802 62			FANNY	MET	P		1790 65	
811	COCHRANE	JOHN				1810			HARRIOT	MET	P		1795	
913	COCHRANE	JOSEPH	MET		RRS	1810		SINCLAIR	MARY	MET	P	RRS	1847	4378
913	COCHRANE	THOMAS				1810			EMMA	IND	P	RRS	1815 34	
913	COCHRANE	THOMAS				1820			CATHERINE				1820	
915	COCHRANE	THOMAS	IND	P	NWT	1790 70		COCHRANE	HARRIET	IND		NWT	1800	

TABLE 1: GENEALOGIES OF RED RIVER HOUSEHOLDS, 1818-1870

ID	MALE HEAD OF FAMILY	RACE	FAITH	BIRTH PLACE	DATES	DADS ID	FEMALE HEAD OF FAMILY	RACE	FAITH	BIRTH PLACE	DATES	DADS ID
808	COCHRANE WILLIAM	MET	P	RRS	1842		STEVENSON ANN	MET	P	RRS	1846 70	4877
917	COCHRANE WILLIAM	MET	P	RRS	1811	815	GIBSON ELIZABETH	MET	P	RRS	1839	
816	COCKS ROBERT	MET	P	RRS	1837		LANDENOR MARY				1835	
821	COLDWELL WILLIAM				1835		ROSS JEMMA				1812	
817	COLLIER ROBERT	EUR	P	IRE	1817 69		RYLIE CATHERINE	EUR	P	IRE	1783	
919	COLLIN ANTOINE	MET	RC	RRS	1780		WAYERS MISHAH	MET	RC	RRS	1847	
920	COLLIN ANTOINE	MET	RC	RRS	1830	921	GODON MARGUERITE	MET	RC	RRS	1805	
921	COLLIN JEAN BTE				1800	919	ALLARY BETSY				1842	
822	COLLIN JOSEPH				1840		GRANDBOIS ANGELIQUE				1840	
923	COMTOIS DAVID	EUR		LC	1826		CATHERINE	IND		USA	1800	
925	COMTOIS ETIENNE		RC	CAN	1771 61		COLLIN MARIE	MET	RC	RRS	1817	
926	COMTOIS ETIENNE	MET	RC	RRS	1819	931	MCKAY CHARLOTTE	MET	RC	RRS	1788 68	3415
8063	COMTOIS ETIENNE				1788		SARCY MARGUERITE				1825	
927	COMTOIS FRANCOIS	MET		NWT	1825		SANDAIVE MARIE	MET	RC	RRS	1820	
930	COMTOIS GILBERT				1815		MARTIN MARGUERITE	MET	RC	RRS	1800	
931	COMTOIS GILBERT				1800		MARIA	MET	RC	RRS	1845	
929	COMTOIS JOSEPH	MET	RC		1848	930	PARISIEN ROSALIE	MET	RC	RRS	1825	3823
823	COMTOIS PIERRE				1825		MARIE				1850	
928	COMTOIS PIERRE	MET	RC	RRS	1845	930	WHITE ELISE	MET	RC	RRS	1818 40	5165
13370	COOK BAPTISTE						SANDERSON NANCY					
833	COOK CHARLES	MET	P	NWT	1815 69	947	LYONS MARY	MET	P		1825	
833	COOK CHARLES	MET	P	NWT	1815 69	947	ANDERSON NANCY	IND		RRS	1810	82
833	COOK CHARLES	MET	P	NWT	1815 69	947	CATHERINE	MET			1825	
932	COOK CHARLES				1826		SPENCE MARGARET	MET		RRS	1850	
935	COOK GILBERT	MET		RRS	1839	936	BRUCE CATHERINE	MET	P	RRS	1819	
936	COOK HENRY	MET	P	NWT	1822	940	GARRIOCH HARRIET	MET		NWT	1842	558
938	COOK JAMES	MET		RRS	1836	940	BRUCE MARY	MET	P	RRS		1826
3619	COOK JAMES						MCKAY NANCY					
3620	COOK JAMES						SINCLAIR JANE					
942	COOK JEREMIAH	MET	P	NWT	1800	947	SPENCE ELLEN	MET	P	NWT	1804	4378
13380	COOK JEREMIAH						CATHERINE					4437
948	COOK JOHN				1810		SANDERSON NANCY				1812	
3621	COOK JOHN		P				SOPHIA					
940	COOK JOSEPH		P	NWT	1792 48	947	SINCLAIR NANCY	MET	P	RRS	1795	947
941	COOK JOSEPH	MET			1820		CATHERINE	MET			1825	
3623	COOK JOSEPH						CHARLOTTE	IND				
3624	COOK JOSEPH						INDIAN					
3626	COOK JOSEPH	IND					SMITH MARY					
937	COOK MATHEW	IND			1840	940	CADOTTE GENEVIVE	MET	P	RRS	1840	3421
829	COOK RICHARD	MET					MCKENZIE MATILDA					
827	COOK ROBERT	MET	P	RRS	1830	942	KIRTON SUSAN J				1851	
943	COOK RODERICK	IND	P	RRS	1845	945	BOUVET CAROLINE	MET	P	NWT	1850	3433
830	COOK SAMUEL	MET		RRS	1846	934	MCLENNAN ELIZA	MET	P	NWT	1847	4368
945	COOK SAMUEL		P		1847	947	FOLSTER ELIZABETH	MET	P	NWT	1815	
945	COOK SAMUEL		P		1804	947	SHORT SUSANNAH				1810 35	
831	COOK THOMAS				1804		GADDY ISABELLA	IND			1837	
3637	COOK THOMAS				1837		MCKAY NANCY	IND		RRS		
13410	COOK THOMAS	IND					BRUCE ANNE					
13420	COOK THOMAS						MCKENZIE CATHERINE					
13430	COOK WILIAM	IND					JANE					
							ELIZABETH					

ID	MALE HEAD OF FAMILY	RACE	FAITH	BIRTH PLACE	DATES	DADS ID	FEMALE HEAD OF FAMILY	RACE	FAITH	BIRTH PLACE	DATES	DADS ID
826	COOK WILLIAM	MET	P	RRS	1839		SMITH MARGARET	MET	P	RRS	1842	4413
934	COOK WILLIAM	IND	P		1810		SPENCE CHARLOTTE	IND			1815	
947	COOK WILLIAM	EUR	P	ENG	1766 46		KAHNAWPAWAMA	IND			1769 13	
947	COOK WILLIAM	EUR	P	ENG	1766 46		COCKING MARY	MET	P		1790 35	
947	COOK WILLIAM	EUR	P	ENG	1766 46		COCKING MARY	MET	P		1818	
3616	COOK WILLIAM	EUR	P	ENG	1766 46		BEARDY MARY	EUR	P		1780	
950	COOPER JEREMI	MET	P	RRS	1842	951	THOMAS CATHERINE	MET	P	RRS	1846	4669
951	COOPER THOMAS				1810		THOMAS CATHERINE	EUR	P		1813	4901
847	CORBETT G O	EUR			1730		BUTT ABIGAIL	EUR	P	UC	1733	
953	CORE JOHN				1820		NANCY	MET			1822	
848	CORNER JOHN	EUR		UC	1736		LISSONS ELIZABETH	EUR	P		1739	
957	CORRIGAL EDWARD	MET	P	NWT	1835	853	MCGILLIVRAY FRANCE	MET	P	RRS	1839	3363
854	CORRIGAL JAMES	MET	P	RRS	1840		SANDERSON ISABEL	MET	P	RRS	1843	4319
853	CORRIGAL JAMES	MET	P	SCT	1795		SUTHERLAND SARAH	MET	P	SCT	1805	4503
853	CORRIGAL JAMES	EUR	P	ORK	1794		MARGARET	IND	P		1803 43	
958	CORRIGAL JAMES	MET	P	NWT	1828	853	FLETT CATHERINE	EUR	P	NWT	1818	4162
958	CORRIGAL JAMES	MET	P	NWT	1828	853	RICHARD MARY	MET	P		1832	
961	CORRIGAL JAMES	MET	P	NWT	1804	849	FIRTH E			NWT	1828 48	77
1680	CORRIGAL JOHN						ANDERSON ANNA	MET			1810	
959	CORRIGAL JOHN	MET	P	RRS	1836	961	STEAD SAIAH	EUR	P	RRS	1847	3091
959	CORRIGAL JOHN	MET	P	RRS	1836	961	MATHESON ALICE	MET	P		1841	2090
962	CORRIGAL JOHN	MET	P	SCT	1821		HALCROW MARIA	MET	P	RRS	1831 75	
1679	CORRIGAL JOSEPH					961	FIRTH ELIZA	EUR	P			
849	CORRIGAL PETER		P	SCT	1782 66		TODD ELIZABETH	IND	P		1751 51	
963	CORRIGAL PETER		P		1819 67		CHRISTIANNA	IND			1822	
8058	CORRIGAL PETER	MET	P			961	MARGARET	IND	P			
850	CORRIGAL THOMAS				1850	958	ELIZABETH	MET	P		1853	2198
964	COTTERELLE LOUIS				1820		DESMARAIS ANN	IND	P		1822	
912	COULOMBRE FRANCOIS		RC		1815 69		HODGSON FRANCI	MET	RC	RRS	1820	3175
966	COULOMBRE FRANCOIS		RC	CAN	1784		MARIE	MET			1786	
856	COULOMBRE JOHNNY	IND			1841		MOREAU JOSEPH	IND	RC		1843	3034
819	COULOMBRE MANATOT	MET	RC	RRS	1842		MARCHAND MARIE	MET		RRS	1844	
970	COURCHENE ALEX	MET	RC	RRS	1835	966	KUWATAYASH WATISQUACUMI	IND		RRS	1839	3841
971	COURCHENE ANTOINE		RC		1823	912	PARISIEN MARGUERITE	MET	RC		1830	1102
968	COURCHENE BAPTISTE			CAN	1820	967	DELORME HELENE	MET	RC		1824	
967	COURCHENE FRANCOIS			CAN	1786		GRANDBOIS GENEVIEVE	IND	RC		1805	51
967	COURCHENE FRANCOIS	MET		RRS	1786		BEAUCHAMP FRANCOISE	MET	RC	RRS	1787	
857	COURCHENE JOSEPH		RC		1819		MADELEINE	IND			1820	
973	COUTETOIS FRANCOIS				1820		BOUCHER MARIE LOUISE	MET	RC		1823	
869	COWAN D	MET			1830		MARIE	IND		RRS	1832	4381
975	COX JOHN	MET	P	RRS	1837	976	SINCLAIR HENRIETTE	MET	P	RRS	1838	
976	COX JOHN	EUR	P	SCT	1799		NANCY	MET	P	NWT	1818	4638
974	COX ROBERT	MET			1836	976	TAYLOR NANCY	MET			1839	4319
980	CROMARTIE JAMES	MET	P	NWT	1826		SANDERSON MARY	MET	P		1826	2404
979	CROMARTIE JOHN		P		1815		INKSTER NANCY	MET	P		1817	
978	CROMARTIE WILLIAM	EUR	P	NWT	1840		HOURIE CATHERINE	EUR	P		1846	2238
981	CROMARTIE WILLIAM	MET	P		1804		HOURIE MARION	IND	P	RRS	1806	
870	CROWLEY T				1835		NORQUAY JANE	MET			1838	3752

TABLE 1: GENEALOGIES OF RED RIVER HOUSEHOLDS, 1818-1870

ID	MALE HEAD OF FAMILY	RACE	FAITH	BIRTH PLACE	DATES	DADS ID	FEMALE HEAD OF FAMILY	RACE	FAITH	BIRTH PLACE	DATES	DADS ID
867	CROWSEN JOSEPH	EUR	RC	ENG	1835	.	CUSSELL HARRIET	EUR	RC	ENG	1834	1908
987	CUMMINGS CHARLES	MET	P	NWT	1810	.	GARRIOCH SARAH	MET	P	NWT	1818	631
986	CUMMINGS CUTHBERT	MET	P	NWT	1824	.	CALDER ELIZABETH	MET	P	NWT	1813	.
3968	CUMMINGS CUTHBERT	MET	.	.	.	.	SUTHERLAND ELIZABETH	MET	P	.	.	2424
990	CUMMINGS DONALD	MET	P	RRS	1842	.	JOHNSTON SARA	MET	.	RRS	1843 66	2959
990	CUMMINGS DONALD	MET	P	RRS	1824	.	LILLIE MARY ANN	.	.	.	1835 66	1954
988	CUMMINGS MALCOLM	MET	.	.	1824	.	GIBSON MARGARET	MET	.	.	1833	.
988	CUMMINGS MALCOLM	.	.	.	1795	.	MOWAT MARY	IND	.	.	1824 45	.
991	CUMMINGS ROBERT	.	.	.	1795	.	ELIZABETH	IND	.	.	1815 45	.
991	CUMMINGS ROBERT	.	.	.	1795	.	CLEMENTINE	IND	.	.	1801 33	.
991	CUMMINGS ROBERT	.	.	.	.	.	MONKMAN JANE	MET	P	RRS	1822	3149
985	CUNNINGHAM ALEXANDER	MET	P	RRS	1852	866	MATHESON CHRISTINE	.	.	.	1850 68	3092
866	CUNNINGHAM JAMES	MET	P	NWT	1826	993	ROSS SARAH	.	.	.	1825	.
866	CUNNINGHAM JAMES	MET	P	NWT	1826	993	PRITCHARD LETITIA	MET	P	RRS	1826	3998
983	CUNNINGHAM JOHN	MET	P	NWT	1820	.	WORK JANE	.	P	NWT	1817	.
993	CUNNINGHAM JOHN	MET	P	NWT	1820	.	LHIRONDELLE	.	P	NWT	1836	.
993	CUNNINGHAM PATRICK	.	.	.	1795	.	BRUCE ANN	MET	.	.	1797	.
874	CURTIS CHARLES	EUR	.	USA	1825	.	ISBISTER C	MET	.	NWT	1837	.
873	CUSITAR DAVID	MET	.	.	1840	.	VIVIER MARGARET	IND	.	.	1842	.
995	CYR FRANCOIS	MET	RC	.	1803	.	MCINTOSH VICTOIRE	MET	RC	.	1813 43	.
994	CYR FRANCOIS	MET	RC	RRS	1840	.	DAUNAIS CHARLOTTE	MET	RC	RRS	1825 65	.
996	CYR GEORGE	MET	RC	RRS	1825	.	BOUCHER ISABELLE	MET	RC	RRS	1844	1023
1000	CYR JOHN	MET	RC	CAN	1832	.	BERARD MARIE	MET	RC	RRS	1827 69	297
997	CYR JOSEPH	EUR	RC	CAN	1797	.	CATHERINE	MET	RC	.	1825	.
1001	CYR LOUIS	EUR	RC	CAN	1797	.	NANCY	MET	RC	.	1799	.
999	CYR LOUIS	MET	RC	RRS	1835	1001	ELISE	MET	RC	.	1805	.
999	CYR PIERRE	MET	RC	RRS	1835	1001	MARTINEAU CATHERINE	MET	RC	CAN	1807	3074
998	CYR PIERRE	MET	RC	.	1801	1001	LAGEMONIER MARIE ANNE	MET	RC	RRS	1842 66	2284
	CYR WILLIAM	MET	RC	.	1823	.	KLYNE ANGELIQUE	MET	RC	RRS	1825	.
1005	DAHL ALEXANDER	EUR	P	UC	1823	1004	FORBISHER JOSEPHTE	MET	P	NWT	1805	5018
1005	DAHL ALEXANDER	EUR	P	UC	1848	1004	VINCENT ELIZABETH	MET	P	NWT	1836	.
1006	DAHL ALEXANDER	MET	P	RRS	1847	1005	FOLSTER JANE	MET	P	RRS	1828 50	.
1003	DAHL JOHN	MET	P	RRS	1781	1005	BIRSTON LETISIA	MET	P	RRS	1851	334
1004	DAHL PETER	EUR	P	OTH	1824	.	CUMMINGS ELIZABETH	EUR	P	NWT	1852	.
1007	DAIGNEAULT JOSEPH	MET	.	CAN	1824 67	1008	MURRAY CATHERINE	MET	RC	RRS	1785 57	.
1008	DAIGNEAULT JOSEPH	MET	.	RRS	1826 64	.	THIBAULT LISETTE	.	P	RRS	1826	.
1012	DANIEL EDWARD	.	P	.	1835	.	CAMERON GENEVIEVE	MET	RC	RRS	1806	640
886	DANIEL GEORGE	MET	P	RRS	1795 69	.	FAVEL ELIZABETH	MET	P	RRS	1838	.
1013	DANIEL GRIFFITH	.	P	RRS	1795 69	.	LAVALLEE MADELEINE	MET	P	RRS	1825 37	.
1013	DANIEL GRIFFITH	MET	P	RRS	1792	.	MCKAY MARGARET	MET	P	.	1797	.
1014	DANIEL JACOB	MET	P	RRS	1825	.	MARGUERITE	MET	P	RRS	1795	.
885	DANIEL JAMES	MET	P	.	1843	1014	GOODWIN JANE	MET	P	RRS	1828	.
883	DANIEL JOHN	MET	.	NWT	1776	1020	MCIVER MARGARET	MET	P	.	1849	.
1015	DANIEL JOHN	MET	P	RRS	1845	1017	JANE	MET	P	.	1778	.
1016	DANIEL JOHN	MET	P	RRS	1810	1013	CALDER ANNIE	MET	P	.	1849	.
1017	DANIEL JOHN	MET	P	RRS	1840	1017	JANE	MET	P	.	1812	.
884	DANIEL JOSEPH	MET	P	RRS	1822	1014	HENDERSON ANN	MET	P	RRS	1841	.
1020	DANIEL WILLIAM	MET	RC	RRS	1822	1020	LINKLATER MARGARET	MET	RC	RRS	1822 46	.
1020	DANIEL WILLIAM	MET	RC	.	.	1020	ROSS BETSY	.	RC	.	1823 48	4246

TABLE 1: GENEALOGIES OF RED RIVER HOUSEHOLDS, 1818-1870

ID	MALE HEAD OF FAMILY	RACE	FAITH	BIRTH PLACE	DATES	DADS ID	FEMALE HEAD OF FAMILY	RACE	FAITH	BIRTH PLACE	DATES	DADS ID
1020	DANIEL WILLIAM	MET	RC	RRS	1822	1014	MITCHELL ISABEL	MET	RC	NWT	1838	3134
880	DAOUST	MET	·	·	1795		MARY	IND	·	RRS	1800	
882	DAOUST ISAAC	MET	RC	·	1845		MARY	MET	RC	RRS	1850	310
1021	DAUNAIS JEAN BTE	MET	RC	RRS	1839	1023	LOGAN ELISE	MET	RC	RRS	1850	
1022	DAUNAIS JEAN BTE	MET	RC	CAN	1810	1026	BERIAULT CATHERINE	MET	RC	RRS	1815	2250
1026	DAUNAIS JOSEPH	MET	RC	RRS	1846	1023	HOURIE ANGELIQUE	MET	RC	RRS	1850	1639
888	DAUNAIS LOUIS	EUR	·	·	1790		FORBISHER ISABEL	EUR	·	·	1795	
1033	DAUPHINAIS ALEXIS	MET	RC	RRS	1841	1031	MAURICE PHILOMENE	MET	RC	RRS	1847	712
890	DAUPHINAIS BAPTISTE	MET	RC	RRS	1828	1035	CARRIERE MARGUERITE	MET	RC	RRS	1838	921
1034	DAUPHINAIS CASIMIR	·	·	·	1838		COLLIN MARIE	MET	·	·	1841	508
1037	DAUPHINAIS JOSEPH	MET	·	·	1813	1035	BRELAND M	MET	·	·	1815	
1032	DAUPHINAIS JOSEPH	MET	·	·	1843	1038	VILLENEUVE DELAGI	MET	·	·	1827	
887	DAUPHINAIS MAXIME	·	·	·	1825		SUTHERLAND ANGELIQUE	MET	·	·	1846	4557
1035	DAUPHINAIS MICHEL	MET	RC	RRS	1826		HOULE MARIE	MET	·	·	1832	
1789	DAUPHINAIS MICHEL	·	RC	CAN	1843		DESCHAMPS MARIE	MET	RC	USA	1845	
897	DAVID BASILE	·	·	·	1781		GREGRISCHE MARIE	MET	·	·	1793	
896	DAVIDSON JOHN	MET	RC	RRS	1829	1044	OUELLETTE VICTOIRE	MET	RC	·	1784	
1044	DAVIS DAVID	MET	RC	RRS	1821		DEFOND THERESE	MET	·	·	1831	
1045	DAVIS DAVID	EUR	·	·	1795		MOWAT MARGARET	·	·	·	1827	
1042	DAVIS GEORGE	MET	·	NWT	1825		DRUANNE JULIE	MET	RC	RRS	1797	
1046	DAVIS JEAN BTE	MET	RC	NWT	1810		JOSETTE	IND	·	·	1836	
895	DAVIS JEAN BTE	MET	RC	NWT	1810		BIRSTON CATHERINE	MET	·	RRS	1814	
1052	DAVIS JOHN	EUR	P	LC	1795		JOSEPHTE	IND	·	·	1827	
1047	DAVIS R A	EUR	P	USA	1839		DESHOMME JULIE	MET	·	·	1804	
1041	DAWSON ANDREW	MET	·	·	1840		NANCY	MET	P	NWT	1848	
	DAYON JACOB	MET	·	·	1827		TRUE SUSAN	EUR	P	USA	1847	
	DAYON JOSEPH	MET	·	·	1790		MORGAN ANNIE	EUR	P	SCT	1829	
1177	DE'SHAW BAPTISTE	·	·	·	1843		DUCHARME ROSALIE	MET	·	·	1790	
1053	DEACON RICHARD	·	·	·	1790		THIBAULT SUZETTE	MET	·	·	1843	
893	DEAN ALEXIS	·	RC	·	1795		ISABELLE	·	·	·	1795	
1054	DEASE CHARLES	·	RC	·	1823		MCBEATH MARY	EUR	·	·	1797	
1056	DEASE JOHN	MET	RC	NWT	1795		SUSANNE	IND	·	RRS	1825	
1057	DEASE JOHN W	EUR	RC	·	1818		DEMONTIGNY LOUISE	IND	·	·	1820	
1058	DEASE PETER	·	·	·	1849		MCMILLAN ANGELIQUE	MET	RC	·	1851	
892	DEASE WILLIAM	MET	RC	RRS	1827	1059	BENOIT GENEVIEVE	MET	RC	·	1827	
1059	DEASE WILLIAM	MET	RC	RRS	1799	1057	CHONINARY	MET	RC	NWT	1806	
1198	DEFOND JOSEPH	MET	RC	RRS	1820	1057	GRANT AGNES	MET	RC	RRS	1851	1930
2083	DEGAIN JOSEPH	IND	P	RRS	1825		GENTHON MARGUERITE	MET	RC	RRS	1832	
899	DEGO MARTIN	EUR	RC	LC	1843		GESBIENS JOSEPHTE	MET	RC	NWT	1822	
715	DEGUIRE JOSEPH	MET	RC	RRS	1825		CHAMPLAIN MARIE	IND	P	RRS	1828	
1067	DEHOMME PIERRE	EUR	RC	RRS	1828		KEKAKIKWONEP ELIZA	IND	·	·	1842	
8011	DELISLE EDMOND	MET	RC	RRS	1850		CHALIFOUX MADELEINE	MET	RC	RRS	1826	
1101	DELORME ALEXIS	EUR	RC	NWT	1802	1102	AMIOTTE ELIZA	·	·	·	1856	
1091	DELORME BAPTISTE	MET	RC	RRS	1845		GAUTHIER HELENE	EUR	RC	RRS	1832	3868
1092	DELORME BAZIL	MET	RC	RRS	1805		PAUL MARGUERITE	MET	RC	·	1853	
1111	DELORME BONIFACE	MET	RC	CAN	1767	1099	ST GEORGE	MET	RC	RRS	1802	
1097	DELORME FRANCOIS	MET	RC	RRS	1833	1102	MCGILLIS MARGUERITE	MET	RC	RRS	1849	
1099	DELORME FRANCOIS						LAFERTE ANGELIQUE	MET	RC	NWT	1805	
1100	DELORME FRANCOIS						MALATERRE CHARLOTTE	IND	RC	·	1775	
							TOURAND ROSALIE	MET	RC	RRS	1845	

TABLE 1: GENEALOGIES OF RED RIVER HOUSEHOLDS, 1818-1870

ID	MALE HEAD OF FAMILY		RACE	FAITH	BIRTH PLACE	DATES	DADS ID	FEMALE HEAD OF FAMILY		RACE	FAITH	BIRTH PLACE	DATES	DADS ID
1100	DELORME	FRANCOIS	MET	RC	RRS	1833	1102	ST GERMAIN	JOSEPHTE	MET	RC	RRS	1850	4592
1128	DELORME	FRANCOIS		RC	NWT	1807	1089	DESMARAIS	MARGUERITE	MET		RRS	1809	3772
1094	DELORME	JEAN BTE	MET	RC		1831		PEPIN	MARGUERITE				1845	
1126	DELORME	JEAN BTE	MET	RC	RRS	1848		ST DENIS	MARGUERITE	MET	RC	RRS	1852	4189
1112	DELORME	JOHN	MET	RC	RRS	1838 69	1113	RITCHOT	LEONILE	MET			1838 60	
1095	DELORME	JOSEPH		RC	CAN	1799	1097	GARIEPY	MARIE ANNE	MET	RC	RRS	1805	5120
1102	DELORME	JOSEPH	MET	RC	NWT	1813	1102	VILLEBRUNE	BRIGITTE	MET	RC		1815	967
1105	DELORME	JOSEPH		RC		1821		BELLISLE	JOSEPHTE	MET	RC		1827	
1108	DELORME	JOSEPH				1822		COURCHENE	ANGELIQUE	MET	RC		1803	
1109	DELORME	JOSEPH				1810		GAURNEAU	ISABEL	MET			1812	
1106	DELORME	LOUIS	MET	RC	RRS	1833	1102	LAFOURNAISE	MARIE	MET	RC		1838	1931
1113	DELORME	LOUIS	MET	RC	RRS	1817	1102	GENTHON	SUZANNE	MET	RC	RRS	1815	553
1114	DELORME	LOUIS	EUR			1795		BRUCE	CECILE	MET	RC	RRS	1797	
1096	DELORME	MOISE	MET	RC	RRS	1837	1097	BELLE	JOSETTE	MET	RC		1844	43
1116	DELORME	NORBERT	MET	RC	RRS	1837	1117	ALLARY	SUSANNE	MET	RC	RRS	1840	1942
1103	DELORME	NORBERT	MET	RC	RRS	1832	1117	GERVAIS	CHARLOTTE	MET	RC	RRS	1838	489
8009	DELORME	PIERRE				1819	1104	DESMARAIS	MARIE	MET	RC	RRS	1835	
1117	DELORME	URBAIN	MET	RC	RRS	1800	1099	BEAUCHEMIN	ADELAIDE	MET	RC		1819 64	
1118	DELORME	URBAIN	MET	RC	RRS	1840		PARISIEN	VICTOIRE	MET	RC	NWT	1815	
1219	DEMONTIGNY	CHARLE	MET			1819	1221	VIVIER	MADELEINE	MET	RC	RRS	1843	1270
1220	DEMONTIGNY	CHARLES	MET			1845		BELANGER	ELISE	MET	RC		1817	4689
1221	DEMONTIGNY	DAVID	EUR			1797		DESJARLAIS	MARIE	MET			1846	
1223	DENNET	ANDREW	MET	P	RRS	1807	1226	THORNE	NANCY	MET			1799	
1134	DENNET	ANDREW	MET	P	RRS	1807	1226	FAGNANT	JOSEPHTE	MET	P	RRS	1825	629
1224	DENNET	WILLIAM	MET	P	RRS	1815	1223	MARTINEAU	MARY	MET			1823	
1226	DENNET	WILLIAM	EUR	P	RRS	1844		MOORE	ELLEN	MET	P	RRS	1849	
1229	DENNING	ANDREW	MET	P	ORK	1780 64		CALDER	MARGARET	MET	P	RRS	1791	
1227	DENNING	EDOUARD			NWT	1840		LOW	ISABEL	IND	P		1845	
1230	DENNING	JAMES	MET			1820		BALLENDINE	SOPHIA	MET	P	RRS	1822	
1234	DENNISON	WILLIAM	EUR	P	ENG	1815		SPENCE	ELIZABETH	IND			1818	
1145	DENOMME	XAVIER	MET			1820		ASSINIBOINE	BETSY	IND	P		1825	
1135	DEOLYNE	BRIAN	EUR	RC	IRE	1830		MCKAY	MARGARET	EUR		RRS	1835	
1138	DEOLYNE	DAN	EUR	RC	OTH	1819	1135	GOUIN	ALICE	MET	P		1824	95
1249	DESAUTELS	JEAN BTE	EUR	RC	LC	1847		FADE	MARGUERITE	EUR	RC	IRE	1845	
1251	DESAUTELS	JEAN BTE	EUR	RC	LC	1830	1251	ANDERSON	JANE	EUR	P	NWT	1826	
								AMIOTTE	MARGARET	EUR	RC	LC	1808	
								LAPORTE	JULIE	EUR	RC		1843	
1151	DESCHAMBAULT	GEORGE	EUR	RC		1805		HAMELIN	LUCIE	MET	RC	RRS	1833	2106
1252	DESCHAMPS	BAPTISTE	MET	RC	USA	1795 70		ALLARY	ISABELLE	MET	RC	NWT	1826	
1253	DESCHAMPS	BAPTISTE	MET	RC	RRS	1819		ALLARY	ISABELLE	MET	RC	RRS	1827	
1254	DESCHAMPS	BAPTISTE		RC		1825		LAPLANTE	CHARLOTTE	MET	RC		1826	2675
1368	DESCHAMPS	FRANCOIS			NWT	1807		MONTOUR	MARIE	MET	RC		1825	
1152	DESCHAMPS	JOSEPH	MET	RC		1824		SAULTEAUX	MARIE	MET	RC		1835	
1153	DESCHAMPS	JOSEPH	MET	RC	RRS	1820		LAFRAMBOISE	ROSE	MET	RC	RRS	1815	
1155	DESCHAMPS	JOSEPH	MET	RC	RRS	1835		BERGER	ROSE	MET	RC		1803	
1255	DESCHAMPS	JOSEPH				1816		HOULE	MARGUERITE	MET			1824 46	
1157	DESCHENAUX	PIERRE	MET	RC	RRS	1800		BEAUDRY	SUZANNE	MET			1825	
1157	DESCHENAUX	PIERRE	MET	RC	RRS	1820		COURCHENE	JOSEPHTE	MET	RC	RRS	1825	967
1256	DESCOLEAUX	ANTOINE				1823		RIVIER	MARIE	MET	RC	RRS	1825	

TABLE 1: GENEALOGIES OF RED RIVER HOUSEHOLDS, 1818-1870

ID	MALE HEAD OF FAMILY	RACE	FAITH	BIRTH PLACE	DATES	DADS ID	FEMALE HEAD OF FAMILY	RACE	FAITH	BIRTH PLACE	DATES	DADS ID
1257	DESCOLEAUX JOSEPH	.	.	.	1785	.	DUMILLE MADELEINE	MET	.	.	1787	.
1260	DESCOLEAUX LOUIS	MET	RC	NWT	.	.	PELLETIER JOSEPHTE	.	.	.	1844	3886
1260	DESCOLEAUX LOUIS	MET	RC	NWT	.	.	AMIOTTE GENEVIEVE	.	.	.	.	.
1258	DESCOLEAUX PIERRE	.	.	.	1816	.	LAPOINTE CHARLOTTE	MET	.	.	1818	.
1158	DESJARDIN ANTOINE	MET	.	NWT	1835	.	GENDRON ANGELIQUE	MET	.	.	1831 67	.
1262	DESJARDIN ANTOINE	.	RC	.	1803 62	.	LAMBERT ISABEL	MET	.	.	1805	.
1070	DESJARDIN BAPTISTE	.	.	.	1845	.	LAFLEUR MADELEINE	MET	.	.	1846	.
1264	DESJARDIN FRANCOIS	MET	RC	RRS	1847	1265	LECLAIR MARGUERITE	MET	RC	RRS	1853	2114
1278	DESJARDIN JEAN BTE	MET	RC	RRS	1799	1265	HAMELIN MARGUERITE	MET	RC	RRS	1819	.
1266	DESJARDIN JOSEPH	MET	.	.	1844	1262	GUIBOCHE GENEVIEVE	MET	.	.	1828	.
1154	DESJARDIN PIERRE	.	.	.	1841	.	WELSH ANGELI	MET	.	.	1841	.
1277	DESJARLAIS ANDRE	MET	.	.	1822	1271	FAGNANT JOSEPHTE	MET	.	.	1826	1461
1284	DESJARLAIS ANDRE	MET	.	.	1843	1276	MORRISETTE ADELAIDE	MET	.	.	1848	3203
2241	DESJARLAIS ANDRE	.	.	.	1819 53	1166	FAGNANT SOPHIE	MET	.	.	1820	.
1270	DESJARLAIS ANTOINE	MET	RC	NWT	1794 64	1271	ALEXIS MARIE	MET	RC	.	1800	.
1270	DESJARLAIS ANTOINE	MET	RC	NWT	1794 64	.	ALLARY CATHERINE	MET	RC	.	.	.
1274	DESJARLAIS ANTOINE	MET	RC	RRS	1818	.	FALCON M	.	.	.	1820	.
1289	DESJARLAIS ANTOINE	MET	.	.	1841	2214	CHARTRAND MARY	MET	.	.	1849	758
1289	DESJARLAIS ANTOINE	MET	.	.	1840	2214	FALCON MARIE	MET	.	.	1846	1483
1290	DESJARLAIS ANTOINE	MET	.	.	1840	1276	PELLETIER JOSEPHTE	MET	RC	.	1844	3886
1275	DESJARLAIS BAPTISTE	MET	RC	NWT	1811	1077	MARTIN MARY	MET	.	NWT	1821	3060
1288	DESJARLAIS BAPTISTE	MET	.	.	1836	1270	GRANT JULIE	MET	.	.	1844	.
1163	DESJARLAIS BENJAMIN	.	.	.	1830	.	KEPEZABAUNID GENEVIEVE	IND	.	.	1832	.
1281	DESJARLAIS CHARLE	MET	RC	RRS	1815	1077	MONTOUR MARGUERITE	MET	RC	.	1820	.
1160	DESJARLAIS D	MET	.	.	1849	.	MCKAY URSULE	MET	.	RRS	1852	.
1078	DESJARLAIS FRANCOIS	.	.	.	1826 67	1269	BONNEAU LOUISE	MET	.	.	1824 46	.
1078	DESJARLAIS FRANCOIS	.	.	.	1826 67	1269	GARIEPY HELENE	MET	.	.	1827	.
1271	DESJARLAIS FRANCOIS	EUR	.	RRS	1795	.	ROY MADELEINE	IND	.	.	1789	.
1276	DESJARLAIS FRANCOIS	MET	.	ORK	1800	.	OTSHIHKAN MARIE	IND	.	ORK	1810	.
1165	DESJARLAIS JEAN BTE	.	.	.	1808	.	CARDINAL CHARLOTTE	.	.	.	1810	.
1282	DESJARLAIS JEAN BTE	MET	.	.	1830	1276	SAULTEAUX GENEVIEVE	IND	.	.	1810	.
1161	DESJARLAIS JEAN BTE	.	.	.	1810	.	FLEURY JOSEPHTE	MET	.	.	1839	1612
1268	DESJARLAIS JOSEPH	MET	RC	NWT	1810	1077	SAYER JOSEPHTE	MET	.	.	1815	4269
1283	DESJARLAIS JOSEPH	MET	.	RRS	1847	1268	RICHARD LOUISE	MET	RC	RRS	1813	.
1285	DESJARLAIS JOSEPH	.	.	.	1845	1275	SLATER MARIE	MET	.	.	1848	4796
2214	DESJARLAIS JOSEPH	.	.	.	1815	.	LAFRENIERE ISABELLE	MET	.	.	1837	2533
1279	DESJARLAIS LOUIS	MET	.	.	1832	1276	RICHARD JOSEPHTE	MET	.	.	1817	.
1190	DESJARLAIS MARCEL	.	.	.	1814	2214	CHARTRAND JULIA	MET	.	.	1831	758
1162	DESJARLAIS MICHEL	MET	.	RRS	1836	1190	CARDINAL BRIGITTE	.	.	.	1816	.
1267	DESJARLAIS MICHEL	MET	.	RRS	1819	1270	DENOMME BETHSY	.	.	.	1838	.
1164	DESJARLAIS PAUL	.	.	.	1830	1270	DAVIS MARGUERITE	MET	RC	.	1819	1190
1168	DESJARLAIS PAUL	MET	.	.	1833	1190	BONNEAU JULIE	IND	.	.	1825	1044
1280	DESJARLAIS PIERRE	MET	.	.	1831	1276	SAULTEAUX SUZANNE	MET	.	.	1832	.
1736	DESJARLAIS STANISLAS	.	.	.	1849	1268	BRABANT GENEVIEVE	IND	.	.	1835	.
1273	DESJARLAIS XAVIER	.	.	.	1822	.	HOULE SARA	IND	.	.	1832	.
							MCKAY VIRGINIE	MET	.	.	1850	.
1086	DESLAURIERS ANTOINE	EUR	RC	LC	1787	.	LACOUTURE MARIE	IND	.	.	1824	.
1122	DESLAURIERS JOSEPH	.	RC	RRS	1814	1316	LAMIRANDE GENEVIEVE	EUR	RC	LC	1801	.
1316	DESLAURIERS JOSEPH	.	.	.	1790	.	ST DENIS GENEVIEVE	EUR	.	.	1795	2586

TABLE 1: GENEALOGIES OF RED RIVER HOUSEHOLDS, 1818-1870

ID	MALE HEAD OF FAMILY	RACE	FAITH	BIRTH PLACE	DATES	DADS ID	FEMALE HEAD OF FAMILY	RACE	FAITH	BIRTH PLACE	DATES	DADS ID
1123	DESLAURIERS NORBERT	EUR	RC	RRS	1839	1086	FORBISHER MARIE	MET	RC	RRS	1844	1639
1235	DESMARAIS BAPTISTE	MET	.	RRS	1812		ERASMUS SOPHIA	MET	.	RRS	1816	
1740	DESMARAIS BAPTISTE		P		1825		PATRICE MARGUERITE	.	P	RRS	1830	
1236	DESMARAIS CHARLES	MET	P	RRS	1806	1236	FAVEL HARRIOT C	.	P	RRS	1816	
1147	DESMARAIS FRANCIS	MET	P	RRS	1831		POCHANT CATHERINE	MET	P		1828	
1238	DESMARAIS FRANCOIS	MET	P	RRS	1804		ANDERSON MARY	MET	P	RRS	1819	
8012	DESMARAIS FRANCOIS				1804		SPENCE HARRIET	.	RC		1815 37	407
1148	DESMARAIS GABRIEL	MET	RC		1838		BOISCLAIR JULIE	MET	RC		1838	
1150	DESMARAIS HENRY C	MET	RC		1845	1235	WHITFORD MARY	MET	.		1851	
1130	DESMARAIS JEAN BTE	MET	RC	RRS	1820		FONTAINE MARIE	IND	.		1825	
1130	DESMARAIS JOHN	MET	RC	RRS	1831	1239	SAULTEAUX MARIE	MET	RC		1837	
1136	DESMARAIS JOHN	MET	RC	RRS	1831	1239	PATENAUDE LOUISE	MET	RC	RRS	1830	
1136	DESMARAIS JOHN	MET	RC	RRS	1841	1241	ROSSELIN HELENE	MET	RC	RRS	1843 66	3850
1189	DESMARAIS JOSEPH	MET	RC		1801		GERVAIS ROSE	.	RC		1844	
1240	DESMARAIS JOSEPH	MET	RC		1798		HAMELIN MARIE	MET	RC		1802	
8015	DESMARAIS JOSEPH	MET	RC	NWT	1810	1191	DUMONT CECILE	MET	RC	RRS	1800	
1241	DESMARAIS JOSEPH	MET			1822		JANNOT ADELAIDE	MET	RC	RRS	1835	
1137	DESMARAIS MICHEL	MET	RC	RRS	1845	1242	CLARMONT ADELAIDE	.	RC		1822 46	
1237	DESMARAIS MICHEL	MET	RC	RRS	1845	1236	GOSSELIN HELENE	MET	RC	RRS	1845	4388
1242	DESMARAIS MICHELL	MET	RC	RRS	1810	1191	SINCLAIR ISABELLA	MET	RC		1843	
1243	DESMARAIS SEVERE	MET	RC	RRS	1822	1189	ROCHON JOSEPHIE	MET	RC	RRS	1815	1262
1171	DESNOYERS EMILE				1851		DESJARDIN MARGUERITE	MET	RC	RRS	1847	
1170	DESNOYERS PIERRE			NWT	1830 66	1292	GREGOIRE MATHILDE	MET	.		1852	
1170	DESNOYERS PIERRE			NWT	1830 66	1292	BOURASSA ANGELIQUE	MET	RC		1837 59	459
1173	DESRIVIERE L				1845		CAPLETTE LOUISE	MET	.		1850	677
1293	DESRIVIERE LOUIS	MET	RC	RRS	1851	1294	NAULT URSULE	.	RC		1851	3711
1294	DESRIVIERE LOUIS	EUR	RC	LC	1814		NAULT MELANIE	EUR	RC	RRS	1834	3698
1295	DESROSIERS JEAN BTE	EUR	RC	LC	1797	2157	LAMBERT MARY	MET	RC	RRS	1826	
2157	DESROSIERS JEAN BTE	EUR		LC	1777		VANDAL MARIE	MET	RC	NWT	1778	5035
1176	DEWIG BOB				1839		BELGARDE SUSANNE	EUR	.		1841 64	
1180	DIONNE LOUIS				1831 58		BRUYERE ISABELLE	.	.		1836	
1178	DIONNE PASCAL	EUR	RC	CAN	1831	1183	ALLARY CATHERINE	.	RC	RRS	1836	
1182	DIVERTISSANT FRANCOIS				1820		MORIN PHILOMENE	MET	.		1818	
1300	DONALD CHARLES	MET	P	RRS	1836		POITRAS EUPHROSINE	EUR	RC	RRS	1828	3195
1306	DONALD GEORGE				1830		INGRAM JANE	EUR	.	ENG	1818	2272
1301	DONALD JOHN	MET	P	RRS	1839	1302	BRASS ELIZABETH	.	.		1836	
1184	DONALD JOSEPH	MET	P	RRS	1843	1305	FIRTH NANCY	MET	P	RRS	1841	
1302	DONALD WILLIAM	MET	P	RRS	1795 69	1302	SINCLAIR CATHERINE	MET	P	RRS	1800	
1303	DONALD WILLIAM	MET	P	RRS	1800	1305	BOLLEN NANCY	MET	P	RRS	1846	
1305	DONALD WILLIAM	MET	P	RRS	1800	1302	FIRTH JANE	MET	P	RRS	1845	
							HARPER MARY	MET	P	RRS	1835	
1192	DONALDSON H T	EUR	RC	LC	1831		HARRIOT ELIZA	MET	.	USA	1805 49	2134
							MARGARET	MET	.		1831	
1309	DONNAIS MICHEL			CAN	1797		ISABELLE	.	.		1800	2137
8017	DOZE LOUIS				1844		DAUPHINAIS CAROLINE	.	.		1844	
1310	DREVER JAMES				1845		MARGARET	.	.		1848	
1311	DREVER WILLIAM	EUR	P	SCT	1802	1311	ROTHNEY HELEN	EUR	.	UC	1802	
1312	DREVER WILLIAM	EUR	P	RRS	1844	1326	HILL JANE	EUR	P		1811 66	
1325	DUBOIS EUGENE	MET	RC	RRS	1847		GEORGE BETSY	MET	RC	RRS	1852	
1322	DUBOIS FRANCOIS	MET	RC	RRS	1775	2649	LARIVIERE ANGELIQUE	MET	RC	RRS	1775	2649

TABLE 1: GENEALOGIES OF RED RIVER HOUSEHOLDS, 1818-1870

ID	MALE HEAD OF FAMILY	RACE	FAITH	BIRTH PLACE	DATES	DADS ID	FEMALE HEAD OF FAMILY	RACE	FAITH	BIRTH PLACE	DATES	DADS ID
1324	DUBOIS FRANCOIS	MET			1850	1326	DESJARDIN ELISE	MET	RC	RRS	1852	1278
1326	DUBOIS FRANCOIS	MET	RC	RRS	1822	1322	LABERGE MADELEINE	MET	RC	RRS	1827	
1319	DUBOIS JEAN BTE	MET	RC	RRS	1849	1320	LAURENCE JOSEPHTE	MET	RC	RRS	1813	
1320	DUBOIS JEAN BTE	MET	RC	RRS	1826	1322	LABERGE MARIE	MET	RC	NWT	1834	
1304	DUBOIS LOUISON	MET	RC	NWT	1825		KIPPLING CATHERINE	MET	RC		1830	5152
1193	DUBOISHUE ALEXANDER				1815	1195	WELLS EMILIE				1820	
1194	DUBOISHUE PASCAL				1816		GRANT MARIE				1820	
1144	DUBOISHUE PETER				1812		SPENCE CATHERINE				1815	
1195	DUBOISHUE PIERRE				1790		BELLYSIS LOUISE				1795	2287
1196	DUBOISHUE ADOLPHUS				1812		KIRKNESS LOUISA	MET		RRS	1847	
1197	DUBRAIL JOSEPH	EUR		LC	1837		HENEAULT MARIE ANNE				1849	961
1335	DUBUC ALEXANDER	EUR	RC	CAN	1840	1336	CORRIGAL CATHERINE	MET	RC		1787 53	
1332	DUCHARME ANTOINE	MET		RRS	1850		RICHARD JOSEPHTE		RC		1780	
1333	DUCHARME ANTOINE		RC		1780		CAROLINE				1793	
1334	DUCHARME ANTOINE			CAN	1776 51		BELLEAU FRANCOISE	MET		RRS	1826	2582
1336	DUCHARME ANTOINE				1793		LAMBERT JANE				1814	
1343	DUCHARME CHARLES				1816 56	1339	PANGMAN ANGELIQUE	MET	RC	RRS	1826	
1344	DUCHARME CHARLES		RC	NWT	1812	1339	LAVALLEE MARIE	IND		NWT	1800	
1346	DUCHARME COLLICH	EUR	RC	LC	1806	1347	HENEAULT CAROLINE	MET	RC	NWT	1818	713
1345	DUCHARME DOMINIQUE	MET	RC	RRS	1803	1346	CARRIERE SOPHIA	MET	RC	RRS	1846	
1347	DUCHARME FRANCOIS				1847		RIVEL JOSEPHTE	EUR			1780	
1349	DUCHARME FRANCOIS		RC	RRS	1770	1350	LAROCQUE LOUISE	MET	RC	RRS	1852	2788
1359	DUCHARME FRANCOIS	MET	P	RRS	1846	1360	HENEAULT CLEMENCE	MET	RC	RRS	1841	
1330	DUCHARME JAMES	MET	RC	RRS	1838	1334	HALCROW CATHERINE	MET	P	NWT	1846	
1338	DUCHARME JEAN BTE	MET			1842	1342	FOYE MARGARET	MET	RC		1827	1576
1341	DUCHARME JEAN BTE	MET			1813	1333	FLAMMAND ANGELIQUE	MET			1850	
1342	DUCHARME JEAN BTE	MET			1848		HOULE VIRGINIE	MET			1825	
1342	DUCHARME JEAN BTE	MET			1826		JOLICOEUR MADELEINE	MET			1825	
1371	DUCHARME JEAN BTE	MET		RRS	1818		ALLARY MARGUERITE	MET		RRS	1825	41
1350	DUCHARME JOSEPH	MET	RC	NWT	1821		RACETTE CATHERINE	MET	RC	RRS	1825	
1353	DUCHARME JOSEPH				1798		MARGUERITE				1800	
1354	DUCHARME JOSEPH	MET	RC	NWT	1810		LAFOURNAISE LISETT	MET	RC	NWT	1820	
1355	DUCHARME JOSEPH	MET	RC	NWT	1829	1354	HOULE MARIE ANN	MET	RC	NWT	1835	2834
1352	DUCHARME LOUIS	MET			1818	1353	LAVERDURE HELENE	MET			1826	1255
1358	DUCHARME LOUIS	MET		USA	1818	1339	DESCHAMPS ISABEL	MET			1823	2510
1337	DUCHARME MOISE	EUR	RC	LC	1830		LAFLEUR JULIA	EUR	RC	RRS	1825	
1339	DUCHARME NICHOLAS				1795		ANGELIQUE	IND			1795	
1360	DUCHARME OLIVER	EUR	RC	LC	1806	1347	GLADU CHARLOTTE	MET	RC	NWT	1816	1969
1356	DUCHARME PIERRE	MET			1827	1339	DESJARLAIS GENEVIEVE				1833	
1362	DUCHARME PIERRE		RC	CAN	1776		SAULTEAUX MARIE	IND			1801	
1363	DUCHARME PROSPER	EUR	RC	RRS	1821	1347	BELLEHUMEUR CATHERINE	MET	RC	RRS	1832	279
1364	DUCHARME ROGER	MET	RC	NWT	1848	1365	TESSIER MARGUERITE	MET	RC	NWT	1849	4654
1365	DUCHARME ROGER	MET			1823		LAFOURNAISE MARIE	MET			1828	
1201	DUFRESNE EDDUARD				1825		MONDION MARGUERITE				1830	
1202	DUFRESNE JOSEPH				1840		VANDAL ISABELLE	MET	RC		1845	5066
1373	DUGANNE JOSEPH				1797		CHATELAIN MARIE				1800	
1203	DUMAINE ALFRED		RC		1846 23	1389	DELIMA ROSE		RC		1845 1	
1375	DUMAS CHARLES			NWT	1824		ST ARNAUD MARIE				1831	
1376	DUMAS CYRILL				1841	1387	VENNE CHARLOTTE	MET			1850	5090

TABLE 1: GENEALOGIES OF RED RIVER HOUSEHOLDS, 1818-1870

ID	MALE HEAD OF FAMILY	RACE	FAITH	BIRTH PLACE	DATES	DADS ID	FEMALE HEAD OF FAMILY	RACE	FAITH	BIRTH PLACE	DATES	DADS ID
1205	DUMAS DAVID	MET	RC	RRS	1847	1387	FARQUARHSON ELISE	MET	RC	RRS	1851	
1378	DUMAS JEAN	MET	RC	RRS	1810		LAFRAMBOISE MARGUERITE	MET	RC	RRS	1805	2586
1384	DUMAS JEAN	MET	RC	RRS	1832	1378	GRAND DOMITILDE	MET	RC	RRS	1834	2541
1380	DUMAS JOSEPH	MET	RC	RRS	1816	1383	LAMIRANDE HENRIETTE	MET	RC		1821	2930
1381	DUMAS MAXIME	MET	RC	RRS	1839	1389	LAGEMONIER MARGUERITE	MET	RC	RRS	1832	
1382	DUMAS MICHEL	MET	RC	RRS	1828	1387	LESPERANCE ADELAIDE	MET			1830	2592
1383	DUMAS MICHEL	EUR	RC	LC	1776		LECLAIR MARGUERITE				1780	
1387	DUMAS MICHEL	EUR	RC	LC	1796	1383	LANDRY HENRIETTE	EUR	RC	RRS	1822	2541
1388	DUMAS PIERRE	MET		CAN	1824		SANCHEAU JOSETTE	MET			1808	
1389	DUMAS PIERRE			RRS	1768	1389	LAGEMONIER JOSETTE				1835	
1206	DUMAS VITAL	MET	RC	RRS	1830		GAGNON JOSEPHTE	MET	RC		1800	
1212	DUMONIER CHARLES	MET			1820		DESJARLAIS JOSEPHE	MET			1837	
1398	DUMONT CECILE	MET			1800	1396	DESMARAIS MARY	MET	RC	RRS	1814	
1391	DUMONT EDOUARD				1845	1394	LETENDRE J	MET			1805	2945
1392	DUMONT ELIE				1847	1394	OUELLETTE SOPHIE	MET			1846	3717
1393	DUMONT ISADORE	MET			1833	1394	PARENTEAU FRANCOISE	IND			1847	3804
1396	DUMONT JEAN BTE	MET			1775		CAREY JUDITH	MET			1780	
1399	DUMONT JEAN BTE	MET			1833	1400	GRAVEL JOSETTE	MET			1835	
1400	DUMONT JEAN BTE	MET			1805	1396	LAFRAMBOISE DOMITILDE	MET			1810	
1402	DUMONT PIERRE				1820		MARGUERITE				1825	
1404	DUMONT VITAL	MET			1844	1402	CAROLINE				1849	
1401	DUMONT XAVIER	MET			1845		LAROCQUE ADELAIDE	MET			1845	
8007	DUPEREY ETIENNE				1839		TREMBLAY CAROLINE	MET			1839	2783
1407	DUPUIS JEAN BTE	MET	RC	RRS	1825	1410	ROCHELEAU MARIE	MET	RC	RRS	1827	4215
1408	DUPUIS JEAN BTE	MET	RC	RRS	1849	1407	PILON EUPHRASINE	MET	RC	RRS	1849	3933
1410	DUPUIS JEAN BTE				1800	1409	HUGHES CECILE	MET	RC	RRS	1805	
1413	DUPUIS PIERRE				1812		BREMNER MARIE	MET			1817	
1414	DURAND JOSEPH				1780		ANGELIQUE	MET			1785	
1386	DURAND ZIPHIRIN				1843		BENDREAU JOSEPHTE	MET			1848	305
8018	DUSSAULT DAVID				1850		GELINAS MADELEINE	MET			1850	
1415	DUVAL ALEXIS	MET			1795	1416	EVELINA	MET			1800	
1181	DYSON	MET			1848		LOUIS FRANCOISE	IND			1853	
1416	DYSON WILLIAM				1823		EMMA	MET	P	RRS	1828	
1419	EASTER JOHN	OTH	P	NWT	1776		NANCY	IND			1796	
1420	ECCLES JOHN	MET	P	RRS	1842		LOGAN MARY	MET	P	RRS	1839	
1167	EDINBURCK HENRY	EUR	P	OTH	1814		STAR CATHERINE	MET	P	RRS	1820	2987
1421	EHRLER JOHN				1800		PLANKIN ROSINA				1803	
1422	ELEMONT EDOUARD	EUR	RC	CAN	1839		LAGEMONIER CAMILLE	MET	RC	RRS	1838	
1423	ELLIOT JAMES				1817		SARAH				1822	
1424	ELLIOT WILLIAM				1822		ELIZABETH				1827	
1208	ELSE HENRY	EUR	P	ENG	1843		FIDLER CATHERINE	MET	P		1841	1532
1209	EMERLING GEORGE	EUR	RC	OTH	1827		MAJOR EMILIE	EUR	RC	OTH	1834	
1435	EMOND JOSEPH	MET	RC	RRS	1843		LAGON ELISE	MET			1848	
1434	EMOND SEPAPHIN	EUR	RC	LC	1822	1434	LARIVIERE MARIE	MET	RC	NWT	1820	2484
1440	ENEAU JEAN BTE	EUR	RC	NWT	1812		HORSEFALL SARAH	MET	RC		1817	
1436	ENGLAND JAMES	EUR			1828		MARGARET	MET			1797	
1215	ENGLISH E			NWT	1827		PRITCHARD ELIZABETH	EUR			1833	
1447	ERASMUS HENRY		P	NWT	1827	1445	ANDERSON MARGARET	MET			1832	
1448	ERASMUS HENRY	EUR	P	OTH	1830		STEAD JANE	MET	P	NWT	1835	3998

TABLE 1: GENEALOGIES OF RED RIVER HOUSEHOLDS, 1818-1870

ID	MALE HEAD OF FAMILY	RACE	FAITH	BIRTH PLACE	DATES	DADS ID	FEMALE HEAD OF FAMILY	RACE	FAITH	BIRTH PLACE	DATES	DADS ID
1445	ERASMUS PETER	EUR	P	OTH	1794 49	1445	BUDD CATHERINE	MET	.	.	1800	.
1443	ERASMUS WILLIAM	MET	.	.	1835	.	SPENCE ISABELLA	.	.	.	1840 70	.
8030	FABIEN HEBERT	.	.	.	1794	.	DEMONTIGNY MARGUERITE	.	.	.	1794 64	.
8019	FAGNANT AMBROISE	.	.	.	1809	.	PELLETIER JOSEPHTE	MET	RC	RRS	1809 56	.
1469	FAGNANT ANTOINE	MET	RC	RRS	1807	1469	PELLETIER JOSEPHTE	MET	RC	RRS	1810 56	.
1470	FAGNANT ANTOINE	MET	RC	RRS	1826	1469	DESJARLAIS BRIGITTE	MET	RC	.	1832 60	.
1467	FAGNANT CUTHBERT	MET	RC	RRS	1823	1460	LEDOUX MARIE	MET	RC	RRS	1837	.
1460	FAGNANT FRANCOIS	MET	RC	RRS	1796	1460	MCGILLIS ISABELLE	MET	RC	.	1825	.
1460	FAGNANT FRANCOIS	MET	RC	RRS	1796	1460	LEMIRE MADELEINE	MET	RC	RRS	1803	.
1476	FAGNANT FRANCOIS	MET	RC	RRS	1842	1460	FALARDEAU CHARLOTTE	MET	RC	NWT	1799 25	.
1461	FAGNANT JEAN	MET	RC	NWT	1801	1461	BONNEAU MARIE	MET	RC	.	1844	3140
1466	FAGNANT JEAN	MET	RC	RRS	1836	1461	MONETTE JOSEPHTE	MET	RC	.	1805	.
1466	FAGNANT JEAN	MET	RC	RRS	1836	1461	ST DENIS JOSEPHTE	MET	RC	.	1836 61	5146
1458	FAGNANT JOSEPH	MET	RC	RRS	1799	1460	WARD ANGELIQUE	MET	RC	.	1842	.
1468	FAGNANT JOSEPH	MET	RC	RRS	1826	1460	HAMEL MARGUERITE	MET	RC	RRS	1800	.
1508	FAGNANT MOISE	MET	RC	RRS	1840	1460	PAGE MARGUERITE	MET	RC	RRS	1831	.
1465	FAGNANT PAUL	MET	RC	RRS	1835	1471	DESMARAIS MARGUERITE	MET	RC	.	1843	.
1465	FAGNANT PAUL	MET	RC	RRS	1835	1471	HOULE MARGUERITE	MET	RC	RRS	1839 66	.
1474	FAILLE GUILLAUME	MET	RC	RRS	1835	1471	BEAUPRE MARIE	MET	RC	RRS	1852	3911
1472	FAILLE PIERRE	EUR	RC	LC	1791	.	PETIT ELIZABETH	MET	RC	.	1848	3772
1471	FAILLE TOUSSAINT	MET	.	.	1827	.	PEPIN MARIE	MET	RC	RRS	1845	5190
1473	FAILLE TOUSSAINT	MET	.	.	1828	.	WILKEY JOSEPHTE	MET	RC	.	1805	.
8020	FALARDEAU JOSEPH	.	.	.	1790	.	RACETTE MARGUERITE	MET	RC	USA	1830	3727
1480	FALARDEAU LOUISON	MET	.	.	1828	.	MARGUERITE	MET	RC	.	1793	.
1483	FALCON BAPTISTE	.	RC	RRS	1826	1487	NOLIN MARIE	MET	RC	RRS	1828	.
1497	FALCON BAPTISTE	MET	RC	NWT	1844	1487	ALLARD JOSEPHTE	MET	RC	.	1846	.
1481	FALCON FRANCOIS	MET	RC	.	1815	.	POITRAS EUPHRASINE	MET	RC	.	1820 56	2837
1484	FALCON MICHEL	MET	.	.	1805	.	MARIE	MET	RC	.	1810	.
1486	FALCON ONESIME	MET	RC	RRS	1851	1485	LAVERDURE MARIE	MET	RC	RRS	1849	.
1485	FALCON PIERRE	MET	RC	RRS	1820	1487	LAVALLEE MARIE	MET	RC	RRS	1830	.
1487	FALCON PIERRE	MET	RC	NWT	1793	.	GRANT MARIE	MET	RC	NWT	1794	.
1496	FARQUARHSON ANTOINE	EUR	RC	RRS	1811	.	MATT ELISE	MET	RC	RRS	1816	.
1506	FARQUARHSON JOHN	MET	RC	.	1818	1506	MORRISETTE JOSEPHTE	MET	RC	.	1820	3206
1507	FARQUARHSON JOHN	MET	RC	RRS	1809 66	.	HAMELIN MONIQUE	MET	RC	RRS	1823	2114
2707	FARQUARHSON JOHN	MET	RC	.	1840	1506	LUSSIER JOSEPHTE	MET	RC	RRS	1839	.
1524	FARQUARHSON JOSEPH	MET	.	.	1845	.	LUSSIER JOSEPHTE	MET	RC	.	1831	.
1107	FAVEL D	.	.	.	1835	.	DONALD ELIZABETH	MET	.	.	1849	.
1737	FAVEL FRANCIS	MET	P	NWT	1846	1517	MARY	.	P	.	1836	.
1518	FAVEL GEORGE	IND	P	.	1725	.	MUNROE ISABEL	MET	.	NWT	1852	3249
1510	FAVEL HUMPHREY	MET	P	NWT	1820	1520	JENNY	IND	P	.	1727	.
1521	FAVEL HUMPHREY	MET	P	NWT	1820	1520	COCHRANE SOPHIE	MET	.	.	1834	.
1521	FAVEL HUMPHREY	.	.	.	1800 70	.	JANE	.	.	.	1816	.
1218	FAVEL JAMES	MET	P	RRS	1848	1517	MARGARET	.	.	.	1810	.
1503	FAVEL JAMES	MET	P	.	1797	1510	SHORT MATHILDA	IND	P	RRS	1850	.
1512	FAVEL JOHN	.	P	.	1825	.	SWAIN ISABEL	MET	P	.	1800	.
1513	FAVEL JOHN	MET	.	NWT	1843	1517	THOMAS MARGARET	MET	P	NWT	1827 69	.
1519	FAVEL JOHN	MET	P	RRS	1828	1520	DUBOIS NANCY	.	P	RRS	1846 56	.
1522	FAVEL JOSEPH	MET	.	.	1828	1520	MOAR MARGARET	MET	.	.	1827	4676
1522	FAVEL JOSEPH	MET	.	.	1828	.	MARGARET	MET	.	.	1830	.

TABLE 1: GENEALOGIES OF RED RIVER HOUSEHOLDS, 1818-1870

ID	MALE HEAD OF FAMILY	RACE	FAITH	BIRTH PLACE	DATES	DADS ID	FEMALE HEAD OF FAMILY	RACE	FAITH	BIRTH PLACE	DATES	DADS ID
1515	FAVEL RICHARD	MET	.	NWT	1812	1520	ANDERSON EUPHINIA	MET	.	NWT	1824	1520
1516	FAVEL RICHARD	MET	.		1842	1515	SAYER MARGUERITE	MET	.		1848	1515
1517	FAVEL SAMUEL	MET	P	RRS	1820	1520	KIPPLING MARGARET	MET	P		1822 45	1520
1675	FAVEL SAMUEL	MET	P	RRS	1820	1520	IRVINE ELIZABETH	IND	P		1829 70	1520
1217	FAVEL THOMAS		.		1840		SPENCE MARGARET	MET	.		1838	
1217	FAVEL THOMAS		.		1815		MARTINEAU CHARLOTTE	IND	.		1817 39	
1498	FAVEL THOMAS	MET	RC	RRS	1836	1517	MADELEINE		.		1821	
1520	FAVEL THOMAS	MET	.	NWT	1781 48	1510	ADAM ANGELIQUE	MET	RC	RRS	1838	1517
1501	FAVEL WILLIAM		.		1845	1515	TROUT SALLY	IND	P	NWT	1780	1510
1514	FAVEL WILLIAM	MET	.		1824		GADDY ANNIE	MET	.		1846	1515
1505	FAWCETT CHARLES	EUR	.	UC	1821		MOODY MARGARET		.		1824 54	
1525	FAYAN PETER	MET	.		1842	1525	COTE CHARLOTTE		.		1830	
1504	FAYAN ST LOUIS		.	RRS	1828		TYLER SAMANTHA	EUR	.	UC	1836	
1526	FAYE TOUSSAINT	MET	.	RRS	1805		PEPIN BETSY	MET	.		1846	
1531	FIDLER ALBAN		.	NWT	1807	1549	ALLARY MADELEINE	MET	.	NWT	1807	3772
1539	FIDLER ALEXANDER	MET	P	RRS	1833	1535	ANGELIQUE		.		1814	
1488	FIDLER AMBROISE		.		1840		HALLET ELIZABETH	MET	P	NWT	1843	2097
1532	FIDLER ANDREW	MET	P	NWT	1807 46	1547	LINKLATER MARY	MET	P	RRS	1843	2963
1535	FIDLER CHARLES	MET	P	NWT	1797		MCGILLIS CAROLINE	MET	RC	RRS	1809	
1540	FIDLER CLEMENT	MET	P		1810 70	1532	HALLET ANN	MET	P	NWT	1807	2097
1533	FIDLER CORNEL	MET	.		1833		SAUNDERS ANN	MET	P	NWT	1805	4301
2455	FIDLER CYRUS		.		1844 69		SLATER CHARLOTTE	MET	P		1833	4391
1537	FIDLER DAVID	MET	P	RRS	1842	1535	BIRSTON JANE	MET	P		1846	
1538	FIDLER EDWARD	MET	P	RRS	1826	1535	COX ELIZABETH	MET	P	RRS	1848	976
1542	FIDLER FRANCOIS	MET	RC	NWT	1838	1541	MCCORRISTER ELIZABETH	MET	P	RRS	1833	
1543	FIDLER GEORGE	MET	RC		1843	1541	BREMNER NANCY	MET	RC	RRS	1844	
1552	FIDLER HENRY	MET	P		1837	1549	LAPLANTE JOSEPHTE	MET	P		1848	2584
1546	FIDLER JAMES	MET	P		1825	1549	LAPLANTE MARIE	MET	RC		1837	2584
1546	FIDLER JAMES	MET	P		1825	1549	PRUDEN NANCY	MET	P		1829 63	
1550	FIDLER JOHN	MET	P		1825	1549	LINKLATER ELIZABETH	MET	P		1828	
1545	FIDLER JOSEPH	MET	RC		1840		THOMAS MARGUERITE	MET	P		1826	2298
1425	FIDLER PETER	MET	P	NWT	1820	1547	KIPPLING SUSAN	MET	RC		1843	
1547	FIDLER PETER	EUR	.		1777		WELLS ANGELIQUE	MET	P		1826	
1536	FIDLER THOMAS	MET	P		1829	1534	BIRD AMELIA	IND	.	NWT	1765 26	
1549	FIDLER THOMAS	MET	P		1798		MARY	MET	P		1836	
1551	FIDLER THOMAS	MET	P		1843	1549	LAMBERT MARGARET	MET	P		1805	2575
1216	FIDLER WILLIAM	MET	RC		1785		KIPPLING JANE	MET	P		1849	
1544	FIDLER WILLIAM	MET	P		1827	1541	CAMPBELL ELISE	MET	P		1788 26	660
1553	FIDLER WILLIAM	MET	P		1845	1549	MARY		RC		1832	
1556	FIDLER WILLIAM	MET	P		1843	1531	MCGILLIS MARGUERITE	MET	P		1848	5213
1850	FIELD HENRY	MET	RC	UC	1840	1558	YOUNG JANE	MET	P	RRS	1844	1626
1849	FIELDING ALEX	MET	RC	RRS	1790		FOULDS ELIZABETH	MET	P	RRS	1832	
1558	FIELDING JOHN	MET	P	NWT	1770		SMITH CAROLINE	MET	P		1849	
1567	FIELDING THOMAS	MET	RC		1828	1563	SANDERSON FLORA	MET	RC		1801 52	
1562	FINLAYSON HECTOR		RC		1840		COOK ELIZABETH		.		1830	
1851	FINNEGAN JAMES	EUR	.	SCT	1829 62		DUCHARME LISETTE	MET	RC	RRS	1842	
1573	FIRTH CHARLES	MET	RC	RRS	1841	1559	MODE ELIZA	MET	P	NWT	1823	
1571	FISHER ALEXANDER	MET	RC	RRS			RACETTE MARGUERITE	MET	RC	RRS	1843	1559

TABLE 1: GENEALOGIES OF RED RIVER HOUSEHOLDS, 1818-1870

ID	MALE HEAD OF FAMILY	RACE	FAITH	BIRTH PLACE	DATES	DADS ID	FEMALE HEAD OF FAMILY	RACE	FAITH	BIRTH PLACE	DATES	DADS ID
1559	FISHER ALEXIS	MET	RC	NWT	1821	1568	DESJARLAIS SUSANNE	MET	.	.	1810	1271
1566	FISHER GABRIEL	MET	RC	RRS	1848	1569	ELIZABETH	MET	.	.	1807	.
1566	FISHER GABRIEL	MET	RC	RRS	1848	1569	LANGEVIN MARIE	MET	RC	RRS	1849	2609
1567	FISHER GEORGE	MET	RC	USA	1830	.	BOYER EMILIE	MET	RC	RRS	1845	308
1568	FISHER HENRY	EUR	RC	RRS	1800	.	BERGIS LOUISE	MET	RC	RRS	1810	.
1569	FISHER JOHN	MET	.	.	1829	1568	BOURDON BETSY	MET	.	.	1830	.
1854	FLAMMAND FRANCIS	MET	RC	RRS	1833	1576	THIBERT MARGUERITE	MET	RC	RRS	1848	561
1856	FLAMMAND JEAN	MET	RC	RRS	1843	1576	BRUCE ALPHONSINE	MET	RC	RRS	1848	5118
1859	FLAMMAND JEAN BTE	.	.	.	1834	.	VILLEBRUNE MARIE	.	.	.	1832	153
1863	FLAMMAND JEAN BTE	.	.	.	1840	.	AZURE MARIE	.	.	.	1843	.
1572	FLAMMAND JOSEPH	.	.	.	1770	.	CREE MARIE	IND	.	.	1772	.
1574	FLAMMAND JOSEPH	MET	RC	CAN	1792	1572	MOREAU MARGUERITE	MET	RC	.	1797 67	.
1576	FLAMMAND JOSEPH	MET	RC	RRS	1817	1574	LAFRENIERE MARGUERITE	MET	RC	RRS	1823	2532
1576	FLAMMAND JOSEPH	MET	RC	RRS	1817	1574	BOUSQUET NANETTE	MET	RC	RRS	1820	472
1852	FLAMMAND JOSEPH	MET	RC	RRS	1841	1576	DUCHARME GENEVIEVE	MET	RC	.	1842	1360
1857	FLAMMAND JOSEPH	MET	RC	RRS	1841	1576	LAFOND MARGUERITE	MET	RC	RRS	1846	.
1577	FLAMMAND LOUIS	.	RC	RRS	1840	1576	BRUCE MARGUERITE	MET	RC	.	1844	561
1858	FLAMMAND LOUISON	MET	RC	RRS	1828	1574	MONETTE JOSEPHTE	.	RC	RRS	1833	.
1853	FLAMMAND OLIVER	MET	RC	RRS	1836	1574	MALATERRE HELENE	.	.	.	1837	.
1855	FLAMMAND PIERRE	MET	RC	RRS	1842	1576	DUCHARME MARGUERITE	MET	RC	RRS	1840	5127
1561	FLAMMAND THOMAS	EUR	.	.	1842	.	VILLENEUVE SCHOLASTIQUE	EUR	.	.	1838 62	.
1578	FLETCHER JOHN	EUR	.	RRS	1829	.	CAMPBELL ANNE	EUR	.	.	1842	.
1870	FLETCHER JOHN	IND	P	RRS	1837	1868	MUNROE ANN	IND	P	RRS	1845	.
1607	FLETT ANTOINE	MET	.	.	1840	1604	WESKIPAKOKOS CHARLOTTE	MET	.	.	1830	.
1872	FLETT ARCHIBALD	MET	.	RRS	1827	1583	WARD NANCY	EUR	P	RRS	1824	.
1594	FLETT DAVID	EUR	P	.	1823	1596	COOK LETTY	EUR	P	.	1840	4504
444	FLETT DONALD	.	.	.	1842	1583	SUTHERLAND ANN	EUR	.	.	1818	.
1583	FLETT GEORGE	EUR	P	SCT	1773 50	.	COOK FRANCES	MET	P	.	1796	.
1584	FLETT GEORGE	MET	P	RRS	1820	.	WHITFORD MARGUERITE	MET	P	.	1824	4228
1585	FLETT GEORGE	MET	P	.	1820	1584	MARY	MET	P	.	1820 40	.
1586	FLETT GEORGE	EUR	P	ORK	1840	.	ROSS CHARLOTTE	EUR	P	.	1846	4565
1631	FLETT JAMES	.	P	.	1813	.	SWAIN SARA	EUR	P	.	1815	.
1866	FLETT JAMES	EUR	P	RRS	1836	1604	BIRD CHLOE	.	.	.	1838	.
2453	FLETT JAMES	MET	.	.	1829	.	MACBEATH MARY	MET	.	.	1838	.
1590	FLETT JAMES	.	P	NWT	1815	.	BIRSTON MARGARET	IND	P	NWT	1822 52	.
1591	FLETT JOHN	.	P	NWT	1816	.	BIRD CATHERINE	.	.	.	1819	.
1592	FLETT JOHN	EUR	P	RRS	1779 69	.	COOK CHARLOTTE	EUR	P	.	1781	.
1596	FLETT JOHN	EUR	P	SCT	1827	.	FRASER JENNY	MET	P	RRS	1827	1596
1605	FLETT JOHN	MET	P	RRS	1784 65	1604	MURRAY ISABELLA	EUR	.	.	1790	.
1861	FLETT JOHN	MET	P	RRS	1825	1868	ATKINSON ISABEL	MET	P	RRS	1837	.
1871	FLETT JOHN	IND	P	RRS	1845	1873	KENNEDY ELEANORE	MET	P	RRS	1848	136
1580	FLETT JOHN	MET	.	.	1825	2453	JOHNSTON JANE	IND	P	RRS	1830	.
1597	FLETT JOSEPH	.	.	.	1835	.	NANCY	.	.	.	1836	.
1874	FLETT JOSEPH	MET	P	.	1822	1604	COOK MARIANNE	MET	P	.	1824 45	.
1598	FLETT JOSEPH	IND	P	.	1830	.	LYDIA	IND	P	.	1838	.
1873	FLETT PETER	MET	P	NWT	1811	.	HARIET	MET	P	NWT	1816	.
1865	FLETT PETER	IND	.	.	1796	.	HALCROW EUPHORIA	IND	.	.	1809	.
1590	FLETT PHILIP	IND	.	.	1835	.	BADGER JANE	MET	.	.	1835	.
1875	FLETT RICHARD	IND	.	.	1815	.	WHITFORD MARY	IND	.	.	1817	.

TABLE 1: GENEALOGIES OF RED RIVER HOUSEHOLDS, 1818-1870

ID	MALE HEAD OF FAMILY	RACE	FAITH	BIRTH PLACE	DATES	DADS ID	FEMALE HEAD OF FAMILY	RACE	FAITH	BIRTH PLACE	DATES	DADS ID
1599	FLETT ROBERT	EUR			1844	1596	BANNERMAN ANN	EUR			1845	182
2454	FLETT ROBERT	IND	P		1831		FOULDS MARIE ANNE			RRS	1828	1623
1860	FLETT THOMAS	MET	P	RRS	1830		PARISIEN ROSALIE	MET	P	RRS	1842	3823
1868	FLETT THOMAS	IND	P	RRS	1810		ISABEL	IND	P		1802	
1869	FLETT THOMAS	MET	P	RRS	1823		NANCY	MET	P	NWT	1817 55	
1493	FLETT THOMAS		P		1763 24	1493	MARY	MET	P		1830 45	
1602	FLETT WILLIAM	EUR	P		1820		MCKAY MARY	MET	P		1825	902
1604	FLETT WILLIAM	EUR	P	NWT	1786 52		WIDOW SARAH		P		1787 47	
1606	FLETT WILLIAM	MET	P	ORK	1817		ATKINSON ISABELLA	MET	P		1832	
1608	FLETT WILLIAM	MET	P		1809		NANCY	MET	P		1807 38	
1608	FLETT WILLIAM	MET	P	NWT	1809		CLOUSTON MARGARET				1809 54	
1825	FLETT WILLIAM			NWT	1826 65		MCNAB MARY		P	RRS	1826	
2449	FLETT WILLIAM				1832		CURTNIR JANE	MET	P		1834	
2450	FLETT WILLIAM				1840		KIRKNESS ELLEN				1842	
1589	FLEURY EDWARD	MET	RC	RRS	1848	1609	MORIN MELANIE	MET	RC	RRS	1850	3172
1588	FLEURY JOSEPH	MET	RC	RRS	1832	1612	PICHE MADELEINE	MET	RC	RRS	1839	3931
1609	FLEURY JOSEPH				1818		BELLE JOSEPHE	IND			1820	276
1613	FLEURY JOSEPH	MET			1829	1612	THORNE MARIE				1837 62	
1616	FLEURY LOUIS	MET		CAN	1818	1612	TROTTIER MARGUERITE	MET	RC	RRS	1825	4711
1612	FLEURY LOUISON		RC	RRS	1775 47	1609	GROSVENTRE JOSEPHTE	IND			1800	
1610	FLEURY MICHEL	MET	RC		1841		PICHE MARIE ANNE	MET	RC		1843	
1614	FLEURY PATRICE	MET			1848	1612	WILKEY AGATHE	MET	RC		1844	5187
1489	FOLSTER JAMES	EUR	P	SCT	1784 41	1495	NANCY				1790 30	
1489	FOLSTER JAMES	EUR	P	SCT	1784 41	1495	PATENAUDE JOSEPHTE	MET	P	NWT	1814	
1630	FOLSTER JAMES	EUR	P	SCT	1730		JANE	EUR	P		1733 34	
1494	FOLSTER JOHN	EUR	P	SCT	1813	1630	BROWN ISABEL	MET	P	SCT	1830	532
1494	FOLSTER JOHN	EUR	P	SCT	1813		MCDONALD FLORA	MET	P		1824 44	
1495	FOLSTER JOHN	EUR	P	SCT	1776		JANE				1811 51	
1491	FOLSTER THOMAS	MET	P	RRS	1828	1489	WALLER NANCY	MET	P		1835	
1491	FOLSTER THOMAS	MET	P	RRS	1827	1489	DANIEL FANNY	MET	P		1829 51	
1490	FOLSTER WILLIAM	EUR	P	OTH	1825	1489	PRUDEN MARIA	MET	P	RRS	1844	4035
1528	FONCECA WILLIAM	EUR			1830 66		LOGAN MARGARET	MET	P	RRS	1831	3765
1618	FONTAINE JEAN BTE			CAN	1798		OUELLETTE ANGELIQUE	MET	P		1818	
1642	FONTAINE JEAN BTE	MET	RC	RRS	1840		ISABEL	MET	P	NWT	1852	
1643	FONTAINE LOUIS	EUR	RC	IRE	1788 66		BLONDIN MARY				1788 63	
1635	FORBES JOHN	EUR	RC		1775		SPENCE ELIZABETH	MET	RC		1778	
1669	FORBISHER ALEXANDER	EUR			1827		MARGUERITE	IND	RC		1833	
1833	FORBISHER JAMES	MET	P	ORK	1792	1834	FOULDS CATHERINE	MET	P		1805	1626
1638	FORBISHER JOHN	EUR	P	SCT	1800		ROBERTSON CATHERINE	MET	P	RRS	1810	
1834	FORBISHER JOHN	EUR		RRS	1814		ROBINSON SCHOLASTIQUE	MET	P	NWT	1824	3935
1639	FORBISHER THOMAS	MET	RC	NWT	1800		PILON MARY	MET	RC	RRS	1804	
1640	FORREST GRANT				1840		MATHILDA				1843	
1581	FORRISTER JOSEPH				1799		ELIZA	MET			1800	
1560	FORTH THOMAS	EUR	P	SCT	1815		BOUCHER CHARLOTTE	EUR	P	RRS	1827	2930
1615	FORTIER BAPTISTE	EUR	P	UC	1844		LESPERANCE HANNAH	EUR	P	RRS	1851	
1554	FORTNEY GEORGE				1831		RICHARD JULIE				1832 51	
1582	FOSSENEUVE BAPTISTE				1831		MORIN JOSETTE	MET	RC		1832	
1582	FOSSENEUVE BAPTISTE				1831		LAFRENIERE ANGELIQUE		RC		1832	
1641	FOUCILLE TOUSSAINT				1805		SANCHEAU ANGELIQUE	MET	P		1807	

TABLE 1: GENEALOGIES OF RED RIVER HOUSEHOLDS, 1818-1870

ID	MALE HEAD OF FAMILY	RACE	FAITH	BIRTH PLACE	DATES	DADS ID	FEMALE HEAD OF FAMILY	RACE	FAITH	BIRTH PLACE	DATES	DADS ID
1624	FOULDS ABRAHAM	MET		RRS	1842	1623	HARKNESS ELIZABETH	MET	P	RRS	1838	2125
1601	FOULDS HENRY	MET	P	RRS	1838	1626	KIRTON JESSIE	MET	P	RRS	1843	
1623	FOULDS JOHN	EUR	P	ENG	1798 68	1623	FIDLER MARY		P	RRS	1805	
1625	FOULDS JOHN	MET	P	RRS	1830 70		ADAM ANN		P	RRS	1835	
1626	FOULDS SAMUEL	EUR	P	ENG	1846	1626	CALDER ANN	EUR	P	RRS	1805	
1629	FOULDS THOMAS	MET	P	RRS	1840	1626	ARMSTRONG CHARLOTTE	MET	P	RRS	1852	
1628	FOULDS WILLIAM	MET	RC	RRS	1835	1644	DANIEL ELIZABETH	MET	P	RRS	1847	
1555	FOURNIER FRANCOIS	MET	P	RRS	1793		LACOUTURE MADELEINE	MET	RC		1840	
1644	FOURNIER FRANCOIS	MET	RC		1845		METHOT ANGELIQUE		RC		1800	3862
1564	FOURNIER MICHEL	MET	RC	NWT	1830		SAULTEAUX MARIE	IND	RC	NWT	1848	4478
1835	FOURON JOSEPH		RC		1820		PAUL JOSEITE			RRS	1831	
1646	FOX CHARLES			NWT	1826	1647	STEVENS THERESA	MET		RRS	1823	
1836	FOYE TOUSSAINT	MET	RC	NWT	1848		JOSEPHTE	MET	RC	RRS	1826	1471
1837	FRANCOIS JOSEPH	MET	RC	RRS	1802		FAILLE MARIANNE		RC	RRS	1846	
1838	FRANCOIS NICHOLAS				1813		ABERLAE MARY		P		1804	
1663	FRANKLIN THOMAS	EUR	P	ENG	1813		FLETT SARA	MET	P	RRS	1831 67	
1650	FRANKS JAMES	EUR	P	ENG	1846		JUSTINA					
1650	FRANKS JAMES	EUR	P	RRS	1843		MATHESON JANET	EUR	P	RRS	1830	
1662	FRANKS JAMES	EUR	P	RRS	1819	1650	MATHESON CATHERINE	EUR	P	RRS	1817 55	
1657	FRANKS ANGUS	EUR		SCT	1789		GAUDRY NANCY	MET	P		1820	
1652	FRASER COLIN	EUR	P	RRS	1819		BANNERMAN ANN	EUR	P	RRS	1846	
1654	FRASER JAMES	MET	P	NWT	1845		MATHESON JANE	MET	P	RRS	1833	3084
1656	FRASER JOHN	MET	RC	RRS	1832	1656	VINCENT SARAH	EUR	P	RRS	1838	
1664	FRASER JOHN	MET	RC	RRS	1830	1654	MCBEATH ANNIE	MET	RC		1824	
1655	FRASER WILLIAM				1791 63		BOISCLAIR JULIE	EUR	RC		1800	407
1840	FREDERICK GABRIEL	EUR	RC	RRS	1840	1652	HAMELIN MARGUERITE	MET	RC	RRS	1837 69	
1665	FREDERICK GABRIEL	MET	RC	IRE	1840	1654	BOURET CATHERINE	MET	P	RRS	1840	
1673	FREDERICK JEAN BTE	EUR			1830		DAUPHINAIS FRISINE	EUR	RC		1840	
1842	FREDERICK LOUIS	MET	RC	RRS	1850		LEDOUX JANE	MET	P	RRS	1850	
1843	FRIDAY ANTOINE	EUR	P	IRE	1840		GIBSON MARY ANN	MET	P	SCT	1842	
1672	FULSHER FREDERICK	EUR			1772							
1845	FULTHORPE GEORGE	EUR	P		1815		CAMPBELL MARGARET	EUR			1775	
1887	GADDY ALEXANDER	EUR			1844		MARY	MET	P	RRS	1840	
1886	GADDY JAMES	EUR	RC		1777							
1883	GADDY WILLIAM	MET	RC	RRS	1815		GARRIOCH MARGUERITE	MET	RC	RRS	1815	3198
1877	GAGNON DAVID	MET	RC	CAN	1839	1881	MORIN HERMINE	EUR	RC	RRS	1840	
1880	GAGNON JOSEPH	MET	RC	NWT	1813		LAPIERRE JOSEPHTE		RC		1785	
1882	GAGNON JOSEPH	MET	RC	RRS	1812	1881	PELLETIER MARIE		RC		1819	
1881	GAGNON LOUIS	EUR	RC	NWT	1786	1877	MCKENZIE MARY	MET	RC	NWT	1828	3421
1889	GAGNON LOUISON	EUR	RC	CAN	1806	1915	MINNIE JOSEPHTE	MET	RC	RRS	1805	
1915	GALARNEAU JOSEPH	EUR	RC	LC	1818		REPENTIGNY MARIE	EUR	RC	CAN	1828	
1890	GALARNEAU JOSEPH	EUR	RC	CAN	1828	1915	ARCHAMBEAULT MARGUERITE	MET	RC	RRS	1787	
1831	GALARNEAU LOUIS	MET			1840		CREBASSA MARIE	MET	RC	LC	1803	
1817	GALIPEAU FRANCOIS	EUR	P	ENG	1820		BRUYERE ANGELIQUE	EUR	RC	USA	1820	
1828	GARDNER JOSEPH	MET	RC		1842		WATSON JANE	MET	P		1833	
1899	GARDNER R		RC				COX ELIZABETH	MET	P	ENG	1846	
1805	GARDUPUIS PIERRE			CAN	1795 70		GRANT MARIE	MET	RC		1822	
1832	GARIEPY ALEXANDER	MET	RC	RRS	1842		CADOTTE GENEVIEVE	MET	RC	RRS	1850	
1892	GARIEPY ALEXIS	MET	RC	RRS	1824	1898	MONTOUR SOPHIE	MET	RC	RRS	1825	
	GARIEPY BAPTISTE		RC	CAN	1795 65	1892	SAULTEAUX MARGUERITE	IND	RC		1790 65	976

TABLE 1: GENEALOGIES OF RED RIVER HOUSEHOLDS, 1818-1870

ID	MALE HEAD OF FAMILY	RACE	FAITH	BIRTH PLACE	DATES	DADS ID	FEMALE HEAD OF FAMILY	RACE	FAITH	BIRTH PLACE	DATES	DADS ID
1893	GARIEPY BONAVENTURE		RC	RRS	1822	1898	LAROCQUE MADELEINE	MET	RC	RRS	1823	2030
1830	GARIEPY FRANCOIS				1835		GRANT CAROLI	MET	P	NWT	1840	1535
1830	GARIEPY FRANCOIS		RC		1835		FIDLER NANCY			RRS	1828	
1895	GARIEPY FRANCOIS				1820	1897	POITRAS HELENE		RC	RRS	1821	
1897	GARIEPY FRANCOIS				1797		GLADU LOUISE				1800	
1808	GARIEPY JEAN BTE	MET	RC	RRS	1840	1898	CARDINAL JUDITH	MET	RC	RRS	1841	
1806	GARIEPY LOUIS	MET	RC	RRS	1836		CARDINAL MARIE	MET	RC	RRS	1836	
1898	GARIEPY LOUIS	EUR	RC	CAN	1782 56	1897	DUCHARME JOSEPHTE	MET	RC	RRS	1785	3804
1894	GARIEPY PHILIP	MET	P	RRS	1843		PARENTEAU ROSALIE	EUR	P	UC	1844	
1814	GARRALT CHARLES	EUR	P	ENG	1816		WHITE SARAH				1817	
1862	GARRIOCH AMOS	MET	P	RRS	1840		SAUNDERS FLORA	MET	P	RRS	1843	
1904	GARRIOCH GAVIN	MET	P	RRS	1819	1908	BOURKE HANNAH	MET	P	RRS	1830	
1813	GARRIOCH JOHN	MET	P		1810		SANSON SOPHIE	MET	P		1810	
1827	GARRIOCH JOHN				1833		CAMPBELL ELIZABETH				1834	
1896	GARRIOCH JOHN			NWT	1832 52	1908	LEDOUX ISABELLE	MET	P	NWT	1834	
1905	GARRIOCH JOHN	MET	P		1809		CAMPBELL ELIZA				1824	
2448	GARRIOCH JOHN				1844		MARGARET				1845	
2451	GARRIOCH JOHN			RRS	1818		SOPHIA				1820	
1903	GARRIOCH PETER	MET	P		1811	1908	MCKENZIE MARGARET	MET	P	NWT	1826	3427
1811	GARRIOCH WILLIAM	MET	P	RRS	1833		MARY				1835	
1907	GARRIOCH WILLIAM	EUR	P	SCT	1828	1908	BROWN MARY	MET	P	RRS	1835	543
1908	GARRIOCH WILLIAM	MET	P	NWT	1779	1910	COOK NANCY	MET	P		1785	
1909	GARTON JOHN				1823		SPENCER MARY	MET	P	NWT	1838	4457
1910	GARTON JOHN	EUR			1809		MARY	MET			1810	
1815	GAUDREAU ANTOINE	MET			1843		MARIANNE				1845	
1923	GAUDRY AMABLE	MET	RC	RRS	1826	1922	DUCHARME HELENE	MET	RC	RRS	1829	
1919	GAUDRY ANDRE	MET	RC	RRS	1833	1922	BURNEAU SARA	MET	RC	RRS	1802	
1920	GAUDRY AUGUSTIN	MET	RC	RRS	1836	1922	LAFOND ELISE	MET	RC	RRS	1845	
1916	GAUDRY FRANCOIS	MET	RC	NWT	1845	1917	SAULTEAUX MELANIE	MET	RC	NWT	1847	2512
1921	GAUDRY ISIDORE	MET	RC		1845	1922	BOUSQUET ELISE	MET	RC		1851	
1917	GAUDRY JOSEPH		RC		1780 63		KAKORWASTE	MET	RC		1819	
1906	GAUDRY LOUIS				1820		BOURBON CHARLOTTE	EUR	RC	RRS	1822	
1918	GAUDRY PIERRE	EUR	RC	LC	1810		HUGHES MARIA	IND		RRS	1812	
1816	GAUTHIER JEAN BTE	EUR			1831		GERMAIN ROSALIE		RC		1836	460
1924	GAUVIN JEAN				1839		MARGARET	EUR		LC	1812	
8022	GAUVIN ANTOINE						PARENT MALVINA		P		1839	
1809	GEDDES JOHN	EUR		SCT	1823		ROTHNEY ISABELLA	EUR		SCT	1830	
1926	GENDRON FRANCOIS	MET	P		1835		MARCELLAIS ELISE	MET	RC		1836	
2461	GENDRON FRANCOIS			NWT	1795 65		LUSSIER ANGELIQUE	MET	RC		1800	
1928	GENTHON CHARLE	MET	RC	RRS	1844	1930	CARRIERE URSULA	MET	RC	RRS	1849	719
1929	GENTHON ELIE	MET	RC	RRS	1830	1930	LAURENCE GENEVIEVE	MET	RC	RRS	1842	2642
1927	GENTHON JOSEPH	MET	RC		1790	1930	MARION JOSEPHTE	MET	RC		1835	
1930	GENTHON MAXIME	EUR	RC	CAN	1818		JEROME MARIE	EUR			1807	
1931	GENTHON MICHEL				1790		OUELLETTE VICTORIA	IND			1820	2349
1932	GENTHON FREDERICK			ENG	1832		JOSEPHTE	EUR			1792	
1936	GEORGE HENRY	EUR			1785		MARY ANNE	IND		RRS	1832	
1937	GEORGE JOSEPH	EUR		RRS	1843		COCHRANE MARY ANNE				1787	
1935	GEORGE PETER		P		1795	1938	PARISIEN JOSETTE	MET	P		1848	
1938	GEORGE PIERRE	MET		RRS	1825	1937	CHATELAIN ISABELLA	MET		RRS	1823 68	
2470	GEORGE PIERRE	MET	RC	RRS			FOUCILLE MARIE	MET	RC	RRS	1829	

TABLE 1: GENEALOGIES OF RED RIVER HOUSEHOLDS, 1818-1870

ID	MALE HEAD OF FAMILY	RACE	FAITH	BIRTH PLACE	DATES	DADS ID	FEMALE HEAD OF FAMILY	RACE	FAITH	BIRTH PLACE	DATES	DADS ID
1934	GEPSON GEORGE	IND	P	RRS	1835		JOHN ELIZABETH	IND	P	RRS	1838	1487
1774	GEPSON FRANCOIS				1815		FALCON MADELEINE				1815	
2056	GEPSON HYPOLITE				1817		GARIEPY CATHERINE				1817	
1901	GERALD A P	EUR	P	USA	1840		ARMSTRONG MARY	EUR	P	ENG	1844	
1939	GEROME MARTIN	MET	RC	RRS	1822		LANDRY ANGELIQUE	MET	RC	USA	1825	
1769	GERVAIS ALEXIS	MET	RC	CAN	1846	1950	FAILLANT MADELEINE	MET	RC	RRS	1837	2113
1942	GERVAIS BAPTISTE	MET	RC	RRS	1826		BOUER CLEMENCE	MET	RC	RRS	1851	
1824	GERVAIS BAPTISTE	MET	RC	RRS	1821	1950	HAMELIN JOSEPHTE	MET	RC	RRS	1824	
1945	GERVAIS BASILE	MET	RC	RRS	1844	1942	LEDOUX FRANCOISE	MET	RC	RRS	1848	4246
1941	GERVAIS CLEOPHILE	MET	RC	RRS	1828	1950	ROSS CATHERINE	MET	RC	RRS	1828	
1948	GERVAIS FRANCOIS	MET	RC	RRS	1828	1950	BRUYERE JOSEPHTE	MET	RC		1825	
1952	GERVAIS FRANCOIS	EUR	RC		1790	1942	KEKEHONS ANGELIQUE	IND	RC	NWT	1805	418
1950	GERVAIS JEAN BTE	EUR	RC		1840	1950	BONNEAU MADELEINE	MET	RC		1842	3886
1949	GERVAIS NORBERT	MET	RC		1835	1951	PELLETIER CECILE	MET	RC	RRS	1836	3780
1951	GERVAIS PAUL	MET	RC	RRS	1820	1950	PAGE MADELEINE	MET	RC		1821	
1953	GERVAIS URBAIN	MET			1805		DEFOND J	MET			1808	
1943	GESBIENS JOSEPH	MET			1850		NOLIN MARGUERITE				1851	3726
1822	GETS CHARLES				1834		SINCLAIR MARGUERITE				1836	4378
1803	GIBEAU DENYS	EUR		LC	1830		SINCLAIR MARGARET				1835	4378
1955	GIBEAU GUILLAUME		P		1775		CHRISTINA		P	NWT	1788	
1954	GIBSON HUGH	EUR	P	ORK	1790		CHALIFOUX CHRISTINA	MET		NWT	1810	735
1821	GIBSON WILLIAM	MET			1825		SINCLAIR ANGELIQUE	MET			1829	
1957	GIBSON WILLIAM	MET	P	ORK	1788		FLETT MARGARET	MET	P		1800	
1820	GIBSON SAMUEL	MET			1845		FAVEL NANCY	MET			1825	
1963	GIDDINGS ANTOINE	MET	RC	NWT	1824		TROTTIER SARAH	MET			1855	
1962	GINGRAS FRANCOIS	MET			1822	1963	MCMURRAY SCHOLASTIQUE	MET	RC		1825	
1807	GIRARD JOSEPH	IND	P	RRS	1795		ASSINIBOINE ANNIE	IND	P	RRS	1800	
1972	GLADMAN GEORGE	MET	RC	NWT	1817		MARGUERITE	MET	RC	NWT	1825	
1964	GLADU ANTOINE	MET	RC	NWT	1817	1969	BOURASSA BETHSY	MET	RC		1823	
1966	GLADU ANTOINE				1776	1969	DESJARLAIS MARIE	MET	RC	RRS	1785	
1969	GLADU CHARLE	EUR	RC		1776	2473	POITRAS JOSEPHTE	MET	RC	NWT	1788	
2473	GLADU CHARLES	EUR	RC		1799		POITRAS MADELEINE	MET	RC		1804	
1977	GLADU CHARLES	MET	RC		1846		ROSS MARIE	MET	RC		1850	
1978	GLADU FRANCOIS	MET	RC		1849	1975	LAURIN MADELEINE	MET	RC	RRS	1810	
1975	GLADU JOSEPH	MET	RC	RRS	1815	1979	WELSH MARGUERITE	MET	RC	NWT	1848	2526
1976	GLADU LOUIS	MET	RC	RRS	1842	1969	LAFOURNAISE ADELE	MET	RC	RRS	1849	1271
1967	GLADU LOUIS	MET	RC	RRS	1840	1975	DESJARLAIS SUSANNE	MET	RC	RRS	1824	3206
1979	GLADU PIERRE	MET	RC		1815		MORRISETTE PHILOMENE	MET	RC		1829	
1944	GLADU PIERRE	EUR	RC	RRS	1845	1973	MOOSSETTE ISABEL	EUR	RC	RRS	1847	1057
1772	GLADU WILLIAM	MET	RC		1840		DEASE NANCY	MET	RC		1842	
1984	GODON JOHN	MET	RC	NWT	1816	1983	JOHNSTON CAROLINE	MET	RC	RRS	1825	2785
1983	GODON JOSEPH	MET			1836		MCCRAE ISABEL	MET		NWT	1827	
1985	GODON LOUIS	MET			1827	1983	LAROCQUE MARIE	MET		RRS	1828	2785
1992	GODON LOUIS	EUR			1838		ISAAC ISABEL	EUR			1846	
1989	GONEVILLE ALEXIS	MET	RC		1838	1990	LAROCQUE MARIE	MET	RC	RRS	1846	3896
1990	GONEVILLE ALEXIS	MET	RC		1817		TROTTIER JOSEPHTE	MET	RC	RRS	1812	4711
1987	GONEVILLE ANTOINE		RC	CAN	1779		LABINE MARGUERITE	MET	RC	RRS	1785	2459

TABLE 1: GENEALOGIES OF RED RIVER HOUSEHOLDS, 1818-1870

ID	MALE HEAD OF FAMILY		RACE	FAITH	BIRTH PLACE	DATES	DADS ID	FEMALE HEAD OF FAMILY		RACE	FAITH	BIRTH PLACE	DATES	DADS ID
1986	GONEVILLE	LOUIS	MET	RC	RRS	1835	1987	MATHEW	MARIE	MET	RC	NWT	1845	
1770	GOOD	JAMES	EUR	P	ENG	1813		SCARF	DELILA	EUR	P	RRS	1815	
1991	GOOD	JAMES	EUR	P	RRS	1847	1770	BROWN	SARAH	MET	P	RRS	1842	2286
1771	GOOD	JOSEPH	EUR	P	RRS	1837	1770	KIRTON	MARIANNE	EUR	P	RRS	1842	4266
1996	GOSSELIN	ANTOINE	MET	RC		1807 62	2001	ROY	MARIE	MET	RC	RRS	1810	
2000	GOSSELIN	ANTOINE	MET	RC	RRS	1840	1996	DELORME	FRANCOISE	MET	RC	RRS	1840	
1994	GOSSELIN	BAPTISTE	MET	RC	RRS	1842	2001	RAINVILLE	ADELAIDE	MET	RC	RRS	1844	4159
1998	GOSSELIN	FRANCOIS	MET	RC	RRS	1817	2001	LAFOURNAISE	SUZANNE	MET	RC	RRS	1848	
1999	GOSSELIN	JOSEPH	MET	RC	RRS	1825	2001	PETIT	ROSALIE	MET	RC	RRS	1833	3910
1995	GOSSELIN	MICHEL	MET		RRS	1833	1996	DESCOLEAUX	MADELEINE	MET	RC	NWT	1840	
2001	GOSSELIN	MICHEL		RC	CAN	1776			MARGUERITE	IND	RC		1796 28	
2007	GOSSELIN	MICHEL		RC	CAN	1812		DESCHAMPS	JOSEPHTE				1809	
8026	GOUIN	ANTOINE		RC	CAN	1830		BOUCHER	FRANCOISE				1812	
1773	GOUIN	OCTAVE	MET			1832		DUCHARME	MARIE				1835	
2009	GOULET	ALEXANDER	MET	RC	RRS	1847	2010	PICHE	SUSANNE				1837	3931
2012	GOULET	ALEXIS		RC	NWT	1812 69	2010	BOYER	MARGUERITE	MET	RC	RRS	1845	
2587	GOULET	ALEXIS				1840		SAVERET	JOSETTE	MET	RC	RRS	1817	4293
8021	GOULET	DAMASE				1843		GOULET	HELENE				1844	2685
2073	GOULET	ELZEAR				1840 69		TARDIF	ADELE				1843	
2010	GOULET	JACQUES		RC	CAN	1779		ST MATHE	HELENE	MET	RC	RRS	1844	
2685	GOULET	JEAN BTE			CAN	1820		VERSAILLES	LOUISE				1811	967
2015	GOULET	LOUIS				1813		COURCHENE	JOSEPHTE				1825	
2008	GOULET	MOISE	MET	RC	RRS	1831	2010	WINSEL	EMILIE				1818	
2014	GOULET	PIERRE	MET		RRS	1840	2015	BEAUCHAMP	MARIE	MET	RC	RRS	1837	
2019	GOURNEAU	FRANCOIS				1800		CHABOYER	MARIE	MET	RC	RRS	1846	728
2011	GOURNEAU	LAWRENCE	MET	RC		1844		MARTINEAU	MARGUERITE				1805	3074
2070	GOWLAR	JOHN	EUR		USA	1813 65	2020	THOMAS	HELEN	MET	P	RRS	1851	
2020	GOWLAR	OLIVIER			RRS	1813		SHARP	MARY	EUR		IRE	1847	
2013	GOWLAR	WILLIAM	EUR	P	RRS	1841		BRAYBROOKE	MARY	EUR	P	ENG	1816	
2024	GRANDBOIS	ISIDOR	MET			1833		MILLER	ANN	MET		RRS	1844	
2021	GRANDBOIS	LOUIS			NWT	1825	2026	CADOTTE	ANGELIQUE				1838	
2026	GRANDBOIS	MICHEL				1785		LANDRY	MARGUERITE				1818	612
2027	GRANDBOIS	MICHEL		RC	NWT	1827		HOULE	EMILIE	MET	RC		1790	
2025	GRANDBOIS	PIERRE				1827		VANDAL	JOSEPHTE	MET			1832	4907
2029	GRANT	CHARLES	MET	RC	NWT	1825		GLADU	EUPHROSINE				1829	
2030	GRANT	CUTHBERT	MET	RC	NWT	1796 54		MCKAY	ELIZABETH				1825	
2030	GRANT	CUTHBERT	MET	RC	NWT	1796 54		DESMARAIS	MARIE				1800 17	
2028	GRANT	JEAN BTE	MET	RC	NWT	1806		MCGILLIS	MARIE				1805 22	
2032	GRANT	JOHN	MET	RC	NWT	1831	2034	DUCHARME	JULIE				1806 56	
2032	GRANT	JOHN	MET	RC	NWT	1831	2034		LOUISE	IND			1810	
2079	GRANT	JOHN				1837		BRUNEAU	CLOTILDE	MET	RC	RRS	1833	
2034	GRANT	RICHARD	EUR		CAN	1806	2038		WANOYESSIE	IND	P	RRS	1850	
2036	GRAVEL	MICHEL				1810			MARIE ANN				1842	
2037	GREEN	JAMES	MET	P	RRS	1846		BRELAND	NANCY	MET	RC		1811	578
2038	GREEN	JAMES		P	USA	1816		KIPPLING	ELIZABETH	MET	P	RRS	1815	
2080	GREGOIRE	LOUIS				1840		STEVENSON	ISABEL				1849	2298
2065	GRENOT	HENRI				1840		ROSS	MARGUERITE	MET		RRS	1820 65	4483
2033	GREY	EYES	MET	P	RRS	1805		PELLETIER	SARA				1846	
								SANSLETTA	NANCY	IND	P	RRS	1810	

ID	MALE HEAD OF FAMILY		RACE	FAITH	BIRTH PLACE	DATES	DADS ID	FEMALE HEAD OF FAMILY		RACE	FAITH	BIRTH PLACE	DATES	DADS ID
2041	GROAT	GEORGE	EUR	P	SCT	1799		SPENCE	CHARLOTTE	MET	P	NWT	1809	
2042	GROUETTE	ANTOINE	EUR	RC	LC	1795	2044	NOLIN	MADELEINE	MET		RRS	1790 69	
2045	GROUETTE	AUGUSTIN	MET	RC	RRS	1835	2042	PERREAULT	ROSE	MET	RC	RRS	1837	3899
2047	GROUETTE	JAMES				1770		MADER	CATHERINE			RRS	1775	
2046	GROUETTE	JEAN BTE	MET	RC	RRS	1828	2042	PERREAULT	JULIA	EUR	RC	RRS	1827	3899
2051	GROUETTE	THEOPHILE	MET	RC	RRS	1830	2042	ST LUC	MADELEINE	MET	RC	RRS	1834	4856
2052	GUIBOCHE	ANDRE	MET		NWT	1840	2052	DESJARDIN	JULIE	MET	RC	RRS	1847	1278
2054	GUIBOCHE	EDWARD				1791 61		LAROCQUE	MARIE	MET	RC	NWT	1795	
2050	GUIBOCHE	LOUIS				1784			ANGELIQUE				1787 62	
2055	GUIBOCHE	NOEL	MET	RC	NWT	1838	2052	DESJARDIN	CAMILLE	MET		NWT	1840 62	
2053	GUILBEAULT	JOSEPH	MET	RC	NWT	1838		SMITH	MARIA	IND	RC		1832	4413
2069	GUILBEAULT	MEDARD	EUR		LC	1784			MARIA				1790 34	
2064	GUNN	ALEXANDER	MET	P	RRS	1837 21		CHRISTIN	PRISCILLE	MET	RC	RRS	1840	
2072	GUNN	ALEXANDER	EUR	P	RRS	1829	2064	MCKENZIE	ANGELICA	EUR		RRS	1832	4569
2067	GUNN	DONALD	EUR	P	SCT	1826	2076	MATHESON	ANN	MET	P	NWT	1830	
2068	GUNN	DONALD	EUR	P	RRS	1797	2076	SWAIN	MARGARET	MET	P	RRS	1802	
2062	GUNN	JAMES	EUR	P	RRS	1832	2064	MATHESON	CATHERINE	EUR	P	RRS	1832	
2075	GUNN	JERIMIAH	MET	P	RRS	1840	2064	BALLENDINE	CAROLINE	MET	P	RRS	1846	172
2063	GUNN	JOHN	EUR	P	RRS	1824	2076	DONALD	MARY	EUR	P	RRS	1818	
2076	GUNN	JOHN	MET	P	RRS	1836		MATHESON	JANE	MET	P	RRS	1839	
2074	GUNN	ROBERT	EUR	P	RRS	1826		GARRIOCH	EMMA	EUR	P	RRS	1824	
2066	GUNN	WILLIAM				1789		SUTHERLAND	ANN	EUR	P		1796	
2078	GUNN	WILLIAM	EUR	P	RRS	1841		MCKAY	BARBARA	EUR	P	SCT	1849	
2082	GUNN	WILLIAM				1834			MAGDELENE			RRS	1839	
2043	GUTHRIE	THOMAS	IND	P	NWT	1818			ISABELLA	EUR	P		1842	
2084	HAGUE	AMABLE		P	SCT	1818		ROSS	ANN	EUR	P		1821 60	
2088	HALCROW	DAVID	MET	P		1825	2087	SUTHERLAND	MARY	IND	P	RRS	1830	
2086	HALCROW	JOSEPH	MET	P	RRS	1759 34	2087	MCBEATH	ISABELLA	MET	P	NWT	1770	947
2091	HALCROW	JOSEPH	MET	P	RRS	1813	2092		MARGUERITE	MET	P		1818	
108	HALCROW	SAMUEL				1832		TAYLOR	ELIZABETH		P		1830	
2087	HALCROW	THOMAS	EUR			1820		CORRIGAL	SOPHIA	MET	P	RRS	1827	961
2090	HALCROW	THOMAS				1837		COOK	MARY ANN	MET	P	RRS	1845	
2092	HALCROW	THOMAS				1823		CORRIGAL	MARGARET	MET		RRS	1830	961
109	HALCROW	WILLIAM				1787 54			MARY	MET	P	NWT	1775 60	
						1814		SUTHERLAND	CHARLOTTE	MET	P		1808	2277
						1823		KNIGHT	SARAH	IND	P	NWT	1825	
1791	HALERO	JOHN							BETSY	MET			1817	
						1812			SARAH	MET			1829	
1775	HALL	ANDREW	EUR	P	UC	1824		OMAND	ANN	MET	P		1835	3759
2107	HALL	WILLIAM		P	NWT	1831		TALBOT	MATHILDA	EUR	P	UC	1830	
2094	HALLET	HENRY	MET			1825		MCNAB	ELLEN	MET		RRS	1775 7	3466
2097	HALLET	HENRY	MET		IND	1772 44		DUNGAS	CATHERINE	IND		NWT	1780	
2098	HALLET	HENRY	MET			1772 44		PARENTEAU	CATHERINE	MET		RRS	1799 57	
2099	HALLET	HENRY JR	MET		NWT	1799	2097	BOURKE	MARIA	MET	P	RRS	1837	
2102	HALLET	JAMES	MET		RRS	1828		FIDLER	SARAH	MET			1802	
2100	HALLET	JOHN	MET		NWT	1800		STODGILL	ANN	MET	P	RRS	1850	
2101	HALLET	WILLIAM	MET		NWT	1851	2097	LUNES	SUZETTE	MET		RRS	1815 40	1547
2101	HALLET	WILLIAM	MET		NWT	1810		PRUDEN	MARIA	MET	P		1820	4489
8028	HAMEL	AMEDEE	MET			1847		LAMY	ODILE		P	NWT	1847	

TABLE 1: GENEALOGIES OF RED RIVER HOUSEHOLDS, 1818-1870

ID	MALE HEAD OF FAMILY	FAMILY	RACE	FAITH	BIRTH PLACE	DATES	DADS ID	FEMALE HEAD OF FAMILY	FAMILY	RACE	FAITH	BIRTH PLACE	DATES	DADS ID
2103	HAMEL	JOSEPH	MET	RC	RRS	1764 46		HOULE	CHARLOTTE	IND			1774 34	
2111	HAMELIN	ALEX	MET	RC	RRS	1841	2113	PINAND	MARGUERITE	MET	RC	RRS	1844	
2111	HAMELIN	ALEX	MET	RC	RRS	1840	2113	PERREAULT	MARGUERITE	MET	RC	RRS	1841 60	3899
1776	HAMELIN	ANTOINE		RC	RRS		2104	BOWETTE	PHILOMENE				1843	
2109	HAMELIN	AUGUSTIN	MET	RC	RRS	1849		PARISIEN	MARIE	MET	RC	RRS	1845	
1777	HAMELIN	BERNARD	MET	RC	RRS	1847	2113	BRELAND	ANGELIQUE	MET	RC	RRS	1852	508
2112	HAMELIN	FIRMIN				1809			CLEMENCE	IND			1849	
1783	HAMELIN	FRANCOIS						LANDRY	MARGUERITE				1814	
2114	HAMELIN	GASPARD		RC	CAN	1841		TOURANGEAU	LOUISE				1846	
1778	HAMELIN	JACQUE				1771		LAROCQUE	ANGELIQUE	MET	RC	RRS	1770 68	
1785	HAMELIN	JEAN BTE	MET			1822	2112	HOULE	JOSEPHTE	MET	RC	RRS	1827	
1785	HAMELIN	JEAN BTE	MET			1820	2112	PIWANOK	THEOTISTE	IND			1825	
2106	HAMELIN	JEAN BTE	MET		RRS	1820	2114	MCKAY	MARGUERITE	MET			1820 43	925
2110	HAMELIN	JEAN BTE		RC		1814		COMTOIS	FRANCOISE	MET	RC	RRS	1819	
2095	HAMELIN	JONAS JR	MET			1805		DAIGNEAULT	MARIANNE				1826	
1779	HAMELIN	JOSEPH	MET	RC	RRS	1829	2113	SAYER	MARIE	MET	RC	RRS	1834 62	2647
1779	HAMELIN	JOSEPH	MET	RC	RRS	1833	2113	LAURENCE	JOSEPHTE	MET			1826	
1781	HAMELIN	JOSEPH				1831		COMTOIS	JULIE				1836	
1787	HAMELIN	JOSEPH				1838		PELERIN	ANABLE				1842	
2105	HAMELIN	JOSEPH	MET		NWT	1840		LAURENCE	ZOE				1844	2641
2115	HAMELIN	JOSEPH	MET			1811		DUCHARME	LOUISE	MET			1812	
2104	HAMELIN	LOUIS	MET	RC		1809		BRUYERE	THERESE	MET			1814	
1788	HAMELIN	NARCISSE			RRS	1818 70	1788	RACETTE	CICILE	MET	RC	RRS	1823 73	
2108	HAMELIN	NARCISSE	MET	RC	RRS	1843	2114	GAUDREAU	MARGUERITE	MET	RC	RRS	1809	
2113	HAMELIN	SOLOMON	MET	RC	RRS	1810		VANDAL	MARGUERITE	MET	RC	RRS	1839	
2118	HAMILTON	DANIEL	EUR	P	SCT	1833		SUTHERLAND	ISABELLE	EUR	P	RRS	1826	
2123	HANCOCK	HARRY				1821		WARD	JANET				1809	
1790	HARBRIDGE	GEORGE				1797		BODEN	MARY ANN	MET	RC	RRS	1802	
2125	HARKNESS	ANDRE	MET		RRS	1795 69		STEVENSON	ELIZABETH	MET	RC	RRS	1809	4481
2444	HARPER	ALEXANDER				1843		MATHESON	SARAH				1848	
2129	HARPER	JAMES	MET	P	RRS	1841	2127	SUTHERLAND	NANCY	EUR	P	RRS	1833 64	4504
2129	HARPER	JAMES	MET	P	RRS	1810	2127	TURNER	HELEN	MET	P	NWT	1843	4728
2133	HARPER	JAMES	MET	P	NWT	1831 64	2134	GIBSON	CHRISTIANA		P		1828	
1796	HARPER	JOHN	EUR	P	SCT	1806	2126	KNIGHT	CHARLOTTE	MET	P	NWT	1840	2277
2127	HARPER	JOHN JR	EUR	P	SCT	1781		FLETT	JANE	MET	P	RRS	1815	
2126	HARPER	JOHN SR	EUR	P	RRS	1835		DANIEL	MARIA	IND	P	NWT	1786	
2130	HARPER	MAGNUS	MET	P	RRS	1840	2132	THOMAS	MARIANN	MET	P	RRS	1844	1012
1792	HARPER	PHILIP	MET	P	RRS	1840		STEVENSON	MARGUERITE	MET	P	RRS	1844	
2131	HARPER	ROBERT	MET	P	RRS	1837		PRINCE	MARGUERITE	IND	P	IND	1845	
2132	HARPER	THOMAS	IND	P	RRS	1846	2126	CUMMINGS	JULIE	IND	P	IND	1848	
1793	HARPER	THOMAS	MET	P	RRS	1807	2133	THOMAS	NANCY	MET	P	RRS	1843	991
1794	HARPER	THOMAS	MET	P	RRS	1848		TAYLOR	ELIZA	MET	P	RRS	1821	
2132	HARPER	WILLIAM	MET	P	RRS	1806		THOMAS	JANE	MET	P	RRS	1853	
1795	HARPER	WILLIAM	MET	P	RRS	1842	2137	TAYLOR	NANCY	MET	P	RRS	1811	
2134	HARRIOT	JOHN E JR	MET	P	NWT	1842		THOMAS	HARRIET	MET	P	RRS	1845	4685
2136	HARRIOT	JOHN EDWARD	EUR			1797 66		PRUDEN	ELIZABETH	EUR	P	RRS	1800	
2137	HARRIOT	JOHN EDWARD	EUR	P	RRS	1797 66		BUNN	NANCY	MET	P	RRS	1810	
2140	HARRISON	AUGUSTIN	MET	RC	RRS	1836	2142	CHAMPAGNE	LUCIE	MET	RC	RRS	1841	739
2141	HARRISON	DOLPHUS	MET	RC	RRS	1839	2142	CYR	ELIZA	MET	RC	NWT	1850	996

TABLE 1: GENEALOGIES OF RED RIVER HOUSEHOLDS, 1818-1870

ID	MALE HEAD OF FAMILY	RACE	FAITH	BIRTH PLACE	DATES	DADS ID	FEMALE HEAD OF FAMILY	RACE	FAITH	BIRTH PLACE	DATES	DADS ID
2142	HARRISON THOMAS JR	MET	RC	NWT	1814 22	2139	LAGEMONIER PAULINE	EUR			1812 65	
2139	HARRISON THOMAS SR		RC	RRS	1768		SARAH	IND			1776	
1800	HARVEL ANDRE				1825		MARGUERITE				1830	
2143	HARVEL JAMES	EUR	P	ENG	1838		MALATERRE NANCY	MET	RC	RRS	1843	1954
2128	HAY EDWARD	MET			1832		JOHNSTON SARAH		P	RRS	1836	
2145	HAY HENRY	MET			1797		GIBSON MARGUERITE				1782	
2124	HAY ROBERT	EUR	P	SCT	1843		ARCUS SARAH	MET	P	RRS	1800	
2144	HAY THOMAS		P	NWT	1816		MCDONALD CHRISTIANA	MET			1840	
2197	HAYWOOD CHARLES				1808		SPENCE LETITIA	MET		RRS	1826	
2149	HEAD ABRAHAM	EUR	P	OTH	1790 45		COOK MARGARET		P	RRS	1816 58	
2152	HECKENBERGER HENRY	EUR	P	ENG	1817 57		SUTHERLAND SARAH	MET			1813	
2153	HEMINGWAY FREDERICK	EUR	P	RRS	1824		JANE				1800 70	
2179	HENDERSON ANGUS	EUR	P	RRS	1835	2174	TAYLOR CATHERINE	EUR	P	RRS	1828	3275
2167	HENDERSON CHARLES	EUR	P	RRS	1831	2164	MCBEATH MARY	MET	P	RRS	1832	
1933	HENDERSON FRANCOIS	MET		RRS	1841		JOHNSTON ANNE	EUR			1835	3245
2175	HENDERSON JOHN	EUR	P	RRS	1799	2174	COOK ANNE	MET	P	RRS	1836	
2447	HENDERSON JOHN				1830		MUNROE MARY	IND		RRS	1848	
2161	HENDERSON NEIL	EUR	P	RRS	1795 63	2174	JANET	EUR			1804	
2164	HENDERSON NEIL	EUR	P	RRS	1823		MCKAY ANN	EUR	P	RRS	1832	
2165	HENDERSON PETER				1835	2164	MATHESON CHARLOTTE	MET			1835	
2176	HENDERSON PETER	MET		RRS	1845	2174	YORKSTON ELEONOR	IND	P	RRS	1806	
2180	HENDERSON PETER	EUR	P	RRS	1818	2164	WHITFORD ANN	EUR		RRS	1829	
2446	HENDERSON PETER	MET		RRS	1799	2164	MCBEATH ANN	MET	P	RRS	1846 74	3267
2174	HENDERSON SAMUEL				1820		HALCROW MARY	IND	P	RRS	1849	
2445	HENDERSON SAMUEL				1820		FLORA	EUR			1823	
2177	HENDERSON WILLIAM	EUR		SCT	1825 70		MARGARET	IND			1801 65	
2178	HENDERSON WILLIAM			RRS	1826		MADELEINE	IND			1824 45	
2151	HENEAULT ANTOINE	EUR	RC	NWT	1833		JANE	IND			1823	1042
1798	HENEAULT CHARLES	MET			1810		MATHESON CATHERINE	EUR	P	RRS	1830	2398
2150	HENEAULT CHARLES				1823 68		DAVIS CATHERINE	EUR	P	RRS	1827	3840
1439	HENEAULT PIERRE				1836	1798	IRIS MARIE	MET	RC	NWT	1832	
2189	HENRY ALEXANDER	MET	RC	RRS	1833	2188	PARISIEN LOUISE	MET	RC	RRS	1810	
2188	HENRY ALEXIS	MET	RC	NWT	1813 68		LAROCQUE MARGUERITE	MET	RC	RRS	1842	
2154	HENRY ALEXIS	MET	RC	RRS	1813 68		BEAUCHAMP MARIE	MET	RC	NWT	1837	
2159	HENRY JOHN	MET	RC	RRS	1810	2154	LYONNAIS MARIE				1818 62	
2190	HENRY JOHN	MET	RC	RRS	1835		CONTRE GENEVIEVE	MET	RC	RRS	1820	13360
2184	HENRY JOHN	MET	RC	RRS	1828		DENAULT JESSIE	MET	RC	RRS	1839	
2186	HENRY JOSEPH				1818		MCKAY MARGARET	MET	RC	RRS	1824	
2213	HENRY LOUIS			RRS	1829 67	2188	PARISIEN JOSEPHTE	MET		RRS	1823	
2187	HENRY MOURICE	MET	RC		1847	2188	CYR MARGUERITE		P		1834	5054
2183	HERMAN PIERRE	MET	RC	RRS	1845		HOGUE MARIE	MET	P	RRS	1852	194
2192	HERON EDOUARD				1821		VANDAL ISABEL				1845	
2148	HERON EDOUARD				1819		BEAUCHEMIN CAROLINE	MET	RC	RRS	1826	
2195	HERON FRANCIS				1810		DAUPHINAIS MARGUERITE	MET			1823 64	
2196	HEYDEN FELIX	MET	RC	RRS	1840		ILLINOIS ELIZA				1815	
2182	HEYDEN PETER	EUR	RC	IRE	1806		CHALIFOUX ISABELLA	MET			1811	2675
	HIGGINS JOHN	EUR	P	IRE	1825		LAPLANTE BETSY	MET	RC	RRS	1846 70	
							LAGEMONIER ANTOINETTE					
							MARGARET					

ID	MALE HEAD OF FAMILY	RACE	FAITH	BIRTH PLACE	DATES	DADS ID	FEMALE HEAD OF FAMILY	RACE	FAITH	BIRTH PLACE	DATES	DADS ID
1228	HIGGS WILLIAM				1797		HOERNER HENRIETTE	MET			1802	
2171	HODGES GEORGE	EUR		USA	1828	2200	DESMARAIS CATHERINE	MET		RRS	1843	
2201	HODGSON JOHN	MET	P	NWT	1795	2201	YORKSTON CHARLOTTE	MET		NWT	1806	
2203	HODGSON JOHN	MET	P	RRS	1826	2201	DAVIS CATHERINE	MET	P	NWT	1822	
2198	HODGSON WILLIAM	MET	P	NWT	1826	2201	COOK NANCY	MET		RRS	1830	945
2205	HOGUE AMABLE	MET			1835		ALLARY MARIANNE	MET		RRS	1830	
2209	HOGUE AMABLE	MET	RC	CAN	1795	2211	MORRISETTE BETSY	MET	RC	RRS	1845	
2211	HOGUE ANTOINE	MET	RC	RRS	1844		TAYLOR MARGUERITE	MET	RC	RRS	1810	
2207	HOGUE JOSEPH	MET	RC	RRS	1835	2211	BROWN CRAWFORD	MET	RC	RRS	1845	
2210	HOGUE LOUIS	MET	RC	RRS	1846	2211	TURCOTTE PELAGIE	MET	RC	RRS	1843	4725
2208	HOGUE THOMAS	MET	RC	RRS	1842	2211	TURCOTTE JULIE	MET	RC	RRS	1851	4725
2212	HOLMES JOHN	EUR	P	ENG	1775 35		MCMILLAN PHILOMENE	MET	RC	RRS	1847	
2169	HOOKEY GEORGE	EUR	P	ENG	1820		THOMAS ELIZABETH	MET	P	NWT	1790	4673
2156	HOOKEY THOMAS				1840		THOMAS JULIA	MET	P	RRS	1847	
2166	HOPE JOHN	IND	P	RRS	1840		AGNES	IND	P	RRS	1822	
2163	HOPE THOMAS	IND	P	RRS	1820		FLETT JANE	IND	P	RRS	1839	
2155	HORN WILLIAM				1834		SPENCE SARAH	IND			1774	
2229	HOULE ANTOINE	EUR		LC	1769		BEAR ELISE	IND		RRS	1830	
2220	HOULE ANTOINE	MET	RC	RRS	1812	2221	LEDOUX ELIZA	IND	RC	RRS	1831	
2220	HOULE ANTOINE	MET	RC	RRS	1812	2221	LAROCQUE MADELEINE	MET	RC		1820	
2221	HOULE ANTOINE	MET	RC	RRS	1812	2221	LOUZON MARIE				1787 45	
2222	HOULE ANTOINE				1787 67		CHARTRAND JOSEPHTE	MET	RC	RRS	1790	2914
2223	HOULE CHARLES				1787 67		LEPINE J	MET			1847	
2228	HOULE CHARLES	MET		RRS	1839	2220	FLEURY JULIE	MET	RC	RRS	1800 33	
2228	HOULE CHARLES	MET	RC	RRS	1847	2220	BRELAND JULIAN	MET		RRS	1820	
2227	HOULE GABRIEL	MET	RC	RRS	1794	2229	FALARDEAU MAGDELEINE	MET	RC	RRS	1844	
2215	HOULE JEAN BTE	MET	RC	RRS	1794	2229	VANDAL CATHERINE	MET	RC	RRS	1836	5073
2218	HOULE JOSEPH	MET			1845	2228	KIPITOWE MARGUERITE	IND			1830	
2234	HOULE JOSEPH				1831	2231	KEJEKOK	IND			1826	
2216	HOULE LOUIS				1829		FAGNANT SOPHIE	MET	RC	RRS	1824	
2226	HOULE LOUIS	MET	RC	RRS	1835	2221	ROSS MARGUERITE	MET	RC	RRS	1849	
1782	HOULE MICHEL	MET	RC	RRS	1824	2228	BERTHELET CAROLINE	MET	RC	RRS	1842	
2233	HOULE PIERRE				1839		HOULE JOSEPHTE	MET		RRS	1811 46	2221
8029	HOULE WILLIAM				1838	2231	LAROCQUE MARIE	MET	RC	RRS	1847	
2217	HOURIE GEORGE	MET	RC	RRS	1811	2243	MCGILLIS DOMITILDE	MET	RC	RRS	1807	
2238	HOURIE GEORGE	MET	RC	RRS	1800	2243	BOISBERT JOSEPHTE	MET	RC	RRS	1826 59	
2242	HOURIE JOHN	MET		RRS	1829	2252	COOK HELEN	MET		RRS	1829	
2244	HOURIE JOHN	MET	P	RRS	1845	2245	KNIGHT ELIZABETH	MET	P	RRS	1850	2277
2248	HOURIE JOHN	MET	P	RRS	1835	2250	MCKENZIE MARGARET	MET	P		1840	3424
2245	HOURIE JOHN	MET		RRS	1852	2243	MCKAY MARGARET	MET			1855	4565
2243	HOURIE JOHN JR	MET		NWT	1810	2243	SWAIN MATHILDE	MET	P	RRS	1815	1226
2236	HOURIE JOHN SR	EUR	P	ORK	1779 57		DENNET JESSIE	IND		NWT	1787 47	
2247	HOURIE PETER	MET		RRS	1830	2250	WHITFORD MARGARET	MET		RRS	1837	4676
2237	HOURIE PETER	MET		RRS	1849	2243	THOMAS SARAH	MET			1840	
2240	HOURIE PHILIP	MET		RRS	1832	2250	COOK MARGARET	MET	P	RRS	1848	
2250	HOURIE ROBERT	MET		RRS	1840	2243	JOHNSTON SARAH	MET		RRS	1845	
2250	HOURIE ROBERT	MET		RRS	1815		RACETTE ANGELIQUE	MET	P	RRS	1840	

TABLE 1: GENEALOGIES OF RED RIVER HOUSEHOLDS, 1818-1870

ID	MALE HEAD OF FAMILY	RACE	FAITH	BIRTH PLACE	DATES	DADS ID	FEMALE HEAD OF FAMILY	RACE	FAITH	BIRTH PLACE	DATES	DADS ID
2250	HOURIE ROBERT	MET	P	RRS	1815	2243	ANDERSON CHRISTINE	MET	P	RRS	1825	82
2249	HOURIE THOMAS	MET	P	RRS	1844	2250	BIRD AGNES	MET	P	RRS	1845	4388
2252	HOURIE THOMAS				1820	2243	SINCLAIR MARY	MET			1825	
1802	HOUSE HENRY			LC	1830		ANDERSON ELIZABETH				1835	
2251	HOUSE JOSEPH	EUR	P	ENG	1814	2254	ANDERSON ELIZABETH	EUR		ENG	1837	78
2147	HOUSE JOSHUA	EUR			1833		BORNES PROCINA				1839	
2253	HUDDLESTONE ADAM				1836		MARGARET				1840	
2257	HUDDLESTONE THOMAS				1822 48		LAFLEUR CHARLOTTE				1827	
2258	HUDSON THOMAS				1780			IND			1785	
5279	HUGHES JOHN				1828		DESJARLAIS MARGUERITE				1830	
2259	HUGHES LEON				1793		GREY MARIE	MET			1805	
2260	HUIREAULT CHARLES				1792		TURNER ANNE	MET			1797	
1735	HUMPHABLE THOMAS				1835		GUNN HENRIETTA				1840	
2268	HUNT FRANK	MET	RC	RRS	1846	2269	ATKINSON SOPHIE	MET	RC	RRS	1850	2142
2264	HUPPE ATHANASE	MET	RC	RRS	1845	2267	HARRISON CATHERINE	MET	RC	RRS	1849	
2269	HUPPE ISADORE				1820 66		CHARBONNEAU ELIZABETH	MET	RC		1824 68	3899
2271	HUPPE JEAN BTE	MET	RC	RRS	1841	2269	PERREAULT AMAGILE	MET	RC	RRS	1845	997
1002	HUPPE JEAN BTE	MET	RC	RRS	1818	2267	CYR JOSEPHTE	MET	RC	RRS	1822	
2266	HUPPE JOSEPH	EUR	RC	RRS	1833		LAYISSE MARIE	MET		RRS	1841	
2267	HUPPE JOSEPH	EUR	RC	CAN	1788		MARCELLAIS MARGUERITE	MET			1793	
2270	HYDE DAVID	EUR		IRE	1840		CAMERON JANE	MET		RRS	1853	
2272	INGRAM JAMES	MET		RRS	1803		SMITH SARAH	EUR			1808	4417
2407	INKSTER GEORGE	EUR	P	RRS	1842	2405	FRANKS ELIZA	MET		RRS	1845	1650
2403	INKSTER JAMES	EUR		ORK	1774 54		MARY	IND			1790	
2405	INKSTER JAMES	MET		SCT	1805 65		SUTHERLAND ELIZABETH	MET		RRS	1821	4520
3014	INKSTER JAMES	MET		SCT	1805 65	2405	LINKLATER ELIZABETH	IND			1815	
2404	INKSTER JAMES JR	MET	P	RRS	1831	2405	WORK JANE	MET		RRS	1843	5201
2400	INKSTER JOHN	EUR		SCT	1798	2403	SUTHERLAND LETITIA	MET		RRS	1815	4520
2402	INKSTER JOHN	MET		NWT	1807 64	2405	SINCLAIR MARY	MET		NWT	1805	4385
2406	INKSTER ROBERT	MET		RRS	1840	2402	SANDERSON ISABELLA	MET		RRS	1813	
2401	INKSTER THOMAS	MET	P	RRS	1836	2396	COOK CHRISTIANA	MET		NWT	1846	933
2398	IRIS CORNELIOUS	MET		RRS	1785		GILL HARRIET	MET		RRS	1838	
1449	IRVINE GEORGE				1843		NEPISSING MARIE	IND	P		1790	
2390	IRVINE GEORGE				1809		LAMBERT CATHERINE	MET		RRS	1843	2582
2390	IRVINE GEORGE				1803 70		FIDLER COLLETE				1814	
2391	IRVINE JAMES				1803 70		FIDLER COLLETE			NWT	1813 42	
2392	IRVINE JAMES	EUR	P	ENG	1817		JANE				1830	
2388	IRVINE JAMES	EUR	P	ENG	1825	2781	TAIT MATILDA				1828 61	
2396	IRVINE JOHN	MET	RC	NWT	1785	2781	JOHNSTON ANN	MET	RC	NWT	1832 69	2428
2781	IRVINE JOHN JR	MET	P	NWT	1820	2781	ST GERMAIN ANGELIQUE	MET	RC	USA	1825	
2138	IRVINE WILLIAM	EUR	P	ORK	1803		LAGARDE LOUISE	MET		NWT	1781	3848
2385	ISAAC MICHAEL	MET	P	RRS	1833		PARK MARGARET	IND			1821	
2376	ISBISTER DAVID	EUR	RC	OTH	1788 38	2375	MARY	IND			1800	
2375	ISBISTER JAMES	MET		NWT	1795 62		LOUIS ELIZABETH	MET	P	RRS	1843	
2378	ISBISTER JAMES				1849	2375	ROY MAGDELEINE	MET	P	RRS	1810	4266
2380	ISBISTER JAMES	MET	P	RRS			BROWN MARGARET	MET	P	NWT	1854	
	ISBISTER JAMES						MCGILLIVRAY MARY	MET	P	RRS	1851	
	ISBISTER						CAPLETTE SARAH	MET	RC			

ID	MALE HEAD OF FAMILY		RACE	FAITH	BIRTH PLACE	DATES	DADS ID	FEMALE HEAD OF FAMILY		RACE	FAITH	BIRTH PLACE	DATES	DADS ID
2380	ISBISTER	JAMES	EUR	p	SCT	1834	.	LIVINGSTON	JESSIE	EUR	p	.	1839	.
2374	ISBISTER	JOHN	EUR	p	NWT	1794	.	IRVINE	FANNY	MET	p	NWT	1816	.
2377	ISBISTER	JOHN	MET	.	.	1841	2375	IRVINE	MARTHA	MET	p	RRS	1840	2390
2372	ISBISTER	THOMAS	.	.	.	1800 40	.	WIDOW	MARY	MET	p	NWT	1804	.
2373	ISBISTER	WILLIAM	EUR	p	USA	1826	.	MUNROE	MARY	MET	.	.	1831	.
2363	JACKSON	ANDREW	.	.	.	1818	.	CORRIGAL	AMELIA	MET	p	NWT	1835	.
1120	JACQUISH	HIRAM	EUR	p	.	1836	.		NANCY	MET	.	.	1844	854
2354	JANNOT	ALEXANDRE	MET	RC	RRS	1838	.	PAGE	MARGUERITE	MET	RC	RRS	1842	3776
2356	JANNOT	FRANCOIS	MET	RC	NWT	1812	.	FALCON	MADELEINE	MET	RC	NWT	1815	1487
2352	JANNOT	GASPARD	MET	RC	RRS	1845	2356	LAVIOLETTE	EMILIE	MET	RC	RRS	1849	2849
2353	JANNOT	PIERRE	MET	RC	RRS	1839	2356	DELORME	ELISE	MET	RC	.	1866	.
522	JEAN	BAPTISTE	MET	.	.	1847	531	ALLARY	BETHSY	MET	.	.	1850	.
2348	JEROME	MARTIN	.	.	.	1820	.	WILKEY	FRANCOISE	IND	.	.	1823	5190
2349	JEROME	MARTIN	.	RC	LC	1783	.	DENOMME	DELPHINE	MET	RC	LC	1785	.
2345	JETTE	THEOPHILE	EUR	RC	LC	1832	2347	MONDEVILLE	MARGUERITE	EUR	RC	NWT	1837	.
2350	JOBIN	AMBROISE	EUR	RC	LC	1817	.	LAPIERRE	CECILE	MET	RC	.	1831	.
2347	JOBIN	JOSEPH	MET	p	RRS	1810	.	BROWN	EMILIE	EUR	p	.	1812	.
2328	JOHNSTON	ANGUS	IND	p	.	1837	2327	LAMBERT	ELIZABETH	MET	p	RRS	1843	.
2432	JOHNSTON	ARCHIBALD	MET	p	NWT	1845	.	MCDONALD	MARGARET	MET	p	NWT	1847	.
2330	JOHNSTON	CHARLES	MET	p	.	1829	2327	THOMAS	ELIZA	MET	p	.	1832	2582
2329	JOHNSTON	CORNELIUS	MET	p	RRS	1843	2327	ANDERSON	CATHERINE	MET	p	RRS	1833	.
2325	JOHNSTON	DAVID	EUR	p	SCT	1846	2336	DANIEL	BETHSY	MET	p	.	1852	.
2334	JOHNSTON	DONALD	MET	p	NWT	1784	.		NANCY	MET	p	NWT	1800 44	.
2332	JOHNSTON	FRANCIS	MET	p	.	1805	2324	MILLS	MARIE LOUISA	MET	.	.	1810	1013
2433	JOHNSTON	GEORGE	EUR	p	ORK	1834	.	THOMAS	FRANCIS	MET	p	.	1836	.
2327	JOHNSTON	GEORGE	MET	p	RRS	1795	2327	MURDO	CATHERINE	MET	p	.	1815	.
2331	JOHNSTON	HENRY	EUR	p	SCT	1836	.	CLOUSTON	MARY	EUR	p	.	1843	.
2438	JOHNSTON	JAMES	IND	p	RRS	1835	2442	WORK	ELIZABETH	IND	p	SCT	1846	5201
2023	JOHNSTON	JAMES	IND	p	NWT	1840	2442	DUNNING	MARY	IND	p	RRS	1835	.
2326	JOHNSTON	JAMES	MET	p	NWT	1810 59	.	FOULDS	MARY				1818 48	.
2326	JOHNSTON	JAMES	MET	p	NWT	1810 59	.	SPENCE	ISABELLA				1828	.
2422	JOHNSTON	JAMES	.	.	.	1847	.	GIBEAU	JULIA				1845 66	1623
2422	JOHNSTON	JAMES	.	.	.	1823	.	BIRD	MARY ANN				1852	.
2426	JOHNSTON	JAMES	.	.	NWT	1810	.		SALLY	IND	p		1825	.
2427	JOHNSTON	JAMES	.	.	NWT	1808	.		POLLY				1814	.
2428	JOHNSTON	JAMES	.	.	.	1785 60	.	ANDERSON	FANNY				1810	.
2429	JOHNSTON	JAMES	IND	p	NWT	1832	.		MARY				1798 69	.
2436	JOHNSTON	JAMES	MET	.	RRS	1846	.	ANDERSON	SARAH	MET	p	RRS	1834	.
2437	JOHNSTON	JAMES	IND	p	RRS	1828	.	ATKINSON	JULIA	IND	p	RRS	1845	.
2440	JOHNSTON	JAMES	IND	p	NWT	1816 65	2442	GIBBON	MARGARET	MET	p	RRS	1851	.
2441	JOHNSTON	JEREMIE	IND	p	.	1825	.	COCHRANE	ELIZABETH	IND	p	RRS	1835	.
2337	JOHNSTON	JOHN	IND	p	NWT	1835	.		MARGUERITE	IND	p	RRS	1826	.
2423	JOHNSTON	JOHN	IND	p	.	1810	.	STEVENSON	SALLY	MET	p	RRS	1820	.
2431	JOHNSTON	JOHN	.	p	.	1810	.	THOMAS	HARRIET	IND	p	.	1839	.
2442	JOHNSTON	JOSEPH	IND	p	NWT	1843	2332		ELIZABETH	IND	p	RRS	1815	.
2336	JOHNSTON	JOSEPH	IND	RC	RRS	1810	.		MARY	IND	p	RRS	1813	.
2339	JOHNSTON	THOMAS	MET	RC	RRS	1843	2332	SANDERSON	SARAH	MET	p	.	1846	588
2324	JOHNSTON	THOMAS	IND	p	NWT	1785	.	BRUYERE	JANE	MET	.	.	1787	.
2435	JOHNSTON	THOMAS	MET	p	NWT	1842 69	.	STAR	ANNABELLA	MET	p	.	1846	.

TABLE 1: GENEALOGIES OF RED RIVER HOUSEHOLDS, 1818-1870

ID	MALE HEAD OF FAMILY		RACE	FAITH	BIRTH PLACE	DATES	DADS ID	FEMALE HEAD OF FAMILY		RACE	FAITH	BIRTH PLACE	DATES	DADS ID
2435	JOHNSTON	THOMAS	MET	P	.	1842 69	.	PEEBLES	MARGARET	MET	P	RRS	1845	.	3877
2323	JOHNSTON	WILLIAM	MET	P	NWT	1803 56	.	BUDD	BETHSY	MET	P	.	1808	.	
2338	JOHNSTON	WILLIAM	IND	P	RRS	1835	.	KENNEDY	MARGUERITE	IND	P	RRS	1840	.	
2424	JOHNSTON	WILLIAM	.	.	.	1827 56	.		MARGARET	MET	P	.	1827	.	
2316	JOLIBOIS	BAPTISTE	EUR	RC	.	1800	.	VERSAILLES	LOUISE	MET	RC	.	1800	.	
2317	JOLIBOIS	JEAN	MET	RC	RRS	1823	2316	ROBILLARD	MARGUERITE	.	RC	RRS	1831 69	.	
2412	JOLICOEUR	JEAN BTE	.	.	.	1780	2321	BELLEAU	ANGELIQUE	.	RC	.	1812	.	
2322	JOLICOEUR	JOSEPH	.	RC	.	1810	.	PRUDEN	S	IND	RC	.	1775	.	
2321	JOLICOEUR	LOUISON	MET	P	CAN	1772	.		SUSETTE	IND	P	RRS	1847	.	
2416	JOLICOEUR	EDWARD	.	.	RRS	1825	.		MARGUERITE	MET	P	.	1845	.	
2411	JONES	JOHN	EUR	P	.	1843	.		MARGARET	.	P	.	1802 36	.	
2320	JONES	REV D J	EUR	P	ENG	1797	.		MARY	.	RC	.	1835	.	
2414	JUSSIAUME	JOSEPH	EUR	P	.	1835	2311	DESJARDIN	ISABELLE	.	RC	.	1840	.	
2310	KAUFFMAN	JACOB	EUR	P	RRS	1833	.	MATHESON	CHRISTIANA	EUR	P	.	1806	.	
2313	KAUFFMAN	JACOB	EUR	P	.	1806	.	MCKAY	ELIZABETH	EUR	P	SCT	1806	.	
2313	KAUFFMAN	JACOB	.	.	.	1833	.	MCKAY	ELIZABETH	.	P	.	1835	.	
1660	KAYOL	VITAL	MET	P	RRS	1815	.	GAGNON	ADELAIDE	MET	P	RRS	1825	.	
2314	KENNEDY	ADAM	.	.	.	1830	.	BIRD	BETSY	.	P	.	1833 55	.	
2409	KENNEDY	ADAM	.	.	.	1830	.	SAYER	NANCY	.	P	.	1834	.	
2409	KENNEDY	ADAM	MET	P	RRS	1847	.	CAMERON	SOPHIA	MET	P	RRS	1850	.	
1745	KENNEDY	ALEXANDER	MET	P	.	1780	.	DENNET	MARGUERITE	IND	P	NWT	1780 63	.	
2306	KENNEDY	ALEXANDRE	MET	P	.	1830	.		AGATHA	MET	P	RRS	1840	.	
1746	KENNEDY	ANDREW	MET	P	RRS	1820	1750	COCHRANE	MARIE	MET	P	RRS	1821	.	
1748	KENNEDY	ANTOINE	IND	P	RRS	1835	.	ASMAS	SARAH	MET	P	.	1837	.	
1753	KENNEDY	HENRY	.	.	.	1825	.	COCHRANE	MARY	.	P	RRS	1828 58	.	
1752	KENNEDY	JAMES	MET	P	.	1825	.	SINCLAIR	MARGARET	MET	P	.	1830	.	
1752	KENNEDY	JAMES	MET	P	RRS	1810	.	SMITH	MARY	MET	P	.	1820	.	
1750	KENNEDY	JOHN	.	.	NWT	1820	.		MARGUERITE	.	P	RRS	1821 63	.	
2307	KENNEDY	PHILIP	MET	P	NWT	1826	2306	MCKENZIE	JESSY	MET	P	.	1845	3644	
1743	KENNEDY	THOMAS	.	.	NWT	1840	.		NANCY	.	RC	NWT	1840	.	
1751	KENNEDY	THOMAS	MET	RC	NWT	1840	.	GARRIOCH	JULIET	MET	P	.	1812	.	
1751	KENNEDY	THOMAS	MET	RC	NWT	1810	.	FLETT	CAROLINE	IND	RC	.	1832 70	.	
1884	KING	WILLIAM	IND	P	NWT	1774 64	.	HUDSON	VICTORIA	.	P	.	1810	.	
2292	KING	WILLIAM	MET	P	.	1831	2298		ELIZABETH	IND	P	.	1815	5217	
2296	KIPPLING	EDWARD	MET	P	NWT	1800	2293	WALLER	MARY	MET	P	.	1820	.	
2300	KIPPLING	EDWARD	IND	P	NWT	1804	2298		NANCY	IND	P	RRS	1852	.	
2298	KIPPLING	GEORGE	MET	P	NWT	1824	.	LANDRY	ISABELLA	MET	P	NWT	1810	.	
2299	KIPPLING	GEORGE	MET	P	RRS	1848	.	SPENCE	CATHERINE	MET	P	.	1815	.	
2294	KIPPLING	JAMES	MET	P	.	1834	2299	COOK	BELLA	MET	P	RRS	1820	2115	
1760	KIPPLING	JOHN	.	.	.	1770	.	HAMELIN	MARGUERITE	MET	RC	NWT	1836 60	.	
2290	KIPPLING	JOHN	MET	P	.	1795 25	.		MARGUERITE	IND	P	NWT	1790	.	
2293	KIPPLING	JOHN	MET	P	RRS	1792	.		NANCY	IND	P	NWT	1772	.	
2291	KIPPLING	THOMAS	MET	P	RRS	1834	2298		NANCY	IND	P	USA	1800	.	
2297	KIPPLING	THOMAS	IND	P	RRS	1810	.	HENRY	JANE	MET	P	RRS	1838	.	
2288	KIRKNESS	ANDREW	MET	P	NWT	1770	2289		SARAH	MET	P	RRS	1820	.	
2289	KIRKNESS	ANDREW	.	.	NWT	1822	.	MOWAT	MARGUERITE	IND	P	NWT	1772 52	940	
2287	KIRKNESS	JOHN	MET	P	.	1845	2289	COOK	ELIZABETH	MET	P	SCT	1822	.	
1762	KIRKNESS	WILLIAM	EUR	P	SCT	1812	.	BROWN	JANE	EUR	P	NWT	1844	947	
2286	KIRTON	JOSEPH	EUR	P	ENG	.	.	COOK	CATHERINE	EUR	P	RRS	1815	.	

ID	MALE HEAD OF FAMILY	RACE	FAITH	BIRTH PLACE	DATES	DADS ID	FEMALE HEAD OF FAMILY	RACE	FAITH	BIRTH PLACE	DATES	DADS ID
8032	KITTSON WILLIAM N	MET	RC	NWT	1833		MARION ELISE	MET	RC	RRS	1833 68	
1757	KLYNE ADAM	MET	RC	RRS	1822		DONALD ANABELLA	MET	RC	RRS	1848	321
2282	KLYNE GEORGE	MET	RC	RRS	1828	2284	BERTHELET MONIQUE	MET	RC	RRS	1847	998
2283	KLYNE JOHN	MET	RC	NWT	1833	2284	CYR MARGUERITE	MET	RC	RRS	1837	489
2285	KLYNE JOSEPH				1816	2284	BRACONNIER LOUISE	MET	RC	NWT	1815	
1761	KLYNE MICHEAL		RC	CAN	1813	2284	MIQUETTE MADELEINE	MET	RC	RRS	1790	
2284	KLYNE MICHEL				1781		LAFRANCE SUZANNE	MET	P		1818	
2280	KNIFE WILLIAM				1851		HAYWOOD ELIZABETH				1845	
1764	KNIGHT JAMES	MET			1845	2275	LOUISA	MET	P		1792	2098
2277	KNIGHT JAMES	EUR	P	ORK	1783 54		HALLET SOPHIA	MET	P	RRS	1834	
2278	KNIGHT JOHN	MET	P	RRS	1830	2277	BIRD SOPHIA	MET	P		1844	
1759	KNIGHT PETER				1840		BIRD NANCY	MET	P	NWT	1847	
2276	KNIGHT PETER	MET	P	RRS	1826	2277	COTE CAROLINE	MET	RC	RRS	1827	
2275	KNIGHT WILLIAM		P	NWT	1827 54	2277	CUMMINGS MARGARET	EUR			1830	991
2281	KNIPE EDWARD				1830		MATHESON ANN	EUR	P	NWT	1848	
2273	KNOTT ALEXANDER	MET	P	NWT	1842	2274	LINKLATER BARBARA	MET	P	NWT	1817	2968
2274	KNOTT JOHN	IND		NWT	1805		HAY MARY	MET	RC	RRS	1849	
1913	LABERGE FRANCOIS	MET	RC	RRS	1833		GLADU MARGUERITE	MET	RC	RRS	1800	
2458	LABERGE NORBERT		RC		1800		VIVIEN MADELEINE	IND			1764	
2459	LABINE BAPTISTE				1760		JOSEPHTE	MET	P		1849	
1768	LABISTON ALEXANDER	MET	P	RRS	1835		GEORGE SUSANNE	MET		RRS	1835	
1713	LABISTON JOHN	EUR	P	SCT	1844		FOLSTER MARGUERITE	MET		RRS	1797	
2462	LABOUCANE JEAN BTE				1832		ALLARD JOSEPHTE				1825	
2468	LACERTE LOUIS	MET	RC	NWT	1780		MARTIN MARIE	MET	RC		1850	3061
2469	LACERTE LOUIS	MET	RC	RRS	1821	2468	VANDAL JOSEPHTE	MET	RC		1824	
2467	LACERTE NARCISSE	MET			1838	2468	CAPLETTE JULIE	MET			1780	681
871	LACOUTURE FABIEN				1820		DEMERS MARGUERITE	IND			1846	
2474	LACOUTURE FRANCOIS				1777		JOSEPHTE	MET	RC		1780	
868	LACOUTURE HENRIE				1844	2474	LAGEMONIER MARIE	MET	RC	RRS	1846	
1714	LACOUTURE JOSEPH	MET	RC	RRS	1810	2474	PICHE MADELEINE	MET	RC	RRS	1810	2546
2490	LADEROUTE CHRYSOSTOME	MET	RC	RRS	1847	2497	LAROCQUE CHRISTINE				1848	2672
2494	LADEROUTE JEAN	MET	RC	RRS	1809	2496	HONORE NANCY	MET	RC	RRS	1814	
2493	LADEROUTE JOSEPH	MET	RC	RRS	1832	2496	LAROCQUE MARIE	MET	RC	RRS	1833	2664
2491	LADEROUTE OLIVIER		RC	RRS	1830	2496	LHIRONDELLE JOSEPHTE				1828	
2488	LADEROUTE PHILIBERT	MET	RC		1824		LEPINE JULIE	MET	RC	RRS	1824	2921
8034	LADEROUTE PHILIBERT				1784		SANSREGRET MARGUERITE				1784 69	
2496	LADEROUTE THIBERT		RC	CAN	1778		SANSREGRET MARGUERITE	MET	RC		1780	
2501	LADOUCEUR AUGUSTIN	MET	RC	RRS	1817	2486	LAMBERT MADELEINE		RC	RRS	1824	2575
2503	LADOUCEUR BASILE	MET	RC	NWT	1835	2486	LOUZON PAULINE	MET	RC	RRS	1839	
2498	LADOUCEUR ISAIE				1844 66		GOSSELIN HELENE	MET	RC	RRS	1846	
2495	LADRON	MET	RC	NWT	1800		ANGELIQUE	EUR			1810	
2507	LAFERTE JOSEPH				1835		GOYETTE MARIE	MET	RC	RRS	1836	
2504	LAFERTE LOUIS	EUR	RC	CAN	1799		CARRON AGATHE	MET	RC	RRS	1800	687
2508	LAFERTE OLIVER	MET	RC		1830	2505	FAILLE MADELEINE	MET	RC	NWT	1814	
2505	LAFERTE PIERRE	MET		NWT	1800 65		GENEREUSE MARIANNE	MET			1829	
2511	LAFLEUR PIERRE	EUR		NWT	1811		MATCHION CHARLOTTE				1805	
2512	LAFOND AMABLE	MET	RC	NWT	1787		RACETTE MARIE		RC		1811 66	
2506	LAFOND BAPTISTE				1832	2512	ARCAND THERESE				1801	
2502	LAFOND BASILE				1846	2512	DURAND ISABELLE				1835	
2509	LAFOND CYRIL	MET		RRS	1844		PEPIN AGATHE	MET	RC	RRS	1843	3073

TABLE 1: GENEALOGIES OF RED RIVER HOUSEHOLDS, 1818-1870

ID	MALE HEAD OF FAMILY	RACE	FAITH	BIRTH PLACE	DATES	DADS ID	FEMALE HEAD OF FAMILY	RACE	FAITH	BIRTH PLACE	DATES	DADS ID
2514	LAFONTAINE ANTOINE	MET	RC	USA	1844	2515	JANNOT PHILOMENE	MET	RC	RRS	1845	2356
2515	LAFONTAINE ANTOINE		RC	NWT	1820	.	GARIEPY ANGELIQUE	IND	RC	.	1822	.
2516	LAFONTAINE BAPTISTE		RC	NWT	1799	.	MARIE	MET	RC	.	1800 24	.
2516	LAFONTAINE BAPTISTE	MET	RC	RRS	1849	2517	MORIN MADELEINE	MET	RC	RRS	1847	1945
2518	LAFONTAINE BAPTISTE	MET	RC	RRS	1849	2517	GERVAIS LOUISE	MET	RC	RRS	1851	.
2520	LAFONTAINE CALIXT	MET	RC	RRS	1826	2516	BAUVIER CLEMENCE	MET	RC	RRS	1830	.
1900	LAFONTAINE FRANCOIS	MET	RC	RRS	1842	.	ADAM CHARLOTTE	MET	RC	RRS	1848	.
2892	LAFONTAINE FRANCOIS		RC	.	1833	.	HUGHES ELIZA	.	RC	.	1833	.
2477	LAFONTAINE JEAN BTE		RC	RRS	1820	2516	PARISIEN MADELEINE	MET	RC	RRS	1828 63	.
2477	LAFONTAINE JEAN BTE	MET	RC	RRS	1820	2516	MARTIN FRANCOISE	MET	RC	RRS	1839	.
2485	LAFONTAINE LOUISON	MET	RC	RRS	1840	.	GARIEPY MATHILDA	MET	RC	RRS	1842	.
2525	LAFONTAINE BAPTISTE	MET	RC	NWT	1813	2527	PELLETIER LOUISE	MET	RC	.	1816	2591
2679	LAFOURNAISE D	MET	RC	RRS	1833	.	GOSSELIN MARGUERITE	MET	RC	RRS	1833	.
2524	LAFOURNAISE ELZEAR	MET	RC	RRS	1843	2525	LANDRY ELIZA	MET	RC	RRS	1845	.
2523	LAFOURNAISE GABRIEL	MET	RC	RRS	1848	2527	GARIEPY AGATHE	MET	RC	RRS	1850	.
2526	LAFOURNAISE GABRIEL	MET	RC	RRS	1820	.	LANDRY ELIZA	MET	RC	RRS	1826	.
1965	LAFOURNAISE GUILLAUME	MET	RC	RRS	1845	.	COLLIN SUZANNE	MET	RC	RRS	1847	921
2678	LAFOURNAISE JEAN BTE	MET	RC	RRS	1828	.	GARIEPY CAROLINE	MET	RC	RRS	1842	.
2527	LAFOURNAISE JOSEPH		RC	CAN	1776	.	LEDOUX JOSEPHTE	IND	RC	RRS	1780	.
2528	LAFRAMBOISE AUGUSTIN	MET	RC	RRS	1844	.	SUZANNE	MET	RC	.	1844	.
2682	LAFRAMBOISE BAPTISTE		RC	RRS	1820	.	LEDOUX LOUISE	MET	RC	RRS	1822	.
2680	LAFRAMBOISE FRANCOIS	MET	RC	RRS	1830	2529	PARENTEAU ANGELIQUE	MET	RC	RRS	1830	.
2680	LAFRAMBOISE FRANCOIS	MET	RC	RRS	1830	2529	CHABOYER LOUISE	MET	RC	RRS	1831 67	.
2529	LAFRAMBOISE JEAN BTE		RC	NWT	1806 70	.	TROTTIER MARIE	MET	RC	NWT	1802	.
							LANDRY SUSANNE	MET	RC	.	1785	.
							HOULE MARGUERITE	MET	RC	.	1817 45	.
2532	LAFRENIERE ANTOINE	MET	RC	CAN	1780 63	.	GONEVILLE MARGUERITE	MET	RC	.	1828 48	.
2533	LAFRENIERE ANTOINE		RC	CAN	1810	2532	WELSH MARIE	MET	RC	.	1832 52	.
2533	LAFRENIERE ANTOINE		RC	CAN	1810	2532	BAUVIER MARIE	MET	RC	RRS	1826	.
2533	LAFRENIERE ANTOINE		RC	CAN	1810	2532	MORIN URSULE	MET	RC	RRS	1834	480
2618	LAFRENIERE ANTOINE	MET	RC	RRS	1810	.	MORIN URSULE	MET	RC	RRS	1829	3172
2534	LAFRENIERE JEAN BTE	MET	RC	RRS	1816	2532	ST GERMAIN MARIAN	EUR	RC	.	1775	4599
2537	LAGEMONIER BAPTISTE	EUR	RC	CAN	1828	.	GABOURY ANGELIQUE	MET	RC	.	1817	1885
2543	LAGEMONIER BENJAMIN	EUR	RC	CAN	1778	2537	CARRIERE SARAH	MET	RC	RRS	1839	707
2540	LAGEMONIER ELZEAR	MET	RC	RRS	1813	2541	GOULET ROSALIE	MET	RC	RRS	1849	.
2552	LAGEMONIER GODFREY	EUR	RC	RRS	1838	2546	LEPINE MARIE	MET	RC	RRS	1806 65	2923
2541	LAGEMONIER JEAN BTE	MET	RC	RRS	1847	2537	HARRISON MARIE	MET	RC	.	1849	.
2548	LAGEMONIER JOSEPH	EUR	RC	RRS	1808	2549	BLONDEAU MARIE	MET	RC	RRS	1829	.
2549	LAGEMONIER JOSEPH	MET	RC	RRS	1849 64	2537	LUSSIER JOSEPHINE	MET	RC	RRS	1843	351
2551	LAGEMONIER LOUIS	MET	RC	CAN	1826	2546	BRUNEAU MARIE	MET	RC	.	1847	.
2545	LAGEMONIER MODEST	MET	RC	RRS	1843 69	2549	DUCHARME BETSY	MET	RC	RRS	1845	578
2547	LAGEMONIER MODESTE	MET	RC	RRS	1842	2549	LARIVIERE CAROLINE	MET	RC	RRS	1849 65	.
2546	LAGEMONIER MODESTE	MET	RC	RRS	1849	.	BRUNEAU AGLAE	MET	RC	RRS	1824	578
2544	LAGEMONIER ROMAN	EUR	RC	RRS	1819	.	VANDRY MARIE	IND	RC	.	1826	.
2484	LAGON LOUIS		.	.	1820	.	CAPTAIN NANCY	MET	RC	.	1824	.
							MINNIE JOSEPHTE	MET	RC	.	1822	.
2553	LALIBERTE ALEXIS	MET	.	.	1825	2555	ROBILLARD MARY	MET	RC	RRS	1826	.
2558	LALIBERTE ANTOINE	MET	RC	RRS	1822	2560	CADOTTE MARIE	MET	RC	RRS	1824	.
2560	LALIBERTE ANTOINE	MET	RC	RRS	1839	2561	NADEAU MARGUERITE	MET	RC	RRS	1844	616

ID	MALE HEAD OF FAMILY	RACE	FAITH	BIRTH PLACE	DATES	DADS ID	FEMALE HEAD OF FAMILY	RACE	FAITH	BIRTH PLACE	DATES	DADS ID
2559	LALIBERTE CYRILL	MET	RC	RRS	1840		SMITH JUDITH	MET	RC	RRS	1840	4411
2557	LALIBERTE JOSEPH	MET			1847		LAFLEUR MARIE	MET	RC		1852	2511
2561	LALIBERTE PIERRE		RC	CAN	1776	2553	GAUDRY JOSEPHTE	MET	RC		1780	
2567	LALLEMAND BAPTISTE	MET	RC	CAN	1824		CHALIFOUX ANGELIQUE		RC		1825	736
2565	LALONDE FRANCOIS		RC	NWT	1766		MARLOT JOSEPHTE	EUR		NWT	1770	
2571	LAMBERT ANTOINE		RC	CAN	1821		HOULE ISABEL	MET			1824	
2573	LAMBERT ANTOINE	MET	RC	RRS	1782		SAULTEAUX MARIE	IND			1787	
2570	LAMBERT CHARLE		RC	CAN	1846	2571	LAURENCE MARIE	MET	RC	RRS	1847	2647
2575	LAMBERT ETIENNE		RC	CAN	1795		GADDY CATHERINE	MET	RC	NWT	1799	1887
2581	LAMBERT ETIENNE	MET	P	RRS	1838		HONORE BETSY	MET	RC		1795 30	
2578	LAMBERT JAMES	MET	RC	NWT	1826		DUCHARME SUSETTE	MET	P	RRS	1830	
2574	LAMBERT JOHN	MET	P	RRS	1834		PRINCE ANN	MET	P	RRS	1822	
2579	LAMBERT JOSEPH	MET	RC	RRS	1826	2582	FIDLER SOPHIA	MET	P	RRS	1837	
2576	LAMBERT JOSEPH	MET	RC	RRS	1790 62	2582	VILLEBRUNE LOUISE	MET	P	RRS	1827 67	
2582	LAMBERT LOUIS	EUR	P	RRS	1792	2575	BELLEAU ANGELIQUE	MET	P	NWT	1800	
2580	LAMBERT MICHEL	MET	RC	NWT	1823	2573	FAVEL MARGUERITE	MET	RC		1803	
2580	LAMBERT THOMAS	MET	RC	NWT	1823	2568	DUCHARME FANNY	MET	RC	RRS	1826 57	
2586	LAMBERT THOMAS	MET	RC	RRS	1839	2582	DESROSIERS MARIE	MET	RC	RRS	1834	
2585	LAMIRANDE ALEXIS	EUR	RC	CAN	1794	2582	PILON MARIE	MET	RC	RRS	1840	3935
8033	LAMIRANDE LOUIS				1845	2586	DAVIS MARGUERITE	MET	RC	RRS	1800	
2569	LAMONTAGNE MODESTE	EUR	P	ENG	1820		MELINA SENEZ	EUR	P	ENG	1845	
2603	LAND CHARLES				1790		GOOD SARAH	IND			1794	1770
2600	LANDRY BAPTISTE	EUR	RC	RRS	1835		BRUNEAU MARGARET	MET	RC	RRS	1836	578
2592	LANDRY ELIE	EUR	RC	CAN	1797	2592	LALONDE GENEVIEVE	EUR	RC	CAN	1801	2565
2590	LANDRY JOSEPH	MET			1798		GENEVIEVE	MET			1799	
2593	LANDRY JULIEN		RC	CAN	1799		JOSEPHTE	EUR			1800	
2597	LANDRY LOUIS	MET	RC	RRS	1795		MARTIN MARIE ANNE	MET	RC		1811 63	
2601	LANDRY LOUIS	MET	RC	RRS	1830		OUELLETTE MARGUERITE	MET	RC	RRS	1832	3765
2591	LANDRY LOUIS	MET	RC	RRS	1816		CHALIFOUX ISABELLE	MET			1819 69	
2684	LANDRY LOUISON	EUR			1845	2591	LAFRAMBOISE PHILOMENE		RC		1847	
2598	LANDRY MOISE	MET			1841	2592	LAGEMONIER MARIE	MET	RC	RRS	1832	2541
2605	LANDRY NORBERT	MET			1831	2597	OUELLETTE MADELEINE	MET			1835	
2606	LANDRY PIERRE	MET			1840	2606	PARK MARY				1840	
2606	LANE ELZEAR				1819		SUTHERLAND GENEVIEVE	MET			1820	
2602	LANE RICHARD				1819		MCDERMOT MARY	MET			1825	
2608	LANE RICHARD	EUR	P	SCT	1840		SPENCE MARY	EUR	P	RRS	1847	
2609	LANG JAMES		RC	CAN	1794		GEORGE MARGUERITE		RC		1796	
2542	LANGER FRANCOIS				1795		SUTHERLAND GENEVIEVE	MET	RC	RRS	1801	4599
2615	LANGEVIN ANTOINE	MET	RC	RRS	1842	2583	ST GERMAIN ANGELIQUE	MET	RC	RRS	1850	
2614	LANGILL JEAN BTE	MET	RC	NWT	1820		MALATERRE MARGUERITE	MET	RC	NWT	1819	
2614	LAPIERRE ANDRE		RC	CAN	1781		JOSEPHTE	IND	RC		1795 35	
2612	LAPIERRE ANTOINE		RC	CAN	1781		GAGNON CATHERINE	MET	RC		1815 50	
2588	LAPIERRE ANTOINE	MET			1832	2614	CREE BETHSY	IND	RC		1838	
2622	LAPIERRE JOSEPH	MET			1840		CHARLOTTE	MET	RC		1845	
2623	LAPINIS JEAN BTE	MET	RC	NWT	1842	2623	FLEURY JULIA	MET			1851	4262
2584	LAPLANTE ANTOINE	MET	RC	NWT	1807 64		ROY JOSEPHTE	MET		NWT	1810	
2695	LAPLANTE BASILE	EUR	RC	CAN	1809 64		GAGNON JOSEPHTE	MET	RC	RRS	1819	
	LAPLANTE ANTOINE						DEFOND MADELEINE	MET				
	LAPLANTE BAPTISTE	EUR			1790		LACOUISE GENEVIEVE	EUR	RC			

TABLE 1: GENEALOGIES OF RED RIVER HOUSEHOLDS, 1818-1870

ID	MALE HEAD OF FAMILY		RACE	FAITH	BIRTH PLACE	DATES	DADS ID	FEMALE HEAD OF FAMILY		RACE	FAITH	BIRTH PLACE	DATES	DADS ID
2620	LAPLANTE	BONIFACE	MET	RC	RRS	1838	2584	LAROCQUE	ANGELIQUE	MET	RC	RRS	1843	2789
2667	LAPLANTE	FRANCOIS	EUR	RC	LC	1833	8001	BELLECOURT	ISABELLE				1834	
2675	LAPLANTE	FRANCOIS	MET	RC	RRS	1790	2584	GAUDRY	LOUISE	MET	RC	RRS	1807	3862
2686	LAPLANTE	JEAN BTE	MET			1835		PAUL	ANGELIQUE				1835	
8037	LAPLANTE	LEON		RC		1840			CEDALIE	MET	RC	CAN	1836	
2627	LAPLANTE	LOUIS	MET	RC	NWT	1792	2675	LAPIERRE	JOSEPHTE	MET	RC	RRS	1809	
2790	LAPLANTE	LOUIS	EUR	RC	RRS	1827	2695	HENRY	MARIE	MET	RC	NWT	1827	3009
2673	LAPLANTE	MAGLOIRE	MET	RC		1828	2627	LOWE	ISABELLE	MET	RC		1829	921
2625	LAPLANTE	OLIVER				1829		COLLIN	ISABEL				1827	
8000	LAPLANTE	PIERRE				1770		LEGRAVE	FRANCOISE				1770	
2628	LAPOINTE	AUGUSTIN	MET	RC		1800			CHARLOTTE	MET			1810	
2631	LAPOINTE	FRANCOIS	MET	RC		1842		BOUSQUET	JULIE	MET	RC		1849	473
2633	LAPOINTE	FRANCOIS	EUR	RC	RRS	1820	2655	COMTOIS	MADELEINE	MET	RC		1822	930
2632	LAPOINTE	JOSEPH	EUR	RC	RRS	1852		FAILLE	JULIE	MET	RC		1846	
2651	LARIVIERE	FRANCOIS	MET	RC	RRS	1838		NAULT	ARSINDE	MET	RC	RRS	1840	3711
2655	LARIVIERE	FRANCOIS	EUR	RC	RRS	1806		LAMBERT	LOUISE	EUR	RC	RRS	1812	2576
2655	LARIVIERE	FRANCOIS	EUR	RC	RRS	1806		ST GERMAIN	MARGUERITE		RC		1818 60	
2653	LARIVIERE	LOUIS	EUR	RC	RRS	1816		WINSEL	EMILIE	EUR	RC		1818 37	
2787	LAROCQUE	ALEXANDRE	MET	RC	RRS	1847	2788	LAMBERT	MARIE	MET	RC	NWT	1828	2573
2663	LAROCQUE	ANTOINE	MET	RC	RRS	1845	2664	TROTTIER	ROSE	MET	RC	RRS	1846	
2664	LAROCQUE	ANTOINE	MET	RC	RRS	1845	2664	DELORME	ELISE	MET			1848	
2782	LAROCQUE	BAPTISTE	MET	RC		1803		LAPLANTE	ROSALIE	MET			1085	
2782	LAROCQUE	BAPTISTE	MET	RC	RRS	1840	2665	DEASE	LOUISE	MET	RC		1815	1054
2665	LAROCQUE	CHARLES	MET	RC	RRS	1840	2665	LEMIRE	JULIE	MET	RC	RRS	1840	
2669	LAROCQUE	CHARLES	RC	RC	NWT	1800		CHARTRAND	LOUISE	MET	RC		1847	
2672	LAROCQUE	CHARLES	MET	RC	CAN	1777		LAFOURNAISE	CATHERINE	MET	RC	RRS	1810	
2671	LAROCQUE	CYRILL	MET	RC	RRS	1819	2669	LABERGE	CECILE	MET	RC		1789 64	2258
2786	LAROCQUE	DANIEL	MET	RC	RRS	1846	2672	LAURENCE	ISABEL	MET	RC	RRS	1826	2641
2668	LAROCQUE	FRANCOIS	MET	RC	RRS	1850	2687	BRASSEAU	ELIZA	MET	RC	RRS	1852	
2674	LAROCQUE	FRANCOIS	MET	RC		1824	2669	SAYER	ANGELIQUE		RC	RRS	1826	2104
2690	LAROCQUE	FRANCOIS	MET	RC	RRS	1823		HAMELIN	ANGELIQUE	MET	RC		1832	
2691	LAROCQUE	FRANCOIS				1810		POIRIER	JOSEPHTE	MET	RC		1815	
2676	LAROCQUE	JEAN	EUR	RC	CAN	1840		MARCUSSON	SARA				1846	
2783	LAROCQUE	JEAN	MET			1783			JOSETTE	MET	RC		1790	
2693	LAROCQUE	JEAN BTE				1820			LIZETTE	MET			1820 50	
2688	LAROCQUE	JEAN BTE				1835		WALLIS	MARGUERITE				1835	
2785	LAROCQUE	JOSEPH	MET	RC	RRS	1829	2792	LEMIRE	JULIE	MET	RC	RRS	1838	
2789	LAROCQUE	JOSEPH	MET	RC	NWT	1816	2669	FAILLANT	MADELEINE	MET	RC		1844	3032
2788	LAROCQUE	LOUIS	MET	RC	RRS	1821	2687	MARCHAND	SOPHIE	MET	RC	RRS	1820	327
2793	LAROCQUE	LOUIS	MET	RC	RRS	1820	2785	GUILBEAULT	JUDITH	MET	RC	USA	1827	
2791	LAROCQUE	MICHEL	MET	RC	RRS	1841	2792	BERTHELET	MARIE	MET	RC	RRS	1824	
2694	LAROCQUE	OLIVER	MET	RC	CAN	1841		LEDOUX	SUZANNE	MET	RC	RRS	1847	
2692	LAROCQUE	OLIVIER	MET	RC	CAN	1797 42		GERVAIS	ROSE	MET	RC		1844	
2687	LAROCQUE	PIERRE		RC	CAN	1835		PICHE	MARGARET	MET	RC	RRS	1800	4565
2795	LAROCQUE	PIERRE	MET	RC		1786	2687	SWAIN	MARGUERITE	MET	RC		1834	
2798	LAROCQUE	PIERRE	MET	RC		1786	2799	CREE	MARGUERITE	MET	RC	RRS	1799 50	1257
	LARONDE	ETIENNE	MET			1803		DESCOLEAUX	JOSEPHE	MET	RC		1794	4368
						1824		SHORT	SUZANNE	MET	RC		1815	

ID	MALE HEAD OF FAMILY		RACE	FAITH	BIRTH PLACE	DATES	DADS ID	FEMALE HEAD OF FAMILY		RACE	FAITH	BIRTH PLACE	DATES	DADS ID
2657	LARONDE	LOUIS	MET	.	.	1825	2799	GAGNON	MARGUERITE	MET	.	.	1820	.
2657	LARONDE	LOUIS	MET	.	.	1825	2799	MORRELLE	JULIA	MET	.	NWT	1825	.
2799	LARONDE	LOUIS	EUR	RC	CAN	1796	.	BOUCHER	MADELEINE	.	RC	.	1810	445
2652	LARONDE	PAUL	.	.	.	1825	2799	CHAMPAGNE	MARGUERITE	MET	RC	.	1827	.
2658	LARONDE	PAUL	MET	RC	USA	1831	.	SINCLAIR	MARGUERITE	MET	.	CAN	1836	4382
2677	LARONDE	PAUL	EUR	P	ENG	1825	.	MASSON	MARIE	MET	RC	RRS	1852	3075
1083	LARSEN	KYDER	.	.	.	1850	.	PRUDEN	CAROLINE	.	P	RRS	1836	.
2800	LATERRGRASS	BAPTISTE	.	RC	CAN	1835	.	DANIEL	NANCY	IND	.	.	1800	.
2637	LAURENCE	BAPTISTE	.	RC	CAN	1790	.	HAMELIN	JOSEPHE	.	RC	.	1837	2113
2638	LAURENCE	BAPTISTE	EUR	RC	CAN	1836 62	.	IROQUOISE	AGATHE	MET	.	RRS	1825	2970
2641	LAURENCE	BAZILE	.	.	.	1795	.	RITCHOT	MADELEINE	MET	RC	.	1845	.
2640	LAURENCE	CHARLES	.	RC	CAN	1840	.	DESJARDIN	JOSEPHTE	MET	.	RRS	1805	.
2642	LAURENCE	CHARLES	MET	.	.	1800 70	.	MILLET	MARIE	EUR	RC	.	1827	3122
2647	LAURENCE	JEAN	.	.	.	1825 64	2637	BEAUCHEMIN	MARIE	MET	RC	RRS	1830	.
2645	LAURENCE	JEAN BTE	MET	RC	RRS	1828	.	FARQUARHSON	CLARA	MET	RC	RRS	1847	1507
2639	LAURENCE	JOSEPH	MET	RC	NWT	1842	2641	PARENTEAU	JOSEPHTE	MET	RC	.	1825	3811
2646	LAURENCE	NORBERT	EUR	P	SCT	1821	2637	CARNEY	MARY	EUR	P	UC	1834	.
1084	LAURIE	P G	EUR	RC	USA	1832	.	BEAUPRE	MARIA	IND	RC	USA	1836	.
2846	LAUSON	GEORGE	MET	.	.	1825	.	CHABOYER	ELIZA	MET	.	RRS	1852	728
2805	LAVALLEE	ANDRE	MET	.	.	1851	.	CHABOYER	ISABEL	MET	RC	.	1848	725
2804	LAVALLEE	ANTOINE	MET	.	.	1835	2806	DUCHARME	JOSEPHTE	MET	RC	.	1841	1358
2804	LAVALLEE	ANTOINE	MET	.	.	1795	2806	DUCHARME	LOUISE	IND	.	.	1805	1332
2806	LAVALLEE	BAPTISTE	MET	.	NWT	1832	2806	COURCHENE	MARGUERITE	MET	.	RRS	1832	.
2812	LAVALLEE	CHARLE	MET	RC	RRS	1840	2810	MORIN	GENEVIEVE	MET	RC	.	1840	.
2643	LAVALLEE	FRANCOIS	MET	RC	NWT	1820	2814	MORIN	JOSEPHTE	MET	RC	.	1823	.
2807	LAVALLEE	FRANCOIS	.	RC	RRS	1845	.	POITRAS	ELIZA	IND	RC	RRS	1844	3959
2829	LAVALLEE	GABRIEL	MET	.	.	1760 36	2820	CREE	JOSEPHTE	.	.	USA	1786	.
2810	LAVALLEE	IGNACE	.	RC	NWT	1800	.	BIRSTON	NANCY	IND	.	NWT	1805	334
5047	LAVALLEE	JAMES	EUR	RC	ENG	1811	.	DUCHARME	SUZETTE	MET	P	.	1815	.
2809	LAVALLEE	JEAN BTE	MET	RC	.	1841	.	OKIMAIKWE	MARGUERITE	IND	.	NWT	1843	.
2828	LAVALLEE	JEAN BTE	MET	.	.	1815	.	KAPLAN	MARIE	.	.	.	1817	.
4999	LAVALLEE	JEAN BTE	.	.	.	1818	5041	CAMPBELL	ANGELIQUE	MET	.	.	1821	655
5000	LAVALLEE	JEAN BTE	.	.	RRS	1829	.	GRANDBOIS	SOPHIA	MET	.	RRS	1837	.
2827	LAVALLEE	JOSEPH	MET	.	.	1843	2814	VILLEBRUNE	MARIE	.	RC	.	1832	.
4996	LAVALLEE	JOSEPH	MET	RC	RRS	1811	2814	PAGE	LOUISE	MET	.	RRS	1815	5118
5040	LAVALLEE	JOSEPH	MET	RC	NWT	1825	2810	PAUL	MADELEINE	MET	RC	.	1829	.
5042	LAVALLEE	JOSEPH	MET	RC	NWT	1820	.	GERVAIS	MARGUERITE	MET	RC	RRS	1832	.
2811	LAVALLEE	LOUIS	MET	RC	.	1828	.	CAPLETTE	CHARLOTTE	.	.	.	1831 61	.
4998	LAVALLEE	LOUIS	.	.	.	1830	.	DURAND	LOUISE	.	.	.	1832	.
5001	LAVALLEE	LOUIS	.	.	.	1823	.	VILLENEUVE	LOUISE	MET	.	RRS	1837	.
5043	LAVALLEE	LOUIS	MET	RC	RRS	1821	.	MARTELLE	JULIE	.	RC	.	1826	5121
5041	LAVALLEE	LOUISON	.	.	.	1806	5038	GAUDRY	JOSETTE	MET	RC	NWT	1814	.
2817	LAVALLEE	MICHEL	.	RC	CAN	1845	.	DAVIS	REIN	.	.	.	1848	.
4707	LAVALLEE	MOISE	MET	RC	NWT	1829	2814	ROBERT	MARIE	MET	.	.	1800	.
2815	LAVALLEE	PIERRE	MET	RC	NWT	1811	2814	DESLAURIERS	ELISE	MET	RC	RRS	1836	.
2819	LAVALLEE	PIERRE	MET	RC	RRS	1805	2810	BERCIER	MARGUERITE	MET	RC	RRS	1811	.
2822	LAVALLEE	PIERRE	MET	RC	.	1828	2822	GAUDRY	CATHERINE	MET	RC	.	1808	.
2826	LAVALLEE	PIERRE	MET	RC	NWT	1831	.	LAPLANTE	MARIE	IND	.	RRS	1831	5121

TABLE 1: GENEALOGIES OF RED RIVER HOUSEHOLDS, 1818-1870

ID	MALE HEAD OF FAMILY	RACE	FAITH	BIRTH PLACE	DATES	DADS ID	FEMALE HEAD OF FAMILY		RACE	FAITH	BIRTH PLACE	DATES	DADS ID
2830	LAVALLEE	PIERRE	MET			1829	2820	FAGNANT	GENEVIEVE	MET	RC		1841	
2834	LAVERDURE	ALEXIS	MET	RC	CAN	1756		MONTOUR	ANGELIQUE	MET	RC	NWT	1806	
2837	LAVERDURE	JOSEPH	MET	RC	CAN	1785	2840	DUCK	NANCY	MET	RC		1806	
2838	LAVERDURE	JOSEPH		RC	NWT	1816		PLOUF	THERESE				1825	
2840	LAVERDURE	JOSEPH				1760			LISETTE				1765	
2836	LAVERDURE	PIERRE	MET	RC	RRS	1836	2837	DELORME	ANGELIQUE	MET	RC	RRS	1833	
2845	LAVIOLETTE	ALEXIS		RC	CAN	1815		GRANDBOIS	GENEVIEVE	MET	RC		1817	
2847	LAVIOLETTE	ANTOINE	MET	RC	NWT	1836	2848	CAYEN	MARIE	MET	RC	NWT	1842	
2849	LAVIOLETTE	BAPTISTE	MET	RC	NWT	1826	2848	PAUL	NANCY	IND	RC	NWT	1828	3870
2848	LAVIOLETTE	CHARLES		RC	CAN	1795 67			LISETTE	MET	RC		1806 48	
2851	LAVIOLETTE	CHARLES		RC	CAN	1795 67		MOREAU	THERESE	MET	RC	NWT	1815	3174
2650	LAVIOLETTE	DAMASE				1810		TOURAND	ISABEL	MET			1818	
2852	LAWSON	THOMAS				1837		BECK	MARY				1840	
2853	LAYER	EDWARD	MET	P	RRS	1839	2854	DELORME	MADELEINE	MET	P	RRS	1840	
2854	LEASK	WILLIAM	MET	P	RRS	1795	2855	CUMMINGS	ANNE	P			1810	
2835	LEASK	WILLIAM		P		1810		COOK	MARY	P		RRS	1820	
1914	LEBENSON	LOUIS				1806 56		ELIZABETH	ELIZABETH	MET		RRS	1810	1549
2456	LEBLANC	LOUIS				1829		LAVALLEE	ANGELIQUE				1840	
2856	LEBLANC	JOSEPH	MET			1829		FIDLER	ELIZABETH	MET			1832	
2859	LEBRUN	AMBROISE				1810		LOUISE	MARIE			RRS	1811 66	
2857	LECLAIR	JOSEPH		RC	CAN	1796	2857	CHALIFOUX	MARGUERITE	MET	RC	RRS	1815	
2858	LECLAIR	JOSEPH	MET	RC	RRS	1834		HUPPE	THERESE	MET	RC	NWT	1835	
2478	LECLAIR	MICHEL		RC	CAN	1814		BOUSQUET	LOUISE		RC		1815	
2865	LECUYER	AMABLE	MET			1815		HOULE	JOSEPHTE	IND			1817	
2864	LECUYER	FRANCOIS	MET			1842	2865	SAULTEAUX	MARIE	MET			1830	
2863	LECUYER	MICHEL				1835	2865	MENTREUIL	M	MET			1837	
2866	LECUYER	XAVIER				1843		VIVIER	MARIE				1845	
2890	LEDOUX	ALEXANDRE				1845		VIVIER	JOSEPHTE				1847	
2887	LEDOUX	ALEXIS	MET			1839	2888	THOMAS	MARGUERITE	MET	RC		1840 70	1616
2887	LEDOUX	ALEXIS				1839	2888	CHALIFOUX	MADELEINE	MET	RC		1852	1487
2877	LEDOUX	ANTOINE	MET	RC	CAN	1820	2879	FLEURY	CLEMENCE	MET	RC	USA	1830	
2879	LEDOUX	BAPTISTE		RC	CAN	1773		FALCON	MARIE	MET	RC	NWT	1785	
2881	LEDOUX	BAPTISTE		RC		1805 41		SAULTEAUX	MADELEINE	IND	RC	RRS	1800	2474
2870	LEDOUX	EUSEBE		RC	NWT	1811		LACOUTURE	FRANCOISE	MET	RC		1814 39	
2870	LEDOUX	EUSEBE	MET	RC	NWT	1811	2877	BONNEAU	SUZANNE		RC		1816	
2876	LEDOUX	GREGOIRE	MET	RC	RRS	1830		DESJARLAIS	LOUISE	MET	RC	RRS	1849	1569
2868	LEDOUX	JEAN BTE	MET	RC	RRS	1844	2881	FISHER	CAROLINE	MET	RC	RRS	1834	
2884	LEDOUX	JEAN BTE	MET	RC	RRS	1828	2888	HALOIRE	THEOPHILE	MET	RC	RRS	1839	
2880	LEDOUX	JEROME	MET	RC	RRS	1845		BRELAND	MARGUERITE	MET	RC	RRS	1829	
2833	LEDOUX	JOSEPH	MET	RC	RRS	1833	2881	MORIN	ANGELIQUE	MET	RC	RRS	1849	
2885	LEDOUX	JOSEPH	MET	RC	RRS	1830		BRASSEAU	MARGUERITE	MET	RC	RRS	1835	
2891	LEDOUX	LOUIS				1800	2888	BELANGER	ISABELLE	MET	RC	RRS	1847	
2873	LEDOUX	PIERRE	MET	RC	RRS	1808	2879	DESJARLAIS	LOUISE	MET	RC	RRS	1830	3930
2874	LEDOUX	PIERRE		RC		1804		PICHE	EUPHRASINE	MET	RC	NWT	1822	1269
2888	LEDOUX	PIERRE	MET	RC	RRS	1825	2825	MONATE	MARY	MET	RC	RRS	1806	
2825	LEFORT	FRANCOIS	MET	RC	LC	1825		DESJARLAIS	MARIE	MET	RC	RRS	1839	2584
2897	LEFORT	FRANCOIS						BELLEAU	ISABEL	MET	RC	RRS	1806	
2522	LEFORT	LOUIS	FUR					LAPLANTE	ELISE	MET			1829	
								CARRON	ANGELIQUE	MET		RRS		

ID	MALE HEAD OF FAMILY	RACE	FAITH	BIRTH PLACE	DATES	DADS ID	FEMALE HEAD OF FAMILY	RACE	FAITH	BIRTH PLACE	DATES	DADS ID
2902	LEJOUR BAPTISTE				1825		BRABANT GENEVIEVE	MET	RC		1835	3933
2901	LEJOUR GREGOIRE	MET			1850	2902	PILON CECILE	MET	RC		1843	
2907	LELAND RICHARD		RC	CAN	1809		MCDOUGALL JANE	EUR	RC	CAN	1816	
2900	LEMAY JOSEPH	EUR	RC	CAN	1828		AUGER CAMILLE	MET	RC	RRS	1831	297
2909	LEMIRE JEAN BTE	MET			1829	2908	BERARD MARIE	MET	RC	RRS	1830	
2831	LEMIRE JOSEPH		RC	CAN	1844	2908	LEPINE SUSANNE	MET	RC		1847 67	
2908	LEMIRE JOSEPH		RC		1803		MARTIN JULIE	MET	RC	RRS	1809	
2899	LENNON JEAN				1832		DEGAIN ISABELLE	MET	RC	RRS	1835	
2832	LENOIRE JEAN BTE				1838		YANKOSKINFUR MARIE		RC		1840	
2920	LEPINE AMBROISE	MET	RC	RRS	1840	2921	MARION CECILE	MET	RC	RRS	1842	245
2925	LEPINE ATHANASE			RRS	1849	2912	BELANGER MARIE	MET	RC	NWT	1852	
2912	LEPINE BAPTISTE	MET	RC	CAN	1792 69	2914	SAULTEAUX CHARLOTTE	IND	RC		1794 54	
2914	LEPINE BAPTISTE	MET	RC	NWT	1820	2921	GARIEPY SUSANNE	MET	RC		1821 48	
2913	LEPINE JEAN BTE	EUR	RC	LC	1840	2912	FLEURY JULIE	MET	RC		1849	1616
2921	LEPINE JEAN BTE	MET	RC	RRS	1792	2921	HENRY JULIE	MET	RC	USA	1805	
2923	LEPINE JEAN BTE	MET	RC	NWT	1825		PARENTEAU ISABELLE	MET	RC	RRS	1830	3811
2922	LEPINE JOSEPH	MET	RC	RRS	1813		SHORT BETSY	MET	RC	RRS	1815	
2916	LEPINE MAXIME	MET	RC		1837		LAVALLEE JOSEPHTE	MET	RC	RRS	1838	2815
8052	LERODEUR BAPTISTE	EUR	RC	LC	1844		SAULTEAUX		RC			
2930	LESPERANCE ALEXIS	MET	RC	RRS	1797		GRENOT MARGUERITE	MET	RC	UC	1845	
2928	LESPERANCE ANDRE	MET	RC	RRS	1835	2930	FALCON BALSOMINE	MET	RC	RRS	1838	2815
2929	LESPERANCE JEAN	MET	RC	RRS	1837	2930	LAVALLEE EMILIE	MET	RC	RRS	1827	2815
2932	LESPERANCE JOSEPH		RC		1822	2930	L'AVALLEE MARIE	MET	RC	NWT	1846	4725
2935	LESPERANCE LOUIS				1840 67		TURCOTTE GENEVIEVE	MET	RC		1841	1992
2898	LETENDRE A				1839		GODON CATHERINE	MET	RC		1822	
2939	LETENDRE BAPTISTE	MET	RC	RRS	1819	2945	LYONNAIS MARGUERITE	MET	RC		1835	
2943	LETENDRE LOUIS		RC	RRS	1833	2945	BEAUGRAND CHAMPAGNE		RC		1810	2097
2945	LETENDRE LOUISON	MET	RC	RRS	1805		HALLET MARIE JULIE	MET	RC	RRS	1844	3807
2942	LETENDRE XAVIER		RC		1838		PARENTEAU MARGARET	MET	RC		1838	
2894	LEVERGE FRANCOIS	MET		NWT	1838		BERTHELET MARGUERITE	MET	RC		1806	
2949	LEWIS JAMES	EUR	P	ENG	1805		GIBSON BARBARA	MET	P	NWT	1802	171
2951	LEWIS JOHN	EUR	P	ENG	1791		BALLENDINE JANE	MET	P		1792	
2952	LHIRONDELLE ALEXANDER	MET	RC	NWT	1849	2954	MARGARET	MET	RC		1852	
2953	LHIRONDELLE JOSEPH	MET			1844	2954	FOSSENEUVE PHILOMENE	MET	RC	RRS	1850	
2954	LHIRONDELLE JOSEPH				1820		THORNE ELISE	MET			1824	4689
2959	LILLIE DANIEL	EUR	P	ENG	1790		NEPISSING MARGUERITE	MET			1812 47	
2958	LILLIE JAMES	MET	RC	RRS	1841	2959	RICHARD MARY ANNE	MET	P		1848	
2957	LILLIE WILLIAM	MET	RC	NWT	1830	2959	MORIN MARIE	MET	RC	RRS	1837	1881
2961	LINGAN EDOUARD				1820		GAGNON ELIZA	MET	RC	NWT	1821	
2886	LINGAN FRANCOIS				1844	2961	LAROCQUE MARGUERITE	MET	RC		1847	
2962	LINGAN JEAN				1842	2961	ST GERMAIN PHILOMENE	MET	RC		1850	4599
2621	LINKLATER ANDREW	EUR		ORK	1810		ST GERMAIN ANGELIQUE	MET	RC		1812	4599
2967	LINKLATER ANDREW		P	NWT	1802 37		SWANSTONE ELIZABETH	MET	P		1807	
2696	LINKLATER HUGH	MET		NWT	1825		LONGMORE CATHERINE	MET			1825	
2963	LINKLATER HUGH		P	RRS	1823	2964	CORRIGAL BETSY	MET	P	NWT	1824	853
2964	LINKLATER HUGH	MET	P	RRS	1782 65		CHARLOTTE	IND			1790	
2816	LINKLATER JOHN	MET	P	RRS	1800		PEEBLES HELENE	MET	P		1805	
2816	LINKLATER JOHN	MET	P		1800		SAUNDERS ELIZABETH	EUR	P	RRS	1800 47	
2969	LINKLATER MAGNUS		P		1820		FLETT JANE	EUR	P	RRS	1823	1596

TABLE 1: GENEALOGIES OF RED RIVER HOUSEHOLDS, 1818-1870

ID	MALE HEAD OF FAMILY		RACE	FAITH	BIRTH PLACE	DATES	DADS ID	FEMALE HEAD OF FAMILY		RACE	FAITH	BIRTH PLACE	DATES	DADS ID
2821	LINKLATER	WILLIAM	MET	P		1832	2816	MCKAY	CAROLINE	EUR	P	RRS	1835	
2966	LINKLATER	WILLIAM	EUR	P	ORK	1842	2621	SPENCE	JEMINA	MET	P	NWT	1850	4169
2968	LINKLATER	WILLIAM	EUR	RC		1820		RICHARD	ELLEN	MET	P	RRS	1835	
2701	LISK	SAMUEL	EUR		SCT	1834		LINKLATER	CATHERINE	IND	P	NWT	1835	
2702	LISK	THOMAS	EUR		SCT	1830			ELIZA	EUR	P	ENG	1841	
2697	LITTLE	JOSEPH	EUR		ENG	1832		FORRISTER	ELIZABETH	EUR	P		1836	
2973	LIVINGSTON	DONALD		P	SCT	1791			ANNE		P		1795	
2974	LIVINGSTON	HUGH	EUR	P	CAN	1808		ROSE	ISABELLA		P		1810	
2976	LIVINGSTON	JOHN	EUR	P	SCT	1808		MCDONNELL	SOPHIA		P	NWT	1811 35	
2972	LIVINGSTON	NEIL	EUR	P	RRS	1813	2973	MARCHAND	MARGARET	MET	RC	SCT	1815 45	3032
2972	LIVINGSTON	NEIL	EUR	P	RRS	1813	2973	MASSON	CATHERINE	EUR	P	RRS	1836	
2982	LIZOTTE	PIERRE	EUR	RC	RRS	1821		MCDONALD	CATHERINE	MET	RC	RRS	1822	
2981	LODEL	WILLIAM				1820		DENNET	ISABEL		P		1842	
1080	LOGAN	ALEXANDER		P		1842		LANE	MARIA		P	RRS	1853	
2986	LOGAN	JOHN	MET	P	RRS	1842	2988	SETTER	GEORGINA	MET	RC	RRS	1831	1410
2989	LOGAN	JOHN		P		1840	2987	DUPUIS	MARIE	MET	P	RRS	1834 59	
2988	LOGAN	KENNET	EUR	P	SCT	1827 59			SUSAN		RC		1800 38	
2988	LOGAN	ROBERT	EUR	P	SCT	1783 66		INGRAM	MARY	IND	P	NWT	1818	
2987	LOGAN	ROBERT	MET	P	RRS	1783 66	2988	CUMMINGS	SARAH	EUR	P	ENG	1806 33	
2987	LOGAN	THOMAS	MET	P	RRS	1812	2988	DEASE	MARGARET	MET	P	RRS	1812 65	
2985	LOGAN	THOMAS	MET	P	RRS	1841	2987		MARY ANNE	MET	P	RRS	1845	4680
2994	LONSDALE	WILLIAM	EUR	P	ENG	1838		THOMAS	JULIETTE	EUR	P		1842	644
2700	LOUIS	ANDREW	MET	P	RRS	1835		CAMERON	ANN	MET	P	RRS	1832	
2521	LOUIS	EDWARD		P		1835		LINKLATER	CHARLOTTE		P	RRS	1837	
2948	LOUIS	JAMES	MET	P	NWT	1807	2947		MARY	MET	P		1813	
2980	LOUIS	JAMES				1835		SPENCE	ISABELLA		P	NWT	1837	
2990	LOUIS	JAMES	MET	P	RRS	1840		SANDERSON	ROBINA	MET	P		1848	
2992	LOUIS	JAMES	MET	P	RRS	1834		MCKAY	JULIA	MET	P		1843	
2993	LOUIS	WILLIAM	MET	P	RRS	1840		LINKLATER	MARY	MET	P		1840	
3009	LOWE	WILLIAM				1805		HAMELIN	ELIZA	MET	RC	RRS	1807	
2704	LOWTED	JOHN	MET	P	NWT	1841		STEVENS	MARGUERITE	MET	P	RRS	1845	4478
2703	LOWTED	LOUIS	EUR	P	SCT	1819 65	2703	HARPER	NANCY	MET	P	RRS	1817 57	
2703	LOWTED	LOUIS	EUR	P	SCT	1819 65		MCDOUGALL	JANE	MET	P		1826	
2538	LOYER	JEAN	MET	P	RRS	1843	2539	MOORE	CATHERINE	MET	P	RRS	1846	758
3001	LUSSIER	AMABLE	MET	RC	RRS	1845	3003	CHARTRAND	ROSALIE	MET	RC	RRS	1848	2849
3002	LUSSIER	BASILE	MET	RC	RRS	1839	3003	LAVIDLETTE	ANGELIQUE	MET	RC	RRS	1838	
3000	LUSSIER	TOUSSAINT	MET	RC	RRS	1835	3003	BOYER	LOUISE	MET	RC	RRS	1835	
2999	LUSSIER	TOUSSAINT	MET	RC	RRS	1828		FAVEL	LOUISE	MET	RC	RRS	1826	1217
3003	LUSSIER	TOUSSAINT	MET	RC	CAN	1798 70		BRASSEAU	JOSEPHTE	MET	RC	CAN	1815	
3004	LUSTED	THOMAS		P		1800		LACHEVROTIER	NANCY	MET	P	NWT	1800	2471
3006	LUSTED	HENRI	EUR	P	ENG	1840			HESSER	IND	P	UC	1843	
2709	LYONS	JAMES		RC		1833 68		HADSKIS	MARY	EUR	P	RRS	1833	
3011	LYONS	JOHN	MET	P	NWT	1815 47	3008	STEVENS	CATHERINE	MET	RC		1816	4478
3008	LYONS	JOHN	MET	P	NWT	1786		COOK	MARGARET		P	NWT	1791	947
3010	LYONS	THOMAS	MET	P	NWT	1816 50	3008	KIPPLING	MARGARET	MET	P		1817	
3012	LYONS	THOMAS	MET	P	RRS	1848	3013	GIBSON	ELIZA	MET	P	RRS	1851	
3013	LYONS	THOMAS	MET	P	RRS	1820	3008	ISBISTER	CHARLOTTE	MET	P	RRS	1815	
3274	MACCABER	JULIAS	EUR	P	OTH	1836		PRUDEN	ISABEL	MET	P	RRS	1841	2373
	MCCABE							SINCLAIR	ISABEL	MET	P	RRS	1841	

ID	MALE HEAD OF FAMILY		RACE	FAITH	BIRTH PLACE	DATES	DADS ID	FEMALE HEAD OF FAMILY		RACE	FAITH	BIRTH PLACE	DATES	DADS ID
3568	MACTAVISH	WILLIAM	EUR			1818		MCDERMOT	SARA	EUR			1824	
2710	MAIR	CHARLES	MET	RC	RRS	1835			ELIZA	MET	RC	NWT	1844	
3016	MALATERRE	ALEXIS	MET	RC	NWT	1825	3018	WARK	MARGUERITE	MET			1830	
3018	MALATERRE	BAPTISTE	MET	RC	NWT	1780 53		ADAM	ANGELIQUE	MET			1796 56	
3019	MALATERRE	BAPTISTE	MET	RC	NWT	1815 51	3018	COMTOIS	THERESE	MET	RC	RRS	1819 46	
3017	MALATERRE	BAPTISTE	MET	RC	NWT	1815 51	3018	MORSON	LISETTE	MET	RC	RRS	1825	
3020	MALATERRE	BASILE	MET	RC	NWT	1830	3018	BERARD	MARIE	MET	RC	RRS	1835	
2714	MALATERRE	JOSEPH	MET	RC	NWT	1823	3018	VIVIER	MARIE	MET	RC	RRS	1823 63	301
2716	MALATERRE	LOUIS	MET	RC	RRS	1828		LAPIERRE	EUPHROSINE		RC	LC	1820	
2717	MALOUIN	LEANDRE	MET	RC	NWT	1836		CHALIFOUX	MARIE	EUR	RC	RRS	1850 70	
2718	MANCEAU	ONEGIME	EUR	RC	LC	1830		PERREAULT	ADELINE	IND	P	RRS	1825	
2715	MARAGOUIN	WILLIAM	IND	P	RRS	1820			SALE	IND	RC	RRS	1848	
2721	MARCELLAIS	ANTOINE	EUR	RC	RRS	1842			MARIANNE	IND	RC	RRS	1852	
3024	MARCELLAIS	BAPTISTE	MET	RC	LC	1843		ST ARNAUD	ROSALIE	MET	RC	LC	1785	4579
3027	MARCELLAIS	FELIX	MET	RC	CAN	1767	3028	ASSINIBOINE	ANGELIQUE	IND			1844	
3026	MARCELLAIS	JEAN BTE	MET	RC	RRS	1847	3024	VANDAL	ELISE	MET	RC	RRS	1823	5065
3025	MARCELLAIS	JOHN	MET	RC	NWT	1820 60	3024	BOUCHER	FRANCOISE	MET	RC	LC	1848	
3028	MARCELLAIS	LOUIS	MET	RC	RRS	1844		HOGUE	ELISABETH	MET	RC	RRS	1810 50	2211
3032	MARCHAND	BENJAMIN	MET	RC	CAN	1805			SOPHIE	IND	RC		1795	
3034	MARCHAND	BENJAMIN	MET	RC	RRS	1780 68	3032	NADEAU	MARGUERITE	MET	RC	RRS	1829	
3031	MARCHAND	CYRILL	MET	RC	RRS	1822	3032	DUNNAIS	NANCY	MET	RC	RRS	1832	
8040	MARCOUX	NARCISSE	MET	RC	RRS	1826		VILLENEUVE	SOPHIE	MET	RC		1834	5127
3044	MARION	EDOUARD	MET	RC		1834		NORMAND	ANASTASIE	MET	RC		1833	
3039	MARION	FRANCOIS	MET	RC	RRS	1834		MCDDUGALL	ELIZA	MET	RC	RRS	1810	
3040	MARION	FRANCOIS	MET	RC		1810		MOREAU	ANGELIQUE	MET	RC		1785	
3030	MARION	JOSEPH	MET	RC	CAN	1781 63		MARTELLE	LISETTE	EUR			1848	
3033	MARION	JOSEPH	MET	RC	RRS	1847		LAURENCE	ANNIE	MET	RC	RRS	1850	
3042	MARION	LOUIS	MET	RC	RRS	1846		MCDERMOT	ESTHER	MET	RC	RRS	1849	
3043	MARION	MAXIME	MET	RC	RRS	1840		JEROME	MARIE	MET	RC	RRS	1843	2647
3045	MARION	NARCIS	MET	RC	CAN	1838	3045	BOUCHARD	ELISE	MET	RC	RRS	1814	
2726	MARON	SIMON	MET	RC		1805		MORRISEAU	MARIE	MET	RC		1848	2348
8039	MARROTOUR	ROBERT	MET	RC	CAN	1799		SPENCE	ISABELLE				1799 39	
3036	MARSAND	ANTOINE	MET	RC		1812	3057	MASKEGON	JOSEPHTE				1793 53	
3058	MARTELLE	JEAN BTE	MET	RC	RRS	1765 62		LYONS	LOUISE	MET	RC		1800	
3059	MARTELLE	JOSEPH	MET	RC	RRS	1826		RITCHOT	MARGUERITE	MET	RC	RRS	1832	4184
3066	MARTELLE	JOSEPH	MET	RC	CAN	1805			MARIE	MET	RC		1810	
3063	MARTIN	ABRAHAM	MET	RC	RRS	1833	3064		MARGUERITE					
3064	MARTIN	ABRAHAM	MET	RC	CAN	1798 66		GERVAIS	ROSE	MET	RC	RRS	1844	
3062	MARTIN	ALPHONSE	MET	RC	RRS	1838	3064	GARIEPY	EUPHRISINE	MET	RC	NWT	1825	
3060	MARTIN	FRANCOIS	MET	RC		1790 36		RACETTE	ISABEL	MET	RC	RRS	1834	
3065	MARTIN	FRANCOIS	MET	RC		1770		RACETTE	MADELEINE	MET			1787 57	4147
3069	MARTIN	LAURENT	MET			1821	3060	CREE	LOUISE				1772	
3061	MARTIN	SIMON	MET	RC	CAN	1775		CHALIFOUX	ANGEL	MET			1830	736
3074	MARTINEAU	AMBROISE	MET	RC	CAN	1761		LISETTE	JOSEPHTE	IND	RC		1777	
3074	MARTINEAU	AMBROISE	MET	RC	CAN	1761			CHARLOTTE	MET	RC		1785	
3075	MASSON	FRANCOIS	EUR	P	ENG	1800			THERESE	MET	RC		1787	
3071	MASSY	ROBERT	MET	RC		1823		DUCHARME	SARAH	MET	P		1812	
3073	MATCHION	LOUISON	MET	RC		1791		SMITH	MARIE	MET		RRS	1827	
3076	MATHESON	ALEXANDER	EUR	P	SCT	1781		LEBLANC	JANE	EUR	P		1783 25	4417

TABLE 1: GENEALOGIES OF RED RIVER HOUSEHOLDS, 1818-1870

ID	MALE HEAD OF FAMILY	RACE	FAITH	BIRTH PLACE	DATES	DADS ID	FEMALE HEAD OF FAMILY	RACE	FAITH	BIRTH PLACE	DATES	DADS ID
3077	MATHESON ALEXANDER	EUR	P	SCT	1767 45		ANN JOHNSTON	EUR	P		1779 69	
3081	MATHESON ALEXANDER	EUR	P	RRS	1827	3099	VICTORIA GUNN	EUR	P	SCT	1837	
3080	MATHESON ANGUS	EUR	P	SCT	1813		MARGARET LIVINGSTON	EUR	P		1816	
3082	MATHESON ANGUS	EUR	P	SCT	1810 36		ISABELLA	EUR	P	SCT	1816	
3084	MATHESON ANGUS	EUR	P	SCT	1784		CHRISTIANNA		P			
1721	MATHESON DONALD				1840		FLORA	EUR	P		1843	
3087	MATHESON DONALD	EUR	P	RRS	1835 67	3084	CHRISTINE SUTHERLAND		P	RRS	1845	4494
3090	MATHESON HUGH	EUR	P	SCT	1811 67		BARBARA FRASER	EUR	P		1818 54	3998
3090	MATHESON HUGH	EUR	P	SCT	1811		CHRISTIANA		P		1815 50	
3091	MATHESON HUGH	EUR	P		1808		MARGARET ROSS	EUR	P		1819	
3092	MATHESON HUGH	EUR	P	SCT	1823 64		LETITIA PRITCHARD	EUR	P	RRS	1826 28	3998
3105	MATHESON JAMES	EUR	P		1803		JANE		P			
3105	MATHESON JAMES	EUR	P		1803		MARGARET SUTHERLAND	EUR	P		1810	
3037	MATHESON JOHN	EUR	P	RRS	1841	3099	ANN FRASER	EUR	P	RRS	1840	
3078	MATHESON JOHN	EUR	P		1842		MARY GUNN	EUR	P		1846	
3083	MATHESON JOHN	EUR	P	RRS	1837	3084	CATHERINE MCKAY	EUR	P	RRS	1852 53	
3094	MATHESON JOHN	EUR	P	SCT	1815		CATHERINE PRITCHARD	EUR	P	SCT	1820 53	
3099	MATHESON JOHN	EUR	P	SCT	1798	3084	ANN POLSON	EUR	P	RRS	1805	2445
3107	MATHESON SAMUEL	EUR	P	RRS	1829		MARGARET HENDERSON	EUR	P	RRS	1839	
3098	MATHESON WILLIAM	EUR	P	RRS	1836		CHRISTIE MCBEATH	EUR	P	NWT	1843	
3121	MATHEW HECTOR	IND	P	NWT	1839		JANE DREVER	MET	P		1830	
2731	MATHEW THOMAS		P		1844		SUSAN LAPLANTE		P	UC	1835	
3054	MAXWELL		P		1825 69		ELIZABETH MCINTOSH	MET	P	RRS	1813	
3261	MCAULAY RODERICK	EUR	P	SCT	1846		HARRIET MCDONALD	MET	P	SCT	1821	
3262	MCBAIN KENNETH	EUR	P	SCT	1803		ELIZABETH URQUHART	MET	P		1841	
3259	MCBEATH ADAM	EUR	P		1816		MARY	EUR	P	RRS	1831 65	
3282	MCBEATH ADAM	EUR	P	RRS	1834	3275	GEORGINA MATHESON	EUR	P		1845	
3271	MCBEATH ALEXANDER	EUR	P	RRS	1826	3272	MARGARET SETTER	EUR	P	RRS	1762 53	
3271	MCBEATH ALEXANDER	EUR	P	RRS	1826	3272	CATHERINE HALCROW		P		1805	
3276	MCBEATH ALEXANDER	EUR	P	SCT	1757 48		CATHERINE	MET	P	RRS	1810	
3279	MCBEATH GEORGE	EUR	O	SCT	1800		HELEN		P		1805	
3272	MCBEATH JOHN	EUR	P	SCT	1791		CHRISTIANNA MATHESON	EUR	P	SCT	1819 48	189
3270	MCBEATH MORRISSON	EUR	P	RRS	1814	3272	CHRISTIANNA BANNERMAN	EUR	P	RRS	1835	
3277	MCBEATH MORRISSON	EUR	P	RRS	1832	3276	ISABELLA GUNN	EUR	P	SCT	1815	
3275	MCBEATH ROBERT	EUR	P	SCT	1813		MARY MCLEAN		P		1812 63	
3280	MCBEATH RODERICK	EUR	P	SCT	1807	3267	MARY LIVINGSTON	MET	P		1806	
3287	MCBEATH WILLIAM	EUR	P	RRS	1804		ELLEN HERON	EUR	P		1848	
3649	MCCLAREN WILLIAM	EUR	P		1838		MAGDELEINE SAVOYARD	MET	P	UC	1845	4291
3292	MCCORRISTER ALEX	EUR	P	NWT	1840		CATHERINE JONES	IND	P		1795	
3246	MCCORRISTER ALEXANDER	MET	P	RRS	1783		JANE COCKS	MET	P	RRS	1842	
3250	MCCORRISTER CHARLES	MET	P	RRS	1835		CHARLOTTE ATKINS	MET	P	RRS	1826	
3294	MCCORRISTER HENRY	IND	P		1824		MARIE TAIT	MET	P		1820	
3242	MCCORRISTER JAMES	MET	P	NWT	1817	3292	ELIZABETH SMITH	MET	P	NWT	1820	
3291	MCCORRISTER JAMES	IND	P	NWT	1810	3296	SARAH ATKINSON		P	NWT	1825	
3295	MCCORRISTER JAMES		P	NWT	1816		LETTIE SPENCE	MET	P		1843	
3296	MCCORRISTER JAMES	MET	P	NWT	1840		SOPHIA SINCLAIR		P	NWT	1822	
3241	MCCORRISTER JOHN	MET	RC	RRS	1829	3290	ANN DONALD	MET	P	RRS	1831	
3289	MCCORRISTER THOMAS	MET	P	RRS	1847		MARY STEVENS	MET	P	RRS	1851	4474

ID	MALE HEAD OF FAMILY	RACE	FAITH	BIRTH PLACE	DATES	DADS ID	FEMALE HEAD OF FAMILY	RACE	FAITH	BIRTH PLACE	DATES	DADS ID
2776	MCCRAE ALEXANDER	EUR	P	RRS	1848		ARCUS ELIZABETH	MET	P	RRS	1850	
2777	MCCRAE DUNCAN	EUR	P	SCT	1818		SMITH CHARLOTTE	EUR	P	ENG	1825	
3300	MCDERMOT ANDREW	MET	P	IRE	1837	3301	TRUTHWAITE NANCY	MET	P	RRS	1809	4719
3304	MCDERMOT ANDREW	EUR	P	RRS	1793		MCNAB SARAH	MET	P	RRS	1803	3464
3303	MCDERMOT HENRY	MET	P	RRS	1830	3304	HARRIOT FLORA		P	RRS	1840 58	
1717	MCDERMOT HENRY	MET	P	RRS	1830	3304	LOGAN SARAH	MET		RRS	1827	2988
3302	MCDERMOT JOHN	MET	P		1839		DELORME MADELEINE	MET	RC	RRS	1847	
3322	MCDERMOT MILES	MET	P	RRS	1832	3324	GOULET GUILLEMINE	MET	P	NWT	1839	
3308	MCDONALD ADAM				1800		MCKAY MARY	MET			1802	
3320	MCDONALD ALEX	MET	P	RRS	1828		LAURIN SUSETTE	MET	P		1836	
3331	MCDONALD ALEX	EUR	P	SCT	1826		TAIT ANN	MET	P	NWT	1837	4577
1716	MCDONALD ALEX	EUR	P	SCT	1836	3333	ROBILLARD ISABELLA	MET	RC	RRS	1845	4211
3329	MCDONALD ALEXANDER	EUR	P	SCT	1840		MCCRAE MARIANNE	EUR	P	RRS	1850	
3315	MCDONALD ALEXANDER	MET	P	RRS	1840	3318	WHITEWAY SARAH	IND	P	RRS	1848	5183
3273	MCDONALD CHARLES	MET	P	SCT	1829	3333	SMITH MARYANN	MET			1806 66	
3318	MCDONALD DONALD	EUR	P	SCT	1797		FARQUARHSON ANN		P		1796	
3324	MCDONALD DONALD	EUR	P	SCT	1794	3328	BEAUDRY NANCY	MET			1840	
3327	MCDONALD DONALD	MET	P		1831		SETTER JANE	MET	P	RRS	1850	
3485	MCDONALD DONALD				1848		LAURENGEAU CAROLINE		P		1832	
3314	MCDONALD DUNCAN	MET	P	RRS	1825	3318	TAIT CATHERINE	MET	P	RRS	1774 64	4577
3487	MCDONALD FRANCOIS				1772		DEMONTIGNY ELIZABETH	EUR	P		1820	
3263	MCDONALD HUGH	EUR	P	SCT	1808		MCPHIE CATHERINE	MET	P	SCT	1839	
3269	MCDONALD JOHN	MET	P	RRS	1812		INKSTER MARGARET	MET	P	RRS	1837	2402
3316	MCDONALD JOHN	EUR	P	SCT	1831	3318	ANDERSON CHARLOTTE	MET	P	RRS	1836	78
3319	MCDONALD JOHN	MET	P	RRS	1825	3324	MCDONALD ELIZABETH	MET	P	RRS	1838	
3326	MCDONALD JOHN	MET	P	RRS	1834	3328	FLETT NANCY	MET	P	RRS	1791 44	1584
3328	MCDONALD JOHN	EUR	P	SCT	1789		SWAIN MARY	MET			1849	
3332	MCDONALD JOHN	MET	P	RRS	1834	3333	SETTER SARAH	MET	P	RRS	1849	
3336	MCDONALD JOHN	EUR	P		1842	3342	TURNER NANCY	MET	P		1839	
3488	MCDONALD JOHN				1847		MCKAY ISABELLA	MET	P		1845	
3323	MCDONALD JOSEPH	MET	P	RRS	1837	3324	FRASER MARGARET	MET	P	RRS	1839	1652
3264	MCDONALD KENNETH	MET	P	SCT	1845	3333	SETTER NANCY	MET	P	RRS	1845	2936
3333	MCDONALD KENNETH	IND	P		1796 69		CALDER ELIZABETH	MET	P	NWT	1808	633
3330	MCDONALD MURDOCH				1830		MCCORRISTER FRANCOISE	MET	P	RRS	1830	
3334	MCDONALD NEIL	EUR	P	SCT	1799		LOGAN ANN	MET	P		1809 56	
3266	MCDONALD WILLIAM	MET	P	RRS	1839	3334	MCKAY CHRISTIANE	EUR	P	RRS	1847	
3342	MCDONALD WILLIAM	EUR	P	SCT	1805		GUNN CATHERINE	MET	P	SCT	1822	
3480	MCDOUGALL ALEX				1823		MOWAT MARGARET	MET	P		1825	3234
3345	MCDOUGALL COLLIN	MET	RC	RRS	1841	3346	IRVINE MARIA	MET	RC	RRS	1838	
1718	MCDOUGALL DANIEL	MET	RC	RRS	1837		LAGEMONIER MATHILDE	MET	RC	RRS	1839	
3351	MCDOUGALL DANIEL	MET	RC	RRS	1843	3352	BRUNEAU MARGUERITE	MET	RC	NWT	1850	578
3344	MCDOUGALL DUNCAN	MET	RC	RRS	1837	3346	LESPERANCE ROSALIE	MET	RC	RRS	1838	2930
3346	MCDOUGALL DUNCAN	MET	RC	LC	1800 70		MCDONALD MARGARET	MET	RC	RRS	1820	
3350	MCDOUGALL GEORGE	EUR			1825		JASPER JENNIE	MET			1827	
3352	MCDOUGALL JOHN				1810		GASPARD GENEVIEVE	MET	P	SCT	1813	
3593	MCDOUGALL JOHN				1840		MCKAY HARRIET	MET	P	RRS	1843	
3353	MCGILLIS ALEXANDER	EUR			1825		DELORME ANGELIQUE		RC		1828	
3356	MCGILLIS ALEXANDER	MET	RC	RRS	1811		BATENEAU MARGUERITE	MET	RC	RRS	1811	
3594	MCGILLIS ALEXANDER	MET	RC	RRS	1842		JANNOT MARIE	MET	RC	RRS	1847	2356

TABLE 1: GENEALOGIES OF RED RIVER HOUSEHOLDS, 1818-1870

ID	MALE HEAD OF FAMILY	RACE	FAITH	BIRTH PLACE	DATES	DADS ID	FEMALE HEAD OF FAMILY	RACE	FAITH	BIRTH PLACE	DATES	DADS ID
3354	MCGILLIS ANGUS	MET	RC	RRS	1838		FAGNANT ISABELLE	MET	RC	RRS	1838	1461
3357	MCGILLIS ANGUS	EUR	RC		1775 42	3357	DELORME MARGARET	MET	RC	RRS	1779	
3358	MCGILLIS CUTHBERT	MET	RC	NWT	1822 69		BLEUVE MARGARET	MET	RC	RRS	1822	353
3597	MCGILLIS DANIEL				1809 69		ALLARD JULIE	MET			1810	
3598	MCGILLIS JEROME		RC		1842		BRELAND MARIE				1845	
3595	MCGILLIS JOHN		RC	RRS	1840 69		POITRAS MARIE	MET	RC	RRS	1840	507
3596	MCGILLIS MODESTE	MET	RC		1848		CAMPBELL ISABELLE	MET	RC	RRS	1847	
3360	MCGILLIS WILLIAM	MET	RC		1814 68	3357	ROY MARIE	MET	RC	RRS	1816	661
3362	MCGILLIVRAY SAMUEL				1804		RAEFE THERESE	MET			1806	
3363	MCGILLIVRAY SIMON				1792 40		RAEFE THERESE	MET			1819 66	
3599	MCGUIRE PETER	EUR	RC	IRE	1825		HUGH MARY	EUR	RC	IRE	1829	
3364	MCINTOSH CHRISTOPHER	EUR	P	SCT	1822		GUNN ANN	EUR		RRS	1835	
3600	MCINTOSH WILLIAM	MET			1816		GLADU SARAH	MET			1818	
3365	MCIVER ALLAN	EUR	P	SCT	1816		BEADS ELIZABETH	EUR	P	NWT	1835	
3373	MCIVER DONALD	EUR	P	SCT	1828		MUNROE MARION	EUR	P	RRS	1831	3245
3373	MCIVER DONALD	EUR	P	SCT	1828		CATHERINE	MET			1828	
3601	MCIVER MURDOCH		RC		1840		MUIR FRANCE	EUR			1845	
3445	MCIVER WILLIAM				1817 62		GUIBOCHE GENEVIEVE	EUR	RC	SCT	1794	
3376	MCKAY ALEXANDER	MET	P	RRS	1790		BANNERMAN CHRISTIE	MET	RC	RRS	1852	
3401	MCKAY ALEXANDER	MET	P	NWT	1844		LAROCQUE VIRGINIE	MET	P	RRS	1831	1626
3377	MCKAY ALEXIS			RRS	1826		MCCORRISTER CATHERINE	IND	P	RRS	1788	
3378	MCKAY ALEXIS	MET			1785	3377	SAULTEAUX MARGUERITE	IND		NWT	1817	
3381	MCKAY ALEXIS				1814		FLAMMAND MARIE	MET		NWT	1840 57	
3372	MCKAY ANGUS	MET			1836		MARGUERITE	MET			1816	
3384	MCKAY ANGUS	EUR			1813		BERCIER SUZETTE	EUR			1783	
3394	MCKAY ANGUS	MET	RC	SCT	1780		ELIZABETH	EUR		RRS	1837	
3400	MCKAY ANGUS	EUR	RC	NWT	1832		FOULDS FLORA	MET	P	RRS	1849	
3390	MCKAY CHARLE	MET	P		1836	3393	BOULETTE VIRGINIE	MET	RC		1857	
3386	MCKAY CHARLES	MET	P	NWT	1847		LAROCQUE CAROLINE	MET	P	RRS	1809	
3662	MCKAY DAVID				1807		BIRD LAETITIA	MET	P	RRS	1813	
3388	MCKAY EDWARD	MET	P	RRS	1809	3411	MARY				1827	
3409	MCKAY EDWARD R	MET	P	RRS	1826	3411	COOK CAROLINE	MET	P	RRS	1851	940
3389	MCKAY GEORGE	EUR	O	SCT	1847		VALEUR CAROLINE	MET	P	RRS	1800	
3395	MCKAY GEORGE	MET	P	RRS	1797	3398	HELEN	IND	O	NWT	1851	
3393	MCKAY IGNACE	MET	RC	RRS	1833	3377	TAIT SARAH	MET	P	RRS	1818	
3370	MCKAY JAMES	MET	RC	NWT	1808	3398	BERCIER JOSEPHTE	MET	RC	NWT	1800	4625
3397	MCKAY JAMES	EUR	P	SCT	1816	3384	ELIZABETH	IND	RC		1825	
3398	MCKAY JAMES	EUR	P	SCT	1827		ROWAND MARGARET	MET	P	NWT	1808	
3403	MCKAY JAMES	IND			1800		GLADU MARGUERITE	MET	P		1840	4256
3661	MCKAY JERRY	MET	P	NWT	1831		MATHESON JANE	EUR	P	RRS	1823	
3369	MCKAY JOHN	MET	P	RRS	1820	3382	HALCROW MARGARET	IND			1847	
3383	MCKAY JOHN	MET	P	NWT	1837		DREVER MARGARET	MET	P	RRS	1838	
3396	MCKAY JOHN	MET	P	NWT	1842	3398	MCKAY ELIZABETH	MET	P	RRS	1836	
3405	MCKAY JOHN	MET	P	RRS	1832	3407	MCBEATH CHRISTINE	EUR	P	RRS	1817	
3407	MCKAY JOHN	MET	P		1816		ENGLAND MARIE	EUR	P	RRS	1830	
3411	MCKAY JOHN				1827		HARRIET	MET	P		1816	
3650	MCKAY JOHN	MET		NWT	1814		FAVEL MARY	MET		RRS	1838	3275
3651	MCKAY JOHN	MET			1832		MCCORRISTER MARY	MET	P	RRS	1838	1436

TABLE 1: GENEALOGIES OF RED RIVER HOUSEHOLDS, 1818-1870

ID	MALE HEAD OF FAMILY	RACE	FAITH	BIRTH PLACE	DATES	DADS ID	FEMALE HEAD OF FAMILY	RACE	FAITH	BIRTH PLACE	DATES	DADS ID
3667	MCKAY JOHN				1820		LAVALLEE SOPHIA				1822	
3664	MCKAY JOHN AMABLE				1812		SMITH LIZETTE				1814	
3408	MCKAY JOHN R	MET			1832		WHITE CATHERINE	MET			1836	
3412	MCKAY JOHN RICHARD	MET	P	NWT	1791		BALLENDINE HARRIET	MET	P	NWT	1800 60	
3412	MCKAY JOHN RICHARD	MET	P	NWT	1791	3411	POITRAS MARGUERITE	MET	RC	RRS	1849	
3404	MCKAY JOSEPH	MET	RC	RRS	1842	3407	BIRD BETSY	MET			1818	
3410	MCKAY JOSEPH	MET			1815	3415	LEPINE CHARLOTTE	MET			1844	
3391	MCKAY MICHEL	MET			1839		MCDONALD MARY	MET	P		1827	2922
3382	MCKAY NEIL	EUR	P	SCT	1822		LAROSE ROSE	MET	O	RRS	1843	
3392	MCKAY PIERRE	MET			1840	3393	CHRISTIANA	EUR			1812	
3413	MCKAY ROBERT	EUR	O	SCT	1773 53		ELIZABETH	EUR	P		1822 46	
3414	MCKAY SELKIRK	EUR	P	SCT	1814	3418	ISABELLE	IND	P	NWT	1846	
3659	MCKAY SEVERE				1843		MASKEGON FRANCOISE	IND	RC		1800	
3415	MCKAY SIMON	MET	RC		1790		SARAH				1828	
3665	MCKAY THOMAS				1826							
3416	MCKAY WILLIAM	MET	P	RRS	1793 64		BUNN MARY	MET	P	NWT	1796	1134
3418	MCKAY WILLIAM	EUR	P	SCT	1769 49		SUTHERLAND BARBARA	EUR	P	SCT	1772 61	
3574	MCKAY WILLIAM	EUR			1775		SUSETTE	IND		NWT	1780	
3652	MCKAY WILLIAM	MET		RRS	1842		DENNET SOPHIA	MET	P	RRS	1850	
3653	MCKAY WILLIAM	MET	RC	RRS	1845		LAMBERT SARAH	MET	RC	RRS	1847	
3654	MCKAY WILLIAM	MET			1820		VERSAILLES SUSAN	MET			1832	
3655	MCKAY WILLIAM	MET		NWT	1794	3658	MATHESON JANET	EUR	P	RRS	1819	5111
3657	MCKAY WILLIAM				1817		MATHESON CHARLOTTE				1817	
3660	MCKAY WILLIAM				1828		GRANT BETSY				1833	
3669	MCKAY WILLIAM				1805		JULIA				1806	
3668	MCKAY WILLIAM				1840		CHRISTY				1814	
3656	MCKAY XAVIER	MET	P		1840		ELIZABETH	IND	P		1840	
3638	MCKEEVER MORDO	EUR		SCT	1828		MUIR FRANCOISE	MET	P	RRS	1847	2969
3419	MCKENNY JOHN	EUR	P		1845		LINKLATER ISABELLA	EUR	P		1845	
3428	MCKENZIE JOHN	EUR			1783		MARIE	MET			1787	
3426	MCKENZIE ALEXANDER	MET	P	NWT	1828	3427	BELLE CHRISTIANA	MET	P	NWT	1829 69	276
3420	MCKENZIE BENJAMIN	MET	P	NWT	1838	3421	OMAND MARY		P		1827	
3645	MCKENZIE BENJAMIN	MET			1837		FIDLER HARRIET				1840	
3642	MCKENZIE CHARLES				1778 55		MCKAY MARY	MET	P	NWT	1795	552
3421	MCKENZIE DONALD	MET	P	NWT	1800		BRUCE MATILDA	MET	P	NWT	1810	
3421	MCKENZIE DONALD	MET	P	NWT	1800		DROZ ADELGONDE		P	NWT	1805 34	
3422	MCKENZIE HECTOR	MET			1818		CAMERON JANE	MET	P	LC	1842	639
3423	MCKENZIE HECTOR				1798	3642	BIRD MARY	MET	P		1800	
3424	MCKENZIE JAMES	MET			1826		SETTER NANCY	MET	P		1830	
3429	MCKENZIE PHILIP				1808		LINKLATER NANCY	MET	P		1813	
3427	MCKENZIE RODERICK	EUR			1772 59		SUTHERLAND SARAH	MET	P		1777 27	
3427	MCKENZIE RODERICK	EUR			1772 59		ANGELIQUE	MET	P		1784 59	
3644	MCKENZIE RODERICK				1833		JANE	MET	P		1836	
3643	MCLAUGHLAN PETER	EUR	P	IRE	1821		LILLIE ELIZABETH	MET	P		1835 69	
3449	MCLEAN ALEXANDER	EUR	O	SCT	1800		GRACE	EUR	O	SCT	1808	
3432	MCLEAN DONALD	EUR	P	SCT	1793		MCKAY CHRISTIANA	MET	P	RRS	1793	4669
3646	MCLEAN DUNCAN	EUR			1838		THOMAS HELENA	MET			1838	
3511	MCLEAN FARQUARSON	EUR			1840		MUIR MARGARET	MET			1843	
3512	MCLEAN HECTOR	EUR			1836		MCBAIN MARGARET	EUR	P	RRS	1846	
3515	MCLEAN HECTOR			SCT	1788		CATHERINE	EUR		UC	1793	

TABLE 1: GENEALOGIES OF RED RIVER HOUSEHOLDS, 1818-1870

ID	MALE HEAD OF FAMILY	RACE	FAITH	BIRTH PLACE	DATES	DADS ID	FEMALE HEAD OF FAMILY	RACE	FAITH	BIRTH PLACE	DATES	DADS ID
3431	MCLEAN JOHN	EUR	P	SCT	1794		LIVINGSTON CATHERINE	EUR	P	SCT	1800	
3450	MCLEAN JOHN	EUR		SCT	1818		RHODA	EUR		UC	1821	
3514	MCLEAN JOHN	EUR	P	SCT	1828		FLOOD CATHERINE	MET	P	RRS	1839	
3452	MCLEAN MORDO	EUR	P	SCT	1826		BIRD ANN	MET	P	RRS	1849	
3516	MCLENNAN JAMES	MET	P	NWT	1842		FLETT BARBARA	MET	P	NWT	1840	
3433	MCLENNAN JOSEPH				1845		HUMPHABLE MARIE				1817	
3513	MCLENNAN JOSEPH				1845		HAYWOOD ELIZABETH	MET			1847	
3647	MCLENNAN JOSEPH				1835		FLETT BARBARA	MET	P		1839 73	1598
3648	MCLENNAN MURDOCK				1845		BIRD ANNE	MET			1848	
3434	MCLEOD ABRAHAM	MET		NWT	1825	3435	LARIVIERE CECILE	MET	P	NWT	1835	2655
3551	MCLEOD ALEXANDER	EUR		SCT	1841		INKSTER ISABELLA	MET	P	RRS	1847	2402
3544	MCLEOD ANGUS	MET	P	NWT	1840		MATHESON MARGARET	MET			1848 69	
3443	MCLEOD ANTOINE	MET	RC		1824		VERSAILLES MARIE	MET	RC	RRS	1837	
3549	MCLEOD ANTOINE				1845		GOULET JOSEPHTE	MET	RC		1838	
3552	MCLEOD ANTOINE				1845		DELORME ELISE	MET			1848	
3437	MCLEOD DONALD	MET	P	RRS	1831	3439	FIDLER MATILDA	MET	P	RRS	1833	1549
3543	MCLEOD DONALD	EUR	P	SCT	1845		MCCORRISTER CATHERINE				1852	
3553	MCLEOD DONALD				1835		JOHNSTON MARIE	MET			1837	
3439	MCLEOD JOHN	MET	P	RRS	1799		SWAIN ELIZABETH	MET	P	RRS	1820	4569
3547	MCLEOD JOHN	MET	P	RRS	1821		FRANKS GEORGINA	EUR	P	RRS	1841	
4038	MCLEOD JOHN	EUR	P	SCT	1835	3439	HARPER CLEMENCE	MET	P	RRS	1838	2132
3441	MCLEOD JOSEPH				1805		LESSARD ANGELIQUE				1810 50	
3442	MCLEOD JOSEPH				1816		LAPIERRE LOUISE				1821	
3444	MCLEOD JOSEPH	MET			1829		MCKAY HELENE				1821	
3546	MCLEOD KENNETH	EUR		SCT	1834		DELORME ISABEL	MET	RC	RRS	1834	2332
3447	MCLEOD MALCOLM				1820		JOHNSTON MATHILDA	MET		RRS	1826	4478
3440	MCLEOD MOISE	MET	RC	RRS	1849	3441	STEVENS ISABELLA	MET	RC	SCT	1845	2959
3453	MCLEOD MURDOCK	EUR	P	SCT	1834		LILLIE JANE	EUR	P	NWT	1833	3248
3548	MCLEOD NEIL		RC		1819		MUNROE FRANCES	MET	RC	RRS	1821	1054
3448	MCLEOD PIERRE	MET	RC	RRS	1849	3441	DEASE LOUISE	MET	RC	RRS	1852	
3545	MCLEOD RODERICK	EUR	RC	SCT	1834		DELORME ROSINE	EUR	RC	RRS	1840	
3461	MCMILLAN JAMES	EUR	RC	NWT	1790		FLETT MARGARET	MET	RC	NWT	1790	
3456	MCMILLAN JOSEPH	EUR	RC	RRS	1850		LETENDRE MARIE	MET			1795	
3462	MCMILLAN PIERRE	MET		RRS	1785 40	3457	BELLISLE JOSEPHTE	MET	RC	RRS	1853	555
3120	MCMILLAN WILLIAM				1790		BRUCE PAULINE	IND			1804	
3457	MCMILLAN WILLIAM	MET	RC	NWT	1800		SUZETTE	MET	RC		1820	
3458	MCMURRAY WILLIAM				1815	3461	DEASE MARGUERITE	MET		NWT	1820	1057
3466	MCNAB CHARLES	MET		NWT	1806		DEASE MARGARET	MET	RC		1824	1057
3454	MCNAB JAMES	MET		RRS	1820		NANCY	MET			1635 70	
3467	MCNAB JAMES	MET	P	NWT	1835	3464	MCLEOD MARIE ANNE	MET			1834	
3455	MCNAB JOHN	EUR		UC	1815		CARRIERE CATHERINE	EUR	P	RRS	1820	
3460	MCNAB JOHN	MET	P	RRS	1840		MICHEAL SARAH	MET			1850	
3463	MCNAB JOHN	EUR			1836		CAMPBELL JANE	MET		UC	1835	
3468	MCNAB JOHN	MET		NWT	1780	3468	WISHART MARY	EUR	P	RRS	1784	
3555	MCNAB JOHN	MET			1806		COOK JANE	MET			1810	
3567	MCNAB THOMAS				1819		SAUNDERS JANE			NWT	1806	
3464	MCNAB THOMAS	MET	P	NWT	1782 66	3464	WALKINGCHIEF BETSY				1819	
3465	MCNAB THOMAS	MET			1807		LIVINGSTON CATHERINE	EUR	P	NWT	1834	2972

TABLE 1: GENEALOGIES OF RED RIVER HOUSEHOLDS, 1818-1870

ID	MALE HEAD OF FAMILY	RACE	FAITH	BIRTH PLACE	DATES	DADS ID	FEMALE HEAD OF FAMILY	RACE	FAITH	BIRTH PLACE	DATES	DADS ID
3558	MCNAB THOMAS				1834		HALLET CHARLOTTE				1837	
3556	MCNAB TIMOTHY				1816 46		ELIZABETH				1826	
3472	MCPHAIL DUNCAN	EUR	P	SCT	1836		INKSTER MATILDA	MET	P	RRS	1846	
3473	MCPHAIL JOHN	EUR	P	SCT	1831		MCKAY ANNE	EUR	P	RRS	1840	
3475	MCPHERSON GEORGE	EUR	P		1800		RACETTE ANGELIQUE	MET			1803	
3477	MCRAE JOHN	EUR	P	SCT	1837		POLSON CATHERINE	EUR	P	RRS	1841	
3470	MCTAVISH JOHN	EUR	RC	UC	1838		ROWAND MARIA	MET	P	RRS	1849	4256
3053	MEADE ROLLIN	EUR	P	UC			ASHFORD MARY	EUR			1849	
3052	MELOIN JEAN BTE	EUR	RC	LC	1832		LESPERANCE MAGDELEINE	MET	RC	RRS	1826	2930
3051	MERCER F C	EUR	P	ENG	1839		DRY ELIZA	EUR		ENG	1840	
3050	MERCREDI FRANCOIS	MET	RC	RRS	1830		LAMIRANDE GENEVIEVE	MET	RC	RRS	1836	2586
3119	MEYERS JOHN	EUR	P	OTH	1800		ABERLAE MARGUERITE				1802	
2734	MIGNEAULT I				1842		LAFERTE MARIE	MET			1847	
2727	MILLER GEORGE	EUR	RC	USA	1866		MOZENY MARGUERITE	MET	RC	RRS	1853	2504
2728	MILLER JOSEPH	EUR	RC	RRS	1838		LACERTE CATHERINE	MET	RC	RRS	1842	3211
3118	MILLER ROBERT				1802 67		SETTER ELIZABETH	MET	P	RRS	1822	2469
2729	MILLER WILLIAM	EUR	P	SCT	1831		HUME JESSIE	EUR		SCT	1870	4358
3122	MILLET ANDRE	EUR			1772 65		DUCHARME MADELEINE	MET	RC		1801	1362
2749	MILLET ANSELME	MET			1840		DUCHARME MADELEINE	MET			1830	
2720	MILLET BENJAMIN				1803 70		PARENTEAU MARIE	MET			1815	3801
2723	MILLET JOSEPH				1820		MASKEGON MARGUERITE				1823	
3123	MILLET JOSEPH				1817		BOURBON MARGUERITE				1822	
2730	MILLHAM CHARLES	EUR	P	ENG	1840		GOWLAR SARAH	IND	P	RRS	1846	
2751	MILLS A				1844		MCBEATH ANNE	EUR			1849	
2750	MILOIS JEAN BTE				1839		LESPERANCE MAGDELEINE	EUR	P		1844	3275
3049	MINNIE CASIMER	MET	RC	RRS	1866	3048	COMTOIS ISABELLE	MET	RC	RRS	1852	926
3048	MINNIE CHARLES				1816 66		OUELLETTE MAGDELEINE	MET		RRS	1825	3765
3128	MINNIE JEAN BTE	EUR		USA	1780		PELLETIER MARGUERITE	MET	P		1785	
3129	MITCHELL	EUR		USA	1816		DESCHAMPS JOSEPHTE	MET			1821	
3134	MITCHELL COLONE	EUR	P	SCT	1813		DESCHAMPS NANCY	MET			1818	
3132	MITCHELL DAVID	EUR	P	SCT	1793		LANGSKIT ANN	EUR	P	SCT	1790	
3133	MITCHELL JOHN	MET	P	NWT	1796		MARY				1791 44	
3125	MODE EDWARD				1830		NORQUAY JANE	MET	P	NWT	1838	3752
3126	MODE EDWARD	MET	P	RRS	1800		MARGUERITE	IND		NWT	1805	
2752	MODE JACOB	MET			1850		SPENCE SARAH	MET	P	RRS	1852	
2753	MODE ROBERT	MET	P	RRS	1825		SMITH CATHERINE	MET	P	RRS	1830	
2754	MODE ROBERT	MET	P	RRS	1828		FORTH CHARLOTTE	MET	P	RRS	1837	4433
2757	MONATE ANDREW	MET		RRS	1805		MARGUERITE	IND		RRS	1809	
3143	MONETTE ANDRE	MET			1805	3140	MARON MARGUERITE	MET	P	RRS	1810	
3141	MONETTE FRANCOIS	MET			1838	3143	MORRISEAU LOUISE	MET			1844	
3142	MONETTE JEAN BTE	MET			1832	3143	DESJARLAIS ANGELIQUE	MET			1830	1272
3140	MONETTE MICHEL	EUR			1780		GRANT MARGUERITE	MET			1790	
3145	MONETTE MICHEL	MET	RC	USA	1802	3140	BRUYERE JOSEPHTE	MET			1790	
3144	MONETTE OLIVER	MET	RC	USA	1827	3145	MILLET JOSEPHTE	MET	IND		1807	
3146	MONJEUNIER FRANCOIS				1790		MARY	MET		NWT		
3146	MONJEUNIER FRANCOIS				1790		CHARLATS TERESA				1800	
3104	MONJEUNIER JOHN			NWT	1850		LAROCQUE MARIA					
2738	MONKMAN EDWARD		P	NWT	1840		KIPPLING SUSETTE				1842	
2744	MONKMAN HENRY				1838		RESSON LOUISA					
2744	MONKMAN HENRY				1838		SPENCE NANCY				1840	

TABLE 1: GENEALOGIES OF RED RIVER HOUSEHOLDS, 1818-1870

ID	MALE HEAD OF FAMILY	RACE	FAITH	BIRTH PLACE	DATES	DADS ID	FEMALE HEAD OF FAMILY	RACE	FAITH	BIRTH PLACE	DATES	DADS ID
2739	MONKMAN JAMES				1805 65	3149	RESSARD MARGUERITE	MET			1820	
2739	MONKMAN JAMES				1805 65	3149	RICHARD MARY	IND		RRS		
2745	MONKMAN JAMES				1809		CHABOYER NANCY					
2746	MONKMAN JAMES				1844		HALCROW MARGARET				1838	
3149	MONKMAN JAMES				1771 65		MARY					
2740	MONKMAN JOHN				1823 61		RESSARD MARY	MET	P		1830	
2741	MONKMAN JOSEPH	MET	P	RRS	1830		HENDERSON ELIZABETH	MET	P		1835	
3154	MONKMAN JOSEPH	MET	P	RRS	1836		LELAND MARY	MET	P		1836	2907
3154	MONKMAN JOSEPH	MET	P	RRS	1836		ANNABELLA					
3156	MONKMAN JOSEPH	MET	P	RRS	1810	3149	SETTER ISABEL	MET	P		1816	
3152	MONKMAN PHILIP	MET	P	RRS	1848	3156	HAPPER CATHERINE	MET	P		1849	
3155	MONKMAN THOMAS	MET	P	NWT	1845	3156	INKSTER MARY	MET	P		1847	2780
2761	MONSIGNE CHARLES	MET	RC	RRS	1844		THORNE NANCY	MET	RC		1845	4689
3117	MONSIGNE CHARLES	MET	RC	RRS	1824		DESJARDIN MARIE	MET	RC		1824	
2770	MONSIGNE FRANCOIS						SAULTEAUX MARIE					
2768	MONTOUR PASCAL						RICHARD MAGDELAINE					
3163	MONTZIN JOHN						KIPPLING MARIA				1851	
3165	MOORE CAESAR	MET	P	RRS	1828		CUMMINGS MARGARET	MET	P		1827	991
3168	MOORE CHARLES	IND	P	NWT	1832		BIRSTON JANE	MET	P		1833	
3136	MOORE GEORGE				1820		EMMA				1815	
3169	MOORE GEORGE				1776		TRUTHWAITE MARY	MET		NWT	1810	
2736	MOORE JOHN	MET	P	RRS	1800	3166	ARCUS NANCY	MET	P	RRS	1805	
3130	MOORE JOHN	MET	P	RRS	1836	3169	MATILDA				1838	
3166	MOORE JOHN				1805		ROSS CLEMENCE				1807	
3166	MOORE JOHN				1805		THOMAS NANCY				1820	
2769	MOOSOO BAZILE	MET		NWT	1840		SPENCE MARGARET				1830	4901
2763	MOOSOO				1825		ANDERSON CATHERINE	MET		RRS	1833	94
2765	MORE JOHN				1833		HELENA				1831	
3162	MOREAU BAPTISTE				1820		BEAUCHAMP FRANCOISE				1822	
3174	MOREAU JEANBAPTISTE	MET	RC	RRS	1824	3175	VENNE MARIE	MET	RC	RRS	1824	5090
3175	MOREAU JEANBAPTISTE	MET	RC	CAN	1795		LAFEVILLE CHARLOTTE				1802	
3176	MOREAU JONAS	MET	P	RRS	1841	3162	DESJARLAIS CECILE	MET	RC	RRS	1840	1281
2747	MORGAN GEORGE	MET	P	RRS	1835		BADGER HARRIET	IND	P	RRS	1838	
2748	MORGAN GEORGE	EUR	P	SCT	1810		HELEN	IND	P	RRS	1820	
3110	MORGAN ROBERT	MET	P	RRS	1825		DENIG MARGARET	IND	P	USA	1842	
3194	MORIN ALEX	MET	RC	RRS	1836	3195	BERTHELET ELISE	MET	RC	RRS	1842	
3193	MORIN ANDRE	MET	RC	RRS	1847	3195	GRANDBOIS ADELAIDE	MET	RC	RRS	1849	
3079	MORIN ANTOINE				1842		HARKNESS MARIE	MET			1844	2125
3180	MORIN ANTOINE	MET	P	RRS	1808		LAROCQUE THERESE	MET			1813	
3171	MORIN BAPTISTE	MET	RC	NWT	1799		BONNEAU FRANCOISE	MET			1801	
3183	MORIN BAPTISTE	MET	RC	RRS	1820		LAFOURNAISE MARIE	MET			1822 67	
3196	MORIN CHARLES	MET	RC	RRS	1838	3198	DAUPHINAIS MARIE	MET	RC		1845	
3187	MORIN ETIENNE	MET	RC	CAN	1777		SARCY MARGUERITE	MET	RC		1779	
3109	MORIN FRANCOIS	MET	RC	RRS	1837	3190	ROBINSON MARGUERITE	MET	RC		1837	4203
3188	MORIN FRANCOIS	MET	RC		1784		GRANT MARIE	MET			1837 45	
3806	MORIN FRANCOIS	MET			1817		BONNEAU ISABEL	MET			1819	
2772	MORIN JEANBAPTISTE	MET			1818		SAULTEAUX CATHERINE	MET			1819 39	
2774	MORIN JEANBAPTISTE	MET			1844		DELORME NANCY	MET		RRS	1846	
3106	MORIN JEANBAPTISTE	MET	RC	RRS	1838	3190	DELORME BETSY	MET	RC		1840	
3172	MORIN JEANBAPTISTE				1806		DUBOIS MARIE	MET	RC	RRS	1808	

TABLE 1: GENEALOGIES OF RED RIVER HOUSEHOLDS, 1818-1870

ID	MALE HEAD OF FAMILY	RACE	FAITH	BIRTH PLACE	DATES	DADS ID	FEMALE HEAD OF FAMILY	RACE	FAITH	BIRTH PLACE	DATES	DADS ID
3186	MORIN JEANBAPTISTE	MET	RC	RRS	1812	3187	JOSEPHE LUSSIER	MET	RC	RRS	1825	
2773	MORIN JOSEPH	MET	RC		1827		JOSEPHE LANG	MET			1829	
3102	MORIN JOSEPH	MET	RC	RRS	1843	3180	HELENE PELLETIER	MET		RRS	1845	
2756	MORIN LOUIS	MET	RC	RRS	1816	3187	CATHERINE DELORME	IND	RC	RRS	1825	
3100	MORIN LOUIS	MET	RC		1842		MARGUERITE MORIN	MET	RC	RRS	1842	
3179	MORIN LOUIS	MET	RC	RRS	1837	3180	MARGUERITE GOSSELIN	MET	RC	RRS	1842	
3192	MORIN LOUIS	MET	RC	RRS	1841	3195	CATHERINE HOULE	MET	RC	RRS	1842	
3195	MORIN LOUIS	MET	RC	RRS	1812		MARIE BEAUCHEMIN	MET	RC	RRS	1821	
3198	MORIN LOUIS	IND	RC		1819		MARGUERITE MALATERRE	IND	RC	NWT	1839	3018
3181	MORIN MAGLOIRE	MET	RC		1834	3182	HENRIETTE SAVOYARD	MET	RC	RRS	1834	
3184	MORIN PIERRE	IND	RC	RRS	1830	3185	LIZETT DESJARLAIS	MET	RC	RRS	1842	1273
3086	MORIN XAVIER	MET			1820		MARIE VERSAILLES	MET		RRS	1830	
8038	MORIN LEOPOLD				1848		ADELE SCHMIDT			OTH	1848 [70]	
2766	MORNEAU HENRY	EUR	P	OTH	1800		SOPHIE FLOTMAN	EUR	P	ENG	1802	
3202	MOROG JOHN			SCT	1836		CAROLINE ARMSTRONG				1830	
3088	MORRELLE JEAN				1848		SOPHIE ABERLAE			RRS	1850	
3093	MORRIS ROBERT			RRS	1826	3216	MARYROLFE LAFOURNAISE				1828	3143
3215	MORRISEAU ANDRE			RRS	1843		CECILE MONETTE	IND	RC	RRS	1843	
3213	MORRISEAU ANTOINE	MET	RC		1781		CHARLOTTE SAULTEAUX	IND		NWT	1783	
3207	MORRISEAU JOSEPH	MET		RRS	1830	3216	MARIE LAUVAGE	IND	RC	RRS	1835	
3214	MORRISEAU JOSEPH	MET	RC		1841	3213	MARIE DESJARLAIS	IND			1842	1276
3216	MORRISEAU JOSEPH	MET	RC		1801	3213	JOSEPHE DESJARLAIS				1815	1271
3204	MORRISEAU JOSEPH	MET	RC		1801	3205	CAROLINE LACERTE				1826 [52]	
3206	MORRISETTE BAPTISTE	MET			1829	3208	PHILOMENE BRACONNIER	MET	RC	RRS	1831	1512
3210	MORRISETTE FRANCO	MET		RRS	1814	3206	LOUISE FAVEL	MET		USA	1822	2856
3212	MORRISETTE FRANCO	MET		RRS	1840	3205	BETSY LEBRUN	MET			1849	
3209	MORRISETTE NORBERT	MET			1838	3206	CATHERINE BRACONNIER	IND	RC	NWT	1840	
3217	MORRISETTE WILLIAM	EUR	P	RRS	1845		ANN COCHRANE	MET		RRS	1833	
1723	MORRISSON ANGUS	MET		SCT	1819		MARY CUNNINGHAM	MET	P	NWT	1827	913
1724	MORRISSON JOSEPH	MET		RRS	1835		MARY DESJARLAIS	MET		RRS	1840	993
1729	MORRISSON JOSEPH	EUR		NWT	1815		ISABEL DESJARLAIS	MET		RRS	1810	
3218	MORRISSON NORMAN	EUR	P	SCT	1834	3217	CHARLOTTE MATHESON	EUR		SCT	1842	4417
1730	MORRISSON NORMAN	MET	P	NWT	1846		ELIZA SMITH	MET		RRS	1842	
3222	MORRISSON THOMAS	MET			1830		MARY STEVENS	MET		RRS	1832	
3225	MORWICK GEORGE	MET	P	RRS	1842		MARGUERITE ATKINSON	MET	P	RRS	1835	
3226	MORWICK JAMES	EUR	P	ORK	1821	3226	SARAH THOMPSON	MET	P	RRS	1837	4692
3221	MORWICK JOHN	EUR	P	ORK	1778 [65]		ISABELLA NORQUAY	MET			1783 [30]	
1731	MOSES JAMES	EUR	P	SCT	1787		LORETTA KING	EUR		IRE	1808 [61]	
1731	MOSES JAMES	EUR	P	SCT	1803		GENEVIEVE BURNS	EUR		RRS	1814	
1732	MOUARD CLAUDE	EUR	RC	OTH	1803		GENEVIEVE ROSSETTE	MET	RC	RRS	1820	
1706	MOUTON JEAN BTE	MET	RC	RRS	1767 [51]		JANE DENIS	MET		RRS	1840	
3227	MOWAT ADAM	EUR	P	ORK	1822	3233	ISABELLA ASHAM	MET	P	NWT	1772	
3232	MOWAT ANDREW	MET	P	NWT	1825		MARY MCDONALD	IND		NWT	1829	
3233	MOWAT EDWARD	EUR	P	ORK	1786 [62]	3233	MARGARET DAVIS	MET	P	NWT	1780	1046
3234	MOWAT EDWARD	EUR		ORK	1787 [57]	3234	FRANCOISE MCDONALD	IND		NWT	1800	
3229	MOWAT JOHN	MET	P	NWT	1820	3233	MARGARET TRUTHWAITE	MET	P	NWT	1818	
3230	MOWAT THOMAS	MET	P	RRS	1843	3233	MARY ANANGGOK	IND		NWT	1822 [64]	4720
3231	MOWAT THOMAS	MET	P	NWT	1821	3234						
1711	MOZENY FRANCOIS	MET			1813							

TABLE 1: GENEALOGIES OF RED RIVER HOUSEHOLDS, 1818-1870

ID	MALE HEAD OF FAMILY	RACE	FAITH	BIRTH PLACE	DATES	DADS ID	FEMALE HEAD OF FAMILY	RACE	FAITH	BIRTH PLACE	DATES	DADS ID
3211	MOZENY JOHN	MET	RC	RRS	1825	1711	KIPPLING MARIA	MET	RC	RRS	1834	
3238	MUIR JOHN	MET	RC	RRS	1848	3239	BIRSTON CHARLOTTE	MET	P	NWT	1848	
3239	MUIR JOHN	EUR	P	SCT	1810		STEWART ELIZABETH	EUR	P	RRS	1820	1342
1708	MULLIGAN JAMES	MET	P	IRE	1841		DUCHARME FRANCOISE	MET	RC	RRS	1846	
1712	MULLOIS JEAN BTE	EUR			1814		MCGEE CATHERINE	EUR	RC	ENG	1824	2930
1704	MULVANY WILLIAM				1823		LESPERANCE MADELEINE	MET			1828	
3251	MUNROE ALEXANDER	EUR	P	SCT	1842		COX CATHERINE	EUR		RRS	1847	
3249	MUNROE FINLAY	MET	P	RRS	1825		BANNERMAN BARBARA	MET	P	NWT	1822	182
3248	MUNROE GEORGE				1820		DENNING JANE				1840	
3245	MUNROE ROBERT	EUR	P	SCT	1797 64	3248	ANNE	EUR	P	RRS	1822	
3252	MURDO THOMAS				1822		FRASER CHRISTIANA				1827	1654
3257	MURRAY ALEXANDER				1750		SINCLAIR MARIE		P	NWT	1823	
1698	MURRAY ALEXANDER	EUR	P	SCT	1815	3254	ISABELLA	EUR	P	NWT	1753 37	658
1699	MURRAY ALEXANDER	EUR	P	UC	1840		CAMPBELL ANNE	MET	P	RRS	1851	
3253	MURRAY DONALD	MET	P	RRS	1839		RODWAY MARY ANN	MET	P	RRS	1839	444
3255	MURRAY JAMES	EUR	P	SCT	1804		FLETT LETITIA	EUR	P	NWT	1814	
3254	MURRAY JAMES	MET	P	RRS	1802		HERON JANE	MET	P	NWT	1807	
3256	MURRAY JOHN	EUR	P	SCT	1840		HOLMES ELIZABETH	EUR	P	NWT	1841	
1697	MURRAY JAMES	MET	P	RRS	1837		MCBEATH CHRISTIE	EUR	P	RRS	1841	2101
3693	NABASE JAMES	MET	P	RRS	1837		POLSON CATHERINE	MET	P	RRS	1839	
3694	NABASE JAMES	MET	P	RRS	1837		HALLET SUZETTE	IND		NWT	1818	
3379	NABASE LEWIS	MET	P	RRS	1840	3559	HARRIOT MARGARET	MET	P	RRS	1840	
3559	NABASE LOUIS	MET			1810	3559	LEDOUX MARY	MET	P	NWT	1815	
3562	NABASE LOUIS	MET			1805	3379	DAOUST NANCY	MET			1810	
3417	NABASE LOUIS	MET			1827	3559	BOUSQUET NANCY	IND	RC	NWT	1837	
3696	NADEAU DENIS	EUR	RC	CAN	1747		MARIE	MET	RC	RRS	1800	
3697	NADEAU DENNIS	EUR	RC		1797		DAZE MADELEINE	EUR	RC		1813	
3695	NADEAU JOSEPH	MET	RC	NWT	1810	3697	BOURDON MADELEINE	MET	RC	RRS	1835	
3560	NADEAU PIERRE	MET	P	RRS	1833		CARDINAL SUSANNE	MET			1840	
3706	NARVEN GEORGE	MET		RRS	1826		COCHRANE JOSEPHTE	EUR	RC	RRS	1832	
3711	NAULD ALEXIS	EUR	RC	CAN	1797 67		BRELAND JANE	EUR	RC	RRS	1812	
3698	NAULT AMABLE	EUR	RC	RRS	1828	3711	LAGEMONIER ANGELIQUE	EUR	RC	RRS	1833	2592
3703	NAULT ANDRE	EUR	RC	RRS	1830	3711	LANDRY JOSEPHTE	EUR	RC	RRS	1835	2113
3715	NAULT BENJAMIN	EUR	RC	RRS	1832	3711	HAMELIN ANASTHASIE	MET	RC	RRS	1845	2592
3713	NAULT BONIFACE	MET	RC	RRS	1834	3711	LANDRY ISABELLE	MET	RC	RRS	1839 67	
3721	NAULT CHARLE	MET	RC	NWT	1840	3711	HAMELIN CHRISTINE	EUR	RC	RRS	1846	3183
3709	NAULT CHARLE	EUR	RC	RRS	1827	3711	HAMELIN MARIE	EUR	RC	RRS	1828	
3710	NAULT JEAN BTE	RC	CAN		1819		MORIN LOUISE	RC		RRS	1825	1347
3705	NAULT JOSEPH		RC	RRS	1779 65		DUCHARME CATHERINE	RC		CAN	1786 46	
3561	NAULT JOSEPH	EUR	RC	CAN	1849	3711	VIVIER LOUISE	EUR	RC	RRS	1844	2592
3702	NAULT ROMAIN	MET			1840		LANDRY JOSEPHTE	MET			1842	1014
3699	NELSON ANGUS	EUR	RC	OTH	1832		DANIEL PHILOMENE	EUR		IRE	1834	
3563	NESS ANTONY	EUR	P	SCT	1843		AIGAN BETSY	MET	P	RRS	1852	
3727	NICOLSON ROBERT				1839		MCDONALD BRIDGETTE				1844	
3729	NISBET JAMES	MET	RC	RRS	1827	3727	MCBEATH ELIZABETH	EUR	RC	RRS	1835	
3731	NOLIN AUGUST	MET	RC	NWT	1781	3727	PERREAULT MARY	MET	RC	NWT	1806	
3733	NOLIN AUGUSTIN	MET	RC	RRS	1838	3727	CAMERON DOMITILDE	MET	RC	RRS	1843	2142
	NOLIN CHARLE	MET	RC	RRS	1840		HARRISON HELENE	MET	RC	RRS	1852	2142
	NOLIN DUNCAN						HARRISON MARIE ANNE					
							HARRISON CAROLINE					

TABLE 1: GENEALOGIES OF RED RIVER HOUSEHOLDS, 1818-1870

ID	MALE HEAD OF FAMILY	RACE	FAITH	BIRTH PLACE	DATES	DADS ID	FEMALE HEAD OF FAMILY	RACE	FAITH	BIRTH PLACE	DATES	DADS ID
3730	NOLIN FRANCOIS	MET	RC	RRS	1832		BERARD MARGUERITE	MET	RC	RRS	1834	300
3734	NOLIN JOHN	MET	RC	NWT	1831		LAVALLEE JULIE	MET	RC	NWT	1839	
3726	NOLIN JOSEPH	.	RC	NWT	1810		FREDERICK LIZETTE	MET	RC	.	1812	
3735	NOLIN JOSEPH	MET	RC	NWT	1842	3727	GAUDRY MARIE ANNE	MET	RC	RRS	1842	
3728	NOLIN NORBERT	MET	RC	RRS	1825		DUCHARME MARIE ANNE	MET	RC	RRS	1835	
3741	NORMAND BONIFACE	MET	RC	RRS	1851		ROY MARIE ROSE	MET	RC	RRS	1851	4265
3742	NORMAND MATHIAS	MET	RC	RRS	1847	3746	LADEROUTE ELISE	MET	RC	RRS	1853	
3723	NORMAND MICHEL	MET	RC	RRS	1821	3746	LAPLANTE ROSE	MET	RC	RRS	1822	2488
3745	NORMAND MICHEL	.	RC	CAN	1781	3745	BELANGER FRANCOISE	MET	RC	.	1790	
3740	NORMAND MOISE	MET	RC	RRS	1841	3746	DESJARDIN MARIE	MET	RC	RRS	1846	1278
3747	NORMAND WILLIAM	MET	RC	RRS	1830		CARRIERE LISETTE	MET	RC	RRS	1811	
3747	NORMAND WILLIAM	MET	RC	.	1830		WHITFORD SARAH	MET	.	.	1805	
3748	NORMAND WILLIAM	MET	RC	.	1805		BIRSTON CATHERINE	MET	P	.	1836	
3754	NORQUAY HENRY	EUR	P	ORK	1801		SPENCE ANNE	MET	P	.	1811	35
3754	NORQUAY HENRY	MET	P	NWT	1810	3756	MONKMAN MARY	MET	P	RRS	1817	3149
3720	NORQUAY JAMES	EUR	P	SCT	1810	3756	MCCORRISTER JANE	MET	P	.	1844	
3752	NORQUAY JOHN	MET	P	NWT	1841		FIRTHWAITE ISABEL	MET	P	RRS	1818	43
3752	NORQUAY JOHN	MET	P	RRS	1837		WARD NANCY	.	.	.	1821	
3753	NORQUAY JOHN	MET	P	.	1843	3754	SETTER ELIZABETH	MET	P	.	1842	4359
3755	NORQUAY JOHN	MET	P	RRS	1837	3754	SANDERSON MARIE	MET	P	RRS	1839	4323
3751	NORQUAY JOSEPH	MET	P	RRS	1843	3756	MILLER JESSIE	MET	P	.	1852	
3756	NORQUAY OMIE	MET	P	RRS	1785		MORWICK JANE	MET	P	RRS	1788	
3722	NORQUAY THOMAS	MET	P	OTH	1824		MILLER ELIZABETH	MET	P	.	1846	
3757	NORTE MARTIN	EUR	RC	OTH	1790		TREATHLY CATHERINE	.	RC	.	1800	
3750	NOTT JOHN	EUR	P	.	1824		MARY	.	.	.	1826	
3739	ODONNEL MICHEL	EUR	P	IRE	1830		JOHNSTON MARY	MET	P	RRS	1835	
3738	ODONNELL JOHN	EUR	.	UC	1838		ROUTLEDGE HANNAH	EUR	P	ENG	1841	
3743	OGLETREE FRANCOIS	EUR	P	IRE	1825		MCLARTY JEANNET	EUR	P	SCT	1822	
4040	OLSEN OLAFF	EUR	P	OTH	1836		JOHNSTON MARTHE	IND	P	NWT	1848	
3732	OLSEN RIAR	EUR	P	OTH	1830		JACKSON HIKISKAWACYA	IND	.	NWT	1832	
3761	OMAND JAMES	MET	P	RRS	1841	3759	BIRSTON JANE	MET	P	RRS	1842	
3719	OMAND JOHN	EUR	P	ORK	1822		MCKAY CATHERINE	EUR	P	ORK	1821	
3760	OMAND JOHN	MET	P	RRS	1828	3759	BROWN JANE	MET	P	NWT	1805	
3760	OMAND JOHN	MET	P	RRS	1836		HEAD RUTH	MET	P	NWT	1833	2149
3744	OMAND THOMAS	MET	P	OTH	1828	3759	MCDONALD SARAH	MET	P	OTH	1837	
3763	OSTERTODE GODOWICK	EUR	.	OTH			CARTON ANNE BARBARA	EUR	.	OTH		
3768	OUELLETTE ANTOINE	MET	RC	RRS	1845		BOTTINEAU ANGELIQUE	MET	RC	RRS	1838	
3708	OUELLETTE FRANCOIS	MET	.	.	1847	3717	DUPUIS MARGUERITE	MET	RC	RRS	1843	429
3769	OUELLETTE FRANCOIS	MET	RC	RRS	1838	3765	DUMONT E	MET	RC	.	1850	1410
3716	OUELLETTE GUILLAUME	MET	RC	RRS	1793	3764	GUIBOCHE SOPHIE	MET	RC	RRS	1840	
3765	OUELLETTE JACQUE	MET	RC	RRS	1840		MARCELLAIS MARIE	MET	RC	RRS	1794	3024
3712	OUELLETTE JEAN BTE	MET	RC	RRS	1834	3717	COURCHENE CECILE	MET	RC	RRS	1837	
3707	OUELLETTE JOSEPH	MET	RC	RRS	1790		PAUL MADELEINE	MET	RC	RRS	1835	
3717	OUELLETTE JOSEPH	MET	RC	RRS	1770		HOULE THERESE	MET	RC	RRS	1795	
3764	OUELLETTE JOSEPH	MET	RC	.	1832	3765	ANGELIQUE	IND	.	.	1773	
3766	OUELLETTE JOSEPH	MET	RC	RRS	1830	3717	LAMIRANDE MARIE ANNE	MET	RC	RRS	1835	
3718	OUELLETTE MOISE	MET	RC	RRS	1835	3765	DUMONT ISABEL	MET	RC	RRS	1844	2586
3564	OUELLETTE PIERRE	MET	RC	RRS	1825		GINGRAS MARGUERITE	MET	RC	RRS	1823	1393
3767	OUELLETTE PIERRE	MET	RC	.	1762	3765	MARGUERITE	MET	RC	RRS	1830	
3671	PACQUET ANTOINE	.	.	.			GRANDBOIS LISETTE	IND	.	.	1765	

TABLE 1: GENEALOGIES OF RED RIVER HOUSEHOLDS, 1818-1870

ID	MALE HEAD OF FAMILY		RACE	FAITH	BIRTH PLACE	DATES	DADS ID	FEMALE HEAD OF FAMILY		RACE	FAITH	BIRTH PLACE	DATES	DADS ID
3771	PACQUET	ANTOINE		RC	CAN	1784	3777	MARCHAND	AUGUSTINE	MET	RC		1786	2921
3782	PAGE	ALEXANDRE	MET	RC	RRS	1831		LEPINE	ADELAIDE	MET	RC		1833	2591
3783	PAGE	CHARLES	MET	RC	RRS	1833	3780	LANDRY	NANCY	MET	RC	RRS	1845	508
3779	PAGE	ELZEAR	MET	RC	USA	1838	3777	BRELAND	MARGUERITE	MET	RC	RRS	1846	
3776	PAGE	HENRY	MET	RC	CAN	1820		GRANT	ELIZABETH	MET	RC		1822	
3777	PAGE	JOSEPH		RC	CAN	1783		POITRAS	MARGUERITE	MET	RC		1785 29	
3778	PAGE	JOSEPH	MET	RC	CAN	1798		LETENDRE	AGATHE		RC		1790	
3780	PAGE	JOSEPH	MET	RC	RRS	1811	3777	PERREAULT	MARGUERITE	MET	RC		1800	
3565	PAGE	THOMAS	MET	RC	RRS	1838	3777	MORIN	MARGUERITE	MET	RC	RRS	1814 44	
3781	PAGE	XAVIER	MET	RC	RRS	1805		PELLETIER	GENEVIEVE		RC	RRS	1830	
3787	PANGMAN	JOSEPH	MET	RC	RRS	1815	3777	PITCHITE	JOSEPHTE		RC		1840	2643
3788	PANGMAN	PETER	MET	RC	NWT	1794		LAVALLEE	PHILOME	MET	RC		1843	
3789	PANGMAN	PETER				1815	3788	CHALIFOUX	ISABELLE		RC	RRS	1808	
4044	PARENT	JOSEPH				1845		SAULTEAUX	MARGUERITE		RC		1800	
3672	PARENTEAU	BAPTISTE	MET	RC		1830		SHORT	MARIE				1820	3034
3805	PARENTEAU	BAPTISTE	MET	RC	RRS	1832	3804	MARCHAND	MARIE ANNE	MET	RC	RRS	1847	1400
3818	PARENTEAU	ELIE	MET	RC	RRS	1835		DUMONT	DELAGIE	MET	RC		1835	
3818	PARENTEAU	ELIE	MET	RC	CAN	1835		BERIAULT	SCHOLASTIQUE	MET	RC		1834	
3800	PARENTEAU	JEAN	RC		CAN	1784 63		BERIAULT	MARIE	MET	RC	RRS	1842 65	
3566	PARENTEAU	JOSEPH		RC	CAN	1776		LEDOUX	FRANCOISE	MET	RC	RRS	1786	934
3801	PARENTEAU	JOSEPH	MET	RC	CAN	1832	3804	LASANSENTE	MARGUERITE	MET	RC		1849	
3803	PARENTEAU	JOSEPH	MET	RC	NWT	1811		COOK	HELENE	MET	RC		1780	3857
3804	PARENTEAU	JOSEPH	RC		RRS	1815			SUZANNE		RC	RRS	1843	
3807	PARENTEAU	JOSEPH		RC	RRS	1837	3811	PATENAUDE	MARIE	MET	RC	RRS	1818	
3810	PARENTEAU	JOSEPH	MET	RC	RRS	1838		GODON	ANGELIQUE	MET	RC	RRS	1817	
3817	PARENTEAU	LOUIS	MET	RC	RRS	1846		DAIGNEAULT	SUZANNE	MET	RC	RRS	1838	
3815	PARENTEAU	MOISE	MET	RC	RRS	1832	3813	HOULE	JULIE	MET	RC	RRS	1840	
3809	PARENTEAU	PIERRE	RC		CAN	1797 67	3811	GRANT	SUSANNE	MET	RC	RRS	1847	4592
3811	PARENTEAU	PIERRE	MET	RC	RRS	1843		ST GERMAIN	VERONIQUE	MET	RC	RRS	1842	3747
3812	PARENTEAU	PIERRE	MET	RC	RRS	1817	3813	NORMAND	HELENE	MET	RC		1800	
3813	PARENTEAU	PIERRE	MET	RC	RRS	1817	3801	LAURIN	JOSEPHTE	MET	RC	RRS	1838	
3838	PARISIEN	ABRAHAM	MET	RC		1837	3839	FARQUARHSON	NANCY	MET	RC	RRS	1832	
3825	PARISIEN	ALEXANDER	MET	P	RRS	1835		CARRON	MARIE	IND	RC	RRS	1823 45	2799
3843	PARISIEN	ALEXIS	MET	RC	RRS	1834	3839	DELORME	JOSEPHTE	MET	RC		1838	
3837	PARISIEN	ANDRE	MET	RC	RRS	1827	3839	LARONDE	MARIE	MET	RC	RRS	1845	930
3823	PARISIEN	AUGUSTIN	MET	RC	RRS	1810	3829	PRINCE	SARAH	MET	RC	RRS	1837	5207
3823	PARISIEN	AUGUSTIN	MET	RC	RRS	1810	3829	COMTOIS	MARGUERITE	MET	RC	RRS	1837	
3823	PARISIEN	AUGUSTIN	MET	RC	RRS	1810	3829	ZASTRE	JULIE	MET	RC	RRS	1819 34	
4097	PARISIEN	AUGUSTIN	MET	RC	RRS	1830		DUCHARME	THERESE	MET	RC	RRS	1819 47	3475
3830	PARISIEN	BAPTISTE		RC	RRS	1814		ALLARD	LOUISE	MET	RC		1820	
3829	PARISIEN	BONAVENTURE	MET	RC	RRS	1797 67	3829	MCPHERSON	ANGELIQUE	IND	RC	RRS	1832	
3841	PARISIEN	BONAVENTURE		RC		1800	3839	ADAM	FRANCOISE	IND	RC		1826	
8041	PARISIEN	FRANCOIS		RC	RRS	1837			MARGUERITE	IND	RC	NWT	1838	4269
3833	PARISIEN	GERMAIN	MET	RC	RRS	1809	3829		ISABEL		RC		1783	
3836	PARISIEN	GILBERT	MET	RC	RRS	1845	3839		MARGUERITE		RC		1805 45	968
3573	PARISIEN	HONORE	EUR	RC	LC	1835		SAYER	ANNIE	MET	RC	RRS	1837	
3839	PARISIEN	HYACINTH		RC	CAN	1781		COLBORNE	LOUISE	MET	RC	RRS	1821	

TABLE 1: GENEALOGIES OF RED RIVER HOUSEHOLDS, 1818-1870

ID	MALE HEAD OF FAMILY	RACE	FAITH	BIRTH PLACE	DATES	DADS ID	FEMALE HEAD OF FAMILY	RACE	FAITH	BIRTH PLACE	DATES	DADS ID
3773	PARISIEN IGNACE		RC		1830		LETENDRE MARGUERITE	MET		RRS	1833	
3821	PARISIEN ISAIC	MET	RC	RRS	1840	3823	LECLAIR CHARLOTTE	MET	RC	RRS	1841	
3819	PARISIEN JEAN BTE	MET	RC	RRS	1840		DESCHAMPS ISABELLA	MET	RC		1845	25
3840	PARISIEN JEAN BTE			CAN	1785		BERCIER LISETTE	MET	RC		1800	
3572	PARISIEN JOSEPH	MET	RC		1847	3828	GARIEPY MARGUERITE				1850	
3828	PARISIEN JOSEPH	MET	RC	NWT	1819	3840	MARTIN MARGUERITE	MET	RC	RRS	1827	
3834	PARISIEN JOSEPH	MET			1835		SPENCE CATHERINE	MET	RC		1840	
8051	PARISIEN JOSEPH			NWT	1847		THOMAS MARY				1847 67	
3826	PARISIEN NARCIS	MET	RC	NWT	1840	3830	SABISTON MARGUERITE	MET	RC	RRS	1845	
3824	PARISIEN PASCAL	MET	RC	RRS	1830	3823	COURCHENE CATHERINE	MET	RC	RRS	1837	
3822	PARISIEN PIERRE	MET	RC	RRS	1839	3823	ADAM MARGUERITE	MET	RC	RRS	1845	
3845	PARK GEORGE	MET	P	RRS	1847		SINCLAIR MARIE	MET	P	RRS	1850	
3846	PARK GEORGE	MET	P	RRS	1822	3848	GUIBOCHE JULIE	MET	P	RRS	1832	
3847	PARK JAMES	MET	P	RRS	1831	3848	INKSTER MARGARET	MET	P	RRS	1831	
3844	PARK JOHN	MET	P	RRS	1847	3846	SABISTON MARIE	MET	P	RRS	1852	
3848	PARK JOHN	EUR	O	SCT	1771 46		SPENCE MARGARET	MET	O	NWT	1786 53	
3795	PASSAGE JOHN	IND		RRS	1840		BERGE JANE	IND		RRS	1842	
3850	PATENAUDE BAPTISTE	MET	RC	NWT	1804		PRITCHARD LOUISE	EUR	RC		1810	
3853	PATENAUDE CHARLE	MET	RC	NWT	1838		PICHE ROSE	MET	RC	RRS	1846	
3852	PATENAUDE CUTHBERT	MET	RC	RRS	1838	3854	PICHE MARIE	MET	RC	RRS	1843	
3851	PATENAUDE MICHEL	MET	RC	RRS	1830	3854	SERPENT THERISE	IND	RC	NWT	1837	3930
3854	PATENAUDE MICHEL			CAN	1784 63		MARGUERITE	MET			1793	
3857	PATENAUDE MICHEL	MET			1808		BOURASSA JOSEPHTE	MET			1810	
3579	PATERSON ALBERT				1785		SUTHERLAND MARIE	MET			1790	
3580	PATERSON MALCOLM	EUR	P	SCT	1835		FIRTH MARIE	MET	RC	RRS	1840	
3856	PATERSON ALEXANDRE	EUR	P		1820		KAUFFMAN BARBARA	EUR			1826	2313
3875	PAUL ALEXANDRE				1840		SAULTEAUX LISETTE		P		1847 64	
3863	PAUL ANTOINE	MET	RC	NWT	1828	3870	NOLIN MARIE	MET			1846 66	
3862	PAUL BAPTISTE	MET	RC	NWT	1794	3874	BEAUVIER FRANCOISE	MET	RC	NWT	1830	1982
3872	PAUL BAPTISTE				1826 52	3862	GODON ANGELIQUE	MET	RC	NWT	1805	1945
3860	PAUL BERNARD	MET	RC		1848	3862	MCGILLIS MARIE	MET			1830	
3867	PAUL DANIEL	MET	RC	RRS	1838	3868	GERVAIS MARIE	MET	RC	RRS	1849	
3866	PAUL FRANCOIS		RC	CAN	1791 56	3862	GUIBOCHE MARGUERITE	MET	RC		1839	
3868	PAUL FREDERICK		RC	CAN	1792		GRANT MARGUERITE	MET	RC		1790	
3865	PAUL JOSEPH	MET	RC	RRS	1843		BRUNET JOSEPHTE	MET	P		1795	933
3873	PAUL JOSEPH		P		1831		COOK ANN	MET		RRS	1849	
3874	PAUL JOSEPH				1770		JOSETTE				1833	
3820	PAUL MARC				1830	3870	CREE LOUISE				1772	
3869	PAUL OLIVIER	MET	RC	NWT	1822	3866	GERVAIS SUSANNE	MET	RC		1830	1950
3861	PAUL PAUL	MET	RC	RRS	1844	3869	GERVAIS MADELEINE	MET	RC	NWT	1824	5207
3870	PAUL PAUL			CAN	1782 67		ZASTRE LOUISE	MET	RC	RRS	1847	
3870	PAUL PAUL		RC	CAN	1782 67		LAVALLEE MARGUERITE		RC		1797 46	
3871	PAUL PIERRE	MET	RC	NWT	1813	3862	GRANT MARGUERITE	MET		RRS	1795	
3859	PAUL WILLIAM	MET	RC	RRS	1833	3869	CREE ANGELIQUE	MET	RC		1849	
3864	PAUL WILLIAM	EUR	RC	RRS	1848		BRELAND ADELAIDE	MET	RC		1833	
3876	PEEBLES JAMES	MET	P		1811 40		PAGE FLAVIE	IND	RC	NWT	1789	507
3877	PEEBLES JAMES	MET	P	RRS	1830 66		MORRISSON ELIZABETH	MET	RC	RRS	1825	3776
3878	PEEBLES ROBERT	EUR	P		1838		THOMAS MARGUERITE	MET	P	RRS	1840	
3880	PEEBLES THOMAS	MET	P	RRS	1835		CUMMINGS CATHERINE	MET	P	RRS	1835	991

TABLE 1: GENEALOGIES OF RED RIVER HOUSEHOLDS, 1818-1870

ID	MALE HEAD OF FAMILY		RACE	FAITH	BIRTH PLACE	DATES	DADS ID	FEMALE HEAD OF FAMILY		RACE	FAITH	BIRTH PLACE	DATES	DADS ID
3879	PEEBLES	WILLIAM	MET	P	NWT	1809	.	ARCUS	CATHERINE	MET	P	NWT	1832	2121
3879	PEEBLES	WILLIAM	MET	P	NWT	1809	.	ARCUS	MARY	MET	P	.	1822 46	.
3879	PEEBLES	WILLIAM	MET	P	NWT	1809	.	ARCUS	NANCY	IND	.	.	1815 41	.
3583	PEEL	WILLIAM	.	.	.	1847	.	.	SARAH	EUR	.	.	1851	.
3892	PELLETIER	ALPHONSE	MET	RC	.	1834	3886	MCDONALD	MADELEINE	MET	.	.	1844	.
3884	PELLETIER	ANASTASIE	MET	RC	.	1841	3886	DESJARLAIS	LOUISE	.	RC	.	1844	.
3884	PELLETIER	ANASTASIE	MET	.	.	1822	.	HOULE	LEANDRE	MET	.	.	1830	.
3882	PELLETIER	ANTOINE	MET	RC	.	1831	.	ST GERMAIN	JULIE	.	RC	.	1835	1644
3578	PELLETIER	BENJAMIN	.	.	NWT	1805	.	FOURNIER	MARGUERITE	MET	.	.	1801	.
3886	PELLETIER	CHARLES	MET	RC	.	1834	.	GONEVILLE	SUZANNE	MET	RC	.	1835	282
3886	PELLETIER	CHARLES	MET	RC	.	1819 61	.	BERCIER	MARIE	.	RC	RRS	1840 65	1541
3889	PELLETIER	EDOUARD	MET	RC	RRS	1830	3886	FIDLER	CATHERINE	.	RC	.	1830	.
3576	PELLETIER	EDOUARD	MET	.	.	1825	.	ROCHEBLAVE	MADELEINE	MET	RC	.	1836	.
3858	PELLETIER	JEAN BTE	MET	RC	NWT	1787	3891	DESCHAMPS	LIZETTE	IND	RC	.	1816	4583
3885	PELLETIER	JOSEPH	MET	RC	.	1819	3886	ST DENIS	GENEVIEVE	.	RC	NWT	1823	.
3891	PELLETIER	JOSEPH	MET	RC	.	1833 55	.	CREE	SUSANNE	MET	.	.	1835	.
3577	PELLETIER	MARTIN	.	RC	.	1820	.	BERCIER	MARIE	.	RC	.	1821	.
3575	PELLETIER	PIERRE	MET	RC	NWT	1820	3886	THORNE	JOSEPHTE	MET	.	.	1824	.
3793	PELLETIER	PIERRE	MET	RC	CAN	1804	3891	DESCHAMPS	ANGELIQUE	.	.	.	1806	.
3890	PELLETIER	PIERRE	EUR	RC	RRS	1791	3893	COMTOIS	ANGELIQUE	.	.	.	1819	.
3893	PELLETIER	PIERRE	MET	.	.	1845	.	AZURE	AGATHE	MET	RC	.	1849	.
3772	PEPIN	ANTOINE	.	RC	CAN	1794	.	DAVIS	MARGUERITE	MET	RC	USA	1847	1044
3894	PEPIN	HENRIE	MET	RC	RRS	1815	3895	GENDRON	MARIE	EUR	RC	RRS	1796	.
3895	PEPIN	JEAN BTE	EUR	RC	.	1817	3899	LANOUILLE	JOSETTE	MET	.	.	1820	.
3896	PEPIN	JOSEPH	MET	.	RRS	1839	.	PATENAUDE	MARY	MET	RC	NWT	1818	.
3897	PEPIN	NARCIS	MET	RC	RRS	1841	3895	BEAULIEU	ANNE	MET	RC	RRS	1847	258
3587	PERREAULT	DAMASE	EUR	RC	.	1831	3899	ST GERMAIN	MADELEINE	MET	RC	RRS	1844	4603
4045	PERREAULT	EDOUARD	MET	RC	UC	1790	.	MILLET	GENEVIEVE	MET	RC	.	1840	.
3898	PERREAULT	EDWARD	MET	RC	RRS	1813	3899	CARRIERE	MARIE	MET	RC	RRS	1794	712
3902	PERREAULT	FRANCOIS	EUR	.	.	1799	.	GRANT	MARGUERITE	EUR	.	.	1814	58
3904	PERREAULT	FRANCOIS	EUR	RC	.	1824	3902	ALLARD	CATHERINE	MET	RC	UC	1804	1347
3899	PERREAULT	JEAN BTE	EUR	RC	.	1797	3899	DUCHARME	MADELEINE	MET	RC	USA	1826	.
3901	PERREAULT	JEAN BTE	EUR	RC	RRS	1819	.	GROUETTE	MARGUERITE	MET	RC	.	1801	.
3906	PERREAULT	LOUIS	EUR	RC	RRS	1823	.	DUCHARME	MARGARET	MET	RC	.	1822	.
3907	PERREAULT	LOUIS	MET	RC	RRS	1830	.	MALATERRE	JUDITH	EUR	RC	RRS	1832	1362
3908	PERREAULT	NORBERT	EUR	RC	.	1835	.	HAMELIN	ELIZABETH	MET	RC	RRS	1838	3018
3900	PERREAULT	REGIS	MET	RC	RRS	1848	3904	VILLENEUVE	JANE	MET	RC	RRS	1832	2113
3903	PERREAULT	XAVIER	MET	.	RRS	1840	.	BONNEAU	ARABELLA	MET	.	RRS	1849	5128
3914	PETER	JOHN	.	RC	.	1824 44	.	CAMERON	MARY ANNE	MET	P	.	1843	.
3916	PETER	JOHN	MET	RC	RRS	1805	.	MCKENZIE	MARIE	MET	RC	.	1828	.
3590	PETERSON	ANDREW	.	P	.	1844	.	ERASMUS	JOSEPHTE	MET	RC	NWT	1822 67	.
3910	PETIT	THOMAS	EUR	RC	CAN	1837	.	BEAULIEU	CHARLOTTE	MET	P	.	1847	2582
3911	PETIT	THOMAS	EUR	RC	CAN	1800	.	OUELLETTE	ELIZA	MET	RC	SCT	1810	.
3588	PHILIPS	WILLIAM	EUR	P	SCT	1850	.	LAMBERT	ANGELIQUE	MET	P	RRS	1848	.
3589	PICARD	JAMES	MET	RC	RRS	1841	.	DESBORNE	JOSEPHTE	MET	RC	.	1853	.
3921	PICARD	JOSEPH	MET	RC	NWT	1834	3931	BERCIER	MARIE	MET	RC	.	1837	.
3923	PICHE	BONIFACE	MET	RC	RRS	1810	.	LEPINE	JANE	MET	RC	RRS	1818	2922
4043	PICHE	EDWARD	MET	RC	RRS	1840	.	BARRON	MADELEINE	MET	RC	NWT	1840	212
3905	PICHE	FRANCOIS	.	RC	NWT	.	.	.	MARIE	MET	RC	NWT	.	.
3931	PICHE	FRANCOIS	MET	RC	RRS	.	3926	HOULE	MADELEINE	MET	RC	RRS	.	.
4042	PICHE	FRANCOIS	MET	RC	RRS	.	.	ROSS	NANCY	MET	RC	RRS	.	.

TABLE 1: GENEALOGIES OF RED RIVER HOUSEHOLDS, 1818-1870

ID	MALE HEAD OF FAMILY	RACE	FAITH	BIRTH PLACE	DATES	DADS ID	FEMALE HEAD OF FAMILY	RACE	FAITH	BIRTH PLACE	DATES	DADS ID
3927	PICHE JEAN	MET	.	RRS	1846	3930	DESMARAIS ELIZABETH	MET	.	RRS	1839	.
3929	PICHE LOUIS	MET	RC	RRS	1834	3930	DESMARAIS CECILE	MET	RC	RRS	1839	.
3930	PICHE LOUIS	MET	RC	RRS	1806	.	DAUPHINAIS CHARLOTTE	MET	.	RRS	1825 44	.
3930	PICHE LOUIS	MET	RC	RRS	1806	.	LEPINE ANGELIQUE	MET	.	RRS	1824	2921
3933	PILON ANTOINE	MET	RC	RRS	1821	3935	HARKNESS CECILE	MET	RC	RRS	1805	2125
3935	PILON ANTOINE	.	.	.	1789	.	LISETTE ANGELIQUE	MET	RC	RRS	1839	.
3934	PILON JOSEPH	MET	RC	RRS	1837	3935	NORMAND ANGELIQUE	MET	RC	RRS	1842	3746
3936	PILON PIERRE	MET	RC	RRS	1829	3938	SAUVE HELENE	MET	RC	RRS	1849	4296
3939	PINKMAN WILLIAM	EUR	P	.	1843	.	DREVER JEAN	EUR	.	.	1847	.
3796	POCHA CHARLES	MET	.	RRS	1843	3943	TATE MARY	MET	P	.	1838	.
3945	POCHA JOHN	MET	.	RRS	1835	3943	SPENCE HARRIET	MET	.	RRS	1838	.
3945	POCHA JOHN	MET	.	RRS	1833	3943	ANDERSON MARIA	MET	.	RRS	1848	94
3775	POCHA JOSEPH	EUR	.	RRS	1780	3798	HODGSON MATILDA	MET	.	.	1834	.
3798	POCHA JOSEPH	MET	P	NWT	1800	.	DESCOLEAUX MARGARET	IND	RC	NWT	1780	1257
3943	POCHA JOSEPH	MET	P	RRS	1800	3798	LAPOINTE JOSEPHTE	MET	.	RRS	1794	.
3943	POCHA JOSEPH	MET	RC	RRS	1835	.	LAPOINTE MARIE	MET	.	RRS	1810	2628
3797	POCHA THOMAS	MET	.	RRS	1839	3943	FLAMMAND ROSALIE	MET	RC	RRS	1850	.
3592	POISSON JOSEPH	MET	.	.	1849	.	DESCOLEAUX ISABEL	MET	.	RRS	1836	1258
3284	POITIER JOSEPH	.	.	.	1849	.	MARY	.	.	.	1839	.
3953	POITRAS CHARLES	MET	.	.	1836	3952	BRELAND MARIE	MET	RC	RRS	1851	.
3953	POITRAS CHARLES	MET	RC	RRS	1828	3952	LAVERDURE SUZANNE	MET	RC	.	1820	.
3957	POITRAS DAVID	MET	.	RRS	1825	3959	ST DENIS MAGDELEINE	MET	.	.	1831	.
1692	POITRAS FLEURY	.	.	.	1848	.	FAGNANT CATHERINE	MET	.	.	1830	.
3947	POITRAS FRANCO	MET	RC	RRS	1822	3961	FISHER MAGDELEINE	MET	RC	RRS	1849	.
3956	POITRAS FRANCOIS	MET	RC	RRS	1796	3959	DUCHARME CATHERINE	MET	RC	.	1826	.
3951	POITRAS GABRIELLE	MET	RC	NWT	1757	3961	MALATERRE ISABELLE	MET	RC	RRS	1807	.
3950	POITRAS HENRY	MET	RC	RRS	1830	.	GEORGE MARIE	MET	RC	.	1793	.
3961	POITRAS HENRY	MET	RC	CAN	1842	.	GRANT MARGUERITE	MET	RC	.	1832	.
3949	POITRAS IGNACE	MET	RC	RRS	1833	3961	MCGILLIS HELENE	MET	RC	.	1840	.
3260	POITRAS JOSEPH	MET	RC	RRS	1837	.	LAPLANTE NANCY	MET	RC	.	1850	.
3955	POITRAS JOSEPH	MET	RC	RRS	1810	.	BRELAND ELSIE	MET	RC	.	1836	507
1693	POITRAS PIERRE	MET	RC	.	1768	.	LAVALLEE LOUISE	MET	RC	RRS	1843	.
1694	POITRAS PIERRE	MET	RC	RRS	1778	.	BREMNER ISABELLE	MET	RC	NWT	1818	.
3959	POITRAS PIERRE	MET	RC	RRS	1822	.	BRUYERE MARIE	MET	RC	RRS	1900	.
3962	POLANDER JOSEPH	EUR	O	OTH	1768	.	ABERLAE CHRISTY	EUR	O	SCT	1786	.
3964	POLSON ALEXANDER	EUR	O	SCT	1778	.	HENDERSON CATHERINE	EUR	P	RRS	1829	2445
3969	POLSON ANGUS	EUR	P	RRS	1822	.	SUTHERLAND CATHERINE	EUR	P	RRS	1834	.
3972	POLSON DONALD	EUR	P	SCT	1814 69	.	PRITCHARD ANNE	EUR	P	.	1827 46	.
3972	POLSON DONALD	EUR	P	SCT	1814 69	3964	HENDERSON JANET	EUR	P	RRS	1821	2445
3975	POLSON HUGH	EUR	P	SCT	1807	.	CHRISTINE	EUR	.	.	1850	.
3976	POLSON HUGH	EUR	P	.	1846	.	CATHERINE	EUR	.	.	1824	.
3977	POLSON JOHN	EUR	P	SCT	1810	3964	FLETT SARAH	EUR	P	RRS	1851	.
3971	PORTER CHARLES	EUR	RC	USA	1843	.	LAROCQUE MARGUERITE	MET	RC	RRS	1848	2674
3970	POTTINGER GEORGE	.	.	.	1834	.	SINCLAIR FRANCOISE	.	.	.	1836	.
3979	POULET ANTOINE	EUR	RC	IRE	1813	.	BAUVIER ANNIE	EUR	RC	SCT	1823	.
3966	POWERS MICHEAL	IND	P	RRS	1826	.	SCOTT ANNIE	IND	RC	RRS	1837	480
3973	PRATT CHARLES	EUR	RC	RRS	1845	.	STEVENSON CATHERINE	MET	.	.	1845	.
3982	PRIMEAU AGUSTIN	MET	.	.	1818	3984	LAMBERT ELIZABETH	.	.	.	1821	.
4051	PRIMEAU CHARLES	.	.	.	1840	.	LAVALLEE ANGELIQUE	.	.	.	1818	.
4052	PRIMEAU FRANCOIS	.	.	.	.	.	PAIENAN CAROLINE	.	.	.	1840	.

TABLE 1: GENEALOGIES OF RED RIVER HOUSEHOLDS, 1818–1870

ID	MALE HEAD OF FAMILY	RACE	FAITH	BIRTH PLACE	DATES	DADS ID	FEMALE HEAD OF FAMILY	RACE	FAITH	BIRTH PLACE	DATES	DADS ID
3981	PRIMEAU JEAN BTE	MET			1841	3984	SMITH ROSALIE	MET			1844	
3985	PRIMEAU JEAN BTE	MET		RRS	1840	3986	LAROCQUE MARIE LOUISE	MET	RC	RRS	1845	2665
3983	PRIMEAU JERIMIE				1844	3984	MORIN MARIE	MET	RC		1846	3195
3980	PRIMEAU JOSEPH	MET	RC	NWT	1785		DURAND JOSEPHTE	MET	RC	RRS	1787 67	
3984	PRIMEAU JOSEPH	MET	RC	USA	1802		STEVENSON CHARLOTTE	MET		RRS	1807	
3986	PRIMEAU LOUIS	MET	RC		1817			IND	P		1820	
4053	PRINCE				1808		MARIE	IND	P		1810	
4054	PRINCE ANDRE	IND	P	RRS	1842		KIPPLING JANE	IND	P	RRS	1843	
4055	PRINCE ANGUS	IND	P	RRS	1830		STEVENS MARY	IND	P	RRS	1840	
3989	PRINCE ASHAM	MET			1800		LEASK ANN	MET			1804	
4066	PRINCE BAPTISTE				1842		NANCY				1845	
4056	PRINCE DAVID	IND	P	RRS	1840		ANNE	IND	P	RRS	1842	
4057	PRINCE GEORGE	IND	P	RRS	1800		BEARDY NANCY	IND	P	RRS	1820	
4065	PRINCE HENRY	IND	P	RRS	1819		BADGER SARAH	IND	P		1823	
4061	PRINCE JOHN	IND	P		1830		MAEGUERITE				1830	
4063	PRINCE JOHN	IND	P	RRS	1805		MARGARET	IND	P		1808	
4060	PRINCE JOSEPH	IND	P	RRS	1842		HOURIE ELIZABETH	IND	P	RRS	1843	
4059	PRINCE THOMAS	IND	P	RRS	1844		SINCLAIR ANNE	IND	P	RRS	1846	
4058	PRINCE WILLIAM	IND	P	RRS	1830		BEAR MARY	IND	P	RRS	1835	
4064	PRINCE WILLIAM	IND	P		1848		CATHERINE	IND	P	RRS	1852	
4073	PRINER HENRI	MET	RC	RRS	1815		BADGER CATHERINE	IND	P	RRS	1816	2922
4010	PRITCHARD CHARLE	MET	P	RRS	1843		SARA	MET	P		1845	
3996	PRITCHARD HUGH	EUR	O	ENG	1831		LEPINE BETHSY	EUR	P	RRS	1836	
3998	PRITCHARD JOHN	EUR	P	ENG	1777		ELSE EMILY	EUR	O	ENG	1798 54	
4002	PRITCHARD JOHN	EUR	P	NWT	1815		MCGILLIVRAY CATHERINE	EUR	P	RRS	1818	
4004	PRITCHARD JOHN	EUR	P	NWT	1840		MATHESON JANET				1843	
4005	PRITCHARD JOHN	MET	RC	RRS	1778		MATHESON ANNE	IND	P		1790	
4007	PRITCHARD JOHN		RC	RRS	1843		SAUVAGE MARIE				1815	
4006	PRITCHARD JOSEPH	EUR	RC		1809		DELORME ROSE	MET		RRS	1849	
3997	PRITCHARD RICHARD	EUR	RC	RRS	1835		PARENT LOUISE		RC		1815	
4014	PRITCHARD SAMUEL	EUR	RC	RRS	1827		MATHESON CATHERINE	MET	RC	RRS	1839	
4009	PRITCHARD WILLIAM	MET	RC	NWT	1849		BANNERMAN JOHANNAH	EUR	P	RRS	1843	
4011	PRITCHARD WILLIAM		RC	NWT	1800 61		LEPINE ELIZABETH	MET	RC	RRS	1848	189
4011	PRITCHARD WILLIAM	EUR	RC	NWT	1800 61		BEAULIEU LOUISE	EUR	RC		1810 35	258
4019	PROULX MICHEL	EUR	RC	LC	1818		FLEURY MARIE	MET	RC	NWT	1826	1612
4018	PROULX PAUL	EUR	RC	CAN	1839		GUIBOCHE ANGELE	EUR	RC	RRS	1831	
4020	PROULX PIERRE		RC	RRS	1794		NAULT ANGELIQUE	EUR	RC		1849	
3994	PRUDEN ALBERT	MET	P	RRS	1842		LACROIX FRANCOISE	EUR	RC		1798	3711
4016	PRUDEN ARTHUR	MET	P		1833		THOMPSON CATHERINE	MET	P	RRS	1842	
4024	PRUDEN CORNELIUS	MET	P	NWT	1819		GUIBOCHE ARCHANGE	MET	P	NWT	1835	
4034	PRUDEN CORNELIUS	MET	P	NWT	1839		MCKENZIE NANCY		P		1825	
4031	PRUDEN EDWARD	MET	P	NWT	1835		ISBISTER ISABELLA	MET	P	USA	1846	
4027	PRUDEN JAMES		P		1820		SMITH MARY	MET	P	NWT	1843	
4027	PRUDEN JAMES				1820		NANCY				1824 46	
4036	PRUDEN JAMES				1846		GENEVIEVE				1830 68	
4000	PRUDEN JOHN	MET	P	RRS	1830		MILLER CATHERINE	MET	P	RRS	1850	
4022	PRUDEN JOHN	MET	P	RRS	1820		ROSS SARAH				1834	
4028	PRUDEN JOHN	MET	P		1829		SETTER BETHSY	MET	P	RRS	1840	
4026	PRUDEN JOHN PETER	EUR	P	ENG	1778 68		ROWLAND ANN	MET	P		1850	
4026	PRUDEN JOHN PETER	EUR	P	ENG	1778 68		NANCY ANN	MET	P		1787 39	4260
4026	PRUDEN JOHN PETER						ARMSTRONG ANNE	EUR	P		1795	

ID	MALE HEAD OF FAMILY	RACE	FAITH	BIRTH PLACE	DATES	DADS ID	FEMALE HEAD OF FAMILY	RACE	FAITH	BIRTH PLACE	DATES	DADS ID
4017	PRUDEN LOUIS	MET	P	RRS	1840	4032	FANNY ISBISTER		P	RRS	1845	2374
4021	PRUDEN PETER	MET	P	RRS	1842	4032	MARY DUCHARME	MET	P	RRS	1842	1342
4032	PRUDEN PETER	MET	P	NWT	1807	4026	JOSEPHTE JOLICOEUR	MET	P		1810	2321
4029	PRUDEN WILLIAM	MET	P	RRS	1832		SARAH TRUTHWAITE	MET	P	RRS	1835	1549
4033	PRUDEN WILLIAM	MET	P	RRS	1830 44	4035	MARIA FIDLER	MET	P	RRS	1836	
4035	PRUDEN WILLIAM				1804 44		NANCY OGDEN	MET			1805	
4774	PURCELL JAMES				1803		NANCY CAMPBELL		P		1794	662
4074	PURCELL WILLIAM				1782		MARGARET BARRON				1786 61	
4075	PURCELL JOHN				1828		JULIA				1832	
3974	PURDY CHARLES						HANNAH				1852	2948
4145	RACETTE AUGUST	MET	RC	NWT	1833	4146	MADELEINE PARENTEAU	MET	RC	RRS	1833	
4146	RACETTE AUGUSTIN	EUR	RC	CAN	1796		SUSANNE GOUIN	MET	RC	RRS	1826	
4150	RACETTE AUGUSTIN				1847		ARCHANGE GUIBOCHE				1850	
3999	RACETTE CHARLES	MET	RC	NWT	1807		ANGELIQUE LAVALLEE	IND	RC		1811 61	
3999	RACETTE CHARLES	MET	RC	NWT	1807		JOSEPHTE SAULTEAUX	MET	RC	RRS	1832	1067
4025	RACETTE CHARLES	MET	RC	NWT	1833		HELENE BOYER	MET	RC	RRS	1847	
4148	RACETTE CHARLES	MET	RC	NWT	1850	4147	CATHERINE DEHOMME	IND	RC	NWT	1780	
4149	RACETTE CHARLES		RC	NWT	1766		JOSEPHTE	MET	RC	RRS	1820	2669
4013	RACETTE GEORGE	MET	RC	RRS	1819	4147	MARIE LAROCQUE	MET	RC	RRS	1830	
4147	RACETTE GEORGE	MET	RC	NWT	1800	4149	ANGELIQUE MOREAU	MET	RC		1802 62	
4147	RACETTE GEORGE	MET	RC	NWT	1800		FRANCOISE GUILBEAULT		RC		1845	
4008	RACETTE GILBERT		RC	RRS	1843		ROSALIE LHEUREUX	MET	RC	RRS	1834	
4003	RACETTE JEAN BTE	MET	RC	NWT	1832		EUPHROSINE	MET	RC	RRS	1842	
4012	RACETTE JOSEPH	MET	RC	RRS	1830		SARAH FISHER	MET	RC	RRS	1835	
3993	RACETTE WILLIAM		RC	RRS	1843 67		MARGUERITE PARENTEAU				1847	3811
4151	RAINE MICHEL		P	OTH	1784 29		NANCY BUDD		P		1790	
4158	RAINVILLE FRANCOIS	MET	RC	RRS	1837	14013	MARIE GOSSELIN	MET	RC		1837	
4159	RAINVILLE FRANCOIS		RC	NWT	1807		MARGUERITE DEMERS	MET	RC		1807	
4159	RAINVILLE FRANCOIS		RC	NWT	1807		MARGUERITE BELGARDE	MET	P		1811 40	
3991	RAMSAY ROBERT	EUR	P	SCT	1800		AGNES TRODDEN	EUR		SCT	1816	
4071	RAMSAY ROBERT				1853		SARA PERREAULT				1856	
3990	RAT LOUISON	IND	P	RRS	1835		HARRIET TAKKOKWEYAN	IND	P	RRS	1838	
4067	RAT NORBERT	IND	RC	RRS	1839		ROSALIE	MET	RC	RRS	1840	
4068	RAT PIERRE	IND	RC	RRS	1837		GENEVIEVE RICHARD	MET	RC	RRS	1842	
4070	REID MURDOCK	EUR	P	SCT	1845		ISABELLE BIRD	MET	P	RRS	1850	
8053	REPENTIGNY GILBERT				1845		MARGUERITE SUTHERLAND				1847 65	
4160	RICHARD ANTOINE	MET	RC	RRS	1818	4170	JOSEPHTE LAPOINTE	MET	RC	RRS	1830	2628
4163	RICHARD FRANCOIS	EUR	RC		1770		MARGUERITE	IND	RC		1788	
4165	RICHARD FRANCOIS	MET			1836		MARGUERITE LEDOUX	MET			1836	
4166	RICHARD FRANCOIS	MET	RC	RRS	1843	4167	ANNIE BRACONNIER	MET	RC	RRS	1844	
4167	RICHARD FRANCOIS	MET	RC		1810	4163	MARGUERITE SAULTEAUX	IND	RC		1820	490
4168	RICHARD JAMES	EUR	P	ENG	1845	4175	MARY IRVINE	EUR	P	ENG	1849	
4172	RICHARD JAMES	EUR	P	ENG	1813		HANNAH WILLSTEDD	MET	P	RRS	1809	
4175	RICHARD JAMES			NWT	1821 70		ELIZABETH TRUTHWAITE	MET			1825	
4162	RICHARD JEAN BTE		P	NWT	1797		MARGARET	IND			1800	
4173	RICHARD JOSEPH				1808		SOPHIE OKAPEKAMOK	MET	RC		1812	
4171	RICHARD LOUIS	MET	RC	RRS	1835	4170	LUCIE LAROCQUE	MET		RRS	1843	2788
4161	RICHARD MICHEL	MET			1849	4160	ISABELLE BRUYERE	MET	RC		1851	587
4170	RICHARD MICHEL		RC	NWT	1790		COLLIN		RC		1789 64	

TABLE 1: GENEALOGIES OF RED RIVER HOUSEHOLDS, 1818-1870

ID	MALE HEAD OF FAMILY	RACE	FAITH	BIRTH PLACE	DATES	DADS ID	FEMALE HEAD OF FAMILY	RACE	FAITH	BIRTH PLACE	DATES	DADS ID
4164	RICHARD PIERRE	MET		RRS	1817	4163	CHARTRAND ISABELLE	MET		NWT	1826	
4169	RICHARD THOMAS	MET	P		1793		FIDLER MARGARET	MET	P	NWT	1795 60	
4174	RICHARD WILLIAM		P	NWT	1826	4162	FARQUARHSON JANE	MET	RC	RRS	1842	1549
4088	RICHARDSON ALFRED	EUR			1843		ADSHEAD ELISA	EUR	RC	ENG	1845 67	
4077	RIDSDALE	EUR			1810		CHALIFOUX MARY	EUR			1813	
4079	RIEL FRANCOIS	MET	RC	NWT	1833		BOUCHER MARIE		RC		1836	736
4080	RIEL JEAN BTE	EUR	RC	NWT	1809		LAGEMONIER MARGUERITE	EUR	RC	LC	1812	
4155	RIEL LOUIS	MET	RC	NWT	1816 64	4080	FAILLANT JULIE	MET	RC	RRS	1822	2537
2630	RIEL PIERRE	MET	RC	RRS	1828	2572	LADOUCEUR GENEVIEVE	MET	RC	RRS	1834	
4185	RITCHOT ANDRE		RC	RRS	1828		ST LUC MARGUERITE	MET	RC		1839	2486
4177	RITCHOT ANTOINE	MET	RC	RRS	1822		LAURENCE CATHERINE	MET	RC	RRS	1825	
4178	RITCHOT BASILE	MET	RC	RRS	1834	4184	HENEAULT CATHERINE	MET	RC	RRS	1847	
4180	RITCHOT JEAN BTE	MET	RC	NWT	1848		CHATELAIN ELISE	MET	RC	RRS	1851	789
4189	RITCHOT JEAN BTE		RC	NWT	1823		AMIOTTE MARIE ANNE	MET	RC		1831	
4184	RITCHOT JOSEPH A	MET	RC	CAN	1785		NAULT JOSEPHE	MET	RC	RRS	1797 67	
4179	RITCHOT LOUIS	MET	RC	RRS	1851	4189	MARTELLE ISABEL	MET	RC		1853	
4187	RITCHOT MICHEL		RC	NWT	1815		SUTHERLAND SUZANNE	MET	RC		1818	3703
4188	RITCHOT PIERRE	MET	RC		1843	4187	VANDRY LOUISE	MET	RC		1838	4557
4190	RITCHOT PIERRE		RC		1837		BELANGER ROSALIE	MET	RC		1839	5078
4192	RIVARD BAPTISTE	MET			1772		OUELLETTE THERESE	MET	RC		1778	
4193	RIVARD BAPTISTE		RC	NWT	1817	4192	MARIE				1827 67	
4194	RIVARD PIERRE	MET			1798		ROCHELEAU THERISE	MET	RC		1800	
4195	RIVARD PIERRE	MET	RC	RRS	1820	4194	BOUVET MARIE	MET	RC	RRS	1822	3765
4082	RIVET JOHN	EUR	RC	OTH	1835		MORPES MARY	MET	RC		1837	
4081	ROBERTS JOHN	MET	RC	NWT	1835		ATKINSON NANCY	MET		ENG	1845	
4198	ROBERTSON ANDREW	EUR	P	NWT	1809 36		VICTORIA NANCY	EUR	RC	NWT	1840	
4086	ROBERTSON GEORGE	EUR	P	SCT	1771 55						1809 38	
4202	ROBERTSON GEORGE	EUR	P	SCT	1771 55		JOHNSTON JANE	IND	P	NWT	1815	
4089	ROBERTSON JAMES	MET		USA	1815		MCKAY LOUISA		P		1816	
4087	ROBERTSON WILLIAM	MET		USA	1835		LILLIE FRANCES				1837	
4084	ROBILLARD ANDREW	MET	RC	CAN	1827	4209	MARGUERITE	MET	RC		1841 62	
4084	ROBILLARD ANDREW	MET	RC	CAN	1827		HAGUE MARGUERITE	IND	RC	RRS	1838	
4206	ROBILLARD JEAN BTE			CAN	1824	4209	DUCHARME CATHERINE	MET	RC		1828	
4209	ROBILLARD JEAN BTE	EUR	P	CAN	1781		ANTOINETTE	IND	RC		1785	1347
4211	ROBILLARD PETER	MET	P	CAN	1796	4209	MARGARET	IND	P		1800	
4200	ROBINSON FRANCOIS	MET	RC	NWT	1806		MASKEGON SOPHIE	IND	RC		1821 46	
4200	ROBINSON FRANCOIS	MET	RC	NWT	1806		BRUYERE ANGELIQUE	MET	RC	NWT	1801	586
4203	ROBINSON JAMES		P	NWT	1813 39		ATKINSON MARGUERITE			RRS	1814	
4090	ROBINSON JOHN				1844	4200	LOGAN MARY	IND	RC	NWT	1848	
4207	ROBINSON ROBERT	IND	P	RRS	1835		AWASSI	IND	P	RRS	1848	
4085	ROBINSON THOMAS	IND	P	RRS	1845		ISABEL	MET	RC	RRS	1852	
4201	ROBINSON XAVIER	MET	RC	RRS	1842		MORIN MARGUERITE	IND	RC		1844	
4093	ROCHEBLAVE ANTOINE				1840		PELLETIER NANCY				1805	
4091	ROCHEBLAVE FRANCOIS				1802 59		DESJARLAIS JUDITH	MET		RRS	1837	
4094	ROCHEBLAVE FRANCOIS				1834 59	4091	PICHE MADELEINE			RRS	1835	3198
4092	ROCHEBLAVE THOMAS	MET	RC		1833 53	4091	DESMARAIS JOSEPHE				1848	
4213	ROCHELEAU GUILLAUME	MET	RC	RRS	1837	4215	GAUDRY PAULINE	MET	RC	RRS	1792	
4215	ROCHELEAU GUILLAUME	MET	RC	CAN	1790 70		ADAM MARIE	MET	RC		1833	
4214	ROCHELEAU JEAN	MET	RC	RRS	1824	4215	CARRIERE MARIE	MET	RC	RRS	1824	712

TABLE 1: GENEALOGIES OF RED RIVER HOUSEHOLDS, 1818-1870

ID	MALE HEAD OF FAMILY		RACE	FAITH	BIRTH PLACE	DATES	DADS ID	FEMALE HEAD OF FAMILY		RACE	FAITH	BIRTH PLACE	DATES	DADS ID
4100	ROCHWAY	JOSEPH	.	.	.	1825	.	STANLEY	BETSY	.	P	.	1827	.
4225	RODWAY	JOSEPH	.	P	.	1808 69	.	STANLEY	ELIZABETH	EUR	O	.	1829	.
4223	ROSE	ALEXANDER	EUR	O	SCT	1779	.	MONTZINI	JANE	.	.	.	1785	.
4096	ROSE	FRANCOIS	MET	P	.	1840	4223	STEVENS	CAROLINE	MET	P	NWT	1844	.
4224	ROSE	WILLIAM	EUR	P	NWT	1820	.	SINCLAIR	NANCY	MET	P	RRS	1825	.
4228	ROSS	ALEXANDER	MET	P	SCT	1785 56	.	.	SARAH	IND	P	.	1790	.
4231	ROSS	ALEXANDER	.	.	.	1842	4228	MURRAY	CATHERINE	MET	RC	RRS	1848	3255
4248	ROSS	BERNARD	.	.	.	1837	.	ROSS	CHRISTINA	EUR	P	NWT	1840	4232
4245	ROSS	CHARLES	MET	RC	.	1836 46	4246	ALLARD	MARGUERITE	MET	RC	.	1846	48
4232	ROSS	DONALD	.	.	.	1804	.	MCBEATH	MARY	EUR	RC	.	1803	.
4236	ROSS	DONALD	MET	RC	RRS	1822	.	DELORME	CATHERINE	IND	.	.	1825	.
4237	ROSS	GEORGE	EUR	P	.	1835	4246	PEEBLES	CHARLOTTE	MET	.	RRS	1842	3876
4249	ROSS	GEORGE	EUR	P	ORK	1797	4239	BRELAND	CATHERINE	MET	.	SCT	1813	.
4246	ROSS	HUGH	MET	RC	SCT	1793 63	.	SHORT	SARAH	MET	RC	.	1795	4368
4241	ROSS	JAMES	MET	P	RRS	1836 71	4228	SMITH	MARGARET	EUR	RC	.	1835	.
4226	ROSS	JOHN	MET	RC	.	1832	4246	GRANT	MARGUERITE	MET	RC	.	1836	.
4101	ROSS	JOHN	MET	.	.	1838	4239	PEEBLES	MARGARET	MET	.	.	1844	3876
4238	ROSS	RODERICK	MET	RC	RRS	1839	4246	HARRIOT	VICTORIA	MET	.	RRS	1843	.
4243	ROSS	RODERICK	MET	RC	RRS	1829	4246	DELORME	MARIE	MET	RC	RRS	1833 70	1942
4242	ROSS	WILLIAM	MET	RC	RRS	1840	4232	GERVAIS	ISABELLE	MET	RC	LC	1841	2897
4247	ROSS	WILLIAM	.	P	NWT	1849	4228	LEFORT	MARY	MET	P	.	1852	3644
13280	ROSS	WILLIAM	MET	.	.	1825 56	.	MCKENZIE	JEMINA	MET	.	.	1825	687
4235	ROUSSEAU	EUSTACHE	.	.	.	1823	.	CARRON	MARGUERITE	IND	.	.	1832	.
4252	ROUSSIN	BAPTISTE	.	.	.	1772	.	.	JOSEPHTE	MET	.	.	1775	.
4254	ROUSSIN	CHARLE	.	.	.	1809	.	.	THERESE	MET	.	.	1812 34	.
4253	ROUSSIN	CHARLE	MET	RC	NWT	1833	.	DUCHARME	BETSY	MET	.	.	1820	972
4256	ROWAND	FRANCOIS	MET	RC	.	1812 65	4257	HOULE	ELISE	MET	RC	NWT	1838	.
4257	ROWAND	JOHN	EUR	.	NWT	1802 54	.	COURCHENE	MARGUERITE	MET	.	.	1815	.
4251	ROWAND	WILLIAM	MET	P	.	1847	.	HARRIOT	LOUISA	MET	.	.	1806	.
4258	ROWLAND	GEORGE	MET	.	.	1827	.	.	MARY	MET	.	NWT	1846	.
4730	ROWLAND	JOHN	.	.	.	1830	.	ROSS	NANCY	MET	.	.	1828	.
4259	ROWLAND	ROBERT	.	P	ORK	1784	.	BIRSTON	ISABELLA	MET	.	.	1833	.
4260	ROWLAND	WILLIAM	.	RC	NWT	1827	.	FRASER	ELIZABETH	MET	P	.	1799 31	.
4255	ROY	AUGUSTIN	MET	RC	RRS	1845	.	FLETT	SUSANNE	MET	RC	RRS	1846	.
4240	ROY	FRANCOIS	.	P	.	1840	4267	.	PAULINE	IND	.	.	1843	.
4244	ROY	FRANCOIS	MET	RC	RRS	1820	.	NORMAND	MARIE YVONNE	IND	P	RRS	1830	.
4265	ROY	FRANCOIS	MET	P	RRS	1810	.	SAULTEAUX	MARGUERITE	IND	RC	RRS	1815	2532
4267	ROY	FRANCOIS	.	P	.	1789	.	PAKON	ISABELLE	MET	.	.	1792	.
4263	ROY	JEAN	MET	RC	RRS	1841	4265	LAFRENIERE	LISETTE	MET	RC	RRS	1843	3173
4266	ROY	JEAN BTE	.	.	.	1783	.	COLLIN	CATHERINE	IND	RC	.	1788	.
4262	ROY	JOSEPH	EUR	RC	LC	1818	4265	MORIN	HENRIETTE	EUR	P	.	1835	724
4264	ROY	MARCEL	MET	RC	RRS	1838	.	CAYEN	URSULE	MET	RC	NWT	1845	.
4345	SABINE	HERBERT	EUR	P	ENG	1830	.	VENNE	MARGARET	EUR	P	RRS	1831	.
4341	SABISTON	ALEXANDER	.	P	.	1828	.	CAMERON	SARAH	MET	.	RRS	1832	.
4342	SABISTON	ALEXANDER	.	P	NWT	1804 46	.	FLETT	NANCY	MET	P	.	1820	.
4353	SABISTON	ALEXANDRE	.	P	.	1820	.	CAMPBELL	NANCY	EUR	.	RRS	1825	.
4344	SABISTON	JOHN	.	.	.	1846	.	FOLSTER	MARGARET	MET	.	.	1851	.
4338	SALTER	RICHARD	EUR	P	ENG	1818	.	SMITH	MARIE ANNE	MET	P	NWT	1823	1494
4234	SALTER	WILLIAM	.	P	.	1840	.	COMTOIS	SOPHIE	MET	.	.	1843	4417

TABLE 1: GENEALOGIES OF RED RIVER HOUSEHOLDS, 1818-1870

ID	MALE HEAD OF FAMILY	RACE	FAITH	BIRTH PLACE	DATES	DADS ID	FEMALE HEAD OF FAMILY	RACE	FAITH	BIRTH PLACE	DATES	DADS ID
4268	SANDERSON ALEXANDER	MET	P	RRS	1838		HENDERSON MARIE	MET	P	RRS	1838	
4337	SANDERSON ALEXANDRE				1820		KENNEDY NANCY	MET			1824	
4306	SANDERSON DAVID	MET	P	RRS	1834	4735	ARCUS JANE	MET			1843	
4328	SANDERSON DAVID		P	NWT	1824		MARY		P		1830	
4734	SANDERSON DAVID	MET			1806 37		GUIBOCHE LOUISA	MET	P		1808	
4330	SANDERSON GEORGE	MET	P		1790		LAGEMONIER LISETTE	MET	P	RRS	1803	
4335	SANDERSON GEORGE	IND	P	RRS	1843		ADAM ELIZABETH	IND	P	RRS	1850	
4733	SANDERSON GEORGE	MET		RRS	1800		NANCY	MET	P		1810	
4323	SANDERSON JAMES	EUR			1816	4324	ANDERSON ELIZABETH	IND	P		1820	
4324	SANDERSON JAMES	MET	P		1750	4324	ELIZABETH	IND	P		1755	
4327	SANDERSON JAMES	MET	P		1784 73	4324	SALLY				1787 27	
4327	SANDERSON JAMES	MET	P		1784 73	4324	MARGARET LOUIS		P		1806 31	
4327	SANDERSON JAMES	MET	P		1784 73		NANCY ANN WHITFORD		P		1801 42	
4327	SANDERSON JAMES	MET	P		1784 73		MARY FAVEL	MET	P	NWT	1823	
4320	SANDERSON JOHN	MET		RRS	1840		FANNY SINCLAIR	MET	P	RRS	1838	
4326	SANDERSON JOHN	MET		RRS	1843	4323	ANNE ELIZA SMITH	MET	P	RRS	1846	
4736	SANDERSON JOHN	IND			1810		HARRIET SMITH	MET		RRS	1814	
4325	SANDERSON RICHARD	MET	P	RRS	1835	4330	NANCY COOPER	MET			1840	
4230	SANDERSON ROBERT	MET	P		1828		JANE MCNAB	MET			1826	
4322	SANDERSON ROBERT			NWT	1796 68		MARY LINNECAFSO	MET			1800	
4331	SANDERSON ROBERT	MET	P		1812		MARY BEAR	IND			1815	
4321	SANDERSON RODERICK	MET	P	RRS	1826		MARY SMITH	MET	P	RRS	1835	
4229	SANDERSON WILLIAM	MET	P		1830		MARY MCNAB	MET	P		1831	
4319	SANDERSON WILLIAM			NWT	1803		MARY ALDER	MET	P		1810	
4735	SANDERSON WILLIAM	MET	RC	RRS	1804 34		MARGARET COOK	MET		NWT	1808 27	
4735	SANDERSON WILLIAM	MET	RC	RRS	1804 34		JANE BADGER	MET			1809 31	
4738	SANSON GEORGE			RRS	1815		SARAH GILL	MET			1841	
4738	SANSON GEORGE	MET		RRS	1815		JANE HENDERSON	MET	P	RRS	1825	2445
4316	SANSREGRET BAPTISTE		RC		1800		LISETTE	IND			1804 24	
4316	SANSREGRET BAPTISTE	MET	RC	RRS	1800		MARGUERITE LAFOURNAISE	MET	P		1805	
4318	SANSREGRET JEAN	MET	RC	RRS	1824	4316	MARIE GERVAIS	MET	RC	RRS	1830	1950
4317	SANSREGRET LOUIS	MET		RRS	1825	4316	GENEVIEVE CARRIERE	MET	RC	RRS	1826	
4739	SANSREGRET REINE	EUR			1832		CAROLINE PARENTEAU	MET	RC	RRS	1835	
4311	SARGENT ALBERT	MET	P	NWT	1826		CAROLINE PRUDEN	MET			1830	
4314	SAUCIER JEAN BTE	EUR			1844		JUSTINE MCKAY	MET		RRS	1847	
4304	SAUNDERS DAVID		P	NWT	1818		JANE			RRS	1822	
4303	SAUNDERS GEORGE	EUR			1779 53		MARY	MET		RRS	1785	
4299	SAUNDERS JACK		P		1807		SOPHIE	MET			1810	
4301	SAUNDERS JOHN	MET		NWT	1797		ISABEL	IND			1790	
4308	SAUNDERS JOHN	EUR			1803		SOPHIE	IND	P		1805	
4741	SAUNDERS PALM				1801 31		HARRIET FAVEL				1809	
4740	SAUNDERS ROBERT				1819 64		JANE MOWAT				1822	
4298	SAUNDERS WILLIAM	MET	P	NWT	1832		MARY	MET			1834	3234
4305	SAUNDERS WILLIAM		P		1806		MARY ALDER	MET			1810	
4310	SAUNDERS WILLIAM		P		1799	4303	FLORA HOPE	IND	P	NWT	1820	
4343	SAUNDERS WILLIAM	MET		NWT	1819		CATHERINE LAFERTE	MET	P		1839	
4744	SAUVAGE FRANCOIS				1825		MADELEINE LAPOINTE	MET	P		1829	
4747	SAUVE FRANCOIS	MET		RRS	1840		ELIZA CAPLETTE	MET	P		1844	
4296	SAUVE JOSEPH		RC	NWT	1819	4295	SUSANNE DEASE	MET	RC	RRS	1824	2505
4757	SAUVE NORBERT		RC		1837		MARGUERITE	MET	RC	RRS	1843	2628

ID	MALE HEAD OF FAMILY		RACE	FAITH	BIRTH PLACE	DATES	DADS ID	FEMALE HEAD OF FAMILY		RACE	FAITH	BIRTH PLACE	DATES	DADS ID
4293	SAVERET	JOHN				1797		ROUSSIN	LOUISE	MET			1800	
4289	SAVOYARD	ALEXIS	MET	RC		1822		DUBOIS	MARGUERITE	MET	RC		1820	
4287	SAVOYARD	AUGUSTIN	MET	RC		1845	4285	BOUCHER	MARGUERITE				1846	
4290	SAVOYARD	FRANCOIS	MET	RC	RRS	1849	4291	RIVARD	MARIE	MET	RC	RRS	1848	
4291	SAVOYARD	FRANCOIS	MET	RC	USA	1808	4292	COMTOIS	MADELEINE	MET	RC	NWT	1822	930
4292	SAVOYARD	JOSEPH				1784			MARGUERITE		RC		1788	
4759	SAVOYARD	NORBERT				1819		DEMONTIGNY	S				1821	
4745	SAVOYARD	PIERRE	MET	RC	NWT	1840	4284	COULOMBRE	ROSALIE	MET			1843	966
4285	SAVOYARD	PIERRE	MET			1800	4285	DUBOIS	LOUISE	MET	RC		1805	1322
4286	SAVOYARD	CLEOPHILE		RC		1831	4274	BERARD	LOUISE	MET			1837	
4275	SAYER	EDOUARD				1849		CAPLETTE	MARIE				1850	
4763	SAYER	EDWARD	MET	RC		1824		DELORME	MADELEINE	MET	RC	RRS	1827	
4764	SAYER	FRANCOIS	MET			1827		FORBISHER	MARGUERITE	MET			1829	
4269	SAYER	FRANCOIS	MET	RC	RRS	1791	4269	VERSAILLES	MARGUERITE	IND	RC	RRS	1795	5104
1527	SAYER	GEORGE	MET	RC	NWT	1826		CAPLETTE	GENEVIEVE	MET	RC	NWT	1833	677
4270	SAYER	GEORGE	MET			1803		CAPLETTE	MARIE	MET		RRS	1805	
4278	SAYER	GUILLAUME	MET			1825	4277	CAPLETTE	CATHERINE	MET	RC	NWT	1827	
4282	SAYER	HENRY	MET	RC		1828	4274	PANGMAN	CATHERINE	MET	RC		1831	
4276	SAYER	JEAN BTE	MET	RC	RRS	1841	4274	BREMNER	MARY	MET		RRS	1838	
4761	SAYER	JOHN	MET		NWT	1800			MARGUERITE	IND		NWT	1790	
4277	SAYER	JOHN	MET	RC		1805			MARIE	IND			1808	
4280	SAYER	JOHN	MET			1847	4278	CAMPBELL	EMMA	MET	RC	RRS	1848	660
4280	SAYER	JOHN	MET			1847	4278	FIDLER	MARIE	MET			1835	1541
4760	SAYER	JOSEPH	MET		NWT	1840	4274	CHARTRAND	SUSANNE	MET		NWT	1848	
4273	SAYER	LOUIS	MET			1843	4274	DESJARLAIS	EUPHRASINE	MET			1833	1276
4272	SAYER	WILLIAM	MET		NWT	1826		FLEURY	SUZANNE	MET		RRS	1795	1612
4274	SCHEIDEGAN	SAMUEL	EUR	RC	NWT	1796		FORBISHER	JOSEPHTE	IND	RC		1802	
4349	SCHMIDT	ALFRED		P	OTH	1769	4753	LESPERANCE	NELLY	MET	RC	RRS	1826	
4347	SCHMIDT	ALFRED	MET	RC	NWT	1825		VIVIER	MARGUERITE		RC		1844	
4347	SCHMIDT	BERNARD		RC	NWT	1825	4753	ABERLAE	EMILIE		RC		1804	2930
4297	SCHMIDT	MATTHEW				1800		SCHEIDECHER	SUSANNAH				1804	
4753	SCHULTZ	JOHN	EUR		UC	1839		FARQUARHSON	MARIANNE				1846	
4755	SCHULTZ	WILLIAM	EUR		RRS	1815		SETTER	AGNUS	EUR	P	SCT	1824	
4352	SCOTT	PAUL	MET		SCT	1829		THORNE	ANN	MET	P	NWT	1829	
4748	SEINEZ	ANDREW	EUR		ENG	1807		SCARTH	CECILE	EUR	P	ENG	1811	
4751	SELLWOOD	JOHN			ORK	1781		SPENCE	DELILAH	MET	P		1790	
2918	SETTER	GEORGE	IND	P	NWT	1808 43		KENNEDY	MARGARET	MET	P	NWT	1810	
4358	SETTER	GEORGE	EUR	P	ORK	1800	4358	CAMPBELL	MARGARET	MET	P		1832	940
4359	SETTER	GEORGE	MET	P	NWT	1815			ISABEL	MET		NWT	1820 46	
4362	SETTER	GEORGE	EUR	P	SCT	1789 68		COOK	JESSIE	MET	P	NWT	1815	
4836	SETTER	JAMES	MET		RRS	1816	4836	TODD	MARGARET	MET	P	RRS	1820	
2917	SETTER	JAMES	MET	P	RRS	1837		MORWICK	SARA	MET	P	RRS	1843	
2919	SETTER	JAMES		P	NWT	1816		COOK	LIZIE	MET	P	NWT	1817	3226
2936	SETTER	JAMES	MET	P		1837		GOWLAR	JANE	MET	P	RRS	1820	
4838	SETTER	JOHN	MET	P		1816		COOK	SARAH	MET	P	RRS	1839	
4360	SETTER	JOHN	MET	P		1837		MCKENZIE	ELIZA	MET	P	NWT	1835 13	940
4839	SETTER	JOHN	MET	P		1823		MOORE	ANN	MET	P	RRS	1846	
4872	SETTER	JOHN JAMES	MET	P	RRS	1845		MATHESON	LOUISE	EUR	P	RRS	1828	3421
4361	SETTER	WILLIAM	MET	P	RRS	1833		MOORE	ANN	MET	P	RRS	1828	
4797	SHANNON	WILLIAM	EUR	P	IRE	1837		HOURIE	CATHERINE	MET		RRS	1845	

TABLE 1: GENEALOGIES OF RED RIVER HOUSEHOLDS, 1818-1870

ID	MALE HEAD OF FAMILY	RACE	FAITH	BIRTH PLACE	DATES	DADS ID	FEMALE HEAD OF FAMILY	RACE	FAITH	BIRTH PLACE	DATES	DADS ID
4802	SHARON JOHN	EUR	RC	USA	1846	.	BRACONNIER PHILOMME	MET	RC	RRS	1853	.
4798	SHARP EDWARD	EUR	.	.	1801	.	SHARP SARAH	EUR	RC	RRS	1811	.
4799	SHARP WILLIAM	EUR	.	.	1845	4798	BIRD SARAH	MET	RC	RRS	1841	.
4801	SHERIDDON JOHN	.	.	.	1806	.	LEWIS MARY	.	.	.	1810	.
4367	SHORT JAMES	MET	RC	NWT	1809 70	.	SAULTEAUX ANGELIQUE	IND	RC	NWT	1830 47	.
4367	SHORT JAMES	MET	RC	NWT	1809 70	.	GLADU CHARLOTTE	MET	RC	.	1805 63	.
4368	SHORT JAMES	EUR	P	ORK	1767	4367	SAULTEAUX BETHSY	.	P	.	1783	1252
4370	SHORT JAMES	MET	.	.	1834	.	MCGILLIS MATHILDE	MET	.	.	1847	.
4805	SHORT JAMES	MET	RC	.	1820	.	GLADU MARIE	MET	.	RRS	1824	.
4369	SHORT JOSEPH	MET	RC	RRS	1845 48	4805	HOULE MARGUERITE	MET	RC	RRS	1831	.
4806	SHORT WILLIAM	EUR	P	RRS	1830	.	DESCHAMPS MARIE	MET	RC	RRS	1844	.
4375	SIMON GEORGE	.	.	OTH	1796	.	BUNSLEY CATHERINE	MET	P	.	1800	.
3492	SIMPSON DAVID	.	.	.	1840	.	FAVEL MARGARET	.	.	.	1848	.
4374	SIMPSON GEORGE	.	.	.	1809	.	HOGUE MARGARET	.	.	.	1811	.
4373	SIMPSON JOHN	MET	P	NWT	1827	.	FIDLER EMILIA	MET	RC	RRS	1840	.
4800	SIMPSON THOMAS	.	.	.	1809 41	4374	SUTHERLAND JANE	.	.	.	1817	.
4773	SINCLAIR BAKIE	EUR	P	SCT	1850	.	JANE	MET	.	.	1853 55	.
4378	SINCLAIR CHARLES	MET	P	RRS	1842	.	SWAIN ELIZABETH	MET	P	RRS	1805	.
4762	SINCLAIR DAVID	IND	P	.	1846	.	THOMAS VICTORIA	MET	P	.	1844	.
4781	SINCLAIR DONALD	EUR	P	SCT	1796	.	PARISIEN NANCY	MET	P	.	1846	.
4379	SINCLAIR FRANCOIS	IND	P	.	1839	.	GIBBS ANNE	.	.	.	1804	.
4768	SINCLAIR FRANCOIS	IND	P	NWT	1839	.	STEVENSON ANNABELLA	IND	P	.	1845	.
4768	SINCLAIR FRANCOIS	IND	.	NWT	1820	.	HARRIET	IND	P	NWT	1832	.
4782	SINCLAIR GEORGE	.	.	.	1820	.	MARIA	MET	.	.	1830	2582
4380	SINCLAIR GEORGE	MET	P	RRS	1831	.	JOHNSTON NANCY	.	P	RRS	1822	.
4386	SINCLAIR JACOB	.	P	RRS	1834	4388	LAMBERT MARIA	IND	P	RRS	1833	.
4769	SINCLAIR JAMES	IND	P	RRS	1830	.	HECKENBERGER MARGARET	.	.	.	1836	.
4783	SINCLAIR JAMES	IND	P	NWT	1810	.	JOHNSTON ISABELLA	IND	P	RRS	1845	.
4381	SINCLAIR JAMES	.	.	.	1845	.	BIRD ELIZABETH	.	.	.	1811	.
4770	SINCLAIR JAMES	.	.	.	1828	.	TROTTIER CATHERINE	.	.	.	1848	.
4771	SINCLAIR JAMES	.	.	.	1828	.	WHITFORD JANE	MET	.	.	1830	.
4772	SINCLAIR JAMES	MET	.	RRS	1848	.	CAMPBELL MARY	MET	.	.	1830	.
4784	SINCLAIR JAMES	MET	.	RRS	1825	4378	WALLER MARIA	IND	RC	RRS	1853	.
4785	SINCLAIR JOHN	MET	RC	RRS	1835	.	SAUVE MARGARET	MET	P	RRS	1831	.
4786	SINCLAIR JOHN	IND	P	RRS	1834	.	DANIEL JANE	IND	P	RRS	1837	.
4787	SINCLAIR JOHN	MET	P	RRS	1825	.	ATKINSON CATHERINE	MET	P	RRS	1835	.
4788	SINCLAIR JOHN	MET	RC	NWT	1820	.	MARY	MET	P	RRS	1830	1898
4789	SINCLAIR JOHN	.	.	.	1815	.	GARIEPY MARIE	IND	RC	RRS	1825	.
4843	SINCLAIR PETER	MET	.	.	1790	.	MARIA	MET	.	.	1820	.
4382	SINCLAIR ROBERT	.	.	.	1850	.	ROUSSIN MARGUERITE	IND	.	.	1795	4252
4775	SINCLAIR SAMUEL	IND	.	.	1825 55	.	JEANIE	.	.	.	1853	.
4776	SINCLAIR SAMUEL	.	.	.	1835	.	ELIZABETH	.	.	.	1828	.
4777	SINCLAIR SAMUEL	.	.	.	1846	.	HARRIET	.	.	.	1837	.
4778	SINCLAIR THOMAS	.	.	.	1842	.	LAMBERT KITTY	.	.	.	1848	.
4371	SINCLAIR THOMAS	.	P	NWT	1812 70	.	SUSETTE	.	.	.	1844	.
4384	SINCLAIR THOMAS	.	P	.	1828	.	CUMMINGS HANNAH	MET	P	RRS	1812 46	.
4389	SINCLAIR THOMAS	.	P	.	1835	.	PRUDEN CAROLINE	MET	P	.	1829	.
4793	SINCLAIR WILLIAM	MET	.	.	1836	.	MCDONALD MARY	MET	.	RRS	1844	.
4804	SINCLAIR WILLIAM	MET	.	.	1836	.	ELIZABETH	MET	.	RRS	1838	.

ID	MALE HEAD OF FAMILY	RACE	FAITH	BIRTH PLACE	DATES	DADS ID	FEMALE HEAD OF FAMILY	RACE	FAITH	BIRTH PLACE	DATES	DADS ID
4383	SINCLAIR WILLIAM	MET	P	RRS	1832	4384	MCDONALD JANE	MET	P	RRS	1839	
4385	SINCLAIR WILLIAM	EUR	O	SCT	1784		MARGARET	MET	O		1786	
4388	SINCLAIR WILLIAM				1788		ANDERSON ELIZABETH	MET		NWT	1802	77
4766	SINCLAIR WILLIAM	MET	P	RRS	1839		DENNET MARIA	MET	RC	RRS	1845	
4815	SINCLAIR WILLIAM				1785		CHARLOTTE	IND	P	RRS	1790	
4816	SINCLAIR WILLIAM				1837		HAMELIN ELIZA		P	NWT	1839	
4818	SINCLAIR WILLIAM				1830		KENNEDY JANE				1837	
4391	SLATER JAMES	EUR	P	ORK	1777 56		GARIEPY MARIE				1833	1549
4393	SLATER JAMES	MET	P	RRS	1824	4391	FIDLER MATILDA	MET	P	RRS	1836	
4796	SLATER JOHN	MET	RC	SCT	1810		ROSE MARY	MET	P	RRS	1780 60	4224
4394	SLATER THOMAS	EUR	P	RRS	1800		MORRISETTE HARRIET	MET	RC	NWT	1848	1226
4364	SLATER THOMAS	MET	P		1829		DENNET JOSEPHTE	MET	P	RRS	1811	
4795	SLATER WILLIAM	MET		RRS	1843	4394	BRUCE ELIZABETH	MET		RRS	1812	
4392	SLATER WILLIAM	MET	P	NWT	1834	4391	COOK FRANCES	MET	P	RRS	1839	
4395	SLATER WILLIAM	MET			1820		ROWLAND MARIA	MET		NWT	1847	
4397	SMALL PATRICK		RC	NWT	1800		HUGHES CATHERINE		RC		1844	
4406	SMITH ALEXANDER	IND	P		1789 60		SANDERSON NANCY	IND		RRS	1825	
4809	SMITH ANDRE				1830		COLUMBIA NANCY	MET	P	RRS	1803	
4810	SMITH ANDREW		P		1837 68		JOHNSTON JEMINA	MET	P	RRS	1808	2442
4811	SMITH ANGUS	EUR		SCT	1836	4417	INKSTER JEMIMA	MET	P	RRS	1832	
4102	SMITH CHARLES				1830		STEVENSON MARY				1840	
4812	SMITH EDWARD	MET	P	RRS	1846		SABISTON SARAH	MET	P	RRS	1836	
4415	SMITH EUGENE				1832		FINLAYSON ANNE	MET	P	RRS	1834	1562
4103	SMITH FLEURY				1825	4417	DESJARLAIS NANCY				1847	
4813	SMITH GILBERT	MET	P	RRS	1835		MCLEOD MARIE	MET	P	RRS	1833	
4127	SMITH HENRIE				1824		WELLS SARA	MET		RRS	1840	3439
4128	SMITH HENRIE				1831		STEVENS MARGUERITE	MET			1825	5153
4412	SMITH JACKSON	MET	P	NWT	1827	4413	COOK MARIE	MET		RRS	1832	
4408	SMITH JACOB	IND	P	RRS	1800		MCNAB ELIZABETH		P		1839	
3495	SMITH JAMES	MET			1840		JANE	MET			1800	
4401	SMITH JAMES	IND	P		1841	4409	NANCY				1844	
4416	SMITH JAMES	MET		RRS	1825	4408	NANCY	IND		RRS	1845	
3493	SMITH JEAN BTE	MET	P	RRS	1830	4411	SMITH HARRIET	MET	P	RRS	1835	152
3496	SMITH JOHN	EUR	RC	IRE	1816		THOMAS MARIE ANNE	EUR	RC	ENG	1833	
4130	SMITH JOHN		RC		1833		AZURE HANNAH		RC		1830	
4130	SMITH JOHN				1831		MASTERS MADELEINE	IND			1838	
4131	SMITH JOHN				1832		BUBUE ANN				1835	
4133	SMITH JOHN				1814		CATHERINE	IND			1832	
4134	SMITH JOHN		P	NWT	1848	4403	JANE				1834	
4399	SMITH JOHN	MET	P	RRS	1835		IRVINE HARRIET	IND	P	NWT	1816	
4400	SMITH JOHN	MET			1820		INKSTER MARGARET	MET		RRS	1851	
4403	SMITH JOHN	MET	P	RRS	1825	4417	MOORE JANE	MET	P	RRS	1836	2396
4808	SMITH JOHN	EUR	RC	ENG	1798 50		FOULDS ELIZABETH	MET	P	NWT	1824	
4409	SMITH JOHN JAMES	EUR	P	ENG	1798 50		MARGARET	IND	RC		1830	
4409	SMITH JOHN JAMES	EUR	P	ENG	1821 45		FAVEL MARY	MET	RC	RRS	1794 32	1626
4135	SMITH JOSEPH	IND			1759 70		NANCY	IND			1816	
4844	SMITH LESPERANCE	IND			1821		ANNE	IND		RRS	1825	
4411	SMITH LOUIS	MET	P	NWT	1810		PARENTEAU MARGUERITE	MET	P	RRS	1812	

TABLE 1: GENEALOGIES OF RED RIVER HOUSEHOLDS, 1818-1870

ID	MALE HEAD OF FAMILY		RACE	FAITH	BIRTH PLACE	DATES	DADS ID	FEMALE HEAD OF FAMILY	RACE	FAITH	BIRTH PLACE	DATES	DADS ID
4136	SMITH	PATRICK	IND	P		1850		IRVINE GRACE	MET	P		1852	
3498	SMITH	PETER	IND	P	RRS	1830		MCNAB MARY	MET	P	RRS	1840	
4413	SMITH	PETER	MET	P		1795 51		PEYSONETTE SUSAN	MET	P	NWT	1805	
3499	SMITH	RICHARD	MET	P	RRS	1818	4408	ROBINSON ANN	MET	P		1820	4901
4499	SMITH	RICHARD	MET	P	RRS	1818	4409	THOMAS CATHERINE	MET	P		1820 68	
3510	SMITH	ROBERT				1814		CHARLOTTE	IND			1816	
4137	SMITH	ROBERT	MET	P		1825 59	4409	MARY	MET	P		1834	
3501	SMITH	SAMUEL	MET	P		1849		BEAR MARY ANN	MET	P		1850	
3503	SMITH	THOMAS	MET	P		1843	4409	DESMARAIS MADELEINE	MET	P		1850	
3504	SMITH	THOMAS				1824		LIZOTTE ELIZABETH	MET	P		1825 54	
3505	SMITH	THOMAS	MET	P	NWT	1830		SANDERSON MARY	MET	P	NWT	1835	
4138	SMITH	THOMAS				1838	4413	BEAR HARRIET	MET	P		1840	
4418	SMITH	THOMAS				1778		SUSANNE	MET	P		1783	
4419	SMITH	THOMAS				1848		DUMONT MARGARET	EUR	P	RRS	1850	
3506	SMITH	WILLIAM	MET	P	RRS	1825		SMITH ANN	MET	P		1827	
3507	SMITH	WILLIAM	MET	P	RRS	1830		OMAND CHARLOTTE	MET	P	RRS	1830 65	
3507	SMITH	WILLIAM*				1830		MOWAT LOUISA	MET	P	RRS	1828	
4139	SMITH	WILLIAM	EUR	P	ENG	1827		THOMAS JANE	MET	P		1830	
4417	SMITH	WILLIAM	EUR	P	ENG	1795 69		ASHAM MARY ANNE	MET	P		1805 51	
13279	SMITH	WILLIAM	EUR	RC	OTH	1812 53		SWAIN PATIENCE	EUR	RC	OTH	1845	
3674	SOUNDERMAN	J G				1827		HOWELL BERTHA				1849	
4122	SPARROUR	CHARLES	IND			1839		HAMDORY CHARLOTTE	IND	P		1813	
4110	SPENCE	ANDREW	MET	P	RRS	1810		COOPER SARAH	MET	P	RRS	1838	
3675	SPENCE	ANDREW				1838		HARPER JANE				1843	
3689	SPENCE	ANDREW				1840		CHARLOTTE				1807	
3690	SPENCE	ANDREW				1800 51		SUSETTE				1850	
3691	SPENCE	ANDREW		P	NWT	1842		LEUNAY NANCY	MET	P		1804	
4424	SPENCE	ANDREW		P	NWT	1789 51		WHITFORD MARGARET	IND	P		1806	
4425	SPENCE	ANDREW	MET	P	RRS	1805		PEGGY	MET	P	RRS	1838	933
4426	SPENCE	ANDREW	MET	P	RRS	1837		COOK LETITIA	MET	P	RRS	1833	
4427	SPENCE	ARCHIBALD	EUR	P	ORK	1834	4431	INKSTER ELIZABETH	IND	P	NWT	1806 27	
13281	SPENCE	ARCHIBALD	EUR	P	SCT	1800	4431	PEGGY	MET	P	RRS	1824	2098
3491	SPENCE	DAVID	MET	P	NWT	1824		HALLET CATHERINE	MET	P		1827	
4428	SPENCE	DONALD	MET	P	RRS	1823	4439	ARCUS NANCY	MET	P	NWT	1800	
4431	SPENCE	DONALD	EUR	O	NWT	1815	4437	HALCROW CATHERINE	IND	O	NWT	1791	
4435	SPENCE	GEORGE	EUR	P	SCT	1790 45		WARD NANCY	MET	P		1843	
4819	SPENCE	GEORGE				1773		CATHERINE	IND			1836	
4820	SPENCE	GEORGE				1840		JANET				1824	
4433	SPENCE	GEORGE	MET	P	RRS	1834	4435	SARAH	MET	P	RRS	1830	
4433	SPENCE	JACOB	MET	P	RRS	1830	4435	STEVENS MARGUERITE	MET	P	RRS	1795	334
4437	SPENCE	JACOB	EUR	O	SCT	1781		BIRSTON SARAH	IND	O	NWT	1794	
4439	SPENCE	JAMES	EUR	O	NWT	1805	4441	MARY	MET	P	RRS	1829	
4440	SPENCE	JAMES	MET	P	NWT	1820		MORWICK JANE	IND	O	NWT	1800	
4441	SPENCE	JAMES	MET	P	NWT	1787		LEWIS MARGARET	MET	P	RRS	1813	
4443	SPENCE	JAMES				1810		MARGARET	IND			1823	
4446	SPENCE	JAMES	EUR	P	ORK	1814		MARY	EUR	P		1840	
4471	SPENCE	JAMES				1839		MCKAY MARY		P	RRS	1820	
4821	SPENCE	JAMES				1818		WHITFORD ANN					
	SPENCE	JAMES						SAUNDERS MARGARET					

ID	MALE HEAD OF FAMILY	RACE	FAITH	BIRTH PLACE	DATES	DADS ID	FEMALE HEAD OF FAMILY	RACE	FAITH	BIRTH PLACE	DATES	DADS ID
4824	SPENCE JAMES				1815		WHITEWAY NANCY				1820	
3677	SPENCE JEAN BTE	MET		NWT	1840	3678	CAMERON ELIZABETH				1843	
3678	SPENCE JEAN BTE	MET			1812		MATWEWENIN MARGARET	MET		RRS	1816	593
4467	SPENCE JEAN BTE				1825		MARIE	IND			1830	
4593	SPENCE JEAN BTE				1840		KIYIPAYASIK NANCY	IND			1846	66
4825	SPENCE JEAN BTE				1821		EMMA				1825	
4826	SPENCE JEAN BTE				1850		LOUISA				1852	
3680	SPENCE JOHN	MET			1825		WHITFORD CHARLOTTE	IND			1810	
4429	SPENCE JOHN	MET			1848	4430	MCNAB ELLEN	MET			1849	
4434	SPENCE JOHN	MET	P	NWT	1811	4435	COOK CHARLOTTE	IND	P	RRS	1822	
4447	SPENCE JOHN	IND			1809		NANCY	IND	P		1818	
4448	SPENCE JOHN		P	NWT	1812		FAVEL JANE		P		1814	
4450	SPENCE JOHN	EUR	P	NWT	1810		CATHERINE	IND	P		1815	
4451	SPENCE JOHN		P	NWT	1809		MCKENZIE ANNABELLA		P		1812	
4452	SPENCE JOHN	IND	P	RRS	1792	4435	TAIT JANE	IND	P	RRS	1795	
4454	SPENCE JOHN		P	NWT	1810		ASHAM ISABELLA	MET	P	RRS	1810	
4827	SPENCE JOHN				1818		CHARLOTTE				1820	
4829	SPENCE JOHN				1811		DENNET MARGARET				1814	
4830	SPENCE JOHN				1818	4454	MARY				1820	
3681	SPENCE JOSEPH	MET			1830		BUBBIE ELIZABETH	MET			1843	
4117	SPENCE JOSEPH	EUR	D	SCT	1789		MCKENZIE ANNABELLA	IND	O		1792	
4455	SPENCE JOSEPH			SCT	1773		SOPHIA	IND			1794	
4831	SPENCE JOSEPH				1839		JANET				1842	
4832	SPENCE JOSEPH				1803		HALLET SALLY				1806	
4833	SPENCE JOSEPH	IND	P	NWT	1831		JEFFERSON SARAH	IND	P	NWT	1833	
4834	SPENCE MAGNUS				1814		KIPPLING SALLY				1818	
4835	SPENCE MAGNUS				1829		FAVEL SARAH				1832	
4779	SPENCE MILES				1843		MARY				1842	
4104	SPENCE NICHOLAS				1829		LOUIS HARRIET		P		1832	
4105	SPENCE NICHOLAS		P		1838		MARGUERITE				1844	961
4106	SPENCE NICHOLAS				1839		CORRIGAL MARY		P		1841	
4459	SPENCE NICHOLAS	MET	P	RRS	1824	4424	SOPHIA	MET	P	NWT	1830	
3683	SPENCE PETER				1815		PEEBLES THERESA				1817	
4436	SPENCE PETER	MET	P	NWT	1813	4437	BRUCE ANNE		P		1835	
4449	SPENCE PETER	MET	P		1833	4450	DUNCAN CLARISA	MET	P		1832	
4458	SPENCE PETER	MET			1820		SABISTON GENEVIEVE	MET			1822	4342
4107	SPENCE ROBERT				1847		SAUNDERS ELLEN				1832	
4108	SPENCE SAMUEL				1820		CARIOLE AZELIK				1820	
4109	SPENCE SAMUEL				1818		WHITFORD JANE				1822	
4460	SPENCE SAMUEL	MET	P	NWT	1829		SANDERSON SARAH	MET	RC	RRS	1825	
3685	SPENCE THOMAS	EUR	RC	SCT	1831		COOK CHARLOTTE	EUR		ENG	1833	4733
4111	SPENCE THOMAS				1833		BADGER ANNE				1835	
4112	SPENCE THOMAS				1832		JULIET				1835	
4113	SPENCE THOMAS				1837		MARY				1840	
4456	SPENCE THOMAS	MET	P	NWT	1812		BIRD CATHERINE	MET	P	RRS	1829	
4114	SPENCE WILLIAM				1836		MOWAT MARY		P		1838	
4115	SPENCE WILLIAM			NWT	1813		TRUCHE LORRAINE		P		1815	
4463	SPENCE WILLIAM	EUR	P	NWT	1806		ANNE		P		1810	
4457	SPENCER JOHN	EUR	RC		1790	4579	SINCLAIR ANN	MET		RRS	1800	
4470	ST ARNAUD ALEXANDRE	MET	RC	RRS	1841		LADOUCEUR PHILOMENE	MET	RC	RRS	1845	2501

TABLE 1: GENEALOGIES OF RED RIVER HOUSEHOLDS, 1818-1870

ID	MALE HEAD OF FAMILY		RACE	FAITH	BIRTH PLACE	DATES	DADS ID	FEMALE HEAD OF FAMILY		RACE	FAITH	BIRTH PLACE	DATES	DADS ID
4579	ST ARNAUD	BONAVENTURE	EUR	RC	CAN	1798		CONTRE	GENEVIEVE	MET	RC		1817	13360
4468	ST ARNAUD	CHARLES	MET	RC	RRS	1840	4579	RAINVILLE	GENEVIEVE	MET	RC	RRS	1843	4159
4469	ST ARNAUD	JEAN BTE	MET	RC	CAN	1847	4579	LADEROUTE	MARGUERITE	MET	RC		1843	2488
4581	ST CYR	JEAN BTE	MET	RC	CAN	1766 64		MERCREDI	JULIE	MET	RC		1790	
4848	ST CYR	JEAN BTE	MET	RC	NWT	1824		MCKAY	JUSTINE	MET	RC	NWT	1824	
4851	ST DENIS	CELESTIN	MET			1851	5082	HOULE	JOSEPHTE				1854	
4846	ST DENIS	CUTHBERT	MET	RC	RRS	1844		LAVIOLETTE	CECILE	MET	RC	RRS	1850	
4583	ST DENIS	FRANCOIS	MET	RC	RRS	1787	4589	LYONS	SOPHIA	MET	RC	RRS	1807	
4589	ST DENIS	FRANCOIS	MET			1767			LISETTE	IND			1770	
4752	ST DENIS	FRANCOIS	MET			1828	4583	MARTIN	THERESE	MET			1832	
5082	ST DENIS	JACOB	MET			1820		CARRIERE	GENEVIEVE	MET	RC	RRS	1826	4215
4587	ST DENIS	JACQUE	MET	RC	RRS	1836	5588	ROCHELEAU	CHARLOTTE	MET	RC	RRS	1835	
4588	ST DENIS	JACQUE	MET		CAN	1794		DURAND	GENEVIEVE	MET	RC		1805	1414
4582	ST DENIS	MOISE	MET		RRS	1841	4583	KLYNE	MARGUERITE	MET	RC	USA	1849	2285
4584	ST DENIS	PAUL	MET	RC	RRS	1828	4585	THORNE	CECILE	MET	RC	NWT	1827	
4585	ST DENIS	PAUL	MET	RC	RRS	1802 72		GARIEPY	CATHERINE	MET	RC	RRS	1806	
4845	ST DENIS	PIERRE	MET	RC	RRS	1830		DAUPHINAIS	ADELAIDE	MET	RC	RRS	1835	
4140	ST GERMAIN	ANDRE	MET		RRS	1815		BOUCHER	MADELEINE	MET	RC	RRS	1820	4367
4595	ST GERMAIN	ANDRE	MET	RC		1838	4599		ELISE	MET	RC	RRS	1847	
4853	ST GERMAIN	AUGUSTIN	MET		RRS	1840	4855		CATHERINE	MET	RC	RRS	1842	
4592	ST GERMAIN	ETIENNE	MET	RC	RRS	1824		PRIMEAU	JOSEPHTE	MET	RC	RRS	1825	3980
4410	ST GERMAIN	ETIENNE	MET	RC		1835		LANGILL	ROSE	MET	RC	RRS	1847	
4854	ST GERMAIN	FRANCOIS	MET		RRS	1844		ALLARD	CHARLOTTE	MET	RC	RRS	1846	
4597	ST GERMAIN	FRANCOIS	EUR	RC	LC	1833	4599	BONNEAU	THERISE	MET	RC	RRS	1837	415
4599	ST GERMAIN	FRANCOIS	MET	RC	RRS	1782		SAUCIER	LOUISE	MET	RC	NWT	1810	
4601	ST GERMAIN	FREDERICK	MET	RC	RRS	1850	4603	NAULT	MARGUERITE	MET	RC	RRS	1852	507
4598	ST GERMAIN	HYACINTHE	MET		RRS	1846	4599	BRELAND	REBECCA	MET	RC	RRS	1846	
4600	ST GERMAIN	JOSEPH	MET	RC	CAN	1796	4603	CADOTTE	MARIE	MET	RC		1800	
4602	ST GERMAIN	JOSEPH	MET	RC	RRS	1846	4600	GENTHON	CAROLINE	MET	RC	RRS	1838	1930
4603	ST GERMAIN	JOSEPH	MET	RC	RRS	1820	4599	MCGILLIVRAY	ANNIE	MET	RC	RRS	1826	
4596	ST GERMAIN	LEANDRE	MET	RC	RRS	1839	4600	PELLETIER	ANASTASIE	MET	RC	RRS	1841	
4604	ST GERMAIN	PIERRE	MET	RC	RRS	1830		GOSSELIN	GENEVIEVE	MET	RC	RRS	1825	
4605	ST GERMAIN	PIERRE	MET		RRS	1800	4605	SUTHERLAND	LIZETTE	MET	RC	RRS	1801	
4606	ST GERMAIN	PIERRE	MET	RC	RRS	1817		LAROCQUE	CHARLOTTE	MET	RC	RRS	1818	1337
4855	ST GERMAIN	PIERRE	MET			1848		DUCHARME	SARA	MET			1850	
4856	ST LUC	D ARPENTIGNY	EUR	RC	CAN	1822		BOUCHER	MARIE	MET			1824	
4609	ST LUC	FRANCOIS	MET	RC	RRS	1797	4609	BOUCHER	CATHERINE	MET	RC	RRS	1805 63	
4608	ST LUC	GILBERT	MET	RC	RRS	1836	4609	BERIAULT	MARIE	MET	RC		1847	
4610	ST MATHE	ANDRE	MET	RC	NWT	1833	4611	SUTHERLAND	MARGUERITE	MET	RC	RRS	1835	
4611	ST MATHE	MARTIN		RC	NWT	1827		GOSSELIN	MARGUERITE	MET	RC	RRS	1829	
4614	ST PIERRE	FRANCOIS	EUR		RRS	1798	4614	LETENDRE	ANGELIQUE	MET	RC		1805	
4615	ST PIERRE	FRANCOIS	MET	RC		1802		LAVERDURE	MARIE	MET	RC		1810	
4616	ST PIERRE	FRANCOIS	EUR		SCT	1768			ANGELIQUE				1797	
4613	ST PIERRE	LOUIS	EUR		RRS	1795	4614	HOULE	MARGUERITE	MET	RC	RRS	1835	4494
4466	STALKER	ROBERT	EUR	P	SCT	1838		DUCHARME	MARIE	EUR	P		1839	
4125	STANLEY	JOSEPH	EUR	P	SCT	1832		SUTHERLAND	ELLEN	EUR	P	RRS	1833	
4124	STAR	JAMES	IND	P	RRS	1820		ADAM	GENEVIEVE	EUR	P	RRS	1822	
4165	STAR	ABRAHAM		P	RRS	1795 45		CAMERON	MARIE	IND	P	RRS	1800	

ID	MALE HEAD OF FAMILY		RACE	FAITH	BIRTH PLACE	DATES	DADS ID	FEMALE HEAD OF FAMILY		RACE	FAITH	BIRTH PLACE	DATES	DADS ID
4475	STEVENS	GEORGE	MET	P	RRS	1821	.	MCKENZIE	SARAH	MET	P	RRS	1830	3429
4478	STEVENS	JOHN	MET	P	ENG	1787	.		MARY	MET	.	NWT	1789	.
4476	STEVENS	RICHARD	EUR	P	NWT	1793	.		MARY	IND	.	.	1792	.
4473	STEVENS	ROBERT	MET	P	RRS	1838	4476	CRAMER	MARY ANNE	MET	P	RRS	1845	1623
4474	STEVENS	WILLIAM	MET	P	RRS	1829	4476	FOULDS	MARIE	MET	P	RRS	1828	.
4870	STEVENSON	ANGUS	IND	P	.	1838	.		MARY	MET	P	.	1840	.
4858	STEVENSON	CHARLES	IND	.	.	1840	.	JOHNSTON	CAROLINE	IND	P	RRS	1848	2441
4871	STEVENSON	CHARLES	MET	P	.	1842	.	BALFOUR	ADELAIDE	.	.	.	1850	.
4480	STEVENSON	EDMUND	IND	P	RRS	1810	.	CADOTTE	SUSSETTE	MET	P	RRS	1820	.
4859	STEVENSON	GEORGE	.	.	.	1848	.	KENNEDY	MARY	IND	P	RRS	1850	.
4873	STEVENSON	GEORGE	IND	.	.	1833	.		JULIET	.	.	.	1836	.
13278	STEVENSON	GEORGE	.	.	.	.	.		JANE	.	.	.	1843	.
4482	STEVENSON	JAMES	MET	P	RRS	1841	4483	SINCLAIR	SARAH ANNE	MET	P	RRS	1849	989
4860	STEVENSON	JAMES	IND	.	RRS	1845	.	CUNNINGHAM	MARY	IND	P	RRS	1835	.
4481	STEVENSON	JOHN	MET	.	.	1840	.	BEADS	MARY	IND	.	.	1790	.
4861	STEVENSON	JOHN	IND	.	.	1845	4874	DANIEL	ELIZABETH	MET	P	RRS	1847	.
4874	STEVENSON	JOHN	IND	.	.	1827	4883		JULIA	.	.	.	1830	.
4877	STEVENSON	JOHN	IND	.	.	1789	.		BETSY	.	.	.	1820	.
4879	STEVENSON	JOHN	IND	.	.	1818 68	.		MARGARET	.	.	.	1852	.
4878	STEVENSON	JOHN THOMAS	IND	P	RRS	1850	4480		BETSY	IND	.	.	1820	.
4862	STEVENSON	PETER	IND	P	RRS	1818	.	JOHNSTON	MARGARET	MET	P	RRS	1838	.
4479	STEVENSON	PHILIP	MET	P	NWT	1830	4877	BALLENDINE	ADELAIDE	MET	P	RRS	1850	.
4863	STEVENSON	RODERICK	MET	P	RRS	1836	.	SAYES	MARY	.	.	.	1817 55	787
4864	STEVENSON	SAMUEL	MET	P	RRS	1847	.	CHATELAIN	MARY	.	.	.	1837	.
4865	STEVENSON	THOMAS	.	.	RRS	1790	.		CHRISTIANA	IND	P	RRS	1845	.
4866	STEVENSON	THOMAS	IND	P	RRS	1838 66	.	FAVEL	MARY	EUR	P	NWT	1815	.
4483	STEVENSON	WILLIAM	EUR	P	ORK	1840	.	ASHAM	ELIZABETH	MET	P	RRS	1822	.
4869	STEVENSON	WILLIAM	IND	P	RRS	1810	.	HOLMES	FANNY	IND	P	RRS	1831	7535
4868	STEVENSON	WILLIAM	MET	P	RRS	1810	.	HOPE	MARIE	MET	P	RRS	1826	.
4880	STEVENSON	WILLIAM	MET	P	RRS	1821	.	SPENCE	ELIZABETH	.	.	.	1824	.
4487	STEWART	JAMES	.	.	.	1824	.	MURRAY	MARGARET	MET	P	SCT	1834	3233
4488	STEWART	JAMES	EUR	P	SCT	1820	.	MOWAT	ROBINA	EUR	P	.	1855	.
4508	STODGILL	JOSEPH	EUR	P	ENG	1827	.	MCKAY	ISABELLA	EUR	.	.	1820	.
4489	STOCKS	CHARLES	EUR	P	RRS	1853	.	DENNIS	MARGARET	MET	P	RRS	1851	467
4486	STRANGE	ANDREW	MET	P	RRS	1824	4912	BOURKE	ANN	MET	P	RRS	1844	4389
4485	STRANGE	DAVID	IND	P	LC	1848	4912	SINCLAIR	ELIZABETH	IND	P	RRS	1842	.
4910	STRANGER	LEVY	IND	P	RRS	1836	.	HOPE	MARGUERITE	MET	P	RRS	1812 68	.
4912	STRANGER	ROBERT	IND	P	RRS	1844	.	BEAR	NANCY	IND	P	.	1811 41	.
4913	STRANGER	THOMAS	IND	.	.	1806	.		ELIZABETH	IND	P	.	1851	.
4529	STRONG	ANDREW	.	.	.	1810	.	SINCLAIR	ANNE HARRIET	.	.	.	1844	4389
4499	STUART	TACITUS	MET	.	SCT	1850	.	MCCORRISTER	JANE	MET	.	.	1800	.
4484	STRUTHERS	ANDREW	EUR	.	.	1841	.	THOMAS	FRANCE	EUR	O	.	1800	.
4495	SUTHERLAND	ALEX	EUR	O	SCT	1796	.	MCPHERSON	CATHERINE	EUR	P	.	1850 69	4002
4493	SUTHERLAND	ALEXANDER	EUR	P	RRS	1782	4494	PRITCHARD	CATHERINE	EUR	P	NWT	1816	.
4494	SUTHERLAND	ALEXANDER	EUR	P	SCT	1848	.	MCBEATH	CHRISTIANA	MET	P	.	1847	.
4507	SUTHERLAND	ALEXANDER	EUR	O	SCT	1808	4504	MCBEATH	MARY	.	.	.	1800	.
4496	SUTHERLAND	ALEXIS	EUR	P	RRS	1845	.		JANE	.	.	.	1816	.
4557	SUTHERLAND	ALEXIS	MET	RC	SCT	1792	4543	LAPIERRE	JOSEPHE	MET	.	.	1855	.
4519	SUTHERLAND	ANTOINE	MET	.	.	1814	.	RITCHOT	JEAN BTE	MET	P	.	1847	.
4501	SUTHERLAND	DONALD	EUR	P	SCT	1806	.	MATHESON	ANNE	.	.	.	1810	.

ID	MALE HEAD OF FAMILY	RACE	FAITH	BIRTH PLACE	DATES	DADS ID	FEMALE HEAD OF FAMILY	RACE	FAITH	BIRTH PLACE	DATES	DADS ID
4525	SUTHERLAND DONALD	EUR			1847	4528	MATHESON CHRISTY	EUR			1852	
4558	SUTHERLAND DONALD				1795		LIVINGSTON ANNE	IND			1800 32	
4558	SUTHERLAND DONALD	EUR	P	SCT	1804		BUNN SARAH		P	RRS	1809	
4502	SUTHERLAND EBENEZER	EUR	P	RRS	1839	4494	MATHESON MARGARET	EUR	P	SCT	1844	633
4491	SUTHERLAND GEORGE	EUR	P	SCT	1801	4494	GUNN HENRIETTA	EUR	P		1820	
4504	SUTHERLAND GEORGE	IND			1810		NANCY				1815 46	
4511	SUTHERLAND GEORGE	IND			1810		ELLEN				1820	
4514	SUTHERLAND GEORGE	IND			1824		HARRIET				1821	
4515	SUTHERLAND HUGH	EUR	P	RRS	1843 69	4494	BADGER BARBARA	EUR	P	RRS	1848	
4497	SUTHERLAND JAMES	MET	P	NWT	1833	4555	FRASER MARY ANNE	MET	P	RRS	1843	
4516	SUTHERLAND JAMES	MET	P	NWT	1816		LETTY MARIA	MET	P	RRS	1821	
4518	SUTHERLAND JAMES	MET	P	ORK	1800 44		BIRD ELIZABETH	MET	P	NWT	1808	
4520	SUTHERLAND JAMES	EUR			1777 44		CALDER JANE	MET	P		1785 35	
4523	SUTHERLAND JAMES			SCT	1796		FLETT NANCY	IND	P		1800	
4539	SUTHERLAND JEREMIAH	EUR	O	RRS	1800	4504	COOK MARGARET		O		1805	
4500	SUTHERLAND JOHN	EUR	P	SCT	1837	4494	HARPER ELIZABETH	MET	P	RRS	1849	2127
4522	SUTHERLAND JOHN	EUR	O	SCT	1837		POLSON FLORA	EUR	P	RRS	1845	3975
4524	SUTHERLAND JOHN	EUR	O	SCT	1768		MCBEATH CHRISTIANA	EUR	O		1770	
4526	SUTHERLAND JOHN	EUR	O	SCT	1792		PEGGY		O		1800 23	
4526	SUTHERLAND JOHN	EUR	O	SCT	1792		MARGARET		O		1802	
4527	SUTHERLAND JOHN	EUR	P	SCT	1808	4543	POLSON JANE	MET	P	RRS	1808 44	
4527	SUTHERLAND JOHN	EUR	P	SCT	1808		TAIT MARGARET	EUR	P		1824	4625
4528	SUTHERLAND JOHN	EUR	P	SCT	1794		MATHESON CATHERINE	MET	P	RRS	1809	
4536	SUTHERLAND JOHN	EUR	P	RRS	1821		MCBEATH JANET	MET	P		1822	
4538	SUTHERLAND JOHN	MET	P	NWT	1818	4540	CUNNINGHAM CATHERINE	MET	P		1832	
4540	SUTHERLAND JOHN				1796		ASSINIBOINE ANGELIQUE	IND	P		1800	
4541	SUTHERLAND PIERRE	MET	RC	RRS	1843	4520	GALARNEAU MARIE	MET	RC	RRS	1848	1889
4543	SUTHERLAND PIERRE	MET	RC	RRS	1820		MCMULLEN SUZANNE	MET	RC	RRS	1821	
4537	SUTHERLAND RICHARD	EUR	P	RRS	1838		MARIANNE		P		1840	
4552	SUTHERLAND ROBERT	EUR	P	RRS	1825	4518	ASHAM ANNE	EUR	P	RRS	1826 49	
4552	SUTHERLAND ROBERT	EUR	P	NWT	1825		HENDERSON JANE	EUR	P		1830	
4553	SUTHERLAND RODERICK	MET		NWT	1821		LOWMAN MARY EMILY		P		1829	
4498	SUTHERLAND WILLIAM	EUR	P	RRS	1833	4552	ANDERSON ELIZABETH	MET	P	RRS	1827	2400
4517	SUTHERLAND WILLIAM	EUR	O	SCT	1758 38		INKSTER MARGARET		P		1783 48	
4554	SUTHERLAND WILLIAM	MET	P	NWT	1808		TROCHIE SUSETTE		O		1812	
4555	SUTHERLAND WILLIAM		P	NWT	1806		ISABELLA	MET	P		1807	
4556	SUTHERLAND WILLIAM	MET	P		1847		LOGAN ELIZABETH	MET		UC	1847	
4908	SWAIN ANTOINE	MET	RC	RRS	1836		DESJARLAIS BETHSY	MET	RC	NWT	1838	
4917	SWAIN CHARLE	MET	P	RRS	1843	4567	DESMARAIS CATHERINE	MET	P	RRS	1846	
4562	SWAIN CHARLE	MET	P	NWT	1840	4565	THIBERT FRANCOISE	MET	RC	NWT	1847	
4566	SWAIN CHARLES		P	RRS	1813	4561	MCCORRISTER MARGARET	IND	P		1817	
4560	SWAIN CHARLES	MET	O	NWT	1789		HAY MARGARET	MET	P		1792	
4561	SWAIN CHARLES	MET	P		1835		MARGARET	MET			1840	
4575	SWAIN JAMES	MET	P	RRS	1799	4569	ARCUS MARGUERITE	MET	P	RRS	1810	
4565	SWAIN JAMES	MET	P	RRS	1808		RACETTE MARGUERITE	IND	P	RRS	1794	
4567	SWAIN JAMES				1797		DESCOLEAUX JOSEPHTE	IND	RC		1806	
4568	SWAIN JAMES		RC		1829 51		HENRY NANCY	MET	RC	RRS	1840	1257
4572	SWAIN JAMES						DESMARAIS ELIZABETH	MET	RC		1840	

ID	MALE HEAD OF FAMILY	RACE	FAITH	BIRTH PLACE	DATES	DADS ID	FEMALE HEAD OF FAMILY	RACE	FAITH	BIRTH PLACE	DATES	DADS ID
4564	SWAIN JOHN	MET	.	.	1829	4567	LILLIE ELIZABETH	MET	RC	NWT	1833	.
4570	SWAIN JOHN	MET	P	NWT	1814		ALLARY MARY	MET	RC	NWT	1820	
4914	SWAIN JOHN	MET	RC	RRS	1832		LAVERDURE LOUISE	MET	RC	NWT	1830	2837
4574	SWAIN THOMAS	MET	P	RRS	1800	4570	SABISTON ELIZABETH	IND	P	NWT	1807 60	
4915	SWAIN THOMAS	MET	RC	RRS	1838	4570	DUMAS MARGUERITE	MET			1803 30	
4563	SWAIN THOMAS	MET	RC	RRS	1834		DUCHARME BETSY	MET	RC	RRS	1839 63	
4916	SWAIN WILLIAM	MET	.	RRS	1830		BREMNER ELLEN	MET			1825	492
4919	SWAIN WILLIAM	MET	RC	.	1836		BRUYERE ANGELIQUE	MET	RC	RRS	1831	587
4571	SWANSON JONAS	EUR	.	ORK		7500	HAMELIN ANGELIQUE	EUR			1839	2115
4921	SWINFORD HERBERT		P	.	1814		FRANKS MARIANNE	MET	P	NWT	1840	
4925	SYMESON WILLIAM	MET	.	RRS	1840		LINKLATER MARIE ANNE			RRS	1822	88
4631	TAILLEFER JOSEPH		P	.	1841		SPENCE JANE	MET		RRS	1847	
4926	TAIT ANDREW	MET	.	RRS	1837		MCDERMOT JANE				1845	
4619	TAIT CHARLES		P	.	1830		ANDERSON ELIZA	MET		RRS	1845	1226
4927	TAIT DAVID	EUR	.	ORK	1780		KNIGHT BARBARA	MET	P	RRS	1851	
4621	TAIT GEORGE	EUR	P	ORK	1780	4621	DENNET ELIZABETH	EUR			1833	
4622	TAIT JAMES	MET	P	NWT	1809	4625	TAIT SABRINA	IND		NWT	1780	2582
4627	TAIT JAMES	MET	P	RRS	1828		LAMBERT CATHERINE	MET		RRS	1782	
4920	TAIT JAMES	MET	P	RRS	1832		GUNN SARAH	MET	P	RRS	1822	
4924	TAIT JAMES		.	.	1800		POCHA MARY	MET	P	RRS	1825	
4577	TAIT JOHN	EUR	P	SCT	1801	4621	TAIT ELLEN	MET	P	NWT	1837	542
4617	TAIT JOHN	IND	P	NWT	1822		BROWN MARGARET	IND	P	NWT	1804	
4923	TAIT JOHN	EUR	P	SCT	1828		WILLIAMS CAROLINE	EUR	P	ENG	1803	
4618	TAIT JOHN	MET	P	RRS	1828		RICHARD ELIZABETH	MET	P	RRS	1835	
4578	TAIT JOSEPH	MET	P	RRS	1831	4630	COOK JANE	MET	.	NWT	1838	853
4624	TAIT JOSEPH		.	.	1829	4577	CORRIGAL ISABELLA				1831	
4928	TAIT PETER		.	.	1813		DESJARLAIS CATHERINE				1832	
13277	TAIT PHILIP		.	RRS	1828		SANDERSON MADELEINE				1833	
4576	TAIT ROBERT	MET	P	NWT	1830	4630	MONKMAN MARGUERITE	MET	P	RRS	1817	
4930	TAIT SAMUEL	EUR	P	ORK	1826	4625	INKSTER JENNY				1832	
4625	TAIT WILLIAM	MET	P	RRS	1795		AULD MARY	MET	P		1839	
4626	TAIT WILLIAM	MET	P	NWT	1826	4625	GUNN JANE		.	RRS	1830	
4630	TAIT WILLIAM	MET	P	RRS	1792		BEAR SARAH	IND			1804	
4931	TAIT WILLIAM	IND	P	SCT	1827	4630	PEEBLES MARY	MET			1830	
4623	TALLOCH JOHN	EUR	P	RRS	1840		GIBSON JOHANNA	EUR	P	RRS	1815	1954
4629	TANNER JAMES	MET	.	RRS	1805	4629	DUMAS MARY	MET		RRS	1831	
4628	TANNER JOHN	MET	.	RRS	1840	4639	GUNN CATHERINE	MET		RRS	1846	
4635	TAYLOR ALEXANDER	MET	.	RRS	1844	4646	MCDONALD BARBARA	MET	P	RRS	1830	
4634	TAYLOR DAVID	MET	.	RRS	1837	4646	BIRD MARGARET	MET			1825	
4633	TAYLOR EDWARD	MET	P	NWT	1840	4638	SABISTON CATHERINE	MET		RRS	1846	
4636	TAYLOR GEORGE	MET	P	RRS	1829	4638	COOPER MARY	MET	P	RRS	1835	4341
4638	TAYLOR GEORGE	MET	P	NWT	1800 44		PRINCE NANCY	IND		NWT	1808	
4932	TAYLOR GEORGE		.	RRS	1848	4934	MCNAB MARY	MET	P	RRS	1849	
4639	TAYLOR JAMES	EUR	P	ORK	1798		INKSTER MARY	MET		NWT	1808	
4640	TAYLOR JAMES	MET	.	RRS	1838	4639	THOMAS SARAH	MET	P	RRS	1831 55	
4934	TAYLOR JAMES	MET	P	RRS	1825	4646	BIRD AMELIA	MET		RRS	1826	

ID	MALE HEAD OF FAMILY	RACE	FAITH	BIRTH PLACE	DATES	DADS ID	FEMALE HEAD OF FAMILY	RACE	FAITH	BIRTH PLACE	DATES	DADS ID
4641	TAYLOR JOHN	MET	P	RRS	1834	4639	CAMPBELL FLORA	MET	P	NWT	1833	658
4943	TAYLOR PETER	MET	P	RRS	1840	4639	MCDONALD CATHERINE	MET	P	RRS	1843	
4637	TAYLOR ROBERT	MET	P	RRS	1837	4638	VALEUR ELISE	MET	P	RRS	1850	
4936	TAYLOR ROBERT	EUR	P	SCT	1837	4639	CROMARTIE MARGARET	MET	P	NWT	1843	
4937	TAYLOR SAMUEL	EUR	P	SCT	1816			NANCY			RRS	1828	
4642	TAYLOR THOMAS	MET	P	NWT	1807	4642	KIETH MARY	MET	P		1811	
4643	TAYLOR THOMAS	MET	P	RRS	1831	4638	KENNEDY CAROLINE	MET	P	RRS	1843	
4940	TAYLOR WILLIAM	MET	P		1843		YOUNG MARIANNE	MET	P	RRS	1852	
4942	TAYLOR WILLIAM	EUR			1832	68	GUNN MARGARET	MET	P	RRS	1847	
4652	TELLEFSON PETER	EUR	P	ENG	1835		THOMPSON ISABELLE	EUR	P		1851	5213
4650	TELLIER JOSEPH				1830		DELORME CHRISTINE			RRS	1828	
4647	TEMPLETON ALEXANDER	EUR	P	SCT	1830		MCKAY ELIZABETH	EUR	P	RRS	1832	4692
4969	TESSIER JOHN				1825		JANE				1828	
4654	TESSIER TOUSSAINT				1840		LACHENSTIERE JOSEPHE				1844	
4944	TETREAULT JOSEPH				1845		GLADU NANCY				1856	
4945	TETU C A D				1845		BARRON MELANIE				1804	
4644	THEROUX CHARLES	EUR	P	OTH	1766		SABISTON SARAH	MET	P	NWT	1848	714
4644	THEROUX CHARLES	MET	RC	RRS	1825		CARRIERE ANGELIQUE				1832	
4656	THEURERE MICHAEL	EUR			1790		ANNE	EUR	P		1793	
4939	THIBAULT FRANCOIS	MET	RC	NWT	1844		DAIGNEAULT HELENE	MET	RC	NWT	1846	1008
4659	THIBAULT JEAN BTE	MET	RC	NWT	1849	4661	CARRIERE CHARLOTTE	EUR	RC	RRS	1851	4796
4664	THIBERT CHARLES	MET	RC	NWT	1840	4661	CARRIERE ELIZABETH	MET	RC	RRS	1843	
4663	THIBERT ELZEAR	MET	RC	LC	1812		SLATER ELISE	MET	RC	NWT	1835	4796
4662	THIBERT FRANCOIS	EUR	RC		1790	4661	ZASTRE SOPHIE	MET	RC	RRS	1792	4796
4661	THIBERT PIERRE		RC		1795	4665	SLATER LOUISE	MET	RC	NWT	1800	4146
4665	THIBERT PIERRE				1806		RACETTE PHIMOMENE	EUR		RRS	1806	
4438	THOMAS ALEXANDER	IND	P	RRS	1815		MAHEW SARAH	IND	P	NWT	1845	
4549	THOMAS ALEXANDER				1836		HELENA	MET	P	RRS	1837	
4547	THOMAS CELESTIN	EUR	RC	OTH	1839		STEVENSON MARIE	IND	P	RRS	1836	
4668	THOMAS CHARLES				1838		TAYLOR VICTOIRE	EUR	RC	OTH	1847	4638
4546	THOMAS CHARLES	MET	P	RRS	1820		MAGER CYDONIA	MET	P		1849	
4420	THOMAS CHARLES	MET	P	NWT	1844		CLOUSTON CATHERINE	MET	P		1817	904
4545	THOMAS CHARLES				1815		VINCENT CHARLOTTE	MET	P	RRS	1823	
4669	THOMAS DANIEL	IND	P	RRS	1810		BAUVIER MARY	MET	P	NWT	1846	
4886	THOMAS EDWARD				1847	4672	CALDER MARGARET	MET	P		1814	629
4671	THOMAS GEORGE	MET	P	RRS	1810		SINCLAIR ELIZABETH	MET	P	RRS	1851	4388
4670	THOMAS HENRY	IND	P	RRS	1795	4676	MARY	IND	P		1815	
4678	THOMAS JAMES	IND	P		1835		PARISIEN CHARLOTTE	MET	P	RRS	1800	
4672	THOMAS JEFFERY	IND	P	RRS	1820		HARRIET	IND	P	RRS	1828	3830
4673	THOMAS JOHN	IND	P	RRS	1815		ANNE	MET	P		1825	
4532	THOMAS JOHN	IND	P	NWT	1820		BALLENDINE SARAH	MET	P	RRS	1818	
4674	THOMAS JOHN	MET	P	RRS	1839		TOM JANE	IND	P	RRS	1825	
4887	THOMAS JOHN				1827		JANE			NWT	1846	
4888	THOMAS JOHN	IND		NWT	1840	4887	WILLIAM JANE	MET	P		1829	
4895	THOMAS JOHN				1848		STEVENSON MARY				1844	
4896	THOMAS JOHN	MET	P				MARY				1846	
4897	THOMAS JOSEPH				1840		CORRIGAL MARGUERITE			RRS	1844	
4890	THOMAS JOSEPH	IND	P	RRS	1848	4887	SYDNEY CHARLOTTE	IND	P	RRS	1848	961

ID	MALE HEAD OF FAMILY	RACE	FAITH	BIRTH PLACE	DATES	DADS ID	FEMALE HEAD OF FAMILY	RACE	FAITH	BIRTH PLACE	DATES	DADS ID
4676	THOMAS RICHARD		P	NWT	1800	4676	THOMAS ELEONOR	MET			1807	4670
4677	THOMAS RICHARD	MET	P	NWT	1834		THOMAS MARY	MET	P	NWT	1834	
4679	THOMAS SIMON		P	NWT	1815		LINKLATER CATHERINE		P		1818	
4680	THOMAS THOMAS	MET	P	NWT	1820		STEWART HARRIET	IND	P	NWT	1817	
4681	THOMAS THOMAS		O	ENG	1819	4679	HOPE FANNY	IND	P		1822	
4682	THOMAS THOMAS	EUR		RRS	1765		SARAH	MET	P	NWT	1786	
4892	THOMAS THOMAS	MET	P	RRS	1844		MOORE MARGARET	IND	P	RRS	1848	
4893	THOMAS THOMAS	IND	P		1832		SANDERSON NANCY		P	RRS	1835	
4899	THOMAS THOMAS			NWT	1828		CATHERINE	IND			1831	
4900	THOMAS THOMAS	IND			1810		JANE		P	RRS	1810	
4902	THOMAS THOMAS			RRS	1808		SARAH				1812	
4675	THOMAS WILLIAM	IND	P		1845	4674	SMITH ELIZA	MET	P	RRS	1842	
4685	THOMAS WILLIAM		P	RRS	1804		BUNN ELEANOR		P		1809	
4894	THOMAS WILLIAM	MET			1844		STEVENS MARY ANN	IND	P	RRS	1849	
4901	THOMAS WILLIAM				1795		BESS CATHERINE	MET			1800	
4903	THOMAS WILLIAM				1845		ROSE CHARLOTTE				1850	
4904	THOMAS WILLIAM			NWT	1840		DAHL ISABELLA H				1843	
4905	THOMAS WILLIAM		P		1824		SOPHIA				1826	
4692	THOMPSON ANDREW				1802	4692	DANIEL MARY	MET	P	NWT	1807	1013
4953	THOMPSON ANDREW	MET	P	RRS	1855		SAUNDERS FRANCES				1857	
4952	THOMPSON JOHN				1843		FOX SARAH	MET	P	RRS	1847	
4954	THORNE DAVID				1837 62	4689	AUGER MADELEINE				1840	
4689	THORNE GEORGE	EUR	RC	LC	1816		LEMIRE MARY	MET	RC	NWT	1805	
4690	THORNE GEORGE	MET	RC	NWT	1830		MCLEOD NANCY	MET	RC	RRS	1832	3442
4955	THORNE GEORGE				1805		MCKAY MARIE				1810	
4691	THORNE JOHN	EUR		NWT	1772	4955	LAROCQUE MARY	EUR		NWT	1777	
4948	TIAMANG LOUIS	IND		NWT	1821	4947	MACKOUTEPWAN ANGELIQUE	IND		NWT	1826	
4949	TIEBOWAJAM ALBERT	IND	P	RRS	1812		DEAN NANCY	MET		NWT	1815	
4957	TODD JAMES	MET		RRS	1847	4697	MCKAY MARIE			RRS	1856	
4959	TODD JOHN			NWT	1825	4960	DESLAURIERS JOSEPHINE				1827	
4281	TODD JOHN			NWT	1833		DUCHARME MADELEINE				1830	
4698	TODD WILLIAM	MET	P		1800	4697	WILLIAMS MATILDA	MET	P	NWT	1825	
4697	TODD WILLIAM			NWT	1824		DENNET ISABEL	MET	P		1805	5197
4958	TODD WILLIAM	MET	P		1845		HENRY ANNE	MET		RRS	1840	
4961	TODD WILLIAM			RRS	1810 69		FANNY				1850	
4968	TOURAND CALIXTE	MET			1853		COMTOIS GENEVIEVE	MET	RC	RRS	1813	4236
4702	TOURAND HENRI				1855	4700	ROSS MARGUERITE				1855	
4967	TOURAND ISADORE	MET	RC	RRS	1846	4701	CORRIGAL LOUISE				1859	5098
4704	TOURAND JACQUES	MET	RC	RRS	1836	4701	VERMETTE ANNIE	MET	RC	RRS	1857	
4706	TOURAND JEAN BTE	MET	RC	RRS	1838	4701	COCHRANE MARIE	MET	RC	RRS	1831	
4705	TOURAND JEAN BTE	MET	RC	RRS	1846	4699	DELORME ANGELIQUE	MET	RC	RRS	1845	
4965	TOURAND JOSEPH				1780		LADEROUTE MARGUERITE	MET	RC	RRS	1851	
4699	TOURAND JOSEPH	MET	RC	RRS	1826		GLADU CHARLOTTE	MET			1800	3862
4700	TOURAND JOSEPH	EUR	RC	LC	1782		PAUL JOSEPHTE	MET	RC	RRS	1831	2496
4701	TOURAND JOSEPH	MET	RC	NWT	1830		LADEROUTE ROSALIE	MET	RC	LC	1816	
4962	TOURANGEAU ANTOINE	MET	RC	RRS	1805	4964	LAROCQUE MADELEINE	MET	RC	NWT	1830	
4964	TOURANGEAU JEAN BTE		RC	RRS	1846		VADNAIS MARIE			RRS	1809	
4963	TOURANGEAU LOUIS	IND	RC	RRS	1838	4964	LALIBERTE FANNY	MET	RC	RRS	1847	
4714	TRAVELLER DUNCAN		P	RRS	1838		THOMAS	MET	P	RRS	1845	
4718	TRESTON JAMES	EUR	RC	IRE			LAPIERRE LOUISE	MET	RC	NWT	1830	2614

TABLE 1: GENEALOGIES OF RED RIVER HOUSEHOLDS, 1818-1870

ID	MALE HEAD OF FAMILY	FAMILY	RACE	FAITH	BIRTH PLACE	DATES	DADS ID	FEMALE HEAD OF FAMILY	RACE	FAITH	BIRTH PLACE	DATES	DADS ID
4711	TROTTIER	ANDRE	MET	RC	RRS	1791		PACQUET MARGUERITE	MET	RC	RRS	1787	3671
4712	TROTTIER	ANDRE	MET	RC	NWT	1816	4711	FALCON ISABEL	MET	RC	NWT	1819	1487
4975	TROTTIER	ANDRE				1820		LOUISE	IND			1821	
4976	TROTTIER	ANDRE				1808		ST DENIS MARGUERITE				1811	
4970	TROTTIER	ANTOINE	MET	RC	RRS	1835	43	LAFRAMBOISE ANGELIQUE	MET	RC	RRS	1833	
4716	TROTTIER	BAZILE		RC	RRS	1820	4711	FAGNANT MAGDELEINE	MET	RC	RRS	1825	
4715	TROTTIER	JEAN BTE	MET	RC		1825	55	CHALIFOUX LOUISE	MET	RC	NWT	1818	
4971	TROTTIER	JEAN BTE		RC	RRS	1841	4716	MCGILLIS ROSE	MET	RC	RRS	1847	
4977	TROTTIER	JEAN BTE	MET	RC		1821	4716	ST DENIS PAULETTE	MET			1826	
4717	TROTTIER	JOSEPH	MET	RC	NWT	1797		ELIZABETH	MET			1786	66
4972	TROTTIER	JOSEPH	MET	RC	RRS	1825		LAVALLEE THERESE	MET		NWT	1835	
4978	TROTTIER	JOSEPH	MET	RC		1840		ST DENIS JULIE	MET			1842	
4973	TROTTIER	MICHEL	MET	RC	RRS	1825	4720	DESJARLAIS ANGELIQUE	MET	RC	RRS	1852	4752
4974	TROTTIER	PASCAL	MET	P	NWT	1846	4722	ST GERMAIN ROSE	MET	RC	NWT	1802	
4719	TROTTIER	JACOB			NWT	1790		VINCENT ELIZABETH	IND	P	NWT	1770	4599
4720	TRUTHWAITE	MATTHEW	MET	P	NWT	1768	4719	ELIZABETH	MET		NWT	1853	
4721	TRUTHWAITE	THOMAS	MET	RC	NWT	1847		PRUDEN CAROLINE		P		1830	
4722	TRUTHWAITE	THOMAS	IND	RC		1820		MCDERMOT CATHERINE	IND		NWT	1833	
4980	TSIPIS	THOMAS	EUR	RC	CAN	1830		KIWEKAPAN SUSANNE	MET			1790	
4724	TURCOTTE	JEAN BTE	MET	RC		1784		DUBEY ANGELIQUE	MET		NWT	1840	
4726	TURCOTTE	JEAN BTE	MET	RC	RRS	1837	4725	POCHA SARAH				1854	3457
4727	TURCOTTE	JOSEPH	MET	RC	RRS	1849	4725	MCMILLAN MAGDELEINE	MET	RC	RRS	1818	677
4725	TURCOTTE	VITAL				1818	4724	CAPLETTE OLYMPE	MET	RC	RRS	1855	8
4987	TURNER	ADOLPH				1846	98	MONDOR KITTY				1840	
4988	TURNER	CHARLES				1838		MARY ANN				1849	
4989	TURNER	CORNELIUS	IND		NWT	1845		BEARDY HARRIET				1815	
4986	TURNER	FRANCIS				1812		MARY				1815	
4990	TURNER	FRANCIS	IND		NWT	1810		ELISABETH				1820	
5214	TURNER	FRANCIS				1817		ANN				1815	
4983	TURNER	GEORGE	EUR	P	ENG	1808	67	OBRIEN MARY ANN	EUR	RC	IRE	1852	88
4984	TURNER	GEORGE	EUR	RC	ENG	1835		SANDERSON BRIDGET	MET	P	RRS	1846	
4985	TURNER	JOHN				1844		KENNY EMMA	EUR	RC	IRE	1808	
4728	TURNER	JOSEPH				1805		JANE	MET			1843	
4991	TURNER	JOSEPH ALEX				1840		TODD JANE				1837	
4992	TURNER	MARTIN	MET	RC		1832		ANDERSON HARRIET				1849	
4993	TURNER	PHILIP	EUR	RC		1845		GARNOT MARGARET				1847	
4982	TURNER	RICHARD	EUR	RC		1842		MARGARET				1821	
4729	TWAT	MAGNUS				1762		LEDOUX ELMIRE	MET			1823	
4995	URTUBISE	JEAN BTE	MET			1815		NANCY	MET			1804	
5037	VALEUR	JAMES	EUR	RC	LC	1820		GRENIER URSULE	EUR	RC	RRS	1810	
4997	VALIQUETTE	JEAN BTE	EUR	RC	CAN	1805		SAYER MARGUERITE	MET			1851	
5034	VANDAL	ANTOINE				1784		HENRY ALPHONSINE				1831	
5048	VANDAL	ANTOINE				1848	5035	PERREAULT EMILIE	EUR	RC	RRS	1843	3899
5051	VANDAL	ANTOINE	MET	RC	RRS	1831	5057	FORBISHER SCHOLASTIQUE	MET	RC	RRS	1825	1639
5053	VANDAL	ANTOINE	MET	RC	RRS	1833	5056	BEAUCHEMIN ISABEL	MET	RC		1799	
5054	VANDAL	ANTOINE	MET	RC	NWT	1819	5055	ZASTRE CHARLOTTE	MET		NWT	1780	
5055	VANDAL	ANTOINE				1795		ANGELIQUE	IND			1817	
5056	VANDAL	ANTOINE	EUR	RC	RRS	1771	70	BERTHELET MARGUERITE	MET	RC	RRS	1817	327
5057	VANDAL	ANTOINE	MET	RC	RRS	1819	5055						

ID	MALE HEAD OF FAMILY	RACE	FAITH	BIRTH PLACE	DATES	DADS ID	FEMALE HEAD OF FAMILY	RACE	FAITH	BIRTH PLACE	DATES	DADS ID
5058	VANDAL AUGUSTINE	MET			1775		LECLAIR CATHERINE	EUR			1778	
5068	VANDAL BENJAMIN	MET	RC	RRS	1820		ALLARY MARGUERITE	MET		RRS	1836	4604
5061	VANDAL FRANCOIS	MET	RC	RRS	1832	5057	ST GERMAIN GENEVIEVE	MET	RC	RRS	1852	
5002	VANDAL GABRIEL	MET					TURNER SARAH	MET			1844	
5059	VANDAL JEAN BTE	MET	RC	RRS	1830	5071	PRIMEAU MARIE	MET	RC	RRS	1843	3984
5060	VANDAL JEAN BTE	MET	RC	RRS	1846	5065	BRACONNIER HENRIETTE	MET	RC	RRS	1843	490
5004	VANDAL JEROME	MET			1838		CYR VICTOIRE	IND			1845	995
5062	VANDAL JOHN	MET	RC	RRS	1839	5035	LAMBERT ELIZABETH	MET	RC	RRS	1850	
5063	VANDAL JOHN	MET	RC	RRS	1846	5073	VIVIER MARGUERITE	MET	RC	NWT	1809	5138
4907	VANDAL JOSEPH	MET			1804		ANGELIQUE	MET			1805	
5035	VANDAL JOSEPH	MET			1798		CHARETTE MARIE	MET	RC		1853	743
5064	VANDAL JOSEPH	MET	RC	RRS	1851	5067	CYR ISABEL	MET	RC	RRS	1815	
5065	VANDAL JOSEPH		RC	NWT	1810		DUPUIS LOUISE	MET			1825	
5066	VANDAL JOSEPH	MET	RC	LC	1820		POITRAS SOPHIA	MET			1835	
5067	VANDAL JOSEPH	EUR	RC	RRS	1798	5058	CHARBONNEAU ADELAIDE	MET	RC	RRS	1843	749
5069	VANDAL JOSEPH	MET	RC	RRS	1839	5034	BRACONNIER JULIENNE	MET	RC	RRS	1839	
5070	VANDAL LOUIS	MET	RC	NWT	1834	5035	HAMELIN MARIE	MET	RC	RRS	1790	
5071	VANDAL PIERRE	MET	RC	RRS	1785	5056	HUGHES CHARLOTTE	MET	RC	RRS	1818	
5073	VANDAL PIERRE	MET	RC	RRS	1814		HAMELIN ROSALIE	MET	RC	RRS	1848	
5076	VANDAL MAXIME	MET	RC	RRS	1852	5078	VANDRY CLEMENTINE	MET	RC	RRS	1838	
5077	VANDRY TOUSAINT	MET	RC	RRS	1826		MCDOUGALL LOUISE	MET	RC	RRS	1812	2114
5078	VANDRY TOUSAINT	MET	RC	RRS	1799		CREBASSA MARIE	MET	RC	RRS	1847	5075
5080	VANNERMAN HENRI				1842		FLETT MARGARET	MET			1852	
5005	VAREY THOMAS	MET			1850		DANIELS MARIE ANNE				1800	
5006	VENNE DAVID	MET	RC	RRS	1800		LAURENCE CECILE	MET			1842	
5084	VENNE DAVID	MET	RC	RRS	1843	5090	BEAUCHAMP JOSEPHTE	MET	RC	RRS	1822	
5085	VENNE JEAN BTE	EUR	RC	RRS	1832	5090	HOULE ISABEL	MET	RC	RRS	1778	743
5087	VENNE JEAN BTE	EUR	RC	CAN	1773		RAYMOND CHARLOTTE	EUR			1768	
5088	VENNE JOSEPH	EUR			1765	5088	LEACOURSE MARGUERITE	EUR			1804	
5090	VENNE PIERRE	EUR	RC	RRS	1786	5090	CHARETTE MARIE	MET	RC	RRS	1834	4579
5091	VENNE SOLOMON	MET	RC	RRS	1837		ST ARNAUD JOSEPHTE	MET	RC	RRS	1857	
5007	VENNE WILLIAM				1852		JOLIBOIS ROSALIE				1856	
5008	VERMETTE ALEXANDER	MET	RC	RRS	1837		LAURENCE ANGELE	MET	RC	RRS	1845	194
5095	VERMETTE ALEXIS	MET	RC	RRS	1833	5099	BEAUCHEMIN PHILOMENE	MET	RC	RRS	1838	
5094	VERMETTE ANTOINE				1850	5099	LAROCQUE CECILE	MET			1855	
5009	VERMETTE AUGUSTINE	MET			1810		FORBISHER MELANIE				1837	
5096	VERMETTE JOSEPH	MET			1788	5097	CYR MARGUERITE	MET			1790	998
5097	VERMETTE JOSEPH	MET			1830		PLOUF JOSEPHTE	MET			1830	
5098	VERMETTE JOSEPH	MET	RC	RRS	1806	5099	LALIBERTE ANGELIQUE	MET	RC	RRS	1811	2561
5099	VERMETTE JOSEPH	MET	RC	RRS	1839	5099	LALIBERTE ANGELIQUE	MET	RC	RRS	1845	
5100	VERMETTE LOUIS	MET	RC	RRS	1847	5099	CADOTTE JULIE	MET	RC	RRS	1840	616
5101	VERMETTE NORBERT	MET	RC	RRS	1838	5099	ROCHELEAU GENEVIEVE	MET	RC	RRS	1840	4215
5102	VERMETTE PIERRE	MET	RC	RRS	1845	5107	ST DENIS CAROLINE	MET	RC	RRS	1835	4588
5106	VERSAILLES DAVID	MET	RC	RRS	1810		BOYER SCHOLASTIQUE	MET	RC	RRS	1809	
5104	VERSAILLES JEAN BTE	MET	RC	RRS	1820		SHORT GENEVIEVE	MET	RC	RRS	1825	
5107	VERSAILLES JOSEPH				1791		GENEVIEVE	MET			1798	
5111	VERSAILLES PIERRE	MET	RC	NWT	1800		LETENDRE JOSEPHTE	MET	RC		1800	66
5115	VERSAILLES WILLIAM				1820		CELESTE	MET				
5013	VESTRO FRANCOIS				1800		FALCON MAGDELEINE				1823	
5014	VIDAL WILLIAM				1850		HALLET MARIE				1852	

TABLE 1: GENEALOGIES OF RED RIVER HOUSEHOLDS, 1818-1870

ID	MALE HEAD OF FAMILY	RACE	FAITH	BIRTH PLACE	DATES	DADS ID	FEMALE HEAD OF FAMILY	RACE	FAITH	BIRTH PLACE	DATES	DADS ID
5010	VILLEBRUNE ANTOINE	MET	RC	RRS	1807		MARCELLAIS ARCHANGE	MET	RC	RRS	1816	
5117	VILLEBRUNE JOSEPH	MET			1838	5118	ROBILLARD MARIE	MET	RC	RRS	1847	297
5011	VILLEBRUNE LOUIS				1835	67	BERARD ISABEL	MET	RC	NWT	1832	
5118	VILLEBRUNE LOUIS	MET	RC	NWT	1805		COLLIN LOUISE	MET		NWT	1815	
5120	VILLEBRUNE LOUIS	EUR		LC	1780		MARIAN	IND		NWT	1785	
5122	VILLENEUVE CHARLES				1843		DEMONTIGNY MARGUERITE	MET			1848	
5123	VILLENEUVE FRANCOIS				1825		LAVALLEE HELENE	MET			1828	
5124	VILLENEUVE FRANCOIS	MET			1830	5124	LAPLANTE PHILOMENE	MET			1832	
5125	VILLENEUVE HYACINTHE	MET			1852	5123	LAURENCE PAULINE				1854	
5126	VILLENEUVE ISADORE				1848		HENRY MATILDA	MET			1847	2188
5121	VILLENEUVE JEAN BTE	EUR	RC	CAN	1810		MORIN JULIE	MET			1814 49	
5045	VILLENEUVE MICHEL				1805		DAUPHINAIS JOSEPHTE	MET	RC	RRS	1813	4232
5019	VILLIERS FRANK				1840		ROSS MARIE	EUR			1843	
5020	VINCENT FRANCOIS	MET			1827		MARIE YVONNE	IND		NWT	1831	
5129	VINCENT GEORGE	MET	P	RRS	1851		WORK HARRIET	MET	P	RRS	1851	
5015	VINCENT JOHN	IND	P	NWT	1830	5018	SLATER ELIZABETH	MET	P	NWT	1836	
5017	VINCENT JOHN	MET	P	RRS	1838	5131	GREY MARIE	IND	P	RRS	1845	7029
5018	VINCENT JOHN	MET	P	NWT	1796	5130	THOMAS CHARLOTTE	MET	P	NWT	1805	
5130	VINCENT THOMAS	MET			1771		JEAN	MET			1776	
5016	VINCENT WILLIAM	MET	P	RRS	1836		ROSS CATHERINE	MET	P	RRS	1839	
5028	VISIGNEAULT JOSEPH	MET			1834	5132	PEPIN JULIENNE	MET			1839	3896
5027	VIVIER ALEXANDER	MET			1845	5135	WELLS JULIE	MET			1846	5148
5022	VIVIER ALEXIS	EUR	RC	CAN	1817		MALATERRE J	MET			1820	
5029	VIVIER ALEXIS	MET	RC	RRS	1810		MARIE ANNE	IND		NWT	1814	
5135	VIVIER ALEXIS	MET		NWT	1790	5132	MARIA	IND		NWT	1791	
5136	VIVIER ALEXIS	MET		NWT	1845		BOUSQUET ELISE	MET		NWT	1851	
5132	VIVIER ALEXIS JR				1800	5132	SHORT ISABEL	MET	RC		1810	
5132	VIVIER ALEXIS JR			RRS	1800		CHALIFOUX ANGELIQUE	MET			1812	
5026	VIVIER CHARLES	MET		RRS	1842	5132	PARENTEAU MARGUERITE	MET		NWT	1842	
5030	VIVIER FRANCOIS				1840		LAVERDURE LOUISE				1850	
5137	VIVIER FRANCOIS				1780		SUZANNE	IND		NWT	1785	
5138	VIVIER FRANCOIS				1828		JOSEPHTE	MET			1830	2838
5021	VIVIER JOSEPH	MET	RC	RRS	1811	5135	DUBOIS MARGUERITE	MET	RC	RRS	1837	2115
5025	VIVIER JOSEPH	MET		RRS	1825	5132	HAMELIN CAROLINE	MET	RC	RRS	1833	4574
5031	VIVIER JOSEPH				1800		SWAIN MARGUERITE	MET	RC	NWT	1805	3074
5033	VIVIER MICHEL	MET	RC	RRS	1845	5135	MARTINEAU MARGUERITE	MET	RC	RRS	1852	
5140	VIVIER MICHEL	MET	RC	RRS	1830		DESCHAMPS ELISE	MET		RRS	1823	1644
5228	WABIKINIU JEAN BTE	IND		NWT	1815		FOURNIER MAGDELEINE	MET			1810	1013
5229	WAGNER JAMES E				1852		DANIEL NANCY	MET			1857	
5149	WAGNER MICHEL	EUR	P	OTH	1826		COCHRANE RACHEL	EUR		RRS	1834	4565
5145	WAKETCH JOHN	IND	P	NWT	1812		SWAIN ELIZABETH	IND		NWT	1815	
5216	WAKER JAMES	EUR		SCT	1800		MCINTYRE MARY	EUR	P	SCT	1798	
5230	WALKER WILLIAM				1850		LANDRY MARGUERITE	MET			1853	
5146	WARD JOHN	MET	RC	NWT	1778		BRUYERE ANGELIQUE	MET	RC	NWT	1780	
5219	WARD JOHN	MET	RC	NWT	1830		DUCHARME MARGUERITE	MET	RC	RRS	1840	
5220	WARD JOSEPH				1840		WELLS ANGELIQUE	MET	RC	RRS	1841	
5235	WARRING JOHN				1800		FOURNIER LYDIA				1801	
	WASSALOSKI JOHN				1800		FOURNIER JUSTINE				1801	

ID	MALE HEAD OF FAMILY	RACE	FAITH	BIRTH PLACE	DATES	DADS ID	FEMALE HEAD OF FAMILY	RACE	FAITH	BIRTH PLACE	DATES	DADS ID
8056	WELCH FRANCOISE				1840		HOGUE MARIE ANN				1844	1770
5158	WELLS ANTOINE	MET	RC	RRS	1844	5160	GOOD MARIE ANNE	MET	P	RRS	1836	
5159	WELLS ANTOINE	MET	RC	RRS	1835		BROWN ELIZABETH	MET			1817	
5231	WELLS DANIEL	MET	RC	NWT	1815		COLLIN LOUISE				1828	
5150	WELLS EDWARD	MET	RC		1825		MCGILLIS ELIZABETH	MET		NWT	1820	
5160	WELLS GEORGE	EUR	RC	CAN	1819		SHORT ANNE				1791 41	
5148	WELLS JEAN BTE	MET	RC	NWT	1785		CHALIFOUX ANGELIQUE	MET			1820	
5154	WELLS JEAN BTE	EUR	RC	ENG	1815		CREE MARIE	MET		RRS	1790	
5151	WELLS JOHN	MET	RC		1788		MCKAY MARY	MET	RC		1805	
5152	WELLS JOHN	EUR			1800		GRANT JOSEPHTE	MET			1844	
5153	WELLS JOHN	EUR			1844		LAFRAMBOISE LOUISE	MET	RC	NWT	1829	
5225	WELLS JOHN	MET	RC	RRS	1825		THORNE MARIE ANNE	MET	RC	RRS	1843	
5233	WELLS LOUIS				1844		PELLETIER MADELEINE	MET	RC	NWT	1853	
5157	WELLS NORBERT	MET	RC	RRS	1850		BOYER CECILE	MET	RC		1850	
5239	WELLS WILLIAM P				1842		HOPE ELIZABETH	MET	RC	RRS	1809	
5156	WELSH FRANCOIS	MET	RC	RRS	1797	5155	HOGUE MARY	MET	RC	RRS	1833	2505
5155	WELSH FRANCOIS XAV	EUR	RC	CAN	1801 66		SAUVE CHARLOTTE	MET	RC	NWT	1847	
5236	WENSELL ALEXANDER				1851		LAFERTE MARIE ANNE				1827	
5237	WENSELL ALEXANDER				1825	5236	MORIN ROSALIE				1838	
5241	WEWEBASS PIERRE				1820		THOMAS LOUISE				1830	
8055	WHELAN JOHN	MET	RC	RRS	1823		MCKENNY MARGARET	MET	RC	RRS	1803	1665
5165	WHITE JAMES	MET	RC	NWT	1800	5163	FREDERICK JULIE	IND		RRS	1803	109
5240	WHITE JAMES J	MET			1848		JENNY				1850 73	
5163	WHITE JOSEPH				1806		GENEVIEVE	MET		NWT	1824	
5242	WHITE PHILIP	EUR	P	IRE	1788		CUNNINGHAM CATHERINE	IND		RRS	1790	993
5255	WHITE THOMAS				1798		JANE	MET		RRS	1800	
5256	WHITEHEAD				1826		JANE	IND	P	RRS	1837	
5183	WHITEHEAD	MET		RRS	1778 38	5182	SPENCE CHLOE	IND	P	NWT	1807 39	
5185	WHITEWAY JAMES	EUR	O	SCT	1830		MONKMAN ANNE	MET	P	RRS	1842	
5184	WHITEWAY JAMES	MET	P	RRS	1815	5185	HAMELIN ELIZABETH	EUR	P	LC	1819	
5171	WHITEWAY JOSEPH				1845		JANE		P	NWT	1820	
5254	WHITFORD FRANCOIS	MET		RRS	1840		JEAN		P	RRS	1851	
5179	WHITFORD ALEXANDER				1837	5180	COOK ELIZABETH J	MET		RRS	1845	
5243	WHITFORD ANDREW	MET		RRS	1796 60	5180	GILL ELIZABETH				1840	
5244	WHITFORD CHARLES C				1835		ANDERSON ANNE	MET	RC	NWT	1805	78
5174	WHITFORD FRANCOIS				1810		GLADU MARIE				1843	
5245	WHITFORD FRANCOIS			NWT	1822		ANDERSON JANE	IND		NWT	1795 70	
5072	WHITFORD GEORGE	IND		NWT	1795 60		SANDERSON SARAH	MET	P	RRS	1825	
5166	WHITFORD GEORGE	MET	P	RRS	1800 72		JOKE CATHERINE				1800	
5167	WHITFORD GEORGE	MET	P	RRS	1827 72		SPENCE MARY				1802	
5169	WHITFORD JAMES	MET			1815	5167	ROBILLARD MARY	MET	RC	NWT	1824	
5170	WHITFORD JAMES	MET		RRS	1806 46	5169	FAGNANT MARGUERITE	MET			1826	
5175	WHITFORD JAMES	MET	RC	NWT	1836	5174	CHARLOTTE				1817	
5251	WHITFORD JOSEPH				1836	5180	KENNEDY ELLEN				1821	
5173	WHITFORD MAGNUS				1771		SARAH				1838 61	
5247	WHITFORD MAGNUS				1795		BEADS MARY	IND		NWT	1842	
5168	WHITFORD PETER	EUR	P	ENG	1776 46	5180	SARAH				1776 46	
5180	WHITFORD PETER	MET		NWT	1795		SPENCE CHRISTY	MET			1800	

TABLE 1: GENEALOGIES OF RED RIVER HOUSEHOLDS, 1818-1870

ID	MALE HEAD OF FAMILY	RACE	FAITH	BIRTH PLACE	DATES	DADS ID	FEMALE HEAD OF FAMILY	RACE	FAITH	BIRTH PLACE	DATES	DADS ID
5248	WHITFORD PHILIP				1840	5180	HENDERSON MARY	MET			1843	
5172	WHITFORD SAMUEL	MET	P	NWT	1822		SPENCE MARY				1826	2164
5249	WHITFORD SIMON				1828		DESJARLAIS MARIA				1830	
5250	WHITFORD WILLIAM				1830	5174	JOHNSTON LOUISE	EUR			1835	
5261	WILD GEORGE	EUR		ENG	1803		ELIZABETH	EUR		ORK	1817	
5187	WILKEY JEAN BTE				1822		AZURE ELISE	MET			1824	
5189	WILKEY JEAN BTE	MET			1833		LAFRAMBOISE MARIE	MET			1836	
5269	WILLIAMS JOSEPH				1808		CATHERINE				1810	
5260	WILLIAMS THOMAS	MET	P	RRS	1830	5269	PARISIEN ELISE	MET	P	RRS	1838	
5197	WILLIAMS WILLIAM				1800		FIDLER SARAH				1805	1547
5270	WILLIAMS WILLIAMS		P	NWT	1786 51		MARY				1790 55	
5259	WILLIAMSON JOHN	EUR	P	SCT	1833		NORQUAY ANNE	MET	P	RRS	1845	
5258	WILSON DANIEL	EUR		ORK	1824		BUBBIE MARIE C	MET		NWT	1832	
5257	WILSON JAMES	EUR		SCT	1841		SINCLAIR MARY	MET		RRS	1827	4388
5265	WINIFORD SAMUEL				1832		MARY				1837	
5266	WINTERS WESLEY I	IND		NWT	1845		PRITCHARD CATHERINE	EUR			1848	
5267	WISAWOK JEAN BTE	MET	P	RRS	1828		PELLETIER ANGELIQUE	MET		RRS	1830	
5194	WISHART JAMES	EUR		SCT	1830	5195	FLETT ELIZABETH	MET			1834	
5195	WISHART THOMAS	IND		RRS	1797		SPENCE BARBARA	MET		RRS	1800	
5271	WITIMASE EUSTACHE	EUR	P	ORK	1785 50		MARY	IND		NWT	1840	
5200	WORK ALEXANDER	EUR	P	ORK	1807		BRUYERE ISABELLA	MET			1786 46	
5198	WORK JACK		RC	NWT	1817 61		WELLS ANGELIQUE				1810	
5202	WORK JOSEPH				1840		DESMARAIS ANGELIQUE				1820	
5276	WRAY J FINLAY	EUR	P	SCT	1841		FRANCES				1843	
5274	WRIGHT ARCHIBALD	EUR	P	UC	1821		RAMSAY MARY	EUR	P	RRS	1848	
5212	YOUNG GEORGE	EUR		ENG	1822 70		HOLMES MARGE	EUR	P	UC	1821	
5213	YOUNG JAMES	MET	RC	RRS	1839		STEVENS ISABEL	MET	P	RRS	1826	
5278	ZASTRE ALEXIS	EUR			1778		ROSS ANGELIQUE	EUR	RC	RRS	1843	4246
5206	ZASTRE ANDRE	MET			1851	5210	CONTRE MARIE	EUR			1780	
5209	ZASTRE ANDRE	MET	RC	RRS	1836	5210	ROSS MATILDA	MET	RC	RRS	1852	4246
5207	ZASTRE GONZAQUE	EUR	RC	LC	1800	5210	PARISIEN MARIE	MET	RC	RRS	1842	3841
5210	ZASTRE GONZAQUE	MET	RC	RRS	1832	5210	PARISIEN ANGELIQUE	EUR	RC	NWT	1808	3840
5208	ZASTRE JEAN BTE	MET	RC	RRS	1840		RIEL MARGUERITE	MET	RC	RRS	1840	4155

Table 2:

Family Size, Personal Property, and Geographical Location of Land Owners, 1835

ID	MALE HEAD OF FAMILY	FAMILY	PERSONS	HORSES	CATTLE	FARM IMPLEMENTS	CARTS	FARMED ACREAGE	LOT NUMBER	PARISH
47	ALLARD	AMBRO	2	0	4	1	1	2	168	SFX
57	ALLARD	PIERRE	4	0	3	0	0	0	169	ST NORBERT
79	ANDERSON	JAMES	9	2	13	2	1	10	98	ST ANDREW
88	ANDERSON	JOHN	10	3	5	2	2	10	25	ST ANDREW
94	ANDERSON	THOMAS	7	1	3	1	0	3	28	ST ANDREW
105	ARCAN	JOSEPH	4	0	2	0	1	5	154	SFX
168	BALLENDINE	GEORGE	.	.	.	.	.	.	82	ST ANDREW
171	BALLENDINE	JOHN	.	.	.	.	.	.	83	ST ANDREW
177	BALLENDINE	WILLIAM	.	.	.	.	.	.	84	ST ANDREW
177	BALLENDINE	WILLIAM	.	.	.	.	.	.	85	ST ANDREW
120	BEAUCHAMP	CHARLES	1	1	2	0	1	6	51	ST VITAL
190	BEAUCHAMP	PIERRE	4	4	4	1	3	8	119	ST BONIFACE
270	BELGARDE	ALEXIS	9	2	7	1	2	4	143	ST NORBERT
272	BELGARDE	CHARLES	3	0	0	1	0	3	32	ST VITAL
275	BELGARDE	JEAN	.	1	4	0	0	1	96	ST NORBERT
415	BENNEAU	ANDRE	4	5	3	0	3	6	172	SFX
417	BENNEAU	FRANCOIS	7	5	5	0	2	4	173	SFX
182	BENNERMAN	ALEXANDER	5	0	16	2	2	5	21	KILDONAN
189	BENNERMAN	DONALD	4	0	16	3	0	5	20	KILDONAN
204	BENNERMAN	WILLIAM	2	0	16	.	2	5	78	KILDONAN
310	BEREAU	GILBERT	.	.	4	.	.	.	164	ST NORBERT
507	BERLAND	ALEXANDER	6	4	18	2	5	10	192	SFX
297	BERRARD	LOUIS	.	.	.	.	.	.	31	ST BONIFACE
373	BIRD	GEORGE	7	1	9	2	1	3	24	ST PAUL
373	BIRD	GEORGE	7	1	9	2	1	3	25	ST PAUL
379	BIRD	JAMES	7	2	37	4	3	30	100	ST PAUL
379	BIRD	JAMES	7	2	37	4	3	30	101	ST PAUL
379	BIRD	JAMES	7	2	37	4	3	30	102	ST PAUL
379	BIRD	JAMES	7	2	37	4	3	30	103	ST PAUL
379	BIRD	JAMES	7	2	37	4	3	30	105	ST PAUL
379	BIRD	JAMES	7	2	37	4	3	30	106	ST PAUL
379	BIRD	JAMES	7	2	37	4	3	30	107	ST PAUL
379	BIRD	JAMES	7	2	37	4	3	30	108	ST PAUL
379	BIRD	JAMES	7	2	37	4	3	30	109	ST PAUL
387	BIRD	JOSEPH	7	3	11	1	1	10	110	ST PAUL
399	BIRD	WILLIAM	7	2	10	2	2	2	26	ST PAUL
329	BIRSTON	ALEXANDER	4	0	14	1	0	4	16	ST ANDREW
330	BIRSTON	ALEXANDER	4	1	7	1	0	0	89	ST ANDREW
336	BIRSTON	WILLIAM	7	1	4	2	0	7	87	ST ANDREW
406	BOISVERT	JEAN BAPTE	4	.	11	1	1	0	96	ST BONIFACE
408	BOISVERT	LOUIS	3	0	5	0	6	2	221	SFX
467	BOURKE	JEAN BAPTE	7	6	13	2	6	4	35	ST JAMES
467	BOURKE	JEAN BAPTE	7	6	13	2	1	4	36	ST JAMES
2	BOYER	BAPTE	6	1	9	0	1	10	185	ST NORBERT
489	BRASCONNIER	JEAN BAPTE	8	.	10	2	2	6	49	ST JAMES
492	BREMNER	ALEXANDER	10	0	11	0	0	10	7	ST JAMES
492	BREMNER	ALEXANDER	10	1	11	0	0	10	8	ST JAMES
493	BREMNER	JOSEPH	3	.	12	2	1	7	68	KILDONAN
585	BREYERE	BAPTE	5	0	1	.	.	10	203	SFX
524	BRIBANT	AUGUSTUS	5	0	1	0	0	2	33	ST BONIFACE
558	BRUCE	JAMES	6	1	14	3	2	10	16	KILDONAN

TABLE 2: FAMILY SIZE, PERSONAL PROPERTY, AND
GEOGRAPHICAL LOCATION OF LANDOWNERS, 1835

ID	MALE HEAD OF FAMILY	FAMILY	PERSONS	HORSES	CATTLE	FARM IMPLEMENTS	CARTS	FARMED ACREAGE	LOT NUMBER	PARISH
554	BRUCE	WILLIAM	6	5	17	2	6	20	17	KILDONAN
578	BRUNEAU	FRANCOIS	4	1	6	2	1	0	68	ST BONIFACE
578	BRUNEAU	FRANCOIS	4	1	6	2	1	0	69	ST BONIFACE
597	BUNN	THOMAS	4	0	10	1	1	4	12	ST PAUL
611	BUXTON	HENRY	·	·	·	·	·	·	17	ST PAUL
624	CALDER	HARATIO	7	1	12	2	2	3	34	ST ANDREW
645	CAMERON	HUGH	5	1	14	2	2	10	2	KILDONAN
677	CAPLETTE	JOSEPH	23	2	11	2	1	6	4	ST CHARLES
677	CAPLETTE	JOSEPH	23	2	11	2	1	6	5	ST CHARLES
682	CARDINALLE	JEAN BAPTE	5	·	3	1	1	5	183	ST NORBERT
702	CARRIER	ALEXIS	·	·	·	·	·	·	184	ST NORBERT
	CARRON	EUSTACH	8	3	13	2	2	11	174	ST NORBERT
739	CHAMPAIGNE	EMANUEL	7	·	5	0	0	0	15	ST BONIFACE
997	CIRE	LOUIS	9	2	·	2	2	·	285	ST ANDREW
917	COCKRAN	WILLIAM	12	2	7	3	0	3	60	ST ANDREW
917	COCKRAN	WILLIAM	8	1	10	2	1	14	61	ST ANDREW
921	COLLIN	JEAN BAPTE	3	·	8	0	·	10	128	ST NORBERT
940	COOK	JOSEPH	7	3	9	3	0	6	41	ST PAUL
947	COOK	WILLIAM H	7	2	6	2	3	1	44	ST PAUL
853	CORRIGAL	JAMES	4	2	6	2	1	12	19	ST ANDREW
961	CORRIGAL	JAMES	7	0	16	0	0	7	41	ST ANDREW
967	COURCHENE	FRANCOIS	7	6	7	1	6	10	39	ST VITAL
977	CREMER	CHARLES	5	7	11	3	4	24	94	ST ANDREW
1004	DAHAL	PETER	6	0	40	1	0	8	6	ST PAUL
1009	DAIGNEAU	RICHARD	13	2	16	2	0	9	6	ST BONIFACE
1018	DANIEL	PIERRE	2	1	9	2	2	5	113	ST BONIFACE
1032	DAUPHINE	MAX	8	5	4	1	7	3	25	ST BONIFACE
1035	DAUPHINE	MICHEL	9	0	5	2	2	10	98	ST BONIFACE
1040	DAVIES	JEAN BAPTE	9	·	10	1	1	8	41	ST BONIFACE
1262	DEJARDIN	ANTOINE	4	1	14	2	·	3	52	ST VITAL
1102	DELORME	JOSEPH	7	3	·	1	0	4	129	ST NORBERT
1117	DELORME	URBIN	1	0	6	1	2	·	162	SFX
	DELORME	WIDOW	4	1	·	2	7	8	37	ST VITAL
1236	DEMARAIS	CHARLES	7	0	6	2	2	9	40	ST ANDREW
1238	DEMARIS	FRANCOIS	2	·	14	0	·	1	148	ST NORBERT
1241	DEMARIS	JOSEPH	2	2	0	3	4	9	82	ST NORBERT
1270	DESJARLAIS	ANTOINE	2	1	·	·	·	·	8	ST BONIFACE
1302	DONALD	WILLIAM	8	0	6	2	1	6	95	ST ANDREW
1323	DUBOIS	JEAN BAPTE	3	0	14	0	0	6	106	ST BONIFACE
1362	DUCHARME	PIERRE	3	5	0	2	3	17	184	ST BONIFACE
1373	DUGANNE	JOSEPH	6	0	5	2	1	17	53	ST NORBERT
1387	DUMAIS	MICHEL	6	·	·	2	1	16	11	ST VITAL
1403	DUMOND	SAKASTI	5	6	2	2	1	18	40	ST VITAL
1406	DUNORD	ANTOINE	5	4	6	0	1	19	25	ST BONIFACE
1406	DUNORD	ANTOINE	4	4	11	0	1	16	26	ST NORBERT
1409	DUPUIS	BAPTE	6	1	5	0	1	20	18	ST BONIFACE
1409	DUPUIS	BAPTE	6	1	5	0	1	1	19	ST BONIFACE
1409	DUPUIS	BAPTE	6	2	0	1	2	1	20	ST BONIFACE
2115	EMLYN	JOSEPH	5	2	0	1	1	4	85	ST NORBERT
2115	EMLYN	JOSEPH	5	2	0	0	1	1	93	ST NORBERT
1430	EMLYN	LOUIS	4	2	5	2	2	4	24	ST VITAL
2113	EMLYN	SOLOMON	4	3	1	0	1	1	55	ST VITAL

TABLE 2: FAMILY SIZE, PERSONAL PROPERTY, AND
GEOGRAPHICAL LOCATION OF LANDOWNERS, 1835

ID	MALE HEAD OF FAMILY	PERSONS	HORSES	CATTLE	FARM IMPLEMENTS	CARTS	FARMED ACREAGE	LOT NUMBER	PARISH
1487	FALCON PIERRE	11	2	15	0	2	12	190	SFX
1520	FAVEL THOMAS	8	1	3	0	1	2	29	ST ANDREW
1469	FAYGNAND ANTOINE	5	0	3	0	0	6	204	SFX
1458	FAYGNANT JOSEPH	5	0	3	0	0	6	38	SFX
1531	FIDLER ALBAN	6	3	12	2	1	6	59	ST JAMES
1532	FIDLER ANDREW	5	0	6	1	1	8	60	ST JAMES
1535	FIDLER CHARLES	8	2	10	1	1	8	58	ST JAMES
1540	FIDLER CLEMENT	3	0	6	0	1	5	52	ST JAMES
1540	FIDLER CLEMENT	3	0	5	0	1	5	53	ST JAMES
1541	FIDLER GEORGE	9	1	3	1	2	6	83	SFX
1549	FIDLER THOMAS	5	0	3	2	1	3	93	ST CLEMENT
	FIRTH THOMAS	8	0	3	2	1	0	86	ST ANDREW
1574	FLAMMANT JOSEPH	8	0	3	0	0	0	159	SFX
1574	FLAMMANT JOSEPH	3	0	3	0	0	0	160	SFX
2453	FLETT JAMES	11	2	21	3	3	0	26	ST JAMES
1596	FLETT JOHN	6	1	5	3	0	15	22	KILDONAN
1604	FLETT WILLIAM	6	0	5	2	0	3	75	ST ANDREW
1604	FLETT WILLIAM	6	2	11	2	2	3	76	ST ANDREW
1623	FOLDS JOHN	7	0	11	2	1	12	61	ST JAMES
1626	FOLDS SAMUEL	7	1	17	1	1	7	62	ST JAMES
1489	FOLSTER JAMES	2	0	22	2	1	15	6	ST PAUL
1635	FORBES JOHN	3	0	.	2	.	8	53	ST PAUL
1638	FORBISTER JOHN	6	2	20	2	3	.	50	ST ANDREW
1644	FOUMIR FRANCOIS	6	2	10	2	3	10	169	SFX
1654	FRASER JAMES	9	1	5	1	1	12	15	KILDONAN
1886	GADDY WILLIAM	2	2	5	1	1	1	45	ST PAUL
1876	GAGNON FRANCOIS	4	.	6	0	.	9	133	ST NORBERT
1877	GAGNON JOSEPH	2	1	14	2	2	0	2	ST CHARLES
1880	GAGNON JOSEPH	2	1	24	0	4	20	2	ST CHARLES
	GARDIPUIS JEAN BAPTE	10	0	24	6	2	15	193	SFX
1908	GARDIPUIS LOUIS	9	2	17	6	2	20	181	SFX
1908	GARRIOCH WILLIAM	9	2	10	3	1	20	42	ST PAUL
	GARRIOCH WILLIAM	6	3	6	3	1	14	43	ST PAUL
1954	GIBSON HUGH	6	2	6	2	4	10	9	ST ANDREW
1956	GIBSON HUGH	9	5	15	0	4	14	20	ST ANDREW
1969	GLADU CHARLES	9	5	.	.	3	14	141	SFX
1969	GLADU CHARLES	11	1	2	0	.	15	142	SFX
1987	GONVILLE ANTOINE	5	1	2	0	0	.	152	SFX
2001	GOSELIN MICHEL	8	6	24	3	10	2	91	ST NORBERT
2028	GRANT BAPTE	8	5	11	3	4	20	158	ST NORBERT
2030	GRANT CUTHBERT	6	4	16	3	3	12	183	SFX
2054	GRANT LOUIS	6	2	15	1	1	6	48	ST PAUL
2076	GUIBOCHE JOHN	6	1	10	2	1	8	62	KILDONAN
2087	GUNN THOMAS	10	0	8	2	0	6	50	ST PAUL
2100	HALCRO JAMES	8	1	11	0	1	10	50	ST JAMES
2164	HALLETT PETER	7	0	3	0	0	8	16	ST ANDREW
2174	HENDERSON SAMUEL	10	1	4	1	1	4	4	ST PAUL
2152	HENDERSON HENRY	7	1	5	2	3	2	66	ST BONIFACE
2221	HICKENBERGER ANTOINE	10	1	28	4	1	6	191	SFX
2228	HOOLE CHARLES	6	.	5	.	3	3	124	ST NORBERT
2243	HOURIE JOHN	8	1	.	.	1	7	58	ST PAUL
2245	HOURIE JOHN	3	0	.	.	.	.	60	ST PAUL

TABLE 2: FAMILY SIZE, PERSONAL PROPERTY, AND
GEOGRAPHICAL LOCATION OF LANDOWNERS, 1835

ID	MALE HEAD OF FAMILY	FAMILY	PERSONS	HORSES	CATTLE	FARM IMPLEMENTS	CARTS	FARMED ACREAGE	LOT NUMBER	PARISH
1802	HOWSE	HENRY	4	0	5	2	0	3	239	ST ANDREW
2408	INKSTER	GEORGE	1	1	14	.	1	4	34	ST VITAL
2403	INKSTER	JAMES	3	1	7	2	0	7	5	KILDONAN
2390	IRVINE	GEORGE	3	.	.	0	0	7	64	ST JAMES
2372	ISBISTER	THOMAS	2	0	7	2	2	7	12	ST ANDREW
125	ISHAM	THOMAS	2	0	6	3	2	3	55	ST VITAL
2366	JACQUE	FRANCOIS	7	0	6	3	2	3	57	ST VITAL
2366	JACQUE	FRANCOIS	7	2	4	2	1	2	85	ST NORBERT
2351	JEANVENNE	PIERRE	6	.	12	2	0	8	58	ST ANDREW
2327	JOHNSTONE	GEORGE	4	.	3	0	2	3	43	ST ANDREW
2318	JOYAL	TOUSS	5	.	15	0	2	7	63	KILDONAN
2312	KAUFFMAN	WERIC	5	0	15	3	.	.	64	KILDONAN
2312	KAUFFMAN	WERIC	2	0	4	.	0	3	24	KILDONAN
2298	KIPPLING	GEORGE	2	.	15	.	0	.	205	ST CLEMENT
2293	KIPPLING	JOHN	11	1	4	1	0	11	56	ST NORBERT
2277	KNIGHT	JAMES	3	1	1	0	0	3	171	ST PAUL
2870	LADOUX	ESOP	4	1	2	0	.	3	162	SFX
2872	LADOUX	JOSEPH	9	1	2	.	.	.	173	SFX
2504	LAFERTE	LOUIS	8	.	34	2	9	18	112	ST NORBERT
2527	LAFOURNAISE	JOSEPH	8	7	.	.	.	.	14	ST BONIFACE
2573	LAMBERT	ANTOINE	8	1	3	1	1	4	15	ST VITAL
2573	LAMBERT	ANTOINE	13	1	3	1	1	4	32	ST VITAL
2582	LAMBERT	MICHEL	3	0	2	0	0	2	33	ST ANDREW
2582	LAMBERT	MICHEL	6	1	6	2	1	8	135	ST ANDREW
2586	LAMIRANDE	LOUIS	3	1	3	0	0	3	46	ST NORBERT
2592	LANDRIE	JOSEPH	3	0	1	2	1	2	166	ST VITAL
2593	LANDRIE	LOUIS	6	1	3	0	1	8	166	SFX
2597	LANDRIE	LOUIS	3	1	4	1	0	3	194	SFX
2608	LANGER	FRANCOIS	6	1	1	1	2	2	28	ST NORBERT
2654	LARIVIER	LOUIS	3	1	3	2	0	15	12	ST BONIFACE
2659	LAROCQUE	ANDRE	2	1	1	0	2	0	13	ST BONIFACE
2659	LAROCQUE	ANDRE	2	1	1	0	0	0	2	ST BONIFACE
2660	LAROCQUE	ANTOINE	5	.	2	1	1	3	16	ST BONIFACE
2664	LAROCQUE	BAPTE	2	3	8	2	2	6	27	ST BONIFACE
2669	LAROCQUE	CHARLES	9	1	3	2	1	3	24	ST VITAL
2676	LAROCQUE	JEAN BAPTE	7	1	6	1	0	11	177	ST BONIFACE
2792	LAROCQUE	OLIVIER	5	0	8	2	1	0	160	SFX
2687	LAROCQUE	PIERRE	7	0	6	2	0	5	159	ST NORBERT
2795	LAROCQUE	PIERRE	3	0	8	1	1	0	88	ST NORBERT
2834	LAVERDERE	ALEXIS	6	3	4	0	0	2	89	ST NORBERT
2834	LAVERDERE	ALEXIS	6	3	4	0	1	7	54	ST NORBERT
13290	LEBERGE	MICHEL	7	0	7	2	2	1	138	ST VITAL
2857	LECLAIR	JOSEPH	4	0	.	.	.	8	145	ST NORBERT
2906	LEGROS	ANTOINE	7	0	5	1	3	8	8	ST NORBERT
2904	LEITH	WILLIAM	6	0	15	3	1	10	76	ST ANDREW
2537	LEJEMONIER	JEAN BAPTE	5	1	21	3	4	9	263	ST BONIFACE
2949	LEWES	JAMES	3	0	4	1	1	4	14	ST ANDREW
2959	LILLIE	DANIEL	4	.	.	.	.	.	55	ST PAUL
2967	LINKLATER	ANDREW	3	0	7	3	.	2	35	ST ANDREW
2973	LIVINGSTONE	DONALD	7	1	21	2	2	14	3	KILDONAN
2975	LIVINGSTONE	JAMES	10	4	21	2	2	10	36	ST PAUL
2977	LIVINGSTONE	NEIL	2	1	11	2	1	5		KILDONAN

TABLE 2: FAMILY SIZE, PERSONAL PROPERTY, AND
GEOGRAPHICAL LOCATION OF LANDOWNERS, 1835

ID	MALE HEAD OF FAMILY		PERSONS	HORSES	CATTLE	FARM IMPLEMENTS	CARTS	FARMED ACREAGE	LOT NUMBER	PARISH
2977	LIVINGSTONE	NEIL	2	1	11	2	1	5	37	KILDONAN
3003	LUCIER	TOUSSANT	5	0	3	0	0	3	77	ST PAUL
3008	LYONS	JOHN	8	2	8	1	1	4	8	ST CLEMENT
3008	LYONS	JOHN	8	4	8	1	0	8	9	ST CLEMENT
3032	MARCHAND	BENJ	8	4	12	2	3	8	87	ST CHARLES
3040	MARION	FRANCOIS	4	0	1	0	1	9	175	ST NORBERT
2723	MARSELLAIS	BAPTE	4	0				1	1	ST VITAL
3057	MARTELLE	JEAN BAPTE	2	2	3	0	0	0	151	ST NORBERT
3058	MARTELLE	JEAN BAPTE	7	0	12	2	2	7	9	ST BONIFACE
3074	MARTINEAU	AMBROISE	8	0	11	3	1	0	65	ST PAUL
3076	MATHESON	ALEXANDER	6	3	16	2	2	15	34	KILDONAN
3077	MATHESON	ALEXANDER	4	0	13	2	2	6	60	KILDONAN
3084	MATHESON	ANGUS	11	0	21	3	3	15	9	KILDONAN
3279	MCBEATH	GEORGE	6	1	23	3	1	16	32	KILDONAN
3279	MCBEATH	GEORGE	6	1	23	3	1	16	33	KILDONAN
3272	MCBEATH	JOHN	11	0	23	3	2	16	31	KILDONAN
3310	MCDONALD	ANGUS	3	1	17	2	1	12	49	ST VITAL
3324	MCDONALD	DONALD	8	0	6	2	2	0	78	ST ANDREW
3333	MCDONALD	KENNITH	7	0	12	2	1	12	36	ST ANDREW
3357	MCGILLES	ANGUS	4	24	29	4	0	10	184	SFX
3377	MCKAY	ALEXIS	2		5	2	0	0	144	SFX
3393	MCKAY	IGNACE	10		3	0	0	4	81	SFX
3413	MCKAY	ROBERT	4	1	24	3	2	15	19	KILDONAN
3574	MCKAY	WILLIAM	4	2	20	3	2	15	18	KILDONAN
3432	MCLEAN	ALEXANDER	4	0	4	0	2	0	1	KILDONAN
3439	MCLEAN	JOHN	5	0	4	1	0	3	161	ST ANDREW
3468	MCLEOD	JOHN	5	0	5	0	0	1	102	ST CLEMENT
3464	MCNAB	THOMAS	7	0	4	1	0	2	100	ST CLEMENT
3465	MCNAB	THOMAS			6				65	ST BONIFACE
3135	MOAR	JOHN	10	2	20	3	1	17	55	ST PAUL
3149	MONKMAN	JAMES	7	3	22	4	0	17	7	ST PAUL
3149	MONKMAN	JAMES	7	1	22	2	2	17	8	ST PAUL
3161	MONTREL	JOSEPH	7	1	4	0	1	1	86	ST NORBERT
3160	MONTREL	LOUIS	4	0	4	2	1	2	80	ST NORBERT
3180	MORIN	ANTOINE	6	2	6	0	3	9	97	ST BONIFACE
3187	MORIN	ETIENNE	4	2	14	2	2	9	29	ST BONIFACE
3188	MORIN	FRANCOIS	5	2	7	2	1	5	161	ST NORBERT
3226	MORWICH	JAMES	9	2	7	2	1	8	74	ST ANDREW
3205	MOUSETTE	ARSON	6	0	7	2	2	4	123	ST NORBERT
3227	MOWAT	ADAM	3	0	6	2	0	4	64	ST PAUL
3248	MUNRO	GEORGE	6	0	14	2	2	6	67	KILDONAN
3255	MURRAY	DONALD	1	1	5	0	0	6	28	KILDONAN
3254	MURRAY	JAMES	2	0	20	2	2	12	24	KILDONAN
3726	NOLIN	JOSEPH	4	0	4	0	1	1	83	ST NORBERT
3746	NORMIN	BAPTE	3	0					115	ST NORBERT
3745	NORMIN	MICHEL	3	1	25	2	2	8	114	ST NORBERT
3752	NORQUAY	JOHN							90	ST ANDREW
3761	ORMAN	JAMES	5	1	15	3	1	6	57	ST ANDREW
3777	PAGE	JOSEPH	8	1	11	2	1	17	22	ST BONIFACE
3778	PAGE	JOSEPH	5	1	9	1	2	6	201	SFX
3804	PARENTEAU	JOSEPH	5	1	11	2	0	4	114	ST BONIFACE
3808	PARENTEAU	NORBERT	6	3	1	0	1	2	145	ST NORBERT

TABLE 2: FAMILY SIZE, PERSONAL PROPERTY, AND
GEOGRAPHICAL LOCATION OF LANDOWNERS, 1835

ID	MALE HEAD OF FAMILY	FAMILY	PERSONS	HORSES	CATTLE	FARM IMPLEMENTS	CARTS	FARMED ACREAGE	LOT NUMBER	PARISH
3811	PARENTEAU	PIERRE	7	2	13	2	2	15	8	ST VITAL
3811	PARENTEAU	PIERRE	7	2	13	2	2	15	9	ST VITAL
3827	PARISIEN	BAPTE	6	5	5	2	4	3	191	ST NORBERT
3840	PARISIEN	JEAN BAPTE	11	1	7	0	1	5	41	ST VITAL
3854	PARISIEN	LAVENTURE	5	1	7	0	0	0	60	ST NORBERT
3862	PATNAUDE	MICHEL	6	0	4	0	1	8	139	SFX
3584	PAUL	BAPTE	7	1	8	0	0	10	178	SFX
3918	PELTIER	CHARLES	9	2	11	2	0	6	215	SFX
3926	PHILP	MADAME	5	.	5	.	.	.	1	ST BONIFACE
3930	PICHE	JOSEPH	3	3	19	.	3	12	179	SFX
3935	PICHE	LOUIS	4	0	2	0	0	5	53	SFX
13286	PILLON	ANTOINE	7	0	7	2	0	5	130	ST NORBERT
3964	PIVIN	THOMAS	2	.	.	.	.	.	125	ST NORBERT
3950	PLOOFE	ANTOINE	5	0	8	.	.	.	104	ST NORBERT
	POLSON	ALEXANDER	9	2	25	3	4	14	11	KILDONAN
	PORTRAS	HENRIE	4	4	8	2	3	10	200	SFX
	PORTRAS	MARGARET	6	7	12	.	3	10	199	SFX
3998	PRITCHARD	JOHN	11	2	27	3	3	20	53	KILDONAN
3998	PRITCHARD	JOHN	11	2	27	3	3	20	54	KILDONAN
3998	PRITCHARD	JOHN	11	2	27	3	3	20	55	KILDONAN
3998	PRITCHARD	JOHN	11	1	27	3	3	20	56	KILDONAN
4035	PRUDEN	WILLIAM	6	.	10	3	2	8	67	ST ANDREW
4035	PRUDEN	WILLIAM	6	1	10	3	2	8	68	ST ANDREW
4159	RANVILLE	FRANCOIS	9	0	2	0	0	9	94	ST NORBERT
4170	RICHARD	MICHEL	9	1	9	2	0	.	163	SFX
4184	RICHOTTE	JOSEPH	8	0	3	0	2	15	36	ST VITAL
4202	ROBERTSON	GEORGE	7	0	0	0	1	1	169	ST ANDREW
4209	ROBILLARD	JEAN BAPTE	6	0	1	0	0	0	56	ST BONIFACE
4215	ROCHELEAU	GUILLAME	4	0	4	0	0	4	131	ST NORBERT
2785	ROCQUE	JOSEPH	.	.	.	.	.	.	157	ST NORBERT
4223	ROSE	ALEXANDER	6	2	21	3	2	9	13	KILDONAN
4222	ROSIGNALLE	ANDRE	7	1	2	0	1	4	12	ST VITAL
4249	ROSS	GEORGE	3	0	8	2	0	2	79	ST ANDREW
4246	ROSS	HUGH	6	1	10	2	3	25	148	SFX
4305	SANDERS	WILLIAM	5	0	7	1	0	5	97	ST ANDREW
4733	SANDISON	GEORGE	7	2	3	3	0	7	45	ST ANDREW
4733	SANDISON	GEORGE	7	2	3	3	0	7	46	ST ANDREW
4322	SANDISON	ROBERT	6	0	16	4	0	27	3	KILDONAN
4295	SAUVE	JEAN BAPTE	10	2	12	2	2	9	35	ST BONIFACE
4288	SAVOYARD	JOSEPH	3	0	13	1	0	0	56	ST VITAL
4285	SAVOYARD	PIERRE	5	1	5	1	0	2	167	ST NORBERT
4284	SAVOYARD	TOUSSANT	4	0	8	0	0	12	165	ST NORBERT
4875	SAYER	PIERRE	5	0	5	0	1	7	82	SFX
4348	SCARTH	WIDOW	.	.	4	.	.	.	46	ST PAUL
2918	SETTEE	GEORGE	5	0	2	1	0	0	229	ST ANDREW
4358	SETTEE	ANDREW	10	7	37	5	3	20	233	ST ANDREW
4365	SHAW	WILLIAM	.	.	.	.	.	.	60	ST VITAL
4365	SHAW	WILLIAM	.	.	.	.	.	.	61	ST VITAL
4367	SHORT	JAMES	3	0	4	0	0	0	149	SFX
4379	SINCLAIR	DONALD	5	2	15	2	2	10	37	ST ANDREW
4384	SINCLAIR	THOMAS	5	2	14	3	1	7	59	ST ANDREW
4385	SINCLAIR	WILLIAM	1	0	11	2	0	9	54	ST PAUL

TABLE 2: FAMILY SIZE, PERSONAL PROPERTY, AND GEOGRAPHICAL LOCATION OF LANDOWNERS, 1835

ID	MALE HEAD OF FAMILY		PERSONS	HORSES	CATTLE	FARM IMPLEMENTS	CARTS	FARMED ACREAGE	LOT NUMBER	PARISH
4409	SMITH	JOHN JAMES	9	0	10	2	0	12	102	ST ANDREW
4411	SMITH	LOUIS	5	1	6	2	0	2	118	ST BONIFACE
4417	SMITH	WILLIAM ROB	10	3	8	0	2	3	15	ST PAUL
	SPENCE	ANDREW	3	4	2	0	3	2	13	ST ANDREW
4424	SPENCE	ANDREW	6	0	11	3	2	11	13	ST ANDREW
4431	SPENCE	GEORGE	7	3	8	3	2	8	5	ST CLEMENT
4431	SPENCE	GEORGE	7	3	8	4	2	8	6	ST CLEMENT
4441	SPENCE	JAMES	14	4	10	4	3	5	51	ST JAMES
4450	SPENCE	JOHN	3	2	6	1	3	0	4	ST CLEMENT
4452	SPENCE	JOHN	2	3	6	0	2	0	23	ST ANDREW
4463	SPENCE	WILLIAM	7	0	2	0	0	0	41	ST ANDREW
4581	ST CIRE	JEAN BAPTE	3	0	8	2	1	3	134	ST NORBERT
	ST DENNIS	FRANCOIS	4	0	4	0	1	4	165	SFX
4585	ST DENNIS	PAULETTE	7	1	0	0	1	4	207	SFX
4605	ST GERMAIN	PIERRE	6	0	7	2	2	2	47	ST VITAL
4609	ST LUC	ARPENLIGNIER	7	0	3	2	1	2	80	ST BONIFACE
4476	STEVENS	RICHARD	8	1	16	2	0	8	100	ST ANDREW
4518	SUTHERLAND	JAMES	4	1	6	0	0	1	20	ST PAUL
4518	SUTHERLAND	JAMES	4	1	6	0	0	1	21	ST PAUL
4518	SUTHERLAND	JAMES	4	1	6	0	0	1	22	ST PAUL
4518	SUTHERLAND	JAMES	13	5	18	2	3	25	23	ST PAUL
4520	SUTHERLAND	JOHN	4	1	15	2	2	8	39	ST ANDREW
	SUTHERLAND	WILLIAM	2	0	10	2	1	20	27	KILDONAN
4554	SWAIN	JAMES	6	0	2	0		1	6	KILDONAN
4565	SWAIN	JAMES	2	0					163	ST ANDREW
4568	SWAIN	JAMES	2	0					9	ST JAMES
4568	SWAIN	JOHN	5	0	10	1	1	3	118	ST CHARLES
4577	TAIT	WILLIAM	9	1	13	3	1	10	56	ST ANDREW
4625	TAIT	JAMES	5	2	24	2	1	15	14	KILDONAN
4639	TAYLOR	WILLIAM	9	3	11	3	1	22	27	ST PAUL
4646	TAYLOR	WILLIAM	7	2	22	3	1	16	28	ST PAUL
4687	THOMAS	WILLIAM	3	0	7	1	1	5	9	ST PAUL
4694	THYFAULT	BASIL	3	1	8	0	1	5	116	ST BONIFACE
4695	THYFAULT	LOUIS	3	0	9	2		6	38	ST VITAL
4701	TOURON	JOSEPH	3	3	7	2	2	6	62	ST BONIFACE
4709	TROTTIER	ADOTTE	10	0	14	2	2	2	164	ST BONIFACE
4711	TROTTIER	ANDRE	6	0	8	2		9	96	SFX
4719	TRUTHWAITE	JACOB	3	0	5	2	1	6	63	ST ANDREW
4724	TURCOTTE	BAPTE	2	0	9	1	1	5	95	ST BONIFACE
5045	VALLENNEUVE	MICHEL	8	0	5	2	1	6	166	ST BONIFACE
5034	VANDALE	ANTOINE	3	0	6	2	2	6	45	ST NORBERT
5050	VANDALE	ANTOINE	6	0	0	2	0	4	280	ST VITAL
5035	VANDALE	JOSEPH	6	1		0	0	2	136	ST ANDREW
5104	VERSAILLES	BAPTE	4	0	2	2	0	1	140	ST NORBERT
5109	VERSAILLES	LOUIS	5	1	6	0			180	ST NORBERT
5137	VIVIER	ALEXANDER	4	1	2	2	1	6	53	SFX
5078	VIVIER	FRANCOIS	6	0	6	1		3	288	ST VITAL
5174	VOUDRIE	TOUSSANT	5	0	7	2	2	10	146	ST ANDREW
5180	WHITFORD	FRANCOIS	7	2	4	1	2	2	30	SFX
5185	WHITFORD	PETER	6	0		1			13	ST ANDREW
	WHITWAY	JAMES	6	5	24	3	2	18		ST ANDREW
5186	WILKIE	JEAN BAPTE	7	2	6	1	2	6	13	ST VITAL

TABLE 2: FAMILY SIZE, PERSONAL PROPERTY, AND
GEOGRAPHICAL LOCATION OF LANDOWNERS, 1835

ID	MALE HEAD OF FAMILY		PERSONS	HORSES	CATTLE	FARM IMPLEMENTS	CARTS	FARMED ACREAGE	LOT NUMBER	PARISH
5049	WILLETTE	JOSEPH	6	1	6	2	2	10	139	ST NORBERT
5236	WINTZEL	ALEXANDER	.	0	.	1	1	.	30	ST BONIFACE
5195	WISHART	THOMAS	7	.	7	1	1	11	29	ST JAMES
5210	ZASTRE	GONSACQUE	6	1	13	2	3	11	48	ST VITAL

Table 3:

Contract Employees of the HBC

ID	NAME OF EMPLOYEE		JOB AT FIRST CONTRACT	DATE	JOB AT RETIREMENT	DATE
13	ABELL	EDMUND	ENGINEER	1865		1868
27	ADAMS	JEAN BAPTIST	INTERPRETER	1825	INTERPRETER	1828
·	ADIN	JOSEPH	LABOURER	1845	BOWSMAN	1853
·	ADIN	JOSEPH	BOWSMAN	1850		1853
·	AIDEESON	JOSEPH	MILLER	1850		1853
·	ALEXANDER	JOHN	MIDDLEMAN	1867	MIDDLEMAN	1869
72	AMOS	SERAPHIM	MIDDLEMAN	1855		1858
74	ANDERSON	CALEB	MIDDLEMAN	1854		1855
90	ANDERSON	DAVID	LABOURER	1846	LABOURER	1849
90	ANDERSON	PETER	LABOURER	1845	BOWSMAN	1852
94	ANDERSON	PETER	BOWSMAN	1852	INTERPRETER	1862
95	ANDERSON	THOMAS	LABOURER	1832	LABOURER	1834
·	ANDERSON	THOMAS	LABOURER	1865		1870
·	ANDERSON	WILLIAM	MIDDLEMAN	1855		1858
·	ANNAL	JAMES	LABOURER	1878		1881
101	ARCAN	ALEXANDER	MIDDLEMAN	1857		1860
103	ARCAN	BAPTISTE	MIDDLEMAN	1864		1867
102	ARCAN	FRANCOIS	MIDDLEMAN	1864		1867
105	ARCAN	JOSEPH	LABOURER	1826	LABOURER	1831
104	ARCAN	JOSEPH	MIDDLEMAN	1855		1859
·	ASHBURNE	PIERRE	MIDDLEMAN	1849	MIDDLEMAN	1851
·	ASSINIBOINE	LOUIS	MIDDLEMAN	1844	MIDDLEMAN	1846
·	ATKINSON	GEORGE	STEERSMAN	1851		1851
·	ATKINSON	GEORGE	STEERSMAN	1851		1854
142	ATKINSON	HENRY	MIDDLEMAN	1841		1852
·	ATKINSON	RICHARD	LABOURER	1832	BOWSMAN	1838
·	ATKINSON	WILLIAM	LABOURER	1852	MIDDLEMAN	1855
143	AUBICHON	PIERRE	MIDDLEMAN	1852		1854
6001	BADGER	JEAN BAPTIST	LABOURER	1833	LABOURER	1836
160	BADGER	WILLIAM	MIDDLEMAN	1857		1860
·	BAILLIE	WILLIAM	TINSMITH	1851	TINSMITH	1862
173	BALLENDINE	JAMES	BOWSMAN	1827	STEERSMAN	1831
175	BALLENDINE	JOHN	BOATBUILDER	1856		1859
175	BALLENDINE	JOHN	BOATBUILDER	1866		1868
177	BALLENDINE	JOHN	MIDDLEMAN	1860		1862
·	BALLENDINE	WILLIAM	GUIDE	1837	INTERPRETER	1851
·	BARCLAY	JOHN	LABOURER	1833	LABOURER	1838
238	BEADS	JACOB	MIDDLEMAN	1846	BOWSMAN	1852
238	BEADS	JACOB	STEERSMAN	1854		1857
240	BEADS	JACOB	CARPENTER	1863	CARPENTER	1865
·	BEADS	JOHN	CARPENTER	1851		1854
·	BEADS	THOMAS	CARPENTER	1867		1868
6005	BEAR	HENRI	MIDDLEMAN	1861		1864
6006	BEAR	JACOB	MIDDLEMAN	1860		1863
·	BEAR	JAMES	MIDDLEMAN	1856		1860
·	BEAR	JOHN JAMES	LABOURER	1875		1878
195	BEAR	THOMAS	STEERSMAN	1862	STEERSMAN	1866
201	BEAR	WILLIAM	CARPENTER	1856		1859
·	BEARDY	JOHN	MIDDLEMAN	1862		1865
120	BEAUCHAMP	CHARLES	MIDDLEMAN	1828	MIDDLEMAN	1835
838	BEAUCHAMP	JOSEPH	MIDDLEMAN	1849		1852
838	BEAUCHAMP	JOSEPH	BOWSMAN	1852	STEERSMAN	1860
264	BEDDOME	HENRY B	SURGEON	1852	SURGEON	1864

ID	NAME OF EMPLOYEE		JOB AT FIRST CONTRACT	DATE	JOB AT RETIREMENT	DATE
	BEDDS	JOHN	CARPENTER	1851		1854
266	BEGG	CHARLES	SLOOPER	1841	LABOURER	1846
251	BELL	GEORGE	LABOURER	1862		1867
.	BENARD	PIERRE JR	MIDDLEMAN	1841		1844
	BERENS	SAMUEL	MIDDLEMAN	1861		1864
297	BERRARD	LOUIS	CARPENTER	1831	CARPENTER	1834
	BETURNE	PIERRE	LABOURER	1829	MIDDLEMAN	1838
	BIAS	JOHN	JOINER	1853	JOINER	1862
	BIRD	DAVID	SAILOR	1829	SAILOR	1847
	BIRD	JAMES J	CLERK	1833	INTERPRETER	1838
	BIRD	THOMAS	MIDDLEMAN	1865		1868
	BIRSTON	MAGNUS	MIDDLEMAN	1855		1857
	BIRSTON	MILES	LABOURER	1832	STEERSMAN	1849
	BIRSTON	WILLIAM	SAILMAKER	1853		1856
356	BLONDIN	PAUL	MIDDLEMAN	1846		1849
	BLONDIN	PAULET	MIDDLEMAN	1857		1860
357	BLONDIN	PIERRE	MIDDLEMAN	1828	STEERSMAN	1848
	BLONDIN	PIERRE	MIDDLEMAN	1840		1843
	BLONDIN	PIERRE	STEERSMAN	1845		1848
402	BLONDIN	SIMON	MIDDLEMAN	1853	MIDDLEMAN	1857
	BLOYAN	TIMOTHEE	MIDDLEMAN	1851		1854
	BLUNT	HENRY	LABOURER	1875		1878
	BODREAU	FRANCOIS	MIDDLEMAN	1832	BOWSMAN	1842
406	BOISVERT	JEAN BAPTIST	MIDDLEMAN	1828	BOWSMAN	1832
	BOIVIN	PIERRE	MIDDLEMAN	1862		1865
	BONAMIS	ALEXIS	GUIDE	1826	GUIDE	1835
415	BONNEAU	ANTOINE	LABOURER	1829	LABOURER	1831
422	BONNEAU	PIERRE	LABOURER	1832	LABOURER	1834
	BORIEN	FELIPPE	BOWSMAN	1845	MIDDLEMAN	1852
473	BOSQUET	MICHEL	MIDDLEMAN	1828	MIDDLEMAN	1847
	BOUCHARD	FRANCOIS	MIDDLEMAN	1833	MIDDLEMAN	1836
439	BOUCHE	JEAN BAPTIST	BOWSMAN	1828		1843
436	BOUCHER	IZIDORE	MIDDLEMAN	1866		1869
439	BOUCHER	JEAN	CARPENTER	1828	CARPENTER	1836
437	BOUCHER	JEAN BAPTIST	MIDDLEMAN	1842	BOWSMAN	1850
	BOUCHER	JOSEPH	MIDDLEMAN	1852	STEERSMAN	1861
446	BOUCHER	PAUL	MIDDLEMAN	1841	MIDDLEMAN	1848
445	BOUCHERA	PAUL	FISHERMAN	1854	STEERSMAN	1859
	BOUCHEZ	JOSEPH	MIDDLEMAN	1868		1870
456	BOURASSA	J BAPTISTE	STEERSMAN	1861		1864
	BOURASSA	PIERRE	MIDDLEMAN	1868		1871
	BOUSQUET	GUILLAUME	MIDDLEMAN	1857		1860
479	BOUVIER	ANTOINE	MIDDLEMAN	1841		1844
	BOUVIER	JOSEPH	BOWSMAN	1839	STEERSMAN	1853
482	BOYD	ANDREW	LABOURER	1883		1886
4	BOYER	JEAN BAPTIST	MIDDLEMAN	1839	STEERSMAN	1850
792	BRACONNIER	AMABLE	MIDDLEMAN	1826	FISHERMAN	1844
	BRASS	JAMES	INTERPRETER	1883		1892
	BRASS	JOHN	STEERSMAN	1862		1864
	BRASS	JOHN	LABOURER	1868		1871
	BRASS	PETER	BOWSMAN	1851		1857
	BRAZEAU	JOSEPH	POST MASTER	1846	GUIDE	1849
	BREBANT	SIMON	BOWSMAN	1826	BOWSMAN	1833

RECRUITED

TABLE 3: CONTRACT EMPLOYEES OF THE HBC
FROM OR RETIRED TO THE RED RIVER COLONY, 1821-1870

ID	NAME OF EMPLOYEE		JOB AT FIRST CONTRACT	DATE	JOB AT RETIREMENT	DATE
.	BRIDGES	DAVID	BOATBUILDER	1868	.	1873
.	BRILLANT	ANTOINE	STEERSMAN	1835	.	1837
541	BROWN	JOSEPH	MIDDLEMAN	1862	.	1862
544	BROWN	WILLIAM	LABOURER	1830	LABOURER	1839
556	BRUCE	ANTOINE	STEERSMAN	1840	.	1843
555	BRUCE	BAPTISTE	MIDDLEMAN	1828	GUIDE	1849
553	BRUCE	PIERRE	INTERPRETER		.	1843
813	BUDD	HENRY	LABOURER	1832	LABOURER	1835
.	BUNN	JOHN	CLERK	1867	.	1870
.	CADIEN	APETIT	MIDDLEMAN	1847	.	1849
.	CADIEN	HENRY	MIDDLEMAN	1872	.	1875
613	CADOTTE	JOSEPH	LABOURER	1836	.	1839
616	CADOTTE	LAURENT	STEERSMAN	1826	.	1829
616	CADOTTE	LAURENT	STEERSMAN	1836	.	1839
.	CADOTTE	PIERRE	BOWSMAN	1857	BOWSMAN	1862
627	CALDER	JAMES	LABOURER	1846	.	1849
.	CAMERON	ADOLPHUS	LABOURER	1875	.	1878
.	CAMERON	ALEXANDER	HORSE KEEPER	1853	.	1856
.	CAMERON	JOSEPH	BOWSMAN	1856	.	1860
.	CAMERON	PETER	MIDDLEMAN	1858	MIDDLEMAN	1862
.	CAMERON	THOMAS	MIDDLEMAN	1853	.	1859
.	CAMERON	THOMAS	MILLER	1856	.	1859
.	CAMERON	WILLIAM	MIDDLEMAN	1861	MIDDLEMAN	1866
660	CAMPBELL	ALEXANDER	MIDDLEMAN	1868	.	1869
671	CAMPBELL	DUNCAN	MIDDLEMAN	1831	.	1834
.	CAMPBELL	NEIL	LABOURER	1841	MIDDLEMAN	1848
.	CANADA	CHARLES	BOWSMAN	1849	.	1850
.	CANADA	CHARLES	BOWSMAN	1853	.	1856
.	CANADA	PIERRE	MIDDLEMAN	1858	.	1861
.	CANTARAH	MODESTE	MIDDLEMAN	1826	.	1845
.	CARDINAL	NARCISSE	MIDDLEMAN	1853	MIDDLEMAN	1857
.	CARDINALLE	JOSEPH	MIDDLEMAN	1857	.	1860
685	CARDINALLE	RENNIS	MIDDLEMAN	1826	MIDDLEMAN	1830
.	CARRIERE	ELIE	MIDDLEMAN	1866	.	1867
719	CARRIERE	LOUIS	STEERSMAN	1840	.	1843
719	CARRIERE	LOUIS	LABOURER	1849	.	1852
.	CARRIERE	THEODORE	BLACKSMITH	1867	.	1868
.	CATFISH	JOHN	MIDDLEMAN	1865	.	1866
.	CHAINE	MARGUERITE	MIDDLEMAN	1867	.	1867
.	CHALEFOUX	JOSEPH	MIDDLEMAN	1838	.	1841
.	CHAMBERS	DAVID	LABOURER	1833	.	1838
.	CHARBONNEAU	CHARLES	MIDDLEMAN	1868	.	1873
749	CHARBONNEAU	JEAN BAPTIST	BOWSMAN	1835	STEERSMAN	1840
.	CHARLES	BENJAMIN	LABOURER	1827	.	1831
.	CHARLES	WILLIAM	BOWSMAN	1887	.	1890
.	CHARTIER	JOSEPH	MIDDLEMAN	1870	.	1873
.	CHARTIER	JOSEPH	STEERSMAN	1836	.	1847
.	CHARTIER	JOSEPH	MIDDLEMAN	1855	.	1858
.	CHASTELLAIN	DAVID	LABOURER	1889	.	1872
788	CHASTELLAIN	LOUIS	MIDDLEMAN	1877	.	1888
.	CHIEF	ALBERT	LABOURER	1833	.	1846
.	CHIEF	JOSEPH	LABOURER	1875	.	1878
.				1875	.	1878

TABLE 3: CONTRACT EMPLOYEES OF THE HBC
RECRUITED FROM OR RETIRED TO THE RED RIVER COLONY, 1821-1870

ID	NAME OF EMPLOYEE		JOB AT FIRST CONTRACT	DATE	JOB AT RETIREMENT	DATE
.	CHIEF	THOMAS	MIDDLEMAN	1862		1864
.	CIRE	FRANCOIS	MIDDLEMAN	1853		1856
.	CIRE	JOHN	LABOURER	1846	STEERSMAN	1852
.	CIRE	JOSEPH	CARPENTER	1854		1857
.	CIRE	JOSEPH	BOWSMAN	1857	MIDDLEMAN	1862
.	CIRE	PIERRE	MIDDLEMAN	1866		1867
.	CLARKE	RICHARD	MIDDLEMAN	1867		1868
904	CLOUSTON	WILLIAM	LABOURER	1838	LABOURER	1845
.	COCKRAN	JOHN	BOWSMAN	1861		1863
912	COLOMBE	FRANCIS				1828
.	COMPTOIS	GILBERT	MIDDLEMAN	1865		1868
.	COMPTOIS	LOUIS	MIDDLEMAN	1853		1856
.	CONTOIS	ANDRE	MIDDLEMAN	1839	MIDDLEMAN	1849
.	COOK	BAPTISTE	MIDDLEMAN	1859		1862
.	COOK	JEREMIAH	MIDDLEMAN	1865		1868
.	COOK	JOSEPH	INTERPRETER	1853		1855
.	COOK	JOSEPH	INTERPRETER	1873	INTERPRETER	1889
.	COOK	SAMUEL	MIDDLEMAN	1865		1868
.	CORK	WILLIAM	MIDDLEMAN	1861		1864
.	CORRIGAL	EDWARD	MIDDLEMAN	1855		1858
.	CORRIGAL	JAMES	LABOURER	1878		1881
.	CORRIGLE	JAMES	MIDDLEMAN	1830		1834
.	COURCHENE	ANTOINE	LABOURER	1847	LABOURER	1850
.	COURCHENE	BAPTISTE	STEERSMAN	1861	STEERSMAN	1866
.	COURCHENE	FRANCIS	MIDDLEMAN	1827	LABOURER	1841
.	COURCHENE	FRANCIS	MIDDLEMAN	1850		1853
.	COURCHENE	FRANCOIS	MIDDLEMAN	1836	MIDDLEMAN	1854
857	COURCHENE	JOSEPH	LABOURER		MIDDLEMAN	1841
.	COUTEREILLE	OLIVIER	APPRENTICE INTERPRETER	1870	INTERPRETER	1871
.	COWAN	WILLIAM	SURGEON	1849		1856
.	COWLEY	GEORGE	APPRENTICE CLERK	1866		1867
.	COX	GEORGE	MIDDLEMAN	1868		1870
.	CRATE	JAMES	FISHERMAN	1887		1888
862	CREMER	GEORGE	APPRENTICE COOPER	1833	COOPER	1843
.	CROMARTIE	JAMES	INTERPRETER	1851	INTERPRETER	1864
.	CROMARTIE	WILLIAM	LABOURER	1858		1861
.	CROMARTIN	JOHN	INTERPRETER	1839	POST MASTER	1849
.	CROSBIE	JOHN	HOUSE SERVANT	1843		1846
.	CUMMINGS	CHARLES	APPRENTICE	1836		1840
.	CUMMINGS	JOHN	POST MASTER	1851		1854
.	CUMMINGS	JOHN	LABOURER	1882		1885
983	CUNNINGHAM	JOHN	LABOURER		MIDDLEMAN	1844
.	CUNNINGHAM	JOHN	LABOURER	1850	POST MASTER	1854
.	DAIGNEAU	BAPTISTE	MIDDLEMAN	1835		1840
.	DANIEL	EDWARD	STEERSMAN	1864		1866
.	DANIEL	GEORGE	MIDDLEMAN	1861		1864
.	DANIEL	JAMES	LABOURER	1874		1877
.	DANIEL	JOHN	LABOURER	1861		1862
.	DANIEL	JOHN	LABOURER	1874		1877
.	DANIEL	JOSEPH	INTERPRETER	1877		1878
.	DANIEL	ROBERT	LABOURER	1852		1855
.	DANIEL	SAMUEL	APPRENTICE SERVANT	1879		1882
335	DANIEL	WILLIAM	LABOURER	1841	STEERSMAN	1852

TABLE 3: CONTRACT EMPLOYEES OF THE HBC
RECRUITED FROM OR RETIRED TO THE RED RIVER COLONY, 1821-1870

ID	NAME OF EMPLOYEE		JOB AT FIRST CONTRACT	DATE	JOB AT RETIREMENT	DATE
.	DANIEL	WILLIAM	BOWSMAN	1852	STEERSMAN	1857
.	DANIELS	WILLIAM	STEERSMAN	1854		1856
1023	DAUNAIS	JEAN BAPTIST	CARPENTER	1839	JOINER	1849
.	DAUPHINE	JOSEPH	MIDDLEMAN	1844	BOWSMAN	1850
.	DAVIDSON	JOHN	LABOURER	1848		1851
.	DAVIS	CHARLES	LABOURER	1868		1869
.	DAVIS	GEORGE	INTERPRETER	1852		1855
.	DECHAMP	ANTOINE	MIDDLEMAN	1826		1831
108	DELORME	BAPTISTE	MIDDLEMAN	1841		1844
.	DELORME	PIERRE	MIDDLEMAN	1853		1856
1242	DEMARRAIS	MICHEL	BLACKSMITH	1839	LABOURER	1844
.	DESCHAMBEAU	LOUIS	APPRENTICE POST MASTER	1864		1867
.	DESCHAMPS	FRANCOIS	STEERSMAN	1857		1859
.	DESCHAMPS	FRANCOIS	MIDDLEMAN	1865		1872
.	DESJARDINS	ANTOINE	MIDDLEMAN	1857		1860
.	DESJARDINS	ANTOINE	MIDDLEMAN	1861		1861
.	DESJARDINS	BAPTISTE	MIDDLEMAN	1858		1861
.	DESJARDINS	BAPTISTE	MIDDLEMAN	1858		1870
1278	DESJARDINS	F BAPTISTE	MIDDLEMAN	1826	STEERSMAN	1859
.	DESJARDINS	JOSEPH	LABOURER	1867		1870
.	DESJARLAIS	ANTOINE	INTERPRETER	1853		1855
1262	DESJARLOIS	ANTOINE	GUIDE	1833	STEERSMAN	1843
1150	DESJRRDINS	ANTOINE	MIDDLEMAN	1827	STEERSMAN	1833
.	DESMARAIS	BAPTISTE	MIDDLEMAN	1840		1849
1238	DESMARAIS	BAPTISTE	MIDDLEMAN	1841	MIDDLEMAN	1846
.	DESMARAIS	FRANCOIS	MIDDLEMAN	1840	MIDDLEMAN	1848
.	DESMARAIS	FRANCOIS	MIDDLEMAN	1853		1855
.	DESMARAIS	JOHN	MIDDLEMAN	1852		1854
.	DESMARAIS	JOSEPH	MIDDLEMAN	1841	BLACKSMITH	1851
.	DESMARAIS	JOSEPH	MIDDLEMAN	1856		1859
.	DESRIVIERES	LOUIS	BOWSMAN	1845		1848
.	DESRIVIERS	LOUIS	BOWSMAN	1854	MIDDLEMAN	1861
.	DESROSIERS	F BAPTISTE	MIDDLEMAN	1827	CARPENTER	1842
1306	DONALD	CHARLES	MIDDLEMAN	1857		1858
.	DONALD	GEORGE	APPRENTICE BLACKSMITH	1833		1839
.	DONALD	GEORGE	BLACKSMITH	1850		1852
.	DONALD	JOHN	BLACKSMITH	1852	CARPENTER	1857
.	DONALD	WILLIAM	LABOURER	1876		1879
.	DORION	JOHN	LABOURER	1832	STEERSMAN	1840
.	DREVER	WILLIAM	MIDDLEMAN	1830	STEERSMAN	1839
1327	DUBOIS	BAPTISTE	CARPENTER	1842		1844
.	DUBOIS	JOSEPH	MIDDLEMAN	1851		1854
1343	DUCHARME	BAPTISTE	MIDDLEMAN	1843		1848
.	DUCHARME	CHARLES	MIDDLEMAN	1855		1858
.	DUCHARME	CHARLES	BOWSMAN	1833	MIDDLEMAN	1847
.	DUCHARME	FRANCOIS	FISHERMAN	1838	STEERSMAN	1851
1375	DUMAIS	CHARLES	MIDDLEMAN	1854		1859
.	DUMAIS	CHARLES	STEERSMAN	1842	MIDDLEMAN	1850
.	DUMAS	CHARLES	MIDDLEMAN	1855		1859
.	DUMAS	MICHEL	BOWSMAN	1853		1856
.	DUMOND	EKABDOR	MIDDLEMAN	1829	11	1855
.	DUNNING	JAMES	HARPOONER	1828	HARPOONER	1849

ID	NAME OF EMPLOYEE		JOB AT FIRST CONTRACT	DATE	JOB AT RETIREMENT	DATE
	DUPRES	PIERRE	MIDDLEMAN	1865		1868
	DURAND	LEPHERIN	BOWSMAN	1868		1871
	DYER	JOHN	LABOURER	1866		1871
1419	EASTER	JOHN	LABOURER	1829	COOPER	1839
	EINHELLY	ANTHONY	LABOURER	1875		1876
	EMERSON	SAMUEL	ENGINEER	1885		1893
	EMLYN	BAPTISTE	MIDDLEMAN	1861		1869
	EVANS	JACOB	HOUSE SERVANT	1887		1890
	EVERETTE	JOSEPH	MIDDLEMAN	1843		1848
1471	FAILLE	TOUSS T	MIDDLEMAN	1827	MIDDLEMAN	1827
	FAILLE	TOUSSAINT	STEERSMAN	1865		1868
	FAVEL	CHARLES	MIDDLEMAN	1858		1861
	FAVEL	CHARLES	MIDDLEMAN	1861		1864
1503	FAVEL	JAMES	MIDDLEMAN	1870		1873
1513	FAVEL	JOHN	MIDDLEMAN	1853		1854
1522	FAVEL	JOSEPH	STEERSMAN	1859		1862
1516	FAVEL	RICHARD	MIDDLEMAN	1861		1864
1517	FAVEL	SAMUEL	LABOURER	1849		1852
1517	FAVEL	SAMUEL	BOWSMAN	1852		1854
1498	FAVEL	SAMUEL	STEERSMAN	1856	STEERSMAN	1860
1844	FAVEL	THOMAS	MIDDLEMAN	1855	BOWSMAN	1866
	FAVEL	WILLIAM	STEERSMAN	1858		1858
1542	FERGUSON	JOHN	MIDDLEMAN	1854		1859
1535	FIDDLER	FRANCOIS	MIDDLEMAN	1849		1856
	FIDLER	CHARLES	MIDDLEMAN	1833		1853
	FILY	FRANCOIS	STEERSMAN	1825	GUIDE	1836
	FIRTH	THOMAS	INTERPRETER	1849		1852
1569	FISHER	JOHN	INTERPRETER	1851		1854
1569	FISHER	JOHN	MIDDLEMAN	1866		1869
1575	FLAMMAND	ANTOINE	LABOURER	1875		1878
1867	FLETT	ANDREW	MIDDLEMAN	1870		1873
	FLETT	CHARLES	BOATBUILDER	1856		1859
1585	FLETT	GEORGE	MIDDLEMAN	1856		1859
1631	FLETT	JAMES	APPRENTICE BLACKSMITH	1833		1840
1590	FLETT	JOHN	LABOURER	1876		1879
1861	FLETT	JOHN	LABOURER	1887		1890
	FLETT	JOSEPH	LABOURER	1876		1879
	FLETT	WILLIAM	LABOURER	1835	INTERPRETER	1849
	FOLEY	JOHN	LABOURER	1864		1871
	FOLSTER	WILLIAM	MIDDLEMAN	1859	LABOURER	1865
	FONTAGNE	MOYSE	MIDDLEMAN	1850		1851
	FONTAIGNE	JEROME	MIDDLEMAN	1866		1868
	FONTAIGNE	MOYSE	MIDDLEMAN	1850		1862
1643	FONTAINE	LOUIS	MIDDLEMAN	1861	STEERSMAN	1863
	FORCIER	J BAPTISTE	MIDDLEMAN	1842		1848
	FORREST	CHARLES	MIDDLEMAN	1825		1828
	FOSSENEUVE	BAPTISTE	MIDDLEMAN	1835		1841
1582	FOSSENEUVE	BAPTISTE	GUIDE	1866	STEERSMAN	1869
	FRANK	ALFRED	LABOURER	1884	APPRENTICE SERVANT	1893
	FRANK	DONALD	LABOURER	1881		1884
1650	FRANKS	JAMES	FARM SERVANT	1836		1841
1653	FRAZER	HUGH	BOWSMAN	1828	LABOURER	1846

TABLE 3: CONTRACT EMPLOYEES OF THE HBC
RECRUITED FROM OR RETIRED TO THE RED RIVER COLONY, 1821-1870

ID	NAME OF EMPLOYEE		JOB AT FIRST CONTRACT	DATE	JOB AT RETIREMENT	DATE
	FREDERIQUE	BAPTISTE	MIDDLEMAN	1843	BOWSMAN	1851
	FREDERIQUE	DANIEL	FISHERMAN	1868		1875
145	FREEMAN	SAMUEL	LABOURER	1887		1887
	GADDY	ALEXANDER	BOWSMAN	1855		1856
1888	GADOUA	JEAN BAPTIST	MIDDLEMAN	1830	HORSE KEEPER	1850
1880	GAGNON	JOSEPH	LABOURER	1861		1864
1878	GAGNON	LOUIS	MIDDLEMAN	1835		1838
	GALLARNEAUX	JEAN BAPTIST	INTERPRETER	1826	INTERPRETER	1831
1828	GARDINER	ROBERT	LABOURER	1881		1884
1829	GARDINER	THOMAS	LABOURER	1849		1854
	GARDINER	THOMAS	LABOURER	1879		1882
	GARDNER	ANDREW	STEERSMAN	1873		1879
	GARDUPUIS	BAPTISTE	MIDDLEMAN	1852	MIDDLEMAN	1857
	GARDUPUIS	BONAVENTURE	MIDDLEMAN	1858	BOWSMAN	1857
	GARRIOCH	JOHN	LABOURER	1837		1840
	GARRIOCH	JOHN	MIDDLEMAN	1860	LABOURER	1866
	GAUBIN	JOSEPH	STEERSMAN	1825	STEERSMAN	1836
	GEHRCKE	JOHAN	LABOURER	1856		1861
1926	GENDRON	FRANCOIS	STEERSMAN	1871	STEERSMAN	1873
	GENDRON	PIERRE	LABOURER	1859		1862
2054	GIBOCHE	LOUIS	CLERK	1828	INTERPRETER	1831
1819	GILLIES	ANGUS	LABOURER	1869	STEERSMAN	1877
	GIRARD	ANTOINE	LABOURER	1867		1868
	GIRARD	JOSEPH	BOWSMAN	1856		1861
	GIRARD	PIERRE	MIDDLEMAN	1868	BLACKSMITH	1873
	GLADSTON	WILLIAM	APPRENTICE BOATBUILDER	1855		1859
	GODREAU	EUSTACHE	MIDDLEMAN	1866		1857
1987	GONVILLE	ANTOINE	MIDDLEMAN	1855	MIDDLEMAN	1867
1986	GONVILLE	LOUIS	MIDDLEMAN	1855		1858
1770	GOODE	JAMES	FARM SERVANT	1836		1841
	GORDON	ALEXANDER	LABOURER	1863		1868
1917	GOUDRIE	JOSEPH	MIDDLEMAN	1829	MIDDLEMAN	1842
	GOUDRIE	LOUISON	BOWSMAN	1855		1858
	GOUIN	ANTOINE	MIDDLEMAN	1864	MIDDLEMAN	1865
8026	GOUIN	ANTOINE	BOWSMAN	1826		1849
2017	GOULAIT	CHARLES	INTERPRETER	1847	INTERPRETER	1849
2017	GOULAIT	CHARLES	INTERPRETER	1829		1833
2015	GOULET	LOUIS	MIDDLEMAN	1836	MIDDLEMAN	1841
2020	GOWLER	OLIVER	FARM SERVANT	1827		1837
2026	GRANDBOIS	MICHEL	MIDDLEMAN	1846	MIDDLEMAN	1849
2029	GRANT	CHALES	INTERPRETER	1858		1863
	GRANT	COLIN	LABOURER	1862		1871
	GREEN	JOSEPH	LABOURER	1838	LABOURER	1841
4997	GRENIER	URSULE				1841
	GUILBOCHE	MARCELLAIS	STEERSMAN	1852		1854
	GUILLOCHE	MARCELLAIS	MIDDLEMAN	1844		1849
	GUN	PATRICK	LABOURER	1848		1851
	GUNN	DUNCAN	LABOURER	1875		1893
	GUNN	JOHN	APPRENTICE BLACKSMITH	1881	BLACKSMITH	1889
	HALCROW	JOSEPH	LABOURER	1876		1879
	HALCROW	THOMAS	MIDDLEMAN	1870		1873
	MARCUS	JOHN	LABOURER	1852	FISHERMAN	1859

ID	NAME OF EMPLOYEE		JOB AT FIRST CONTRACT	DATE	JOB AT RETIREMENT	DATE
2125	HARKNESS	ANDRE	ASSISTANT SHOPKEEPER	1833		1836
1796	HARPER	JOHN	LABOURER	1825	LABOURER	1833
	HARPER	JOHN	APPRENTICE TINSMITH	1847	TINSMITH	1860
	HARPER	JOHN	MIDDLEMAN	1870		1873
2130	HARPER	MAGNUS	APPRENTICE COOPER	1849	COOPER	1859
1794	HARPER	THOMAS	APPRENTICE JOINER	1853		1860
1794	HARPER	WILLIAM	LABOURER	1867		1868
2136	HARRIOTT	JOHN E	APPRENTICE POST MASTER	1858		1863
	HAY	ROBERT	BLACKSMITH	1870		1875
	HEBERT	FABIEN HENRI	MIDDLEMAN	1827	MIDDLEMAN	1849
	HEBERT	JEAN	BRICKMAKER	1833		1837
2152	HECKENBURGR	HENRY	LABOURER	1852		1855
	HENDERSON	ANGUS	BOWSMAN	1871		1874
	HENDERSON	EDWARD	MIDDLEMAN	1867		1870
1933	HENDERSON	FRANCIS	LABOURER	1862		1867
2445	HENDERSON	SAMUEL	BOWSMAN	1849		1852
2445	HENDERSON	SAMUEL	GUIDE	1859		1862
	HODGSON	GEORGE	LABOURER	1870	.	1871
	HOOLE	FRANCOIS	INTERPRETER	1841	INTERPRETER	1847
	HOPE	JAMES	MIDDLEMAN	1832	BOWSMAN	1840
	HOPE	JOHN	BOWSMAN	1843		1846
2166	HOPE	JOHN	FISHERMAN	1862		1865
2166	HOPE	JOHN	FISHERMAN	1862		1865
6043	HOPE	JOSEPH	MIDDLEMAN	1867	MIDDLEMAN	1871
2163	HOPE	THOMAS	MIDDLEMAN	1844	MIDDLEMAN	1873
	HOULE	ANTOINE	LABOURER	1840	BOWSMAN	1848
	HOURIE	JOHN	STEERSMAN	1867	GUIDE	1872
	HOURIE	JOHN	LABOURER	1869		1874
2237	HOURIE	PHILIP	LABOURER	1850		1851
2237	HOURIE	PHILIP	LABOURER	1850		1854
2240	HOURIE	ROBERT	MIDDLEMAN	1859	BOWSMAN	1866
2252	HOURIE	THOMAS	MIDDLEMAN	1840		1843
2252	HOURIE	THOMAS	MIDDLEMAN	1859		1862
	HOURSTON	JOHN	LABOURER	1871		1883
1802	HOWSE	HENRY	BOWSMAN	1856	STOREKEEPER	1859
	HOWSE	JAMES	MIDDLEMAN	1856		1859
1002	HUPPE	JOSEPH	STEERSMAN	1849		1852
	HUPPE	JOSEPH I	MIDDLEMAN	1835		1838
	HUPPEE	DAMAS	MIDDLEMAN	1868		1871
2263	HUPPIE	JOSEPH	MIDDLEMAN	1861		1870
2405	INKSTER	JAMES	LABOURER	1824	CARPENTER	1831
2390	IRVINE	GEORGE	LABOURER	1824	LABOURER	1832
2391	IRVINE	JAMES	MIDDLEMAN	1841		1846
	IRVINE	JAMES	BOATBUILDER	1852		1854
	ISAACS	JACQUES	BOWSMAN	1856		1859
	ISBISTER	ADAM	LABOURER	1855		1858
	ISBISTER	EDWARD	MIDDLEMAN	1865		1868
	ISBISTER	JAMES	POST MASTER	1864		1867
	JAMES	VALENTINE	LABOURER	1876		1879
	JARVOIS	FRANCOIS	MIDDLEMAN	1859		1862
	JEANVENNE	J BAPTISTE	LABOURER	1868		1870
2350	JOBIN	AMBROISE	MIDDLEMAN	1839	MIDDLEMAN	1852

TABLE 3: CONTRACT EMPLOYEES OF THE HBC RECRUITED FROM OR RETIRED TO THE RED RIVER COLONY, 1821-1870

ID	NAME OF EMPLOYEE	JOB AT FIRST CONTRACT	DATE	JOB AT RETIREMENT	DATE
2347	JOBIN JOSEPH	MIDDLEMAN	1868	MIDDLEMAN	1872
2329	JOHANSEN AUGUST	LABOURER	1857		1862
	JOHNSTON CHARLES	LABOURER	1853	LABOURER	1856
2326	JOHNSTON JAMES	LABOURER	1835	LABOURER	1844
	JOHNSTONE GEORGE	MIDDLEMAN	1862		1863
2339	JOHNSTONE JAMES	LABOURER	1866		1849
	JOHNSTONE JAMES B	MIDDLEMAN	1860		1863
	JOHNSTONE JOSEPH	STEERSMAN	1862	CARPENTER	1865
	JOHNSTONE WILLIAM	MIDDLEMAN	1855		1868
	JOHNSTONE WILLIAM	MIDDLEMAN	1862		1867
2314	JOHNSTONE WILLIAM	LABOURER	1869	MIDDLEMAN	1875
2318	JONES DAVID	BLACKSMITH	1835	BOWSMAN	1842
	JOSE J BAPTISTE	LABOURER	1853		1857
	JOYAL TOUSSAINT	LABOURER	1826		1833
	JUISSAUME ALEXANDRE	MIDDLEMAN	1865		1868
	JULIA THOMAS	MIDDLEMAN	1875		1878
	KEARNEY HUGH	MIDDLEMAN	1837		1840
	KENNEDY ALEXANDER	LABOURER	1887		1890
1753	KENNEDY HENRY	LABOURER	1852		1857
1752	KENNEDY JAMES	LABOURER	1852		1855
1751	KENNEDY THOMAS	BOWSMAN	1862		1867
	KING WILLIAM	MIDDLEMAN	1866		1872
	KING JOSEPH	APPRENTICE INTERPRETER	1861	INTERPRETER	1864
2299	KIPPLING GEORGE	MIDDLEMAN	1849		1851
	KIPPLING GEORGE	STEERSMAN	1851	GUIDE	1854
	KIPPLING JAMES	GUIDE	1868		1871
	KIPPLING JOHN	LABOURER	1893		1896
2295	KIPPLING PETER	FISHERMAN	1841		1846
2297	KIPPLING THOMAS	MIDDLEMAN	1857	MIDDLEMAN	1862
	KIPPLING WILLIAM	MIDDLEMAN	1861		1864
	KIPPLING WILLIAM	MIDDLEMAN	1877		1881
2286	KIRTON JOSEPH	LABOURER	1836		1841
2276	KNIGHT PETER	FARM SERVANT	1846		1849
1913	LABERGE FRANCOIS	MIDDLEMAN	1856		1859
2469	LACERTE LOUIS	BLACKSMITH	1848		1847
	LACUILLERE MICHEL	MIDDLEMAN	1853		1856
	LADEROULE JEAN	MIDDLEMAN	1865		1868
2486	LADOUCEUR JOSEPH	MIDDLEMAN	1828		1835
	LAFERTE ALFRED	STEERSMAN	1857		1860
2504	LAFERTE LOUIS	STEERSMAN	1849	FISHERMAN	1852
2508	LAFERTE OLIVIER	FISHERMAN	1854		1863
2505	LAFERTE PIERRE	FISHERMAN	1851		1854
2505	LAFERTE PIERRE	FISHERMAN	1851		1858
2506	LAFONDE BAPTISTE	MIDDLEMAN	1858		1861
2683	LAFRAMBOISE FRANCOIS	MIDDLEMAN	1826		1838
	LAFRETAY PIERRE	FISHERMAN	1838		1842
2536	LAGARDE JOSEPH	BOWSMAN	1836		1836
2536	LAGARDE JOSEPH	MIDDLEMAN	1850		1854
2536	LAGARDE JOSEPH	MIDDLEMAN	1850	MIDDLEMAN	1856
2553	LALIBERTE ALEXIS	BOWSMAN	1853		1858
	LALIBERTE ANTOINE	MIDDLFMAN	1857		1867

ID	NAME OF EMPLOYEE		JOB AT FIRST CONTRACT	DATE	JOB AT RETIREMENT	DATE
2557	LALIBERTE	JOSEPH	MIDDLEMAN	1866	COW HERD	1872
	LALIBERTE	LOUIS	MIDDLEMAN	1868		1871
2561	LALIBERTE	PIERRE	STEERSMAN	1851	INTERPRETER	1857
.	LALIBERTE	PIERRE LACHT	MIDDLEMAN	1838		1848
	LALLEMOND	ANTOINE	MIDDLEMAN	1865		1868
	LAMBERT	AUGUSTIN	BOWSMAN	1836	STEERSMAN	1844
	LAMBERT	JOHN	MIDDLEMAN	1870		1873
2582	LAMBERT	MICHEL	STEERSMAN	1832		1833
	LAMBERT	WILLIAM I	MIDDLEMAN	1870		1873
	LAMOUREUX	BAPTISTE	CARPENTER	1869		1872
	LANDRIE	ALEXANDER	LABOURER	1833		1852
	LANDRIE	ALEXANDRE	MIDDLEMAN	1857		1858
	LANGE	EDOUARD	MIDDLEMAN	1841		1844
	LANGE	FRANCOIS	MIDDLEMAN	1835		1838
	LAPIE	BAPTISTE	MIDDLEMAN	1852	BOWSMAN	1857
2614	LAPIERRE	ANTOINE	FISHERMAN	1825		1828
2614	LAPIERRE	ANTOINE	LABOURER	1829		1843
	LAPIERRE	IRVINE	MIDDLEMAN	1836		1838
2612	LAPIERRE	JOSEPH	MIDDLEMAN	1866		1869
2613	LAPIERRE	LOUIS	MIDDLEMAN	1868		1869
	LAPIERRE	LOUIS BRILLT	MIDDLEMAN	1835		1838
2561	LAPIERRE	PIERRE	INTERPRETER	1862		1864
2610	LAPIERRE	PIERRE	MIDDLEMAN	1861		1872
2622	LAPLANTE	ANTOINE	MIDDLEMAN	1861	BOWSMAN	1864
2627	LAPLANTE	LOUIS	STEERSMAN	1827		1847
2641	LARANCE	BAZIL	STEERSMAN	1827		1844
2641	LARANCE	BAZIL	STEERSMAN	1857		1860
	LARANCE	LOUIS	MIDDLEMAN	1857		1835
2656	LARIVIE	HYCTHE	BOWSMAN	1827		1848
	LAROCQUE	FRANCOIS	MIDDLEMAN	1841		1849
2657	LARONDE	LOUISON	MIDDLEMAN	1846		1857
	LARONDE	LOUISON	INTERPRETER	1854		1856
2658	LARONDE	PAUL	MIDDLEMAN	1853		1859
2658	LARONDE	PAUL	STEERSMAN	1857		1858
2693	LAROQUE	BAPT PIERRE	LABOURER	1855		1838
2782	LAROQUE	BAPTISTE	MIDDLEMAN	1835	LABOURER	1862
2672	LAROQUE	BAPTISTE	MIDDLEMAN	1857		1861
	LAROQUE	CHARLES	STEERSMAN	1858		1854
	LAROQUE	FRANCOIS	MIDDLEMAN	1851		1861
	LAROQUE	MOYSE	MIDDLEMAN	1858		1860
	LARPENTIGNR	JOSEPH	MIDDLEMAN	1857		1843
	LASERTE	ALFRED	MIDDLEMAN	1838		1846
	LATENDRE	JOSEPH	MIDDLEMAN	1839		1831
2591	LAUNDRIE	LOUISSON	LABOURER	1829		1843
2818	LAVALLE	MICHEL	MIDDLEMAN	1825		1871
	LAVALLEE	ELIE	MIDDLEMAN	1868		1872
	LAVALLEE	LOUIS	MIDDLEMAN	1864		1853
2837	LAVERDURE	FRANCOIS	MIDDLEMAN	1850		1828
2804	LAVERDURE	JOSEPH	MIDDLEMAN	1825		1871
	LAVIOLETTE	ANTOINE	STEERSMAN	1868		1858
	LAVIOLETTE	J BAPTISTE	MIDDLEMAN	1856		1856
	LAWRENCE	DAVID	MIDDLEMAN	1871		1874
	LEASK	JOHN	LABOURER	1866		1873

TABLE 3: CONTRACT EMPLOYEES OF THE HBC
RECRUITED FROM OR RETIRED TO THE RED RIVER COLONY, 1821-1870

ID	NAME OF EMPLOYEE		JOB AT FIRST CONTRACT	DATE	JOB AT RETIREMENT	DATE
.	LEASK	JOHN	LABOURER	1870	.	1875
.	LEASK	JOSEPH	LABOURER	1875	.	1878
.	LEASK	SAMUEL	LABOURER	1851	CARPENTER	1860
1914	LEBLANC	DONALD	LABOURER	1879	.	1882
2456	LEBLANC	LOUIS	INTERPRETER	1833	.	1836
.	LEBLANC	LOUIS	MIDDLEMAN	1859	.	1871
.	LEBLANC	LOUIS	LABOURER	1871	LABOURER	1884
.	LEBLANC	PIERRE	POST MASTER	1832	.	1834
.	LECLAIRE	JEAN	MIDDLEMAN	1866	MIDDLEMAN	1869
2891	LECREE	FRANCOIS	MIDDLEMAN	1868	MIDDLEMAN	1874
.	LEDOUX	LOUIS	MIDDLEMAN	1865	STEERSMAN	1872
.	LEFEVRE	LOUIS	STEERSMAN	1828	.	1834
.	LEFRENIERE	LOUIS	LABOURER	1826	.	1829
2896	LEGAULT	ANTOINE	MIDDLEMAN	1826	.	1834
.	LEPINE	BAPTISTE	STEERSMAN	1849	.	1852
.	LETENDRE	JOSEPH	MIDDLEMAN	1853	MIDDLEMAN	1857
.	LETENDRE	PIERRE	MIDDLEMAN	1860	MIDDLEMAN	1866
.	LETOURNEAU	HILAIRE	MIDDLEMAN	1856	.	1859
.	LEVEILLER	FRANCOIS	MIDDLEMAN	1856	.	1859
.	LEVEILLER	JOSEPH	MIDDLEMAN	1852	.	1855
.	LEVEILLER	LOUIS	LABOURER	1849	.	1852
.	LEVEILLER	LOUIS	BOWSMAN	1852	.	1855
.	LEVEILLER	PIERRE	LABOURER	1849	.	1852
.	LEVEILLER	PIERRE	MIDDLEMAN	1852	.	1855
2949	LEWIS	JAMES	LABOURER	1865	.	1866
.	LINKLATER	ALEXANDER	RUNNER	1889	.	1896
.	LINKLATER	ARCHIBALD	LABOURER	1878	.	1881
.	LINKLATER	CHARLES	MIDDLEMAN	1862	.	1869
2969	LINKLATER	MAGNUS	STOREKEEPER	1843	WAREHOUSEMAN	1852
2536	LINKLATER	WILLIAM	LABOURER	1851	.	1854
.	LINKLATER	WILLIAM	LABOURER	1851	.	1854
.	LINKLATER	WILLIAM	LABOURER	1852	.	1865
.	LINKLATER	WILLIAM	INTERPRETER	1868	INTERPRETER	1872
.	LINKLATER	WILLIAM D	LABOURER	1862	.	1867
2986	LOGAN	JOHN	LABOURER	1866	.	1869
2988	LOGAN	ROBERT	LABOURER	1866	.	1869
902	LOUSTON	ROBERT	LABOURER	1828	.	1843
.	LOUTTIT	LOWE	MIDDLEMAN	1866	.	1869
.	LOUTTIT	PETER	APPRENTICE CLERK	1843	.	1849
2705	LOWMAN	MAURICE	STEERSMAN	1857	.	1858
3013	LYONS	THOMAS	STEERSMAN	1825	STEERSMAN	1835
.	MACDONALD	DONALD	BOWSMAN	1856	.	1859
.	MACKLIN	THOMAS	MIDDLEMAN	1833	FISHERMAN	1852
.	MACREDI	FRANCOIS	MIDDLEMAN	1846	MIDDLEMAN	1851
.	MACREDI	FRANCOIS	MIDDLEMAN	1857	.	1870
.	MAGDALEN	DANIEL	MIDDLEMAN	1853	.	1856
3017	MALATER	BAZIL	MIDDLEMAN	1856	.	1859
.	MALETTE	ARSEN	MIDDLEMAN	1831	MIDDLEMAN	1846
.	MALETTE	JOSEPH	MIDDLEMAN	1858	.	1859
.	MALETTE	JOSEPH	MIDDLEMAN	1866	.	1869
.	MALLETTE	JOSEPH	MIDDLEMAN			
3020	MANGOSIT	PASCAL	MIDDLEMAN			

ID	NAME OF EMPLOYEE		JOB AT FIRST CONTRACT	DATE	JOB AT RETIREMENT	DATE
3025	MARCELLAIS	JOHN	MIDDLEMAN	1865		1868
	MARCELLAIS	PIERRE	BOWSMAN	1856		1867
	MARCELLAIS	PIERRE	MIDDLEMAN	1860		1862
3029	MARCHAND	FELIX	MIDDLEMAN	1861		1864
3040	MARION	FRANCIS	BLACKSMITH	1827	BLACKSMITH	1833
3045	MARION	NARCISSE	BLACKSMITH	1827	BLACKSMITH	1835
	MARSELLOIS	BAPTISTE I	MIDDLEMAN	1835	GUIDE	1848
	MARTIN	JOHN	LABOURER	1874		1875
3061	MARTIN	NORMAN	LABOURER	1870		1875
	MARTIN	SIMON	MIDDLEMAN	1826		1829
	MARWICK	JAMES	LABOURER	1870		1875
	MASRREASE		MIDDLEMAN	1859		1864
3071	MASSEY	ROBERT	LABOURER	1848	APPRENTICE SERVANT	1858
	MCAULAY	ALEXANDER	LABOURER	1867		1872
	MCAULAY	RODERICK	LABOURER	1862		1870
3294	MCCORRISTER	HENRY	MIDDLEMAN	1870		1873
1716	MCDONALD	ALEXANDER	LABOURER	1851		1853
	MCDONALD	ALEXANDER	LABOURER	1851		1853
	MCDONALD	ALEXANDER	LABOURER	1862		1869
	MCDONALD	ANGUS	LABOURER	1869		1875
	MCDONALD	DAVID	LABOURER	1868		1873
3314	MCDONALD	DUNCAN	APPRENTICE BLACKSMITH	1844		1849
	MCDONALD	JOHN	CARPENTER	1849		1852
	MCDONALD	JOHN	LABOURER	1852		1857
	MCDONALD	JOHN	LABOURER	1868		1873
	MCDONALD	JOHN	INTERPRETER	1885		1888
3317	MCDONALD	JOSEPH	POST MASTER	1866		1869
	MCDONALD	PHILIP	POST MASTER	1865		1868
	MCDONALD	WILLIAM	LABOURER	1831	MIDDLEMAN	1839
	MCDONALD	WILLIAM	MIDDLEMAN	1868		1871
	MCDOUGALL	NEIL	LABOURER	1858		1862
3365	MCGILLIVRAY	EDWARD	INTERPRETER	1839	INTERPRETER	1852
	MCIVER	ALLAN	LABOURER	1850	LABOURER	1857
	MCIVER	FRANCIS	LABOURER	1871	STEERSMAN	1877
	MCIVER	JOHN	MIDDLEMAN	1865		1867
	MCIVER	MALCOLM	LABOURER	1850	LABOURER	1864
	MCIVER	NEIL	LABOURER	1878		1879
	MCIVER	RODERICK	LABOURER	1864	FISHERMAN	1867
	MCIVER	RODERICK	LABOURER	1872		1873
3401	MCKAY	ALEXANDER	INTERPRETER	1853	INTERPRETER	1857
3378	MCKAY	ALEXIS	GUIDE	1849		1852
	MCKAY	ALEXIS	STEERSMAN	1864		1866
3394	MCKAY	ANGUS	LABOURER	1859		1864
3385	MCKAY	BAPTISTE	FISHERMAN	1859	FISHERMAN	1863
	MCKAY	CHARLES	INTERPRETER	1861		1864
	MCKAY	CHARLES	MIDDLEMAN	1860	MIDDLEMAN	1868
3388	MCKAY	EDWARD	MIDDLEMAN	1848		1848
	MCKAY	EDWARD	CLERK	1866		1869
3393	MCKAY	IGNACE	GUIDE	1866	STEERSMAN	1867
	MCKAY	ISIDORE	MIDDLEMAN	1864		1867
	MCKAY	JACOB	LABOURER	1861		1864
3403	MCKAY	JAMES	STEERSMAN	1835	COAST GUIDE	1839
	MCKAY	JAMES	LABOURER	1849	GROOM	1860

TABLE 3 : CONTRACT EMPLOYEES OF THE HBC
RECRUITED FROM OR RETIRED TO THE RED RIVER COLONY, 1821-1870

ID	NAME OF EMPLOYEE	JOB AT FIRST CONTRACT	DATE	JOB AT RETIREMENT	DATE
3397	MCKAY JAMES	POST MASTER	1853	POST MASTER	1859
.	MCKAY JOHN	LABOURER	1835		1843
.	MCKAY JOHN	LABOURER	1864	INTERPRETER	1869
	MCKAY JOHN D	INTERPRETER	1851	MIDDLEMAN	1857
	MCKAY JOHN MCNAB	MIDDLEMAN	1853	POST MASTER	1859
3408	MCKAY JOHN R	POST MASTER	1836		1839
	MCKAY JOHN RICHARD	CLERK	1844		1847
3410	MCKAY JOSEPH	MIDDLEMAN	1833		1838
3410	MCKAY JOSEPH	MIDDLEMAN	1849	MIDDLEMAN	1856
3410	MCKAY JOSEPH	LABOURER	1854		1856
3410	MCKAY JOSEPH	MIDDLEMAN	1857		1860
3382	MCKAY NEIL	COOK	1853		1855
3665	MCKAY THOMAS	MIDDLEMAN	1861		1864
	MCKAY WILLIAM	MIDDLEMAN	1865		1868
3422	MCKENZIE HECTOR A	POST MASTER	1844	MIDDLEMAN	1847
	MCKENZIE JAMES	APPRENTICE	1827		1840
	MCKENZIE JOHN	INTERPRETER	1869		1878
	MCKENZIE JOHN DUNCAN	LABOURER	1867		1869
3641	MCKENZIE KENNETH	LABOURER	1852	MIDDLEMAN	1857
3640	MCKENZIE MURDO	FISHERMAN	1863		1870
	MCKINNON ROBERT	LABOURER	1851	FISHERMAN	1867
	MCLEAN DONALD	MIDDLEMAN	1850		1855
3646	MCLEAN DONALD	LABOURER	1857		1860
3646	MCLEAN DONALD	LABOURER	1866		1872
3511	MCLEAN DUNCAN	LABOURER	1867		1870
3512	MCLEAN FARQUHAR	LABOURER	1860		1865
	MCLEAN JOHN	LABOURER	1868		1873
3452	MCLENNAN MURDOCH	LABOURER	1852		1855
	MCLEOD ALEX ROD	APPRENTICE CLERK	1837		1842
	MCLEOD ANGUS	LABOURER	1831		1836
3544	MCLEOD ANGUS	MILLER	1860		1862
3550	MCLEOD ANGUS	LABOURER	1862		1867
	MCLEOD JAMES	MIDDLEMAN	1855		1858
4039	MCLEOD JOHN	LABOURER	1859		1864
3546	MCLEOD KENNETH	BOWSMAN	1864		1867
3447	MCLEOD MALCOLM	SAWYER	1868		1869
	MCLEOD RODERICK	LABOURER	1869		1876
	MCLEOD THOMAS	MIDDLEMAN	1865		1868
	MCLEOD WILLIAM	LABOURER	1863	CARPENTER	1871
	MCLEOD WILLIAM	MIDDLEMAN	1865	FISHERMAN	1871
	MCLEOD WILLIAM	CARPENTER	1867		1872
	MCLOUGHLIN JOHN	SURGEON	1837		1842
3457	MCMILLAN WILLIAM	MIDDLEMAN	1826	BOWSMAN	1835
3458	MCMURRAY WILLIAM	CLERK	1853		1856
	MCNAB ANDREW	MIDDLEMAN	1857		1860
3466	MCNAB CHARLES	MIDDLEMAN	1859		1863
3454	MCNAB JAMES	GUIDE	1848		1851
3454	MCNAB JAMES	GUIDE	1856		1856
3465	MCNAB THOMAS	BOWSMAN	1857		1861
3556	MCNAB TIMOTHY	LABOURER	1833		1860
3472	MCPHAIL DUNCAN	LABOURER	1853	LABOURER	1863

ID	NAME OF EMPLOYEE	JOB AT FIRST CONTRACT	DATE	JOB AT RETIREMENT	DATE
2777	MCRAE DONALD	LABOURER	1879		1892
	MCRAE DUNCAN	MASON	1837		1842
3050	MERCREDI ABRAHAM	MIDDLEMAN	1853	FISHERMAN	1861
	MERCREDI FRANCOIS	MIDDLEMAN	1853	BOWSMAN	1868
3118	MILLAR JOHN	MIDDLEMAN	1854		1856
	MILLAR ROBERT	LABOURER	1840	MIDDLEMAN	1846
3048	MILLER JAMES	COOPER	1831		1836
	MINIE CHARLES	BOWSMAN	1844	STEERSMAN	1850
	MOAR HEBRON	LABOURER	1849		1852
	MOAR HEBRON	MIDDLEMAN	1853		1854
	MOAR ROBERT	MIDDLEMAN	1870		1873
	MOAR WILLIAM	LABOURER	1868		1873
2738	MONJEUNIER JOHN	MIDDLEMAN	1838	MIDDLEMAN	1846
	MONKMAN EDWARD	MIDDLEMAN	1860		1863
	MONKMAN JOSEPH	LABOURER	1849		1851
	MONKMAN JOSEPH	MIDDLEMAN	1854		1857
	MONTJEUNIER FRANCOIS J	LABOURER	1832	LABOURER	1836
	MORAIS FRANCOIS	LABOURER	1836		1839
	MORIN ALEXANDRE	MIDDLEMAN	1866		1869
	MORIN ANTOINE	BOWSMAN	1852		1867
	MORIN JOSEPH	STEERSMAN	1866	GUIDE	1869
3217	MORRISON ANGUS	LABOURER	1841		1849
3212	MORRISETTE NORBERT	LABOURER	1859	BLACKSMITH	1862
	MORRISON ANGUS	SAILOR	1874		1880
	MORRISON JOSEPH	FISHERMAN	1851		1855
3232	MOWANCE BAPTISTE	FISHERMAN	1861		1862
	MOWAT ANDREW	LABOURER	1842	BOATBUILDER	1850
3229	MOWAT JACOB	MIDDLEMAN	1870		1875
3239	MOWAT JOHN	INTERPRETER	1850		1853
	MUIR JOHN	LABOURER	1833	LABOURER	1836
3249	MUNRO FINLAY	COOPER	1856	POST MASTER	1864
1698	MURRAY ALEX HUNTER	CLERK	1845		1848
	NAULT ALEXIS	MIDDLEMAN	1838	STEERSMAN	1850
	NEPAPINAISE	STEERSMAN	1866		1868
	NERRON GEREMIE	MIDDLEMAN	1840	CARPENTER	1845
	NORN WILLIAM	LABOURER	1848		1854
3754	NORQUAY HENRY	MIDDLEMAN	1829		1831
3752	NORQUAY JOHN	MIDDLEMAN	1833		1838
	OBICHON PIERRE	MIDDLEMAN	1826	MIDDLEMAN	1848
3739	ODONELL MICHEL	LABOURER	1859		1864
	OGDEN PETER	APPRENTICE	1835		1840
	OIG CHARLES	APPRENTICE SERVANT	1887	CARPENTER	1890
4040	OLSEN JOHANNES	LABOURER	1855	CARPENTER	1860
3732	OLSEN OLAF	LABOURER	1856	APPRENTICE JOINER	1862
	OLSEN REIER	LABOURER	1851	MIDDLEMAN	1862
	PAGE ANTOINE	LABOURER	1841		1846
	PAMBRUN P C	APPRENTICE POST MASTER	1853		1856
	PAMBRUN PETER C	CLERK	1826		1842
	PAPIN PIERRE	BLACKSMITH	1861		1864
	PAPPIN PIERRE	MIDDLEMAN	1849	BOWSMAN	1862
	PAQUETTE JOSEPH	CARPENTER	1868		1870
3819	PARANTEAU BAZIL	MIDDLEMAN	1868	CARPENTER	1871
	PARANTEAU JOSEPH	MIDDLEMAN			

TABLE 3: CONTRACT EMPLOYEES OF THE HBC
RECRUITED FROM OR RETIRED TO THE RED RIVER COLONY, 1821-1870

ID	NAME OF EMPLOYEE		JOB AT FIRST CONTRACT	DATE	JOB AT RETIREMENT	DATE
3830	PARISIEN	BAPTISTE	MIDDLEMAN	1857	.	1857
3827	PARISIEN	FRANCOIS	BOWSMAN	1851	.	1854
.	PARISIEN	J BAPTISTE	INTERPRETER	1827	POST MASTER	1833
.	PARISIEN	JEAN	MIDDLEMAN	1860	.	1860
.	PARISIEN	JOSEPH	LABOURER	1865	INTERPRETER	1866
.	PARISIEN	JOSEPH	TRADER	1866	MIDDLEMAN	1869
.	PARISIEN	JOSEPH	MIDDLEMAN	1866	.	1867
.	PARISIEN	NORBERT	MIDDLEMAN	1868	.	1869
3824	PARISIEN	PASCAL	LABOURER	1851	.	1854
.	PARISIEN	WILLIAM	LABOURER	1875	.	1876
.	PARK	ARCHIBALD	LABOURER	1879	.	1882
.	PARK	LOUIS	LABOURER	1881	.	1884
3856	PATERSON	MALCOLM	LABOURER	1841	MIDDLEMAN	1849
.	PATNAUDE	AUGUST	MIDDLEMAN	1832	BOWSMAN	1846
.	PAUL	LOUISON	MIDDLEMAN	1865	BOWSMAN	1870
3871	PAUL	PAULET	GUIDE	1852	.	1855
3870	PAUL	PAULET	MIDDLEMAN	1826	STEERSMAN	1847
.	PAYETTE	J BAPTISTE	BOWSMAN	1850	POST MASTER	1862
.	PECHE	FRANCOIS	STEERSMAN	1826	GUIDE	1831
.	PEDERSON	HALVOR	LABOURER	1856	.	1861
.	PELLETIER	DOCITE	MIDDLEMAN	1866	.	1867
3888	PELLETIER	JOSEPH	MIDDLEMAN	1868	.	1871
.	PELLY	JOHN	CARPENTER	1867	CARPENTER	1873
.	PELTIER	PIERRE	LABOURER	1842	.	1843
3912	PETERSON	JOHN	LABOURER	1864	.	1869
.	PICHE	FRANCOIS	STEERSMAN	1849	.	1852
.	PICHEE	FRANCOIS	MIDDLEMAN	1857	.	1860
3591	PICHEE	FRANCOIS	BOWSMAN	1860	BOWSMAN	1863
.	PIERPONT	ALONZO	SALESMAN	1868	.	1869
.	PLANTE	ANTOINE	STEERSMAN	1855	.	1858
.	PLANTE	FRANCOIS	MIDDLEMAN	1828	MIDDLEMAN	1845
.	POITRAS	MEDARD	MIDDLEMAN	1826	CARPENTER	1833
3970	POMBRILLANT	LOUIS	MIDDLEMAN	1851	MIDDLEMAN	1856
.	POTTINGER	GEORGE	LABOURER	1862	LABOURER	1871
.	POTTINGER	JAMES	LABOURER	1863	.	1868
.	PRATT	CHARLES	MIDDLEMAN	1835	STEERSMAN	1848
3983	PRIMEAU	BAPTISTE	MIDDLEMAN	1861	.	1864
4056	PRIMEAU	JEREMIE	MIDDLEMAN	1861	.	1864
.	PRINCE	DAVID	BOWSMAN	1859	.	1862
.	PRINCE	FREDERICK	LABOURER	1876	.	1879
4065	PRINCE	HENRY	MIDDLEMAN	1865	.	1869
.	PRINCE	JAMES	HOUSE SERVANT	1888	.	1891
.	PRINCE	WILLIAM	HOUSE SERVANT	1888	.	1891
4016	PRUDEN	ARTHUR	CLERK	1860	.	1863
4024	PRUDEN	CORNELIUS	MIDDLEMAN	1855	.	1859
4027	PRUDEN	JAMES	APPRENTICE POST MASTER	1842	.	1847
4027	PRUDEN	JAMES	CLERK	1860	.	1863
.	PRUDEN	PATRICK	MIDDLEMAN	1861	.	1862
.	PURCELL	THOMAS	LABOURER	1862	.	1874
4146	RACETTE	AUGUSTIN	INTERPRETER	1854	BOWSMAN	1856
4146	RACETTE	AUGUSTIN	MIDDLEMAN	1855	.	1858

RECRUITED FROM OR RETIRED TO THE RED RIVER COLONY, 1821-1870

ID	NAME OF EMPLOYEE		JOB AT FIRST CONTRACT	DATE	JOB AT RETIREMENT	DATE
	RICHARD	FRANCOIS	INTERPRETER	1828	.	1839
	RICHARD	LESAEZ	LABOURER	1870	.	1871
	RICHOTTE	ANDRE	BOWSMAN	1854	.	1857
4180	RICHOTTE	BAPTISTE	MIDDLEMAN	1865	.	1870
4178	RICHOTTE	BAZIL	BOWSMAN	1867	STEERSMAN	1869
	RICHOTTE	FRANCOIS	MIDDLEMAN	1860	.	1862
	ROBERTSON	FRANCOIS	STEERSMAN	1835	.	1840
4089	ROBERTSON	GEORGE	MIDDLEMAN	1855	.	1858
	ROBERTSON	JAMES	LABOURER	1832	.	1834
	ROBERTSON	JOHN	LABOURER	1833	.	1840
	ROBILLARD	ALEXIS	MIDDLEMAN	1856	MIDDLEMAN	1865
4206	ROBILLARD	BAPTISTE	STEERSMAN	1849	.	1852
4206	ROBILLARD	BAPTISTE	FISHERMAN	1852	GUIDE	1860
	ROBILLARD	LOUIS	MIDDLEMAN	1868	.	1871
4215	ROCHELEAU	GUILLAUME	STEERSMAN	1827	.	1840
4215	ROCHLEAU	GUILLAUME	STEERSMAN	1837	.	1840
	ROCQUEBRUN	OLIVIER	MIDDLEMAN	1855	.	1858
	ROLPH	GEORGE	BLACKSMITH	1876	.	1879
4245	ROSS	CHARLES	MIDDLEMAN	1855	.	1857
4249	ROSS	GEORGE	BOWSMAN	1832	.	1834
	ROWLAND	FRANCIS	STEERSMAN	1862	.	1864
4730	ROWLAND	JOHN	LABOURER	1844	.	1850
4730	ROWLAND	JOHN	INTERPRETER	1869	.	1870
4262	ROY	JOSEPH	BOWSMAN	1852	.	1855
	RUELLE	FELIX	MIDDLEMAN	1861	.	1867
4342	SABISTON	ALEXANDER	MIDDLEMAN	1862	.	1866
4344	SABISTON	JOHN	LABOURER	1861	.	1867
4340	SABISTON	JOSEPH	LABOURER	1862	LABOURER	1865
	SABISTON	WILLIAM	INTERPRETER	1844	.	1847
	SAHYS	BAPTISTE	MIDDLEMAN	1849	.	1852
	SANDERS	THOMAS	LABOURER	1835	.	1835
	SANDERSON	GEORGE	CARPENTER	1873	.	1876
4335	SANDESON	THOMAS	MIDDLEMAN	1844	.	1849
	SANDIN	CARL ERIK	LABOURER	1857	LABOURER	1860
4333	SANDISON	GEORGE	MIDDLEMAN	1840	.	1843
4327	SANDISON	GEORGE	MIDDLEMAN	1864	BOWSMAN	1869
	SANDISON	JAMES	MIDDLEMAN	1826	.	1829
	SANDISON	JOHN	LABOURER	1871	LABOURER	1881
4737	SANDISON	THOMAS	BOWSMAN	1852	.	1854
4332	SANDISON	WILLIAM	BOWSMAN	1856	.	1860
4317	SANSREGRET	LOUIS	MIDDLEMAN	1851	.	1854
4740	SAUNDERS	PALM	FISHERMAN	1856	.	1857
4747	SAUVE	FRANCOIS	MIDDLEMAN	1859	.	1862
4295	SAUVE	JEAN	LABOURER	1831	.	1833
4296	SAUVE	JOSEPH	STEERSMAN	1848	.	1851
4296	SAUVE	JOSEPH	STEERSMAN	1855	.	1858
4296	SAUVE	JOSEPH	LABOURER	1862	.	1865
4421	SAUVE	NORBERT	MIDDLEMAN	1844	.	1847
	SAUVE	NORBERT	STEERSMAN	1851	.	1858
	SAUVE	PETER	LABOURER	1862	.	1865
4291	SAVOYARD	FRANCOIS	LABOURER	1845	.	1849
4291	SAVOYARD	FRANCOIS	MIDDLEMAN	1852	BOWSMAN	1856
4763	SAYER	EDOUARD	MIDDLEMAN	1844	STEERSMAN	1852

TABLE 3: CONTRACT EMPLOYEES OF THE HBC
RECRUITED FROM OR RETIRED TO THE RED RIVER COLONY, 1821-1870

ID	NAME OF EMPLOYEE		JOB AT FIRST CONTRACT	DATE	JOB AT RETIREMENT	DATE
4764	SAYER	EDWARD	STEERSMAN	1852	INTERPRETER	1857
1527	SAYER	GEORGE	BOWSMAN	1838	STEERSMAN	1848
487	SAYER	PIERRE GUILM	BOWSMAN	1828	STEERSMAN	1832
	SCOTT	EDWARD	BLACKSMITH	1867	LABOURER	1876
4352	SCOTT	WILLIAM	LABOURER	1835	MIDDLEMAN	1844
	SETTEE	HENRY GEORGE	LABOURER	1875	.	1878
	SETTEE	WILLIAM	LABOURER	1875	.	1878
	SETTER	GEORGE	LABOURER	1883	.	1886
	SEVIELLEZ	PIERRE				
	SHORT	JAMES	MIDDLEMAN	1825	.	1830
	SHORT	JAMES	GUIDE	1855	MIDDLEMAN	1862
	SIMPSON	ALEXANDER	MIDDLEMAN	1855	.	1858
4373	SIMPSON	JOHN	LABOURER	1861	.	1864
	SINCLAIR	ANDREW	APPRENTICE JOINER	1849	BOATBUILDER	1865
4378	SINCLAIR	BAKIE	BOWSMAN	1860	BOWSMAN	1863
	SINCLAIR	COLIN	LABOURER	1826	BLACKSMITH	1843
4780	SINCLAIR	CUTHBERT	LABOURER	1866	LABOURER	1871
	SINCLAIR	DAVID	POST MASTER	1864	.	1867
	SINCLAIR	GEORGE	MIDDLEMAN	1853	.	1856
	SINCLAIR	GEORGE	STEERSMAN	1827	COAST GUIDE	1839
	SINCLAIR	GEORGE	INTERPRETER	1852	INTERPRETER	1856
	SINCLAIR	JAMES	LABOURER	1874	.	1877
	SINCLAIR	JAMES	LABOURER	1851	.	1853
	SINCLAIR	JAMES	LABOURER	1851	.	1853
	SINCLAIR	JAMES	MIDDLEMAN	1853	.	1856
	SINCLAIR	JAMES	LABOURER	1865	.	1872
	SINCLAIR	JAMES	LABOURER	1869	.	1876
	SINCLAIR	JOHN	MIDDLEMAN	1840	LABOURER	1848
	SINCLAIR	JOHN	LABOURER	1870	.	1876
	SINCLAIR	JOHN	INTERPRETER	1874	.	1877
	SINCLAIR	NICOL I	POST MASTER	1867	.	1870
4382	SINCLAIR	PETER	INTERPRETER	1839	.	1853
4382	SINCLAIR	PETER	INTERPRETER	1850	INTERPRETER	1857
	SINCLAIR	THOMAS	MIDDLEMAN	1851	BOWSMAN	1855
	SINCLAIR	THOMAS	MIDDLEMAN	1860	.	1863
	SINCLAIR	THOMAS	LABOURER	1887	.	1890
	SINCLAIR	WILLIAM	MIDDLEMAN	1866	.	1869
	SINCLAIR	WILLIAM	POST MASTER	1866	.	1869
4796	SLATER	JAMES	LABOURER	1833	.	1849
4811	SMITH	ANGUS	LABOURER	1853	MIDDLEMAN	1859
	SMITH	GEORGE	LABOURER	1863	.	1868
4127	SMITH	HENRY	MIDDLEMAN	1846	.	1851
	SMITH	HENRY	MIDDLEMAN	1852	.	1855
	SMITH	JAMES	MIDDLEMAN	1864	CARPENTER	1871
	SMITH	JOHN	LABOURER	1861	.	1864
	SMITH	JOHN	LABOURER	1870	STEERSMAN	1890
	SMITH	JOHN	BLACKSMITH	1874	ENGINEER	1884
	SMITH	THOMAS	MIDDLEMAN	1865	.	1868
13279	SMITH	WILLIAM	FARM SERVANT	1836	.	1841
	SMITH	WILLIAM	LABOURER	1869	.	1882
	SMITH	WILLIAM ROBT	MIDDLEMAN	1856	.	1859
.	SMITH	SAM	LABOURER	1850	.	1864

ID	NAME OF EMPLOYEE	JOB AT FIRST CONTRACT	DATE	JOB AT RETIREMENT	DATE
	SOULIER WILLIAM	MIDDLEMAN	1833		1845
	SOULIER WILLIAM	STEERSMAN			1853
	SOUPARENS BAPTISTE	BOWSMAN	1850		1853
3491	SOUPARONS BAPTISTE	BOWSMAN	1850		1853
	SPENCE DONALD	MIDDLEMAN	1856		1859
	SPENCE GEORGE	MIDDLEMAN	1854		1859
	SPENCE JAMES	COOPER	1839		1844
	SPENCE JAMES	MIDDLEMAN	1841		1843
	SPENCE JOHN	LABOURER	1868		1871
	SPENCE JOSEPH	LABOURER	1876		1879
4834	SPENCE MAGNUS	LABOURER	1829	BOWSMAN	1832
	SPENCE NICOL	BOWSMAN	1860	BOWSMAN	1868
3498	SPENCE PETER	MIDDLEMAN	1863		1870
	SPENCE ROBERT	MIDDLEMAN	1867		1870
	SPENCE WILLIAM	LABOURER	1823		1831
4470	ST ARNAUD ALEXANDRE	MIDDLEMAN	1861	FISHERMAN	1864
4579	ST ARNAUD BONAPARTE	MIDDLEMAN	1828		1846
	ST ARNAUDE LOUIS	MIDDLEMAN	1853		1856
	ST CYR FRANCOIS	INTERPRETER	1878		1879
4848	ST CYR JEAN BAPTIST	MIDDLEMAN	1864	INTERPRETER	1869
	ST CYRE J BAPTISTE	MIDDLEMAN	1839		1844
	ST DENIS LOUIS	MIDDLEMAN	1834		1838
4588	ST DENNIS JACQUES	MIDDLEMAN	1827	MIDDLEMAN	1839
	ST GERMAIN PIERRE	STEERSMAN	1866		1869
	ST GERMAINE PIERRE	INTERPRETER	1827		1832
4605	ST LUC GILBERT	MIDDLEMAN	1851		1854
4608	ST LUC GILBERT	MIDDLEMAN	1851	BOWSMAN	1861
4608	STANGER JAMES	LABOURER	1862		1867
	STANGER WILLIAM	LABOURER	1869		1875
	STAR WILLIAM	MIDDLEMAN	1867		1870
4475	STEVENS GEORGE	MIDDLEMAN	1842		1846
	STEVENSON EDWARD	MIDDLEMAN	1865		1868
	STEVENSON JOHN	LABOURER	1852	STEERSMAN	1862
	STEVENSON JOHN	FISHERMAN	1874	LABOURER	1891
4488	STEWART JAMES	LABOURER	1850	50	1859
	STOUT ALEXANDER	LABOURER	1861	INTERPRETER	1872
	SUHYS FRANCOIS	MIDDLEMAN	1841		1849
	SUISSAUME LAURENT ALEX	MIDDLEMAN	1836	FISHERMAN	1854
	SUPRENANT BAPTISTE	BOWSMAN	1853		1854
	SUTHERLAND ALEXANDER	LABOURER	1887		1890
	SUTHERLAND JAMES R	MIDDLEMAN	1853	MIDDLEMAN	1861
	SUTHERLAND JOHN	ENGINEER	1891		1894
4552	SUTHERLAND ROBERT	LABOURER	1851		1854
4552	SUTHERLAND ROBERT	LABOURER	1851		1854
	SUTHERLAND WILLIAM	LABOURER	1883		1886
4919	SVENSEN JONAS	LABOURER	1857		1862
	SWAIN ALEXANDER	LABOURER	1866		1869
	SWAIN ALEXANDER	LABOURER	1874		1876
	SWAIN JAMES	MIDDLEMAN	1855		1858
4921	SYMISON WILLIAM	MIDDLEMAN	1851		1853
4921	SYMISON WILLIAM	MIDDLEMAN	1851		1853
4922	TATE JOHN	BOWSMAN	1858	SAWYER	1870
4578	TATE JOSEPH	LABOURER	1851		1854

TABLE 3: CONTRACT EMPLOYEES OF THE HBC
RECRUITED FROM OR RETIRED TO THE RED RIVER COLONY, 1821-1870

ID	NAME OF EMPLOYEE		JOB AT FIRST CONTRACT	DATE	JOB AT RETIREMENT	DATE
	TATE	JOSEPH	MIDDLEMAN	1851		1854
13277	TATE	PHILIP	LABOURER	1849		1852
13277	TATE	PHILIP	BOWSMAN	1858	INTERPRETER	1857
4695	TAYFAULT	LOUIS	MIDDLEMAN	1826		1831
4637	TAYLOR	ROBERT	MIDDLEMAN	1855		1858
4936	TAYLOR	ROBERT	LABOURER	1863		1868
4661	THIBERT	PIERRE	MIDDLEMAN	1835		1842
	THICKFOOD	GEORGE	MIDDLEMAN	1869		1871
	THOMAS	ALBERT	LABOURER	1875		1878
	THOMAS	CHARLES	LABOURER	1832	INTERPRETER	1871
	THOMAS	JAMES	STEERSMAN	1864		1851
	THOMAS	JOHN	MIDDLEMAN	1857	MIDDLEMAN	1866
	THOMAS	LOUIS	MIDDLEMAN	1869		1868
	THOMAS	RODERICK G	HOUSE SERVANT	1888		1871
	THOMAS	THOMAS	MIDDLEMAN	1865		1891
4951	THOMPSON	JOHN	LABOURER	1874		1868
	THOMPSON	ROBERT	MIDDLEMAN	1868		1877
	THOMSON	ROBERT	LABOURER	1862		1871
	TODD	DONALD	APPRENTICE BOATBUILDER	1856		1867
	TOMISON	WILLIAM	LABOURER	1860		1859
4962	TOURANGEAU	ANTOINE	MIDDLEMAN	1851		1865
4962	TOURANGEAU	ANTOINE	MIDDLEMAN	1859	BOWSMAN	1858
4964	TOURANGEAU	J BAPTIST SR	BOWSMAN	1852		1864
4964	TOURANGEAU	JEAN BAPTIST	MIDDLEMAN	1827	STEERSMAN	1862
4964	TOURANGEAU	JEAN BAPTIST	GUIDE	1847	INTERPRETER	1842
4964	TOURANGEAU	JEAN BAPTIST	GUIDE	1852		1850
4714	TRAVELLER	DUNCAN	MIDDLEMAN	1867	GUIDE	1862
	TRINDELL	CHARLES	MIDDLEMAN	1867		1870
	TRINDELL	CHARLES	BOWSMAN	1873		1870
	TRINDELL	KENNETH	MIDDLEMAN	1857		1875
	TRINDELL	PETER	MIDDLEMAN	1856	MIDDLEMAN	1870
	TRINDELL	RICHARD	MIDDLEMAN	1867		1859
	TROTTIER	J BAPTISTE	MIDDLEMAN	1851		1869
	TROTTIER	JEAN BAPTIST	MIDDLEMAN	1851		1853
4982	TURNER	RICHARD	CARPENTER	1850		1853
	TURON	JOSEPH	MIDDLEMAN	1825	TRADER	1866
	VALETTE	GUILLAUME	MIDDLEMAN	1860		1835
	VALLE	JOSEPH	MIDDLEMAN	1864		1863
5068	VANDALLE	BENJAMIN	MIDDLEMAN	1850		1867
5061	VANDALLE	FRANCOIS	MIDDLEMAN	1861		1853
5002	VANDALLE	GABRIEL	MIDDLEMAN	1865		1864
5070	VANDALLE	LOUIS	MIDDLEMAN	1866		1868
5095	VERMETTE	ALEXIS	MIDDLEMAN	1865		1869
	VERNETTE	MAXIME	MIDDLEMAN	1868		1868
5104	VERSAILLES	PIERRE	MIDDLEMAN	1850		1871
5116	VILLEBRUN	DANIEL	MIDDLEMAN	1866		1854
	VILLEBRUN	FRANCIS	MIDDLEMAN	1864		1870
	VILLEBRUN	GUILLAUME	MIDDLEMAN	1864	STEERSMAN	1867
5117	VILLEBRUN	JOSEPH	MIDDLEMAN	1866		1870
	VILLEBRUN	LEON	MIDDLEMAN	1866		1869
	VILLENEUVE	DAVID	MIDDLEMAN	1865		1868

ID	NAME OF EMPLOYEE	JOB AT FIRST CONTRACT	DATE	JOB AT RETIREMENT	DATE
5126	VILLENEUVE IZIDORE	MIDDLEMAN	1866	MIDDLEMAN	1871
.	VINCENT JOHN	FARMER	1867		1869
	VIVIER ALEXIS	BOWSMAN	1856		1859
	VIVIER JOSEPH	MIDDLEMAN	1833		1836
5021	VIVIER JOSEPH JNR	MIDDLEMAN	1833		1838
5140	VIVIER MICHEL	BOWSMAN	1850		1851
	VIVIER MICHEL	MIDDLEMAN	1857		1857
	VIVIER OLIVIER	MIDDLEMAN	1833	INTERPRETER	1851
5149	WAGNER MICHAEL	LABOURER	1862		1865
5145	WAKETCH	STEERSMAN	1831		1834
5238	WALKINGCHIF JOHN	BOWSMAN	1860		1863
	WARDS JAMES	LABOURER	1862	COOK	1869
5223	WATTS FREDERICK	LABOURER	1851		1854
5242	WHITE PHILIP	LABOURER	1860		1871
5174	WHITFORD FRANCIS	GUIDE	1859		1858
	WHITFORD FRANCIS	MIDDLEMAN	1858		1859
	WHITFORD JAMES	STEERSMAN	1832		1835
5249	WHITFORD SIMON	MIDDLEMAN	1846		1849
5249	WHITFORD SIMON	STEERSMAN	1857		1859
	WILLIAMS JAMES	LABOURER	1875		1878
5192	WILLIAMSON JAMES	LABOURER	1862	MIDDLEMAN	1871
5258	WILSON ANDREW	INTERPRETER	1852	POST MASTER	1834
5174	WILSON DANIEL	BOWSMAN	1852		1855
	WNITFORD FRANCIS	GUIDE	1838	STEERSMAN	1848
	WOOD JOHN	LABOURER	1868		1873
	YOUNG JAMES	LABOURER	1871		1878
5210	YOUNG PASCAL	LABOURER	1858		1863
	ZASTRE GONZ	BOWSMAN	1829		1832

Table 4:

Geographical Location and Children of Manitoba Families, 1870

TABLE 4: GEOGRAPHICAL LOCATION AND
CHILDREN OF MANITOBA FAMILIES, 1870

ID	FAMILY	PARISH	AT OR BETWEEN		CHILDREN AND AGES AT NEXT BIRTHDAY
90	ANDERSON	PORTAGE	92	·	WILLIAM 18, ELIZA 14, HARRIET 14, PETER 12, JOHN 9, JOHN 6
90	ANDERSON	PORTAGE	92	·	MARY 5, LYDIA 3, HARRIET 6, DANIEL 5
91	ANDERSON	PORTAGE	133	70	MARGARET 8, DAVID 8, CHARLES 6, JOSHUA 9, BETSY 5
92	ANDERSON	PORTAGE	111	92	HENRY 13, CALET 13, RICHARD 11, LOUISA 4
92	ANDERSON	PORTAGE	111	92	MARY 14, JANE 11
93	ANDERSON	ST ANDREW	97	98	JAMES 19, JAMES 16, CHARLES 16, JOHN 8
94	ANDERSON	PORTAGE	111	92	GEORGE 6, NANCY 18, MARIANNE 4, MARIA 10
97	ANGER	ST JAMES	9	13	NANCY 16, SARAH 6, WILLIAM 4
97	ANGER	ST JAMES	9	13	JAMES 7, THOMAS 7
98	ANNAL	ST ANDREW	24	·	JANE, NANCY, MARIANNE 14, BARBARA 4
98	ANNAL	ST ANDREW	24	·	THOMAS
3501	ANTILL	ST JAMES	44	45	
101	ARCAND	BAIE S PAUL	219	244	MARIE 5, GENEVIENE 3, J BAPTISTE 1
102	ARCAND	SFX	120	126	NAPOLEON 7, SUZETTE 4, GASPARD 2
103	ARCAND	BAIE S PAUL	245	·	MARY 9, FLORESTINE 5, GREGOIRE 3
104	ARCAND	BAIE S PAUL	219	244	LUCIA 1
106	ARCHIBALD	ST JOHN	4	13	
107	ARCROW	ST ANDREW	150	155	THOMAS 22, JOSEPH 18, FINNIA 18, ELIZABETH 14
108	ARCROW	ST PETER	56	74	DAVID 9, GEORGE 13, JANE 11, MARGUERITE 11, MAGNUS 2
112	ARKISS	ST ANDREW	96	·	CATHERINE 15
115	ARKISS	ST ANDREW	76	·	JOHN 2, CATHERINE 15, GEORGE 13, CHARLOTTE 6
115	ARKISS	ST ANDREW	76	·	
116	ARKLAND	ST JOHN	13	6	
117	ARMIT	ST JAMES	8	17	
121	ARMSTRONG	ST JAMES	70	73	MARY 6, MARGARET 4, SARAH 2
123	ARMSTRONG	ST JAMES	70	73	MARIANNE 1
123	ARMSTRONG	POPLAR PT	52	41	
125	ASHAM	ST ANDREW	264	267	MARY
126	ASHAM	ST PETER	133	167	MARIANNE 1
132	ASHDOWN	ST JOHN	6	33	
127	ASHIM	ST PETER	8	17	NATHANIEL 18, WILLIAM 16, MARIANN 11, RACHEL 11, EDITH 5
127	ASHIM	ST PETER	8	17	NATHANIEL 18, WILLIAM 16, MARIANN 11, RACHEL 11, EDITH 5
128	ASHIM	ST PETER	56	74	ELISE 4, MATHILDA 1, WILLIAM 1
129	ASHIM	ST PETER	8	17	
135	ATKINSON	ST ANDREW	264	267	ELIZA 1
137	ATKINSON	POPLAR PT	63	62	JAMES 10, JOHN 9, DONALD 9, MARGARET 7, MARGARET 3
139	ATKINSON	POPLAR PT	68	·	
145	AYOTTE	SFX	31	32	
157	BADGER	ST CLEMENT	77	·	JOSEPH 22, CATHERINE 22, MARY 18, THOMAS 16, ELIZABETH 11
157	BADGER	ST CLEMENT	77	·	BENJAMIN 3, JANE 3, JANE 1
158	BADGER	ST PETER	133	167	SARA 14, SOPHIE 8, WILLIAM 8, WILLIAM 4
159	BADGER	ST PETER	83	85	SAMUEL 24
160	BADGER	ST PETER	133	167	HARIET 19
175	BALLENDEN	ST PAUL	35	·	EMMA 15, MARY 13, MARGARET 13, JOSEPH 7, CAROLINE 5
175	BALLENDEN	ST PAUL	35	·	CHRISTIE 3, FLORA 1
1140	BALLENDEN	ST PAUL	110	115	
167	BALLENDIN	ST ANDREW	66	67	ANNE 4, CATHERINE 2
168	BALLENDIN	ST ANDREW	113	·	GEORGE 36, ELISE 27, GEORGE 25
172	BALLENDIN	ST ANDREW	66	67	JOHN 35, JOHN
173	BALLENDIN	ST ANDREW	66	67	ISABELLA 3, JAMES 17, ALEXANDER 17, ANNE 17
177	BALLENDIN	ST ANDREW	82	85	CHARLES 23, CHARLES, ROBERT 18
180	BALLSOLIE	ST JOHN	6	33	ANGUS 1

TABLE 4: GEOGRAPHICAL LOCATION AND
CHILDREN OF MANITOBA FAMILIES, 1870

ID	FAMILY	PARISH	AT OR BETWEEN		CHILDREN AND AGES AT NEXT BIRTHDAY									
179	BANNANTYNE	ST JOHN	7	.	JAMES	14	ELIZA	12	RODERICK	10	LAURA	8	WILLIAM	6
179	BANNANTYNE	ST JOHN	7	.	ROBERT	3	ANNIE	1		.		.		.
182	BANNERMAN	KILDONAN	21	.	JOHN	38	ALEXANDER	31	SELKIRK	26	JAMES	21	DONALD	19
189	BANNERMAN	KILDONAN	20	.	BARBARA	29	JAMES	27	WILLIAM	25	BELLA	22	ANN	19
189	BANNERMAN	KILDONAN	20	.	HUGH	15		.		.		.		.
191	BANNERMAN	KILDONAN	1	.		.		.		.		.		.
192	BANNERMAN	ST JOHN	49	.	ARCHIBALD	9	MARGARET	7	ALEX	3	HARRIET	1		.
198	BANNERMAN	POPLAR PT	64	.	ELIZABETH	10	WILLIAM	7	D	5	SAMUEL	4	JOHN	2
205	BARBEAU	ST CLEMENT	91	97	MARGUERITE	18		.		.		.		.
206	BARBER	ST JOHN	9	25	HARRIET	8	ALBERT	6	JOHN	4	ALEXANDER	3		.
392	BARNES	ST JAMES	9	13		.		.		.		.		.
211	BARRON	SFX	140	141		.		.		.		.		.
212	BARRON	SFX	140	.	MELANIE	15	OLIVIER	14	NAPOLEON	10		.		.
215	BARRON	ST JAMES	47	.		.		.		.		.		.
224	BAUVEH	ST JOHN	28	55	LOUIS	8	CAROLINE	5	VIRGINIA	2		.		.
226	BAUVEH	ST JOHN	28	55		.		.		.		.		.
235	BAXTER	ST PAUL	13	14		.		.		.		.		.
233	BEADRY	ST BONIFACE	26	25	PAULINE	20	AUGUSTIN	14	MARIE	13		.		.
238	BEADS	ST JAMES	22	23	JAMES	12	WILLIAM	10	ELIZABETH	8	MARGARET	6		.
195	BEAR	ST PETER	8*	.	ISABEL	28	SOPHIE	23	PETER	18	MARY	12		.
201	BEAR	ST PETER	.	.	ALBERT	12	ALEXANDER	10	WILLIAM	4	NANCY	1		.
193	BEAUCHAMP	ST NORBERT	72	67	MARIE	10	JOSEPHTE	5	CECILE	2		.		.
196	BEAUCHAMP	SFX	133	115	J BAPTISTE	17		15	ANDRE	12	ELISE	10	ROSINE	8
196	BEAUCHAMP	SFX	133	115	MARIANNE	5		.		.		.		.
174	BEAUCHEMIN	ST VITAL	40*	.	LEON	23	ANDRE	18	FAISELLE	11	MARIE	8	ADELAIDE	5
174	BEAUCHEMIN	ST VITAL	40*	.	ALEXANDRE	3		.		.		.		.
197	BEAUCHEMIN	ST CHARLES	59	.	WILLIAM	11	VIRGINIE	9	ADELAIDE	7	MARGUERITE	4	MARIA	2
202	BEAUCHEMIN	ST VITAL	38*	.		.		.		.		.		.
186	BEAUCHENE	STE ANNE	38	46	ISABELLE	8	OLIVIER	6	ALEXANDRE	3		.		.
253	BEAUDRY	SFX	183	190	ALFRED	2		.		.		.		.
264	BEDDOM	ST ANDREW	.	.	FRANCES	11	ANNIE	8	WILLIAM	7	JOHN	5		.
265	BEGG	ST JOHN	25	28	MARION	2		.		.		.		.
266	BEGG	ST CLEMENT	5	.	MARGUERITE	21	CATHERINE	17	CHARLES	20	JOHN	16	ROBERT	11
267	BEGG	ST CLEMENT	5	2	WILLIAM	5	JAMES	1		.		.		.
210	BELANGER	ST NORBERT	76	75		.		.		.		.		.
245	BELANGER	ST NORBERT	94	.	JOHN	19	NORBERT	14	BERNARD	7	JOSEPH	2	JOSEPHTE	16
245	BELANGER	ST NORBERT	94	.	HELENE	13		.		.		.		.
251	BELL	ST JOHN	25	28		.		.		.		.		.
278	BELLEFEVILL	ST NORBERT	81	76	JOSEPH	2		.		.		.		.
280	BELLEHUMEUR	PORTAGE	.	.	MARY	10		.		.		.		.
281	BELLHUMEUR	SFX	150	159	PATRICE	27	ELIZABETH	24	MARGUERITE	22	LOUISE	20	CUTHBERT	18
281	BELLHUMEUR	SFX	150	159	MICHEL	16	ROSE	9	JOSEPHTE	7	J BAPTISTE	5	CALIXTE	4
303	BELLY	ST ANDREW	114	115	NANCY	22	ALEXANDER	20	HELEN	17	CATHERINE	11	WILLIAM	8
303	BELLY	ST ANDREW	114	115	GEORGE	2		.		.		.		.
290	BERARD	ST BONIFACE	31	.	PIERRE	20	MARIE	18	ROSALIE	16	ALEXANDRE	12	JOSEPHINE	9
291	BERARD	ST JAMES	65	.	HARRIET	16		.		.		.		.
292	BERARD	ST BONIFACE	.	.	CATHERINE	9	VIRGINIE	8	FLORANT	5	ALFRED	3	MARGUERITE	1
293	BERARD	ST NORBERT	122	.	GUSTAVE	16	MARGUERITE	13	CATHERINE	11	ROSALIE	9	ETIENNE	7
293	BERARD	ST NORBERT	122	.	CHARLES	5	MARIE	4	ADELAIDE	1		.		.
294	BERARD	STE ANNE	31	38	JEREMIE	9	ALFRED	8	VIRGINIE	4	ADELE	2		.
296	BERARD	ST BONIFACE	81	87		.		.		.		.		.
297	BERARD	ST BONIFACE	94	.	LOUIS	40	ANDRE	31	PIERRE	29	AMBROISE	22	MARIE	35

TABLE 4: GEOGRAPHICAL LOCATION AND
CHILDREN OF MANITOBA FAMILIES, 1870

ID	FAMILY	PARISH	AT OR BETWEEN	CHILDREN AND AGES AT NEXT BIRTHDAY
297	BERARD	ST BONIFACE	94	JOSEPHTE 28
300	BERARD	STE ANNE	49 66	
301	BERARD	ST JAMES	21 22	
302	BERARD	STE ANNE	51	JULIE 14
284	BERCIER	SFX	176 181	MARIE 11, MARGUERITE 8
285	BERCIER	SFX	176 181	ALEXIS 11, MARIE 4, WILLIAM 17
286	BERCIER	SFX	176 181	LOUISE 7, THIBAULT 4, MARIE 2
287	BERCIER	SFX	76	MOISE 23, FRANCOIS 1, PAUL 19, J BAPTISTE 1
288	BERCIER	SFX	76	NAPOLEON 11, CUTHBERT 9, HYACINTHE 4, MARIE 2
289	BERCIER	SFX	54	ELIE 8, MARGUERITE 7, JOSEPH 5
309	BERIAU	STE ANNE	65 68	ROSALIE 12, MELANIE, PHILOMENE 3
310	BERIAU	STE ANNE	65 68	LOUIS 29, LOUIS 17, CELESTIN 1
315	BERIAU	STE ANNE	13 6	MARGUERITE 17, JOSEPH 1
312	BERIAULT	ST NORBERT	22	ANTOINE 6, ALEXANDRE 4, JOACHIM 14
320	BERTHELET	STE AGATHE	589 577	BRUNEAU 18, ELIZA 16, PATRICE 9, ELIZA 2
321	BERTHELET	STE AGATHE	579 577	ANTOINE 2, JOSEPHINE 13, ISABELLE 11, CHARLES 8, PHILOMENE 5
322	BERTHELET	STE AGATHE	585	MARIE 15, MARGUERITE 11, EDWARD 11
322	BERTHELET	STE AGATHE	585	VICTORINE 1, JEAN 1
324	BERTHELET	STE AGATHE	265 124	JOSEPH 15, TOUSSAINT 8, ROGER 4
326	BERTHELET	STE AGATHE	265 124	NORBERT 22, ELISE 18, FRANCOIS 16, ELLEN 1, FREDERICK 4
364	BIAS	POPLAR PT	55	ISABELLA 4, CHARLES, MARGARET 2
367	BIRD	POPLAR PT	60 63	CHARLES 2, MARY 4, ALFRED 3, GEORGE 1
370	BIRD	ST JOHN	6 33	JAMES 7, EMMA 19, CLARA 14, CATHERINE 10, MARIA 8
372	BIRD	PORTAGE	66	EMMA 19, HENRY 2
372	BIRD	PORTAGE	66	HENRY 2
374	BIRD	ST PAUL	25	SOPHIA 2
375	BIRD	ST PAUL	111	SOPHIA 2
377	BIRD	POPLAR PT	41	SOPHIE 15
378	BIRD	ST ANDREW	287 280	SOPHIE 15, SOPHIE, CHARLES 10
380	BIRD	ST PETER	100 133	CHARLES 15
384	BIRD	ST PETER	56 74	SARAH 3
385	BIRD	ST ANDREW	69	
387	BIRD	POPLAR PT	60 63	
389	BIRD	ST ANDREW	69 70	SARAH 3
390	BIRD	POPLAR PT	40 43	
391	BIRD	*ST PAUL	63	JOHN 1
393	BIRD	ST CHARLES	105	ANN 8, CHARLES 4, THOMAS 1
395	BIRD	ST PAUL	92 104	JOHN 8
397	BIRD	ST PAUL		WILLIAM 2
398	BIRD	POPLAR PT	36 38	WILLIAM 2, CHARLES
399	BIRD	POPLAR PT	40	HENRY 24, JOHN 18
1143	BIRD	PORTAGE	263 268	
334	BIRD	ST ANDREW	7	BARBARA 4, MARY 16
335	BIRSTON	SFX	159	HENRI 21, MARY 16, CLEMENCE 20, PHILOMENE 16
338	BIRSTON	ST CLEMENT		ELISE 19, CHARLES 25, ALEXANDRE 23
338	BIRSTON	SFX		WILLIAM 25, NANCY 13
341	BLACK	SFX	146 147	NANCY 13
343	BLACK	ST ANDREW	280 260	SAMUEL 9, ANGELIQUE 7, JOHN 5
345	BLACK	KILDONAN	25 28	WILLIAM 16, SARAH 15, JAMES 12, JOHN, ANN 2
348	BLAVUNNE	SFX	77 85	LOUIS 1

TABLE 4: GEOGRAPHICAL LOCATION AND
CHILDREN OF MANITOBA FAMILIES, 1870

ID	FAMILY	PARISH	AT	BETWEEN	CHILDREN AND AGES AT NEXT BIRTHDAY				
351	BLONDEAU	ST BONIFACE	8		LOUIS 28	ISABELLE 15	VERONIQUE 13	ELISE 11	MARGUERITE 3
403	BODDIE	PORTAGE	24						
404	BODDY	HEADINGLY	55	57					
414	BONHOMME	BAIE S PAUL	207	215	BAZILE 23	PETER 16	JULIAN 13	ELMIRE 18	GENEVIEVE 16
415	BONNEAU	SFX	127	130					
416	BONNEAU	SFX	198	203					
419	BONNEAU	SFX	133	115	MAGLOIRE 18	NORBERT 16	FRANCOIS 13	WILLIAM 11	MADELEINE 9
419	BONNEAU	SFX	133	115	JUSTINE 7				
421	BONNEAU	SFX	172						
422	BONNEAU	SFX			BAZILE 24	PIERRE 22	JULIEN 19	ELMIRE 15	GENEVIEVE 12
424	BONNEAU	SFX	127	130					
425	BONNEVILLE	BAIE S PAUL	194	207	J BAPTISTE 5	LAROSE 2	SUZETTE 33	ELIZA 32	MARGUERITE 21
426	BONNEVILLE	BAIE S PAUL	194	207	ANTOINE 35	ELIZABETH 33	MARY 10	CAROLINE 10	NORBERT 2
426	BONNEVILLE	BAIE S PAUL	194	207	LUCY 18	ADELAIDE 13			
426	BONNEVILLE	BAIE S PAUL	194	207	CHRISTIAN 12				
436	BOUCHER	SFX	42		CAROLINE 12	ALEXANDRE 6	SOLOMAN 8	CHARLES 6	ROSE 5
437	BOUCHER	SFX	34		MARIE 11	J BAPTISTE 10			
437	BOUCHER	SFX	34		MARGUERITE 4	CAROLINE 1			
439	BOUCHER	SFX	34	42	HILAIRE 21				
441	BOUCHER	SFX	43						
442	BOUCHER	ST BONIFACE	41	31					
443	BOUCHER	SFX	42	53					
445	BOUCHER	ST BONIFACE	41	31	LOUIS 3	NANCY 1			
446	BOUCHER	ST LAURENT			JULIA 17	ROGER 15	CAROLINE 13	PAUL 9	ALEXANDRE 6
446	BOUCHER	ST LAURENT			ANNIE 2				
448	BOUDREAU	SFX			ALEXANDRE 18	JOSEPH 16	FRANCOIS 15	MARGUERITE 13	ADELAIDE 11
448	BOUDREAU	SFX			MARIE 9	ELISE 7	ISABEL 4		
451	BOUDREAU	ST JOHN	7	2	BAPTISTE 17	PIERRE 20	FRANCOIS 13	ANTOINE 6	JOSEPH 5
451	BOUDREAU	ST JOHN	7		ROSALIE 11	PHILOMENE 10			
457	BOURASSA	ST BONIFACE	8	9					
463	BOURIER	SFX	191		CASIMIR 23	ANTOINE 15			
464	BOURKE	ST JAMES	30		JOHN 9	EDWIN 8	ALEXANDER 6	SARAH 3	ANDREW 1
465	BOURKE	ST JAMES	37	39	WILLIAM 8	EDMOND 4	MARIA 3	FLORENCE 1	
466	BOURKE	ST JAMES	37		ANN 15	ELLEN 13	HARRIET 10	VICTORIA 7	ISABELLA 3
466	BOURKE	ST JAMES	37		MARY 1				
467	BOURKE	ST JAMES	37	39	WILLIAM 31				
468	BOURKE	ST JAMES	34		CATHERINE 9				
469	BOUSQUET	ST BONIFACE	117	113	NAPOLEON 4				
470	BOUSQUET	ST CHARLES	68	75		HENRI 2	DOMITILDE 13		
471	BOUSQUET	ST BONIFACE	117	113	MARGUERITE 17	CHRISASTOME 15			
473	BOUSQUET	ST LAURENT	111		CYRILLE 16	J BAPTISTE 13			
474	BOUSQUET	ST BONIFACE	117		JULIE 12	JOHN 17			
481	BOYD	POPLAR PT	46	45	MARTHA 2	WILLIAM 1			
482	BOYD	ST ANDREW	85	86	MARGUERITE 1				
483	BOYDEN	ST BONIFACE	110	107	CLEMENCE 20				
2	BOYER	SFX	172	175					
3	BOYER	ST NORBERT	166		NARCISSE 22	MARIE 24	ELISE 20	THEOPHILE 16	CAROLINE 14
4	BOYER	ST NORBERT	166		JOSEPH 12	AUGUSTIN 10	LOUISE 7	LOUIS 10	ALBERT 8
4	BOYER	ST LAURENT	24		FULGINA 19	JOSEPHINE 17	DAMASE 12		
7	BOYER	ST LAURENT	24		R 6	ALEXANDRE 3			
7	BOYER	ST LAURENT			VIRGINIE 6	ALEXANDRE 5	CHRISASTOME 3		
9	BOYER	ST BONIFACE	117	113					

TABLE 4: GEOGRAPHICAL LOCATION AND
CHILDREN OF MANITOBA FAMILIES, 1870

ID	FAMILY	PARISH	AT OR BETWEEN	CHILDREN AND AGES AT NEXT BIRTHDAY
11	BOYER	ST BONIFACE	110 107	ELIZA 6, RAPHAEL 4, ALEXANDRE 2
486	BRACONNIER	ST NORBERT	124 119	JUSTINE 19, ISABELLE 16, ELIZA 14
488	BRACONNIER	ST NORBERT	124 119	MARIE 3, AMABLE 1
496	BRAMNER	ST CHARLES	78 73	JAMES 1
496	BRAMNER	ST CHARLES	73	JAMES 1
489	BRANCONNIER	SFX	86 93	
520	BRAZEAU	SFX	134 122	JULIE 19, BERNARD 17, NAPOLEON 11, ROSE 8, JOSEPH 3
507	BRAZEAU	SFX	134 122	WILLIAM 2
508	BRELAND	SFX	192	
510	BRELAND	SFX	183	JOSIE 16, ELIZA 16, GREGOIRE 12, JUSTINE 10
511	BRELAND	SFX	194	CONSTANCE 9, EULALIE 7, MOISE 5, XAVIER 2
512	BRELAND	SFX	204 195	MARIE 10, ERNESTINE 7, PATRICE 5, EMILIE 3
513	BRELAND	SFX	194	ADELINE 6, VIRGINIE 4, CECILE 1, VIRGINIE 1
514	BRELAND	SFX	193	
515	BRELAND	SFX	183 190	PASCHAL 6, NORBERT 6, OLIVE 3
13350	BRELAND	SFX	193 194	
492	BREMNER	HEADINGLY	43	JOHN 50
494	BREMNER	HEADINGLY	41	ALEXANDRE 6, MARIA 5, JEMIMA 3, ELIZABETH 2
497	BREMNER	ST CHARLES	116	THOMAS 23, ANNIE 20, MARGARET 14, ALEXANDER 13, WILLIAM 12
499	BREMNER	HEADINGLY	45	HARRIET 11, JOSEPH 10, MOISE 8, MARIA 7, ALBAN 17
500	BREMNER	HEADINGLY	44	ALEXANDRE 13, FLORA 12, ELLEN 10, JAMES 4, ROBINA 2
504	BREMNER	POPLAR PT	82 88	ANDREW 9, MARGARET 7, ELLEN 4, CHRISTIANA 2
521	BRENNAN	ST JAMES	52	SUSANNAH 8, EDWARD 5, MARY 3, M 8
522	BRIERE	BAIE S PAUL	158 182	J BAPTISTE 1
523	BRIERE	BAIE S PAUL	158 182	PETER 4, MARY 2
587	BRIERE	BAIE S PAUL	158 182	LUCY 19, JEREMIAH 17, CLEOPHAS 14, CAROLINE 12
529	BRISTOW	ST ANDREW	87	AMBROISE 6
530	BROOKS	POPLAR PT	44	DAVID 19
532	BROWN	POPLAR PT	44	GEORGE 19, ANNIE 13
533	BROWN	ST CHARLES	116 117	WILLIAM 15
536	BROWN	ST CHARLES	63	JOHN 1
539	BROWN	ST ANDREW	46 47	JANE 5, MARGARET 3, JOSEPH 1
540	BROWN	ST ANDREW	47	JAMES 21, ELIZABETH 17, PHILIP 15, MARIANNE 13
543	BROWN	ST JOHN	55*	
545	BROWN	ST JOHN	6 33	
546	BROWN	POPLAR PT	43	HENRY 6, ELIZABETH 4, JOHN 2, DAVID 1
547	BROWN	POPLAR PT	42	JAMES 11, THOMAS 9, MARY 3, FRANCES 17
548	BROWN	HEADINGLY	39	JOHN 23, MAGNUS 21, JAMES 19, WILLIAM 15
548	BROWN	HEADINGLY	39	MARGARET 13
549	BROWNSEL	ST CLEMENT	18 21	ELIZABETH 11, CHRISTINE 9, NIEL 4, ANGUS 2
550	BRUCE	ST JOHN	48	
551	BRUCE	ST JOHN	48	GEORGE 13, JOHN 10, ELIZABETH 6, COLIN 3
555	BRUCE	ST BONIFACE	97	PIERRE 15, VIRGINIE 9, ZACHARIAS 19, ELISE 16, MODESTE 13
556	BRUCE	ST BONIFACE	31 29	JOSEPH 21, FREDERICK 23
556	BRUCE	ST BONIFACE	31 29	JULIET 9
558	BRUCE	KILDONAN	17	DONALD 24, JOSEPH 20, JANE 18, DAVID 14
560	BRUCE	POPLAR PT	50	LETITIA 17, JAMES 15, MARY 11, JOHN 8
561	BRUCE	ST VITAL	39*	CECILE 18, CLEMENCE 17, J BAPTISTE 11
567	BRUCE	ST JAMES	27	ANN 5, BENJAMIN 5, ALICE 4, ADELAIDE 1

TABLE 4: GEOGRAPHICAL LOCATION AND
CHILDREN OF MANITOBA FAMILIES, 1870

ID	FAMILY	PARISH	AT OR BETWEEN	CHILDREN AND AGES AT NEXT BIRTHDAY				
568	BRUCE	ST JAMES	24	JAMES 13	WILLIAM 10	THOMAS 7	MARY 5	HARRIET 3
568	BRUCE	ST JAMES	24	CATHERINE 3				
570	BRUCE	ST BONIFACE	31 29	JEAN 1	RENIE 13	JOSEPH 9		MARIE ROSE 1
571	BRUCE	ST BONIFACE	.	MARIE 3	ARCHIBALD 1			
573	BRUCE	POPLAR PT	71	JEMIMA 1				
574	BRUCE	ST NORBERT	11	PIERRE 1	HENRIETTA 2			
575	BRUCE	POPLAR PT	72	ALICE 5				
576	BRUCE	KILDONAN	28 29					
579	BRUNEAU	ST VITAL	10	NAPOLEON 12	ADELAIDE 10	ELISE 10	MARGUERITE 8	ATHANASE 3
579	BRUNEAU	ST VITAL	10	MARIE 1				
580	BRUNELL	ST JOHN	9					
582	BRUNNER	ST BONIFACE	63					
3162	BRUNNER	ST BONIFACE	63					
590	BRYANT	HEADINGLY	12					
591	BUBAR	SFX	176 181					
593	BUBBIE	POPLAR PT	53 54	BAPTISTE 24	JANE 19	CAROLINE 16	MARGUERITE 2	MARY 19
598	BUNN	ST CLEMENT	97	JOHN 15	ISABEL 14	FLORA 8		
599	BUNN	ST PAUL	29	PHEBE 24	THOMAS 22	FRANCOISE 21	ALFRED 20	MARY 19
599	BUNN	ST PAUL	29	HELEN 17	MAGDELEINE 15	COLIN 15	ALICE 10	FLORA 8
599	BUNN	ST PAUL	29	ALBERT 6	ROBERT 2			
584	BURNELL	ST JAMES	64					
603	BURR	POPLAR PT	88 83	ESTELLE 10	EUGENE 7	HERMINE 7	ROSALIE 6	ANDREW 5
604	BUSHEN	BAIE S PAUL	194 207	J BAPTISTE 12	ELIZA 11			
604	BUSHEN	BAIE S PAUL	194 207	MARY 3	MARGUERITE 1			
609	BUTTS	SFX	139 142					
616	CADOTTE	ST NORBERT	113 101	FELIX 23	ELIZA 19			
617	CADOTTE	ST NORBERT	113*	J BAPTISTE 12	JOSEPH 9	SARAH 7	PHILOMENE 5	PATRICE 3
617	CADOTTE	ST NORBERT	113*	ELZEAR 1				
618	CADOTTE	ST NORBERT	127	FREDERICK 9	ROSALIE 8	DOMITHILDE 3	VIRGINIE 1	
619	CADOTTE	ST PETER	.	JAMES 12				
620	CADOTTE	ST NORBERT	113 101	EDWARD 18				
621	CADOTTE	PORTAGE	.					
623	CALDER	ST CLEMENT	11	JOHN 6	MARIA 2			
626	CALDER	ST CLEMENT	10	CATHERINE 18	ALBERT 15	MILES 10	MATHILDA 8	JOSEPH 6
626	CALDER	ST CLEMENT	10	MARY 3				
627	CALDER	ST CLEMENT	41	WILLIAM 11	MARGUERITE 17	MARIA 14	MARY 9	GEORGE 6
634	CALDWELL	ST JOHN	6 33					
635	CALDWELL	ST JOHN	9*	MARY 8	GEORGE 6			
636	CAMERON	*KILDONAN	4 6	MARY 10	WILLIAM 7			
638	CAMERON	HEADINGLY	57*	MARY 1	CATHERINE 3			
640	CAMERON	ST PETER	46*					
644	CAMERON	HEADINGLY	59*	JOHN 34	DONALD 32			
648	CAMERON	POPLAR PT	.	THOMAS 14	ELIZA 12	ISABELLA 7	WILLIAM 1	
649	CAMERON	ST PETER	171 174	MARGUERITE 12	MARIE 10	ELISE 8	SARA 2	ELIZA 4
650	CAMERON	POPLAR PT	.	THOMAS 17	JAMES 10	MARGARET 7	HENRY 6	
650	CAMERON	POPLAR PT	.	CHARLES 2				
651	CAMERON	ST ANDREW	104 106					
652	CAMERON	ST PETER	31 46	MARGUERITE 29				
657	CAMPBELL	ST PAUL	11 13	EDITH 5	ELLEN 2			
660	CAMPBELL	ST CLEMENT	28					
663	CAMPBELL	ST JOHN	45 46					
664	CAMPBELL	ST JAMES	20 21	JOHN 12	MARY 10			

TABLE 4: GEOGRAPHICAL LOCATION AND
CHILDREN OF MANITOBA FAMILIES. 1870

ID	FAMILY	PARISH	AT OR BETWEEN		CHILDREN AND AGES AT NEXT BIRTHDAY
665	CAMPBELL	POPLAR PT	44	47	ELIZA 3, WILLIAM 2
666	CAMPBELL	ST ANDREW	21		MALCOLM 6, JESSIE 2, RODRIC 1
667	CAMPBELL	ST PETER	85	95	
668	CAMPER	ST LAURENT	20		
669	CANADY	ST ANDREW	63		ALEXANDER 26, ISABELLA 24, ALBERT 16, JOHN 8, EMMA 12
669	CANADY	ST ANDREW	63		CAROLINE 9
670	CAPISISET	ST CHARLES	105	113	JOHN 10, MARIE 8, ROSE 6, EMILIE 4
675	CAPLETTE	ST CHARLES	113		PATRICE 17, ELIZABETH 16, ALEXANDRE 15, LOUIS 15, JOHNNY 10
675	CAPLETTE	ST CHARLES	113		DENIS 8, WILLIAM 6, ADELAIDE 4, ROSINE 1
1600	CAPLETTE	ST BONIFACE	62*		PETER 23, PAUL 7, MARIE 19, ISABELLE 16, J BAPTISTE 11
1600	CAPLETTE	ST BONIFACE	62*		HELENE 10, MARIE 11, FRANCISE 5, ALPHONSE 2, ELIZA
688	CARDINAL	ST NORBERT	209	202	MARIE 11, CHARLES 8, FRANCOIS 5
689	CARDINAL	ST NORBERT	213		JOSEPH 3, VIRGINIE 3
695	CARDINAL	SFX			CHARLES 8, OCTAVIE 6, VIRGINIE 3
699	CARDINAL	ST BONIFACE	44	41	
697	CARON	ST NORBERT	113	101	JEAN 8, ANGELIQUE 9, THEOPHILE 5, PATRICE 3, ANTOINE 1
766	CARRIE	HEADINGLY	12	14	
709	CARRIER	ST NORBERT	244		ALFRED 10, NAPOLEON 8, WILLIAM 8, CYRIAE 3, JUSTINE 5, LOUISA 1
710	CARRIER	ST NORBERT	124		PATRICE 3, ADELAIDE 3, CYRIAE 1
710	CARRIER	ST NORBERT	41		PATRICE 3, ADELAIDE 3, CYRIAE 1, AUGUSTIN 3
711	CARRIER	ST BONIFACE	101		ADELAIDE 5, VIRGINIE 3, AUGUSTIN 2, ALEXIS 17, VITALINE 6
714	CARRIER	ST BONIFACE	102		DANIEL 21, ANGELIQUE 23, MELANIE 22, PLACIDE 22
714	CARRIER	ST BONIFACE	102		HENRY 13, CAMILLE 12, MARIE 10, FRANCIS 6
717	CARRIER	ST VITAL	10		MATHILDE 22, DUMAS 22, LOUIS 19, EULALIE 17, NAPOLEON 12
717	CARRIER	ST VITAL	10		BRUNO 10, MARGUERITE 10, ATHANASE 7, ANGELIQUE 5
720	CARRIER	ST BONIFACE	15		ANDRE 27, MOISE 27, SEDHSINE 22, PAUL 20, LEONIDE 15
720	CARRIER	ST BONIFACE	15		ALEXANDRE 10, MARIE 10, MAXIME 7, PAUL 5
702	CARRIERE	ST BONIFACE	118	117	NAPOLEON 9, SARAH 7, ALFRED 5, YVES 3, WILLIAM 1
703	CARRIERE	ST BONIFACE	118		SUZANNE 7
703	CARRIERE	ST BONIFACE	118		
704	CARRIERE	ST BONIFACE	62	58	
705	CARRIERE	ST NORBERT	137		JULIEN 5, WILLIAM 19, ALFRED 3, ROGER 13, AMABLE 10
708	CARRIERE	ST BONIFACE	81		ANGELIQUE 19, JULIEN 17, FRANCOIS 7, LEON 16
708	CARRIERE	ST BONIFACE	81		ALPHONSE 8, ALEXANDRE 8
712	CARRIERE	ST NORBERT	118	117	DANIEL 27, LOUIS 23, LEOCADIE 23, CECILE 20
713	CARRIERE	ST BONIFACE	114	58	
716	CARRIERE	ST VITAL	62	58	
767	CASITAR	PORTAGE	114		MARIE 6, NANCY 4, LEON 4, JEMIMA 2, WILLIAM 6
767	CASITAR	PORTAGE	114		JOHN 13, JAMES 11, ANN 9, MARGARET 1
768	CAUTU	ST JOHN	13	6	JANE 4, MARY 3, VICTOR 3
768	CAUTU	ST JOHN	13	6	DANIEL 8, GEORGE 6, ALEX 4, WILLIAM 2
769	CAVALLIER	ST NORBERT	37	35	
771	CHABOIS	ST LAURENT	11		ELIZA 1
772	CHABOIS	ST LAURENT	16		
773	CHABOIS	ST LAURENT	12		PETER 5, PHILOMENE 4, ELIZA 2
774	CHABOIS	ST LAURENT	15		
775	CHABOIS	ST LAURENT	13		
776	CHABOIS	ST LAURENT	11	9	
736	CHALIFOUX	SFX	103		MICHEL 24, LOUIS 17, ROSE 26, BLANDINE 15
779	CHAMBERLAIN	ST CHARLES	9	14	MARIA 9, MARY 9, JOHN 4, CLOUSTINE 10
780	CHAMBERS	ST JOHN	13	6	

TABLE 4: GEOGRAPHICAL LOCATION AND
CHILDREN OF MANITOBA FAMILIES, 1870

ID	FAMILY	PARISH	AT OR BETWEEN	CHILDREN AND AGES AT NEXT BIRTHDAY
737	CHAMPAGNE	STE ANNE	68 .	JOSEPH 19, JULIENNE 15, FRANCOIS 14, ALEXANDRE 11, CHARLES 7
737	CHAMPAGNE	STE ANNE	68 .	ANDRE 5, MAXIME 1
738	CHAMPAGNE	STE ANNE	68 69	MARIE 3, VIRGINIE 2, CELESTE 1
739	CHAMPAGNE	ST BONIFACE	14 .	DAVID 23, CAROLINE 20, ESTER 16
749	CHARBONNEAU	ST BONIFACE	87 77	
782	CHARBONNEAU	STE ANNE	20 22	
745	CHARETTE	ST NORBERT	27 .	J BAPTISTE 4, JOSEPH 4, MOISE 2
745	CHARETTE	ST NORBERT	95 .	MARIE ANN 10, MARIE 7, DANIEL 6, HELENE 4
746	CHARETTE	ST NORBERT	17 .	BAPTISTE 5
747	CHARETTE	ST NORBERT	90 .	PIERRE 24, FRANCOIS 23, WILLIAM 19, SOLOMAN 15, MARGUERITE 13
747	CHARETTE	ST NORBERT	90 .	MARIE 11, ALEXANDRE 9, PATRICE 6, NORBERT 2
3653	CHARETTE	ST NORBERT	27 17	J BAPTISTE 4, JOSEPH 4, MOISE 2
783	CHARTIER	SFX	187 185	
784	CHARTIER	SFX		
785	CHARTIER	SFX	187 185	BONIFACE 10, ISABELLE 8, LOUISA ... , PETER 8, PATRICK 5
754	CHARTRAND	ST LAURENT		ANTOINE 15, MARY 13, ELLEN 1, ...
754	CHARTRAND	ST LAURENT		ANGELIQUE 3, LAROSE 10, H 9, ALEXANDRE 3, URSULE 2
755	CHARTRAND	ST LAURENT		MARY 9, MARY 10, MOSES 7, ADELAIDE 5, E 3
756	CHARTRAND	ST LAURENT		WILLIAM 1, H 8, CAROLINE 7
756	CHARTRAND	ST LAURENT		ANGELIQUE 4, LOUIS 2
757	CHARTRAND	ST LAURENT		PETER 18, NORBERT 15, MICHEL 12, ROSALIE 5
758	CHARTRAND	ST LAURENT	202 .	MARIE 11, HELENE 9, ROGER 2
761	CHARTRAND	ST NORBERT	2 .	
764	CHARTRAND	ST LAURENT	9 2	MICHEL 21, R 16, CATHERINE 16, ALEXANDRE 5, PATRICK 4
797	CHARTRAND	ST LAURENT	116 133	
798	CHARTRAND	SFX	196 199	
799	CHARTRAND	SFX		
786	CHATLAIN	ST PETER	56 74	ELIZABETH 3, MARGARET 1, MARIE 1, NANCY 16, FLORA 7
787	CHATLAIN	ST PETER	56 74	DAVID 12, WILLIAM 4, THOMAS 4, WILLIAM 1
788	CHATLAIN	ST CLEMENT	48 53	ELISE 8, JOHN 6
792	CHISHOLME	ST JAMES	4 13	
792	CHISHOLME	ST JOHN	85 95	PETER 8, CHRISTINE 6, CLARA 3
793	CHISHOLME	ST PETER	58 59	JAMES 9, ARTHUR 5
794	CHRISTIANSO	ST ANDREW		ESTHER 4, LEONARD 1
795	CLARE	ST LAURENT	164 168	
801	CLARK	ST ANDREW	46 56	
802	CLARK	ST PETER	1 8	
803	CLEMENS	ST PETER		JOHN 22, JOHNNY 3
804	CLEMENS	ST ANDREW	155 .	BERNARD 4, SARAH 1
806	CLOUSTON	KILDONAN	58 61	JAMES 2, JAMES 24
807	CLOUSTON	HEADINGLY	12 .	ANNIE 24
903	CLOUSTON	HEADINGLY	60 .	ELLEN 12
904	CLOUSTON	HEADINGLY	60 .	
904	CLOUSTON	ST PAUL	24 .	MARY 18, FLORA 21, SARAH 14
905	CLOUSTON	ST CLEMENT	70 .	MILES 5
808	COCHRANE	ST CLEMENT	35 44	ELIZABETH 4, NANCY 2, ANNE 1
809	COCHRANE	ST PETER	171 174	ALEXANDER 3, ALICE 1
810	COCHRANE	ST PETER	171 174	JOHN 36, ADAM 20, WILLIAM 18, JOHN 7
811	COCHRANE	ST CLEMENT	58 .	RACHEL 13, THOMAS 11, WILLIAM 11, FRANCOISE 4
812	COCKS	ST ANDREW	148 .	HENRI 2
816	COCKS	ST ANDREW	148 .	ROBERT 11, NANCY 9, WILLIAM 6, GEORGE 2
816	COCKS	ST BONIFACE	58 44	ELIZABETH 1
817	COLLIER	ST BONIFACE		

TABLE 4: GEOGRAPHICAL LOCATION AND
CHILDREN OF MANITOBA FAMILIES, 1870

ID	FAMILY	PARISH	AT OR BETWEEN	CHILDREN AND AGES AT NEXT BIRTHDAY				
818	COLLIN	ST NORBERT	31 27	JUSTINE 12	BASTIEN 10	MARGUERITE 8	ISABELLE 5	JOSEPH 3
920	COLLIN	STE AGATHE	108 80	SARAH 10	WAWESA 4	WIPICHIAUSE 1		
819	COLOMBE	STE AGATHE	108 80	FRANCOIS 27	SAMUEL 20	JOSEPH 9	GILBERT 6	
912	COLOMBE	STE AGATHE	108 80					
916	COLOMBE	STE AGATHE	108 80					
820	COLUMBIA	ST PETER	133 167	MARIE 14	JOSEPH 11	CHARLES 8	EMILIE 5	DAVID 1
923	COMTOIS	POPLAR PT	88 83	GEORGE 13	FRANCOIS 13	MARIE 11		
926	COMTOIS	KILDONAN	65 67	ANGELIQUE 16	PIERRE 1			
928	CONTOIS	ST NORBERT	218 210	JULIEN 3	PAULINE 1			
929	CONTOIS	KILDONAN	58 61	MARIE 4				
930	CONTOIS	ST NORBERT	218 210	ELISE 20				
825	COOK	ST JOHN	48 45					
826	COOK	ST JOHN	48 7					
827	COOK	ST ANDREW	117 120					
828	COOK	ST CLEMENT	4 6					
829	COOK	ST JAMES	63 64					
830	COOK	ST PETER	56 74	ANN 1	MARY 8			
831	COOK	ST PETER	16*	JAMES 15				
833	COOK	ST PETER	16 31					
935	COOK	POPLAR PT	58	ADELAIDE 2	EDITH 1			
936	COOK	ST JAMES	23					
937	COOK	POPLAR PT	75	WILLIAM 6	CATHERINE 1			
938	COOK	POPLAR PT	76	MARY 10	RUBINA 9	CHRISTIE 7	MARTHA 5	EDWIN 3
942	COOK	HEADINGLY	63	GEORGE 26	HARRIET 22	LETITIA 19		
943	COOK	ST PAUL	91	RICHARD 2				
944	COOK	POPLAR PT	72 71					
945	COOK	ST PAUL	44	JOSEPH 21	MARGARET 19	JOHN 17	MARIA 15	BENJAMIN 13
945	COOK	ST PAUL	44	SAMUEL 27				
950	COOK.	HEADINGLY	170	ISABEL 2				
847	COOPER	HEADINGLY	55	MARGARET 15	DAVID 13	FRANCIS 10	MARY 8	
848	CORBETT	PORTAGE	51 53	FRANCIS 7	CATHERINE 3			
854	CORNER	PORTAGE	116	FANNY 22	JOSEPH 19	HENRY 17	RODERICK 15	FLORA 13
854	CORRIGAL	PORTAGE	116	ANNABELLA 11				
962	CORRIGAL	ST ANDREW	85	ELIZABETH 18	MARIANNE 15	NANCY 11	ROBIN 9	CATHERINE 4
850	CORRIGAL	ST ANDREW	85	FRANCOISE 1	VICTORIA 1	WILLIAM 20	JOHN 7	
851	CORRIGALL	PORTAGE	67 66					
957	CORRIGALL	ST ANDREW	145	ISABEL 9	CATHERINE 7	CLARA 5	WILLIAM 3	RODRIC 1
853	CORRIGALL	ST ANDREW	50 52					
958	CORRIGALL	ST ANDREW	50 52					
959	CORRIGALL	ST ANDREW	52	CATHERINE 21	JAMES 16	ELIZA 13	JOHN 10	WILLIAM 8
961	CORRIGALL	ST ANDREW	41	HENRY 10	WILLIAM 8	MARGARET 8	JOHN 3	
855	CORRIGALL	ST ANDREW	42	JAMES 40	GEORGE 30	WILLIAM 30	THOMAS 20	BELLA 17
857	COSGROVE	ST JOHN	13					
970	COURCHAINE	ST NORBERT	64	JOSEPH 13	FRANCOIS 13	NORBERT 10	MARIE J 6	MARIE B 1
971	COURCHAINE	ST NORBERT	65	BRIGITTE 17	FRANCOISE 17	J BAPTISTE 15	MARIE 11	NORBERT 5
971	COURCHAINE	ST NORBERT	75	JULIE 3	ROSE 1			
972	COURCHAINE	ST NORBERT	159 157					
858	COUTELLE	ST NORBERT	9 16					
859	COWLAND	ST JAMES	23 24					
860	COWLAND	ST JAMES	23 24					
861	COX	ST JAMES	70 73					

ID	FAMILY	PARISH	AT OR BETWEEN	CHILDREN AND AGES AT NEXT BIRTHDAY
975	COX	ST ANDREW	120	BARBARA 6, WILLIAM 18, ELIZABETH 26
976	COX	ST ANDREW	117 120	GEORGE 24
3202	COX	ST JAMES	70 73	
862	CRAMER	ST ANDREW	93	
863	CREE	SFX	120 126	
2826	CREE	SFX	120 126	
864	CROMANTIE	ST ANDREW	6 7	
980	CROMANTIE	ST ANDREW	13	JAMES 9, MARGARET 5, JOHN 2, JOHN 1
978	CROMATIE	ST ANDREW	280 260	HELEN 8, ELIZABETH 5, WILLIAM 4
867	CROWSEN	ST JOHN	2 4	ELISA 13, SUSAN 10
986	CUMMINGS	ST ANDREW	39	
987	CUMMINGS	PORTAGE	63	CHARLES 24, JOHN 22, WILLIAM 20, CUTHBERT 18, SAMUEL 1
988	CUMMINGS	PORTAGE	63	WALTER 14, PHILIP 12, FLORA 10, THOMAS 8, JAMES 16
988	CUMMINGS	PORTAGE	51	ELIZA 14, DAVID 11, JANE 9, BELLA 7
991	CUMMINGS	ST PAUL	51	CATHERINE, ANN 2
992	CUMMINGS	PORTAGE	92 104	
4675	CUMMINGS	PORTAGE	1 8	ALEXANDER 2
866	CUNNINGHAM	HEADINGLY	33	ALEXANDER 18, JAMES 18, JOHN 12, CHARLES 10, LETITIA 2
875	CURATER	ST PETER	25 28	
994	CYR	ST JOHN	79 99	CATHERINE 9, JOSEPH 9, JOHN 5, PIERRE 3
996	CYR	STE ANNE	65 124	JOHNNY 23, CAROLINE 23, ELZEAR 15, MELANIE 10
999	CYR	STE AGATHE	265 124	VIRGINIE 10, VIRGINIE 19, MARIE 17, JOSEPH 12, EUPHROSINE 9
1000	CYR	ST BONIFACE	79 99	JOSEPHTE 19, MARGUERITE 10, MARIE 15
1000	CYR	ST BONIFACE	79 99	PIERRE 7, MARGUERITE 7
1001	CYR	ST BONIFACE	79 99	PATRICE 23, ISABELLE 19, EULALIE 15
1003	DAHL	ST PAUL	4	WILLIAM 22, CATHERINE 22, CHARLOTTE 19, THOMAS 13
1005	DAHL	ST PAUL	4	ALEXANDER 1
1005	DAHL	ST PAUL	37	NANCY 2, DONALD 5
1008	DAIGNEAU	ST CLEMENT	77 79	PIERRE 30, MAGDELEINE 35, SUZANNE 32, BAPTISTE 18
883	DANIEL	PORTAGE	65 58	ELIZABETH 1
884	DANIEL	ST CLEMENT	106	ADAM 6, THOMAS 6, JANE 4
885	DANIEL	ST CLEMENT	105	JACOB 26, JAMES 26, JOHN 20
886	DANIEL	ST ANDREW	88 89	CAROLINE 4
1012	DANIEL	ST JAMES	68 67	PHILIP 20, JAMES 17, HELENA 17, MARY 26
1013	DANIEL	ST ANDREW	72	
1014	DANIEL	ST CLEMENT	91 97	THOMAS 20
1016	DANIEL	ST CLEMENT	10 11	MOISE 15, ELIZABETH 15
1017	DANIEL	ST CLEMENT	105 106	ALEXANDRE 13, JOSEPH 13
1020	DANIEL	SFX	133 115	JOSEPH 10, WILLIAM 8, CATHERINE 5
880	DAOUST	BAIE S PAUL	158 182	MARIE 2, WILLIAM 2
882	DAOUST	BAIE S PAUL	158 182	ELZEAR 4, MARIE 1
1021	DAUNAIS	ST BONIFACE	79 99	
1022	DAUNAIS	ST BONIFACE	79 99	
1023	DAUNAIS	ST BONIFACE	79 99	
888	DAUPHINAIS	SFX	21	VERONIQUE 5, ALEXANDRE 2
1031	DAUPHINAIS	SFX	214 218	FRANCOIS 27, CASIMIRE 24, PIERRE 22, WILLIAM 21, FLAVIE 19
1031	DAUPHINAIS	SFX	214 218	PATRICE 13, CLEMENCE 10, MARGUERITE 7
1032	DAUPHINAIS	SFX	218	MARIE 15, CAROLINE 13, ELZEAR 11, EMERISE 9
1033	DAUPHINAIS	ST NORBERT	31	
894	DAVIS	ST JOHN	13 6	ST PIERRE 2

TABLE 4: GEOGRAPHICAL LOCATION AND
CHILDREN OF MANITOBA FAMILIES, 1870

ID	FAMILY	PARISH	AT	BETWEEN	CHILDREN AND AGES AT NEXT BIRTHDAY				
895	DAVIS	ST JOHN	4	13	J BAPTISTE 23	ALEXANDRE 19	LOUIS 16	MARGUERITE 21	MARIE 14
896	DAVIS	ST VITAL	35	28	VIRGINIE 10	MARIE 9	EDITH 11		GEORGE 5
896	DAVIS	ST VITAL	35	28	JOHN 15	MATILDA 13			
1045	DAVIS	PORTAGE			MARGARET 3	WILLIAM 2			
1045	DAVIS	PORTAGE		33					
1049	DAVIS	ST JOHN	6						
1048	DAWSON	ST JOHN	7	2					
1052	DAWSON	SFX	220						
1041	DAYON	ST LAURENT			MARY 21	HENRY 17	LOUISA 15	WILLIAM 11	LUCIEN 8
1041	DAYON	ST LAURENT			JOSEPH 4	FRANCOIS 1			
1047	DAYON	ST LAURENT			JOSEPH 8	PETER 6	GENEVIEVE 3		
892	DEASE	ST NORBERT	9						
1059	DEASE	ST NORBERT	15		ELIZA 20	MARGUERITE 17	VIRGINIE 14	ALFRED 13	NELSON 5
1060	DECARIE	STE ANNE	69		ALEXANDER 12	JOSEPHTE 7	JOSEPH 5		
899	DEGO	ST PETER	122	139	CAROLINE 1				
715	DEGUIRE	SFX	44	41					
1071	DELARONDE	ST BONIFACE	44	41					
1121	DELARONDE	ST BONIFACE	27	31					
1086	DELORIER	SFX	27	31	ISABELLE 9	PIERRE 8	MELANIE 5	MARIE ROSE 3	MARIE 3
1123	DELORIER	SFX	27	31	CLOTILDE 1				
1123	DELORIER	SFX	158		MARY 13	DAVID 10	JULIAN 8	ROSALIE 3	FRANCOIS 3
1094	DELORME	BAIE S PAUL	158		ROGER 1				
1094	DELORME	BAIE S PAUL	11	13					
1095	DELORME	SFX	161	148					
1096	DELORME	SFX	13		SARA 3				
1097	DELORME	SFX	45		CASIMIRE 25	URBAIN 19	HELENE 16	SARAH 13	FRANCOIS 11
1100	DELORME	ST NORBERT	45		MARIE 8	FRANCOIS 2	JOSEPHTE 1		
1101	DELORME	ST NORBERT	76	75	JOSEPH 20	ALEXIS 18	JOSEPHTE 17	URBAIN 12	
1101	DELORME	ST NORBERT	21		PATRICE 7	MARIE 5	MELANIE 4	NORBERT 1	
1102	DELORME	ST NORBERT	47		ADELAIDE 16	PIERRE 16	CELINA 12	PATRICE 5	ALFRED 2
1103	DELORME	ST NORBERT	47		SARAH 22	JULIEN 18	JOSEPH 16	ANGELIQUE 14	FRANCOIS 12
1105	DELORME	ST NORBERT	76	75	ADELE 10	MARIE 8	CHARLES 6	ALPHIE 3	URBAIN 2
1105	DELORME	ST NORBERT	76	75	LOUISON 12	URBAINE 10	MARIE 1	ELIZE 8	MAGLOIRE 5
1106	DELORME	ST NORBERT	117	113	ELZEAR 4	LAURENT 1			
1106	DELORME	ST NORBERT	117	113	MODESTE 4				
1111	DELORME	ST BONIFACE	117	113	ELIZA 2				
1112	DELORME	ST BONIFACE			ELIZA 18				
1113	DELORME	ST BONIFACE	162	179	WILLIAM 11	MARIE 9	FRANCOIS 9	MADELEINE 4	URBAIN 2
1113	DELORME	ST BONIFACE	181	179	ELIZA 11	ALEXANDRE 10	JOSEPH 10		
1115	DELORME	SFX	181		WILLIAM 12				
1116	DELORME	SFX	37	35	JOSEPH 22				
1117	DELORME	SFX	4		ELISE 3	COLIN 1			
1118	DELORME	ST NORBERT	195	196	ISABELLE 17	PIERRE 9			
1130	DEMARAIS	ST BONIFACE	58	52	JOSEPH 12	MARGUERITE 13	MARIE 4	ALFRED 1	
1241	DEMARAIS	SFX	18	20	MARIE 18	OLIVIER 14	ETIENNE 2		
1243	DEMARAIS	ST VITAL	36						
1131	DENICK	HEADINGLY			JANE 3	PETER 2	JOHN 1		
1224	DENNETH	ST CLEMENT	22		MARGUERITE 22	JANE 19	JEREMIE 18	CATHERINE 17	SARA 15
1223	DENNETT	ST PETER	13		SOPHIE 13	GILBERT 11	SAMUEL 9	MARIE 7	
1223	DENNETT	ST PETER	264	267	RICHARD 1				
1229	DENNING	ST ANDREW	62		ANNE 21	ROBERT 21	DONALD 18	CHRISTIE 15	WILLIAM 13
1234	DENNISON	HEADINGLY	62		JANET 10	JOHN 10	GRIFFITH 7	ALICE 5	MARY 2

TABLE 4: GEOGRAPHICAL LOCATION AND
CHILDREN OF MANITOBA FAMILIES, 1870

ID	FAMILY	PARISH	AT OR BETWEEN		CHILDREN AND AGES AT NEXT BIRTHDAY
1134	DENNITH	ST CLEMENT	36	.	GILBERT 18
1135	DEOLYNE	ST JOHN	2	4	WILLIAM 18
1138	DEOLYNE	ST JOHN	2	4	
1249	DESAUTELS	STE ANNE	57	.	
1151	DESCHAMBAUL	ST BONIFACE	77	.	
1152	DESCHAMPS	SFX	133	115	LUCIE 21, AMILA 15, DENISE 12, EUGENE 9, CAROLINE 8
1153	DESCHAMPS	SFX	133	115	ALEXANDRE 24, EUGENIE 6, JOSEPH 2, ELISE 12, LOUISE 10
1252	DESCHAMPS	POPLAR PT	82	88	MARIE 22, SUZANNE 14, AGNES 2, MARIE 11, ROSE 8
1252	DESCHAMPS	POPLAR PT	82	88	ANNE 16, HELENE 14, MADELEINE 12, JOSEPH 10, CECILE 6
1253	DESCHAMPS	SFX	133	115	JOHN 23, J BAPTISTE 19, JOSEPH 17, PIERRE 17, ISABELLE 15
1253	DESCHAMPS	SFX	133	115	CHARLES 2, MARIE 12, MADELEINE 8, HELENE 5
1264	DESJARDINS	ST VITAL	58	52	JOHN 23, J BAPTISTE 21, JOSEPH 19, PIERRE 17, ISABELLE 15
1278	DESJARDUNS	ST VITAL	244	245	PIERRE 22, MONIQUE 17, SOLOMAN 15, ROSALIE 12
1160	DESJARLAIS	BAIE S PAUL	227	219	GREGOIRE 25, FRANCOIS 22, BERNARD 20, J BAPTISTE 18, LAROSE 16
1268	DESJARLAIS	BAIE S PAUL	227	219	MADELEINE 14, CHARLES 9, SUZETTE 7, FRISINE 14
1275	DESJARLAIS	BAIE S PAUL	215	207	XAVIER 25, THOMAS 20, MATHEW 16, FRANCOIS 15, ISABELLA 7
1279	DESJARLAIS	BAIE S PAUL	194	207	LOUIS 15, ANTOINE 9, JULIA 15, MARY 13
1282	DESJARLAIS	BAIE S PAUL	227	.	FRIZINE 5, ELIZABETH 13, AMABLE 11, ELIZA 9, SUZETTE 7
1283	DESJARLAIS	BAIE S PAUL	227	.	FRANCOIS 13, J BAPTISTE 5, ANTOINE 1
1285	DESJARLAIS	ST LAURENT	215	224	MARY 5, ALEXANDRE 3, J BAPTISTE 1
1289	DESJARLAIS	BAIE S PAUL			MARY 3, ANTOINE 2
1289	DESJARLAIS	ST LAURENT			JOHN 6, LOUISE 4
1136	DESMARAIS	SFX	162	172	CAROLINE 4
1148	DESMARAIS	SFX			CHARLES 3, ELIZABETH 2
1236	DESMARAIS	PORTAGE			ELIZA 2, MARGUERITE 17
1237	DESMARAIS	PORTAGE			JOSEPH 15, JAMES 13
1242	DESMARAIS	PORTAGE			NAPOLEON 15, J BAPTISTE 13, HONORE 12, ISABELLE 10, JOHN 9
1294	DESRIVIER	POPLAR PT			ANTOINE 23, FRANCOIS 18, MARGUERITE 4, MARY 9
1294	DESRIVIER	POPLAR PT			PAUL 6
1293	DESRIVIERE	ST VITAL	50	45	MARGARET 23, MARIANNE 23, LOUIS 20, JOSEPH 18, JULIE 17
1295	DESROSIERS	*ST PAUL	65	.	MADELEINE 14
1295	DESROSIERS	**ST PAUL	65	.	
1297	DESROSIERS	ST ANDREW	1	.	
1175	DEVLIN	ST JOHN	13	6	ELIE 1
1179	DION	SFX			JOSEPH 8, ELIE 1
1178	DIONNE	STE AGATHE	565	.	REMIE 5, BAPTISTE 4, MARIE 2
1181	DISON	ST ANDREW	263	268	
1184	DONALD	ST ANDREW	94	.	SARA 6, JOSEPH 4, JOHN 3, MARIE 2
1300	DONALD	ST CLEMENT	18	21	CHARLES 12, ALEXANDER 8, JOHN 4, ELISE 3
1301	DONALD	ST PETER	100	133	JOHN 13, ELIZABETH 11, ALFRED 4, WILLIAM 6
1302	DONALD	ST ANDREW	177	.	ELIZABETH 46, ISABEL 33, MARGUERITE 9, SARA 2
1303	DONALD	ST ANDREW	156	160	ROBERT 9, WILLIAM 7, SARA 5, JESSIE 3
1305	DONALD	ST ANDREW	156	160	NANCY 16, CATHERINE 14, JANE 12, ELISE 10
1305	DONALD	ST ANDREW	156	160	ROBERT 6, VICTOR 4, GEORGE 2
1192	DONALDSON	ST JOHN	4	*	M J 4
1311	DREVER	ST JOHN	4	13	CHRISTIAN 15, FRANCIS 2
1312	DREVER	ST JOHN	78	73	MARIE 16, PIERRE 14, LOUISON 10, WILLIAM 8, ELISE 6
1304	DUBOIS	ST CHARLES	78	73	

TABLE 4: GEOGRAPHICAL LOCATION AND
CHILDREN OF MANITOBA FAMILIES, 1870

ID	FAMILY	PARISH	AT OR BETWEEN	CHILDREN AND AGES AT NEXT BIRTHDAY				
1304	DUBOIS	ST CHARLES	78 73	JOSEPH 5				
1319	DUBOIS	STE AGATHE	589 585					
1320	DUBOIS	STE AGATHE	579	NORBERT 19	ALEXANDRE 16	JULIEN 14	ROSALIE 12	FRANCOIS 8
1322	DUBOIS	STE AGATHE	579 577	MARIE 6	NAPOLEON 3			
1325	DUBOIS	ST VITAL	58 52					
1326	DUBOIS	ST VITAL	58*	MAXIME 19	AMBROISE 16	JEAN 13	MAGDELEINE 10	ALPHONSINE 9
1326	DUBOIS	ST VITAL	58*	ALEXANDRE 6	JOHNNY 6	FREDERICK 3	ANTOINE 1	FRANCOIS 21
1196	DUBRELL	POPLAR PT	82 88	ELISE 9	ELIZABETH 3	ADOLPHUS 1		
1197	DUBUC	ST BONIFACE		ALEXANDRE 7	SARAH 1			
1330	DUCHARME	ST ANDREW		MARY 1				
1335	DUCHARME	ST VITAL	42 43	ANN 1				
1337	DUCHARME	ST VITAL	34	MOISE 18	PHILOMENE 17	LAURENT 16	FRANCOIS 14	MARIE ROSE 12
1337	DUCHARME	ST JAMES	34	ELIZA 10	MARIE 2			
1338	DUCHARME	ST VITAL	9 13	J BAPTISTE 20	JOSEPHTE 17	MARGUERITE 14	TOUSSAINT 12	PIERRE 4
1343	DUCHARME	ST BONIFACE	10	JONAS 24	ANTOINE 21	CATHERINE 19	MARGARET 9	JEAN 6
1345	DUCHARME	STE ANNE	26					
1346	DUCHARME	STE ANNE	27	JOHNNY 19	ROGER 17	JOSEPH 13	MARIE 12	PHILOMENE 6
1349	DUCHARME	SFX	139 142	FRANCOIS 24	MARGUERITE 24	ELZEAR 14	ANDRE 12	EDWARD 5
1350	DUCHARME	ST CHARLES	94	DOMITILDE 20	ELIZA 8	CAROLINE 5	MARIE 8	
1354	DUCHARME	STE AGATHE	124 73	NORBERT 12	PIERRE 11	ALEXANDRE 10		
1355	DUCHARME	STE AGATHE	124 73	FRANCOIS 12	DOMONIQUE 1			
1358	DUCHARME	ST LAURENT	7	FRIGINE 3				
1359	DUCHARME	STE ANNE						
1359	DUCHARME	STE ANNE	60	ALEXANDRE 20	AMABLE 14	ANTOINE 14		
1360	DUCHARME	STE ANNE	45 42	REINE 18	MARI ROSE 16	MELANIE 8		
1363	DUCHARME	ST VITAL	124 73					
1364	DUCHARME	STE AGATHE						
1371	DUCHARME	ST LAURENT	9	J BAPTISTE 23	LUCIE 23	JACOB 16	CUTHBERT 14	LOUISA 12
1371	DUCHARME	ST LAURENT	9	ANTOINE 9	MARY 18	ISABELLA 6	ELIZA 4	CATHERINE 2
1157	DUCHESNEAU	ST NORBERT	159 157	CHARLES 20	MARIE 15	WILLIAM 8	CELINA 6	THEO 3
1157	DUCHESNEAU	ST NORBERT	159 157	JOSEPH 23	ANGELIQUE 19			
1064	DUFFIN	ST JAMES						
1198	DUFOND	SFX	150 159					
1200	DUGAS	ST BONIFACE	87 77	MARIE 3	MAXIME 2			
1381	DUMAIS	ST BONIFACE	99 111					
1205	DUMAIS	ST VITAL	26 29					
1206	DUMAS	SFX	226 180	LOUIS 18	JOSEPH 18	HENRI 12	FRANCOIS 16	ALPHONSE 5
1378	DUMAS	ST BONIFACE	113 107					
1380	DUMAS	ST NORBERT	98					
1382	DUMAS	ST BONIFACE	58 44	MICHEL	JULIETTE 19	MARGUERITE 17	PIERRE 15	VIRGINIA 13
1382	DUMAS	ST BONIFACE	58 44	CELINA 11	JOSEPHINE 10	JOSEPH 8	PASCHAL 5	ALPHONSE 4
1384	DUMAS	ST BONIFACE	113 107	AMBROISE 14	ELIZABETH 12	JEAN 10	ALEXIS 8	DOMITILDE 6
1384	DUMAS	ST BONIFACE	113 107	J BAPTISTE 2				
1387	DUMAS	ST VITAL	11	ISADORE 20	LOUIS 18	PIERRE 16	GENEVEINE 12	CHRISTINE 9
1387	DUMAS	ST VITAL	11	ADELINE 7	PATRICE 5	PATRICK 13		
1212	DUMONTIER	BAIE S PAUL	227 219	HERMAS 19	ELLEN 16			
1213	DUNNAVAN	ST JAMES	29 13					
1214	DUPUIS	ST BONIFACE	81 87	MAGDELEINE 19	MARGUERITE 16	CLEOPHAS 16	JOSEPHTE 9	GENEVIENE 7
1407	DUPUIS	ST NORBERT	21 1	ADELAIDE 5	HERMINE 2			
1407	DUPUIS	ST NORBERT	21 1					

TABLE 4: GEOGRAPHICAL LOCATION AND
CHILDREN OF MANITOBA FAMILIES, 1870

ID	FAMILY	PARISH	AT OR BETWEEN		CHILDREN AND AGES AT NEXT BIRTHDAY
1408	DUPUIS	ST NORBERT	21	1	GUILLAUME 4, MARIE 2
1410	DUPUIS	ST NORBERT	218	.	
1420	ECCLES	ST NORBERT	209	.	
1444	EDGAR	ST ANDREW	.	.	
1167	EDINBURCK	ST PETER	16	31	
1422	ELLEMOND	ST BONIFACE	113	107	ANABELLA 6, SAMUEL 4, LOUISA 1, MARY 8
27404	ELLWOOD	ST JOHN	2	4	
1208	ELSE	ST JAMES	39	.	
1209	EMERLING	ST BONIFACE	.	.	
1434	EMOND	*SFX	1	3	EDWARD 5, BENJAMIN 4, ANGELIQUE 2
1434	EMOND	*SFX	1	3	SOPHIA 7, CAROLINE 4, FRANCIS 1
1435	EMOND	*SFX	1	3	FRISINE 19, ALEXANDRE 17, JANE 14, SARA 12, ADELE 8
1439	ENEAULT	STE ANNE	27	31	NANCY 6
1439	ENEAULT	STE ANNE	27	31	MARIE 2
1448	ERASMUSON	ST ANDREW	264	.	ROGER 14
1210	EVERLY	POPLAR PT	46	45	PIERRE 2
1460	FAGNANT	SFX	133	115	MARIA 11, JOHN 4, SOPHIE 9
1461	FAGNANT	SFX	197	.	WILLIAM 17, MARGUERITE 12, JAMAIMA 6
1465	FAGNANT	SFX	133	115	ELISE 30, PIERRE 2, ANGELE 23
1466	FAGNANT	SFX	202	.	PAUL 10, SOPHIA 9, ELISE 7
1467	FAGNANT	SFX	133	115	NAPOLEON 10, PHILOMENE 27, LUCIE 1
1467	FAGNANT	SFX	133	115	JEREMIE 22, WILLIAM 9, WILLIAM 19
1468	FAGNANT	SFX	199	202	ADELE 11, ROSALIE 10, ROSE 6
1470	FAGNANT	SFX	.	.	
1470	FAGNANT	SFX	.	.	
1476	FAGNANT	SFX	133	115	WILLIAM 24, CHARLES 22
1508	FAGNANT	SFX	133	115	ADELE 4, MELANIE 11
1471	FAILLE	STE AGATHE	80	87	FRANCOIS 6, JEAN 22, ANTOINE 17
1474	FAILLE	STE AGATHE	87*		ELZEAR 8, MELANIE 1
1481	FALCON	SFX	166	.	LEON 19, CUTHBERT 3, CECILE 20, JULIEN 6, MARIE 4
1483	FALCON	SFX	44	.	ROSALIE 2, GABRIEL 5, ROSE 18, HENRY 4, SARAH 1
1483	FALCON	SFX	44	.	CUTHBERT 27, TOUSSAINT 1, MADELEINE 8, JOHN 17, CUTHBERT 15
1485	FALCON	SFX	190	.	MELANIE 21, ELIE 24, J BAPTISTE 13, JOSEPH 15, PHILOMENE 6
1485	FALCON	SFX	190	.	JOSEPH 12, PIERRE 20, ATHANASE 23, EMILIE 17, ALPHONSINE 15
1486	FALCON	ST CHARLES	90	94	JOB 18, FRANCOIS 9, MARGUERITE 3, CHARLES 3, ISABELLE 2
1487	FALCON	SFX	190	.	PIERRE 4, GREGOIRE 15, JOSEPHTE 11, JULIE 10, VERONIQUE 7
1500	FARMER	HEADINGLY	18	.	ELEONOR 1, CATHERINE 2
1496	FARQUAHSON	ST VITAL	26	29	JULIE 40, CATERINE 38
1507	FARQUAHSON	ST VITAL	26	.	ELEONOR 6, NANCY 4
1502	FARQUHARSON	ST JOHN	2	4	JOACHIM 17, LEON 14
1495	FAULSTER	ST ANDREW	55	59	MARGARET 10, RODERICK 6, THOMAS 3
1498	FAVEL	ST ANDREW	287	280	WILLIAM 4
1501	FAVEL	PORTAGE	58	51	DAVID 18, HARRIET 11, VICTORIA 9
1503	FAVEL	ST ANDREW	270	285	JOHN 3, SARAH 1
1515	FAVEL	PORTAGE	113	119	MARY 15, WILLIAM 12, CORNELIUS 3
1516	FAVEL	PORTAGE	113	119	JOHN 2, ALEXANDER 1, GEORGE 5
1517	FAVEL	ST ANDREW	270	285	RICHARD 4, HENRY 2
1518	FAVEL	ST ANDREW			
1519	FAVEL	ST CLEMENT	108	110	SARAH 19, WILLIAM 17, ANN 14, HARRIET 12, HUMPHREY 9
1520	FAVEL	ST ANDREW	33	34	MARY 8
1521	FAVEL	ST ANDREW	29	.	
1521	FAVEL	ST ANDREW	29	.	

ID	FAMILY	PARISH	AT OR BETWEEN		CHILDREN AND AGES AT NEXT BIRTHDAY
1505	FAWCETT	PORTAGE	133	111	JAMES 15, ROBERT 13, CLARICE 13, ALBERT 10, ANGELE 6
1505	FAWCETT	PORTAGE	133	111	CHESTER 4, MARY 3, ISABELLA 1
1504	FAYAN	POPLAR PT	82	88	HARRIET 4, PETER 3
1525	FAYANT	BAIE S PAUL	143	158	ELIZA 6, ROSALIE 4
1488	FIDDLER	BAIE S PAUL	207	215	ELIZABETH 10, ALEXANDRE 6, JOSEPH 4, DOMITILDE 2
1531	FIDDLER	ST JAMES	58	63	JEMIMA 24, GEORGE 20, JOHN 18, DORCAS 17
1533	FIDDLER	ST JAMES	57	58	ANDREW 18, CHARLES 15, HARRIET 11, HENRY 9, JOSEPH 7
1533	FIDDLER	ST JAMES	41		CYRUS 5, MAGNUS 4, ALBERT 3, MARY 1
1535	FIDDLER	ST JAMES	41		CATHERINE 31, EMILY 25, CATHERINE 3
1536	FIDDLER	HEADINGLY	58		THOMAS 11, MARY JANE 9, MARY 5
1537	FIDDLER	ST JAMES	25		JAMES 16, CHARLES 14, PETER 12, WILLIAM 10, SARAH 8
1538	FIDDLER	HEADINGLY	58	63	THOMAS 6, JOHN 4, DAVID 2, JOHN 2
1538	FIDDLER	HEADINGLY	46		CHRISTINA 1
1539	FIDDLER	HEADINGLY	46		CAROLINE 11, J BAPTISTE 9, MAXIME 8, FRANCOIS 6, URSULE 3
1542	FIDDLER	ST JAMES	57	58	CATHERINE 7, CATHERINE 1
1542	FIDDLER	SFX	75		MARIE 19, MARGUERITE 17, JOSEPH 15, NORBERT 5, JOHN 12
1543	FIDDLER	SFX	75		MARIE 9, JAMES 9, WILLIAM 3, JULIE 1
1544	FIDDLER	SFX	82		XAVIER 6, ALEXANDER 6, JOSEPH 2
1544	FIDDLER	SFX	147		JOSEPH 4, NORBERT 1
1545	FIDDLER	SFX	147		HARRIET 4, LOUISA 4, JOHN 1
1556	FIDDLER	HEADINGLY	161	148	
13273	FIDDLER	BAIE S PAUL	39	41	
1425	FIDLER	ST PAUL	207	215	SARAH 20, THOMAS 20, MARY 17, WILLIAM 13, PETER 11
1546	FIDLER	ST CLEMENT	106		JAMES 22, ALBERT 20, JOHN 20, JOSEPH 18, CHARLES 16
1549	FIDLER	ST CLEMENT	96		JOHN 20, GEORGE 13, ANDREW, THOMAS 10
1550	FIDLER	ST CLEMENT	94		
1551	FIDLER	ST CLEMENT	25		CAROLINE 17, THOMAS 14, WILLIAM 14, ANN 9
1552	FIDLER	ST CLEMENT	93		PETER 3, JOHN 3
1552	FIDLER	ST CLEMENT	14		JANE 3, WILLIAM 2
1553	FIDLER	ST CLEMENT	14		FLORA 11, MARY 7, JAMES 1, JOHN 6
1850	FIELD	HEADINGLY	170	197	WILLIAM 7, JOHN 4, HENRY
1558	FIELDING	ST ANDREW	21		MARY 2, JAMES 2
1849	FIELDING	ST PETER	50	52	
1851	FINNEGAN	STE ANNE	8	17	
1529	FISHER	SFX	113		
1566	FISHER	ST BONIFACE	117	113	GEORGE 20, ALEXANDRE 2, MICHEL 10, CHARLES 8, HENRY 5
1567	FISHER	SFX	151		VIRGINIE 12
1568	FISHER	SFX	151		JOSEPH 1
1570	FISHER	ST BONIFACE	110	107	ADELAIDE 8, LEON 10
1571	FISHER	SFX	150	159	
1853	FLAMAND	STE AGATHE	161	148	
1857	FLAMAND	ST VITAL	73	108	PIERRE 7, PIERRE 6
1576	FLAMMAND	ST BONIFACE	107	102	VIRGINIE 1, ELISE 17, MAGDELEINE 20, JOSEPH 9, FRIZINE 7
1852	FLAMMAND	STE ANNE	31	38	HENRI 9, SARA 12
1852	FLAMMAND	STE ANNE	31	38	ISABELLE 10, DANIEL 1
1854	FLAMMAND	ST BONIFACE	81	87	JOSEPH 5, PIERRE 3, MARIE 1, JOSEPH 1
1855	FLAMMAND	ST BONIFACE	79	99	ALEXANDRE 2, ELIZABETH 21, MARIE 15, LAURENT 14, MELANIE 5
1856	FLAMMAND	ST BONIFACE	107	102	SARAH 1
1594	FLEET	KILDONAN	23		
1595	FLEET	KILDONAN	22		

ID FAMILY PARISH · AT OR BETWEEN · CHILDREN AND AGES AT NEXT BIRTHDAY

ID	FAMILY	PARISH	AT	BETWEEN	\<children and ages at next birthday\>				
1598	FLEET	ST PAUL	37		ANNY 26	MARGARET 23	ELIZABETH 20	FLORA 15	JOHN 12
1598	FLEET	ST PAUL	37		GEORGE 8	FLORA 7	JAMES 3		
1583	FLETT	POPLAR PT	63	62					
1584	FLETT	ST JAMES	22	23					
1585	FLETT	ST ANDREW	139	46	JOHN 3	WILLIAM 1			
1592	FLETT	ST JOHN	45	46	WILLIAM 12	JOHN 10	ANNY 7	JAMES 3	CHRISTIE 2
1599	FLETT	PORTAGE	122		JOHN 1				
1605	FLETT	ST ANDREW	198		JOHN 15	JOSEPH 12	ANN 11	CATHERINE 10	CARRY 8
1605	FLETT	ST ANDREW	198		MARIE 6	HELEN 2			
1606	FLETT	ST ANDREW	120	122	NANCY 25	WILLIAM 19	JAMES 15	JANE 13	ALFRED 8
1606	FLETT	ST ANDREW	120	122	LEWELLIN 5	ANNE 3			
1607	FLETT	ST ANDREW	196		JOHN 20	JOSEPH 18	ARCHIBALD 14	GEORGE 12	MARGUERITE 10
1607	FLETT	ST ANDREW	196		ALEXANDER 8				
1825	FLETT	ST PETER	46	56	CHARLES 21	ANDREW 16	MARIA 13	GEORGE 6	
1860	FLETT	ST PETER			JOHN 6	MARGUERITE 4	MARIE 3	CHRISTINE 3	
1861	FLETT	ST PETER	1	8	JOHN 3				
1865	FLETT	POPLAR PT	88	83	ALBERT 14	ELIZA 5	DAVID 3		
1866	FLETT	ST ANDREW	75		WILLIAM 15	JAMES 13	JANE 11	MARGUERITE 9	DAVID 6
1866	FLETT	ST ANDREW	75		SARA 3	ELIZABETH 2			
1868	FLETT	ST PETER	133	167	THOMAS 23	CHARLES 21	DAVID 19		
1869	FLETT	ST ANDREW	119		MARIANNE 3	HENRIE 1			
1870	FLETT	ST PETER	133	167	EDWARD 9	ROBERT 7	WILLIAM 5	MARIE 3	
1871	FLETT	ST PETER	175*		JANE 17	JOHN 14	NANCY 9		
1874	FLETT	ST PETER	133	167	MARIE 18	ANDRE 15	J BAPTISTE 12	JOSEPH 7	SARA 3
1587	FLEURY	STE AGATHE	124	73					
1588	FLEURY	SFX	85		EDWARD 9	MARIE	WILLIAM	ANDRE 3	
1589	FLEURY	SFX	142		MARIE 1				
1609	FLEURY	SFX	85						
1610	FLEURY	SFX	139	142	NORBERT 5	JOSEPH 2	MARIE 6	MARGUERITE 11	
1616	FLEURY	BAIE S PAUL	194	207	J BAPTISTE 19	BAZILE 15	WILLIAM 13	LOUIS 10	JOHN 7
1616	FLEURY	BAIE S PAUL	194	207	CLEMENCE 17				
1490	FOLSTER	ST CLEMENT	34		WILLIAM 17	HARRIET 15	JOHN 12	JAMES 10	THOMAS 8
1490	FOLSTER	ST CLEMENT	34		CHARLES 6				
1491	FOLSTER	ST CLEMENT	17		NANCY 15	ANDRE 2			
1494	FOLSTER	ST ANDREW	109	111	WILLIAM 19	GEORGE 17	HENRIE 16	THOMAS 11	ANNE 10
1494	FOLSTER	ST ANDREW	109	111	ALEXANDER 7	CHARLES 6	ISABEL 4		
1528	FONCECA	ST JOHN	28*		RACHEL 7	BENJAMIN 4	ALBERT 2		
1643	FONTAIN	ST JOHN	28	55					
1639	FORBISHER	ST NORBERT	137		ROSALIE 24	THOMAS 22	FRANCOIS 20	ELISE 18	MARGUERITE 16
1639	FORBISHER	ST NORBERT	137		MELANIE 14	NANCY 12	HARRY 10	JULIEN 7	ALEXANDRE 6
1833	FORBISTER	POPLAR PT	88	83	JAMES 13	ANDREW 16	CAROLINE 16	CATHERINE 11	FLORA 9
1834	FORBISTER	POPLAR PT	88	83	JOHN 7	SAMUEL 5	EMMA 4		
1446	FORBISTER	PORTAGE	107	114					
1560	FORTH	ST ANDREW	86						
1573	FORTH	ST ANDREW	89	91	NANCY 15	THOMAS 13			
1554	FORTNEY	ST CHARLES							
1601	FOULDS	ST JAMES	63		JESSIE 1				
1624	FOULDS	POPLAR PT	50	51	ALEXANDER 9	ELIZA 4	EMILY 1		
1625	FOULDS	HIGH BLUFF	59		ROBERT 15	WILLIAM 13	JOHN 11	ALEXANDER 9	MARTHA 7
1625	FOULDS	HIGH BLUFF	59		ELIZABETH 5	SARAH 3			
1626	FOULDS	ST JAMES	58	63	DAVID 13	FLORA 3			

TABLE 4: GEOGRAPHICAL LOCATION AND
CHILDREN OF MANITOBA FAMILIES, 1870

ID	FAMILY	PARISH	AT OR BETWEEN		CHILDREN AND AGES AT NEXT BIRTHDAY				
1628	FOULDS	ST JAMES	68	67	MARGARET 2				
1629	FOULDS	ST JAMES	58	63					
1627	FOULS	ST ANDREW	104	106					
1555	FOURNIER	SFX	161	148					
1564	FOURNIER	SFX	195	196					
1644	FOURNIER	SFX	133	115					
1646	FOX	ST ANDREW	107			MARIE 9	MADELEINE 11		ELIZABETH 5
1836	FOYE	SFX	116						
1837	FRANCOIS	STE AGATHE	87	92	ANTOINE 13	FRANCOIS 11			
1650	FRANK	ST ANDREW	114	97	MARY 20	WILLIAM 15	JOHN 10		
1662	FRANK	KILDONAN	50		EDWARD 20	JOSEPH 10			
1663	FRANKLIN	KILDONAN	70		ALEXANDRE 3	JOSEPH 1			
1661	FRANKS	*KILDONAN	83	82	DONALD 14	SARA 12	ALFRED 10		
1655	FRASER	KILDONAN			JACOB 10	CAROLINE 6			
1656	FRASER	ST JOHN	9	25	JAMES 21	HUGH 13	CHRISTIE 24	JEANNET 18	ISABELLA 16
1657	FRASER	ST PAUL	115		GEORGE 5	CATHERINE 5	JOHN 1		
1664	FRASER	ST PAUL	114		JOHN 4	HENRY 2			
1840	FREDERICK	ST VITAL	22	21	SOLOMAN 10	VIRGINIE 11	MELINA 4		
1841	FRENCH	HEADINGLY	39	41					
1842	FRIDAY	SFX	134	122	ISABELLE 1				
1843	FULSHER	ST ANDREW	19		HELEN 2				
1844	FURGUSON	HIGH BLUFF	26						
1847	GAGNIER	STE ANNE	49	66					
1881	GAGNON	SFX	10		MICHAEL 18				
1882	GAGNON	SFX	226		DONALD 7				
1883	GAGNON	SFX	11		NAPOLEON 6	MARY 5	PATRICE 5	ANGELE 3	ROGER 1
1889	GALARNEAU	ST BONIFACE	26		JOSEPH 20	SUSANNE 18	SARAH 18	ADELAIDE 11	MAGDELEINE 5
1889	GALARNEAU	ST BONIFACE	26						
1890	GALARNEAU	ST BONIFACE	26		WILLIAM 1				
1916	GANDRY	ST CHARLES	66	68	ADELAIDE 5	MARIE 1	GODEFRAIE 4		
1919	GANDRY	ST BONIFACE	99	111	MARGUERITE 2	ANDRE 1	ELISA 2		
1920	GANDRY	ST BONIFACE			MELINA 10	JOSEPH 9			
1921	GANDRY	ST BONIFACE	99	111	AMABLE 21	EMILIE 20	ANDRY 18	LEON 16	ROSALIE 15
1923	GANDRY	ST VITAL	6	15	MELINA 13	HELENE 11	LOUIS 11	OCTAVE 5	MODEST 3
1923	GANDRY	ST VITAL	6	15					
1817	GARDINER	ST ANDREW	6	15	GUILLAUME 1	FRANCES 9	AUGUSTA 7	MARIA 4	ELLA 2
1805	GARIEPY	SFX			BONAVENTURE 2				
1806	GARIEPY	SFX			LOUIS 15	ELIE 13	PAUL 12	MARIE 10	ROSE 8
1808	GARIEPY	SFX			MELANIE 6				
1848	GARIEPY	SFX			ELIE 16	JEAN 14	CHARLES 11	EMELIA 9	MADELEINE 9
1893	GARIEPY	SFX			MARIE 14	ELISE 12	ROSE 11	MATHILDE 7	ANDRE 8
1894	GARIEPY	SFX			LOUIS 26	BERNARD 24	J BAPTISTE 21	MOISE 18	HELENE 16
1893	GARIEPY	SFX			MARGUERITE 14	EUPHROSINE 12	PHILIPPE 3	ROSE 10	MATHILDE 7
1894	GARIEPY	SFX			FRANCOIS 5				
1899	GARIEPY	SFX			CALIXTE 28	CHARLES 26	CUTHBERT 23	DANIEL 23	R 21
1899	GARIEPY	SFX			PATRICE 16	FRANCOIS 14	ALEXANDRE 12	LOUIS 11	ANDRE 9
1899	GARIEPY	SFX			ELISE 7	MARIE 4			
1813	GARRALT	ST JOHN	13	6					
1848	GARRIC	ST CLEMENT	48	53					

CHILDREN OF MANITOBA FAMILIES, 1870

ID	FAMILY	PARISH	AT OR BETWEEN	CHILDREN AND AGES AT NEXT BIRTHDAY
1903	GARRIOCH	PORTAGE	61	WILLIAM 3, ALICE 1, EDWIN, ANN 15, — 12, HENRY 6
1904	GARRIOCH	PORTAGE	61	ANDREW 19, CYRUS 17, FLORA 20, ELLEN 15, — 13, JESSIE 11
1905	GARRIOCH	PORTAGE	109	GEORGE 25, MARY 20, WILLIAM 6, HARRIET 1, — 7, MARGARET 5
1905	GARRIOCH	PORTAGE	109	SCOTT 9, MARIA 6, WILLIAM 11, MARY 9
1907	GARRIOCH	PORTAGE	65	JEREMINA 13, GILBERT 11, MARY 2
1907	GARRIOCH	PORTAGE	65	ALBERT 4, ALICE 2, GEORGE 12
1909	GARTON	ST JOHN	45 46	JOHN 13, GEORGE 12, CHARLES 12, WILLIAM 10, ANNY 8
1909	GARTON	ST JOHN	45 46	MARY 3
1816	GAUTHIER	STE ANNE	49 66	ELIZA 15, PAUL 13, ALPHONSINE 13, LEONARD 11, PIERRE 7
1816	GAUTHIER	STE ANNE	49 66	JOSEPH 4, LEONIDE 2, PAUL 2, JOSEPH 9
1809	GEDDES	KILDONAN	43	
1927	GENTON	ST BONIFACE	24	PHILOMENE 19, ELISE 17, FREDERICK 17, VIRGINIE 15, LUCIE 8
1927	GENTON	ST BONIFACE	24	ROSALIE 1
1928	GENTON	ST BONIFACE	100	AGNES 1
1929	GENTON	ST NORBERT	143	HELENE 9, CLARA 5, PHILOMENE, MAXIME 3
1930	GENTON	ST BONIFACE	25	
1934	GEORGE	ST PETER	95 97	ROBERT 4, PETER 1
1935	GEORGE	ST PETER	83 85	MARIE 5
1936	GEORGE	PORTAGE	107	ANN 14, WILLIAM 12, EDMUND 10, MARIA 10, MARY 7
1936	GEORGE	PORTAGE	107	JANE 2
2470	GEORGE	ST BONIFACE	44 41	NORBERT 20, HYACINTHE 15
1901	GERALD	ST JOHN	4 13	ELLEN 5, J A 1, MARY, ELIZA
1824	GERVAIS	ST VITAL	58 52	MARIE 8, JOSEPH 6, ELIZA 5, WILLIAM 2
1941	GERVAIS	SFX	62	VERONIQUE 4, WILLIAM 2, WILLIAM 1
1942	GERVAIS	SFX	64	CUTHBERT 22, JOSEPHTE 20, PATRICE 17, ELISE 15, ELZEAR 13
1942	GERVAIS	SFX	64	CATHERINE 7, MARIE 6
1945	GERVAIS	SFX	150 159	LOUISE 24, MARIE 21, MARIE 20, J BAPTISTE 19, ALEXIS 17, NOEL 14
1945	GERVAIS	SFX	150 159	NAPOLEON 12, ELZEAR 9, ST PIERRE 7, ALEXIS
1948	GERVAIS	ST BONIFACE	176	MARGUERITE 13, MELANIE 11, ATHALIE 9, NAPOLEON 2
1949	GERVAIS	SFX	58 51	CAROLINE 13, MARY 9, ELEONOR 7
1803	GIBAUD	PORTAGE	6	FRANCOIS 36, ELIZABETH 36
1823	GIBBONS	ST JOHN	16 19	FRANCOIS 36, ELIZABETH 36
1954	GIBSON	ST ANDREW	16 19	ELIZABETH 18
1956	GIBSON	ST ANDREW	113 119	WILLIAM 4, ELIZABETH 18
1820	GIDDINGS	PORTAGE		
1819	GILLIS	ST JAMES	7 2	WILLIAM 4, JAMES 1
1962	GINGRAS	ST JOHN	87 77	JOHN
1818	GIROUX	ST BONIFACE	167 175	PETER
1972	GLADMAN	ST PETER	21 22	
1964	GLADU	ST JAMES		JOSEPH 18, ELIZA 12, ISABELLE 8, JUSTIN 19, JOSEPH
1975	GLADU	POPLAR PT	61	PASCHAL 24, FRANCOIS 23, CUTHBERT 21
1975	GLADU	POPLAR PT	61*	ANDRE 16, MADELEINE 13
1976	GLADU	POPLAR PT	87 77	CHARLES 2
1978	GLADU	ST VITAL	87 77	
1979	GLADU	ST VITAL	80*	WILLIAM 13, ALEXANDRE 11, ELISE, PIERRE 6, ALFRED 3
1968	GLENOT	ST BONIFACE	152	GILBERT 24, DAVID 20, JUSTINE, JUSTIN, ELLEN 8
1988	GODARD	ST BONIFACE	152	AUGUSTIN 12, LOUIS 11, THEOPHILE 11, MARIE 5
1983	GODON	STE AGATHE	54	J BAPTISTE 2, PATRICE 1
1986	GONVILLE	SFX		PETER 10, ALEXANDER 7, JAMES 4, ELIZA
1986	GONVILLE	SFX		
1771	GOOD	ST JAMES		

TABLE 4: GEOGRAPHICAL LOCATION AND
CHILDREN OF MANITOBA FAMILIES, 1870

ID	FAMILY	PARISH	AT OR BETWEEN	CHILDREN AND AGES AT NEXT BIRTHDAY
1991	GOOD	ST JAMES	9	THOMAS 3
1772	GORDON	ST JOHN	6 33	
1994	GOSSELIN	STE AGATHE	108 80	
1995	GOSSELIN	STE AGATHE	108	ADELAIDE 8, CAROLINE 6, J BAPTISTE 4, FREDERICK 1
1996	GOSSELIN	STE AGATHE	124 73	ROSALIE 8, LOUIS 23, STANISLAS 21, ANGELIQUE 32, CHARLOTTE 19
1996	GOSSELIN	STE AGATHE	124 73	PAUL 25, AUGUSTIN 23, ANTOINE 4
1997	GOSSELIN	STE ANNE	13	NANCY 13, WILLIAM 11, WILLIAM 4
1998	GOSSELIN	ST NORBERT	91	GUILLAUME 16, BETSY 22, ISADORE 13, JOSEPHE 11, JOSEPH 7
1999	GOSSELIN	STE AGATHE	92	ROSALIE 18, JOSEPH 17, ALEXANDRE 15, MARIE 12, ELIZA 10
1999	GOSSELIN	STE AGATHE	92	LOUIS 8, HENRI 5, MARGUERITE 2
2000	GOULET	ST NORBERT	72	ANTOINE 10, JOSEPH 6, MARIE 5
2008	GOULET	ST NORBERT	67	MAURICE 14, ROGER 12, LOUIS 10, ALEXANDRE 3, ROSALIE 1
2008	GOULET	ST NORBERT	67	JUSTINE 4, NAPOLEON 1, ALEXANDRE 8, MARIE 7
2009	GOULET	ST NORBERT	64	MARIE 5
2012	GOULET	ST BONIFACE	101 97	ROGER 35, LEONIDE 19, MAXIME 16, FLORA 3, SARAH 3
2014	GOULET	ST LAURENT	101	PETER 8, LOUISA 5, MADELEINE 3, ROGER 7
2073	GOULET	ST BONIFACE	101 97	ALFRED 11, ELISE 9, ALBERT 7
2073	GOULET	ST BONIFACE	101 97	ELISE 1
2011	GOURNEAU	ST ANDREW	96 97	VICTOIRE 7, ELIZABETH 5, JEMIMA 3
2013	GOWLAR	POPLAR PT	46	MARGARET 7, MARY 3, JOHN 1
2070	GOWLAR	POPLAR PT	78 73	MARY 3
2070	GOWLAR	POPLAR PT	46 45	MARY 3
2020	GOWLER	HEADINGLY	66	GRIFFITH 17, GEORGE 15, JAMES 13, OLIVIER 22, PAUL 9
2027	GRANDBOIS	STE AGATHE	541 535	ISADORE 18, MICHEL 15, JOSEPH 13, WILLIAM 11
2027	GRANDBOIS	STE AGATHE	541 535	PATRICE 7
2022	GRANT	ST JAMES	9 13	MARGUERITE 6, SARA 3
2079	GRANT	ST PETER	9	
2037	GREEN	HEADINGLY	6 33	
2058	GREEN	ST JOHN	133*	WITCHINEPAN2O
2033	GREEN	ST JOHN	6	PETER 33
2041	GREY EYES	ST PETER	40*	
2042	GROAT	ST JOHN	16	ANGELIQUE 28, JEAN 11, MALVINA 9, THEOPHILE 7, AUGUSTIN 4
2045	GROUETTE	ST JAMES	16	JAMES 13
2045	GROUETTE	STE ANNE	22	JOSEPH 2, ALEXANDRE 5, MAGDELEINE 14, ELZEAR 3, NAZAIRE 1
2046	GROUETTE	STE ANNE	20	ANTOINE 8, MAGDELEINE 17, ANTOINE 15, JULIE 12, J BAPTISTE 10
2047	GROUETTE	STE ANNE	20	MARIE 19
2047	GROUETTE	STE ANNE	140 141	JOSEPH 8, DAMASE 5, MARGUERITE 3
2055	GUILBAULT	SFX	66	VIRGINIE 10, ELISE 1
2050	GUILBOCHE	ST CHARLES	65	ANDRE 4
2051	GUILBOCHE	ST CHARLES	66	
2052	GUILBOCHE	ST CHARLES	68	MARGUERITE 7
2062	GUNN	ST ANDREW	116	MARGUERITE 7
2063	GUNN	ST ANDREW	165	MARGUERITE 15, WILLIAM 14, DONALD 12, JOHN 10, EMMA 9
2063	GUNN	ST ANDREW	165	MARY 7, HENRY 5, GILBERT 3
2064	GUNN	ST ANDREW	108 109	JANET 24, WILLIAM 22
2067	GUNN	KILDONAN	58	ANN 16, CATHERINE 15, MARY 13, JANE 10, JOHN 7
2067	GUNN	KILDONAN	58	ALEXANDER 5, WILLIAM 3
2068	GUNN	ST ANDREW	109	DONALD 3, GEORGE 1
2069	GUNN	ST ANDREW	127	BENJAMIN 15, ELISE 12, DONALD 3, VICTORIA 2
2072	GUNN	*KILDONAN	7	ANN 12, CATHERINE 10, JOHN 4
2074	GUNN	KILDONAN	61 65	ANN 2

ID	FAMILY	PARISH	AT OR BETWEEN	CHILDREN AND AGES AT NEXT BIRTHDAY
2076	GUNN	KILDONAN	61 66	ALEXANDER 22, CHRISTIE 20, WILLIAM 16, MARGARET 10
2077	GUNN	*KILDONAN	7	
2081	GUNN	POPLAR PT	86	JOHN 22, HENRIETTA 9
2082	GUNN	KILDONAN	37	
2082	GUNN	KILDONAN	37	
1804	HACKS	ST JOHN	25 28	
2086	HALCROW	HIGH BLUFF	66 70	JEMIMA 18, BARBARA 18, MARY 16, ELIZABETH 12, SOPHIA 9
2086	HALCROW	HIGH BLUFF	66 70	MARGARET 2, CHARLES 2, ANNABELLA 2
2091	HALCROW	*ST PAUL	75	CATHERINE 9, MARGARET 6, JOSEPH 4, JULIA 3
1775	HALL	HEADINGLY	1	WILLIAM 13
2099	HALLET	ST JAMES	49	MARIA 19, WILLIAM 15, ALBERT 13, CHARLES 9, JOHN 6, FLORA 6, JAMES 1
2101	HALLET	ST JAMES	40	
2102	HALLET	ST JAMES	40	
2117	HALLET	POPLAR PT	52 41	
2094	HALLETTE	POPLAR PT	61 79	HENRY 16, MARY 19, ROBERT 14, ALEXANDER 6, ELLEN 4
2094	HALLETTE	POPLAR PT	61 79	ANNIE 1
2098	HALLETTE	POPLAR PT	65 68	JANE 23, ELEONORE 7, ANGELE 5, ADELEINE 2
1776	HAMELIN	ST VITAL	22	ELEONORE 9, LEON 1
1777	HAMELIN	ST VITAL	23 20	
1778	HAMELIN	ST VITAL	26 29	J BAPTISTE 22, JOSEPH 1
1779	HAMELIN	ST NORBERT	84	NAPOLEON 15, ROSE 13, ELEONOR 6, JOSEPH 1
2108	HAMELIN	ST VITAL	10 5	MARGUERITE 4, ALEXANDRE 3
2109	HAMELIN	KILDONAN	58 61	FRANCOIS 19, DOMITILDE 16, PAUL 11, LOUIS 8
2110	HAMELIN	KILDONAN	54 56	WILLIAM 9, ELIZA 7, LOUIS 2, LOUISA 6
2110	HAMELIN	KILDONAN	54 56	EULALIE 3
2111	HAMELIN	ST VITAL	20	SARA 25, ST ANN 4, LOUIS 2
2113	HAMELIN	ST VITAL	23	JOHN 8, JAMES 6, MARIANNE 3
2118	HAMILTON	ST JOHN	45 46	ISABELLA 40, JANE 40, CATHERINE 1
2122	HARCUS	ST ANDREW	7	
2116	HARGRAVE	ST JAMES	18	
2137	HARIOTT	ST CLEMENT	41	
2125	HARKNESS	ST BONIFACE	41	CATHERINE 40
1792	HARPER	ST ANDREW	143 160	ALEXANDER 40, GEORGE 30, PIERRE 26, JESSY 23, MARY 6
1793	HARPER	ST PETER	175 171	THOMAS 5, THOMAS 1
1794	HARPER	ST PETER	111 112	ISAAC 2, GEORGE 4
1795	HARPER	ST ANDREW	19 18	
1796	HARPER	ST ANDREW	30	
2127	HARPER	KILDONAN	29	CATHERINE 19, MAGNUS 19, PETER 18, PETER 16
2129	HARPER	KILDONAN		JOHN 6, MAGNUS 3, JOHN 1
2130	HARPER	ST PETER		ELIZABETH 7, WILLIAM 6, MARY 2
2131	HARPER	ST PETER		JOSEPH 9, JANE 11
2132	HARPER	ST PETER	83*	WILLIAM 18, JANE 19
2133	HARPER	ST ANDREW	111	EMMA 19, ROBERT 16, JOSEPH 13, SARA 11, ALEXANDER 10
2133	HARPER	ST ANDREW	111	THOMAS 8, EDWARD 4
2136	HARPER	ST CLEMENT	18	ANN 4, VICTOIRE 4, MARGUERITE 6, REMIE 5, MELANIE 3
2140	HARRIOTT	STE ANNE	66	MARIE 2
2141	HARRISSON	STE ANNE	61 65	PAULINE 7, DAMASE 32, SUZETTE 25, LEONIDE 2
2142	HARRISSON	STE ANNE	23	PORPHIRE 32, JOSEPH 16, SUZANNE 16, EDWARD 11
2142	HARRISSON	STE ANNE	23	MARGUERITE 13, ANNE 9, WILLIAM 4
2138	HARVEN	ST CLEMENT	73 74	PHILOMENE 18
2143	HARVEN	ST ANDREW	73 74	ALEXANDER 6, GEORGE 3
2135	HASTIE	POPLAR PT	79 80	

TABLE 4: GEOGRAPHICAL LOCATION AND
CHILDREN OF MANITOBA FAMILIES, 1870

ID	FAMILY	PARISH	AT	BETWEEN	CHILDREN AND AGES AT NEXT BIRTHDAY
2124	HAY	ST ANDREW	109	111	JOHN 1
2144	HAY	ST ANDREW	270	285	
2146	HAYS	ST ANDREW	165	164	
2128	HAYS	ST ANDREW	194		
1799	HEATH	ST JOHN	13	6	EDWARD 6, WILLIAM 5
1798	HENAULT	STE ANNE			SUZETTE 28, LOUISE 5, CHARLES 14, JUDITH 13, ISABELLE 12
2150	HENAULT	ST VITAL	35	28	CAROLINE 8, WILLIAM 2, LEANDRE 8, J BAPTISTE 6, J 2
2150	HENAULT	ST VITAL	35	28	PIERRE 6, ALEXANDRE 12, VIRGINIE 6, JANE 13, ANGUS 9
2151	HENAULT	ST VITAL	35	28	ANTOINE 14, MARGUERITE 16, CHRISTIANA 15
2151	HENAULT	ST VITAL	35	28	JOSEPHTE 18, FLORA 17
2161	HENDERSON	KILDONAN	42		ROBERT 19, MARY 9
2161	HENDERSON	KILDONAN	42		HELEN 6
2165	HENDERSON	PORTAGE	120		MARIA 23, CHARLES 21, JAMES 19, MARGARET 15, ELIZA 13
2165	HENDERSON	PORTAGE	120		WILLIAM 11, MARY 9, HENRY 9, AMELIA 8, EDWARD 6
2167	HENDERSON	ST ANDREW	16		ANN 13, CHARLOTTE 11, GEORGE 10
2167	HENDERSON	ST ANDREW	16		MARY 5, MARIA 4, MARTHA 1
2175	HENDERSON	KILDONAN	39		FLORA 1
2176	HENDERSON	KILDONAN	44		SAMUEL 5, ANGUS 3, MORRISSON 3, WILLIAM 18, TEBISHKOKIJ20 16
2177	HENDERSON	ST PETER	49		SAMUEL 22, CHARLES 20, PETER 20, NEIL 11, ANNA 11
2178	HENDERSON	KILDONAN	49		ANGUS 17, DONALD 13, SAMUEL 15, ADAM 8, VICTORIA 4
2178	HENDERSON	KILDONAN	25	28	FLORA 8, ELLEN 7, CHRISTIANA 7
2179	HENDERSON	ST JOHN	121		CATHERINE 14, SAMUEL 8, JEANNET 12
2180	HENDERSON	PORTAGE	127	125	ELLEN 3, MARGARET 2, ELIZA 2
2187	HENRI	ST NORBERT	561	541	NORBERT 5, MARIE 6, ELIZA 3, JOSEPHTE 3
2189	HENRI	STE AGATHE	197	166	NARCISSE 11, MARIE A 8, MOISE 17, JOSEPH 15
2190	HENRI	ST NORBERT	197	166	JOHN 19, SARAH 22, XAVIER 17
2190	HENRI	ST NORBERT	13*		CHARLES 11, ROSALIE 9, MARIE 4
2154	HENRY	ST CLEMENT	114	116	OLIVER 10, ELIZABETH 8, GEORGE 8, FRANCOIS 2
2159	HENRY	ST CLEMENT	158	182	JOHN 1
2182	HIGGINS	ST JOHN	6	33	
2181	HILL	PORTAGE			
2173	HINDE	BAIE S PAUL	67		
2172	HIVET	ST JOHN	69	67	
2171	HODGES	PORTAGE	40		WILLIAM 8, ADELINE 8, JAMES 5, ADELAIDE 4, EDWARD 4
2198	HODGESON	PORTAGE	43		MARY 15, JOSEPH 10, ALBERT 10
2201	HODGESON	PORTAGE	43		
2202	HODGSON	ST ANDREW	105		JOHN 21, ALBERT 20, JOSEPH 18, EDWIN 14, CHARLES 12
2203	HODGSON	ST ANDREW	56		HENRY 9, ELIZABETH 9, LOUIS 5
2203	HODGSON	ST ANDREW	61		ROSINE 3, WILLIAM 10
2206	HOGG	ST CHARLES	60		ROSALIE 11, MARY 3, PHILOMENE 10, SARAH 4
2210	HOGG	ST CHARLES	57		ELIZABETH 5, ALBERT 1, ALEXANDRE 2
2207	HOGUE	ST CHARLES	60		CLARA 5, ADELAIDE 3, SARAH 4
2208	HOGUE	ST CHARLES			WILLIAM 10, AMABLE 8, VIRGINIE 6, PHILOMINE 5
2209	HOGUE	ST CHARLES	4	61	CATHERINE 1
2209	HOGUE	ST CHARLES	44	13	
2211	HOGUE	ST CHARLES			
2170	HOLLAND	ST JOHN			
2169	HOOKEY	ST JAMES			ANN 5, ELISE 5, ROBERT 5
2249	HOORIE	ST PETER			SARA 8, PHILIP 16, HENRI 16, ABARIA 10
2250	HOORIE	ST PETER			ISABEL 14, JOSEPH 8

ID	FAMILY	PARISH	AT OR	BETWEEN										CHILDREN AND AGES AT NEXT BIRTHDAY
2163	HOPE	ST PETER	46		FRANCOISE	4	HENRI	2							
2166	HOPE	ST PETER	56		MARY	4	ELIZABETH	4							
2216	HOULE	SFX	115		LOUIS	20	WILLIAM	18	MARGUERITE	16	EMERISE	13	CHARLOTTE	12	
2216	HOULE	SFX	115		MARIE	9					LOUISE	11	EMERISE	9	
2220	HOULE	SFX	120		EMILIE	20	ELISE	16	GUILLAUME	13					
2220	HOULE	SFX	120		J BAPTISTE	5	ETIENNE	3	LOUISON	1					
2221	HOULE	SFX	116	133											
2223	HOULE	BAIE S PAUL	194	207	J BAPTISTE	2	MARY	1							
2226	HOULE	STE AGATHE	559	557	NAPOLEON	5	PATRICE	3	EMILIE	2					
2227	HOULE	STE AGATHE	565		DAMASE	3									
2228	HOULE	STE AGATHE	561		ALEXANDRE	20	ONESIME	13							
2232	HOULE	SFX	115												
2233	HOULE	SFX	127	130	ALEXANDRE	4	PIERRE	3							
2234	HOULE	SFX	69		JOSEPH	15	NORBERT	12	JOHN	10	CUTHBERT	9	LOUISE	1	
2236	HOURIE	HIGH BLUFF	69		MARGUERITE	15	THOMAS	13	ALEXANDRE	11	EDWIN	9	ALBERT	5	
2236	HOURIE	HIGH BLUFF	69		ELIZABETH	13	FLORA	1							
2237	HOURIE	HIGH BLUFF	70		JEMIMA	13	JAMES	11	SARAH	9	MARY	7	WILLIAM	5	
2237	HOURIE	HIGH BLUFF	70		MAGDELEINE	3	ANDREW	1							
2238	HOURIE	ST ANDREW	280	260	JANE	23	JOSEPH	3							
2240	HOURIE	ST CLEMENT	80		CORNELIUS	4	JANE	4	ALBERT	1					
2242	HOURIE	SFX	222	227	MARY	2									
2251	HOUSE	SFX	116	133											
2255	HOUSE	SFX	116	133											
2219	HOWARD	ST ANDREW	71	72	HELEN	2									
2230	HOWARD	ST PAUL	110	115	HENRY	20	JOHN	18	CHARLES	15	EDWARD	5	THOMAS	3	
2147	HUDDLESTON	PORTAGE	107	114	ANNIE	12	ADAM	10	JAMES	8					
2147	HUDDLESTON	PORTAGE	107	114	HENRY	1									
1002	HUPPE	ST BONIFACE	99	111	JOHN	19	JEAN	21							
2263	HUPPE	STE ANNE	2	18											
2264	HUPPE	STE ANNE	64		VIRGINIE	3	ANNE	2							
2265	HUPPE	STE ANNE	2	18											
2268	HUPPE	ST BONIFACE	79	99	MARIE	2	AZILDA	1							
2271	HUPPE	STE ANNE	11												
2195	HYDE	POPLAR PT	31	29	ALEXANDER	4	CHRYSOSTONI	3	MARIE ROSE	1					
1738	HYDEN	ST BONIFACE	37												
2399	INKSTER	*KILDONAN	2	4	MARY	14	JOHN	12	HARRIET	10	ELLEN	8	FLORENCE	6	
2399	INKSTER	*KILDONAN	2	4	ANGUS	4	ALFRED	4							
2400	INKSTER	*KILDONAN	6		MARY	38	COLIN	28	GEORGE	21	WILLIAM	12	JOHN	10	
2400	INKSTER	*KILDONAN	6		JAMES	14	RICHARD	6							
2401	INKSTER	HIGH BLUFF	54	56	WILLIAM	10	ANNIE	5	ELIZA	2					
2403	INKSTER	POPLAR PT	60	63	JOHN	25	JANE	22							
2404	INKSTER	*KILDONAN	4												
2405	INKSTER	POPLAR PT	35												
2406	INKSTER	HIGH BLUFF			ALBERT	3	JAMES	1	JEMIMA	3	ELIZABETH	1			
2407	INKSTER	POPLAR PT	38		ARCHIBALD	6	JOHN	5	JOSEPH	4	BARBARA	2			
3014	INKSTER	POPLAR PT	37	39	MARGARET	8	JOHN	6							
2388	IRVINE	*ST PAUL	61												
2389	IRVINE	STE ANNE	38	46											
2392	IRVINE	ST ANDREW	287	280	JAMES	18	JOHN	14							
2396	IRVINE	ST ANDREW	5	6	SARAH	5	JOHN	1	GEORGE	12	CATHERINE	10	ANNABELLA	7	
2397	IRVINE	ST ANDREW	5	6											

TABLE 4: GEOGRAPHICAL LOCATION AND
CHILDREN OF MANITOBA FAMILIES, 1870

ID	FAMILY	PARISH	AT OR BETWEEN	CHILDREN AND AGES AT NEXT BIRTHDAY
2391	IRWINE	ST JOHN	13 6	CHRISTIANA 17, MATILDA 13, MARIA 11
2385	ISAAC	STE AGATHE	108 80	
2374	ISBISTER	ST PAUL	45	FANNY 28, ALEXANDER 19, GEORGE 24, BENJAMIN 14, MARGARET 12, HENRY 9
2375	ISBISTER	ST JAMES	13 13	EDWARD 27, MARY 5
2376	ISBISTER	ST JAMES	13 9	SUSANNAH 9, MARY 5, HARRIET 5, MARIA 4
2377	ISBISTER	ST JAMES	14	SARA 6, JAMES 4
2378	ISBISTER	ST CHARLES	103	WILLIAM 7, MARIE 1, JANE 2
2364	JACK	HIGH BLUFF		
2363	JACKSON	ST JOHN	29 26	HUGH 17, MARY 15, WILLIAM
2383	JAMESON	ST CLEMENT	48 7	SARA 6
2386	JAMIESON	ST JAMES	45 46	
2352	JANNOT	SFX	187 185	GUILLELEMIN 11, JOSEPH 9
2353	JANNOT	SFX	195 196	FREDERICK 11, GASPARD 8
2354	JANNOT	SFX	199 202	MARIE 11, LEON 6, XAVIER 3
2356	JANNOT	SFX	195	J BAPTISTE 17
2343	JEFFERSON	ST JAMES	44 45	
2344	JEFFREY	ST JOHN	7 2	
2345	JETTE	ST NORBERT	82	JOSEPH 21, AMBROISE 20, MADELEINE 20, PIERRE 15, PATRICE 3, CAROLINE 12
2350	JOBIN	ST CHARLES	55	LOUIS 10, MARIE 8
2350	JOBIN	ST CHARLES	55	
2346	JOCHIAM	ST PAUL	2	
2355	JOHN	ST PETER	95 97	THOMAS 15, JANE 9, ANDRE 9, MILES 7
2023	JOHNSTON	ST CLEMENT	1 8	JOHN 2
2325	JOHNSTON	ST ANDREW	55	
2327	JOHNSTON	ST CLEMENT	58 59	CATHERINE 9, GEORGE 2, ANN 8, CATHERINE 5
2328	JOHNSTON	ST ANDREW	53	ANN 3
2329	JOHNSTON	ST ANDREW	58 59	SARAH 15, FRANCOISE 12, CATHERINE 5, ALEXANDER 3
2330	JOHNSTON	ST ANDREW	58	
2330	JOHNSTON	ST ANDREW	58	
2331	JOHNSTON	ST CLEMENT	53 55	VICTORIA 6, MARIANN 4, GEORGE, ELIZABETH 26, HARRIET 2, MARGUERITE 15, SARAH 1
2332	JOHNSTON	ST ANDREW	73	JOHN 40, WILLIAM 26, ELIZA 15, HARRIET 10
2336	JOHNSTON	ST CLEMENT	54	JANE 19, ANN 15, HARRIET 17
2337	JOHNSTON	ST PETER	167 175	NANCY 13, HELENE 10, ALFRED 2
2338	JOHNSTON	ST PETER	1 8	ELIZABETH 8, ALEXANDER 2
2339	JOHNSTON	ST BONIFACE		
2435	JOHNSTON	ST ANDREW	69 70	ELIZABETH 3, ISABELLE 2
2436	JOHNSTON	PORTAGE	113 119	
2437	JOHNSTON	POPLAR PT	63	JOHN 2
2438	JOHNSTON	ST JOHN	28 55	MARY 6, WILLIAMIENA 4, JOHN 10, COLLIN 5, MATHILDA 3, SAMUEL
2440	JOHNSTON	ST PETER	17* 8	MORDO 14, ELISE 12, SAMUEL 9
2441	JOHNSTON	ST PETER	1	DAVID 16, JEREMIE 9
2442	JOHNSTON	ST PETER	6 8	
2335	JOHNSTONE	*KILDONAN	6 7	
2317	JOLIEBOIS	ST NORBERT	41	J BAPTISTE 20, ROSALIE 15, CELINA 15, MARGUERITE 8, MARIE 6
2317	JOLIEBOIS	ST NORBERT	41 94	JULIEN 3, VIRGINIE 1
2416	JONES	ST CLEMENT	111	ELISE 16, MARIANNE 12, ISIDORE 10
2415	JORDAN	*KILDONAN	12 14	
2414	JUSSIAUME	ST VITAL	58 52	ROGER 13, FRANCOIS 10, ISIDORE
2291	KEEPLING	ST CLEMENT	23 24	MARIAN 11, CATHERINE, FLORA 9, MARGUERITE 4, JESSIE 1

ID	FAMILY	PARISH	AT	BETWEEN	CHILDREN AND AGES AT NEXT BIRTHDAY				
2300	KEEPLING	ST PETER	83	85	THOMAS 12				
1745	KENNEDY	ST PETER	175	171	WILLIAM 4	ALEXANDER 3	JOHN 1		
1746	KENNEDY	ST PETER	175	171	JOHN 8	MARIE 6	EMMA 4	JANE 2	SARA 1
1748	KENNEDY	ST PETER	1	8	ANN 19	JOHN 15	CATHERINE 12		
1749	KENNEDY	ST ANDREW	104	106					
1750	KENNEDY	ST PETER	175	171					
1751	KENNEDY	ST CHARLES	61	65	CAROLINE 6	MARY 4	ELISE 1		
2314	KENNEDY	ST PETER	1	8					
2294	KIPLING	ST ANDREW	266	267					
2299	KIPLING	ST ANDREW	264	267	GEORGE 21	ANDREW 15	MARIAN 12		
1756	KIPPLING	ST CHARLES	16	57					
2295	KIPPLING	ST JAMES	12	9					
1762	KIRKNESS	ST ANDREW	155	156	SARA 17				
2287	KIRKNESS	POPLAR PT	82	88	WILLIAM 22	ALEXANDER 20	MARGARET 18	GEORGE 16	CATHERINE 13
2287	KIRKNESS	POPLAR PT	82	88	RACHEL 10				
2288	KIRKNESS	ST CLEMENT	48	53	MARY 19	JOSEPH 17	JOHN 15	ABRAHAM 13	ELISE 5
2288	KIRKNESS	ST CLEMENT	48	53	JAMES 5				
2286	KIRTON	ST JAMES	53		ELIZABETH 5				
1763	KITTSON	PORTAGE	51	53	THOMAS 6	KATY 4	ANNA 1		
1757	KLYNE	ST JOHN	6	33	HENRY 2				
2282	KLYNE	STE AGATHE	469*		ALEXANDRE 8	MICHEL 5	MARIE 4	ROSALIE 2	HELENA 3
2283	KLYNE	STE AGATHE	265	124	JOHN 14	EDWARD 9	ELIZA 8	ALFRED 5	
2283	KLYNE	STE AGATHE	265	124	FREDERICK 1				
2284	KLYNE	STE AGATHE	265	124	CHARLOTTE 11	GEORGE 10	MARGARET 8		
1758	KNIGHT	ST PAUL	2	4	THOMAS 2				
1759	KNIGHT	ST ANDREW	287	280	MARIA 13	JAMES 20	SOPHIA 14	WILLIAM 6	ANN 4
2276	KNIGHT	ST ANDREW	67		CATHERINE 2				
2277	KNIGHT	ST ANDREW	280	260	WILLIAM 31	MARY 2	ALBERT 14	JOHN 5	
2278	KNIGHT	ST ANDREW	280	260	ALEXANDER 3				
2278	KNIGHT	ST ANDREW	280	260					
2279	KNIGHT	ST PAUL	110	260					
1766	KNIPE	*KILDONAN	82	81					
1767	KNIPE	KILDONAN	42	43					
2273	KNOTT	ST ANDREW	48	48	MATILDA 23	FRANCOISE 16	ROSALIE 2		
2274	KNOTT	KILDONAN	63	66	CHRISTIE 5	ROGER 6			
2310	KUFFMANN	ST ANDREW	48	48					
1913	LABERGE	STE AGATHE	589	585	JOSEPHINE 9	JOHN 1	ANDREW 1		
2458	LABERGE	STE AGATHE	589	585					
1713	LABISTON	ST ANDREW	155	156	MARGUERITE 2	JOHN 1			
1768	LABISTON	ST CLEMENT	111	94	NANCY 12	CLARASSA 3			
2464	LABISTON	ST ANDREW	155	156	MARGUERITE 2				
2469	LACERTE	ST NORBERT	24		MARIE 26	LOUIS 24	JOSEPHTE 22	OCTAVE 16	ISABELLE 15
2469	LACERTE	ST NORBERT	24		PIERRE 13	JOSEPH 12	MARIE M 9	ALPHONSINE 5	CHRISTINE 3
2469	LACERTE	ST NORBERT	24		JUSTINE 3	MARIE L 1			
1714	LACOUTURE	SFX	161	148	JOSEPH 15				
2488	LADEROUT	ST BONIFACE	17		PHILIBERT 22	PHILOMENE 16	MAXIME 13	JOSEPH 7	ZEPHIRIN 4
2489	LADEROUT	ST BONIFACE	17		ALICE 1				
2489	LADEROUTE	ST BONIFACE	12		JOSEPHTE 8	MARGUERITE 6	JOSEPH 4	ROSALIE 2	
2490	LADEROUTE	ST BONIFACE	13	12	MAXIME 1				
2493	LADEROUTE	ST BONIFACE	1						
2494	LADEROUTE	ST BONIFACE	77	79	JOSEPH 13	ELISE 4	APPOLINE 1		
2497	LADEROUTE	ST BONIFACE	13						

TABLE 4: GEOGRAPHICAL LOCATION AND
CHILDREN OF MANITOBA FAMILIES, 1870

ID	FAMILY	PARISH	AT OR BETWEEN	CHILDREN AND AGES AT NEXT BIRTHDAY				
2501	LADOUCEUR	ST NORBERT	30	WILLIAM 12	BAPTISTE 11	JOSEPH 7	JULIE 18	MARIE 15
2503	LADOUCEUR	ST BONIFACE		OLIVER 15	LOUIS 13	HENRI 12	JULIEN 10	SARAHZINE 2
2504	LAFERTE	STE AGATHE	616	MARIE 24	JEAN 19	JOSEPH 10		
2508	LAFERTY	*STE AGATHE	616 589	PIERRE 13	ELISE 11	CAROLINE 9	LOUIS 7	VERONIQUE 4
2508	LAFERTY	*STE AGATHE	616 589	AGATHE 2				
2509	LAFOND	ST VITAL	35 28	DAVID 1				
1900	LAFONTAINE	SFX		ELIZA 2				
2477	LAFONTAINE	SFX		THOMAS 25	BERNARD 23	EMILIE 20	MATHILDA 12	ELIZA 10
2485	LAFONTAINE	SFX		ANASTASIE 8	MARIE 5			
2514	LAFONTAINE	SFX		LOUIS 4	PIERRE 2			
2518	LAFONTAINE	SFX	40	NAPOLEON 8	LOUIS 7	GASPARD 4	PHILOMENE 2	
2520	LAFONTAINE	SFX	191 192	CALIXTE 23	ANTOINE 21	M 19	BERNARD 16	ELZEAR 14
1965	LAFONTAINE	SFX		CUTHBERT 11	PHILOMENE 9	VIRGINIE 7	MARIE 5	
2523	LAFORNAISE	SFX		J BAPTISTE 4	LOUISE 2	ADELE 1		
2524	LAFORNAISE	SFX		JOSEPH 5	ALEXANDRE 3	HYACINTHE 3		
2678	LAFORNAISE	SFX		ELZEAR 7	NAPOLEON 5	FRANCOISE 16		
2679	LAFOURNAIS	SFX	195 196	NAPOLEON 21	FRANCOIS 18	ELIZA 6		
2526	LAFOURNAISE	ST NORBERT	31 27	GUILLAUME 1	DANIEL 2	NAPOLEON 13	MAXIME 9	SARAH 7
2526	LAFOURNAISE	ST NORBERT	31 27	WILLIAM 19	CECILE 17			
2528	LAFRAMBOISE	SFX		CHARLES 5	J BAPTISTE 3			
2529	LAFRAMBOISE	SFX		EDWARD 8	DANIEL 8	ROSALIE 3	CATHERINE 1	FRANCOIS 12
2680	LAFRAMBOISE	SFX		GABRIEL 15	ELISE 13	LOUISE 11		
2680	LAFRAMBOISE	SFX		JOHNNY 21	WILLIAM 19	NORBERT 17		
2682	LAFRAMBOISE	ST BONIFACE	117 113	CATHERINE 9	CAROLINE 21	GABRIEL 4	NAPOLEON 15	CUTHBERT 10
2534	LAFRENIERE	SFX	130 134	ELISE 11	JOSEPH 11	LEON 14	MARIE 12	
2534	LAFRENIERE	SFX	130 134	J BAPTISTE 18	GUILLAUME 18	ALEXANDRE 3	ELIE 1	
2547	LAGEMONIER	ST BONIFACE	29 26	VERONIQUE 8	ROSE 3			
2548	LAGEMONIER	STE ANNE	16 17	MODESTE 2				
2544	LAGER	ST CLEMENT	113 107	JOSEPH 3				
2543	LAGIMONIERE	ST BONIFACE	99	WILLIAM 12	VIRGINIE 12	MICHEL 10	LUCIE 1	
2541	LAGIMONIERE	ST BONIFACE	79 99					
2545	LAGIMONIERE	ST BONIFACE	99 111	JOSEPH 20	ROMAIN 20			
2546	LAGIMONIERE	ST BONIFACE	99 111	JOSEPH 7	ELEONOR 7	EUPHROSINE 15	DANIEL 10	HENRI 6
2551	LAGIMONIERE	ST BONIFACE	99 111	ETIENNE 17	THERESE 16	COLLIN 1		
2552	LAGIMONIERE	ST BONIFACE	99 111	ANGELIQUE 2	MARIE 6	LAZARUS 11		
2553	LALIBERTE	BAIE S PAUL	207	TOUSSAINT 6	MARIE 3	HELENE 3		MODESTE 5
2553	LALIBERTE	BAIE S PAUL	207	PIERRE 4	MARIE 2			
2558	LALIBERTE	ST NORBERT	148	LIN 21	LOUIS 21	THERESE 1		
2559	LALIBERTE	ST NORBERT	148 144					
2560	LALIBERTE	ST NORBERT	148*					
2554	LAMB	ST JAMES						
2550	LAMBERT	ST ANDREW	31 32	JOHN 13	EMILY 13	SAMUEL 2		
2570	LAMBERT	ST NORBERT	84 81					
2575	LAMBERT	HEADINGLY	23					
2578	LAMBERT	HEADINGLY	23 24	ANDREW 21	WILLIAM 21			
2578	LAMBERT	ST ANDREW	32	CATHERINE 7	BELLA 7	MARGARET 16	MICHEL 16	MARIANNE 9

ID	FAMILY	PARISH	AT OR BETWEEN	CHILDREN AND AGES AT NEXT BIRTHDAY
2580	LAMBERT	ST ANDREW	31	LOUISA 5, SARAH 3, MARIANNE 1
2581	LAMBERT	ST ANDREW	248	MARGARET 13, SARAH 11, JOHN 9, CHARLOTTE 7, ANDREW 4
2581	LAMBERT	ST ANDREW	248	MICHEL 1
2582	LAMBERT	ST ANDREW	33	ELIZABETH 21, FRANCOISE 18, JOSEPH 8, ALEXIS 6, ANGELIQUE 4
2585	LAMIRANDE	ST NORBERT	94 91	MARIE 12, LOUIS 10
2586	LAMIRANDE	ST NORBERT	94 91	VIRGINIE 2
2569	LAND	ST JAMES	73*	ANN 18, JAMES 16, CHARLES 14, GEORGE 11, JOSUA 8
2569	LAND	ST JAMES	73*	ELIZA 5, JOSEPH 2
2591	LANDRY	SFX	195 196	PIERRE 17
2592	LANDRY	ST NORBERT	142	BAPTISTE 40
2595	LANDRY	SFX		
2600	LANDRY	ST VITAL	10 5	ALPHONSINE 11, WENCESLAS 9, NORBERT 7
2684	LANDRY	SFX	195 196	MOISE 2
2597	LANDRY LOUI	ST NORBERT	256 250	MARGUERITE 17
2601	LANDRY LOUI	ST NORBERT	256 250	
2604	LANE	SFX	139	ELIZA 8
2602	LANG	ST JAMES	70 73	JAMES 2
2609	LANGEVIN	ST BONIFACE	117 113	MARY 3
2542	LANGILL	SFX	93 99	MARIE 1
2613	LAPIERRE	ST BONIFACE	117 113	BONIFACE 8, WILLIAM 3, MARIE 1
2615	LAPIERRE	SFX	213 214	TOUSSAINT 14, PATRICE 7, MOISE 5, JUSINE 3, JOSEPH 2
2588	LAPINIS	BAIE S PAUL	194 207	MARY 16, CUTHBERT 13, MADELEINE 10, J BAPTISTE 3
2620	LAPLANTE	STE AGATHE	575	MELANIE 16, FRISINE 14, LUCIE 10, MARIE 8, GUILLAUME 6
2686	LAPLANTE	SFX	150 159	PIERRE 6
2686	LAPLANTE	SFX	150 159	
2618	LAPRENIERE	ST BONIFACE	150 159	JOHN 19, ADELE 16, MADELEINE 14
2663	LAP/CQUE	SFX	16 15	MARIE 5, FRANCOIS 4, CHARLES 3
2572	LAREILLE	SFX	42 53	ELISE 20
2630	LAREILLE	STE AGATHE	42 43	FRANCOISE 5, MARIE 4
2651	LARIVIERE	ST VITAL	454*	FRANCOIS 17
2655	LAROCQUE	ST VITAL	50 45	ELISE 20, CHARLES 17, MARGUERITE 14, PIERRE 12, NAPOLEON 9
2672	LAROCQUE	ST VITAL	35 28	FRANCOISE 5
2672	LAROCQUE	ST BONIFACE	35 28	FRANCOIS 17, BARBE 15, J BAPTISTE 12, WILLIAM 9, JULIEN 7
2674	LAROCQUE	ST BONIFACE	44 41	MARGARET 2
2674	LAROCQUE	ST VITAL	44 41	MARIE 4, ADELAIDE 3, J BAPTISTE 1
2782	LAROCQUE	SFX	19 28	ROSE 1
2787	LAROCQUE	STE AGATHE	127 130	SOPHIE 19, ELISE 15, JOSEPH 15, PIERRE 10, ALEXANDRE 8
2789	LAROCQUE	STE AGATHE	571	MELINA 5, JULIENNE 5, JOSEPH 2
2789	LAROCQUE	SFX	571	
2791	LAROCQUE	SFX	67	
2793	LAROCQUE	SFX		LOUISON 9, MARIE 7, ISABELLE 2, CHARLES 2
2652	LARONDE	ST BONIFACE	139 142	PHILOMENE 16
2657	LARONDE	ST LAURENT	14 13	ELIZA 18, LOUIS 16, GASPARD 16, CHARLES 14, J BAPTISTE 12
2657	LARONDE	ST LAURENT	24 19	JOSEPH 8, SUZETTE 6, ALEXANDRE 4, PELAGE 4, M 2
2658	LARONDE	ST LAURENT	24 19	JOHN 14, ELIZA 12, PHILOMENE 10, PAUL 10, ALEXANDRE 6
2658	LARONDE	ST LAURENT		JUDITH 1
2677	LARONDE	STE AGATHE	87 92	ANTOINE 18, JOSEPH 15, MADELEINE 8
2798	LARONDE	ST LAURENT	24 19	PHILOMENE 11, ETIENNE 9, MARY 6, MARGUERITE 1
1083	LARSEN	ST JOHN	6 33	MARY 1
1085	LAUDIE	ST PAUL	31 33	MARY
2641	LAURANCE	ST VITAL	21	DAVID

TABLE 4: GEOGRAPHICAL LOCATION AND
CHILDREN OF MANITOBA FAMILIES, 1870

ID	FAMILY	PARISH	AT OR BETWEEN	CHILDREN AND AGES AT NEXT BIRTHDAY
2639	LAURENCE	ST VITAL	25	MARIE 6, JOSEPH 4, JOHN 1
2642	LAURENCE	ST BONIFACE	77	JULIE 33, MARGUERITE 18
2645	LAURENCE	ST VITAL	45*	ELIZA 17, SARAH 14, JOSEPH 10, JULIEN 6
2646	LAURENCE	ST NORBERT	97	DAVID 23, DANIEL 21, CECILE 18, ANGELE 15, LAROSE 13
2646	LAURENCE	ST NORBERT	97	DUMAS 10, DIDYME 7, MARIE 5, CLARICE 2
1084	LAURIE	ST JOHN	2	WILLIAM 15
2643	LAVALLEE	SFX	133 115	EMERISE 12, MARIE 10, HELENE 7, MARGUERITE 5, FRANCOIS 3
2802	LAVALLEE	ST LAURENT	8 4	PETER 9, JOSEPH 8, JOHN 6
2802	LAVALLEE	ST LAURENT	8 4	ANTOINE 1
2804	LAVALLEE	ST LAURENT	6*	ANDREW 2, J BAPTISTE 1
2805	LAVALLEE	ST LAURENT	10	MICHEL 2, MARY 1
2806	LAVALLEE	ST LAURENT	8	JOHN 18, JOSEPH 16, CHARLES 12, PIERRE 10, LOUIS 8
2812	LAVALLEE	SFX	26	MARIE 4, HELENE 2
2812	LAVALLEE	SFX	26	
2815	LAVALLEE	SFX	32	PIERRE 17, ALEXANDRE 7, ELIE 5, NAPOLEON 3, MARIE 1
2817	LAVALLEE	ST BONIFACE	31 29	ISABELLA 27, MICHEL 31, PIERRE 22
2818	LAVALLEE	ST BONIFACE	41 31	
2819	LAVALLEE	SFX	32	FRANCOIS 26, PIERRE 23, MICHEL 20, JULIENNE 17, MARGUERITE 15
2828	LAVALLEE	ST LAURENT	4*	J BAPTISTE 5, MARY 3
2839	LAVATTE	ST JAMES	9 13	
2836	LAVERDURE	ST CHARLES	90 94	
2837	LAVERDURE	ST CHARLES	90 94	
2847	LAVIOLETTE	SFX	186	JUSTINE 18, MODESTE 16, CHARLES 13, JONAS 10, PAULINE 7
2848	LAVIOLETTE	SFX	187	CHARLES 20, ELISE 12, NORBERT 9, FLORENCE 7, GUILLELMINE 5
2849	LAVIOLETTE	SFX	187	JEROME 3
2849	LAVIOLETTE	SFX	9 13	
2846	LAWSON	ST JAMES	100*	THOMAS 7, JAMES 2
2853	LEASK	ST PETER	100*	SOPHIE 12, WILLIAM 10, CAROLINE 8, MARIE 6, ALFRED 5
2853	LEASK	ST PETER	97 100	ELISE 3, ALEXANDER 1
2854	LEASK	ST PETER	1 8	JOSEPH 15
2835	LEBENSON	ST BONIFACE		
2857	LECLAIRE	ST BONIFACE	69	MARIE 22, ELIZA 14, FRANCOIS 10, LAURENT 12, ANDRE 10
2857	LECLAIRE	ST BONIFACE	69	ANTOINE 4, ANDRE 14, PHILOMENE 13, ROSE 12, JULIE 10
2858	LECLAIRE	ST CHARLES	94 91	AMBROISE 15, VIRGINIE 6, CHARLES 2
2858	LECLAIRE	ST CHARLES		ISABELLE 8
2860	LECLAIRE	ST BONIFACE		
2885	LEDEAUX	ST NORBERT	133 115	MARIE ROSE 2, MARGUERITE 3, EMILIE 1
2833	LEDOUX	SFX	104 102	MODESTE 5, MARIE 2
2873	LEDOUX	SFX	219 244	PIERRE 3
2874	LEDOUX	BAIE S PAUL	189 191	JEREMIAH 1
2876	LEDOUX	SFX	189 191	GREGOIRE 1
2877	LEDOUX	SFX	104	CHRYSOSTOME 22, ISABELLE 17, MARIE 13, JOSEPH 13
2880	LEDOUX	SFX	150 159	MAGLOIRE 2
2881	LEDOUX	SFX	133 115	LOUISON 27, VICTOIRE 14, ALEXIS 7, VICTOIRE 10
2884	LEDOUX	SFX	133 115	J BAPTISTE 17, NAPOLEON 15, FRANCOIS 12
2884	LEDOUX	SFX	120 126	MARGUERITE 1
2888	LEDOUX	SFX	148 150	
2897	LEFORT	SFX	148 150	J BAPTISTE 16, BONIFACE 15, SARAH 12, DELIMA 10, MAXIME 9
2897	LEFORT	SFX	85	EUSTACHE 6, CUTHBERT 4, ELISE 4
2900	LEMAY	ST NORBERT		GEORGE 14, JOSEPHINE 12, ALVINA 12, ALFRED 11, WILFRID 6

ID	FAMILY	PARISH	AT	BETWEEN	\ Child 1	\ Child 2	CHILDREN AND AGES AT NEXT BIRTHDAY Child 3	\ Child 4	\ Child 5
2909	LEMIRE	STE ANNE	49	66	ELZEAR 1	CELESTINE 10	MAXIME 5	PATRICE 3	VIRGINIE 1
2916	LEPINE	SFX	22		JOSEPHTE 12	CLEOPHACE 3			
2920	LEPINE	ST BONIFACE	119		LOUIS 6				
2921	LEPINE	SFX	21	22					
2922	LEPINE	SFX	145		GEORGE 19	CHARLES 18	DANIEL 13	MARGUERITE 10	MARIE 7
2923	LEPINE	ST NORBERT	35		CAROLINE 17	ANACLET 12	MARGUERITE 8	JOSEPH 5	JUDITH 3
2925	LEPINE	ST NORBERT	35		MARIE 1				
2928	LEPINE	ST NORBERT	35	31					
2929	LESPERANCE	SFX	41	31	PIERRE 4	MARGARET 2	MARIE 2		
2930	LESPERANCE	ST BONIFACE	41	31	LOUIS 10	PIERRE 5			
2932	LESPERANCE	ST BONIFACE	41	31	ALEXIS 20				
2935	LESPERANCE	ST BONIFACE	63	62	MARGUERITE 10				
2927	LETENDRE	ST BONIFACE	113	107					
2942	LETENDRE	ST NORBERT	132	131					
2911	LETTER	ST ANDREW	7	9	HELENE 3	ALEXANDRE 1			
2915	LETTER	ST PETER	133	167	GEORGE 21	JAMES 19	MATHILDA 17	BENJAMIN 13	RODERICK 11
2917	LETTER	ST PETER	133	167	JOHN 4	LEODIE 4	JAMES 2	ANNE 11	GEORGE 30
2917	LETTER	ST PETER	133	167	ALBERT 23	ELIZABETH 16	LEODIE 14		
2918	LETTER	ST ANDREW	9	10	JOHN 4	CHARLES 4	MARIE 2		
2919	LETTER	ST PETER	133	167	MARGARET 13	MARY 9	HARRIET 5	ISABELLA 3	
2924	LETTER	*ST PAUL	64		JANE 24	BELLA 19	ALEXANDER 14		
2936	LETTER	ST ANDREW	29	31	ALBERT 23	GEORGE 21	JAMES 19	LEODIE 14	
4838	LETTER	ST PETER	133	167	GEORGE 21	JAMES 19	MATHILDA 17	BENJAMIN 13	RODERICK 11
4838	LETTER	ST PETER	133	167	JOHN 4	CHARLES 4	MARIE 2		
4839	LETTER	ST ANDREW	9		MARGARET 13	MARY 9	HARRIET 9	ISABELLA 3	
4840	LETTER	ST PETER	133	167	JOHN 4	LEODIE 4	JAMES 2	ANNE 11	GEORGE 30
4841	LETTER	*ST PAUL	64	65	JANE 24	BELLA 19	ALEXANDER 14		
4872	LETTER	ST PETER	133	167	MARGARET 13	MARY 9	HARRIET 5	ISABELLA 3	
2811	LEVEILLE	SFX	189	191	PIERRE 14	PAUL 11	MARIE 7	ELIZA 1	
2829	LEVEILLE	SFX	209		PATRICE 5	FLORISTINE 3			
2951	LEWIS	ST ANDREW	63	66	JOHN 40	ELIZA 29	ANNE 25	MAGDELEINE 5	GABRIEL 3
2952	LHERONDELLE	SFX							
2893	LILLIE	ST ANDREW	33	34	DAVID 7	JAMES 5	MARY 3		
2957	LILLIE	SFX	12	21	DANIEL 6	ZACHARIE 4	JAMES 3		
2958	LILLIE	SFX	3	4	EMILIE 13	MARGUERITE 11	ALEXANDER 4		
2816	LINKLATER	ST CLEMENT	105	106	CATHERINE 24	ELIZA 22	ELIZABETH 17	JAMES 14	EDWARD 12
2824	LINKLATER	ST CLEMENT	5	2	DAVID 10	JOSEPH 4			
2963	LINKLATER	ST ANDREW	49		CATHERINE 24	ELIZA 22	ELIZABETH 17	JAMES 14	EDWARD 12
2963	LINKLATER	ST ANDREW	49		DAVID 10	JOSEPH 4			
2965	LINKLATER	ST CLEMENT	5	2	DAVID 10	JOSEPH 4			
2966	LINKLATER	ST JAMES	70	73	MARY 25	JAMES 17	ISABELLA 18	CHARLES 10	
2968	LINKLATER	ST ANDREW	116	117	WILLIAM 16	ISABELLA 18			
2969	LINKLATER	ST ANDREW	4	13	MARY 2	WILLIAM 12	JOHN 7		
2701	LISK	ST JOHN	55						
2701	LISK	ST ANDREW	55		JOHN 12	WILLIAM 7			
2702	LISK	ST ANDREW	51	53					
2698	LISSONS	PORTAGE	81	87					
2699	LISSOT	ST BONIFACE							
2697	LITTLE	PORTAGE	24	26	JANE 14	GEORGE 13	MARTHA 12	MARY 11	
2697	LITTLE	PORTAGE	28	55	ELIZABETH 8	MARGARET 6	CATHERINE 4	JOSEPH 2	
2971	LIVINGSTONE	ST JAMES	24	26	JANE 14	GEORGE 13	MARTHA 12	MARY 11	ROBERT 10
2972	LIVINGSTONE	ST JOHN	28	55	ELIZABETH 8	MARGARET 6	CATHERINE 4	JOSEPH 2	

TABLE 4: GEOGRAPHICAL LOCATION AND
CHILDREN OF MANITOBA FAMILIES, 1870

ID	FAMILY	PARISH	AT OR BETWEEN	CHILDREN AND AGES AT NEXT BIRTHDAY
2982	LIZOTE	ST NORBERT	32*	23	PIERRE 10, MARIE 9, LOUIS 8, JOSEPH 4, VIRGINIE 1
2979	LOGAN	ST JAMES	22	23	
2985	LOGAN	ST JOHN	28	55	GEORGE 5, ROBERT 4, ANN 2
2986	LOGAN	ST NORBERT	246		
2987	LOGAN	ST NORBERT	209	202	THOMAS 32, FRANCIS 23, ROBERT 24, NATTY 21, ALEXANDER 15
2988	LOGAN	ST NORBERT	209	202	ELIZABETH 13
2994	LONSDALE	ST JOHN	9	25	
2700	LOUIS	HEADINGLY	6		WILLIAM 9, LYDIA 3, HORACE 2
2990	LOUIS	ST ANDREW	268	266	WILLIAM 12, ANDREW 9, JAMES 1
2992	LOUIS	BAIE S PAUL	194	207	JAMES 11, BELLA 4, MARIA 8
2993	LOUIS	ST ANDREW	268		CATHERINE 12, WILLIAM 10, JOSEPH 4, FINLAY 1
2996	LOUIS	ST ANDREW	267		
4556	LOUIS	ST ANDREW	10	11	
2705	LOWMAN	ST JAMES	10	11	
2703	LOWTED	ST ANDREW	22	23	CATHERINE 17, THOMAS 10
2704	LOWTED	ST ANDREW	104	106	JANE 2, MARGUERITE 1
2998	LUNN	ST BONIFACE	106		
2707	LUSSIER	SFX	67	71	JOSEPH 13, MARIE 11, MOISE 11, CHARLES 9, ADELINE 5
2999	LUSSIER	SFX	71		LOUISE 16, BAZILE 11, MODESTE 11, DANIEL 9, PHILOMENE 7
2999	LUSSIER	SFX	71		ROGER 2
3000	LUSSIER	SFX	172	175	MARIE 9, LOUISON 7, ANASTASE 5, ELEONOR 5, NAPOLEON 3
3002	LUSSIER	SFX	187	185	VICTOIRE 7, AMABLE 4, CECILE 2
3003	LUSSIER	ST BONIFACE	174		ANTOINE 19, FELIX 13, ADELAIDE 25, LEANORA 3
3003	LUSSIER	ST JOHN	29	26	CHARLES 7, LAURA 5, DAVID 3
3004	LUTED	*ST PAUL	33*		
2706	LYNCH	PORTAGE	64	65	
2708	LYON	ST JOHN	69	67	
2709	LYONS	ST ANDREW	13	6	JOHN 17, RICHARD 13
3008	LYONS	ST CLEMENT	99	101	
3012	LYONS	ST CLEMENT	8	9	JOHN 16, WILLIAM 14, HENRI 14, MILES 12, EDWARD 9
3013	LYONS	ST CLEMENT	8		JAMES 1, CATHERINE 8, JOHN 6, FANNY 4, WILLIAM 2
3013	LYONS	ST ANDREW	8		JOLIAS 8
3274	MACCABER	ST ANDREW	89	91	ISABELLA 5, ALEXANDER 1
3258	MACKRAY	ST JOHN	48	45	LOUISA 1
3477	MACRAY	ST PAUL			
2710	MAIR	PORTAGE	81	87	
2711	MAISONNEUVE	ST BONIFACE	87		
2712	MAISONNEUVE	ST BONIFACE			
2713	MAJOR	ST BONIFACE			
2714	MALATERRE	SFX	203		JOSEPH 23, JOHN 18, LOUIS 16, BAZILE 13, ALEXIS 11
2714	MALATERRE	SFX	203		EUPHROSINE 8, MARIE 6, JUSTINE 4, ZACHARIE 16, ALEXIS 8
3016	MALATERRE	SFX	3		JEREMIE 20, ELIZA 8, ADELE 4
3016	MALATERRE	SFX			NAPOLEON 6, CELINA 4, MARIE 2
3017	MALATERRE	SFX			ADELAIDE 11, ELIZA 8, MARIE 4
3020	MALATERRE	SFX	181	190	JOSEPH 24, GREGOIRE 13, MARIE 16, ROGER 1
3022	MALBOEUF	SFX	162	172	
2716	MALOUIN	SFX	61		
2717	MANCEAU	STE ANNE			ADELE 6, OLIVE 6, ONEGIME 6, ANNE 3

ID	FAMILY	PARISH	AT OR	BETWEEN	CHILDREN AND AGES AT NEXT BIRTHDAY
2721	MARCELLAIS	ST NORBERT	87		
3025	MARCELLAIS	ST BONIFACE	41	31	
3026	MARCELLAIS	ST BONIFACE	41	31	
3027	MARCELLAIS	ST NORBERT	245		
3028	MARCELLAIS	STE ANNE	40	45	PHILOMENE 23, HENRY 18, W F 10
3031	MARCHAND	ST NORBERT	52		JOSEPH 20, VERONIQUE 22, SIMEON 17, ISADORE 14, JULIEN 12
3031	MARCHAND	ST NORBERT	52		ESTHER 10, PHILOMENE 7, CELINA 4, ELIZA 1
3034	MARCHAND	STE AGATHE	124		BENJAMIN 22, ISABELLE 20, GUILLAUME 18, FRANCOIS 16, PHILOMENE 13
3034	MARCHAND	STE AGATHE	124		MARIE 11, JOSEPH 10, EULALIE 8, CAMILLE 6, JUSTINE 4
3034	MARCHAND	STE AGATHE	124		ROSALIE 2
2722	MARCHAND	ST BONIFACE	119	118	
3030	MARION	ST BONIFACE	45	42	MARIE 3, PATRICE 1
3033	MARION	ST VITAL	64	66	MARIE 1
3042	MARION	SFX	64	60	MAXIME 7, MARIE 5, JOSEPH 3, LOUIS 1
3043	MARION	ST NORBERT	37		MARIE 12, LOUISE 11, JOSEPH 9, WILLIAM 6, JULE 3
3044	MARION	ST NORBERT	81	87	ROGER 24, NARCISSE 21, NORMAN 19, PHILOMENE 16, JOSEPH 9
3045	MARION	ST BONIFACE	9		
3059	MARTEL	ST BONIFACE	9		MARIE 21, ISABELLE 20, JULIE 18, ELISE 6, FRANCOISE 4
3059	MARTEL	ST BONIFACE	161		ALEXANDER 6, LOUIS 4, ANDRE 1, JOSEPH 2
3062	MARTIN	SFX	159	161	PIERRE 12, GILBERT 10, MARIE 8
3063	MARTIN	SFX	159	162	THARSILE 11, ELISE 9, LOUIS 5
3064	MARTIN	SFX	219		THEOPHILE 23, FELIX 19, CHARLES 11, CAROLINE 8, MODESTE 4
3069	MARTIN	BAIE S PAUL	219		THERESE 19, JULIA 13
3069	MARTIN	BAIE S PAUL	150	159	THOMAS 2
13450	MASSON	SFX	102	104	
3071	MASSY	ST ANDREW	102	104	HENRY 22, ROBERT 15, JAMES 13, JOHN 11, MARIANNE 9
3071	MASSY	ST ANDREW	31	33	THOMAS 6, SAMUEL 4, ALEXANDER 2, MARGARET 2
3072	MASTERS	ST PAUL	12	14	
3037	MATHESON	*KILDONAN	11	12	CATHERINE 9, JOHN 7, JANE 5
3076	MATHESON	*KILDONAN	83	82	MARGARET 2, ANN 1
3078	MATHESON	*KILDONAN	65		ALEXANDER 22, JAMES 19, MARIANNE 17, CATHERINE 13, HUGH 11
3080	MATHESON	KILDONAN	92		DUNCAN 1
3083	MATHESON	ST PAUL	83	82	ALICE 30, ANGUS 2
3084	MATHESON	*KILDONAN	45*		ALEXANDER 5, MARGARET 21
3087	MATHESON	ST JOHN	45*		NORMAN 23
3089	MATHESON	ST JOHN	12	14	
3091	MATHESON	*KILDONAN	11	12	ALEXANDER 21, SAMUEL 19, ANN 24, MARY 22
3094	MATHESON	*KILDONAN	45	46	ALEXANDER 8, ANNY 4, ISABELLA 3, JOHN 2
3098	MATHESON	ST JOHN	83		CHRISTIE 19
3099	MATHESON	*KILDONAN	33	35	
3103	MATHESON	HEADINGLY	82		JOHANNAH 10, FLORA 8, CHRISTIANA 6, SAMUEL 4, ALICE 2
3107	MATHESON	ST JOHN	47	48	JOHN 5, MARGARET 3, ALEXANDER 1
3121	MATTHEIR	*KILDONAN	162		
3054	MAXWELL	ST JOHN	150	155	
3246	MCALSTER	ST ANDREW	116	117	JANE 8, MARIANN 6, CATHERINE 3, BARBARA 1
3250	MCALSTER	ST ANDREW	150	160	
3288	MCALSTER	ST ANDREW	4	13	EDWARD 2
3289	MCALSTER	ST ANDREW	156		
3294	MCALSTER	ST ANDREW	156		HENRIE 22, JAMES 20, MARIE 17, HARRIET 14, CHARLES 8
3268	MCARTHUR	ST JOHN	4	13	
3262	MCBAIN	PORTAGE	70		ROBERT 25, JAMES 22, ELIZABETH 21, RONALD 18, CATHERINE 16
3262	MCBAIN	PORTAGE	70		JANE 12

TABLE 4: GEOGRAPHICAL LOCATION AND
CHILDREN OF MANITOBA FAMILIES, 1870

ID	FAMILY	PARISH	AT OR BETWEEN	CHILDREN AND AGES AT NEXT BIRTHDAY									
3271	MCBEATH	ST ANDREW	280	GEORGE	18	JOHN	17	HUGH	12	CHRISTIANA	9	HELEN	6
3275	MCBEATH	KILDONAN	33	ALEXANDER	26	ROBERT	22	ANNIE	20	JOHN	16	RODERICK	12
3277	MCBEATH	KILDONAN	34	ADAM	25	MARY	19	ALEXANDER	16	GEORGE	14	JOHANNAH	12
3282	MCBEATH	KILDONAN	34 34	RODERICK	10								
3287	MCBEATH	KILDONAN	33 36										
13272	MCBEATH	KILDONAN	34	ELIZA	1								
3270	MCBETH	SFX	31	JOHN	40								
1696	MCBRIDE	ST ANDREW	196	JAMES	10	MARGARET	9	WILLIAM	6	ELLEN	5	ISABELLE	2
1695	MCCARTHY	ST BONIFACE	288										
3261	MCCAULAY	ST ANDREW	87 77	GEORGE	3	ANN	1						
3516	MCCLENNAN	ST PAUL	34 38										
3516	MCCLENNAN	ST PAUL	33										
3545	MCCLENNAN	ST ANDREW	35										
4038	MCCLOUD	ST CLEMENT	137	MORDO	11	JOHN	9	MARY	8	ELISE	7	MARGARET	4
4038	MCCLOUD	ST CLEMENT	66	CHRISTINE	2								
4039	MCCLOUD	ST ANDREW	66										
3241	MCCORRISTER	ST ANDREW	137										
3242	MCCORRISTER	ST JOHN	168	FRANCOISE	20	PETER	13	GEORGE	11	WILLIAM	9	CATHERINE	4
3291	MCCORRISTER	PORTAGE	47 51	ALEXANDER	8								
3295	MCCORRISTER	ST ANDREW	58 285										
3240	MCCRAR	ST LAURENT	270										
2776	MCCRAY	ST ANDREW	112 110	CHARLOTTE	15	DUNCAN	13	ELIZABETH	11	MALLUM	9	WILLIAM	7
2777	MCCRAY	ST ANDREW	112	CHRISTINE	5	MARGUERITE	2						
3328	MCCRAY	ST ANDREW	110										
3300	MCDERMOT	ST JAMES	12	SARA	10	ANDREW	7						
3302	MCDERMOT	ST CHARLES	12	HENRY	3	MILES	1						
3303	MCDERMOT	ST CHARLES	122	ROBERT	7	ALICE	5	CHARLES	2				
2475	MCDERMOTT	ST JOHN	117										
3304	MCDERMOTT	ST JOHN	6* 33										
1716	MCDONALD	ST ANDREW	6*	JANE	27	JOHN	5	DUNCAN	3	ISABEL	2		
3263	MCDONALD	PORTAGE	125	CHARLES	23								
3264	MCDONALD	ST ANDREW	46	GEORGE	31	ANNIE	4	ANNA	2				
3266	MCDONALD	PORTAGE	29 31	ROBERT		ROSALIE	1						
3269	MCDONALD	ST ANDREW	132	DONALD	7			ANNA	3				
3273	MCDONALD	ST ANDREW	22 24										
3286	MCDONALD	ST ANDREW	48 45										
3307	MCDONALD	ST ANDREW	81 82										
3314	MCDONALD	ST ANDREW	81 82	MARIANNE	19	JOHN	16	DONALD	16	HANNAH	13	MARTHA	11
3314	MCDONALD	ST ANDREW	50	SARAH	9	MARGARET	9	ELIZABETH	7	CATHERINE	3		
3316	MCDONALD	ST ANDREW	50	CATHERINE	10	DONALD	10	JANE	8				
3318	MCDONALD	ST ANDREW	26	ANNA	40	BELLA	40	CUTHBERT	30				
3319	MCDONALD	ST ANDREW	22	JANE	14	ISABELLA	12	MARGUERITE	10				
3322	MCDONALD	ST ANDREW	76 81	FRED	7	MARY	3	MATHILDA	1				
3326	MCDONALD	ST ANDREW	16 19	ISABELLA	10	CHRISTINE	6	JESSIE	6	CATHERINE	4	FLORA	2
3327	MCDONALD	PORTAGE	164			COLLIN	15	JOSEPH	12	JOHN	8	RODRIC	6
3329	MCDONALD	PORTAGE	129 127										
3330	MCDONALD	ST ANDREW	53	ALEXANDER	17			WILLIAM	12	JOHN	8		
3330	MCDONALD	ST ANDREW	148 150	WILLIAM	4								
3331	MCDONALD	ST ANDREW	148 150	JOHN	16	ALEXANDER	16	WILLIAM	14	CHARLES	12	MARY	8

TABLE 4: GEOGRAPHICAL LOCATION AND
CHILDREN OF MANITOBA FAMILIES, 1870

ID	FAMILY	PARISH	AT OR BETWEEN	CHILDREN AND AGES AT NEXT BIRTHDAY
3332	MCDONALD	ST CLEMENT	48	JANE 12, ELIZABETH 10, WILLIAM 6, ANN 4, HELEN 2
3334	MCDONALD	ST JOHN	28 55	MARY 42, JANE 22, KENNETH 20
3336	MCDONALD	KILDONAN	36 40	
3337	MCDONALD	ST ANDREW	81	
3342	MCDONALD	KILDONAN	36	WILLIAM 26, DONALD 24, ANGUS 22, SARAH 20, ALEXANDER 18
3342	MCDONALD	KILDONAN	36	MARY 9, JEREMIAH 7, CHRISTOPHER 4
1718	MCDOUGALL	ST BONIFACE	99 111	ELISE 8, ELZEAR 4, ALBERT 2
1719	MCDOUGALL	SFX	179	
3344	MCDOUGALL	SFX	24	AMEDE 12, EMILIE 11, MARGUERITE 10, ALEXANDRE 8, WILLIAM 5
3344	MCDOUGALL	SFX	24	LOUIS 4, ALFRED 2, ROSALIE 1
3345	MCDOUGALL	ST JAMES	68	MARTHA 4, ALEXANDER 2
3346	MCDOUGALL	ST BONIFACE	44 41	JOSEPH 23, WILLIAM 21, MARGARET 18, SAMUEL 16, CHARLES 13
3346	MCDOUGALL	ST BONIFACE	44 41	MARY 10, GREOIRE 8, ANGUS 5
3351	MCDOUGALL	ST BONIFACE	99 111	ISABELLE 4, ALEXANDRE 3, MARGUERITE 3
3354	MCGILLIS	SFX	202 204	MARIE 10, ALEXANDRE 7, NAPOLEON 6, TOBIE 3, SASE 1
3356	MCGILLIS	SFX		PAUL 16
3358	MCGILLIS	SFX	181 190	ELIZABETH 17, J 15, MELANIE 13, MARGUERITE 11, DANIEL 8
3358	MCGILLIS	SFX	181 190	EMILIE 3
3360	MCGILLIS	SFX		
3594	MCGILLIS	SFX	195 196	JULIE 5, THEOPHILE 4, THERESE 2
3595	MCGILLIS	SFX	183 190	FLORISTINE 10, WILLIAM 8, DANIEL 6, MICHEL 4
3596	MCGILLIS	SFX		MARIE 2
3599	MCGUIRE	ST JAMES	58 63	MARY 20, ELIZABETH 18, FRANCIS 16, PHILIP 14, CATHERINE 12
3599	MCGUIRE	ST JAMES	58 63	THOMAS 10, MARGARET 8, RICHARD 6, JANE 1
3364	MCINTOCH	KILDONAN	56	ISABELLA 9, JOANNA 4, ELIZABETH 4
3365	MCIVER	PORTAGE	65 58	CATHERINE 18, DONALD 16, ELIZABETH 4, JOHN 6, CHRISTIE 3
3373	MCIVER	KILDONAN	45	MARGARET 12, ANN 11, ANGUS 9, GEORGE 7, CHRISTIANA 5
3373	MCIVER	KILDONAN	45	ALEXANDER 4, DANIEL 2, LOUISA 1
3370	MCIVER	ST ANDREW	56 57	ELLEN 5, MARY 1
3372	MCKAY	ST CHARLES	61 65	
3371	MCKAY	SFX	223	CHARLES 24, GUILLAUME 24, ELLEN 14, JAMES 7
3372	MCKAY	BAIE S PAUL	219 244	CATHERINE 14, JOHN 12, CHRISTY 10, JAMES 7, SARA 5
3376	MCKAY	SFX	214	MARY 3
3378	MCKAY	BAIE S PAUL	194	JOHN 18, CHARLES 1
3382	MCKAY	ST ANDREW	108	CATHERINE 14, CHRISTY 10
3382	MCKAY	ST ANDREW	108	MARY 3, JOHN 3
3383	MCKAY	ST CLEMENT	23	JOHN 3
3388	MCKAY	SFX	213 214	COLIN 18, SAMUEL 16, MARIA 15, JEMIMA 13, RACHAEL 11
3388	MCKAY	SFX	213 214	CLARA 9, EMMA 7, WILLIAM 4, BETSY 2
3391	MCKAY	BAIE S PAUL	244 245	LAROSE 5, J BAPTISTE 9, CHARLES 5, CHARLES 2
3392	MCKAY	BAIE S PAUL	244 245	PETER 7, FRANCIS 7, DONALD 2
3394	MCKAY	SFX	227	ISABELLA 5, JEMIMA 4, DONALD 2
3395	MCKAY	POPLAR PT	77	MARY 2, MARY 2
3396	MCKAY	KILDONAN	33 34	JANE 8, CHRISTIE 8, JESSIE 6, JOHN 2
3397	MCKAY	ST JAMES	21	MARY 8, JAMES 8, JOHN 5, JOHN 1
3398	MCKAY	POPLAR PT	61	
3400	MCKAY	ST JAMES	21 22	
3401	MCKAY	SFX	214 218	MARY 18, CATHERINE 16, MARGARET 16, ANDREW 8, HARRIET 6
3401	MCKAY	SFX	214 218	MARIA 4, MARGUERITE 11, ANGUS 9, ISABELLA 6
3403	MCKAY	KILDONAN	68	DONALD 13, ANNA 2, ANGUS 9, JOHN 3
3404	MCKAY	SFX	208 209	JOSEPH 5
3405	MCKAY	ST CLEMENT	85	HARIET 21, ALEXANDER 19, MARIE 16, CHARLES 12

TABLE 4: GEOGRAPHICAL LOCATION AND
CHILDREN OF MANITOBA FAMILIES, 1870

ID	FAMILY	PARISH	AT OR BETWEEN		CHILDREN AND AGES AT NEXT BIRTHDAY											
3409	MCKAY	ST ANDREW	88	89	THOMAS	3	AMELIA	8								
3412	MCKAY	SFX	213	214	ALBERT	6	CHRISTIE	8	WILLIAM	18	ROBINA	17	JAMES	15		12
3414	MCKAY	KILDONAN	18		DOROTHE	25	SELKIRK	8	JAMES	6						
3414	MCKAY	KILDONAN	18		ELIZABETH	10										
3445	MCKAY	HEADINGLY	62	63												
3650	MCKAY	SFX	214	218	SARAH	11	GEORGE	9	ARCHIBALD	18	JOHN	3	ALEXANDER	1		
3651	MCKAY	PORTAGE	58		JOSEPH	14	WILLIAM	12	JULIA	12	JOHN	5	HENRY	3		
3651	MCKAY	PORTAGE	58		FRANCIS	1										
3652	MCKAY	ST CLEMENT	82		SOPHIE	5	NANCY	2								
3654	MCKAY	HIGH BLUFF	26	52	JOSEPH	20	ABSOLON	17	MARY	17	WILLIAM	15	K	9		
3654	MCKAY	HIGH BLUFF	26	52	KAVANNAPAC	7										
3655	MCKAY	ST ANDREW	19	18												
3656	MCKAY	BAIE S PAUL	219	244	ABRAHAM	5	COLLIN		MARGARET	1						
3638	MCKEEVER	ST CLEMENT	58	61	JOHN	7	DUNCAN	5								
3420	MCKENZIE	SFX	223	226	MATHILDA	3										
3422	MCKENZIE	ST JAMES	1													
3426	MCKENZIE	ST CLEMENT	16		JANE	16	CHRISTIE	12	PETER	10	ALEXANDER	8				
3426	MCKENZIE	ST CLEMENT	16		ARABELLA	4										
3639	MCKENZIE	ST JAMES														
3640	MCKENZIE	ST ANDREW	122													
3641	MCKENZIE	PORTAGE	133	111	ANN	21	KENNETH	19	JAMES	17						
3642	MCKENZIE	ST JAMES	1	20												
3315	MCKONALD	ST ANDREW	260		PHILIP	2										
3643	MCLAUGHLIN	HEADINGLY	21	23	MILES	12	MARY	9	MICHAEL		MARGARET	7	PETER	5		
3643	MCLAUGHLIN	HEADINGLY	21	23	HARRIET	3	ABRAHAM	2								
3450	MCLEAN	PORTAGE	133	70	CLEMENTINA	29	ALEXANDER	23	MARGARET	23	DANIEL	18	RHODA	16		
3450	MCLEAN	PORTAGE	133	70	JOHN											
3451	MCLEAN	ST ANDREW	120	122	ANN	4	CHRISTINE	13	JAMES	13	RODERICK	12	WILLIAM	10		
3452	MCLEAN	ST CLEMENT	64	70	DONALD	6	MORDO	2	ANNIE	1						
3452	MCLEAN	PORTAGE	69		H	5	ISABELLA	3								
3512	MCLEAN	ST JOHN	48	45	JESSIE	9	FRANCIS	8	WILHELMINA	8	ROBERT	4	JOHN	2		
3514	MCLEAN	ST ANDREW	177	170	MARIANN	12	FINLEY	9	CHRISTINE	2						
3646	MCLEAN	ST PAUL	91	92	EMMA	15										
3433	MCLENNAN	ST LAURENT			ABRAHAM	23	PETER	15	ALEXANDRE	8	PATRICK	6	J BAPTISTE	4		
3434	MCLEOD	ST LAURENT			MARY	2										
3434	MCLEOD	ST LAURENT			JOHN	6	ELIZABETH	1								
3440	MCLEOD	SFX	5		ANTOINE	16	JOSEPH	14	FRANCOIS	13	ALEXIS	11	ELISE	8		
3443	MCLEOD	SFX	207		MAGLOIRE	6	CAROLINE	3	MOISE	10	ABRAHAM	6	ESTHER	4		
3443	MCLEOD	SFX	207		VITRONILE	12	JOSEPH	10								
3444	MCLEOD	*SFX	1		ROSS	2										
3444	MCLEOD	*SFX			AMBROISE	2										
3448	MCLEOD	SFX	12		GEORGE	11	JANNET	9	DONALD	7	ROBERT	5	ALEXANDER	3		
3453	MCLEOD	KILDONAN	67		MARY	11	WILLIAM	4	ANNABELLA	2	JOHN	1				
3546	MCLEOD	POPLAR PT	85		JUSTINE	10	JOHN	8	WILLIAM	6	ELIZABETH	2				
3547	MCLEOD	*ST ANDREW	137		MARGUERITE	20										
3548	MCLEOD	ST BONIFACE	16		MARY	18	ROSALIE	15	J BAPTISTE	10						
3549	MCLEOD	ST LAURENT														
3550	MCLEOD	ST JAMES														
3551	MCLEOD	HIGH BLUFF	57		DONALD	6	MARY	4	WILLIAM	3	CHRISTIAN	1				
3437	MCLOUD	ST CLEMENT	91		WILLIAM	14	JOHN	12	JANE	10	SARA	8	MARIE	6		
3437	MCLOUD	ST CLEMENT	91		FRANCOIS	4										
3439	MCLOUD	ST ANDREW	161		MALUNER	24	THOMAS	23	MARY	23	JANE	20	DUNCAN	19		17

TABLE 4: GEOGRAPHICAL LOCATION AND
CHILDREN OF MANITOBA FAMILIES, 1870

ID	FAMILY	PARISH	AT OR BETWEEN	CHILDREN AND AGES AT NEXT BIRTHDAY
3439	MCLOUD	ST ANDREW	161	CAROLINE 14, MATHILDE 9
3543	MCLOUD	ST CLEMENT	91	
3544	MCLOUD	ST ANDREW	160	
3456	MCMULLEN	ST JAMES	16	ELIZABETH 11, VIRGINIE 19
3457	MCMULLEN	ST JAMES	16 19	
3461	MCMULLEN	ST JAMES	16	MARY 2
3454	MCNAB	POPLAR PT	82	PATRICE 14, JOHN 12
3455	MCNAB	ST ANDREW	124 119	
3460	MCNAB	POPLAR PT	81	JOHN 9, ANDREW 7, COLIN 5, MARY 2
3460	MCNAB	POPLAR PT	82 88	ROBERT 1
3465	MCNAB	POPLAR PT	82 88	SARAH 14, MARY 11, JAMES 9, MARGARET 7
3465	MCNAB	POPLAR PT	81	DAVID 2
3466	MCNAB	POPLAR PT	88	CHARLES 26, CATHERINE 19, MARIA 18, HARRIET 17
3466	MCNAB	POPLAR PT	88	MILES 11
3468	MCNAB	POPLAR PT	80	JANE 19, JAMES 17, DAVID 15, THOMAS 12
3554	MCNAB	ST JOHN	47 48	ALEXANDER 5, MARGARET 38, CHARLES, ANN 32
3472	MCPHAIL	HIGH BLUFF	56	HARRIET 8, CATHERINE 4, ISABELLA 2
3471	MCPHERSON	ST JOHN	4 13	MARGARET 5
3470	MCTAVISH	ST JAMES		
3469	MCVICAR	KILDONAN	45 49	MARGARET 5, GEORGE 3
3557	MCVICAR	PORTAGE	133 111	
3053	MEADE	ST PAUL	11 13	ROLLIN 2
3052	MELOIN	SFX	27 31	J BAPTISTE 9, ADELE 6, LEON 4, MARIE 3
3051	MERCER	ST PAUL	2 4	EMILY 15, FRED 4, FRANK 3
3050	MERCREDI	ST NORBERT	94 91	SOPHIE 4, FRANCOIS 15, MARGUERITE 11, HENRIETTA 9
3050	MERCREDI	ST NORBERT	94 91	
3048	MEUNIER	ST NORBERT	256 250	FRANCOIS 20, VIRGINIE 16, ELIZA 12
3049	MEUNIER	ST NORBERT	256 218	CHARLES 18
2727	MILLER	ST CHARLES	78 73	ALFRED 8, EMMA 4, HERMINE 2
2728	MILLER	ST NORBERT	23	LOUISA 12, MARGARET 11, RICHARD 8
2729	MILLER	ST JOHN	6 33	GEORGE 22, ALEXANDER 16, ROBERT 15, JOHN 13, ANNA 6
3118	MILLER	*ST PAUL	77	MARY 7, ANGUS 5, JOHN 6
3118	MILLER	*ST PAUL	77	OLIVIER 5, GEORGE 3, JOSEPH 13
2730	MILLHAM	HEADINGLY	15	
3132	MITCHELL	ST PAUL	104	
3133	MITCHELL	ST JAMES	26 27	
2752	MITCHELL	ST PETER	46 56	
2753	MODE	ST ANDREW	89 91	JANE 12, THOMAS 15, ROBERT 12, HARIET 8
2754	MODE	ST ANDREW	86 87	MARIANNE 16, CAROLINE 4
2755	MODE	ST ANDREW	86 87	MARGUERITE 2, CATHERINE 22, EDWARD 20, ELIZABETH 17, JOHN 14
2755	MODE	ST ANDREW	82 85	SARA 8
3125	MODE	ST ANDREW	82 85	CATHERINE 14, JOHN 12, ISABEL 10, THOMAS 6
3126	MODE	ST ANDREW	89 91	MARY 1
3125	MODE	ST ANDREW	89 91	
2756	MONANT	ST NORBERT	81 76	CAROLINE 25, FRANCOIS 22, ELMISE 20, JOSEPH 17
2756	MONANT	ST NORBERT	81 76	MARIE 11, ROSALIE 11, ELISE 8, ROGER 13
2757	MONANT	ST NORBERT	219 244	JEREMIAH 19, MARY 11
2758	MONATE	BAIE S PAUL	13 6	
2759	MONCHAMP	ST JOHN	2 4	
3144	MONCRIFF	ST JOHN	194	CLEMENCE 19, MARIE 14, FLORISTINE 2
	MONETTE	SFX	195	
2739	MONKMAN	ST LAURENT		WILLIAM 30, FRANCOIS 24, JANE 20, CATHERINE 18, ANNIE 16

TABLE 4: GEOGRAPHICAL LOCATION AND
CHILDREN OF MANITOBA FAMILIES, 1870

ID	FAMILY	PARISH	AT OR BETWEEN	CHILDREN AND AGES AT NEXT BIRTHDAY
2739	MONKMAN	ST LAURENT		MARGUERITE 14, ALEXANDRE 12, JAMES 16, ELLEN 16, CHARLOTTE 10
2740	MONKMAN	ST LAURENT	97*	MARY 20, NANCY 18, JOHN 12
2741	MONKMAN	ST PETER		MARIANNE 18, MARGUERITE 16
2742	MONKMAN	POPLAR PT	42	
2743	MONKMAN	ST LAURENT	53	
3137	MONKMAN	ST PETER		
3152	MONKMAN	ST PETER	83 85	WILLIAM 9, ALEXANDER 7, DAVID 5
3154	MONKMAN	ST ANDREW	85*	WILLIAM 1, ISABEL 5, DAVID 1
3155	MONKMAN	ST PETER	280 260	JAMES 23, ANDRE 19, ALBERT 15, MARIE 15, ANNE 11
3156	MONKMAN	ST PETER	95*	JOHN 39
3156	MONKMAN	SFX	95*	MAXIME 1
2761	MONSIGNE	SFX		
3117	MONSIGNE	SFX	148 150	
2762	MOONEY	PORTAGE	133 115	
2736	MOORE	ST CLEMENT	28	ROBERT 22, CHARLOTTE 18
2737	MOORE	ST CLEMENT	105 106	
2779	MOORE	ST CLEMENT	36 34	
3130	MOORE	ST PETER	23 24	CLEMENTINE 12, JOHN 10, CHARLES 10, MARGUERITE 8, LOUISA 3
3165	MOORE	ST PETER	133 167	GEORGE 7
3168	MOORE	ST ANDREW	1 8	
3169	MOORE	ST ANDREW	89 91	CATHERINE 8, MARGARET 6, WILLIAM 6, NANCY 4, ELIZA 1
2763	MOOSOO	PORTAGE	89 92	
2764	MORE	ST ANDREW	111 120	MARIE 23, ELISE 21, GUILLIMINE 19, CLEMENSE 19, OCTAVE 14
3174	MOREAU	STE AGATHE	117 120	SOLOMAN 10, ALPHONSINE 6, CAROLINE 6, CAROLINE 3, FRANCOIS 1
3176	MOREAU	STE AGATHE	108 80	ANGELIQUE 5, WILLIAM 2
2747	MOREAU	ST NORBERT	108 80	
2748	MORGAN	ST PETER	197 166	FREDERICK 21, MARGARET 18, CAROLINE 8
3110	MORGAN	ST PETER	1 8	DAVID 10, ROBERT 8, ELIZA 8, ANDREW 6, ANNIE 2
3095	MORGAN	SFX	220 222	
3096	MORIN	SFX	29 26	
3100	MORIN	ST BONIFACE	213	ALFRED 6, MARGUERITE 5, VIRGINIE 4, LOUIS 4, ELIZA 8
3101	MORIN	ST BONIFACE	29 26	
3102	MORIN	ST BONIFACE	29 26	
3106	MORIN	ST BONIFACE	29 26	BAPTISTE 5
3108	MORIN	ST BONIFACE	29 26	
3109	MORIN	SFX	185 189	MELANIE 12, FLORISTINE 10, PHILOMENE 8, SARAH 4
3179	MORIN	ST NORBERT	91 86	ALFRED 15, MARGUERITE 6, LOUIS 4
3181	MORIN	ST BONIFACE	81 87	CELINA 5, PATRICE 3
3186	MORIN	ST BONIFACE	29 26	ISABELLE 24, NANCY 23, CECILE 19, VIRGINIE 16, NAPOLEON 13
3186	MORIN	ST BONIFACE	29	ETIENNE 8, JOSEPHINE 2
3192	MORIN	STE AGATHE	559 561	ELISE 7, CELINA 1, J BAPTISTE 2
3193	MORIN	STE AGATHE	557	ANDRE 2, ISADORE 1
3194	MORIN	STE AGATHE	575	ROGER 8, WILLIAM 6, PIERRE 1
3195	MORIN	STE AGATHE	577	ABRAHAM 20, SARAH 19, ROSE 19, MARIE 15
3196	MORIN	SFX	210*	DANIEL 3, MARIE 2
3207	MORISEAU	ST PETER	95 97	THOMAS 4
3206	MORISSETTE	*BAIE S PAUL	144	JOHN 18, SUZETTE 23, CAROLINE 15, RODERICK 14, ISABELLA 8
3209	MORISSETTE	BAIE S PAUL	143	ABRAHAM 4, MARY 2
3210	MORISSETTE	*BAIE S PAUL	146	FRANCOIS 8, MARY 5
1722	MORRISON	ST ANDREW	129	
1723	MORRISON	BAIE S PAUL	224	PATRICK 8, MARY 5, SUZETTE 5, SUZETTE 3, JOSEPH 1

TABLE 4: GEOGRAPHICAL LOCATION AND
CHILDREN OF MANITOBA FAMILIES, 1870

ID	FAMILY	PARISH	AT	BETWEEN	CHILDREN AND AGES AT NEXT BIRTHDAY
1724	MORRISON	POPLAR PT			
1725	MORRISON	BAIE S PAUL	224	222	PHILOMENE 19, MARGUERITE 16, MARIE 16, ROSE 12, ADELAIDE 10
3204	MORRISSETTE	ST CHARLES			PIERRE 3
3204	MORRISSETTE	ST CHARLES			
1726	MORRISSON	ST JOHN	9	25	
1727	MORRISSON	ST ANDREW	34	38	
1728	MORRISSON	ST ANDREW	34	38	
1729	MORRISSON	ST ANDREW	129		MARGUERITE 5, JESSIE 3, DONALD 2
3217	MORRISSON	HEADINGLY	28		JOHN 18, JAMES 16, DONALD 14, ANGUS 12, CATHERINE 10
3217	MORRISSON	HEADINGLY	28		EDWARD 7, MARGARET 4, BENJAMIN 2
3218	MORRISSON	HEADINGLY	29		MARY 2, CATHERINE 1
3220	MORRISSON	ST ANDREW	34	38	JAMES 5, MARGARET 1
1731	MOSES	ST JAMES	48		
3211	MOSIGNE	ST CHARLES	78		JOHN 20, MARIE 16, NANCY 15, SAMUEL 13, PASCAL 11
3211	MOSIGNE	ST CHARLES	78		GEORGE 7, MARIE ANN 3, GENEVIENE 1
1732	MOUARD	ST BONIFACE	20		JOSEPH 1
1705	MOUSSEAU	PORTAGE	69	67	
1706	MOUTON	ST NORBERT	117	120	ELIZA 10, ROGER 6, ANNIE 3
2775	MOWAT	ST ANDREW	117		MARY 10
3229	MOWAT	ST ANDREW	45		MARY 13
3230	MOWAT	ST ANDREW	60		JAMES 10
3232	MOWAT	ST ANDREW	60		
1707	MUCKLE	ST ANDREW	280	260	
3238	MUIR	ST ANDREW	124		
1708	MULLIGAN	SFX	116	133	JUSTINE 10
1709	MULLIGAN	ST JOHN	2	4	JAMES 30, GEORGE 22, ROBERT 20, EDWARD 16, ALEX 14
1709	MULLIGAN	ST JOHN	2	4	WILLIAM 5, ELIZABETH 18, HARRIET 15, MARY 8, AGNES 6
1710	MULDIHILL	ST LAURENT	20	16	GEORGE 22, JAMES 20, DONALD 16, JOHN 3
3245	MUNROE	ST JOHN	25	28	JOHN 19, NANCY 17, ELLEN 13, FINLAY 13
3245	MUNROE	ST JOHN	25	28	ANN 13, JEANNET 7, GEORGE 9, BARBARA 7
3247	MUNROE	KILDONAN	61	65	MARION 12, BARBARA 9
3249	MUNROE	ST ANDREW	287	280	JAMES 24, MARY 20, ANDREW 18, ELIZABETH 16
3251	MUNROE	ST JOHN	45	46	JANE 10
3221	MUNWICK	ST CLEMENT	58	61	ISABELLA 5, ALEXANDER 1
3239	MURE	ST ANDREW	115		MARGUERITE 20, ALEXANDER 18, JAMIMA 14, ELIZABETH 18, FREDERIC 15
3239	MURE	KILDONAN	115		ALEXANDER 12
1698	MURRAY	ST CLEMENT	38		ANNE 14, ARCHIBALD 10
1699	MURRAY	ST BONIFACE	2		
3253	MURRAY	ST JAMES	58	44	JAMES 8, DONALD 8, ISABELLA 5, LAURA 3
3255	MURRAY	KILDONAN	4		FRANCIS 25, JOHN 20, DAVID 16, THOMAS 15, CHARLES 12
3256	MURRAY	KILDONAN	28		DONALD 6, JULIA 10, LAURA 3
3692	MURRAY	PORTAGE	133		MARY 3, CATHERINE 1
1700	MURWICK	ST ANDREW	74	75	MARIE 12, ELIZABETH 10, THOMAS 8
1701	MURWICK	ST ANDREW	74	75	
1703	MURWICK	ST ANDREW	74	75	
3222	MURWICK	ST ANDREW	197	75	THOMAS 4, GEORGE 1
3223	MURWICK	ST ANDREW	74	75	JANE, SARA
3224	MURWICK	ST ANDREW	74		
3225	MURWICK	ST ANDREW			WILLIAM 14, ALEXANDER 1
3559	NABASE	ST LAURENT	203		PIERRE 16, ANTOINE 23, ISABEL 12, ROBERT 12

TABLE 4: GEOGRAPHICAL LOCATION AND
CHILDREN OF MANITOBA FAMILIES, 1870

ID	FAMILY	PARISH	AT OR BETWEEN	CHILD 1	CHILD 2	CHILD 3	CHILD 4	CHILD 5
3693	NABASE	ST LAURENT		WILLIAM 8	MARY 6	MARIA 5	JOSEPHINE 2	MARY
3694	NABASE	ST LAURENT		PETER 12	CATHERINE 14	ROGER 10	CHARLES 7	
3694	NABASE	ST LAURENT	74					
3560	NARVEN	ST PETER	56	ISAAC 20	JAMES 8	EMMA 5	MARGARET 2	ANDRE 11
3698	NAULT	ST VITAL	12	ELIZA 9	JOSEPH 17	ELMINE 15	NAPOLEON 13	
3703	NAULT	ST VITAL	12	ELIE 17	MARTIN 5	MARIE 4	CELINA 1	
3703	NAULT	ST VITAL	28	JACQUE 8	LEON 16	AMABLE 14	JOSEPHTE 12	VITAL 10
3705	NAULT	ST VITAL	28	FILICITE 10	PATRICE 8	JOSEPH 5	AGNES 3	ALBERT 1
3711	NAULT	ST VITAL	42	PHILOMENE 16	NOEBERT 6	DENISE 4	WILLIAM 2	
3713	NAULT	ST VITAL	50 / 45	ALFRED 16				
3714	NAULT	ST VITAL	52*	J BAPTISTE 2	CHARLES 1			
3715	NAULT	ST VITAL	42* / 15	VIRGINIE 10	MELANIE 8	JOSEPH 5	ANDRE 4	MARTIN 1
3721	NAULT	ST VITAL	15 / 13	GROSPER 1	ANDRE 17	MARIE 8	ELISE 5	AZILDA 3
3702	NESS	SFX	139 / 142	ROSINE 13	FRANK 11	WILLIAM 11	JOSEPH 4	
3701	NEWCOME	HEADINGLY	/ 6					
3700	NICOL	ST JOHN	33 / 8					
3699	NICOLSON	ST ANDREW	247					
3730	NOLIN	STE ANNE	49	DOLPHIS 10	AUGUSTIN 9	THOMAS 7	MARIE 5	CAROLINE 4
3731	NOLIN	STE ANNE	59 / 40	PAULINE 2	MELANIE 12	JOHNNY 11	ELIE 7	
3731	NOLIN	STE ANNE	59 / 40	ROSE 14	ALEXANDRE 2			
3734	NOLIN	SFX	27 / 31	CHRYSOSTOME 2				MARIE 5
3734	NOLIN	SFX	27 / 31	JOSEPH 4				
3735	NOLIN	STE ANNE	45	ANGELIQUE 37	MARGUERITE 48			
3727	NOLIN	STE ANNE	17	EULALIE 19	NANCY 18	NORBERT 16	MARGUERITE 14	JOSEPH 12
3728	NOLIN	STE ANNE	17 / 16	ALPHONSINE 10	AUGUSTIN 8	FRANCOIS 3	MARIE 1	
3728	NOLIN	STE ANNE	17 / 16	MARGUERITE 18	JOSEPH 15	FRANCOIS 13		
3729	NOLIN	STE ANNE	17	ALEXANDRE 5	ADELE 3		JOACHIM 10	DOMITILDE 7
3733	NOLIN	STE ANNE	38					
3744	NORMAND	ST CLEMENT	35 / 44	SARAH 9	JAMES 6	JANE 4	CHRISTINE 2	
3723	NORMAND	ST NORBERT	153 / 148	ANNE 9	LOUISA 2			
3740	NORMAND	ST NORBERT	153 / 148	PAULINE 5				
3741	NORMAND	ST NORBERT	153 / 148	BONIFACE 4				
3742	NORMAND	ST BONIFACE	81 / 87	MARIE 2				
3746	NORMAND	ST NORBERT	153	JOSEPH 19	NAPOLEON 16	JOHN 16		
3720	NORQUAY	ST ANDREW	143	JAMES 1	SARA 2		WILLIAM 4	
3722	NORQUAY	ST ANDREW	181	ISABEL 4	MARY 1			
3751	NORQUAY	ST PETER	56 / 74	ROBERT 3	DONALD 13	THOMAS 13		
3739	ODONNEL	ST ANDREW	73 / 74	JOHN 15	JOHN 2			
3738	ODONNELL	ST JOHN	13 / 6	F G 9	MARY 9			
3743	OGLETREE	PORTAGE	51 / 53	ANNABELLA 22	ARCHIBALD 6	ISABELLA 13	HENRY 13	SARAH 8
3743	OGLETREE	PORTAGE	51 / 53	FRANCIS 6	BARBARA 3			
3732	OLSEN	HEADINGLY	18 / 20	EWIN 11	JOHN 5	MARY 2		
4040	OLSEN	ST PETER	133 / 167	ELVIRE 4	MARY 14	JAMES 13	WILLIAM 12	
3719	OMAND	ST JAMES	45	JOHN 16				
3760	OMAND	ST ANDREW	57	THOMAS 6	CHARLOTTE 4	CATHERINE 3		
3761	OMAND	ST ANDREW	250 / 57	MARIE 4	JOSEPH 3			
3708	OUELLET	ST NORBERT	250	J BAPTISTE 11	ANGELE 9	BERNARD 6	ABRAHAM 4	WILHELMINA 10
3712	OUELLET	ST NORBERT	159 / 157					
3765	OUELLET	ST NORBERT	256 / 250					
3766	OUELLET	ST NORBERT	91 / 86					

TABLE 4: GEOGRAPHICAL LOCATION AND
CHILDREN OF MANITOBA FAMILIES, 1870

ID	FAMILY	PARISH	AT OR	BETWEEN	CHILDREN AND AGES AT NEXT BIRTHDAY
3564	OUILLET	ST NORBERT	31	27	JOHN 10, CHARLES 7, ELIZA 4, PIERRE 1
3716	OUILLET	ST NORBERT	21	1	MARIE 10, ANGELE 7, VIRGINIE 5, RAPHAEL 2
3717	OUILLET	ST NORBERT	31	27	
3718	OUILLET	ST NORBERT	31	27	
3767	OUILLET	ST NORBERT	17	14	ELISE 8, MARRIANNE 5, THERESE 3, MARIE 1
3767	OUILLET	ST NORBERT	17	14	MARGUERITE 15, MARIE 13, FRANCIS 12, ROSALIE 11, ELISE 10
13282	OUILLETTE	ST NORBERT	98	94	ISABELLE 7, JOSEPHE 5, ISADORE 2, SUPPLIANT 14
3707	OVELLETTE	SFX			JULIEN 22, CHARLES 19, JOSEPH 17, PATRICE 17
3707	OVELLETTE	SFX			CECILE 12, EMILIE 10
3736	OWENS	STE ANNE	15		PATRICK 16, JAMES 14, PETER 14, PIERR 11, JOHN 9
3736	OWENS	STE ANNE	15		MARTIN 7, MARGUERITE 7, JOSEPH 1
3776	PAGE	SFX	199		XAVIER 25, CUTHBERT 18, JUSTINE 15
3779	PAGE	SFX	161	148	JOSEPH 8, NAPOLEON 6, MARIE 4, GUILLEMINE 2
3780	PAGE	SFX			HENRI 21, ROSE 19, ISABELLE 16, ADELE 14, LUCIE 12
3780	PAGE	SFX			MARIE 10
3781	PAGE	SFX	27		ALEXANDRE 20, ELZEAR 9, CECILE 5, J BAPTISTE 3, ALFRED 1
3782	PAGE	SFX	23		MICHEL 1, CLEOPHIE 17, ERNESTINE 13, AIMOND 5, ALFRED 3
3782	PAGE	SFX	23		JOSEPH 7
3783	PAGE	SFX			
3809	PARANTEAU	ST NORBERT	132		PATRICE 8, ELIZA 5, EMILIE 4, JOSEPHTE 2
3810	PARANTEAU	ST NORBERT	98	94	ROSALIE 12, MATHAIS 4, MARIE 8, VIRGINIE 1, JEREMIE 2
3812	PARANTEAU	ST NORBERT	98	94	ANNIE 14, NAPOLEON 10, JOHN 10, ALEXANDRINE 5, MARIE 7
3812	PARANTEAU	ST NORBERT	98	94	ALFRED 14, JOSEPHTE 12, JOHN 2, JOSEPH 8
3903	PAREAU	BAIE S PAUL	207	215	LADADIE 14, MARY 12, CAMILLE 9, J BAPTISTE 6
3903	PAREAU	BAIE S PAUL	207	215	PHILOMENE 1
3904	PAREAU	BAIE S PAUL	207	215	MARGUERITE 20
3802	PARENTEAU	ST BONIFACE	117	113	PATRICE 12, MARGUERITE 11, WILLIAM 8, LAURA 6, ALEXANDRE 3
3805	PARENTEAU	ST BONIFACE	27	17	
3807	PARENTEAU	ST BONIFACE	117	113	
3813	PARENTEAU	ST NORBERT	134		DANIEL 38, ANTOINE 20, COLOMBE 18, SARAH 16, NAPOLEON 14
3813	PARENTEAU	ST NORBERT	134		CELINA 12, LOUIS 10, MELANIE 8, ADELAIDE 2
3815	PARENTEAU	ST NORBERT	135		VERGINIE 6, MOISE 2
3816	PARENTEAU	ST BONIFACE	117	113	WILLIAM 3, CHRYSOSTOME 1, JULIET 1
3818	PARENTEAU	ST BONIFACE	117	113	ALEXIMA 5, VIRGINIE 3, HARRIET 6, JOSEPH 2
3573	PARISEAU	POPLAR PT	24	20	MARGUERITE 10, SARAH 8, MARIE 5, PATRICE 2
3819	PARISIEN	ST NORBERT	82	88	JEAN 7, MARIE 7, JULIEN 3, JOSEPH 2
3821	PARISIEN	ST NORBERT	183		PIERRE 10, WILLIAM 8, HENRI 5, JOSEPH 13, PAULINE 1
3822	PARISIEN	ST NORBERT	197		CECILE 21, CAROLINE 18, SOLOMAN 17, ROSALIE 13, ADELAIDE 11
3823	PARISIEN	ST NORBERT	198		EDWARD 8, ESTHER 5, CLEMENCE 14, ELZEAR 11
3823	PARISIEN	ST NORBERT	198		ATHANASE 9, MARIE 7, MARIE 4
3824	PARISIEN	ST NORBERT	198		CATHERINE 13, PASCHAL 11, MARIE 9, ADELE 8, ADOLPHISE 5
3824	PARISIEN	ST NORBERT	197	166	CAROLINE 1
3825	PARISIEN	ST PETER	197	166	VICTOIRE 7, HENRI 5, ANNE 3, JOSEPH 1
3826	PARISIEN	ST ANDREW	83	85	JOHN 11, MARGUERITE 6, ALEXANDER 4
3830	PARISIEN	ST PETER	77		JOHN 17, WILLIAM 15, GEORGE 13, ANDRE 13
3833	PARISIEN	ST NORBERT	59		ELISE 11, CATHERINE 4, JOHN 2
3834	PARISIEN	ST CLEMENT	4	6	MARGUERITE 7, CATHERINE 4
3835	PARISIEN	ST NORBERT	197	166	SEVERE 8, ANNIE 5, MARIE 5, MARIE 2
3836	PARISIEN	ST NORBERT	197	166	ROGER 13, MARGUERITE 11, SOPHIE 8, WILLIAM 4
3837	PARISIEN	ST NORBERT	219		ANGELIQUE 1

TABLE 4: GEOGRAPHICAL LOCATION AND
CHILDREN OF MANITOBA FAMILIES, 1870

ID	FAMILY	PARISH	AT	BETWEEN	CHILDREN AND AGES AT NEXT BIRTHDAY				
3838	PARISIEN	ST NORBERT	197	166					
3839	PARISIEN	ST NORBERT	197	166					
3841	PARISIEN	ST NORBERT	60		PHILOMENE 18				
3843	PARISIEN	ST NORBERT	218	210	ALEXANDRE 13	HENRI 5			
3844	PARK	ST ANDREW	114	97					
3845	PARK	ST CLEMENT	87		CATHERINE 15		MARIE 4	RAPHAEL 2	
3846	PARK	ST CLEMENT	87		JOHN 14	WILLIAM 12	LOUIS 8	MARGUERITE 6	
3847	PARK	ST ANDREW	4		HENRY 2		CATHERINE 10	LATITIA 8	ISABELLA 4
3847	PARK	ST ANDREW	4						
3849	PARK	PORTAGE	111	92	MARIE 6	NANCY 4			
3794	PAROLIE	ST LAURENT	20	16					
3795	PASSAGE	ST PETER	133	167					
3579	PATERSON	ST BONIFACE	117	113					
3856	PATERSON	KILDONAN	41		ROBERT 9	MARIANNE 7	ELIZABETH 5	GILBERT 9	ROGER 4
3851	PATTENAUDE	SFX	141		MICHEL 13	ADELAIDE 11	CHARLES 9		
3851	PATTENAUDE	SFX	141		FRANCOIS 2				
3852	PATTENAUDE	SFX	100		LOUISON 11	MARIE 10	FRANCOIS 8	CHARLES 4	ADELAIDE 2
3853	PATTENAUDE	SFX	93		ELIZA 7	ADELAIDE 5	MARIE 2		
3854	PATTENAUDE	SFX	141	146	EMILIE 11				
3859	PAUL	SFX	68		JOSEPH 3	ELISE 10	PHILIPPE 8	PIERRE 7	SAMSON 5
3859	PAUL	SFX	68		ERNESTINE 7	ADELAIDE 5	GONZAGUE 3	JOSEPHTE 2	JOSEPH 3
3861	PAUL	SFX	45		BERNARD 23	MARGUERITE 18	ANTOINE 14	VERONIQUE 6	MAGLOIRE 8
3862	PAUL	SFX	159	162	CHARLES 20	ANTOINE 18	ELZEAR 15	PATRICE 13	ANDRE 1
3863	PAUL	SFX	185	191	LEONIDE 20				
3864	PAUL	SFX	189		MARGUERITE 4				
3869	PAUL	SFX	189		JOSEPH 6				
3869	PAUL	SFX	189		JOSEPHTE 8				
3870	PAUL	SFX	185	189					
4392	PAUL	ST PAUL	91	92					
3867	PAULFRICK	ST CHARLES	105	113					
3877	PEEBLES	ST ANDREW	82		ANDREW 23	FRANCOISE 20	RICHARD 19		
3878	PEEBLES	ST CLEMENT	108		ROBERT 8	ANN 4	SAMUEL 2		
3879	PEEBLES	ST ANDREW	53		SARAH 16	ELIZABETH 14	THOMAS 9		
3880	PEEBLES	ST CLEMENT	61		MARGARET 10	MARY 3	PIERRE 4		
3582	PEERS	ST PAUL	19	22					
3858	PELLETIER	SFX	133	115	J BAPTISTE 20	CHRYSOSTOME 18	JOSEPH 15	ISABELLE 12	MARIE 10
3887	PELLETIER	BAIE S PAUL	222		LEONIE 5	MARY 4	FRANCOIS 2	GREGOIRE 1	
3892	PELLETIER	BAIE S PAUL	215	224	JOSEPH 18	SOLOMAN 15	ETIENNE 14	ARCHANGE 12	
3772	PEPIN	ST VITAL	25						
3897	PEPIN	BAIE S PAUL	194	207	BENOIT 13	AMBROISE 11	ADELAIDE 8	JULIAN 6	ALEXIS 2
3587	PERON	STE ANNE	2	18	MARIE 2				
3899	PERON	STE ANNE	2	18	EULALIE 17				
3901	PERON	STE ANNE	49	66	MARGUERITE 24	J BAPTISTE 22	DAMASE 18	MAGDELEINE 16	CATHERINE 15
3901	PERON	STE ANNE	49	66	WILLIAM 13	MARIE 12	ROSALIE 10	ANTOINE 8	BONIFACE 7
3901	PERON	STE ANNE	49	66	EDWARD 1				
3908	PERON	STE ANNE	15	13	OCTAVE 21	JULIENNE 19	EUCARISE 17	SARA 15	ANARGILE 12
3908	PERON	STE ANNE	15	13	MARIE 9	PIERRE 6	OLIVIER 3	SARAH 9	AZILDA 1
3900	PERON	ST NORBERT	40		JULIE 11				
3898	PERRAULT	ST VITAL	13		ROSE 15	JOACHIM 14	EUSTACHE 12		
3916	PERREAULT	ST PETER	46	56	JOSEPH 2	SARAH 1			
3912	PETERSON	ST JOHN	6	33					
3588	PHILIPS	ST ANDREW	234		MARGARET 3				

TABLE 4: GEOGRAPHICAL LOCATION AND
CHILDREN OF MANITOBA FAMILIES, 1870

ID	FAMILY	PARISH	AT OR BETWEEN	CHILDREN AND AGES AT NEXT BIRTHDAY
3589	PICARD	ST JOHN	13 6	WILLIAM 6
3905	PICHE	POPLAR PT	58 60	HENRIETTE 3
3923	PICHE	SFX	120 126	ISABELLE 12
3929	PICHE	SFX	97	HELENE 18, FLORISTINE 5, PHILOMENE 4, ANATALE 2
3930	PICHE	SFX	122	NORBERT 25, ELISE 16, MARGUERITE 14, NORBERT 12, ROSE 10
3931	PICHE	SFX	114	CHARLOTTE 15, BAZILE 14, THERESE 10, CHARLOTTE 8
4042	PICHE	SFX	134 122	SARAH 5, ELIZABETH 11, MARIE 9, WILLIAM 7, VERONIQUE 5
4042	PICHE	SFX	134 122	LOUISE 4, ANATHALIE 2
4043	PICHE	ST JOHN	96	MADELEINE 2
3591	PIERPONT	ST JOHN	13 6	
3933	PILON	ST NORBERT	256 250	WILLIAM 18, TOUSAINT 16, ABRAHAM 16, JOSEPH 12, ALEXIS 9
3933	PILON	ST NORBERT	256 250	CHARLES 7, ROSALIE 4, CHRISTINE 4, MARIE 2
3934	PILON	ST NORBERT	131	JOSEPH 11, BARTHELEINY 9, ALEXANDRE 6, MARIE 4, ALFRED 3
3934	PILON	ST NORBERT	131	MARJILDE
3935	PILON	ST NORBERT	130	ANGELIQUE 28, ANNIE 25, WILLIAM 22, ANDRE 23, GENEVIEVE 30
3935	PILON	ST NORBERT	130	CASIMIRE 24, ALFRED 6, WILLIAM 2
3936	PILON	ST NORBERT	119 97	MARIE 11
3939	PINKHAM	ST JAMES	41 44	
2622	PLANTE	SFX	211	JOSEPH 2, MARIE 20, ANTOINE 4, CUTHBERT 10
2673	PLANTE	SFX	32 34	MAGLOIRE 20, BAZILE 17, CAROLINE 15, FRANCOISE 13, ELISE 11
2673	PLANTE	SFX	32 34	JOHNNY 4, PIERRE 1
2675	PLANTE	ST BONIFACE	31 29	MARIE 11, ROSALIE 9, JOHN 5, JOSEPH 2
2790	PLANTE	ST BONIFACE	31 29	
3937	PLEASE	ST JOHN	6 33	
3775	POCHA	HIGH BLUFF	68	JOHN 10, JOSEPH 8, CHARLOTTE 6, WILLIAM 4, MARIA 3
3775	POCHA	HIGH BLUFF	68	CHARLES 1
3796	POCHA	HIGH BLUFF	66	MARIA 2, GEORGE 1
3797	POCHA	HIGH BLUFF	63	HENRY 1, THOMAS 1
3943	POCHA	HIGH BLUFF	66 70	HENRI 22, GEORGE 18, CATHERINE 14, BETSY 11, GILBERT 25
3944	POCHA	HIGH BLUFF	60	HARRIET 2, JANE 1
3945	POCHA	HIGH BLUFF	64	HARRIET 13, MARY 8, WILLIAM 6, JOHN 1
3592	POISSON	ST JAMES	21 22	
1694	POITRAS	SFX	208	PIERRE 9, MARIE 5, ELZEAR 3, HELENE 1
3260	POITRAS	ST BONIFACE	31 29	MARGUERITE 4, MARY 4, ADELINE 1, JEAN 13, ELIZA 9
3347	POITRAS	ST BONIFACE	113	ELEONOR 20, FRANCOIS 18, ADELAIDE 16, MICHEL 13
3347	POITRAS	ST BONIFACE	113	
3949	POITRAS	SFX		IGNACE 20, MAXIME 18, J BAPTISTE 16, ALEXANDRE 11
3949	POITRAS	SFX	198	ELISE 10, HELENE 7
3951	POITRAS	SFX	198	MODESTE 19, CAROLINE 16, NORBERT 12, WILLIAM 10
3951	POITRAS	SFX	208 209	MARIE 7, EMILIE 5
3955	POITRAS	SFX	95	MARIE 7, GABRIEL 7, FLORISTINE 3, JOSEPH 1
3956	POITRAS	SFX	205 208	ELIZA 4, VIRGINIE 5
3957	POITRAS	SFX	205 208	JUSTINE 12, JEREMIE 10, J BAPTISTE 8, SOLOMAN 3, PAULINE 2
3959	POITRAS	SFX	81	MAXIME 28, CHRYSOSTOME 16, PAULINE 18, ELZEAR 14
3960	POLSON	*KILDONAN	81	
3969	POLSON	ST JOHN	45 46	SAMUEL 24, ALEXANDER 22, ANGUS 18, CATHERINE 16, FLORA 14
3969	POLSON	ST JOHN	45 46	HUGH 11, ANN 11, MARGARET 10, MARY 4
3972	POLSON	*KILDONAN	81	ALEXANDER 15, JOHN 10, JAMES 8, JAMES 6
3975	POLSON	*KILDONAN	2	ALEXANDER 31, JANE 24, SAMUEL 19, CATHERINE 8, MARGARET 5
3977	POLSON	*KILDONAN	11	JEANNET 19
3974	PORDY	ST ANDREW	263 268	
3967	PORTER	ST JOHN	13 6	

TABLE 4: GEOGRAPHICAL LOCATION AND
CHILDREN OF MANITOBA FAMILIES, 1870

ID	FAMILY	PARISH	AT OR BETWEEN	CHILDREN AND AGES AT NEXT BIRTHDAY				
3971	PORTER	ST BONIFACE	44 41	ANDRY 2				
3966	POWERS	ST CHARLES	96	RICHARD 20	JOHN 15	HENRY 13	THOMAS 8	LILLY 5
3973	PRATT	ST PETER	8 17	AGNES 4	THOMAS 2	PHILIPPE 1		
3982	PRIMEAU	ST NORBERT	124 119	MARIE 4	JOSEPHTE 3			
3983	PRIMEAU	STE AGATHE	555	VERONIZUE 3	JOSEPH 1			
3984	PRIMEAU	ST NORBERT	124 119	JOSEPH 30				
4054	PRINCE	ST PETER		SARA 3	ANNE 2	SOPHIE 1		
4055	PRINCE	ST PETER	56 74	JAMES 17	ELIZABETH 14	JOHN 13	ELISE 1	
4056	PRINCE	ST PETER	100 133	ANDRE 12	WILLIAM 10	MARIE 8		
4057	PRINCE	ST PETER		ELISE 19	ISABEL 16			
4058	PRINCE	ST PETER	87*	SARA 16	JESSIE 14	FREDERIC 12	WILLIAM 10	MARIA 3
4059	PRINCE	ST PETER		CHRISTINE 3	ANNE 1			
4060	PRINCE	ST PETER	100 133	MARIE 6	ELISE 4			
4061	PRINCE	ST PETER	100 133					
4062	PRINCE	ST PETER	100 133					
4073	PRINER	ST PETER	83 85	WILLIAM 21	ANDRE 16	JOSEPH 16	HENRY 9	THOMAS 6
3995	PRITCHARD	ST PAUL	108	JOHN 14	ARCHIBALD 12	CATHERINE 11		
3995	PRITCHARD	ST PAUL	108	HUGH 4	LUCY 2			
3996	PRITCHARD	ST PAUL						
3997	PRITCHARD	ST PAUL	19	MARGARET 8	LETTITIA 4	HENRIETTA 2		
4002	PRITCHARD	KILDONAN	54	JOHN 30	CHRISTIE 28	CATHERINE 24	RICHARD 22	ANGUS 20
4002	PRITCHARD	KILDONAN	32	WILLIAM 16	ARCHIBALD 14	JANE 12		
4007	PRITCHARD	KILDONAN	32	SOLOMAN 1				
4009	PRITCHARD	SFX	181 190	WILLIAM 4	ROBERT 4	ADELAIDE 2	MARIE 7	EDWARD 3
4014	PROULX	SFX	84	DONALD 5				
4019	PROULX	ST CHARLES	82	MICHEL 22	ANGILE 18	MODESTE 9		
4019	PROULX	ST CHARLES	67	JOSEPH 1				
4023	PROVIER	POPLAR PT	67					
3994	PRUDEN	ST ANDREW		JOHN 5		WILLIAM 3		
4015	PRUDEN	ST ANDREW	68 69	WILLIAM 19	CHARLES 19	NANCY 17	CAROLINE 13	MARY 9
4016	PRUDEN	ST JAMES	68 69	THOMAS 5	ANNIE 5	CHARLOTTE 4		
4016	PRUDEN	ST JAMES	20					
4017	PRUDEN	ST ANDREW	20	ALFRED 13				
4021	PRUDEN	SFX	68 69	MARY JANE 7	SARAH 5	JOHN 3		
4031	PRUDEN	ST PAUL	226 180	ELIZABETH 26	ALEXANDER 21	JANE 18	KENNETH 17	SOPHIA 15
4034	PRUDEN	ST JAMES	46	EWEN 13	ROBERT 13	ISABELLA 8	CORNELIUS 6	MARY 4
4034	PRUDEN	ST JAMES	26	JOHN 16	SARA 18	GEORGE 14	PAUL 11	ALICE 9
4022	PRUDOM	ST CLEMENT	26	MARIE 2				
4022	PRUDOM	ST CLEMENT						
4029	PRUDOM	ST CLEMENT	88	PETER 15	ANNE 14	MARIE 12	JACOB 10	BELLA 8
4029	PRUDOM	ST CLEMENT	88	JOHN 7	CORNELIUS 1			
4033	PRUDOM	ST ANDREW	67	WILLIAM 16	JOHN 14	ANN 11	JANE 6	CAROLINE 4
4033	PRUDOM	ST ANDREW	67	MARIA 3				
4032	PRUDON	ST ANDREW	68					
4036	PRUDON	ST ANDREW	68 69					
3999	RACETTE	SFX	161 148	JAMES 17	JOSEPH 15	MARIE 13	MARIE ROSE 11	
4001	RACETTE	SFX	180 161	CHARLES 8	JOSEPH 8	MARIE 6		
4003	RACETTE	SFX	161 148	FRANCOIS 5	ALEXANDRE 6	JOSEPH 3		
4008	RACETTE	SFX	180 161	J BAPTISTE 15	JOSEPH 13	ELISE 11	JOSEPH 9	
4012	RACETTE	SFX	180 161	MARGUERITE 23	JULIE 20	JUDITH 17		
4013	RACETTE	ST VITAL	19	WILLIAM 14	JEROME 10	MARIE 10		
4025	RACETTE	ST BONIFACE	110 107		MARIE 10	JOSEPH 9	CHARLES 7	PATRICE 5

ID	FAMILY	PARISH	AT OR BETWEEN	CHILDREN AND AGES AT NEXT BIRTHDAY
4025	RACETTE	ST BONIFACE	110 107	VIRGINIE 3, JOSEPH 4, HENRIETTE 10, PHILOMENE 10, JOSEPH 2
4145	RACETTE	STE ANNE	49 66	BAPTISTE 12, GASPARD 17, ELISE 20
4146	RACETTE	ST BONIFACE	107	MOISE 24
4147	RACETTE	SFX	180	
4148	RACETTE	SFX	180 161	JOSEPH 3, ELIZA 7, JOHN 5
4158	RAINVILLE	STE AGATHE	73	MARIE 9, MARGUERITE 1
3992	RAMSAY	ST JAMES		MARTHA 20, ROBERT 18, THOMAS 14
3991	RAMSEY	STE ANNE	10	ANNE 12, JOSEPH 10, LOUISON 2, LOUISON 3
3990	RAT	ST PETER	83 85	
4067	RAT	SFX	181 179	
4068	RAT	SFX	181 179	
4069	RAYWOOD	ST PAUL	13 14	CATHERINE 4, JOHN 2
4070	REED	ST PETER	100 133	MICHEL 22, ANTOINE 20, ELIZA 18, P 15, BONIFACE 13
4160	RESSARD	BAIE S PAUL	182*	LAZARUS 11, ISIDORE 10, PAULINE 5, ALEXANDRE 13, J BAPTISTE 10
4160	RESSARD	BAIE S PAUL	182*	ANTOINE 21, MICHEL 18, THEOPHILE 16, MARGUERITE 7, FLORA 2
4164	RESSARD	ST LAURENT	18	MOSES 5, MARY 21, LOUISA 12, SUSANNE 10
4164	RESSARD	ST LAURENT	18	PETER 20, ISABELLA 14, PETER 3
4167	RESSARD	ST LAURENT	19	FRANCOIS 7, ROGER 6, THOMAS 9, MARGUERITE 1
4166	RICHARD	SFX	86	MARGUERITE 10, ANNE 8, WILLIAM 6
4174	RICHARD	ST ANDREW	70	ANDREW 16, ANNE 13, JACOB 9
4175	RICHARD	ST ANDREW	70 71	HANNAH 4, MARY 3, JAMES 1
4168	RICHARDS	ST CHARLES	9	MARIE 15, HYACINTHE 8, CLEMENCE 6, FLORISTINE 5
4171	RICHARDS	SFX	105	EMMA 18, THOMAS 18, MARIE 7
4172	RICHARDS	ST PETER		LOUIS 27, MARIE 27, OCTAVIE 18
4078	RIDSDALE	STE ANNE	38 46	JOSEPH 14, HENRIETTE 14, ALEXANDRE 8, EULALIE 17, CHARLES 15
4155	RIEL	ST VITAL	85 95	ALEXANDRE 6, EDWARD 6, ALEXANDRE 8
4155	RIEL	ST VITAL	50*	
4179	RITCHOT	ST VITAL	50*	ANTOINE 1, ANTOINE 1
4178	RITCHOT	ST VITAL	21 15	DOMITILDE 18, VIRGINIE 15, JANNET 11, ANDRY 9, LOUIS 4
4180	RITCHOT	ST VITAL	29 19	DELIMA 2
4185	RITCHOT	ST BONIFACE	29 19	
4185	RITCHOT	ST BONIFACE	36	XAVIER 17, ELIZA 15, ELISE 10
4186	RITCHOT	ST NORBERT	36	
4189	RITCHOT	ST VITAL	81	ALEXANDRE 15, ISABELLE 3
4193	RIVARD	ST JAMES	29	
4195	RIVARD	ST NORBERT		JOHN 10, LORETTA 9, MARY 7, ELEONOR 5, ANN 3
4154	ROBB	ST JOHN	117 114	WILLIAM 1, ALEXANDRE 1
4081	ROBERTS	ST JAMES	4 13	
4081	ROBERTS	ST JAMES	70 73	JOSEPH 5, JOHN 4
4083	ROBERTSON	ST JOHN	70 73	JOHN 4, HENRI 1
4084	ROBILLARD	ST JAMES	4 13	JOSEPHTE 26
4085	ROBINSON	ST PETER	55 57	
4200	ROBINSON	SFX	133 167	
4201	ROBINSON	SFX	212	
4205	ROBINSON	ST JOHN	4	PITASSMI 4
4207	ROBINSON	ST PETER	2 4	MARIE 4
4208	ROBINSON	ST PETER	133 167	JANE 2
4203	ROBISON	ST ANDREW	107 108	MARIE 3
4213	ROCHELEAU	ST NORBERT	113 101	BAPTISTE 19, MODESTE 17, ROSALIE 15, ROGER 12, PIERRE 9
4214	ROCHELEAU	ST NORBERT	133	WILLIAM 7, VIRGINIE 4, MATHILDE 1
4214	ROCHELEAU	ST NORBERT	133	
2688	ROCKBRUNE	SFX	93 99	MARIE 9, AMBROISE 7, CATHERINE 6, JOSEPH 6, CHARLES 2

ID	FAMILY	PARISH	AT	BETWEEN	CHILDREN AND AGES AT NEXT BIRTHDAY				
2694	ROCKBRUNE	SFX	177		MARGUERITE 16	ALPHONSE 14	MARIE 12	OLIVIER 12	ELISE 10
2694	ROCKBRUNE	SFX	177		ANTOINE 8	VERONIQUE 4	JAMES 1		
2786	ROCKBRUNE	SFX	139	142					
2788	ROCKBRUNE	SFX	139	142	NORBERT 19	FLAVIE 16	CAROLINE 14	PIERRE 11	FRANCOIS 7
2788	ROCKBRUNE	SFX	139	142	MARIE 5				
4225	RODWAY	ST JAMES	70	73	JOSEPH 17	WILLIAM 16	ELIZABETH 14	SARAH 13	THOMAS 12
4225	RODWAY	ST JAMES	70	73	JOHN 10	ROSE 7	EDWARD 4		
4096	ROSE	ST PETER					CATHERINE 9		
4224	ROSE	ST LAURENT			CHARLOTTE 21		SARA 14		
4232	ROSS	KILDONAN	16	17					
4236	ROSS	SFX	66		ELISE 20	MARGUERITE 18	BLANDINE 16	ROSINE 14	
4236	ROSS	SFX	66		LOUIS 8	SARAH 5	FLORA 3		JULIE 12
4241	ROSS	ST JOHN	8	9	LOUISA 12	CAROLINE 11	HERBERT 10	HENRIETTA 8	JAMES 6
4242	ROSS	SFX	133	115	JOSEPH 2				
4243	ROSS	SFX	135		MAGDELEINE 18	SARAH 16	ROSE 13	PIERRE 11	PHILOMENE 9
4243	ROSS	SFX	135		RODERICK 7	URBAIN 5	FLORISTINE 3	ELZEAR 2	
4245	ROSS	SFX	134		VERONIQUE 11	AMBROISE 9	MARIE 8	JOHN 4	CHARLES 2
4246	ROSS	SFX	133	115	CELINA 16				
4247	ROSS	SFX	60						
4248	ROSS	KILDONAN	53		ALEXANDER 5	WILLIAM 3			
13280	ROSS	ST JOHN	8*		WILLIAM 21	ALEXANDER 19	MARGARET 18		DAVID 5
4253	ROUSSIN	STE ANNE	31		FRANCOIS 23	JOSEPH 18	LESTANC 12	MARIE 9	
4253	ROUSSIN	STE ANNE	31		NORBERT 3				
4251	ROWAND	ST JOHN			MARY 3				
4233	ROY	ST JOHN	2	4					
4244	ROY	ST PETER	46	56	SUSAN 12	MARIE 8	SARA 5		ELISE 2
4255	ROY	ST NORBERT	72	67	JULIEN 3	ALFRED 1			
4262	ROY	SFX	190	211	J BAPTISTE 17	MARIE 13	LOUIS 11		HENRI 5
4263	ROY	ST NORBERT	76		CATHERINE 2	J BAPTISTE 5	JOSEPH 2		
4264	ROY	STE AGATHE	535		MARIE 10	VIRGINIE 8	LOUIS 5	ELEONOR 1	
4265	ROY	ST NORBERT	149		THERESE 20	CELINA 17	MARGUERITE 15	ROGER 11	FRANCOIS 6
4235	RUSSIN	PORTAGE			CABOT 18	PIERRE 11	EUSTACHE 8	JEANNET 2	
4345	SABINE	HEADINGLY	7		JAMES 10	HERBERT 8	SUZANNA 6		
4338	SALTER	HEADINGLY	17		WILLIAM 19	HENRIETTA 17	THOMAS 14	JANE 14	
4338	SALTER	HEADINGLY	17		MARY 8				
4310	SANDER	ST ANDREW	97		FLORA 30	SARA 16	FRANCIS 14		SAMUEL 10
4229	SANDERSON	POPLAR PT	83		WILLIAM 14	JOHN 13	HARRIET 11	JAMES 8	JANE 9
4229	SANDERSON	POPLAR PT	83		GEORGE 7	ELIZABETH 5	MARY 2		
4230	SANDERSON	POPLAR PT	61	79	FREDERICK 9				
4319	SANDERSON	ST ANDREW	97	92					
4320	SANDERSON	ST ANDREW	91						
4321	SANDERSON	ST ANDREW	92		WILLIAM 15	ISABEL 13	CATHERINE 11	FLORA 8	JAMIMA 6
4321	SANDERSON	ST ANDREW	92		JOHN 4	GEORGE 2	ALEXANDER 4	MARY 2	
4325	SANDERSON	ST ANDREW	96	97	RICHARD 10	CATHERINE 7	JOHN 1		
4326	SANDERSON	HIGH BLUFF	26	52	ANN 4	HARRIET 2			
4330	SANDERSON	ST CLEMENT	46	48					
4334	SANDERSON	ST ANDREW	97	98	THOMAS 6	JANE 5	WILLIAM 3	ROBERT 1	
4335	SANDERSON	HIGH BLUFF	54		JOHN 1				
4733	SANDERSON	ST CLEMENT	46	48					
4268	SANDISON	ST ANDREW	170	197	JAMES 9	JANE 7	GEORGE 5	THOMAS 5	CHARLES 2
4327	SANDISON	ST ANDREW	25	26					
4731	SANDISON	ST JAMES	9	13					

TABLE 4: GEOGRAPHICAL LOCATION AND
CHILDREN OF MANITOBA FAMILIES, 1870

ID	FAMILY	PARISH	AT OR BETWEEN	CHILDREN AND AGES AT NEXT BIRTHDAY
4732	SANDISON	ST JAMES	97 100	HARIET 16, JANE 18, GRACE, CATHERINE 14, CATHERINE 12, ALEXANDER 20
4738	SANSON	ST PETER	5	ANDRE 24, MELANIE 22, JOHN, MATHAIS 19, MICHEL 16
4317	SANSREGNET	ST VITAL	5	HENRI 14, MARGUERITE 12, ADELE, EDWARD, CELINA 7
4317	SANSREGNET	ST VITAL		MARIE 13, CLARA 16
4317	SANSREGNET	ST VITAL		LEOCADIE 21, MARGUERITE 18
4318	SANSREGRET	SFX	5	HELAIRE 6, PIERRE 3, ALPHONSE 18, MARIE, NAPOLEON 7
4739	SANSREGRET	ST BONIFACE	175	FRANCOIS 3
4311	SARGENT	ST JOHN	117 113	J BAPTISTE 4, ALEXANDRE 2
4314	SAUCIER	BAIE S PAUL	2	PIERRE 24, JOSEPH 23, MARIE, MARGUERITE 20, CHARLES 11
4296	SAUVE	ST VITAL	219 244	MARGARET 5
4747	SAUVE	ST JAMES	49*	
4742	SAVAGE	ST JAMES	219 244	
4290	SAVOYARD	KILDONAN	21 22	LOUISE 2, PIERRE 14, JOSEPH, JULIENNE 8, ELIZA 4
4291	SAVOYARD	KILDONAN	29 30	J BAPTISTE 16
4743	SAVOYARD	KILDONAN	54 56	
4763	SAYE	SFX	54 56	EDWARD 25, SAMSON 23, URBAIN, ROSE 18, ELISE 15
1527	SAYER	POPLAR PT	82 88	EDWARD 12, CAROLINE 17
4279	SAYER	ST CLEMENT	28 38	EMMA 2
4280	SAYER	POPLAR PT	82 88	ALICE 6, MARY 8, SUSANNE, JOHN 11
4760	SAYER	ST LAURENT	56 57	PHILOMENE 5, ELIZA 3
4761	SAYER	ST LAURENT	42 44	
4271	SAYIES	POPLAR PT	49	FRANCOIS 18, ELISE 15, CHARLES 15, ROGER 13, JOHN 7
4270	SAYISSE	ST NORBERT	2	HENRY 8, ELLEN 6, MARGARET, CHRISTIANA 3, JOSEPH 1
4276	SAYR	HEADINGLY	46	
4755	SCHULTZ	ST JOHN	46	
4352	SCOTT	ST ANDREW	80 87	MARIAN 24, MALCOLM 19, ANNABELLA, WILLIAM 18, JOHN 11
4352	SCOTT	ST ANDREW		ALICE 2
4754	SCOTT	STE AGATHE	69 67	
4756	SCOTT	PORTAGE	219 244	
4748	SEINEZ	BAIE S PAUL	219 244	ALEXANDRE 17, MARIA 17, LEON 15, ELIZA 12, CATHERINE 6
4748	SEINEZ	BAIE S PAUL		PHILOMENE 5, JOHN 3, J BAPTISTE, ROSALIE 1
4751	SELLWOOD	ST JAMES	55	JOHN 19
4752	SENEZ	BAIE S PAUL	207 215	JULIA 21, ROSALIE 18, FRANCOIS 18, MARY 16, ZACHARIA 9
4752	SENEZ	BAIE S PAUL		ALEXANDRE 7, CUTHBERT 5, THERESE 5, OLIVER 6
4360	SETTER	POPLAR PT	207 215	JOHN 12, ANDREW 10, WILLIAM 10, DAVID 4
4360	SETTER	POPLAR PT		CHARLES 3, CHRISTINA 3
4361	SETTER	PORTAGE	47	MAURICE 5, COLIN 15
4362	SETTER	HIGH BLUFF	47	DUNCAN 16, WILLIAM 1, RODERICK, GEORGE 14, ELLEN 10
4362	SETTER	HIGH BLUFF		ALEXANDER 8
4797	SHANNON	PORTAGE	113	KATE 3, WILLIAM 1
4802	SHARON	ST CHARLES	52 41	ROBERT 1, MATILDA 18, RICHARD 12, GEORGE
4798	SHARP	POPLAR PT	40 43	EDWARD 18
4799	SHARP	POPLAR PT	116 133	WILLIAM 3
4369	SHORT	SFX	105 113	
4806	SHORT	ST CHARLES	20	JOHN 10, MARGUERITE 8, VIRGINIE, WILLIAM 6, CAROLINE 2
4373	SIMPSON	HEADINGLY	35	CHARLES 10, JOHN 8, ALFRED, GEORGE 6, MARGARET 3
4377	SINCLAIR	ST CLEMENT	91	THOMAS 10, ISABEL 9, WILLIAM 7, ALEXANDER 4, NANCY
4378	SINCLAIR	ST ANDREW	58 59	BETSY 33, GEORGE 19, THOMAS, THOMAS 17
4383	SINCLAIR	ST ANDREW	25	ANNA 13, MARGARET 8, HARRIET 8, CHARLES 3
4386	SINCLAIR	ST ANDREW	25	PETER 16, WILLIAM 14, MARY, JAMES 8, JOHNNY 4
4386	SINCLAIR	ST ANDREW		ALEXANDER 2
4387	SINCLAIR	PORTAGE	51 53	

TABLE 4: GEOGRAPHICAL LOCATION AND
CHILDREN OF MANITOBA FAMILIES, 1870

ID	FAMILY	PARISH	AT OR BETWEEN		CHILDREN AND AGES AT NEXT BIRTHDAY				
4389	SINCLAIR	ST ANDREW	58	59	JOHN 17	JAMES 13	CAROLINE 10	FREDERICK 6	LOUISA 3
4762	SINCLAIR	ST PETER	46	56	ROBERT 4	JOHN 2			
4765	SINCLAIR	ST ANDREW	13	14	CATHERINE 9	MARGARET 5	ALEXANDER 2		
4780	SINCLAIR	ST ANDREW	59	60					
4781	SINCLAIR	ST PETER	83	85	MASSE 3				
4782	SINCLAIR	ST PETER	8	17	WILLIAM 15	JOHN 13	ANDRE 12	ALEXANDER 1	
4783	SINCLAIR	ST PETER	1	8					
4784	SINCLAIR	ST ANDREW	88	89					
4785	SINCLAIR	ST BONIFACE			WILLIAM 13	PIERRE 12	JOSEPH 10	MARIE 9	MARGUERITE 8
4785	SINCLAIR	ST BONIFACE			JAMES 6	CHRISASTOME 3			
4786	SINCLAIR	ST PETER	16	17	JOHN 14	MARGUERITE 12	THOMAS 9	ELIZABETH 4	ARABELLA 2
4787	SINCLAIR	ST ANDREW	196	198	EMILIE 8	JOHN 7	ALEXANDER 5	STEVEN 2	
4788	SINCLAIR	ST CLEMENT	43		JANE 9	SAMUEL 13			
4789	SINCLAIR	SFX	133	115	THOMAS 25	JOHN 20	WILLIAM 18	MARGUERITE 15	
4790	SINCLAIR	ST ANDREW	14						
4791	SINCLAIR	ST ANDREW	14	15					
4792	SINCLAIR	ST ANDREW	59						
4793	SINCLAIR	HIGH BLUFF	29		EDWIN 4	MARY 2	CATHERINE 8	WILLIAM 5	GEORGE 1
3865	SLATER	ST PAUL	91	92	JOHN 9	ALBERT 8	MARGARET 10	MARY 7	
4364	SLATER	ST PAUL	31		THOMAS 14	WILLIAM 12			
4393	SLATER	ST PAUL	27	29					
4394	SLATER	ST PAUL	15		ISABELLA 40	JANE 28	JEREMIAH 26	SAMUEL 24	GEORGE 21
4395	SLATER	POPLAR PT	52		JAMES 22	MARGARET 25	MARY 18	CATHERINE 16	SARAH 12
4395	SLATER	POPLAR PT	52		WILLIAM 10	GEORGE 10	JOHN 7		
4795	SLATER	POPLAR PT	52		ELIZABETH 4	CATHERINE 4	JAMES 7		
4796	SLATER	SFX	53		JAMES 25	MARIE 13	LOUISE 11	ALPHONSE 5	
4807	SMALL	ST JOHN	25	28					
3493	SMITH	ST NORBERT	16		MARIE 13	ELIZA 9	ALEXANDRE 7	J BAPTISTE 5	WILLIAM 2
3494	SMITH	ST ANDREW	98	99					
3495	SMITH	POPLAR PT	54		WILLIAM 6	MARY 10	ALEXANDER 4	CAROLINE 2	
3496	SMITH	ST CHARLES	16		JOHN 24	JAMES 22	PATRICK 20	ELIZABETH 18	
3497	SMITH	PORTAGE	51	53					
3498	SMITH	ST PETER	56	74	BENJAMIN 11	JACOB 9	DAVID 6	JOHN 3	
3499	SMITH	ST ANDREW	101						
3500	SMITH	ST JAMES							
3502	SMITH	ST JOHN	48	45					
3503	SMITH	ST ANDREW	102	104	THOMAS 4	JOHN			
3505	SMITH	ST JOHN	52		HARRIET 23	JANE 21	ROBERT 19	WILLIAM 17	DAVID 15
3505	SMITH	ST JOHN	52		ALBERT 10	ELIZABETH 7			
3507	SMITH	ST ANDREW	102		WILLIAM 20	CATHERINE 18	JOHN 16	JANE 15	EDWARD 13
3507	SMITH	ST ANDREW	102		JOSEPH 11	HELENE 6	RICHARD 3	MATHILDE 2	HENRI 1
4399	SMITH	ST ANDREW	117	120					
4400	SMITH	POPLAR PT	39		ELIZABETH 15	ISABELLA 8	WILLIAM 4	MARGARET 2	
4402	SMITH	ST ANDREW	114		ALEXANDER 20	THOMAS 18	RACHEL 13	EDWARD 10	CATHERINE 5
4402	SMITH	ST ANDREW	114		JOHN 2				
4403	SMITH	ST ANDREW	114		WILLIAM 15	SARA 18	JAMES 12	CHARLOTTE 7	SAMUEL 4
4412	SMITH	POPLAR PT	69		WILLIAM 14	JOHN 9	MARY 7	ALFRED 3	GEORGE 1
4416	SMITH	ST PETER	1	8	GILBERT 23	MARIANN 16	JAMES 11	FLORA 3	CATHERINE 1
4551	SMITH	ST CHARLES	16	57	LOUISA 20	GEORGE 19	WILLIAM 18	CAROLINE 16	ROBERT 13
4808	SMITH	ST JAMES	67		MARY 10	SAMUEL 6	ALBERT 2		
4811	SMITH	HIGH BLUFF	55		ALEXANDER 10	ISABELLA 8	CATHERINE 6	MARGARET 4	JOHN 2

TABLE 4: GEOGRAPHICAL LOCATION AND
CHILDREN OF MANITOBA FAMILIES, 1870

ID	FAMILY	PARISH	AT OR BETWEEN	CHILDREN AND AGES AT NEXT BIRTHDAY				
4812	SMITH	ST ANDREW	77 76	MARIE 2				
4813	SMITH	*ST ANDREW	136					
4814	SMITH	ST BONIFACE	94 81					
5280	SMITH	ST ANDREW	102 104					
3674	SOUNDERMAN	ST JOHN	6 33					
3675	SPENCE	ST PETER	56 74	THOMAS 11	SOPHIE 2			
3677	SPENCE	PORTAGE	133 111					
3678	SPENCE	PORTAGE	133 111	LOUIS 18	MARY 16	JOHN 14	ELLEN 8	ELIZA 6
3679	SPENCE	ST CLEMENT	4 6					
3680	SPENCE	PORTAGE		ABRAHAM 19	ABSOLON 11	HENRY 7	CHARLES 2	
3681	SPENCE	POPLAR PT	65	JAMES 12	ALFRED 9			
3682	SPENCE	STE ANNE	2					
3684	SPENCE	ST ANDREW	34 38					
3685	SPENCE	ST BONIFACE	81 87	ISABELLE 14	WILLIAM 5			
3686	SPENCE	ST JAMES						
3687	SPENCE	ST PETER		JOSEPH 30				
4426	SPENCE	HIGH BLUFF	71	GEORGE 13	EMMA 11	EDWIN 9	JOHN 5	RONALD 2
4427	SPENCE	HIGH BLUFF	72	ELIZABETH 14	GEORGE 11	EDWIN 6	ARCHIBALD 2	
4428	SPENCE	ST ANDREW	11	RICHARD 19	MATHEW 17	ADAM 15	MARY 9	
4429	SPENCE	POPLAR PT	63 62					
4430	SPENCE	POPLAR PT	62	ELLEN 18	DAVID 13	JANE 11	MARY 9	HARRIET 7
4430	SPENCE	POPLAR PT	62	WILLIAM 5				
4432	SPENCE	ST PETER	100 133	ALEXANDER 23	CATHERINE 18	CAROLINE 11	CHARLES 6	ELIZABETH 3
4434	SPENCE	ST CLEMENT	4					
4434	SPENCE	ST CLEMENT	6					
4436	SPENCE	ST ANDREW	270					
4440	SPENCE	ST ANDREW	10					
4446	SPENCE	ST JAMES	70 73	ROBERT 17	JAMES 15	ROBINA 13	JANE 11	MARGARET 7
4446	SPENCE	ST JAMES	70 73	ANN 4				
4449	SPENCE	ST CLEMENT	110	ALEXANDER 16	ROBERT 12	SOPHIE 9	NANCY 8	MARIANNE 14
4452	SPENCE	ST PETER	133 167					
4456	SPENCE	ST JOHN	28 55					
4459	SPENCE	PORTAGE		JAMES 18	NICHOLAS 16	WILLIAM 12	CATHERINE 9	DAVID 6
4459	SPENCE	PORTAGE		JOHN 14	ANN 9			
4460	SPENCE	ST ANDREW	59 60	ARABELLA 20				
3688	SPENCER	ST ANDREW	117 120					
4850	SPICE	ST JOHN	4 13					
4468	ST AMAND	ST NORBERT	69	GENEVIENE 9	CHARLES 7	GEORGE 6	JULIE 4	ANNIE 1
4848	ST CYR	SFX		ALEXANDRE 10	J BAPTISTE 4	LIZETTE 3	ROGER 1	
4582	ST DENIS	SFX	140 141	ELZEAR 7	AMBROISE 4			
4583	ST DENIS	SFX	195 196					
4584	ST DENIS	SFX	133	ALEXANDRE 21	GUILLAUME 20	JOHN 18	J BAPTISTE 16	MARIE 15
4584	ST DENIS	SFX	133	ELISE 13	CATHERINE 11	PHILOMENE 7	ROSALIE 4	
4585	ST DENIS	SFX	133	ROSALIE 20	JOSEPH 15			
4587	ST DENIS	ST NORBERT	113 101	MARGUERITE 10	PIERRE 7	PAULINE 5	EMERANCE 1	
4845	ST DENIS	SFX	195 196	FRANCOIS 16	PIERRE 14	ELISE 12	MARIE 11	ROSALIE 9
4846	ST DENIS	SFX	186 187	ADELAIDE 6				
4847	ST DENIS	SFX	148 150	CHARLES 3				
5082	ST DENIS	ST NORBERT	117 114	CELESTIN 20				
4398	ST GERMAIN	ST BONIFACE	87 77					
4410	ST GERMAIN	SFX	100 101	ETIENNE 4	J BAPTISTE 2	MICHEL 1		

TABLE 4: GEOGRAPHICAL LOCATION AND
CHILDREN OF MANITOBA FAMILIES, 1870

ID	FAMILY	PARISH	AT OR BETWEEN	CHILDREN AND AGES AT NEXT BIRTHDAY				
4592	ST GERMAIN	ST NORBERT	151	MARGUERITE 17	FREDERICK 15	PIERRE 12	J BAPTISTE 10	ISABELLE 8
4592	ST GERMAIN	ST NORBERT	151	JOSEPH 7	JOSEPH 6	FRANCOIS 3		
4595	ST GERMAIN	SFX	99	MARIE 7	NORBERT 5	HENRIETTE 4		
4596	ST GERMAIN	SFX	101	EDWARD 10	ROSINE 5			
4597	ST GERMAIN	SFX	127	ROSINE 13	MELANIE 11	PHILOMENE 8	FRANCOIS 5	ST PIERRE 4
4598	ST GERMAIN	SFX	127	MARIE 2		NAPOLEON 1		
4599	ST GERMAIN	SFX	102	MARIE 4	EMILIE 2			
4601	ST GERMAIN	SFX	100 101					
4602	ST GERMAIN	ST NORBERT	140 138	CLARA 3	NAPOLEON 15	SIMON 13	ALEXANDRE 11	VIRGINIE 7
4603	ST GERMAIN	ST NORBERT	165	AUGUSTIN 17	ALFRED 5			
4603	ST GERMAIN	ST NORBERT	141	IDA 3	JULIE 1			
4604	ST GERMAIN	ST NORBERT	141	MARIE 18	PIERRE 17	MARGUERITE 16	J BAPTISTE 13	ADOLPHIS 11
4604	ST GERMAIN	ST NORBERT	140	PIERRE 24	MARIANNE 22	CHARLES 21	JOSEPH 16	AMABLE 13
4606	ST GERMAIN	ST BONIFACE	44 41	LOUIS 3				
4606	ST LUC	STE ANNE	5					
4608	ST LUC	STE ANNE	16 15					
4126	ST MATTE	ST NORBERT	142 140	MARGUERITE 15	BAPTISTE 14	ALEXANDRE 13	ANDRE 12	MARTIN 11
4610	ST MATTE	STE AGATHE		NAPOLEON 3	ROGER 1			
4610	ST MATTE	STE AGATHE	73 108	MARGUERITE 14	RACHEL 12	NORBERT 10	FRANCOIS 8	PATRICE 5
4613	ST PIERRE	STE AGATHE	35	MARGARET 2				
4466	STALKER	*HEADINGLY	44	ISADORE 18	ALEXANDER 14	SARAH 12		
4125	STANLEY	ST BONIFACE	174*	CHRISTINE 19	CAROLINE 15	ELIZABETH 10	JAMES 1	
4124	STAR	ST PETER	28 55	FLORENCE 8	ALICE 8	FANNY 7		
4123	STEEL	ST JOHN	99 101	HENRY 1				
4473	STEVENS	ST ANDREW	99 101	RICHARD 18	SARA 16	GEORGE 13	ROBERT 11	JEREMIE 9
4474	STEVENS	ST ANDREW	99 101	WILLIAM 6	ANNE 5	HARIET 2	JOHN 1	
4475	STEVENS	ST CLEMENT	44	MARIANN 17	SARA 13	ANDRE 8	PHILIP 4	ROBERT 2
4475	STEVENS	ST CLEMENT	44	RICHARD 1				
4476	STEVENS	ST ANDREW	99 101					
4857	STEVENS	ST PETER	133 167					
4868	STEVENS	ST ANDREW	122 129	MARGUERITE 12				
4479	STEVENS	HEADINGLY	26					
4482	STEVENSON	HEADINGLY	61 62			FELIX 6		
4483	STEVENSON	HEADINGLY	61	THOMAS 22	REDERICK 20	BARBARA 19	ISABELLA 16	WILLIAM 12
4483	STEVENSON	HEADINGLY	61	GEORGE 10				
4859	STEVENSON	ST PETER	74*					
4860	STEVENSON	ST PETER	31 46	CAROLINE 2				
4861	STEVENSON	ST PETER	175 171					
4862	STEVENSON	ST PETER	56*	SAMUEL 17	MARY 10	MARGARET 4	RODERICK 2	
4863	STEVENSON	ST PETER	1 8					
4864	STEVENSON	ST PETER	56 74					
4865	STEVENSON	ST PETER	175 171	JOHN 13	FENIA 12	MARY 9	ELIZABETH 8	SAMINA 6
4866	STEVENSON	ST PETER	175 171	SARA 3	EDWARD 1			
4867	STEVENSON	ST PETER	8 17					
4867	STEVENSON	ST PETER	167 175	WILLIAM 20	CATHERINE 17	MARGUERITE 13	ELISE 9	JANE 7
4869	STEVENSON	ST PETER	85 95	CHARLES 6	MAGNUS 3			
4869	STEVENSON	ST PETER	85 95					
4890	STEVENSON	ST PETER	4 13					
4488	STEWART	ST JOHN	29	ROBERT 14	JAMES 12	ALEX 8		
4489	STODGARLL	ST JAMES	6 33	HENRY 16	JAMES 10	ELIE 8		
4486	STRANGE	ST JOHN						

ID	FAMILY	PARISH	AT OR BETWEEN	CHILDREN AND AGES AT NEXT BIRTHDAY
4485	STRANGER	ST CLEMENT	64 70	ELIZABETH 12 · SOPHIA 5
4910	STRANGER	ST PETER	167*	HARIET 2
4911	STRANGER	ST JAMES		
4491	SUTHERLAND	KILDONAN	25 28	CHRISTIE 6 · JOHN 4 · ALEXANDER 3 · CATHERINE 1
4492	SUTHERLAND	KILDONAN	19 20	
4493	SUTHERLAND	KILDONAN	31 32	
4494	SUTHERLAND	KILDONAN	25 28	
4497	SUTHERLAND	ST PETER	133 167	ALEXANDER 9 · ALICE 4 · RODRIC 2 · MARGUERITE 2 · CATHERINE 13
4500	SUTHERLAND	KILDONAN	25 28	JOHN 1
4504	SUTHERLAND	KILDONAN	25	WILLIAM 23 · DONALD 21 · MARY 19 · GEORGE 17
4504	SUTHERLAND	KILDONAN	25	JERIMIAH 10
4507	SUTHERLAND	KILDONAN	25 28	
4515	SUTHERLAND	ST JOHN	9 25	CHRISTIE 2
4516	SUTHERLAND	POPLAR PT	36	THOMAS 22 · EDWIN 17 · CATHERINE 15 · SARAH 9 · CHARLES 5
4517	SUTHERLAND	ST ANDREW	38	GEORGE 9 · MARY 7 · JOHN 6 · ANN 3
4519	SUTHERLAND	ST BONIFACE	117 113	
4522	SUTHERLAND	KILDONAN	24	CHRISTIANA 7 · ANN 5 · ALEXANDER 4
4536	SUTHERLAND	ST JOHN	25*	DONALD 23 · ALEXANDER 21 · MORRISON 19 · HECTOR 18 · ANGUS 17
4536	SUTHERLAND	ST JOHN	25*	WILLIAM 13 · JAMES 10 · RODERICK 10 · MARGARET 16 · CATHERINE 15
4536	SUTHERLAND	ST JOHN	25*	CHRISTIE 11 · MARY 5
4538	SUTHERLAND	ST PAUL	22	JOHN 18 · ALFRED 6 · MARY 2
4541	SUTHERLAND	ST BONIFACE	117 113	JOSEPH 3 · DAMASE 1 · ISAIE 10 · SARAH 18 · MAGDELEINE 13
4543	SUTHERLAND	ST BONIFACE	117 113	JOSEPH 24 · MARIE 19 · ALEXANDER 16 · PETER 14 · ROBERT 12
4552	SUTHERLAND	ST BONIFACE	117 113	CHRISTINE 16 · CATHERINE 18 · WILLIAM 4 · FLORA 2
4552	SUTHERLAND	PORTAGE	133 111	SAMUEL 20 · PIERRE 6 · SIMEON 1
4562	SWAIN	SFX	55	DANIEL 8 · WILLIAM 3 · JULIA 5 · VERONIQUE 3
4563	SWAIN	BAIE S PAUL	158 182	CHARLES 5 · WILLIAM 11 · ISABELLA 7
4565	SWAIN	ST ANDREW	165 164	LAROSE 11
4566	SWAIN	ST ANDREW	141	CHARLOTTE 41 · WILLIAM 18
4573	SWAIN	HEADINGLY	45 49	THERESE 20 · ALEXANDER 18 · FELAIS 18 · ELIZABETH 17 · ELZEAR 15
4574	SWAIN	POPLAR PT		
4575	SWAIN	ST CLEMENT	105 106	JANE 14
4914	SWAIN	ST CHARLES	75	NANCY 13 · JOHN 12 · JOSEPH 11 · MARIE 4
4915	SWAIN	HEADINGLY	50	MARGARET 12 · MARY 6 · HARRIET 4 · JOHN 2 · AMABLE 2
4916	SWAIN	ST CHARLES	16 57	JOHN 14 · WILLIAM 9 · J BAPTISTE 6 · LOUISE 5
4560	SWAN	ST JOHN	7 2	
4921	SYMESON	HEADINGLY	64	
4620	TACHE	ST BONIFACE	81 87	
4576	TAIT	ST JAMES	22	THOMAS 12 · THIMOLEON 10 · COLLIN 10 · ELLEN 9 · MARY 6
4577	TAIT	ST ANDREW		JOHN 33 · FRANCOISE 11 · MARY 13
4578	TAIT	ST ANDREW	2	MARY 13 · WILLIAM 3 · JOHN 10 · ROBERT 8 · ELIZA 5
4578	TAIT	ST ANDREW	2	WILLIAM 3
4617	TAIT	ST PETER	46 56	JOHN 16 · WILLIAM 16 · LIZA 13 · ALEXANDER 8 · BARBARA 3
4618	TAIT	ST JAMES	43	CHRISTIANA 11 · JAMES 9 · ELIZABETH 7 · ANDREW 1
4619	TAIT	POPLAR PT	79	DAVID 3 · HENRY 1
4622	TAIT	ST ANDREW	34	GEORGE 32 · CHARLES 30 · MARY 28 · ELIZABETH 24 · ANN 19
4625	TAIT	*KILDONAN	14	JOHN 19 · WILLIAM 17 · ANN 15 · ROBERT 13 · DAVID 8
4626	TAIT	HEADINGLY	14	MARY 16 · JOSEPH 14 · MARGARET 12 · JOHN 10 · WILLIAM 8
4626	TAIT	HEADINGLY	14	ALEXANDER 4 · GEORGE 1
4627	TAIT	HEADINGLY	16	JANE 6 · ISABELLA 5
4627	TAIT	HEADINGLY	16	

TABLE 4: GEOGRAPHICAL LOCATION AND
CHILDREN OF MANITOBA FAMILIES, 1870

ID	FAMILY	PARISH	AT OR BETWEEN		CHILDREN AND AGES AT NEXT BIRTHDAY
4931	TAIT	ST CLEMENT	61	62	
4623	TALLOCH	ST ANDREW	117	120	
4628	TANNER	POPLAR PT	75	76	
4629	TANNER	POPLAR PT	75	76	
4630	TATE	POPLAR PT	73	74	
4631	TATE	POPLAR PT	74		WILLIAM 2; WILLIAM 16; URBAIN 16; FLORA 8; ELISE 2
4631	TATE	POPLAR PT	74		JOHN 17; CATHERINE 8; MARIA 8; THOMAS 6; GILBERT 1
4920	TATE	HIGH BLUFF	62		CHARLES 10; MARY 6; JAMES 6; FANNY 5
4920	TATE	HIGH BLUFF	62		ALEXANDER 1
4922	TATE	ST PETER	133	167	JOSEPH 9; ANTOINE 10
4923	TAYLOR	POPLAR PT	73		CAROLINE 12; PHILIP 10; COLIN 10; ALFRED 7; MARGARET 2
4633	TAYLOR	ST ANDREW	118		EDWARD 7; ELIZABETH 6; MARIANNE 6; VICTOIRE 4
4634	TAYLOR	POPLAR PT	57		THOMAS 2; CHARLES 1
4635	TAYLOR	POPLAR PT	60	63	GEORGE 15; ISABEL 12; THOMAS 8; LOUISE 8; VICTOR 2
4636	TAYLOR	ST ANDREW	170	197	MARIANNE 2; EDWARD 1
4637	TAYLOR	POPLAR PT	6		DAVID 25; ANNIE 23; HERBERT 23; HARRIET 7; FLORA 5
4639	TAYLOR	POPLAR PT	60		MARY 11; SARAH 10; ELEONORA 10; WILLIAM 4
4640	TAYLOR	ST PAUL	27		EDWARD 3; MARGARET 1; FLORA 10
4641	TAYLOR	ST PAUL	27		JOHN 11; MARY 10; WILLIAM 4
4643	TAYLOR	HEADINGLY	19		ELIZABETH 9; EMMA 4
4932	TAYLOR	ST ANDREW	65	88	
4933	TAYLOR	POPLAR PT	82		
4934	TAYLOR	ST ANDREW	56		WILLIAM 22; JAMES 20; HENRY 20; CHARLOTTE 19; ALEXANDER 17
4934	TAYLOR	POPLAR PT	53		JOHN 12; ELIZABETH 11; ALFRED 11; BENJAMIN 9; DAVID 7
4934	TAYLOR	POPLAR PT	53		ALBERT 3; FLORA 5; ALBERT 3
4935	TAYLOR	POPLAR PT	53		ELIZA 7; MAURICE 5
4936	TAYLOR	ST ANDREW	48	50	CATHERINE 3
4937	TAYLOR	ST CLEMENT	6		WILLIAM 22; JANE 18; MARY 18; ELIZABETH 16
4938	TAYLOR	POPLAR PT	62		
4940	TAYLOR	ST ANDREW	48	50	
4941	TAYLOR	ST JAMES	108	109	
4652	TELLEFSON	ST CLEMENT	58	63	MARIANNE 7; LOUISA 5; ANDREW 5; ANNE 3
4647	TEMPLETON	KILDONAN	94	88	ROBERT 9; JANE 7; WILLIAM 7; ELIZABETH 5
4939	THIBAULT	ST BONIFACE	19		EULALIE 14; MARGUERITE 12; FRANCOIS 12; HELENE 10; JOSEPH 9
4939	THIBAULT	ST BONIFACE	104		MARIE 1
4661	THIBAULT	ST BONIFACE	77	79	MARIE 17; PHILOMENE 13; ANN 13; ELIZABETH 12; PIERRE 5
4662	THIBERT	SFX	77	79	DOMITILDE 6; PIERRE 5; ELISE 5
4663	THIBERT	SFX	146		
4664	THIBERT	SFX	72		ANN 3; JEAN 4
990	THIBERT	SFX	146	147	JAMIMA 15; DOLPHIS 8; VICTOIRE 8; CATHERINE 4
4532	THOMAS	ST PETER	146	147	LOUIS 2
4535	THOMAS	ST PETER	1	8	
4544	THOMAS	*KILDONAN	133	167	
4545	THOMAS	PORTAGE	6	7	
4546	THOMAS	ST PAUL	11		EDWARD 13; ERNESTINE 8; VICTORINE 8; CATHERINE 4
4547	THOMAS	ST PAUL	13		MARGUERITE 24; JANE 16; JANE 16; ALBERT 15
4547	THOMAS	ST PETER	171*		NANCY 9; RODERIC 3; BETHSY 16
4671	THOMAS	ST PETER	171*		JESSIE 3
	THOMAS	ST PETER	8	17	

CHILDREN OF MANITOBA FAMILIES, 1870

ID	FAMILY	PARISH	AT OR BETWEEN	CHILDREN AND AGES AT NEXT BIRTHDAY
4674	THOMAS	ST PETER	31*	BETSY 10, HENRI 7
4677	THOMAS	ST ANDREW	54	CATHERINE 11, MATHILDA 10, ALEXANDRE 2
4678	THOMAS	ST ANDREW	99	MARGUERITE 1
4686	THOMAS	ST PAUL	10	EDWARD 7, WILLIAM 5, JOHN 5
4687	THOMAS	ST PAUL	9	SARAH 28, ALFRED 22, JOHN 16
4858	THOMAS	ST PETER	8 17	EDWARD 2
4888	THOMAS	ST PETER	56 74	FRANCOISE 21, JOHN 19, DAVID 15, MARIAN 12, ARABELLA 8
4888	THOMAS	ST PETER	56 74	NANCY 6
4889	THOMAS	ST CLEMENT	55 58	
4891	THOMAS	ST CLEMENT	92	FANNY 8, JEREMIE 4, JANE 2
4892	THOMAS	ST CLEMENT	133 167	ROBERT 2
4893	THOMAS	ST PETER	20 21	MARIANNE 11, SIMON 8, ALEXANDER 7, ALBERT 5, WILLIAM 4
4894	THOMAS	KILDONAN	16 19	JOHN 3
4951	THOMPSON	ST ANDREW	71	
4952	THOMPSON	ST ANDREW		
4690	THORN	SFX	148	GEORGE 16, JOHN 14, DAVID 11, MARY 39, ROBERT 7
4689	THORNE	SFX	148	MARIA 16, CATHERINE 21, JOHN 26, MARIA 10, FANNY 14
4698	TODD	ST JAMES	33	ELIZABETH 15, WILLIAM 14, SARAH 12
4956	TODD	ST JAMES	33	DONALD 4
4957	TODD	ST JAMES	37 39	
4958	TODD	ST CLEMENT	64	JANE 1, WILLIAM 18, DONALD 16, ISABEL 20
4962	TOURANGEAU	ST VITAL	19 28	BIENAEME 12, HERMENEGILD 12, AMABLE 9, JONAS 7
4963	TOURANJEAU	ST NORBERT	148 144	JOSEPH 4, PIERRE 2
4965	TOURIN	ST BONIFACE	17 16	
4700	TOUROND	SFX	150	DAVID 20, CALIXTE 18, PIERRE 16, PATRICE 14, ELZEAR 12
4700	TOUROND	SFX	150	FRANCOIS 10, CHARLES 8, MARIE 6, ELISE 3, HYACINTHE 1
4704	TOUROND	ST NORBERT	161 159	ELISE 21, JOSEPH 18, HENRI 15
4705	TOUROND	ST NORBERT	42	ELISE 9, ROSALIE 7, REGIS 5, FRANCOIS 3, MARIE 2
4706	TOUROND	ST NORBERT	159	JEAN 14, JOSEPH 11, VINCENT 7, BAPTISTE 6, CLEMENT 4
4706	TOUROND	ST NORBERT	159	JACQUE 2
4966	TRAVELLER	ST BONIFACE	133 167	BAPTISTE 5, ROSALIE 3, ALPHONSINE 1
4714	TRISTEN	ST PETER	222	FLORA 10, JOSEPH 3
4718	TROTTIER	SFX	195 196	SUSANNAH 5, JOHN 3
4711	TROTTIER	SFX	195 196	ALEXANDRE 7
4712	TROTTIER	SFX	195 196	JOHNNY 10, WILLIAM 8, EDWARD 6, MARIE 3
4970	TROTTIER	SFX	202 204	MARIE 4, PATRICE 3, ROSALIE 1
4971	TROTTIER	BAIE S PAUL	182 194	ANDREW 16, JOSEPH 13, MARGUERITE 11, ALBERT 9, CUTHBERT 7
4972	TROTTIER	BAIE S PAUL	182 194	CHARLES 5, MARY 2
4972	TROTTIER	BAIE S PAUL	207 215	
4973	TROTTIER	BAIE S PAUL	127 130	MARY, ANDREW 2, ALEXANDRE, CATHERINE, FRANCOIS
4974	TROTTIER	SFX	6 33	
4723	TRUDEL	ST JOHN		
4719	TRUTHWAIT	ST ANDREW	102 104	THOMAS 23, ANDREW 21, SARA 19, JANE 17, JACOB 15
4722	TRUTHWAIT	ST ANDREW	104	HARIET 13, PASCHAL 14, MODESTE 12, SARAH 9, PATRICE 6
4722	TRUTHWAIT	ST ANDREW	104	NORBERT 16
4725	TURCOTTE	ST BONIFACE	63*	WILLIAM 1
4727	TURCOTTE	ST CHARLES	99	FRANCIS 2
4984	TURNER	ST ANDREW	91 92	
4985	TURNER	ST JAMES	57	
5042	VALETTE	SFX	185 189	JULIEN 20, CECILE 18, CHARLES 16, JOSEPH 13, PATRICE 9

ID	FAMILY	PARISH	AT OR BETWEEN		CHILDREN AND AGES AT NEXT BIRTHDAY
5042	VALETTE	SFX	185	189	EMILIE 6, SUPLIEN 4
4997	VALIQUETTE	STE ANNE	61	60	PHILOMENE 8, JOSEPH 6
4996	VALLEE	ST BONIFACE	81	87	JOSEPHTE 16, LOUISON 13, CUTHBERT 12, CATHERINE 11, ROSE 1
5043	VALLEE	SFX	139	142	ROSE 19, EUCHARISTE 16, MELANIE 14, ANTOINE 10, EULALIE 7
5051	VANDAL	STE ANNE	18		MARIE 4, JUSTINE 1
5051	VANDAL	STE ANNE	18		
5053	VANDAL	STE AGATHE	265*		NANCY 10, VIRGINIE 9, MARIE 8, FREDERICK 6, ELIZA 5
5053	VANDAL	ST NORBERT	265*		JULIEN 3, ANTOINE 20, ISABELLE 19, JOSEPHTE 19, MELANIE 14
5054	VANDAL	ST NORBERT	123		PIERRE 23, JEAN 8, PHILOMENE 3
5054	VANDAL	ST NORBERT	123		MARIE 10
5056	VANDAL	ST NORBERT	84	81	CATHERINE 43, LOUISE 24, ROGER 21, MELANIE 18, MOISE 15
5057	VANDAL	ST NORBERT	138		JOSEPH 13, ROSALIE 11, WILLIAM 11, ANNIE 8, MODESTE 6
5059	VANDAL	ST NORBERT	120		NORBERT 2
5059	VANDAL	ST NORBERT	120		
5060	VANDAL	ST NORBERT	120		MARGUERITE 1
5061	VANDAL	ST NORBERT	140	138	
5063	VANDAL	STE AGATHE	541	535	
5064	VANDAL	ST ANDREW	287		CATHERINE 18, VERONIQUE 12, OLIVIER 10, LOUISE 8, AUGUSTIN 5
5067	VANDAL	ST BONIFACE	82	88	MARGUERITE 2
5067	VANDAL	ST BONIFACE			NORMAN 14
5068	VANDAL	POPLAR PT	113	101	
5069	VANDAL	ST NORBERT	541	535	ROSALIE 29, FRANCOIS 21, JOSEPH 18, ELZEAR 14, BERNARD 11
5073	VANDAL	STE AGATHE	284		JOHN 9, MARGARET 8, LOUIS 8, MARIANNE 6, JULIE 1
5062	VANDALLE	ST ANDREW	285		MARIE 9, LOUIS 8, FIRMIN 7, ANTOINE 5, LOUISE 3
5070	VANDALLE	ST ANDREW	285		ADELE 1
5070	VANDALLE	ST ANDREW	79	99	
5076	VANDRY	ST BONIFACE	79	99	TOUSSAINT 4, ALFRED 2, MARIE 1, JOSEPHTE 1
5077	VANDRY	ST BONIFACE	70		MARIE 5, JULIENNE 5, JUSTINE 3, PIERRE 3
5084	VENNE	STE AGATHE	541		J BAPTISTE 8, JOSEPH 19, PIERRE 17, GUILLAUME 18
5085	VENNE	ST BONIFACE	86	84	MICHEL 23, ALEXANDRE 19, WILLIAM 17, JOSEPHTE 1, VIRGINIE 16
5086	VENNE	ST NORBERT	86		SOLOMAN 14, JOSEPHTE 14, DAVID 12, JOSEPHTE 9, WILLIAM 4
5090	VENNE	ST NORBERT	86		ALEXANDRE 3
5091	VENNE	ST NORBERT	157		JOHN 12, WILLIAM 10, JEAN 9, NAPOLEON 6, ALEXANDRE 5
5091	VENNE	ST NORBERT	157		LAROSE 2
5094	VERMETTE	ST NORBERT	114*		ALEXANDRE 4, JOSEPH 4, VIRGINIE 3, ANGELIQUE 5
5094	VERMETTE	ST NORBERT	150		TOUSSAINT 23, AUGUSTIN 22, FRANCOIS 20, MAXIME 25
5095	VERMETTE	ST NORBERT	119		LOUIS 16, ROGER 10, VIRGINIE 6, ELIZA 5
5099	VERMETTE	ST NORBERT	101		ANNIE 1
5100	VERMETTE	ST NORBERT	157	148	EDWARD 10, JOSEPH 7, NORBERT 6, ROSALIE 4, MARIE 2
5101	VERMETTE	ST NORBERT	94	91	
5102	VERSAILLE	ST NORBERT	165	161	MARIE 9, JOSEPH 7, ROSALIE 19, ELISE 3, CLEMENCE 1
5104	VERSAILLE	ST NORBERT	76	75	BAPTISTE 26, MICHEL 22, PAUL 30, CUTHBERT 13
5106	VILBRUN	ST NORBERT	14		LEON 24, MAXIME 24, GUILLAUME 10, JOHN 5
5010	VILLEBRUN	ST BONIFACE	17		THOMAS 17, FIBBER 14, FRANCIS 10, JOHN 5
5118	VINCENT	ST PAUL	21		DONALD 6, JOHN 3, WILLIAM 1, FLORA 1
5015	VINCENT	ST PAUL	133	167	
5016	VINCENT	ST PAUL	16	57	
5018	VINCENT	ST PAUL			
5129	VINCENT	ST PAUL			ALBERT 4, ELIZABETH 2, CATHERINE 5, MARIE 3
5017	VINSON	ST PETER			JOSEPH 8, MODESTE 7, CAROLINE 2, SOPHIE 2
5021	VIVIER	ST CHARLES			

ID	FAMILY	PARISH	AT OR BETWEEN	CHILDREN AND AGES AT NEXT BIRTHDAY
5026	VIVIER	POPLAR PT	58	ELISE 1
5033	VIVIER	SFX		MARGUERITE 21
5132	VIVIER	POPLAR PT	68	ALEXIS 10, MARY 9, MADELEINE 3, GUILLAUME 1
5136	VIVIER	ST CHARLES	181	BERNARD 16, MARIE 14, ELZEAR 12, MARIE 5
5140	VIVIER	SFX	190	J BAPTISTE 14
5215	VIVIER	POPLAR PT		
5149	WAGNER	*ST ANDREW	138	MARY 12, TUVINS 10, MARGUERITE 8, ELIZABETH 6, CHARLOTTE 4
5149	WAGNER	*ST ANDREW	138	CATHERINE 2
5216	WALKER	PORTAGE		PETER 32
5217	WALLER	ST ANDREW	88	
5219	WARD	SFX	196	MARGUERITE 10, JOHN 7, MARY 6, JAMES 5, JANE 1
5221	WARD	STE ANNE	199	
5227	WASTE	ST PETER	3	
5222	WATT	ST ANDREW	56 74	GEORGE 12, RACHEL 12, HECTOR 7, MATHILDE 4, CHRISTINE 1
5223	WATT	ST CLEMENT	120 122	WILLIAM 10, ELIZABETH 8, ANN 5, JOHN 3
5224	WATT	STE AGATHE	21	
5225	WELLS	SFX	80 87	
5226	WELLS	POPLAR PT		
5156	WELSH	ST CHARLES	14	SARAH 1, CECILE 1
5157	WELSH	ST CHARLES	14 16	WILLIAM 3
5159	WELSH	ST CHARLES	96 105	
5231	WELSH	ST NORBERT	31 27	BETSY 13, MARIE 10, JOSEPH 7, DAMASE 4
5177	WHIMSTER	KILDONAN	20 21	
5164	WHITE	ST JOHN	46	ANN 19, MARY 15, JAMES 13, SARAH 11, JANE 9
5165	WHITE	ST NORBERT	256	ELIZABETH 20, ROGER 14, JULIEN 9, NAPOLEON 8, MARIE 6
5165	WHITE	ST NORBERT	256	GENEVIEVE 5, JUSTINE 1
5166	WHITEFORD	ST CLEMENT	46	JOSEPH 4, SARAH 14, GEORGE 8, ANDREW 10
5170	WHITEFORD	PORTAGE	133 111	JACOB 17, JAMES 14, WILLIAM 12
5175	WHITEFORD	PORTAGE	133 111	UPHENIA 16
5175	WHITEFORD	SFX	202 204	JOHN 18, JAMES 16, MAXIME 14, ELZEAR 11, NAPOLEON 9
5179	WHITEFORD	SFX	202 204	MARIE 4, GENEVIENE 1
5184	WHITEWAY	ST CLEMENT	45	NATHALIE 4, ARCHIBALD 2, WILLIAM 4
5261	WILD	POPLAR PT	84	GEORGE 14, EDWARD 2
5260	WILLIAM	ST PETER	174 189	CHARLES 15, JOHN 14, ANDRE 11, JOSEPH 9, THOMAS 1
5259	WILLIAM	ST PETER	174 189	NANCY 12, JAMES 13, ELISE 3
5258	WILLIAMSON	ST PETER	56 74	HENRY 6, SUSANNAH 5, JOSEPH 3
5194	WILSON	POPLAR PT	56	MARY 20, JOSEPH 13, GEORGE 11, PETER 9
5194	WISHEART	POPLAR PT	48	BARBARA 15, MARY 2, PETER 11, MARGARET 7
5271	WISHEART	POPLAR PT	48	DAVID 5, JOHN 6
5272	WITIMASE	PORTAGE		LIZETTE 7, MARY 4, CHRISTIAN 1
5273	WOOD	PORTAGE	13 6	
5291	WOODDINGTON	ST JOHN	36	JOSEPH 22, PETER 20, ANN 15, CATHERINE 12, WILLIAM 10
5274	WORK	ST PAUL	13 6	ANNABELLA 3
5275	WORK	ST PAUL	36	
5277	WRIGHT	ST JOHN	48 7	
5207	WRIGHTMAN	ST JOHN	94 96	
5208	YOUNG	ST ANDREW	50	NAPOLEON 9, MARIE 5, ROSALIE 3
5210	ZASTE	ST NORBERT	48	EMILIE 10, PAULINE 8, JOSEPH 5
5210	ZASTE	SFX	77	ISIDORE 17, MARIE 19, GUILLELMINE 14, LOUIS 3, ANDRE 22

TABLE 4: GEOGRAPHICAL LOCATION AND
CHILDREN OF MANITOBA FAMILIES, 1870

ID	FAMILY	PARISH	AT OR BETWEEN	CHILDREN AND AGES AT NEXT BIRTHDAY
5278	ZASTRE	SFX	1O7 .	MARIE 5

Table 5:

Recognition of Riverlot Occupants by the Government of Canada

TABLE 5: RECOGNITION OF RIVERLOT OCCUPANTS BY THE GOVERNMENT OF CANADA

OCCUPANT NAMED BY SURVEYORS	PARISH	LOT	AREA	AREA CLAIMED	PATENTEE	YEAR OF PATENT
ADAGH BAPTISTE	SFX	173	78	78	KENNEDY LACKLAN	1877
ADAMS CHARLES	HIGH BLUFF	51	116	116	ADAMS CHARLES	1877
ADAMS GEORGE	HIGH BLUFF	24	479	479	ADAMS GEORGE	1877
ADAMS JAMES	HIGH BLUFF	52	99	99	ADAMS JAMES	1875
ADAMS JOSEPH	HIGH BLUFF	58	132	132	ADAMS JOSEPH	1877
ADAMS ROBERT	HIGH BLUFF	53	99	99	ADAMS ROBERT	1875
ADHMER PAT	ST CLEMENT	111	53	53	MCLENNAN MURDOCK	80
ADHMER PAT	ST CLEMENT	112	51	51		
AITKINS JOHN	ST ANDREW	193	38	38	HAY ROBERT	77
ALCOCK THOMAS	HIGH BLUFF	46	670	112	BISHOP OF RUPERTSLAND	1880
ALCOCK WILLIAM	HIGH BLUFF	50	241	241	ALCOCK WILLIAM	1877
ALLARD BAPTISTE	BAIE S PAUL	6	116	116	H B CO	1880
ALLARD BAPTISTE	SFX	109	81	81	FORGET JOSEPH	85
ALLARD BAPTISTE	SFX	130	100	100	ROSS WILLIA	93
ALLARD MICHEL	SFX	108	188	94	ALLARD MICHEL	1878
ALLARD OCTAVE	ST VITAL	4	132	132	ROBERTS JOHN	1878
ALLARY ANTOINE	BAIE S PAUL	234	92	92	SMITH DONALD	1877
ALLARY FRANCOIS	BAIE S PAUL	232	178	178	BANNATYNE AGB	1878
ALLARY GEORGE	STE AGATHE	88	123	123	ALLEN GEORGE G	81
ALLEN GEORGE	STE AGATHE	90	123	123	ALLEN GEORGE G	81
AMAND JOHN	ST ANDREW	258	44	22	ALLAN JOHN	1877
AMMOND JOHN	ST ANDREW	57	50	50	OMAND JOHN	75
AMSDEN	HEADINGLY	22	218	218	SMITH DONALD A	1875
ANDERSON CHARLES	HIGH BLUFF	38	160	160	ARMSON JAMES	81
ANDERSON ERIC	ST PAUL	175	74	74	THOMPSON CATHERINE	1883
ANDERSON ETAL	ST ANDREW	111	41	41	SAUNDERS WILLIAM	75
ANDERSON HENRY	PORTAGE	98	11	11	ANDERSON HENRY	1877
ANDERSON JAMES	ST ANDREW	92	66	66	ANDERSON JAMES	79
ANDERSON PETER	PORTAGE	174	33	33	MAWHINNEY ISAIAH	78
ANDERSON THOMAS	ST ANDREW	24	40	40	ANDERSON THOMAS	1879
ANNAL JOHN	ST ANDREW	257	43	43		
ANNAL JOHN	BAIE S PAUL	245	16	16	FISHER GEORGE	1878
ARCON BAPTISTE	BAIE S PAUL	242	140	140	CHENIER FELIX	1882
ARCON JOSEPH	POPLAR PT	68	128	128		
ATBINSON JOHN	SFX	2	116	116	AYMOND SERAPHIN	1876
AYMOND SERAPHIN	ST NORBERT	47	170	170	GRAHAM JAMES	1879
AYOTTE GEORGE	ST CLEMENT	49	72	72	BOYD ALFRED	86
BADGER JOHN	ST CLEMENT	77	50	50	COLELEUGH FREDERICK	.
BADGER JOHN	ST CLEMENT	31	169	169	BANNATYNE A G B	82
BAILEY JOSEPH	ST CLEMENT	126	54	54	BAILEY JAMES	
BAILIE WILLIAM	ST ANDREW	79	28	3	TRUSTEES	1887
BALDWIN JAMES	ST CHARLES	84	90	90	MACARTHUR DUNCAN	1881
BALLENDINE CHARLES	ST ANDREW	113	60	60	BALLENDINE CHARLES	77
BALLENDINE GEORGE	ST ANDREW	157	54	54	BALLENDINE GEORGE	75
BALLENDINE GEORGE	ST ANDREW	66	49	49	BALLENTINE GEORGE	75
BALLENDINE JAMES	ST ANDREW	56	59	59	BALLENTINE ELEANO	2
BALLENDINE JOHN	ST PAUL	35	150	150	KENNEDY JOHN	1878
BALLENDINE JOHN	ST PAUL	89	124	124	BALLENDINE JOHN	1878
BALLENDINE A G B	ST VITAL	1	181	181	BANNATYNE A G B	1876
BANNATYNE A G B	HIGH BLUFF	30	145	145	FRASER ALEXANDER	1877

GOVERNMENT OF CANADA

OCCUPANT NAMED BY SURVEYORS		PARISH	LOT	AREA	AREA CLAIMED	PATENTEE		YEAR OF PATENT
BANNATYNE	AGB	PORTAGE	47	161	161	MCCULLOCH	WILLIAM	82
BANNERMAN	ALEXANDER	KILDONAN	21	71	71	BANNERMAN	ALEXANDER	1878
BANNERMAN	ALEXANDER	KILDONAN	87	79	79	BANNERMAN	ALEX	1882
BANNERMAN	DAVID	HIGH BLUFF	28	280	280	BANNERMAN	DAVID	1877
BANNERMAN	DONALD	KILDONAN	20	102	102	BANNERMAN	DONALD	1878
BANNERMAN	DONALD	ST PAUL	38	107	107	BANNERMAN	DONALD	1878
BANNERMAN	DONALD	ST PAUL	86	159	159	BANNERMAN	DONALD	1882
BANNERMAN	GEORGE	ST JOHN	49	39	3	BROWN	MAGNUS	1875
BANNERMAN	GEORGE	KILDONAN	1	95	95	BANNERMAN	GEORGE	1875
BANNERMAN	SAMUEL	POPLAR PT	64	110	110	BANNERMAN	SAMUEL	1877
BARRON	CHARLES	SFX	140	133	133	BARRON	CHARLES	1875
BARRON	PIERRE	ST JAMES	47	36	36	SALTER	FREDERICK	82
BARRON ETAL	BARTHELETTE	STE AGATHE	97	154	154	BARRON	BARTHELETTE	1883
BASKERRIVILL	E J	STE AGATHE	50	115	112	MOFFATT	JOHN	1891
BAUCHEMAN	BENJ	ST NORBERT	126	83	83	HENRY	PIERRE	1882
BAULEE	BATTICE	POPLAR PT	55	67	67	WILSON	DANIEL	1875
BAUPRY	VICTOR	ST NORBERT	168	71	71	BEAUPIE	V J	1884
BAYLIS ETAL	GEORGE	ST CLEMENT	103	53	53	BANNATYNE	A G B	79
BEAUCHAMP	JOSEPH	ST CHARLES	7	45	45	CORREGAU	WILLIAM	1885
BEAUCHAMP	MRS	ST NORBERT	189	156	156	LA CORP ARCH	CR DE ST BO	1880
BEAUCHEMIN	BAPTISTE	ST CHARLES	59	86	86	BEAUCHEMIN	BAPTISTE	1875
BEDFORD	JAMES	STE AGATHE	51	131	131	HORNE	WARREN	1882
BEGG	CHARLES	ST CLEMENT	5	81	81	BEGG	CATHERINE S	82
BELANGER	ABRAHAM	ST NORBERT	94	61	61	BELANGER	ABRAHAM	1876
BELANGER	ABRAHAM	ST NORBERT	99	35	35	BELANGER	ABRAHAM	1876
BELL	ROBERT	STE AGATHE	57	87	87	SPINNING	EDWARD	1883
BELL	ROBERT	STE AGATHE	59	85	85	SPINNING	D	1882
BELLAMONE	FRANCOIS	BAIE S PAUL	235	153	153	BELLAMORE	ANDRE	1879
BELLAMORE	ANDRE	BAIE S PAUL	239	217	217	GOW	JOHN	1903
BENSON	JOHN	STE AGATHE	69	124	124	BERARD	BAPTISTE	1875
BERARD	BAPTISTE	ST BONIFACE	31	149	149	MCDONALD	GEORGINA	1882
BERARD	DANIEL	ST JAMES	65	57	57	TACHE	ALEXANDRE	1878
BERARD	FRANCIS	ST ANNE	67	192	192	CORP ARCH	C R DE ST B	1878
BERARD	LOUIS	ST BONIFACE	94	32	32	BERARD	MAXIME	1878
BERARD	MAXIME	ST ANNE	7	193	193	BERARD	EDOUAR	90
BERARD	PIERRE	ST NORBERT	54	142	142	MARION	SIMON	1879
BERARD	SIMON	ST ANNE	51	110	110	BERARD	AGB	1882
BERARD ETAL	ANDRE	ST NORBERT	122	105	105	BANNATYNE	JOHN	1886
BERCIA	BAPTISTE	SFX	73	89	89	TAYLOR	JEAN BTE	1877
BERCIA	BAPTISTE	SFX	76	144	144	BERCIA	JEAN BTE	1876
BERCIA	BEATRICE	SFX	178	100	100	BERCIA	DONALD A	1882
BERCIER	BAPTISTE	BAIE S PAUL	1	183	92	SMITH	ALEXIS	1884
BERCILER	JOSEPH	SFX	54	190	95	CAMPBELL	WILLIAM	1886
BERIAU	JOSEPH	ST NORBERT	3	181	181	RADFORD	JOHN	1901
BERIAU	JOSEPH	ST NORBERT	22	117	117	MULAIRE	CATHERINE	1885
BERIAULT	JOSEPH	STE AGATHE	630	171	171	BERIAULT	BERNARD	1889
BERLAND	GILBERT	SFX	38	100	100	LAVALLEE	PIERRE	1888
BERTHELET	ANTOINE	STE AGATHE	589	143	143	BERTHELET	ANTOINE	1880
BERTHELET JR	JOSEPH	STE AGATHE	585	218	218	BERTHELET	JOSEPH	1877
BERTHELET ST	JRJOSEPH	STE AGATHE	583	213	213	ROYAL	JOSEPH	1877
BETOURNEY	JUDGE	ST BONIFACE	23	99	99	CAUCHON	HON J E	1882

TABLE 5: RECOGNITION OF RIVERLOT OCCUPANTS BY THE GOVERNMENT OF CANADA

OCCUPANT NAMED BY SURVEYORS	PARISH	LOT	AREA	AREA CLAIMED	PATENTEE	YEAR OF PATENT
BIASS JOHN	POPLAR PT	45	129	129	BIASS JOHN	1875
BIRD DR CURTIS	ST PAUL	101	421	421	BIRD CURTIS J	77
BIRD FREDERICK A	PORTAGE	66	114	114	SCHULTZ JOHN	1879
BIRD GEORGE	ST PAUL	25	86	86	BIRD GEORGE	1883
BIRD GEORGE	ST PAUL	107	46	46	PRITCHARD ARCHIBALD	1877
BIRD HENRY	POPLAR PT	41	128	128	NONE	
BIRD JAMES	ST PAUL	63	126	126	SCHULTZ JOHN	1885
BIRD JOHN	ST ANDREW	69	121	61	BIRD HENRY	1875
BIRD JOHN	ST ANDREW	207	39	39	BIRD JOHN	1877
BIRD MORRIS	ST ANDREW	206	39	39	BIRD MORRIS	1878
BIRD THOMAS	ST PAUL	105	50	50	BIRD THOMAS	1875
BIRD WILLIAM SR	POPLAR PT	40	159	159	BIRD WILLIAM SR	1878
BIRDS L	ST CHARLES	91	104	104	MORRIS ALEXANDER	84
BIRSTON MAGNUS	SFX	159	48	48	BIRSTON MAGNUS	1880
BIRSTON MAGNUS	SFX	163	101	101	CRAWLEY CHARLES	1882
BLACK ALEXANDER	ST PAUL	53	116	116	BLACK ALEXANDER	78
BLACK ROBERT	ST ANDREW	8	133	133	NORQUAY JOHN	1883
BLONDEAU LOUIS	ST BONIFACE	8	76	76	BLONDEAU LOUIS	1883
BOCHETTE BAPTISTE	BAIE S PAUL	200	185	135	SAYER LOUIS	1880
BODDY THOMAS	PORTAGE	24	216	216		
BODDY THOMAS R	PORTAGE	134	334	33	BODDY THOMAS R	1882
BOISSIE ETAL E	STE AGATHE	137	108	108	BOISSY XAVIER	1892
BOITEAU ETAL ALEXIS	STE AGATHE	136	58	58		
BOITEAU ETAL JOSEPH	STE AGATHE	134	51	51	BOITEAU JOSEPH	1878
BONNEAU	SFX	132	113	113	BONNEAU	1903
BONNEAU BAPTISTE	BAIE S PAUL	28	42	42	BREDIN LUCY	1876
BONNEAU BASILE	BAIE S PAUL	27	79	79	BREDIN LUCY	1878
BONNEAU LOUIS	SFX	172	77	77	KENNEDY LACKLAN	1903
BONNEAU PIERRE	BAIE S PAUL	209	225	225	MALONEY DANIEL	1884
BOUCHARDETAL MICHEL	STE AGATHE	131	135	135	BOUCHARD MICHEL	1889
BOUCHER BAPTISTE	SFX	34	81	81	BOUCHER JEAN BTE	1877
BOUCHER ISADORE	SFX	42	81	81	POITRAS JOSEPH	1878
BOUCHER JOSEPH	SFX	43	78	78	MORGAN ROBERT	1877
BOUDREAU BAPTISTE	ST VITAL	8	44	44	BOUDREAU FRANCOIS	1878
BOUILLIER PIERRE	ST LAURENT	24	171	171	BOUILLIER PIERRE	1879
BOURKE ANDREW	ST CHARLES	25	102	102	BOURKE EDWIN	1875
BOURKE ANDREW	ST JAMES	30	105	105	BOURKE EDWIN	1885
BOURKE EDWIN	ST CHARLES	26	102	102	BOURKE EDWIN	1885
BOURKE EDWIN	ST CHARLES	27	101	101	BOURKE EDWIN	1876
BOURKE EDWIN	ST JAMES	36	72	72	BOURKE EDWIN	1876
BOURKE JOHN	ST CHARLES	12	90	90	BOURKE JOHN	1876
BOURKE JOHN	ST CHARLES	13	45	45	CHAMBERLAIN JOHN	1885
BOURKE JOHN	ST CHARLES	15	92	92	BOURKE JOHN	1879
BOURKE JOHN	ST JAMES	37	49	49	BOURKE JOHN	1879
BOURKE JOHN	ST JAMES	46	49	49	BOURKE JOHN	1875
BOURKE WALTER	ST CHARLES	28	99	99	BOURKE WALTER	1875
BOURKE WALTER	ST CHARLES	29	100	100	BOURKE WILLIAM	1880
BOURKE WALTER	ST JAMES	34	52	52	BOURKE WALTER	1878
BOURKE WALTER	ST JAMES	38	49	49	BOURKE WALTER	1883
BOURKE WILLIAM	ST CHARLES	24	102	102	BOURKE WILLIAM	1883
BOURKE WILLIAM	ST CHARLES	25	140	140	BOURKE WILLIAM	

OCCUPANT NAMED BY SURVEYORS		PARISH	LOT	AREA	AREA CLAIMED	PATENTEE		YEAR OF PATENT
BOUSQUETTE	BETSY	ST BONIFACE	111	77	77	BOUSQUETTE	BETTY	1877
BOUVIER	ANTOINE	SFX	191	106	106	BOUVIER	ANTOINE	1881
BOYD	ALFRED	ST CLEMENT	83	25	25	DENNEH JR	WILLIAM	1889
BOYD	ALFRED	ST CLEMENT	86	51	51	SINCLAIR WI	LLIAO3	
BOYD	HDN A	ST ANDREW	117	30	30	YOUNG ETAL	PETER R	77
BOYD ETAL	A	ST CLEMENT	26	49	49	COLCLEUGH	FLORA B	83
BOYD ETAL	ALFRED	ST JOHN	51	47	47	MCMICKEN	GEORGE	1875
BOYER	JOHN B	ST NORBERT	166	132	132	BOYER	JOHN B	1881
BOYER ETAL	BAPTISTE	ST VITAL	9	31	16	BOUDREAU	FRANCOIS	1877
BRACONNIER	BAPTISTE	ST CHARLES	73	98	98	BRACONNIER	BAPTISTE	1881
BRADLEY	F	STE AGATHE	24	129	129	HUDSONS BAY	CO	1880
BRANCONNIER		ST NORBERT	121	103	103	LEMAY	JOSEPH	1877
BRELAND	ALEX	SFX	193	65	65	BRELAND	ALEXAN	85
BRELAND	MOISE	SFX	194	92	92	BRELAND	MOISE	1884
BRELAND	PASCAL	SFX	52	23	23	BRELAND	PASCAL	1883
BRELAND	PASCAL	SFX	183	281	281	BRELAND	PASCAL	1882
BRELAND	PATRICE	SFX	204	112	112	REGNIER	OCTAVE	1885
BRELAND	PATRICE	SFX	206	70	70	JODOIN	ELISE	1884
BRELAND	WIDOW	SFX	192	136	136	BRELAND	EMILIE	85
BREMNAN	PETER	ST CHARLES	52	73	73	CASELMAN	BENJAMIN	1879
BREMNAN	THOMAS	ST CHARLES	53	77		CASELMAN	BENJAMIN	81
BREMNER	ALEXANDER	HEADINGLY	41	88	88	BREMNER	ALEXANDER	1875
BREMNER	ALEXANDER	HEADINGLY	43	72	72	BREMNER	ALEXANDER	1882
BREMNER	CHARLES	HEADINGLY	42	86	86	BREMNER	CHARLES	1875
BREMNER	CHARLES	HEADINGLY	44	72	72	BREMNER	CHARLES	1875
BREMNER	JAMES	HEADINGLY	45	97	97	BREMNER	JAMES	1875
BRENNAN	MICHAEL	ST JAMES	52	24	24	BRENNAN	MICHAEL	1882
BRENNER	WILLIAM	ST CHARLES	116	56	56	BRENNER	WILLIAM	1876
BREWERY CO		ST JAMES	25	49	49	BANNATYNE	ANNIE	1877
BRIDGET ETAL	MARY	ST CHARLES	125	190	190	GIGOT	ROSA	1886
BROWN	HENRY	POPLAR PT	44	116	58	BROWN	GEORGE	1877
BROWN	JAMES	ST CHARLES	62	89	89	BROWN	JAMES	1883
BROWN	JAMES	ST CHARLES	63	240	22	BROWN	JAMES	1883
BROWN	JAMES	POPLAR PT	42	66	66	SPARKS	AMOS	1900
BROWN	JOHN	ST CHARLES	119	65	65	BROWN ETAL	SARAH	1886
BROWN	JOHN	ST JAMES	10	107	107	ISBISTER	DAVID	1882
BROWN	JOHN	ST ANDREW	47	36	36	BROWN	JOHN	1885
BROWN	MAGNUS	POPLAR PT	262	189	189	MUNROE	ROBERT	1881
BROWN	PETER	HEADINGLY	43	293	293	BROWN	PETER	77
BROWN	WILLIAM	HEADINGLY	39	65	65	BROWN	WILLIAM	1877
BROWN ETAL	MAGNUS	ST JOHN	50	37	37	POLSON	JOHN	1875
BRUCE	BAPTISTE	ST BONIFACE	97	171	171	BRUCE	BAPTISTE	1875
BRUCE	BENJAMIN	POPLAR PT	72	179	179	BRUCE	BENJAMIN	1878
BRUCE	GAVIN	POPLAR PT	71	162	162	BRUCE	GAVIN	1875
BRUCE	HERMANGILDE	ST NORBERT	12	160	160	BRUCE	JOHN	1877
BRUCE	JAMES	POPLAR PT	50	147	147	BRUCE	JAMES	75
BRUCE	JAMES	ST JAMES	24	71	71	BRUCE	JAMES	1875
BRUCE	JAMES	KILDONAN	17	123	123	BRUCE	JAMES	1885
BRUCE	JOHN	POPLAR PT	67	200	200	BRUCE	JOHN	1875
BRUCE	JOSEPH	ST NORBERT	11	102		LECOMTE	JOSEPH	1878
BRUCE	PETER	ST JAMES	27	43	43	ALLOWAY	CHARLES W	1878
BRUCE ETAL	JOHN	ST JOHN	48			BANNERMAN	GEORGE	1875

TABLE 5: RECOGNITION OF RIVERLOT OCCUPANTS BY THE GOVERNMENT OF CANADA

OCCUPANT NAMED BY SURVEYORS		PARISH	LOT	AREA	AREA CLAIMED	PATENTEE		YEAR OF PATENT
BUNN	JOHN	ST PAUL	12	264	264	BUNN	WILLIAM R	1882
BUNN	JOHN	ST PAUL	30	80	80	MASTERS	ALFRED	1884
BUNN	JOHN	ST PAUL	70	71	71	BUNN	WILLIAM R	1882
BUNN	THOMAS	ST CLEMENT	97	146	146	BROWN	RACHEL	1886
BUNN	WILLIAM	ST PAUL	29	133	133	BUNN	WILLIAM	1878
BUNN	WILLIAM	ST PAUL	98	104	104	BUNN	WILLIAM	1878
BUNN ETAL	THOMAS	ST CLEMENT	104	71	71	DANIEL	JACOB	1884
BURKE	ANDREW	BAIE S PAUL	161	193	193			
BURKE	ANDREW	BAIE S PAUL	162	125	125			
BURKE	WALTER	BAIE S PAUL	163	119	119	ROBINSON	WILLIAM JOHN	1894
BURKE ETAL	ANDREW	BAIE S PAUL	164	114	114			
BURNELL	MARTIN	ST JAMES	64	48	48	BURNELL	MARTIN	1875
BURSTON	MAGNUS	ST CLEMENT	7	64	64	BURSTON	HENRY	1878
BURSTON	WILLIAM	ST ANDREW	87	59	59	BURSTON	WILLIAM	1885
BURSTON	WILLIAM	ST ANDREW	185	43	43	BERSTON	WILLIAM	75
BURWELL	HAMLIN	ST JAMES	56	40	40	BURNELL	HAMLIN	1878
CADOT	JOSEPH	ST NORBERT	127	96	96	GINGRAS	FRANCOIS	1877
CALDER	GEORGE	ST CLEMENT	10	93	93	CALDER	GEORGE	78
CALDER	JAMES	ST CLEMENT	41	97	97	BANNATYNE	AGB	1877
CALDER	THOMAS	ST CLEMENT	11	46	46	HOURIE SR	JOHN	1883
CALDER	WILLIAM	ST ANDREW	23	87	87	ALLAN	JOHN	77
CALDER	WILLIAM	ST ANDREW	259	44	44	ALLAN	JOHN	1877
CAMERON	ALEXANDER	HEADINGLY	56	214	214	CAMERON	ALEXANDER	1875
CAMERON	DONALD	HEADINGLY	10	86	86	CAMERON	JOHN	75
CAMERON	JAMES	BAIE S PAUL	132	97	99	SCHULTZ	JOHN	1877
CAMERON	JAMES	BAIE S PAUL	133	99	99	KIRTON	JOSEPH	1881
CAMERON	JOHN	HEADINGLY	11	87	87	CAMERON	DONALD	1875
CAMERON	JOHN	HEADINGLY	58	106	106	CAMERON	JOHN	1877
CAMPBELL	ANGUS	ST CLEMENT	68	47	47	BANNATYNE	AGB	1879
CAMPBELL	DUNCAN	STE AGATHE	42	132	132	CAMPBELL	DUNCAN	1883
CAMPBELL	DUNCAN	ST CLEMENT	28	50	50	CAMPBELL	DUNCAN	77
CAMPBELL	JAMES	ST ANDREW	12	44	44	CANIFF	FRANK H	1891
CAMPBELL	JAMES	ST ANDREW	21	43	43	BOSKILL	ALBERT	1886
CAMPBELL	JAMES	ST ANDREW	271	71	71	HARRIS	JOHN	1885
CAMPBELL	NEIL	KILDONAN	91	109	109	CAMPBELL	NEIL	1885
CAMPBELL	ROD	ST CLEMENT	69	63	63	BANNATYNE	AGB	1877
CAMPBELL	RODERICK	ST ANDREW	130	50	31	HBC		1883
CANADA	ANTOINE	ST VITAL	32	116	116	MCDONALD	ARCHIBALD	
CANADA	CHARLES	ST VITAL	32	67	67	YOUNG	REV GEORGE	1877
CANADA	PIERRE	STE ANNE	30	197	197			
CAPLET	DENNIS	ST CHARLES	113	56	56	CAPLET	DENIS	1876
CAPLET	LOUIS	ST CHARLES	5	59	59	CARRIGAU	WILLIAM	1875
CAPLET	LOUIS	ST CHARLES	6	44	44	CORRIGAU	WILLIAM	1885
CARDINAL ETAL	JEREMIE	ST NORBERT	213	107	107	BANNATYNE	A G B	1879
CAREY	DANIEL	ST BONIFACE	33	89	89	ADAMSON	ROBERT	1882
CARRIERE	ANDRE	ST NORBERT	16	267	160	CARRIERE	ANDRE	1875
CARRIERE	ANDRE	ST NORBERT	125	103	103	CARRIERE	ANDRE	1878
CARRIERE	ANDRE	STE AGATHE	628	184	184			
CARRIERE	ANDRIEN	ST NORBERT	137	77	77	CARRIERE	ANDRIEN	1881
CARRIERE	AUGUSTINE	ST BONIFACE	101	6	6	ASHBY	J B	1878

OCCUPANT NAMED BY SURVEYORS	PARISH	LOT	AREA	AREA CLAIMED	PATENTEE	YEAR OF PATENT
CARRIERE DANIEL	ST CHARLES	33	98	98	CARRIERE DANIEL	1882
CARRIERE DANIEL	ST BONIFACE	95	17	17	CARRIERE DANIEL	1877
CARRIERE DANIEL	ST BONIFACE	102	25	25	CARRIERE DANIEL	1875
CARRIERE ELI	ST VITAL	10	101	101	CARRIERE ELI	1876
CARRIERE FRANCOIS	ST BONIFACE	81	45	45	CARRIERE FRANCOIS	1882
CARRIERE LOUIS	ST LAURENT	17	66	66	CARRIERE LOUIS	1878
CARRIERE MOISE	ST BONIFACE	15	36	36	CARRIERE MOISE	1877
CARRIERE SOLOMON	ST BONIFACE	118	36	36	CARRIERE SOLOMON	83
CATHOLIC MISSION	ST NORBERT	20	159	159	CATHOLIC MISSION	1880
CATHOLIC MISSION	ST NORBERT	61	101	101	MISSION CATHOLIC	1880
CATHOLIC MISSION	ST NORBERT	80	713	713	CATHOLIC MISSION	1880
CATHOLIC MIS SION	ST NORBERT	152	136	136	TACHE REV A	1880
CATHOLIC MIS SION	ST NORBERT	162	133	133	SOEURS DE CHARITE DELH	1880
CATHOLIC MIS SION	ST NORBERT	567	203	203	CATHOLIC MIS SION	1881
CEAUSTER DAVID	STE AGATHE	114	116	116	CEAUSTER DAVID	1883
CHABOUILLER BAPTISTE	PORTAGE	11	233	45	CAMPER CLIAS JAS	1882
CHABOUILLER CHARLES	ST LAURENT	13	254	68	CHABOUILLER NORBERT	1878
CHABOUILLER JOSEPH	ST LAURENT	15	78	78	CHABOUILLER JOSEPH	
CHABOUILLER NORBERT	ST LAURENT	12	198	198	CHABOUILLER NORBERT	1878
CHABOUILLER WIDOW	ST LAURENT	14	116	116	CHABOYER AMBROISE	1878
CHABOUILLIER PIERRE	ST LAURENT	16	93	93	CHABOUILLIER PIERRE	1876
CHALIFOUX MICHEL	SFX	103	93	31	CHENIER FELIX	1879
CHAMPAGNE DAVID	ST BONIFACE	14	61	61	CHAMPAGNE DAVID	1877
CHAMPAGNE PIERRE	STE ANNE	68	201	104	CHAMPAGNE PIERRE	1882
CHAMPIONETAL SARGT HJ	ST CHARLES	84	146	146	HALL WB	1881
CHARETTE BAPTISTE	ST NORBERT	17	155	155	BRUNTON THOMAS	1877
CHARETTE DANIEL	ST NORBERT	95	50	50	CHARETTE DANIEL	1885
CHARETTE FRANCES	STE AGATHE	553	229	229	STEPHEN GEORGE	1879
CHARETTE J	STE AGATHE	25	116	116	WELSH JAMES	1883
CHARETTE JOSEPH	ST NORBERT	27	125	125	CHARETTE LOUIS	1875
CHARETTE JOSEPH	ST NORBERT	90	63	63	CHARETTE JOSEPH	1875
CHARETTE JOSEPH	ST NORBERT	96	38	38	CHARETTE JOSEPH	1879
CHARETTE JOSEPH	ST NORBERT	100	41	41	CHARETTE JOSEPH	1880
CHARITY SISTERS OF	ST BONIFACE	32	59	59	CHARITY SISTERS OF	1878
CHARITY SISTERS OF	ST BONIFACE	80	200	200	CHARITY SISTERS OF	1878
CHARTRAND PIERRE	ST LAURENT	2	654	456	CHARTRAND PIERRE	1878
CHARTRAND PIERRE	BAIE S PAUL	202	130	85	SCHULTZ JOHN	1877
CHENIER FELIX	BAIE S PAUL	21	107	107	UNIVERSITY MANITOBA	1898
CHENIER FELIX	ST CLEMENT	206	222	222	CHENIER FELIX	1878
CHRISTIE ALEX	ST CLEMENT	52	49	49	MACFARLANE RODERI	94
CHURCH PRESBYTERIAN	KILDONAN	26	334	334	PRESBYTERIAN CHURCH	1882
CHURCH PRESBYTERIAN	ST ANDREW	123	86	86	PRESBYTERIAN CONGREGATION	82
CHURCH ST ANDREWS	ST ANDREW	62	361	361	RUPERTS LAND BISHOP OF	1876
CHURCH ST JAMES	ST JAMES	42	284	284	RUPERTS LAND LORD BISHOP	1876
CHURCH STEVENS	ST ANDREW	100	126	126	COMM FINANCE RUPERTS LAND	78
CHURCH OF ENGLAND	HEADINGLY	54	189	189	BISHOP OF RUPERTS LAND	76
CLARK T	STE AGATHE	539	209	209	FERRIS ELIZABETH	1876
CLARK HENRY	ST CHARLES	76	95	95	ALLARD REV J	1880
CLARK HENRY	ST CHARLES	77	93	93	ALLARD REV J	1878
CLARK HENRY	STE AGATHE	5	138	138	CLARK HENRY	1878
CLARK HENRY	STE AGATHE	7	145	145		1880
CLARK HENRY	STE AGATHE	9	152	152		

OCCUPANT NAMED BY SURVEYORS	PARISH	LOT	AREA	AREA CLAIMED	PATENTEE	YEAR OF PATENT
CLARKE HON H J	ST BONIFACE	30	108	108	HELLEVILLE A J	1882
CLARKE HON H J	ST BONIFACE	84	7	7	CHARITY SISTERS OF	1880
CLARKE WILLIAM	ST CLEMENT	30	57	57	CLARKE JOHN	1891
CLARKE ALEXIS	HEADINGLY	12	90	90	CLARKE ALEXIS	1875
CLOUSTON ETAL	ST ANDREW	155	106	106	CLOUSTON JOHN	75
CLOUSTON JAMES	ST PAUL	24	52	52	CLOUSTON JAMES	1878
CLOUSTON JAMES	ST PAUL	26	138	138	CLOUSTON JAMES	1878
CLOUSTON JAMES	ST PAUL	76	71	71	CLOUSTON JAMES	1878
CLOUSTON JEANNIE	ST PAUL	23	117	117	CLOUSTON JANE	1884
CLOUSTON JEANNIE	ST PAUL	85	29	29	CLOUSTON JANE	1884
CLOUSTON WILLIAM	HEADINGLY	60	213	213	CLOUSTON WILLIAM	1875
CLOUSTON ETAL JOHN	ST CLEMENT	1	585	340	HUDSONS BAY CO	1881
COCHRANE HENRY	ST CLEMENT	56	81	81	SCHULTZ JOHN	1878
COCHRANE HY	ST CLEMENT	58	62	62	BAIN JOHN F	1877
COCHRANE REV WILLIAM	ST ANDREW	215	290	222	C M S FNCE COMT	1878
COCHRANE WILLIAM	ST CLEMENT	57	62	62	COCHRANE WILLIAM	1878
COCHRANE WILLIAM.	ST CLEMENT	70	70	70	COCHRANE WILLIAM	77
COLSTER JAMES	BAIE S PAUL	134	103	103	MCLEAN LAUGHLIN	1877
COMPANY HB	STE ANNE	71	116	116	COMPANY HB	1881
CONNORS JOHN	PORTAGE	56	627	627	CONNORS JOHN	1878
CONTOIS PIERRE	STE AGATHE	640	168	168	DUFAULT NARCISSE	1902
COOK CHARLES	ST PAUL	81	101	101	SPENCE ANDREW	1885
COOK HENRY	ST JAMES	23	94	94	COOK REV GILBERT	1881
COOK JAMES	POPLAR PT	76	109	109	COOK JAMES	1877
COOK JEREMIAH	HEADINGLY	63	195	195	COOK GEORGE D	1877
COOK MATTHEW	POPLAR PT	75	67	67	COOK MATTHEW	1877
COOK REV GILBERT	POPLAR PT	58	119	119	BISHOP OF RUPERTSLAND	1877
COOK RODERICK	ST PAUL	91	62	62	SCHULTZ AGNES	83
COOK SUSANAH	ST PAUL	44	141	141	GERRIE ROBERT	83
COOK SUSANAH	ST PAUL	78	137	137	SCHULTZ JOHN	1883
COOK ETAL CAROLINE	ST PAUL	41	140	140	FULSHER ETAL JANE	1886
COOK ETAL JONAH	STE AGATHE	67	131	131	COOK JONAH	1883
COOPER JAMES	ST ANDREW	170	39	39	SMITH RICHAR	85
CORBETT ABIGAIL	HEADINGLY	55	107	107	CORBETT ABIGAIL	1878
CORBETT HENRY	PORTAGE	125	562	562	CORBETT HENRY	1885
CORRIGAL GEORGE	ST ANDREW	27	91	91	CORRIGAL GEORGE	77
CORRIGAL JAMES	PORTAGE	116	48	48	CORRIGAL JOHN	1883
CORRIGAL JAMES	ST ANDREW	42	79	79	CORRIGAL JAMES	77
CORRIGAL JAMES	ST ANDREW	52	78	78	CORRIGAL JAMES	1912
CORRIGAL JAMES	ST ANDREW	145	122	122	CORRIGAL JAMES	76
CORRIGAL JAMES	ST ANDREW	226	48	48	CORRIGAL SR JAMES	81
CORRIGAL JAMES	ST ANDREW	255	31	31	CORRIGAL JAMES	76
CORRIGAL JOHN	PORTAGE	115	75	75	CORRIGAL JAMES	1882
CORRIGAL JOHN	ST ANDREW	41	40	40	CORRIGAL JAMES	81
CORRIGAL JOHN	ST ANDREW	85	61	61	CORRIGAL JOHN	76
CORRIGAL JOHN	ST ANDREW	195	38	38	CORRIGAL JOHN	1883
COURCHANE ALEXIS	ST NORBERT	65	107	107	COURCHENE ALEXIS	1879
COURCHENE ANTOINE	ST NORBERT	75	210	105	COURCHENE ANTOINE	1875
COWE ISAAC	PORTAGE	112	23	23	GARRIOCH GEORGE A	1878
COX JOHN	ST ANDREW	120	88	88	ROSS WILLIA	88

OCCUPANT NAMED BY SURVEYORS		PARISH	LOT	AREA	AREA CLAIMED	PATENTEE		YEAR OF PATENT
CRAMER	GEORGE	ST ANDREW	179	35	35	CRAMER	ANNIE	77
CRAWFORD	WILLIAM	PORTAGE	27	240	240	CRAWFORD	WILLIAM	81
CROMARTY	JAMES	ST ANDREW	13	124	124	CROMARTIE	JAMES	77
CROMARTY	WILLIAM	ST PAUL	58	67	67	MAGEE	ROBERT	1879
CUMMINGS		PORTAGE	25	240	240	CUMMINGS		1882
CUMMINGS	CHARLES	PORTAGE	63	109	109	CUMMING	CHARLES	1877
CUMMINGS	CUTHBERT	ST ANDREW	39	62	62	CUMMINGS	CUTHBERT	77
CUMMINGS	CUTHBERT	ST ANDREW	237	43	43	SUTHERLAND	WILLIA	84
CUMMINGS	DONALD	ST PAUL	5	86	86	SCHULTZ	AGNES	78
CUMMINGS	DONALD	ST PAUL	120	79	79	CUMMINGS	DONALD	1878
CUMMINGS	MALCOM	ST ANDREW	227	48	48	MCKAY	JAMES	77
CUMMINGS	WILLIAM	HIGH BLUFF	32	335	335	FRAZER	J	77
CUMMINGSETAL	M	PORTAGE	51	164	164	CUMMINGS	MALCOLM	77
CUNNINGHAM	JAMES	HEADINGLY	31	353	353	CUNNINGHAM	JAMES	1875
CUNNINGHAM	JAMES MPP	HEADINGLY	33	155	155	CUNNINGHAM	JAMES MPP	1875
CUNNINGHAM	JAMES MPP	HEADINGLY	36	93	93	CUNNINGHAM	JAMES	1875
CURTIS	CHARLES	PORTAGE	60	137	137	CURTIS	CHARLES	1877
CURTNESS	JOHN	BAIE S PAUL	104	140	140	CURTNESS	JOHN	1877
CYR	JEAN	STE ANNE	65	141	141	CYR	JEAN	1877
DAHL	ALEX	ST CLEMENT	37	115		HYMAN	ANNA	1884
DAHL	ALEXANDER	ST PAUL	4	85	85	DAHL	ALEXANDER	86
DANIEL	JAMES	PORTAGE	130	338	338	MCDANIELS	JAMES	77
DANIELS	JAMES	ST CLEMENT	105	70	70			
DANIELS	PHILIP	ST ANDREW	72	62	62			
DANIELS	THOMAS	ST CLEMENT	202	38	38	DANIELS	PHILIP	1878
DANIELS	WIDOW	ST ANDREW	106	52	52			
DAUPHINAIS	ALEX	ST ANDREW	265	70	70	FULSHER	FREDERICK	78
DAUPHINAIS	BAPTISTE	SFX	21	111	55	CLARKE	FRANK	1883
DAUPHINAIS	BAPTISTE	ST NORBERT	28	181	181	DAUPHINAIS	BAPTISTE	1877
DAUPHINAIS	FRANCOIS	ST NORBERT	31	100	100	DAUPHINAIS	BAPTISTE	1879
DAUPHINAIS	HON	SFX	17	113	113	HUNT	FRANK	1878
DAUPHINAIS	PIERRE	SFX	218	83	83	DAUPHINAIS	FRANCO	84
DAUPHINAIS	PIERRE	SFX	18	84	84	HUNT	FRANK	1878
DAUPHINAIS	WIDOW	SFX	20	60	60	CLARKE	FRANK	1882
DAUPHINAIS	WIDOW JOSEPH	SFX	124	107	54	DAUPHINAIS	MAXIME	1899
DAUPHINAS		SFX	614	159	159	PERREAULT	JUDITH	1888
DAVIS	GEORGE	ST ANDREW	51	130	78	DAVIS	GEORGE	1875
DAVIS	GEORGE	ST ANDREW	61	63	63	NONE		1875
DAVIS	GEORGE	ST ANDREW	235	45	45	DAVIS	GEORGE	83
DAVIS	GEORGE	ST CLEMENT	32	76	38	ROSS	MALCOLM	1883
DAWSON	ANDREW	SFX	220	136	136	DAWSON	ANDREW	1877
DE LA RONDE	ETIENNE	ST LAURENT	21	61	61	DE LA RONDE	ETIENNE	1883
DE LA RONDE	LOUIS	ST LAURENT	22	101	101	DE LA RONDE	LOUIS	1876
DE MONTIGNEY	CHARLES	BAIE S PAUL	7	135	135	TAYLOR	JOHN	1889
DE MONTIGNEY	CHARLES	BAIE S PAUL	20	272	144	HOFER	ZACHARIES	1927
DE MONTIGNEY	HERMAS	BAIE S PAUL	22	144	144	DUBUC	ALEX JOSEPH	1905
DE RIVIERE	ANTOINE	BAIE S PAUL	155	114	114	DE RIVIERE	ANTOINE	1882
DE RIVIERE	ANTOINE	BAIE S PAUL	156	113	113	DE RIVIERE	ANTOINE	1882
DE RIVIERE	FRANCOIS	BAIE S PAUL	151	96	96	DE RIVIERE	FRANCOIS	1878
DE RIVIERE	LOUIS	BAIE S PAUL	152	99	99	SCHULTZ	JOHN	1878
DE RIVIERE	LOUIS	BAIE S PAUL	153	105	105	DE RIVIERE	LOUIS	1878
DE RIVIERE	LOUIS	BAIE S PAUL	154	112	112	DE RIVIERE	LOUIS	1878

OCCUPANT NAMED BY SURVEYORS	PARISH	LOT	AREA	AREA CLAIMED	PATENTEE	YEAR OF PATENT
DEASE WILLIAM	ST NORBERT	9	202	202	BEAUDRON FRANCOIS	80
DEASE WILLIAM	ST NORBERT	15	156	156	MERCER FREDERICK	1881
DEASE WILLIAM	ST NORBERT	19	374	374	DEASE WILLIAM	1878
DEASE WILLIAM	ST NORBERT	55	135	135	SMITH DONALD A	1877
DEASE WILLIAM	ST NORBERT	58	115	115	SMITH DONALD A	1875
DEASE WILLIAM	ST NORBERT	181	108	108	SMITH DA	1877
DEASE WILLIAM	ST NORBERT	200	96	96	SMITH DA	1877
DEASE WILLIAM	STE AGATHE	569	173	173	SMITH DA	1877
DEBRUE ADOLPHUS	BAIE S PAUL	103	373	73	TAIT CHARLES	79
DECAIRE JEAN	STE ANNE	69	204	204	DECAIRE JEAN	1879
DECEPT MICHAEL	ST NORBERT	146	11	11		
DEUWIE ALEXI	HIGH BLUFF	43	50	50	DIDIER ALEXANDER P	75
DELORME ALEXIE	ST NORBERT	45	120	120	DELORME ALEXIE	1875
DELORME BATTICE	BAIE S PAUL	158	103	103	LANE JOHN A	1878
DELORME BONIFACE	ST NORBERT	233	176	105	HESPELER WILLIAM	1878
DELORME FRANCOIS	SFX	13	79	79	SMITH DONALD	1877
DELORME FRANCOIS	ST NORBERT	44	221	221	DELORME FRANCOIS	1876
DELORME JOSEPH	ST NORBERT	47	138	138	JULIEN ATHANASE	1883
DELORME JOSEPH	ST NORBERT	160	132	132	KITTSON ALEXANDER	1881
DELORME LOUIS	ST BONIFACE	117	54	27	TACHE ALEX	1888
DELORME MAGLOIRE	SFX	37	89	89	PLANTE MAGLOIRE	1876
DELORME NORBERT	SFX	30	70	70	DESLAURIERS	1885
DELORME NORBERT	SFX	65	171	171	TAYLOR JOHN	1878
DELORME PIERRE	ST NORBERT	10	225	225	MACWATT CHARLE	93
DELORME PIERRE	ST NORBERT	21	318	318	DELORME PIERRE	1877
DELORME PIERRE	ST NORBERT	53	148	148	DELORME PIERRE	1879
DELORME PIERRE	ST NORBERT	234	170	170	DELORME PIERRE	1884
DELORME PIERRE	ST NORBERT	235	162	162	DELORME PIERRE	1882
DELORME PIERRE	STE AGATHE	624	149	149	DELORME PIERRE	1885
DELORME URBAIN	SFX	162	306	102	RIPPINTON	1884
DELORME URBAIN	SFX	181	188	188	PROVOST LEON	1877
DELORME WIDOW JOS	ST NORBERT	78	97	97	DELORME BRIGITTE	1890
DEMARIE MARIA	SFX	171	77	77	DELORME URBAIN	82
DENNET ANDREW	ST CLEMENT	84	50	50	BANNATYNE A G B	83
DENNET WILLIAM	ST CLEMENT	36	75		DENNET WILLIA	1875
DENNISON WILLIAM	HEADINGLY	62	315	315	DENNISON WILLIAM	1878
DEROSIERS JEAN BTE	ST PAUL	65	72	72	DESROSIERS JEAN BTE	1882
DESAUTELS J BTE	STE ANNE	57	145	145	DESAUTELS J BTE	1876
DESCHAMBAULT WIDOW	ST BONIFACE	79	15	15	CHARITY SISTERS OF	1878
DESJARDINS FRANCIS	ST CHARLES	64	89	44	DESJARDINS FRANCIS	1876
DESJARLAIS ANDRE	BAIE S PAUL	13	121	121	MCKAY SEVERE	1902
DESJARLAIS ANDRE	BAIE S PAUL	246	112	112	MAGEE ROBERT	1879
DESJARLAIS ANTOINE	BAIE S PAUL	216	90	90	CUNNINGHAM JAMES	77
DESJARLAIS ANTOINE	BAIE S PAUL	230	169	169	DESJARLAIS CHARLES	1880
DESJARLAIS ANTOINE	BAIE S PAUL	231	205	88	HALL WILLIAM	1878
DESJARLAIS BAPTISTE	BAIE S PAUL	14	237	118		
DESJARLAIS BAPTISTE	BAIE S PAUL	15	126	126	TACHE EXTR ALEXANDER	1892
DESJARLAIS BAPTISTE	BAIE S PAUL	215	88	88	FISHER GEORGE	1877
DESJARLAIS BAPTISTE	BAIE S PAUL	227	181	181	DESJARLAIS BAPTISTE	1875
DESJARLAIS BAPTISTE JR	BAIE S PAUL	14	237	118	WHEELER EDWIN J	1907

TABLE 5: RECOGNITION OF RIVERLOT OCCUPANTS BY THE GOVERNMENT OF CANADA

OCCUPANT NAMED BY SURVEYORS		PARISH	LOT	AREA	AREA CLAIMED	PATENTEE		YEAR OF PATENT
DESJARLAIS	FRANCOIS	BAIE S PAUL	19	157	59	DESJARLAIS	ANTOINE	1883
DESJARLAIS	GREGOINE	BAIE S PAUL	229	85	85	DESJARLAIS	GREGOINE	1878
DESJARLAIS	JOSEPH	BAIE S PAUL	25	143	95	FISHER	GEORGE	1878
DESJARLAIS	LOUIS	BAIE S PAUL	225	170	95	BANNATYNE	AGB	1877
DESJARLAIS	PIERRE	BAIE S PAUL	18	101	101	THIBERT	PIERRE	1878
DESJARLAIS	THOMAS	BAIE S PAUL	214	89	89			
DESMARAIS	JOHN	ST BONIFACE	4	85	85	DESMARAIS	JOHN	83
DILWORTH	JOHN	HIGH BLUFF	44	355	355	DILWORTH	JOHN	1875
DIONE	PASCAL	STE AGATHE	565	158	158	DIONE	PASCAL	1877
DIONE ETAL	PASCAL	STE AGATHE	563	159	159	DIONE ETAL	PASCAL	1877
DONALD	ELIZABETH	ST ANDREW	95	63	63	YOUNG	PETER	84
DONALD	JOSEPH	ST ANDREW	94	30	30	YOUNG	PETER	84
DONALD	WILLIAM	ST ANDREW	177	42	42	DONALD ETAL	ISABELLA	77
DONALD ETAL	WILLIAM	ST ANDREW	156	102	51	DONALD	WILLIAM	1876
DREVER	WILLIAM	ST JAMES	66	85	85	DREVER	WILLIAM	1882
DUBIOS	MERCHETTE	ST PAUL	43	103	103	EVANS	ROBERT	1883
DUBOIS ETAL	BAPTISTE	STE AGATHE	579	296	296	SMITH	DA	1877
DUCHARME	BAPTISTE	ST LAURENT	9	88	88	DUCHARME	BAPTISTE	1876
DUCHARME	BAPTISTE	ST CHARLES	42	93	93	DUCHARME	BAPTISTE	1879
DUCHARME	BAPTISTE	ST CHARLES	43	92	92	MCDERMOTT ET AL		1884
DUCHARME	DOMINIQUE	STE ANNE	27	435	435	NONE		
DUCHARME	FRANCOIS	STE ANNE	26	192	192	DUCHARME	FRANCOIS C	78
DUCHARME	JOSEPH	BAIE S PAUL	189	130	87	SMITH	DONALD	1877
DUCHARME	JOSEPH	ST CHARLES	94	193	193	MCPHILLIPS	GEORGE	1876
DUCHARME	LOUIS	ST LAURENT	7	76	76	OBLATES	PERES	1878
DUCHARME	MOISE	ST VITAL	5	177	65	CAMPER	REV CJ	1879
DUCHARME	MOISE	ST VITAL	34	50	50	ROYAL	JOSEPH	82
DUCHARME	OLIVER	STE ANNE	60	323	323	DUCHARME	OLIVER	1880
DUCHARME	ROGER	STE ANNE	29	187	187	GRANGER	HORMIDAS	1882
DUCHARME	WIDOW	ST BONIFACE	10	82	82	DUCHARME	MARIE	1886
DUFFY ETAL	MICHAEL	STE AGATHE	149	166		DESROSIERS	GEORGE	1900
DUHAMEL	IRENE	STE AGATHE	123	144	144			
DUHAMEL	JOSEPH	STE AGATHE	140	107	107	DUHAMEL	JOSEPH	1882
DUHAMEL	TRENEC	STE AGATHE	145	167	167			
DUMAS	JOSEPH	ST NORBERT	93	40	40	DI MARCO	NICHOLAS	1886
DUMAS	JOSEPH	ST NORBERT	98	52	52	DUMAS	JOSEPH	1876
DUMAS	MICHAEL	ST VITAL	11	73	73	DUMAS	MICHAEL	1876
DUMAS	MICHEL	ST CHARLES	54	77	77	DUMAS	MICHEL	1876
DUPUIS	MRS	ST NORBERT	218	100	100	BANNATYNE	AGB	1881
DUPUIS	MRS	ST NORBERT	216	152	152	BANNATYNE	AGB	1877
DUPUIS ETAL	MRS	ST JAMES	39	100	100	ELSE	HENRY	1882
ELSE	HENRY	ST ANDREW	214	143	143	RUPERT LAND	BISHOP	1876
ENGLAND	CHURCH	PORTAGE	49	175	175	BISHOP OF	RUPERTSLAND	1877
EPISCMISETAL		PORTAGE	50	164	164	HARGRAVE	JAMES ETAL	77
EPISCMISETAL		ST ANDREW	264	72	72	ERASMUSSON	HENRY	79
ERASMUSSON	HENRY	SFX	202	140	140	FAGNANT	JOSETTE	
FAGNANT	WIDOW	SFX	197	79	79	MCBEATH	MORRISON	1881
FAIGNANT	JEAN BTE	STE ANNE	47	198	198			1876
FALCO	JB	SFX	44	266	266	INKSTER	COLIN	87
FALCON	BAPTISTE	SFX	166	93	93	BERTRAND	EUTYCH	84
FALCON	FRANCOIS	SFX	217	89	89	MARTIN	P A	1884
FALCON	MARIE	SFX	47	161	161	WELSH	ANTOIN	85

OCCUPANT NAMED BY SURVEYORS		PARISH	LOT	AREA	AREA CLAIMED	PATENTEE		YEAR OF PATENT
FALCON	PIERRE	SFX	46	182	182	LAVALLEE	PIERRE	1893
FALCON	PIERRE	SFX	190	134	134	PERRAS	CONSTANT	
FALCON ETAL	FRANCOIS	SFX	48	218	73	NO INFO		
FARMER	WILLIAM A	HEADINGLY	18	226	226	FARMER	WILLIAM A	1876
FAVAL	HUMPHREY	ST ANDREW	29	45	45	MORGAN	JOSEPH	84
FAVEL	JOSEPH	ST PAUL	71	72	72	BUNN	WILLIAM R	1882
FAVEL	RICHARD	BAIE S PAUL	115	108	108			.
FAVEL	RICHARD	BAIE S PAUL	116	101	101			.
FENAUTE	LOUIS	BAIE S PAUL	119	96	96			.
FENAUTE	LOUIS	BAIE S PAUL	120	96	96			.
FENAUTE	LOUIS	BAIE S PAUL	121	96	96			.
FENAUTE	LOUIS	BAIE S PAUL	122	96	96	GOV CO OF	ADVENTURERS	81
FERGUSSON	JOHN	HIGH BLUFF	26	478	478	MCKENZIE	KENNETH	1886
FERGUSSON	ETAL	ST VITAL	26	13	13			
FIDDLER	CHARLES	ST JAMES	58	48	48	FIDDLER	CHARLES	1882
FIDDLER	WIDOW	ST JAMES	60	48	24	FREEMAN	JOHN	
FIDLER	ALLAN	ST JAMES	59	48	48	FIDLER	ALLAN	1876
FIDLER	CORNELIUS	HEADINGLY	41	101		FIDLER	CORNELIUS	1878
FIDLER	EDWARD	HEADINGLY	46	113	113	FIDLER	EDWARD	1875
FIDLER	FRANCOIS	SFX	75	82	82	SMITH	DONALD A	1877
FIDLER	GEORGE	SFX	82	113	113	SMITH	DONALD A	1879
FIDLER	HENRY	ST CLEMENT	14	52	52	FIDLER	HENRY	85
FIDLER	JOHN	ST CLEMENT	25	49	49	BROWN	WALTER	1882
FIDLER	PETER	HEADINGLY	40	198	198	SCHULTZ	JOHN	1884
FIDLER	PETER	ST PAUL	106	70	70	FIDLER	PETER	1878
FIDLER	THOMAS	HEADINGLY	25	49	49	FIDLER	THOMAS	1876
FIDLER	THOMAS	ST CLEMENT	93	48	48	FIDLER	THOMAS	77
FIDLER	THOMAS	ST CLEMENT	94	49	49	FIDLER	WILLIAM	77
FIDLER	WIDOW	BAIE S PAUL	226	95	95			
FIDLER	WIDOW	SFX	147	88	44	FIDLER	WILLIAM	1885
FIDLER ETAL	JAMES	ST CLEMENT	96	49	49	BUNN	RACHEL	1875
FIELDS	HENRY	HEADINGLY	21	112	112	FIELDS	HENRY	1875
FINLAYSON	HECTOR	ST CLEMENT	60	47	47	BAIN	JOHN	1877
FINLAYSON	JOHN	KILDONAN	13	159	159	POLSON	ALEX	1883
FINNIGAN	JAMES	STE ANNE	9	203	203	FINNIGAN	JAMES	1877
FIRTH	THOMAS	ST ANDREW	86	118	78	NORQUAY	THOMAS	1885
FIRTH	THOMAS	ST ANDREW	187	42	42	MCKAY	JOHN	1882
FISHER	AMBROISE	SFX	113	306	306	MAGEE	ROBERT	1879
FISHER	GEORGE	BAIE S PAUL	2	264	264	SMITH	DONALD A	1877
FISHER	GEORGE	BAIE S PAUL	213	90	90	SPENCE	WILLIAM	1877
FISHER	GEORGE	SFX	79	93	93	FIDLER	FRANCOIS	1877
FISHER	GEORGE	SFX	151	202	202	FISHER	GEORGE	1885
FISHER	WIDOW	ST BONIFACE	5	83	83	DESMARAIS	LOUISE	1883
FLAMAND	JOSEPH	STE ANNE	24	143	143	GIROUX	LRAYMOND	1879
FLATT	PHILIP	BAIE S PAUL	109	253	42	KIRTON	PETER	1883
FLEMING	JAMES	STE AGATHE	127	94	94	FLEMING	JAMES	1882
FLETCHER	WILLIAM	HIGH BLUFF	25	458	458	BURGESS	JOHN	1877
FLETT	ARCHIE	ST ANDREW	196	37	37	FLETT	ARCHIBALD	1877
FLETT	DAVID	KILDONAN	22	83	83	FLETT	DAVID	1883
FLETT	DAVID	ST ANDREW	44	57	57	HODGSON	JOSEPH	1885
FLETT	DONALD	KILDONAN	23	82	82	FLETT	JOSEPH	1885
FLETT	GEORGE	ST ANDREW	139	62	62	FLETT	DONALD	1883

TABLE 5: RECOGNITION OF RIVERLOT OCCUPANTS BY THE GOVERNMENT OF CANADA

OCCUPANT NAMED BY SURVEYORS	PARISH	LOT	AREA	AREA CLAIMED	PATENTEE	YEAR OF PATENT
FLETT JAMES	ST ANDREW	75	21	21	FLETT JAMES	77
FLETT JAMES	ST ANDREW	140	62	62	SMITH JOHN	78
FLETT JOHN	KILDONAN	79	42	42	HAMILTON DANIEL	1884
FLETT JOHN	ST ANDREW	96	150	150	FLETT JOHN	1877
FLETT PETER	ST ANDREW	198	37	37	FLETT JOHN	77
FLETT PETER	ST PAUL	37	109	109	FLETT PETER	1878
FLETT ROBERT	ST PAUL	87	94	94	FLETT PETER	
FLETT THOMAS	PORTAGE	122	208	208	FLETT ROBERT	1877
FLETT WILLIAM	ST ANDREW	119	134	91	FLETT THOMAS	78
FLEURY EDWARD	SFX	3	51	51	FLEURY EDWARD	1875
FLEURY JOSEPH	SFX	142	93	93	FLEURY JOSEPH	1877
FLEURY MICHELLE	SFX	85	91	91	PARADIS BRUNO	1877
FLOWERS WEZAW	BAIE S PAUL	117	229	183	FLEURY LOUIS	76
FOLSTER THOMAS	ST CLEMENT	199	49	49	FOLSTER THOMAS	1883
FOLSTER WILLIAM	ST CLEMENT	17	133	133	BLACK GEORGE	1881
FONSECA WILLIAM	ST CHARLES	34	88	88	HAWKINS AC	77
FORTNAY GEORGE	ST CHARLES	80	60	60	FORTNAY GEORGE	1880
FOULDS HENRY	ST JAMES	8	48	48	FOULDS GEORGE	1876
FOULDS JOHN	HIGH BLUFF	63	128	128	FOULDS HENRY	1879
FOULDS WIDOW	ST JAMES	59	48	24	FOULDS JOHN	77
FOX WILLIAM	BAIE S PAUL	62	59	59	ROBLIN EMILY W	1882
FOY PETER	SFX	107	110	110	FOY PETER	
FOY TOUSSAINT	SFX	157	171	86	PARADIS BRUNO	1878
FRANK JAMES	KILDONAN	116	69	69	MCRAE JOHN	1878
FRANKLIN THOMAS	ST PAUL	50	48	48	FRANKLIN THOMAS	1875
FRASER ANGUS	KILDONAN	70	127	127	MULHOLLAND ROBERT	1878
FRASER JOHN	ST PAUL	115	103	103	FRASER JOHN	1875
FRASER WILLIAM	KILDONAN	16	49	49	MULHOLLAND ROBERT	1878
FRASER WILLIAM	KILDONAN	114	84	84	FRASER WILLIAM	1875
FROBISHER THOMAS	ST NORBERT	15	79	79	FROBISHER THOMAS	1875
FULSHER FRED	ST ANDREW	69	74	74	FULSHER ETAL FRED	1878
GADDY WILLIAM	PORTAGE	136	89	89	GADDY WILLIAM	1885
GAGNE FH	STE ANNE	19	100	100	MORIN ALBERT	1881
GAGNE FH	STE ANNE	65	216	144	GAGNE FH	1905
GAGNON DAVID	SFX	43	224	224	GAGNON DAVID	1878
GAGNON LOUIS	SFX	52	78	78	CLARKE HENRY	1884
GAGNON LOUIS	SFX	11	78	78	MORRIS ALEXANDER	1882
GAGNON LOUIS	SFX	10	120	120	GAGNON LOUIS	1878
GALARNEAU JOSEPH	ST NORBERT	25	177	177	GALARNEAU JOSEPH	1878
GALARNEAU LOUIS	ST BONIFACE	26	185	185	CAUCHON HON J E	1882
GARDNER WIDOW	ST CLEMENT	95	146	146	GARDNER THOMAS	88
GARRELL JOHN	SFX	216	49	49	PERRAS CONSTANT	1884
GARRETT GAVIN H	ST CLEMENT	50	111	111	STRUTTS CHARLES	1882
GARRIOCH JOHN	PORTAGE	61	48	48	GARRIOCH GAVIN H	77
GARRIOCH JOHN	PORTAGE	109	140	140	GARRIOCH JOHN	1876
GARRIOCHETAL WILLIAM	PORTAGE	59	40	40	MCKENZIE GEORGE	1878
GARRIOCHE GEORGE	PORTAGE	54	184	184	GARRIOCH JOHN	1877
GARRIOCK JOHN	PORTAGE	94	172	218	GARRIOCK JOHN	1877
GARTIN JOHN	POPLAR PT	70	149	149	GARTIN JOHN	1877
GAUDRY AMABLE	ST VITAL	15	107	107	GAUDRY AMABLE	1877

OCCUPANT NAMED BY SURVEYORS	PARISH	LOT	AREA	AREA CLAIMED	PATENTEE	YEAR OF PATENT
GEDDES JOHN	KILDONAN	43	98	98	GEDDES JOHN	1877
GEDDINGS CLINTON	PORTAGE	126	367	367	MCKENZIE KENNETH	1877
GENDRON SAUL	STE AGATHE	125	108	108	ROBERT EMERY	1887
GENDRON SAUL	STE AGATHE	126	100	100		
GENTHON HEIRS OF MAX	ST BONIFACE	25	233	233	GENTHON CHARLES	1875
GENTHON JOSEPH	ST BONIFACE	24	189	189	GENTHON JOSEPH	1875
GENTON CHARLES	ST BONIFACE	100	6	6	ALLOWAY WM F	1882
GENTON ELI	ST NORBERT	143	120	120	GENTON ELI	1885
GEORGE HENRY	ST ANDREW	17	83	83	NORQUAY JOHN	82
GEORGE PIERRE	ST NORBERT	109	21	21	GEORGE PIERRE	1875
GEORGE REV HANRY	PORTAGE	107	208	208	GEORGE MARY A	1877
GEORGE REV HENRY	PORTAGE	108	63	63	GEORGE MARY A	1877
GERARD HON M A	ST BONIFACE	106	71	71	GERARD ETAL M A	1876
GERARD HON M A	ST BONIFACE	112	165	165	GERARD MARC A	1877
GERARD HON M A	ST BONIFACE	116	44	44	GERARD HON M A	1876
GERVAIS ALEX	SFX	64	86	86	GERVAIS ALEXIS	1878
GERVAIS BAPTISTE	SFX	158	95	95	GERVAIS FRANCO	85
GERVAIS CLEOPHAS	SFX	62	106	106	STEPHEN GEORGE	1877
GERVAIS CORBET	SFX	63	88	88	LONGBOTTOM FRANK	
GERVAIS FRANCOIS	SFX	50	43	43	BRELAND PASCAL	1883
GERVAIS PAUL	SFX	176	100	100	GERVAIS PAUL	1899
GIBEAULT	SFX	144	72	72	LAROCQUE LOUIS	
GIBEAULT WILLIAM	SFX	143	73	73	FORGET JOSEPH	1885
GIBSON FRANCIS	ST ANDREW	20	160	160	GIBSON FRANCI	85
GILLIS JOHN	HIGH BLUFF	41	167	167	DELWORTH JOHN	1877
GILTREE FRANCIS	PORTAGE	22	717	717	OGILTREE FRANCIS	1877
GINDIPIE PIERRE	SFX	51	30	30	BRELAND PASCAL	1883
GLADU FRANCIS	BAIE S PAUL	135	111	111	MCLEAN LAUGHLIN	1877
GLADU FRANCIS	BAIE S PAUL	136	118	118	SIMESON WILLIAM	77
GLADU PASCAL	BAIE S PAUL	139	109	109	CHENIER FELIX	1878
GLADU SUSIE	BAIE S PAUL	140	105	105	BANNERMAN SAMUEL	1878
GLADU WEZAW	BAIE S PAUL	137	121	121	SYMESON WILLIAM	1884
GLADU WEZAW	BAIE S PAUL	138	117	117	GLADU SR LOUIS	1877
GLADU WEZAW	BAIE S PAUL	141	106	106		
GODON DAVID	STE AGATHE	23	115	115	GODON DAVID	1882
GONVILLE SR ALEX	BAIE S PAUL	195	106	106	CHENIER FELIX	1878
GOOD JAMES	ST CHARLES	120	6	6	BROWN ETAL SARAH	1886
GOOD JAMES	ST JAMES	9	42	42	GRANT JOHN F	1884
GOOD JOSEPH	ST JAMES	54	48	48	GOOD JOSEPH	1875
GOSSELIN ANTOINE	ST NORBERT	72	158	158	LECOMTE JOSEPH	1876
GOSSELIN AUGUSTIN	STE AGATHE	112	112	112	MCCALL ELLA	1886
GOSSELIN CATHERINE	STE AGATHE	44	143	143	GOSSELIN CATHERINE	1877
GOSSELIN DAMASE	STE ANNE	13	205	205	GOSSELIN DAMASE	1878
GOSSELIN FRANCOIS	ST NORBERT	91	82	82	GOSSELIN FRANCOIS	1879
GOSSELIN JOSEPH	STE AGATHE	92	124	124	GOSSELIN JOSEPH	1909
GOSSELIN MARIE	STE AGATHE	35	96	96	GOSSELIN MARIE	1879
GOSSELINETAL AUGUSTE	STE AGATHE	94	125	125	ALLEN REV WC	1882
GOSSELINETAL AUGUSTIN	STE AGATHE	110	118	118		
GOSSELINETAL MICHEL	STE AGATHE	106	109	109	JOHNSON JOHN	1881
GOSSELINETAL MICHEL	STE AGATHE	108	125	125		
GOULET ALEXIS	ST NORBERT	64	99	99	SCHULTZ JOHN	1877
GOULET ELIZ	ST NORBERT	62	102	102	GOULET HELENE	1885

OCCUPANT NAMED BY SURVEYORS		PARISH	LOT	AREA	AREA CLAIMED	PATENTEE		YEAR OF PATENT
GOULET	MOISE	ST NORBERT	67	125	125	GOULET	MOISE	1879
GOULET	ROGER	ST BONIFACE	2	87	87	GOULET	ROGER	1878
GOULET	ROGER	ST BONIFACE	18	105	105	GOULET	ROGER	1878
GOULET	ROGER	ST BONIFACE	88	17	17	GOULET	ROGER	1878
GOULET	ROGER	ST BONIFACE	98	26	26	GOULET	ROGER	1878
GOULET	ROGER	ST NORBERT	180	110	110	GOULET	ROGER	1876
GOWLER	MARY	HEADINGLY	4	103	103	YOUNG	REV GEORGE	1876
GOWLER	MARY	HEADINGLY	66	93	93	YOUNG	REV GEORGE A	1878
GOWLER	WILLIAM	POPLAR PT	46	200	200	GOWLER	WILLIAM	1879
GRAHAM	SAMUEL	PORTAGE	38	160	160	GRAHAM	SAMUEL	1882
GRANT	JOHN	ST CHARLES	118	40	40	GRANT	JOHN	1884
GRANT	JOHN	ST VITAL	7	753	753	GRANT	JOHN FRANCIS	82
GRANT	JOHN	ST NORBERT	102	90	90	GRANT	JOHN	1882
GRANT	JOHN	ST NORBERT	103	91	91	GRANT	CATHER	86
GRANT	JOHN F	ST NORBERT	147	13	13	FROBISHER	THOMAS	1885
GRANT	WILLIAM	STE AGATHE	38	112	112	GRANT	WILLIAM	1883
GREEN	JAMES	ST CHARLES	107	46	46	GREEN	JAMES	1882
GREEN	JAMES	ST CHARLES	109	28	28	GREEN	JAMES	1882
GREEN	JAMES	ST CHARLES	110	28	28	GREEN	JAMES	1882
GREEN	JAMES	HEADINGLY	9	86	86	GREEN	JAMES	1875
GREEN	JAMES	ST JAMES	5	17	17	GREEN	JAMES	1882
GROUETTE	ANGELIQUE	STE ANNE	21	91	91	GROUETTE	ANGELIQUE	79
GROUETTE	AUGUST	STE ANNE	16	184	184	GROUETTE	AUGUSTIN	79
GROUETTE	IB	STE ANNE	20	172	172	GROUETTE	IB	1882
GROUETTE	THEODORE	STE ANNE	22	189	189	GROUETTE	THEODORE	1879
GROVER	J M	STE AGATHE	142	90	90	GROVER	HANNAH	1882
GUIBOCHE	ANDRE	ST CHARLES	65	90	90	GUIBOCHE	ANDRE	1876
GUIBOCHE	NOEL	ST CHARLES	66	95	95	GUIBOCHE	NOEL	1875
GUNN	ALEX	ST ANDREW	127	41	41	GUNN	ALEXANDER	76
GUNN	ALEX	ST ANDREW	146	61	61	THIBERT	PIERRE	76
GUNN	ALEXANDER	KILDONAN	7	75	75	NONE		
GUNN	DON	ST CLEMENT	89	119	119	YOUNG ETAL	DAVID	1883
GUNN	DONALD	KILDONAN	58	159	159	GUNN	D	1885
GUNN	DONALD	ST ANDREW	109	158	158	GUNN	DONALD	1875
GUNN	GEORGE	POPLAR PT	86	192	192	GUNN	GEORGE	77
GUNN	GEORGE	ST CLEMENT	90	161	161	GUNN	GEORGE	75
GUNN	JAMES	ST ANDREW	116	35	35	GUNN	MARY	88
GUNN	JEREMIAH	KILDONAN	61	66	66	GUNN	JEREMIAH	1882
GUNN	JOHN	ST ANDREW	147	60	60	COX	ROBERT	78
GUNN	JOHN	ST ANDREW	165	47	47	GUNN	JOHN	77
GUNN	JOHN	ST ANDREW	167	33	33	GUNN	JOHN	77
GUNN	JOHN	ST CLEMENT	79	156	156	BANNATYNE	A G B	82
GUNN	JOHN	ST CLEMENT	98	146	146	GUNN	JOHN	75
GUNN	JOHN H	ST PAUL	116	95	95	GUNN	JOHN	83
GUNN	ROBERT	ST PAUL	117	94	94	GUNN	JOHN	83
GUNN	WIFE	KILDONAN	37	84	84	GUNN	MARY	1885
GUNN ETAL	JOHN	ST ANDREW	163	120	61	GUNN	DONALD	1875
GUNVILLE	ALEX	BAIE S PAUL	201	125	125	KAVANAGH	REV FRANCOIS	1878
GUNVILLE	ALEX SR	BAIE S PAUL	196	109	109	CHENIER	FELIX	1878
GUNVILLE	LOUIS	SFX	152	47	47	FISHER	GEORGE	1885
HALCRO	JAMES	ST PAUL	50	45	45	HALCRO	WILLIAM	1887
HALCRO	JOSEPH	ST PAUL	75	79	79	HALCRO	JOSEPH	81

TABLE 5: RECOGNITION OF RIVERLOT OCCUPANTS BY THE GOVERNMENT OF CANADA

OCCUPANT NAMED BY SURVEYORS	PARISH	LOT	AREA	AREA CLAIMED	PATENTEE	YEAR OF PATENT
HALETT JAMES	ST JAMES	49	48	24	HALETT JAMES	1878
HALETT WILLIAM	ST JAMES	40	77	77	HALETT ETAL JOHN	1885
HALETT JR JAMES	ST JAMES	50	48	48	HALETT SR JAMES	1879
HALL WILLIAM	HEADINGLY	1	434	434	HALL WILLIAM	1875
HALLETT JULIUS	BAIE S PAUL	159	98	65	MCDERMOT ANDREW	1877
HALLETT ELLEN	POPLAR PT	78	154	154	HUNT ADAM	75
HALLETT JANE	POPLAR PT	66	107	107	BAUBEE JANE	1877
HAMELIN	STE AGATHE	538	189	189		
HAMELIN	STE AGATHE	540	196	196		
HAMELIN	STE AGATHE	542	206	206	GAUTHIER PIERRE	1883
HAMELIN ALEX	ST VITAL	84	71	71	HAMILIN JOSEPH	1885
HAMELIN JOSEPH	ST NORBERT	20	49	49	HAMILIN JOSEPH	1876
HAMELIN JOSEPH	STE AGATHE	543	200	200	MCINDOO WILLIAM	1880
HAMELIN JOSEPH	STE AGATHE	545	172	172	STEPHEN GEORGE	1877
HAMELIN JOSEPH	STE AGATHE	547	196	196	STEPHEN GEORGE	1877
HAMELIN SOLOMAN	ST VITAL	23	130	130	HAMELIN SOLOMAN	1885
HAMELIN SOLOMAN	STE AGATHE	544	193	193		
HAMELIN SOLOMAN	STE AGATHE	587	160	160		
HAMELIN ANTOINE	ST VITAL	22	36	36	SMITH DA	1877
HAMILTON DANIEL	KILDONAN	77	44	22	FLETT DAVID	1883
HAMILTON DANIEL	KILDONAN	95	110	110	HAMILTON DANIEL	1875
HAMILTON DAVID	ST ANDREW	96	56	56	HARCUS DAVID	85
HARCUS GEORGE	ST ANDREW	7	64	64	TAYLOR ROBERT	1877
HARCUS GEORGE	ST ANDREW	76	42	42	HARCUS GEORGE	79
HARKNESS WIDOW SARAH	ST BONIFACE	41	56	56	HARKNESS SARAH	1881
HARPER JAMES	KILDONAN	29	87	87	HARPER JOHN	1875
HARPER JAMES	ST PAUL	66	63	63	HARPER ETALJ AMES	1886
HARPER JOHN	ST ANDREW	111	53	53	HARPER JAMES	75
HARPER JOHN	KILDONAN	30	87	87	HARPER JOHN	1875
HARRISON AUGUST	KILDONAN	75	41	41	PRITCHARD REV S	1878
HARRISON AUGUST	STE ANNE	58	188	188	HARRISON AUGUST	1880
HARRISON SIN	STE ANNE	66	200	200		
HARRISON THOMAS	STE ANNE	63	189	189	HARRISON THOMAS	1878
HAY ROBERT	ST ANDREW	23	231	231	HAY ROBERT	77
HAY ET AL CHARLES	PORTAGE	194	38	38	HAY CHARLES	1877
HAYS CHARLES	BAIE S PAUL	52	197	197	ATKINS ALEX	1880
HAYS CHARLES	BAIE S PAUL	107	235	128	KIRTON PETER	1883
HAYS CHARLES	HIGH BLUFF	108	244	75	BROWN REV NELSON	77
HAYWOOD CHARLES	ST ANDREW	40	184	184	HAYWOOD CHARLES	1878
HBC	ST PAUL	111	82	82	H B CO	1881
HENDERSON ANGUS	KILDONAN	131	94	94	HENDERSON A	1881
HENDERSON CHARLES	ST ANDREW	51	119	119	HENDERSON CHARLE	85
HENDERSON CHARLES	ST ANDREW	16	83	83	HENDERSON JOHN	85
HENDERSON JOHN	KILDONAN	228	48	48	NORQUAY JOHN	1875
HENDERSON NEIL	KILDONAN	39	79	79	HENDERSON JOHN	1875
HENDERSON PETER	PORTAGE	42	98	98	HENDERSON NEIL	77
HENDERSON PETER	PORTAGE	120	81	81	HENDERSON PETER	1877
HENDERSON PETER	KILDONAN	121	101	101	HENDERSON JR PETER	1878
HENDERSON WILLIAM	KILDONAN	44	49	49	HENDERSON PETER	1880
HENRY CATHERINE	KILDONAN	49	121	121	HENDERSON WILLIAM	
HENRY CATHERINE	BAIE S PAUL	117	98	98		
HENRY CATHERINE	BAIE S PAUL	118	96	96	BANNERMAN SAMUEL	1885

OCCUPANT NAMED BY SURVEYORS	PARISH	LOT	AREA	AREA CLAIMED	PATENTEE	YEAR OF PATENT
HEPBURNETAL ANDREW	STE AGATHE	54	112	112	HEPBURN ANDREW	1883
HEPBURNETAL ANDREW	STE AGATHE	56	134	134	JOHN EDWARD	75
HERRIOT JOHN	ST CLEMENT	18	50	50	HARRIOTT JOHN	1877
HIGGINS JOHN	HEADINGLY	37	192	192	HIGGINS JOHN	1879
HODGSON JOHN	ST ANDREW	40	63	63	HODGSON JOHN	1886
HODGSON JOHN	ST ANDREW	43	51	51	HODGSON JOHN	1881
HOGUE AMABLE	ST CHARLES	57	79	79	ROBLIN EMILY	1875
HOGUE ANTOINE	ST CHARLES	61	114	114	HOGUE ANTOINE	1876
HOGUE JOSEPH	ST CHARLES	56	78	78	HOGUE JOSEPH	1876
HOGUE LOUIS	ST CHARLES	105	110	110	HOGUE LOUIS	1876
HOGUE LOUIS	ST JAMES	3	10	10	HOGUE LOUIS	1875
HOGUE THOMAS	ST CHARLES	60	97	97	HOGUE THOMAS	
HOOKEY GEORGE	BAIE S PAUL	160	97	97	HOOKEY GEORGE	1875
HOOKEY GEORGE	ST JAMES	44	95	95	HOULE ANTOIN	85
HOULE ANTOINE	SFX	120	98	98	HAMELIN JOSEPH	1877
HOULE CHARLES	STE AGATHE	561	167	167	SMITH DONALD	1875
HOULE F	SFX	115	169	169	MONCREIFF HENRY	1890
HOULE LOUIS	SFX	137	86	86	HOULE THOMAS	1877
HOULE LOUIS	STE AGATHE	559	162	162	BALLENDINE JANE	1885
HOURIE GEORGE	ST PAUL	57	65	65	BALLENDINE JANE	1885
HOURIE GEORGE	ST PAUL	69	71	36	HOURIE SR JOHN	1883
HOURIE JOHN	ST CLEMENT	12	46	46	BOYD ALFRED	1885
HOURIE PETER	HIGH BLUFF	69	113	113	HOURIE PHILIP	1885
HOURIE PHILIP	HIGH BLUFF	70	152	152	HOURIE A G B	82
HOURIE ROBERT	ST CLEMENT	80	119	119	BANNATYNE RICHARD H	75
HOURIE THOMAS	ST CLEMENT	81	26	26	HUNTER CHARLES	1885
HOUSE CHARLES	SFX	126	94	94	HOUSE JOSHUA M	77
HOUSE HENRY	PORTAGE	68	471	471	HOUSE HENRY	1875
HOUSE JOSHUA M	HIGH BLUFF	49	126	126	HOUSE ROBERT	1882
HOWIE JAMES	BAIE S PAUL	170	121	121	TAIT JAMES	1879
HUDSON BAY CO	HIGH BLUFF	47	282	282	HOWIE BAY CO	79
HUDSON JOHN	BAIE S PAUL	123	786	786	HUDSON JOHN	79
HUDSON WILLIAM	ST ANDREW	230	47	47	HODGSON WILLIAM	1884
HUDSON COMPANY	PORTAGE	67	105	105	HODGSON COMPANY	79
HUDSONBAYCO	SFX	139	325	318	HUDSON BAY ADVENTURERS	1884
HUDSONBAYCO	PORTAGE	23	230	230	COMPANY OF	1884
HUDSONS BAY	PORTAGE	57	305	305	HUDSONBAY CO	1881
HUDSONS BAY	ST BONIFACE	86	19	19	HUDSONS BAY	1881
HUDSONS BAY CO	STE AGATHE	1	116	116	HUDSONS BAY	1879
HUDSONS BAY CO	ST CLEMENT	3	33	33	SMITH DONALD	1885
HUPE ISIDORE	STE ANNE	64	108	108	MORRISON ANGUS	1877
HUPE JOHN	STE ANNE	11	211	106	PARISEAU HONORE	
INDIAN MISSI ON	ST CLEMENT	63	62	62	BISHOP OF RUPERTSLAND	
INKSTER GEORGE	POPLAR PT	38	260	260	INKSTER GEORGE	78
INKSTER JAMES	POPLAR PT	35	286	286	INKSTER JAMES	1875
INKSTER JAMES	KILDONAN	5	59	59	INKSTER JAMES	1882
INKSTER JAMES	KILDONAN	73	41	41	INKSTER JAMES	1882
INKSTER JOHN	ST JAMES	32	173	173	TAIT ROBERT	1882
INKSTER JOHN	KILDONAN	6	291	134	INKSTER MARY	1882
INKSTER JOHN	KILDONAN	85	40	40	INKSTER MARY	1882
INKSTER JOHN	ST PAUL	80	103	103	PRITCHARD SAMUEL	1884
INKSTER MRS	KILDONAN	4	190	190	SMITH THOMAS H	1875

TABLE 5: RECOGNITION OF RIVERLOT OCCUPANTS BY THE GOVERNMENT OF CANADA

OCCUPANT NAMED BY SURVEYORS	PARISH	LOT	AREA	AREA CLAIMED	PATENTEE	YEAR OF PATENT
INKSTER MRS WILLIAM	KILDONAN	3	188	188	INKSTER MARY	1884
INKSTER WILLIAM	POPLAR PT	37	144	144	INKSTER WILLIAM	1875
IRISH ALEX	ST ANDREW	272	71	71	SMITH DONALD A	1880
IRVINE JOHN	ST CHARLES	1	98	98	WRIGHT A	98
IRVINE JOHN	ST ANDREW	5	31	31	PARK MARGAR	1877
IRVINE WILLIAM	ST ANDREW	134	138	138	IRVINE WILLIAM	8
IRVING JAMES	ST PAUL	60	61	61	IRVING JAMES	1886
IRVING JOHN	ST PAUL	61	69	69	ARCHIBALD ETAL L H	1881
ISBESTERS JAMES	ST CHARLES	103	117	117	ISBISTER JAMES	1876
ISBISTER A K	ST ANDREW	212	83	83	ISBISTER ALEX	1876
ISBISTER ALEX	ST ANDREW	64	115	115	ISBISTER ALEX	1876
ISBISTER DANIEL	ST JAMES	8	53	53	GARRETT SARAH	1885
ISBISTER JOHN	ST JAMES	14	135	135	ISBISTER JOHN	1878
ISBISTER JOHN	ST PAUL	45	154	154	ISBISTER JOHN	1878
ISBISTER JOHN	ST PAUL	74	109	36	ISBISTER JOHN	1888
ISBISTER MARY	ST JAMES	13	170	170	SAYER ETAL ALEX	1883
JACOBE MITCHEL	STE AGATHE	122	164	164		
JACOBS MITCHEL	STE AGATHE	121	165	165	MESSNER ANTHONY	
JEANNOT FRANCOIS	SFX	195	84	84	STEWART CHARLES	
JETE THEOPHILE	ST VITAL	3	117	117	JETTE THEOPHILE	1881
JETTE THEO	ST NORBERT	82	97	97	JETTE THEO	1878
JEWETH ETAL BUCK	STE AGATHE	132	135	135		
JOACHIM HENRY	ST PAUL	2	84	84	JOACHIM HENRY	1878
JOACHIM HENRY	ST PAUL	95	123	123	JOACHIM HENRY	1878
JOBIN AMBROSE	ST CHARLES	55	77	77	JOBIN AMBROSE	1876
JOHNSON JOHN	BAIE S PAUL	211	167	167	JOHNSON JOHN	1878
JOHNSTON CORNELIUS	ST CLEMENT	55	37	37	COLELEUGH FLORA	1882
JOHNSTON CORNELIUS	ST CLEMENT	76	169	169	JOHNSTONE DONALD	77
JOHNSTON DAVID	ST ANDREW	201	38	38	JOHNSTONE DONALD	75
JOHNSTON DONALD	ST ANDREW	73	64	64	JOHNSTONE CHARLES	1877
JOHNSTON ETAL	ST ANDREW	58	75	51		
JOHNSTON JAMES	POPLAR PT	63	55	55	JOHNSTON JAMES	1875
JOHNSTON JOHN	STE AGATHE	96	135	135	BELL ABRAHAM	1882
JOHNSTON JOHN	STE AGATHE	98	98	98	SHARMAN THOMAS	1890
JOHNSTON JOSEPH	ST CLEMENT	54	31	31	COLELEUGH FLORA	1882
JOHNSTON WILLIAM	ST CLEMENT	53	67	67	BANNATYNE A G B	79
JOHNSTONE ETAL	ST ANDREW	58	75	24	JOHNSTONE ARCHIBALD	1877
JOHNSTONE GEORGE	ST NORBERT	219	76	51	JOHNSTON CHARLES	1877
JOLIBOIS JEAN BTE	ST VITAL	41	253	253	JOLIBOIS J B	1877
JOLICOCUR A	ST CLEMENT	14	64	64	LALONDE JEAN BTE	1877
JONES EDWARD	ST CLEMENT	113	51	51	GUNN BEN	1903
JOSEPH ALEXANDRE	BAIE S PAUL	127	95	95	PELLY FRANCES ANNA	1887
KARSON JOSEPH	ST JAMES	53	46	46	KENNEDY WILLIAM N	82
KAUFFMAN JACOB	KILDONAN	63	37	37	KAUFFMAN JACOB	1878
KAUFFMAN JACOB	KILDONAN	66	76	76	KAUFFMAN JACOB	1878
KAUFFMAN PETER	KILDONAN	64	111	111	KAUFFMAN PETER	1878
KAVANAGH REV F H	SFX	119	98	98	SCHULTZ JOHN	1883
KENNEDY PHILIP	ST ANDREW	63	108	108		
KENNEDY PHILIP	ST ANDREW	213	87	87	KENNEDY PHILIP	1898
KEPLING GEORGE	ST CLEMENT	24	46	46	KIPPLING JOHN	1884
KEPLING THOMAS	ST CLEMENT	22	49	49	KENNEDY WILLIAM	82
KESSOCK ROBERT	STE AGATHE	130	134	134	KISSICK ROBERT	1909

TABLE 5: RECOGNITION OF RIVERLOT OCCUPANTS BY THE GOVERNMENT OF CANADA

OCCUPANT NAMED BY SURVEYORS		PARISH	LOT	AREA	AREA CLAIMED	PATENTEE		YEAR OF PATENT
KINGSBURY	GEORGE	ST CLEMENT	42	70	70	BANNATYNE	AGB	1877
KIPLING	EDWARD	ST CLEMENT	39	50	50			
KIPLING	THOMAS	ST CLEMENT	38	48	48	KIPLING	JANE	85
KIPLING	WIDOW	ST ANDREW	266	70	70	BIRD	CATHER	84
KNIGHT	JAMES	ST PAUL	110	66	66	KNIGHT	JAMES	1878
KNIGHT	JOHN	ST PAUL	56	68	68	KNIGHT	JOHN	1885
KNIGHT	PETER	ST PAUL	67	69	69	KNIGHT	PETER	1885
KNOTT	JOHN	HIGH BLUFF	27	200	200	KNOTT	JOHN	1885
KNOTTS	JOHN	ST ANDREW	48	53	53	SCHULTZ	JOHN	1876
KOUSSAIN	EUSTACHE	ST NORBERT	174	106	106	STEPHEN	GEORGE	1877
LACERTE	BAPTISTE	ST NORBERT	33	73	49	LANDRY	JOSEPH	1885
LACERTE	LOUIS	ST NORBERT	14	154	154	LACERTE	LOUIS	1875
LACERTE	LOUIS	ST NORBERT	24	98	98	LACERTE	LOUIS	1877
LACERTE	LOUIS	STE AGATHE	114	102	102	LECOMTE	JOSEPH	1879
LACERTE	LOUIS	STE AGATHE	616	162	162	MULAIRE	CATHERINE	1885
LADOUCEUR	AUGUSTE	ST NORBERT	30	43	43	LADOUCEUR	AUGUSTE	1876
LADOUX	LOUIS	SFX	157	92	92	LEDOUX	JOSEPH	81
LAFFERTYETAL		STE AGATHE	591	188	188			
LAFOND		ST VITAL	18	61	61	LAFOND	BENJAM	94
LAFONTAINE	ANTOINE	SFX	40	90	90	MCBEATH	MORRISON	1876
LAFONTAINE	CHARLES	SFX	168	121	36	LUMSDEN	THOMAS	1884
LAFONTAINE	CHARLES	SFX	169	121	86	GERVAIS	ALEXIS	1881
LAFRANCEETAL	ALFRED	STE AGATHE	135	52	52	MOORE	ROBERT WM	83
LAFRENIERE	BAPTISTE	BAIE S PAUL	9	218	218	LAFRENIERE	JEAN BAPTIST	1885
LAFRENIERE	FRANCOIS	SFX	149	83	83	LAFRENIERE	BAPTISTE	1877
LAGIMODIERE	LAZAIRE	ST BONIFACE	99	8	8	LAFORT	FRANCIS	1879
LAGIMODIERE	MODESTE	STE ANNE	6	197	197	LAGIMONIERE	ELZEAR	1889
LAING	THOMAS	STE ANNE	1	250	250	HUDSONS BAY	COMPANY	1878
LALIBERTE	ALEXIS	BAIE S PAUL	207	120	120	CHENIER	FELIX	1912
LALIBERTY	ANT	ST NORBERT	144	22	15	WPG CITY		78
LAMBERT	JOHN	ST ANDREW	32	46	46	LAMBERT	JOHN	1875
LAMBERT	JOSEPH	ST NORBERT	46	185	185	LAMBERT	JOSEPH	1875
LAMBERT	JOSEPH	HEADINGLY	23	102	102	LAMBERT	JOSEPH	85
LAMBERT	MICH	ST ANDREW	33	45	45	LAMBERT	JAMES	85
LAMBERT	MICHEL	ST ANDREW	248	42	42	LAMBERT	JAMES	1879
LAMBERT	THOMAS	ST ANDREW	31	46	46			
LAMBERT	THOMAS	ST NORBERT	249	10	10			
LAMERONDE	ALEXIS	ST NORBERT	92	51	51	BROWN	JOHN	1879
LANDRE	ST PIERRE	SFX	252	145	145	PEPIN DIT LA CHANCEPIERRE	OCTAVE	1885
LANDRY	MOES	BAIE S PAUL	153	94	94	ALLARD	JOSEPH	1878
LANE		BAIE S PAUL	187	211	211	TANNER	JAMES	1877
LANE		ST PAUL	188	134	134	SPENCE	DONALD	1875
LANE	WILLIAM	STE AGATHE	138	161	161	SMITH	WILLIAM	1876
LANE ETAL	JOHN	SFX	100	107	107	LANE	WILLIAM	1882
LAPLANT	ANTOINE	SFX	71	114	114	BALLANTYNE	LUCY	1878
LAPLANTE	ANTOINE	STE AGATHE	211	103	103	HOLLAND	CHARLES	1875
LAPLANTE	BONIFACE	SFX	155	60	60	SMITH	DONALD A	1877
LAPLANTE	JOSEPH	STE AGATHE	573	175	175	LAPLANTE	BONIFACE	1881
LAPOINT	IB	SFX	156	122	122	LAPLANTE	JEAN BTE	1882
LAPOINT	JOSEPH	STE ANNE	12	222	222	LAPOINT	IB	1879
LAPOINT	JOSEPH	STE AGATHE	107	160	160	LAPOINT	JOSEPH	

TABLE 5: RECOGNITION OF RIVERLOT OCCUPANTS BY THE GOVERNMENT OF CANADA

OCCUPANT NAMED BY SURVEYORS	PARISH	LOT	AREA	AREA CLAIMED	PATENTEE	YEAR OF PATENT
LAPOINTE J BTE	ST BONIFACE	78	15	15	LAPOINTE J BTE	1877
LAPOINTE JB	STE ANNE	70	221	221	LAPOINTE JB	1882
LARENTURE LOUIS	STE AGATHE	150	165	82	DESROSIERS GEORGE	1900
LAROCQUE FRANCOIS	ST VITAL	31	68	68	PATTERSON JOHN	1878
LAROKE LOUIS	STE AGATHE	551	139	139		
LAROKE LOUIS	STE AGATHE	571	225	225	LAROKE LOUIS	1877
LARONDE MRS.	ST NORBERT	192	108	108	SCHULTZ JOHN	1878
LAROQUE JOSEPH	ST VITAL	27	24	24	LAROCQUE CHARLES	1897
LAROQUE MICHEL	SFX	67	78	78	LAROCQUE MICHEL	1883
LAROQUE OLIVE	SFX	177	101	101	FORGET JOSEPH	1882
LAROQUE OLIVIA	SFX	49	185	185	TURCOT EUSEBE	1884
LAUNDRY JOSEPH	ST NORBERT	142	210	210	LAUNDRY JOSEPH	1875
LAUNDRY SR JOSEPH	ST NORBERT	194	147	147	LAUNDRY SR JOSEPH	1877
LAURENCE JOSEPH	ST VITAL	25	4	4	ST MARS ABRAHAM	1882
LAURENCE PATRICK	SFX	17	50	50	LAWRENCE PATRICE	83
LAVALETTE BAPTISTE	ST LAURENT	57	107	107	LUMSDEN THOMAS	1878
LAVALLEE BAPTISTE	SFX	8	219	68	LAVALLEE JOSEPH	1878
LAVALLEE CHARLES	SFX	26	86	86	LAVALLEE CHARLES	1881
LAVALLEE ELIE	SFX	25	89	89	MULLOCK WILLIAM	1882
LAVALLEE GREGOIRE	SFX	9	79	79	CLARKE HENRY	1882
LAVALLEE PIERRE	SFX	32	78	78	LAVALLEE PIERRE SR	1887
LAVALLEE PIERRE	SFX	35	80	80	LAVALLEE PIERRE	1880
LAVALLEE PIERRE	SFX	36	197	197	LAVALLEE OBLATE	1878
LAVALLIER ANDREW	ST LAURENT	10	209	46	FATHERS PIERRE	1876
LAVERDIERE PIERRE ETAL	ST CHARLES	90	214	214	LAVERDIERE PIERRE	1885
LAVIOLETTE BAPTISTE	SFX	187	96	96	DAIGNEAULT NARCISSE	84
LAVIOLETTE GILBERT	SFX	165	96	96	BERTRAND CAROLI	85
LAVIOLETTE WIDOW	SFX	186	57	57	PERRAS RAPHAE	1876
LAWRENCE BASILE	ST VITAL	21	76	52	LAURENCE BASILE	1875
LAWRENCE NORBERT	ST NORBERT	97	46	46	LAURENCE NORBERT	81
LAWRENCE WIDOW	ST BONIFACE	77	15	15	LARENCE JOSEPHTE	1878
LEASK SAMUEL	ST ANDREW	222	49	49	LEASK SAMUEL	
LEASK SAMUEL	ST ANDREW	279	63	63	FRAZER JOHN	1878
LEASK THOMAS	ST ANDREW	223	49	49	LEASK SAMUEL	77
LEASK ETAL SAMUEL	ST CLEMENT	55	100	50	BEGG CHARLES	1882
LEBLANCHETAL LEWIS	STE AGATHE	100	203	203		
LECLERC ETAL ARTHUR	ST CHARLES	143	80	80	LECLERC ARTHUR	1882
LECLERE JOSEPH	ST CHARLES	69	110	110	MURRAY LETITIA	1882
LECLERE JOSEPH	ST CHARLES	98	106	106	LECLERE JOSEPH	1875
LECUYER TOUSAINT	STE AGATHE	113	113	113		
LECUYER ETAL ADELARD	STE AGATHE	95	108	108		
LEDEROUTE BAPTISTE	ST BONIFACE	19	52	52	LEDEROUTE BAPTISTE	1877
LEDEROUTE BAPTISTE	ST BONIFACE	21	106	106	LEDEROUTE BAPTISTE	1875
LEDEROUTE JOSEPH	ST BONIFACE	11	80	80	LEDEROUTE MARIE	1885
LEDEROUTE PHILIBERTE	ST BONIFACE	17	156	156	LEDEROUTE PHILIBERTE	1875
LEDEROUTE JR BAPTISTE	ST BONIFACE	13	97	97	LEDEROUTE JR BAPTISTE	1876
LEDEROUTE SR BAPTISTE	ST BONIFACE	12	40	40	LEDEROUTE JOSETTE ETAL	1885
LEDOUX RENE ETAL	SFX	104	190	95	CHENIER FELIX	1879
LEMAY JOSEPH	ST NORBERT	85	214	214	LEMAY JOSEPH	1877
LEPAGE MAJORIE	ST NORBERT	167	97	97	BEAUPIE VICTOR J	1884
LEPINE AMBROISE D	ST BONIFACE	3	92	92	LEPINE AMBROISE D	82
LEPINE AMBROISE D	ST BONIFACE	119	70	70	LEPINE CECIL	1889

TABLE 5: RECOGNITION OF RIVERLOT OCCUPANTS BY THE GOVERNMENT OF CANADA

OCCUPANT NAMED BY SURVEYORS	PARISH	LOT	AREA	AREA CLAIMED	PATENTEE	YEAR OF PATENT
LEPINE BAPTISTE	ST NORBERT	35	228	228	LEPINE BAPTISTE	1875
LEPINE JAMES	SFX	14	82	82	TURCOTTE NORBER	86
LEPINE JOSEPH	SFX	145	74	74	LEPINE MARIE	1882
LEPINE MAXIME	SFX	22	247	247	LEPINE MAXIME	1877
LEPINE ETAL AMBROISE	ST NORBERT	175	112	112	LEPINE AMBROISE D	1882
LERONT ANTOINE	STE AGATHE	101	152	152	CURRAN ROBERT	1878
LESPERANCE ALEXIS	SFX	28	77	77	LESPERANCE ALEXIS	1876
LESPERANCE JEAN	SFX	31	71	71	LESPERANCE JEAN	1879
LESPERANCE JOSEPH	STE AGATHE	531	220	220	HUGHES JAMES	1877
LETUA MICHEL	BAIE S PAUL	130	95	95	BOURKE EDWIN	1877
LEVEILLEE GABRIEL	SFX	209	41	41	LEPINE GABRIEL	1880
LEWIS H	STE AGATHE	26	127	127	HUDSONS BAY CO	1891
LEWIS H	STE AGATHE	34	148	148	CURRAN LUCY	81
LEWIS JAMES	ST ANDREW	263	37	37	ALLAN JOHN	1876
LEWIS JAMES	ST ANDREW	268	47	47	LEWIS JAMES	78
LEWIS JOHN	ST ANDREW	65	59	59	LEWIS NANCY LEE	78
LEWIS JOHN LEE	ST ANDREW	210	40	40	LEWIS JOHN LEE	1876
LEWIS WILLIAM	ST ANDREW	267	23	23	LOUIS JAMES	1894
LEWIS WILLIAM	ST ANDREW	275	38	38	HENDERSON PETER	1907
LINGEN EDWARD	SFX	121	103	52	LAFRENIERE AMBROISE	
LINKLATER HUGH	ST CLEMENT	101	26	26	LINKLATER HUGH	
LINKLATER WILLIAM	ST ANDREW	49	52	52	DEVLIN BRIAN	
LINKLATER ALEXANDER	ST LAURENT	23	103	103	LOGAN ALEX	
LOGAN CHARLES	ST JOHN	53	5	5	BROUSE GEORGE J	75
LOGAN JOHN	HEADINGLY	24	99	99	LOGAN JOHN	1874
LOGAN ROBERT	ST NORBERT	246	116	116	KING PETER	1882
LOGAN ROBERT	ST CHARLES	81	87	87	ALLINGHAUR FRANK A M	1877
LOGAN SARAH	ST CHARLES	82	85	85	JOBIN AMBROISE	1877
LOGAN SARAH	ST CHARLES	44	93	93	BROWN JAMES	1883
LOGAN WILLIAM	ST CHARLES	45	94	94	MORRIS ALEXANDER	1884
LOGAN WILLIAM	ST CHARLES	86	185	185	SMITH D A	1875
LOGAN ETAL WILLIAM	ST NORBERT	172	102		MORRIS ALEXANDER	1883
LOGAN JR ROBERT	ST CHARLES	87	120	120	SMITH DA HON	1878
LONSDALE W T	ST NORBERT	170	212	212	LONSDALE W T	1875
LOUTIT JOHN	HEADINGLY	6	197	197	LOUTIT JOHN	1877
LOUTIT PETER	ST ANDREW	106	58	58	LOUTIT PETER	1875
LOUTIT JOHN	ST ANDREW	169	52	52	LOUTIT HEBER	77
LUCAS ALEX	STE AGATHE	593	148	148	ARCHIBALD THOMAS	77
LUCIA ALEX	SFX	56	110	110	LUMSDEN CHARLES	1880
LUCIA AMABLE	SFX	61	93	93	HOUSE CALINE	1876
LUCIA JOSEPH	SFX	70	101	101	TOURON TOUISSAINT	1885
LUCIA TOUISSAINT	SFX	71	195	195	LUCIER ALEXANDER	1877
LUCIER AMABLE	SFX	174	81	81	LUCIER ALEXANDER	1876
LYONS JOHN	ST CLEMENT	9	47	47	LYONS THOMAS	1883
LYONS THOMAS	ST CLEMENT	8	47	47	LYONS THOMAS	84
MACINTOSH CHRISTOPHER	KILDONAN	48	51	51	MCRAE JOHN	1884
MACINTOSH CHRISTOPHER	KILDONAN	56	83	83	MCINTOSH CHRIS	1881
MACTAVISH IH	STE ANNE	8	463	463	MCTAVISH JOHN H	78
MAGER JEAN	ST BONIFACE	87	38	38	MAGER JEAN	1876
MAGER VICTOR	ST BONIFACE	108	50	50	MAGER VICTOR	1882
MAGUIRE PHILIP	SFX	61	48	48	MCGUIRE PHILIP	1878
MALATERRE ALEX	SFX	203	107	107	BANNATYNE ANDREW G B	1872

OCCUPANT NAMED BY SURVEYORS	PARISH	LOT	AREA	AREA CLAIMED	PATENTEE	YEAR OF PATENT
MALATERRE BASILE	SFX	3	123	123	TAYLOR JOHN	1877
MANSEAU ONESIOME	STE ANNE	61	325	325	MANSEAU ONESIOME	1884
MARCELLAIS ANTOINE	ST NORBERT	87	64	64	VENNE SOLOMON	1878
MARCELLAIS FELIX	ST NORBERT	245	155	155	KENNEDY WILLIAM N	1884
MARCHAND BENJAMIN	STE AGATHE	124	116	116	DANCEREAU MAGLIORE	1888
MARCHAND CYRIL	ST NORBERT	49	141	141	MARCHAND CYRIL	1875
MARCHAND CYRIL	ST NORBERT	52	246	7	ZASTE GONZAGUE	1884
MARCHANDE CYRIL	ST NORBERT	185	104	104	MARCHANDE CYRIL	1878
MARION EDMOND	ST NORBERT	37	160	160	MARION EDMOND	1876
MARION JOSEPH	ST NORBERT	63	98	98	LEMAY JOSEPH	1878
MARION MARCIS	ST NORBERT	176	118	118	MARION ROGER	1879
MARION NARCIS	ST NORBERT	190	62	62	MARION ROGER	1879
MARLATT SAMUEL R	PORTAGE	123	64	11	ROSE FRANCIS	1892
MARTEL MALIN	ST BONIFACE	9	161	161	MARTEL JOSEPH	1877
MARTIN ABRAHAM	SFX	161	151	151	MARTIN ABRAHA	84
MARTIN LAURENT	BAIE S PAUL	219	218	218	ISBISTER THOMAS	78
MARTINETAL WILLIAM	STE AGATHE	46	139	139	CAMPBELL COLIN	1882
MATHESON ANGUS	KILDONAN	60	75	75	MATHESON ANGUS	1878
MATHESON ANGUS	KILDONAN	65	76	76	MATHESON ANGUS	1878
MATHESON DONALD	HIGH BLUFF	34	169	169	MATHESON DONALD	1875
MATHESON DONALD	KILDONAN	84	121	121	BELL JOHN	1875
MATHESON JOHN	KILDONAN	12	157	78	MATHESON JOHN	1875
MATHESON JOHN	KILDONAN	80	41	41	MATHESON JOHN	1875
MATHESON JOHN	KILDONAN	83	41	41	MATHESON JOHN	1875
MATHESON JOHN	ST PAUL	92	92	92	MATHESON JOHN	1881
MATHESON REV ALEX	KILDONAN	59	154	154	MATHESON ALEX	1875
MATHESON SAMUEL	KILDONAN	82	41	41	MATHESON SAMUEL	1878
MATHESON WILLIAM	KILDONAN	52	149	149	MATHESON WILLIAM	1883
MATHESON WILLIAM	KILDONAN	88	76	76	MATHESON WILLIAM	1878
MATHEWSON JAMES	STE AGATHE	36	132	132	MATHEWSON JAMES	1890
MATHEWSON JOHN	KILDONAN	8	73	73	MATHEWSON JOHN SR	1875
MATHEWSON SAMUEL	KILDONAN	9	96	96	MATHEWSON SAMUEL	1884
MAURIE CASSIMERE	STE AGATHE	636	162	162	GREEN GEORGE	1889
MAURIE MAGDELEEN	STE AGATHE	638	166	166	DIMMUCK EVELYN	1885
MAWHINNEY ISAAH	PORTAGE	93	138	138	MAWHINNEY ISAIAH	78
MAY ETAL NARCISSE	STE AGATHE	144	74	74	BOITEAU NAPOLEON	1882
MCALISTER JAMES	ST JOHN	47	46	46	MACARTHUR DAVID	1885
MCBAIN JAMES	PORTAGE	43	161	161	MCBAIN JAMES	1878
MCBAIN ROBERT	PORTAGE	42	161	161	MCBAIN ROBERT	1879
MCBANE KENNETH	PORTAGE	70	214	71	CORRIGAL JOHN	1882
MCBETH ADAM	ST CLEMENT	27	102	102	MCBEATH ADAM	85
MCBETH ALEX	ST ANDREW	280	59	59	MCBEATH ALEXAN	83
MCBETH ALEXANDER	ST PAUL	51	173	173	MCBEATH ALEXANDER	1885
MCBETH JOHN	KILDONAN	31	173	86	MCBETH JOHN	1885
MCBETH JOHN	ST PAUL	118	95	95	MCBETH JOHN	1880
MCBETH MORRISON	SFX	196	79	79	HENDERSON JOHN	1876
MCBETH MORRISON	SFX	215	134	134	MCBEATH MORRISON	1877
MCBETH MORRISON	KILDONAN	34	152	152	MCBEATH ANGUS	1878
MCBETH MORRISON	KILDONAN	74	41	41	ANDERSON THOMAS	1875
MCBETH ROBERT	KILDONAN	33	159	159	HARPER JOHN	1883
MCBETH ROBERT	KILDONAN	46	100	100	MCRAE ROBERT	1878
MCBETH ROBERT	ST PAUL	84	129	129	MCBETH JOHN	1883

TABLE 5: RECOGNITION OF RIVERLOT OCCUPANTS BY THE GOVERNMENT OF CANADA

OCCUPANT NAMED BY SURVEYORS		PARISH	LOT	AREA	AREA CLAIMED	PATENTEE		YEAR OF PATENT
MCBRIDE	JOHN	ST ANDREW	288	65	65	SCHULTZ	JOHN	1877
MCCLENNON		ST PAUL	34	76	76	LYNN	WASHINGTON F	1877
MCCLENNON	JOSEPH	ST PAUL	33	76	76	MCCLENNON	JOSEPH	1878
MCCORRISTER	ALEX	ST ANDREW	162	62	62	MCCORRISTER	ALEXANDER	75
MCCORRISTER	JOHN	ST ANDREW	168	39	39	MCCORRISTER	JOHN	75
MCCORRISTER	WILLIAM	PORTAGE	150	58	58	MCCORRISTER	WILLIAM	81
MCCULLOCK	WILLIAM	PORTAGE	26	240	240	MCCULLOCK	WILLIAM	1881
MCDALLIS ETU	XANGUS	SFX	154	182	182	MCGILLIS	ANGUS	85
MCDEASE JR		ST NORBERT	8	172	172	MCDEASE	JR	1877
MCDEASE SR		ST NORBERT	7	160	160	SCHULTZ	JOHN	1882
MCDERMOT		SFX	15	495	495	SMITH	DONALD	1876
MCDERMOT	A	ST CHARLES	117	78	78	AUGER	JEAN BTE	81
MCDERMOT	A	ST JAMES	2	6	6	MURRAY	A	1882
MCDERMOT	ANDREW	ST CHARLES	92	204	204	MORRIS	ALEX	1878
MCDERMOT	ANDREW	ST CHARLES	104	113	113	MURRAY	ALEX	1882
MCDERMOT	ANDREW	ST CHARLES	122	209	209	MCDERMOT	ANDREW	1875
MCDERMOT	ANDREW	ST JAMES	12	858	858	MCDERMOT	ANDREW	1875
MCDERMOT	ANDREW	ST BONIFACE	6	82	82	MCDERMOT	ALEXANDER	1876
MCDERMOT SR	ANDREW	ST CHARLES	88	114	114	MORRIS	ALEXANDER	1876
MCDERMOTT	JOHN	BAIE S PAUL	202	89	89	MCDERMOTT	JOHN	1876
MCDONALD	A	PORTAGE	53	206	206	MCDONALD	ARCHIE	1877
MCDONALD	ALEX	ST ANDREW	35	46	46	MCDONALD	ALEXANDER	75
MCDONALD	ALEX	ST ANDREW	125	42	42	MCDONALD	ALEX	1875
MCDONALD	ALEX	ST ANDREW	192	39	39	MCDONALD	DONALD	1891
MCDONALD	ARCHIBALD	ST ANDREW	239	40	40	SMITH	DONALD A	79
MCDONALD	CHARLES	HIGH BLUFF	42	152	152	BAILEY	ALFRED	1877
MCDONALD	CUTHBERT	PORTAGE	45	160	160	MCDONALD	JAMES	1878
MCDONALD	D	ST ANDREW	260	46	46	MCDONALD	JOHN	1878
MCDONALD	DONALD	ST ANDREW	22	82	82	MCDONALD	CUTHBERT	1892
MCDONALD	DONALD	ST ANDREW	78	204	204	MCDONALD	JOHN	1878
MCDONALD	DONALD	ST ANDREW	80	127	127	MCDONALD	ADAM	79
MCDONALD	DONALD	ST ANDREW	236	62	62	HEAP	JAMES	1901
MCDONALD	DUNCAN	ST ANDREW	50	44	44	MCDONALD	DONALD	1876
MCDONALD	HUGH	PORTAGE	46	52	52	MCDONALD	DUNCAN	1885
MCDONALD	JOHN	PORTAGE	44	161	161	MCDONALD	HUGH	1878
MCDONALD	JOHN	HIGH BLUFF	31	290	290	MCDONALD	JOHN	78
MCDONALD	JOHN	ST ANDREW	26	92	92	MCDONALD	JOHN	1875
MCDONALD	JOHN	ST ANDREW	110	130	130	MCDONALD	JOHN	1885
MCDONALD	JOHN	ST ANDREW	128	82	82	MCDONALD	DONALD	1875
MCDONALD	JOHN	ST ANDREW	164	56	56	MCDONALD	JOHN	1877
MCDONALD	JOHN	ST ANDREW	254	31	31	MCDONALD	JOHN	1885
MCDONALD	JOHN	ST CLEMENT	48	50	50	MCDONALD	SARAH	85
MCDONALD	WIDOW	ST ANDREW	149	59	59			1885
MCDONALD	WILLIAM	KILDONAN	36	82	82	MCDONALD	ETAL	1885
MCDONALD	WILLIAM	ST ANDREW	36	86	86	MCDONALD	DONALD	1876
MCDONALD	WILLIAM	ST ANDREW	81	62	62			
MCDONALD	WILLIAM	ST ANDREW	191	39	26	FLETT	JAMES	1876
MCDONALD	WILLIAM ETAL	PORTAGE	132	201	181	MCDONALD	WILLIAM ETAL	1878
MCDOUGALL	ALEXANDER	ST JAMES	68	48	48	MCDOUGALL	ALEX	1875
MCDOUGALL	DUNCAN	SFX	24	92	92	MCKENNY	ISABELLA	1878
MCDOUGALL	JOHN	SFX	179	96	96	KAVANAGH		1878

OCCUPANT NAMED BY SURVEYORS	PARISH	LOT	AREA	AREA CLAIMED	PATENTEE		YEAR OF PATENT
MCEWAN WILLIAM	ST CLEMENT	59	47	47	MCIVER	MURDOCK	1875
MCGILLIS	SFX	88	157	157	MCGILLIS	ALEX	1898
MCGILLIS	SFX	89	107	107	PROVENCHER	JOSEPH	84
MCGILLIS	SFX	90	104	104	RYAN	JOSEPH	1881
MCGILLIS	SFX	91	97	97	RYAN	JOSEPH	93
MCGILLIS	SFX	92	95	95	GRANT	JOHN	86
MCGILLIS CORBET	SFX	184	124	124	TACHE	ALEXANDER	
MCGILLIS DANIEL	SFX	170	79	79	LUMSDEN	THOMAS	1884
MCGILLIS HECTOR	BAIE S PAUL	3	209	209	BONNEAU	ANGELIQUE	1883
MCHEAN DUNCAN	ST CLEMENT	78	168	168	BANNATYNE	A G B	82
MCIVER HEIRS OF WM	ST VITAL	2	114	114	BANNATYNE	ANDREW	82
MCIVOR DONALD	KILDONAN	45	148	49	MCIVOR	DONALD	1878
MCKAE BISHOP	ST CLEMENT	19	53	53	MCKAE	BISHOP	1876
MCKAE DUNCAN	ST ANDREW	112	52	52	MCKAE	DUNCAN	1875
MCKAY ALEX	BAIE S PAUL	194	103	103	MCKAY	JAMES	1878
MCKAY ALEX	SFX	214	122	122	BOYLE	LIONEL	85
MCKAY ALEX	PORTAGE	31	240	240	RYAN	JOSEPH	82
MCKAY ALEXANDER	STE AGATHE	55	97	97	SPENCER	JOHN	1882
MCKAY ANGUS	SFX	201	176	176	TURNER	ALEXAN	80
MCKAY ANGUS	SFX	227	168	168	TOOLE	JEMINA	1890
MCKAY GEORGE	POPLAR PT	77	88	88	MCKAY	GEORGE	1878
MCKAY HON JAMES	ST BONIFACE	42	42	42	MCKAY	HON JAMES	1877
MCKAY HON JAMES	ST JAMES	15	97	97	MCKAY	JAMES	1875
MCKAY HON JAMES	ST JAMES	21	186	186	MCKAY	HON JAMES	1875
MCKAY HON JAMES	ST JAMES	28	68	68	MCKAY	HON JAMES	1875
MCKAY JAMES	BAIE S PAUL	167	314	314	MCKAY	JAMES	1878
MCKAY JAMES	BAIE S PAUL	168	376	376	MCKAY	JAMES	1878
MCKAY JAMES	BAIE S PAUL	179	108	108	MCKAY	JAMES	1878
MCKAY JAMES	BAIE S PAUL	218	175	175	MCKAY	JAMES	1877
MCKAY JAMES	ST CHARLES	23	101	101	MCKAY	JAMES	1875
MCKAY JAMES	ST CHARLES	89	444		MCKAY	JAMES	1875
MCKAY JAMES	ST CHARLES	93	100	100	MCKAY	JAMES	1875
MCKAY JAMES	POPLAR PT	112	56	56	MCKAY	JAMES	77
MCKAY JAMES	KILDONAN	61	353	353	MCKAY	JAMES	1878
MCKAY JD	PORTAGE	68	79	79	MCKAY	JD	1877
MCKAY JOHN	PORTAGE	58	147	147	MCKAY	JOHN	1875
MCKAY JOHN	SFX	223	102	102	MOOR	WILLIAM	1885
MCKAY JOHN	ST CLEMENT	23	57	57	BANNATYNE	A G B	82
MCKAY NEIL	ST ANDREW	85	25	25	MCKAY	NEIL	1876
MCKAY PIERRE	BAIE S PAUL	108	113	113	MORRISON	DONALD	
MCKAY SELKIRK	KILDONAN	5	162	162	MCKAY	SELKIRK G	1886
MCKAY WILLIAM	ST ANDREW	18	182	55	MCKAY A	WILLIAM	
MCKAY WILLIAM	ST ANDREW	18	83	83	MCKAY A	WILLIA	77
MCKAY WILLIAM	ST ANDREW	232	46	46	DENNETT	ANDREW	77
MCKAY WILLIAM	ST CLEMENT	256	32	32	MCKAY	WILLIAM	99
MCKAY WILLIAM H	ST ANDREW	82	26	26	BONNEAU	NAPOLEON	1877
MCKAY ET AL JOSEPH	BAIE S PAUL	238	41	41	FISHER	GEORGE	1881
MCKAY ET AL PIERRE	BAIE S PAUL	17	103	103	MCKAY	SEVERE	1886
MCKAY ET AL SEVERE	BAIE S PAUL	244	160	160	COLDEUGH	FREDER	1902
MCKAY ETAL DA	ST CLEMENT	12	71	71	ABBOTT	WILLIAM	98
MCKAYETAL ALEXANDER	STE AGATHE	107	60	60			1882
		53	127	127			

TABLE 5: RECOGNITION OF RIVERLOT OCCUPANTS BY THE GOVERNMENT OF CANADA

OCCUPANT NAMED BY SURVEYORS	PARISH	LOT	AREA	AREA CLAIMED	PATENTEE	YEAR OF PATENT
MCKENZIE ALEX	ST CLEMENT	16	52	52	MCKENZIE ALEXAN	86
MCKENZIE HECTOR	ST JAMES	19	192	192	MCKENZIE HECTOR A	81
MCKENZIE JAMES	SFX	225	92	92	TAYLOR JOHN	1884
MCKENZIE JAMES	ST PAUL	52	60	60	MCKENZIE NANCY	1893
MCKENZIE ROD AND BEN	HEADINGLY	32	158	158	MCKENZIE RODERICK	1875
MCKENZIE SAMUEL	ST ANDREW	122	43	43	BEUTLEY KATHERINE	1882
MCKINNON ANDREW	STE AGATHE	17	108	108	HUDSONS BAY CO	1883
MCLANE FARAQUAHER	PORTAGE	69	623	623	MCLANE FARAQUAHER	1877
MCLEAN DUNCAN	ST CLEMENT	51	55	55	MCLEAN DUNCAN	1879
MCLEANETAL PETER	PORTAGE	40	161	161	MCLEAN PETER	1889
MCLEANETAL PETER	PORTAGE	41	161	161	MCLEAN PETER	1882
MCLEDD ALEXANDER	HIGH BLUFF	57	110	110	SISSONS THOMAS ETAL	1877
MCLEOD ANGUS	ST ANDREW	160	48	48	MCLEOD ANGUS	77
MCLEOD ANTOINE	SFX	207	58	58	JODOIN ELISE	1884
MCLEOD DON	ST CLEMENT	91	93	93	MCLEOD DONALD	75
MCLEOD JOHN	PORTAGE	64	280	280	MCLEAN JOHN	1879
MCLEDD JOHN	ST ANDREW	137	124	62	MCLEOD JOHN	1881
MCLEDD JOHN	ST ANDREW	161	63	63	MCLEOD JOHN	76
MCLEDD JOHN	ST CLEMENT	66	94	94	MCLEOD JOHN	75
MCLEOD JOSEPH	SFX	1	238	119	TRESTON JAMES	1878
MCLEOD KENNETH	POPLAR PT	85	241	241	AITKIN ALEXANDER	81
MCLEOD MALCOLM	ST ANDREW	135	126	126	MCLEOD MALCOLM	76
MCLEOD MOES	SFX	5	29	29	HACKLAND JAMES	1878
MCLEOD MURDOCK	HIGH BLUFF	35	135	135	MCKAY DONALD	1877
MCLEOD MURDOCK	KILDONAN	67	77	77	MCLEOD FRANCES	1885
MCLEOD PIERRE	SFX	12	78	78	SMITH DONALD	1877
MCLEOD WIDOW	ST BONIFACE	16	43	43	LAROCQUE MARGARET	1877
MCLEOD ETAL RODERICK	PORTAGE	124	527	527	MCLEOD ETAL RODERICK	1878
MCMILLAN JOSEPH	ST CHARLES	32	99	99	CARRIER DANIEL	1879
MCMILLAN WILLIAM	ST JAMES	16	146	146	MCMULLEN WILLIAM	1876
MCNABB CHARLES	BAIE S PAUL	105	226	226	MCNABB CHARLES	1875
MCNABB CHARLES	POPLAR PT	88	301	301	MCNABB CHARLES	1875
MCNABB JAMES	POPLAR PT	82	172	172	MCNABB JAMES	1875
MCNABB JOHN JR	POPLAR PT	80	112	112	MCNABB JOHN JR	1877
MCNABB JOHN SR	POPLAR PT	81	132	132	MCNABB JOHN SR	1875
MCPHAIL DUNCAN	HIGH BLUFF	56	113	113	SISSONS THOMAS ETAL	1877
MCPHAIL JOHN	KILDONAN	97	77	77	MCPHAIL JOHN	1875
MCPHERSON ALEXANDER	PORTAGE	129	319	319	MCPHERSON ALEXANDER	1877
MCPHILLIPS FRANK	BAIE S PAUL	221	97	97	TOURON DAVID	1882
MCRAE DUNCAN	ST ANDREW	158	48	48	LILLIE ALEXANDER R	79
MCRAE JOHN	KILDONAN	40	80	80	MCRAE JOHN	1875
MCTAVISH JOHN	ST CHARLES	30	100	100	MCMULLEN JOSEPH	1880
MCTAVISH JOHN	ST BONIFACE	96	16	16	MCTAVISH JOHN HENRY	1878
MCVEIGH ETAL JOHN	STE AGATHE	80	168	168	MCVEIGH JOHN	1882
MEYER CHARLES	PORTAGE	62	154	154	MAIR CHARLES	77
MILHAM CHARLES	HEADINGLY	15	200	200	MILHAM CHARLES	1875
MILLER ELIZABETH	ST PAUL	77	138	52	SUTHERLAND GEORGE	1875
MILLER GEORGE	ST PAUL	48	116	116	MILLER GEORGE	1885
MILLER WIDOW	ST NORBERT	23	93	93	MULAIRE CATHERINE	1885
MINNIE FRANCAIS	ST NORBERT	247	115	115	SCHULTZ JOHN	1880
MISSION CATHOLIC	ST VITAL	6	79	79	NAULT ANDRE	85
MISSION CATHOLIC	STE ANNE	56	196	196	MISSION CATHOLIC	1876

OCCUPANT NAMED BY SURVEYORS	PARISH	LOT	AREA	AREA CLAIMED	PATENTEE	YEAR OF PATENT
MITCHELL DAVID	ST PAUL	104	49	49	MACHRAY REV R	1882
MOFFAT JOHN	STE AGATHE	72	166	166	HEPBURN ANDREW	1882
MONETTE BAPTISTE	BAIE S PAUL	26	82	82	BOUCHER J BAPTISTE	1880
MONETTE MICHEL	BAIE S PAUL	10	120	120	MONETTE MICHEL	1886
MONEYAIS JOHN	ST CHARLES	78	92	92	ALLARD REV J	1878
MONKMAN JAMES	ST PAUL	103	99	99	PRITCHARD HUGH	1883
MONKMAN JOSEPH	ST PAUL	73	47	47	MONKMAN THOMAS	1876
MONKMAN THOMAS	ST PAUL	54	255	255	MONKMAN THOMAS	1875
MOONEY JOHN	PORTAGE	28	160	160	COWAN JAMES	1882
MOONEY JOHN	PORTAGE	29	80	80	COWAN JAMES	81
MOORE CHARLES	ST ANDREW	89	65	65	MOORE JANE	85
MOORE CHARLES	ST ANDREW	159	48	48	MOORE JANE	
MOORE ETAL CHARLES	ST ANDREW	183	43	43	MOORE JANE	85
MOREAU CEASAR	ST PAUL	55	66	66	SCHULTZ JOHN	1877
MOREAU ANTOINE	ST NORBERT	74	110	110	LECOMTE JOSEPH	1877
MOREAU LOUIS	ST NORBERT	79	95	95	MORAND LOUIS	1897
MOREAU LOUISON	ST NORBERT	73	203	203	LECOMTE JOSEPH	1876
MORGAN	SFX	7	166	83	SETTER ELIZA	1887
MORGAN	SFX	221	363	363	MORGAN ROBERT	1877
MORIN ALEX	STE AGATHE	575	181	181	MORIN ALEX	1877
MORIN ANDRE	STE AGATHE	557	156	156	MORIN ANDRE	1877
MORIN ANTOINE	ST VITAL	24	44	44	MORIN ANTOINE	1877
MORIN BAPTISTE	BAIE S PAUL	237	120	120	THIBERT PIERRE	1882
MORIN BAPTISTE	ST BONIFACE	29	65	65	MORIN BAPTISTE	1875
MORIN BATRICE	STE ANNE	19	443	443	PERREAULT JBT	1880
MORIN FRANCOIS	SFX	188	80	80	SMITH DONALD	1877
MORIN GB	STE ANNE	55	367	367	PEAREAULT J BTE	1880
MORIN LOUIS	STE AGATHE	577	193	193	MORIN LOUIS	1877
MORIN NORBERT	STE ANNE	14	194	194	MORIN NORBERT	1878
MORIN OCTAVE	STE ANNE	4	427	171	ANDERSON JAMES	1882
MORIN PIERRE	SFX	213	99	99	MORIN PIERRE	1883
MORIN PIERRE	STE AGATHE	139	111	111	MORIN PIERRE	1883
MORISON ANGUS SR	HEADINGLY	28	204	204	MORRISON ANGUS SR	1875
MORISON JOHN	HEADINGLY	30	114	114	MORISON JOHN	1875
MORISON NORMAN	HEADINGLY	29	216	216	MORISON NORMAN	1875
MORRISEAU JOSEPH	BAIE S PAUL	224	165	83	MORRISEAU JOSEPH	1880
MORRISETTE FRANCIS	BAIE S PAUL	144	125	125	CHENIER FELIX	1883
MORRISETTE FRANCIS	BAIE S PAUL	146	133	133	MORRISETTE FRANCIS	1878
MORRISETTE JOHN	BAIE S PAUL	147	116	116	MCKAY JAMES	1878
MORRISON ANGUS	SFX	8	160	80	MORRISON JAMES	1882
MORRISON JOHN	ST ANDREW	37	64	64	MORRISON JOHN	1875
MORRISON JOHN	ST ANDREW	250	31	31	MORRISON JOHN	1875
MORRISON NORMAN	ST ANDREW	129	43	43	MORRISON NORMAN	77
MORRISSETTE FRANCIS	BAIE S PAUL	145	132	132	MORRISETTE FRANCIS	1878
MORRISSETTE FRANCIS	BAIE S PAUL	149	96	96	FREEMAN JOHN	1878
MORRISSETTE FRANCIS	BAIE S PAUL	150	96	96	MORGAN JOSEPH	81
MORRISSETTE FRANCIS SR	BAIE S PAUL	148	97	97	MCKAY JAMES	1878
MORRISSETTE WILLIAM	BAIE S PAUL	142	110	110		
MORRISSETTE WILLIAM	BAIE S PAUL	143	116	116	CUNNINGHAM JAMES	1877
MORRISSON DONALD	HIGH BLUFF	37	180	180	MORRISON DONALD	1881
MORWICK GEORGE	ST ANDREW	197	37	37	MORWICK GEORGE	75
MORWICK JAMES	ST ANDREW	203	39	39	MORWICK JAMES	77

OCCUPANT NAMED BY SURVEYORS		PARISH	LOT	AREA	AREA CLAIMED	PATENTEE		YEAR OF PATENT
MORWICK	JOHN	ST ANDREW	74	125	125	MORWICK	ROBERT	76
MORWICK	JOHN	ST ANDREW	199	37	37	MORWICK	PETER	1908
MORWICK	JOHN	ST ANDREW	200	38	38			
MOUARD	NICHOLAS	ST BONIFACE	20	53	53	MOUARD	NICHOLAS	1875
MOUTON	BAPTISTE	ST NORBERT	117	74	39	LECOMTE	JOSEPH	1884
MOWAT	ANDREW	ST ANDREW	216	35	35	GEMMEL	ALEXANDER	83
MOWAT	ED	ST ANDREW	90	121	121	MOWAT	EDWARD	77
MOWAT	ETAL	ST ANDREW	60	167	119	MOWAT	THOMAS	1875
MOWAT	JAMES	ST ANDREW	83	60	60	MOWAT	THOMAS	1875
MOWAT	JOHN	ST ANDREW	45	55	55	MOWAT	JOHN	77
MOWAT	THOMAS	ST ANDREW	217	147	147	MOWAT	THOMAS	1876
MOWAT	THOMAS	ST ANDREW	244	35	35	MOWAT	JOHN	77
MOWAT	ROBERT	ST ANDREW	182	43	43	MOWAT	THOMAS	85
MOWAT ETAL	JAMES	ST JAMES	48	37	37	MOYSE	MARY	1882
MOYSE	JOHN	ST JAMES	115	146	146	MUIR	JOHN	76
MUIR	JOHN	ST ANDREW	124	56	56	MUIR	JOHN	1887
MUISEL	WIDOW	STE AGATHE	595	233	233	WINZELL ETAL	ALEXANDER	83
MULLIGAN	JAMES	ST CHARLES	22	102	102	MULLIGAN	JAMES	1876
MULLIGAN	JAMES	ST BONIFACE	28	66	66	MULLIGAN	JAMES	1875
MULLIGAN	JAMES	ST BONIFACE	35	129	129	MULLIGAN	JAMES	1875
MULLIGAN	JAMES	ST BONIFACE	37	50	50	MULLIGAN	JAMES	1875
MULLIGAN	JAMES	ST BONIFACE	43	106	106	BOUCHER	BAPTISTE	1878
MULLIGAN	JAMES	ST BONIFACE	45	87	87	MULLIGAN	JAMES	1877
MULLIGAN	JAMES	ST JAMES	71	96	96	MULLIGAN	JAMES	1876
MULVIN	BAPTISTE	SFX	29	74	74	MULVIN	JEAN BTE	1878
MUNROE	ALEX	KILDONAN	90	110	110	MUNROE	ALEX	1878
MUNROE	ROBERT	KILDONAN	78	42	42	MUNROE	ALEX	1876
MUNROE	ROBERT	KILDONAN	89	111	111	MUNROE	ROBERT	1876
MUNROE	ROBERT	KILDONAN	92	181	181	MUNROE	ROBERT	1876
MURRAY	A	ST CHARLES	106	29	29	GREEN	JAMES	1882
MURRAY	AC	ST CHARLES	108	33	33	GREEN	JAMES	1882
MURRAY	AH	ST CLEMENT	2	95	95	MURRAY	ANNE C	1897
MURRAY	ALEX	ST CLEMENT	15	95	95	MURRAY ETAL	AC	1897
MURRAY	ALEX	ST CHARLES	115	17	17	MURRAY	ALEX	1875
MURRAY	ALEXANDER	ST JAMES	4	8	8	GREEN	JAMES	1882
MURRAY	ALEXANDER	ST CHARLES	39	98	98	BIGGS	EMILY	1887
MURRAY	ALEXANDER	ST CHARLES	40	98	98	BIGGS	EMILY	1887
MURRAY	ALEXANDER	ST CHARLES	41	96	96	DUCHARME	BAPTISTE	1886
MURRAY	ALEXANDER	PORTAGE	133	403	403	MURRAY	ALEXANDER	1882
MURRAY	ALEXANDER	ST JAMES	7	108	108	MURRAY	ALEXANDER	1879
MURRAY	DON	ST JAMES	69	48	48	MURRAY	LETITIA	1882
MURRAY	DON	ST ANDREW	273	73	73	MULHOLLAND	ROBERT	1880
MURRAY	DON	ST ANDREW	282	66	66	MURRAY	DONALD	85
MURRAY	DONALD	ST ANDREW	286	64	64	MURRAY	DONALD	85
MURRAY	DONALD	KILDONAN	28	86	86	MURRAY	DONALD	1885
MURRAY	DONALD	KILDONAN	57	82	82	MURRAY	DONALD	83
MURRAY	DONALD	ST PAUL	97	34	34	MURRAY	DONALD	1885
MURRAY	DONALD	ST PAUL	109	58	58	MURRAY	DONALD	1883
MURRAY	FRANCIS	ST PAUL	7	82	82	MURRAY	FRANCIS	1882
MYRE	JAMES	KILDONAN	38	59	59	MURRAY	JAMES	1885
MYRE	GB	STE ANNE	54	173	173	LEMIPRE	JB	1879
NASH	WH	STE AGATHE	20	131	131	NASH	WH	1878

TABLE 5: RECOGNITION OF RIVERLOT OCCUPANTS BY THE GOVERNMENT OF CANADA

OCCUPANT NAMED BY SURVEYORS		PARISH	LOT	AREA	AREA CLAIMED	PATENTEE		YEAR OF PATENT
NAUD	WIDOW	SFX	167	89	89	LUMSDEN	THOMAS	1884
NAULT	ANDRE	ST VITAL	12	49	49	NAULT	ANDRE	1876
NAULT	BENJAMIN	ST VITAL	28	19	19	NAULT	BENJAMIN	1885
NAULT	IB	STE ANNE	25	342	342	NAULT	IB	1878
NESBITT	JOSEPH	STE AGATHE	100	89	89	CLUXTON	RICHARD	1889
NESS	ANTHONY	BAIE S PAUL	178	116	116	SMITH	DONALD	1885
NESS	ANTHONY	SFX	118	96	96	NESS	MARY	1875
NESS	ANTHONY	ST CHARLES	111	174	174	NESS ETAL	FRANK	1885
NICHOLSON	ROBERT	ST JAMES	6	51	51	SMITH	DONALD A	1885
NOLAN	JOHN	ST ANDREW	247	32	32	NOLAN	JOHN	75
NOLAN	JOHN	STE AGATHE	58	154	154	NOLIN	AUGUST	1882
NOLIN	AUGUST	STE AGATHE	60	156	156			
NOLIN	CHARLES	STE ANNE	17	114	114	DESAUTELS	HONORE	1878
NOLIN	CHARLES	STE ANNE	40	197	98	GIROUX	RAYMOND	1908
NOLIN	CHARLES	STE ANNE	41	206	103	STLAURENT	PHILIPPE	1885
NOLIN	CHARLES	STE ANNE	43	216	72	NOLIN	CHARLES	1888
NOLIN	CHARLES.	STE ANNE	53	220	220	NOLIN	CHARLES	1882
NOLIN	DUNCAN	STE ANNE	59	292	195	PARE	ANGELIQUE	1880
NOLIN	DUNCAN	STE ANNE	38	186	186	NOLIN	DUNCAN	1901
NOLIN	DUNCAN	STE ANNE	39	188	188			
NOLIN	FRANCIS	STE ANNE	48	200	200	NOLIN	FRANCIS	78
NOLIN	JEREMIAH	STE ANNE	49	216	216	BERARD	JERIMIE	1878
NOLIN	JOHN	STE ANNE	50	214	214	NOLIN	JOHN	1879
NOLIN	JOSEPH	STE ANNE	46	97	97	GIRARD	MARC	79
NOLIN	NORBERT	STE ANNE	45	107	107			
NOLIN	NORBERT	STE ANNE	28	191	191	BERNARD	REMI	1878
NOLIN	NORBERT	STE ANNE	35	308	153	NOLIN	NORBERT	1886
NON RESIDENT		STE ANNE	44	223	223	ROYAL	JOSEPH	1878
NORMAND	BAPTISTE	BAIE S PAUL	126	95	95			
NORQUAY	JAMES	ST NORBERT	153	296	199	NORQUAY	JAMES	1880
NORQUAY	JAMES	ST ANDREW	143	62	62	CORRIGAL	JAMES	79
NORQUAY	JOHN	ST ANDREW	144	62	62	MOSS	ANN	1878
NORQUAY	JOHN	HIGH BLUFF	45	132	132			
NORQUAY ETAL	THOMAS	HIGH BLUFF	48	227	227	NORQUAY	THOMAS	1878
OMAND	JOHN	ST ANDREW	181	43	43	OMAND	JOHN	76
OMAND	JAMES	ST JAMES	45	100	100	OMAND	JOHN	1876
OUELETTE	JOSEPH	ST ANDREW	220	50	50	DAUPHINAIS	BAPTISTE	78
OUELETTE	FRANCOIS	ST NORBERT	26	140	140	SPENCER	G B	1877
OUELETTE	WILLIAM	ST NORBERT	250	161	161	HESPELER	WILLIAM	1878
OWENS	JAMES	ST NORBERT	251	156	156	OWENS	JAMES	1877
OWENS	JAMES	STE ANNE	15	203	203	OWENS	JAMES	1877
OWENS	JAMES	STE ANNE	37	198	198	OWENS	JAMES	1877
OWENS	JAMES	STE ANNE	62	198	198	OWENS	JAMES	1877
PAGE	ALEXANDRE	SFX	23	95	95	PAGE	ALEXANDRE	1885
PAGE	HENRY	SFX	199	94	94	PAGE	HENRI	84
PAGE	ISIDORE	SFX	200	95	95	BRELAND	PATRIC	1878
PAGE	JOHN	ST NORBERT	212	133	133	PAGE	JOHN	1882
PAGE ETAL	FRANCOIS	SFX	39	83	83	MCBEATH	MORRISCN	1882
PAJOT	XAVIER	SFX	27	77	77	PAJOT	XAVIER	1882
PARENTEAU	DANIEL	ST NORBERT	128	80	80	PARENTEAU	PIERRE	1880
PARENTEAU	MOISE	ST NORBERT	135	75	75	PARENTEAU	MOISE	

TABLE 3. ACCOUNTING OF RIVERLOT OCCUPANTS BY THE GOVERNMENT OF CANADA

OCCUPANT NAMED BY SURVEYORS	PARISH	LOT	AREA	AREA CLAIMED	PATENTEE	YEAR OF PATENT
PARENTEAU SUSANNE	ST BONIFACE	114	42	42	GERARD M A	1881
PARENTEAU JR PIERRE	ST NORBERT	134	75	75	PARENTEAU JR PIERRE	1879
PARENTEAU SR PIERRE	ST NORBERT	132	117	117	PARENTEAU PIERRE	1879
PARISIEN AUGUSTINE	ST NORBERT	198	99	99	PARISIEN GERMAINE	1875
PARISIEN AUGUSTINE	ST NORBERT	199	98	98	PARISIEN GERMAINE	1875
PARISIEN BONAVENTURE	ST NORBERT	60	104	104	HAMELIN JOSEPH	1877
PARISIEN GERMAIN	ST NORBERT	59	110	110	PARISIEN GERMAIN	1875
PARISIEN ISAAC	ST NORBERT	183	106	106	ALLIANCE TRUST CO LTD	1902
PARISIEN PIERRE	ST NORBERT	197	100	100	MELBOURNE THOMAS	1879
PARISSEAU HENRY	SFX	19	135	135	SMITH DONALD A	1877
PARISSIEN ANDRE	ST NORBERT	219	98	98	ROYAL JOSEPH	
PARISSIEN NARCISSE	ST ANDREW	77	63	63	PARISIEN NARCISSE	79
PARKS GEORGE	ST CLEMENT	87	26	26	SINCLAIR WILLIA	84
PARKS JAMES	ST ANDREW	283	66	66	PARK JAMES	77
PARKS THOMAS	ST ANDREW	4	92	92	PARK JAMES	75
PATROIS ETAL FRANCOIS	ST BONIFACE	7	158	158	PATROIS FRANCOIS	1882
PATTENAUDE CHARLES	SFX	93	173	87	STEPHEN GEORGE	1876
PATTENAUDE CUTHBERTE	SFX	100	106	106	PATTENAUDE CUTHBERT	1878
PATTENAUDE MICHEL	SFX	111	97	97	FORGET JOSEPH	85
PATTENAUDE MICHEL	KILDONAN	141	67	67	PATTENAUDE MICHEL	1877
PATTERSON MALCOM	SFX	41	84	84	PATTERSON MALCOLM	1875
PATTERSON ROBERT	ST BONIFACE	1	88	88	PATTERSON ROBERT	1877
PAUL ANTOINE	SFX	185	89	89	PAUL ANTOINE	1883
PAUL BENARD	SFX	112	97	97	FORGET JOSEPH	85
PAUL BENARD	SFX	160	99	99	PAUL BERNAR	84
PAUL OLIVIER	SFX	189	81	81	PAUL OLIVIER	1880
PAUL PAUL	SFX	45	98	98	PAUL MAGLOIRE	1881
PAUL PIERRE	SFX	68	98	98	PAUL PIERRE	1884
PAYMENT LOUIS	ST NORBERT	89	31	31	PLANTE JR PAYMENT LOUIS	1885
PEATISON ANDREW	HIGH BLUFF	33	217	217	BANNERMAN S	1877
PEEBLES JAMES	ST ANDREW	82	61	61	PEEBLES JAMES	76
PEEBLES JAMES	ST ANDREW	190	40	40	MACDONALD ROBERT	85
PEEBLES MAGGIE	ST CLEMENT	109	51	51	PEEBLES ROBERT	1885
PEEBLES THOMAS	ST CLEMENT	61	78	78	NORQUAY JOHN	1882
PEEBLES THOMAS	ST CLEMENT	108	68	68	FINLAYSEN HECTOR	1885
PEEBLES WILLIAM	ST ANDREW	53	51	51	PEEBLES WILLIA	85
PEEBLES WILLIAM	ST ANDREW	225	49	49	PEEBLES WILLIA	85
PEEL WILLIAM	ST ANDREW	251	31	31	PEEL WILLIAM	75
PEGAN ETAL AP	STE AGATHE	78	166	166	BULLIS JOHN	1882
PELLETIER CHARLES	BAIE S PAUL	222	97	97	TOURON DAVID	1882
PELLETIER WIDOW	BAIE S PAUL	243	109	109	CHENIER FELIX	1878
PELLITIER BOUVETTE	SFX	80	95	95	SMITH DONALD	1877
PEPIN HEIRS OF	ST VITAL	35	66	66		
PERE ALLARD	ST CHARLES	72	50	50	ALLARD REV J	1878
PERE ALLARD	ST CHARLES	74	97	97	ALLARD REV J	1878
PERRAS RAPHAEL	ST CHARLES	85	523		LAVERDURE PIERRE	81
PERRAULT ED	ST NORBERT	115	140	140	PERRAULT ED	1876
PERRAULT REGS	ST NORBERT	40	221	221	PERRAULT REGIS	1875
PHILLIPS WILLIAM	ST ANDREW	234	45	45	CORRIGAL GEORGE	77
PICHE EDWARD	SFX	96	100	100	SMITH DONALD	1877
PICHE FRANCOIS	SFX	106	79	79	SMITH DONALD	1877
PICHE LOUIS	SFX	122	106	53	PICHE LOUIS	1900

OCCUPANT NAMED BY SURVEYORS		PARISH	LOT	AREA	AREA CLAIMED	PATENTEE		YEAR OF PATENT
PICHE ETUX	FRANCOIS	SFX	114	270	180	SMITH	DONALD	1875
PICHI	LOUIS	SFX	97	94	94	PICHIE	LOUIS	1878
PIERRAULT	EDWARD	ST VITAL	13	143	143	PIERRAULT	EDWARD	1875
PILON	ANDRE	ST NORBERT	129	81	55	WELLS	ALFRED	1884
PILON	ANTOINE	STE AGATHE	610	160	160			
PILON	ANTOINE MRS	ST NORBERT	130	81	81	PEPIN	JOSEPH	1878
PILON	FELIX	ST NORBERT	145	11	11	BROUSSEAU	JOEL	88
PILON	JOSEPH	ST NORBERT	131	79	79	PILON	JOSEPH	1878
PIRREAU	ISSADORE	BAIE S PAUL	181	98	98	MCKAY	JAMES	78
PITON	WJ	ST CLEMENT	115	106	106	SMITH	EDGAR	84
POCHA	CHARLES	HIGH BLUFF	66	105	105	POCHA	CHARLES	1871
POCHA	GILBERT	HIGH BLUFF	65	96	96	POCHA	GIBERT	1877
POCHA	HENRY	HIGH BLUFF	67	68	68	POCHA	HENRY	1877
POCHA	JOHN	HIGH BLUFF	64	205	205	POCHA	JOHN	1877
POCHA	JOSEPH	HIGH BLUFF	68	105	105	POCHA	JOSEPH SR	1877
POCHA	THOMAS	HIGH BLUFF	63	65	65	MACHRAY	THOMAS	1889
POCHA JR	JOSEPH	HIGH BLUFF	60	142	142	POCHA	R ETAL	1877
POCHA	WILLIAM	SFX	61	208	208	POITRAS	JOSEPH	1877
POITRAS	FRANCOIS	ST BONIFACE	95	79	79	CORP ARCH	FRANCOIS	1882
POITRAS	FRANCOIS	ST BONIFACE	110	18	18	POITRAS	C R DE ST B	1878
POITRAS	FRANCOIS	SFX	113	65	65	POITRAS	MADELINE	1886
POITRAS	GABRIEL	SFX	198	154	154	STEPHENS	FRANCOIS	1877
POITRAS	JOSEPH	SFX	41	85	85	POITRAS	GEORGE	1876
POITRAS	PIERRE	SFX	205	181	181	LEVEILLEE	PIERRE	1878
POITRAS	PIERRE	SFX	208	82	82	POLSON	GABRIEL	1881
POLSON	ANGUS	KILDONAN	94	145	145	POLSON	ANGUS	1877
POLSON	HUGH	KILDONAN	2	191	191	POLSON	HUGH	1875
POLSON	HUGH	KILDONAN	76	41	41	POLSON	HUGH	1875
POLSON	JOHN	KILDONAN	11	63	32	POLSON	JOHN	1876
POLSON	WIDOW	KILDONAN	10	95	95	POLSON	CATHERINE	1882
POLSON	WIDOW	KILDONAN	81	82	82	POLSON ETAL	JANET	1882
PONTIBRAND	PIERRE	STE AGATHE	105	125	125			
PORTER	CHARLES	ST VITAL	30	11	11	PORTER	CHARLES	1877
PORTER	WILLIAM	ST ANDREW	242	37	37	MULHOLLAND	JOHN H ETAL	77
PORTER	WILLIAM	ST ANDREW	243	36	36	MULHOLLAND	JOHN H ETAL	77
POWERS	MICHAEL	ST CHARLES	70	111	111	MURRAY	LETITIA	1882
POWERS	MICHAEL	ST CHARLES	96	358		POWER	ANNIE	1885
PRIMO	JERIME	STE AGATHE	555	150	150	LEMAY	JOSEPH	1877
PRITCHARD	ARCHIBALD	ST PAUL	108	76	76	PRITCHARD	ARCHIBALD	1878
PRITCHARD	ARCHIBALD	ST PAUL	112	65	65	PRITCHARD	ARCHIBALD	1878
PRITCHARD	HUGH	ST PAUL	19	74	74	PRITCHARD	HUGH	1885
PRITCHARD	HUGH	ST PAUL	42	34	34	PRITCHARD	SAMUEL	83
PRITCHARD	HUGH	ST PAUL	49	85	85	MASTERS	ALFRED	1884
PRITCHARD	HUGH	ST PAUL	102	260	130	PRITCHARD	REV S	1880
PRITCHARD	JANET	KILDONAN	47	101	101	PRITCHARD	JANET	1887
PRITCHARD	MRS JOHN	KILDONAN	32	85	85	PRITCHARD	JANET	1887
PRITCHARD	REV SAM	KILDONAN	55	126	126	PRITCHARD	SAM	1878
PRITCHARD	REV SAM	KILDONAN	71	41	41	INKSTER	COLIN	1883
PRITCHARD	REV SAM	KILDONAN	72	41	41	ALLOWAY	WILLIAM	1881
PRITCHARD	REV SAMUEL	ST PAUL	82	66	66	PRITCHARD	REV SAM	1880
PRITCHARD	RICHARD	KILDONAN	54	104	104	HACKLAND	GILBERT	77
		KILDONAN				PRITCHARD	WIIIA	84

OCCUPANT NAMED BY SURVEYORS		PARISH	LOT	AREA	AREA CLAIMED	PATENTEE		YEAR OF PATENT
PROULX	MICHEL	ST CHARLES	67	105	105	PROULX	MICHEL	1876
PRUDEN		SFX	123	106	53	DAUPHINAIS	MAXIME	1899
PRUDEN	ARTHUR	ST JAMES	20	192	96	PRUDEN	JAMES	1876
PRUDEN	CORNELIUS	ST JAMES	26	93	93	PRUDEN	CORNELIUS	1884
PRUDEN	EDWARD	ST PAUL	46	65	65	PRUDEN	EDWARD	1878
PRUDEN	JOHN	ST CLEMENT	29	101	101	PRUDEN	JOHN	77
PRUDEN	PETER	ST ANDREW	68	60	60	PRUDEN	ALBERT	79
PRUDEN	PETER	ST ANDREW	204	39	39	RICHARDS	ETAL	1886
PRUDEN	PETER	ST ANDREW	205	39	39	NONE		
PRUDEN	WILLIAM	ST ANDREW	67	60	60	PRUDEN	WILLIAM	1875
PRUDEN	WILLIAM	ST ANDREW	209	40	40	PRUDEN	WILLIAM	77
PRUDEN	WILLIAM	ST ANDREW	211	41	41	PRUDEN	WILLIAM	76
PRUDEN	WILLIAM	ST CLEMENT	33	122	122	PRUDEN	WILLIAM	1875
PRUDEN	WILLIAM	ST CLEMENT	88	53	53	PRUDEN	EDWARD	82
QUELETTE	WILLIAM	ST NORBERT	255	154	76	WILLIAMS	ROBERT	1880
R C MISSION		BAIE S PAUL	205	425	425	R C MISSION	KAVANAGH	1878
R C MISSION		SFX	129	101	101	REV FRANCIS	REV F	1878
R C MISSION		SFX	182	136	68	KAVANAGH	OBLATES	1878
R C MISSION		ST CHARLES	71	262	262	PERES	ARCHBISHOP	1876
R C MISSION		ST BONIFACE	22	100	100	TACHE		1878
R C MISSION		ST BONIFACE	34	192	192	R C MISSION		1878
R C MISSION		ST BONIFACE	76	340	340	CORP ARCH	C R DE ST B	1881
R C MISSION		ST BONIFACE	93	93	94	CORP ARCH	C R DE ST B	1878
R C MISSION		ST BONIFACE	109	203	203	CORP ARCH	C R DE ST B	1878
RACETTE		ST BONIFACE	107	28	11	RACETTE	VIRGINII	1885
RACETTE	AUGUSTINE	SFX	180	93	93	PROVOST	LEON	1884
RACETTE	GEORGE	ST VITAL	19	48	48	RAMAGE	JOHN	1884
RAMAGE ETAL	GEORGE	STE AGATHE	63	88	88	RAMAGE	STEPHEN	1884
RAMAGE ETAL	JOHN	STE AGATHE	61	85	85	RAMSAY	THOMAS	1885
RAMSAY	ROBERT	STE ANNE	10	199	199	PERES	OBLATES	1876
RC MISSION		ST CHARLES	95	178	178	FALLS ET AL	ELIZABETH	1887
REID	JANE	HEADINGLY	13	63	274	BANNATYNE	A G B	83
REID	MURDOCK	ST CLEMENT	67	108	63	BELL ETAL	SAMUEL	83
RENVILLE	FRANCOIS	BAIE S PAUL	73	95	108	RICHARD	ANTOINE	1878
RESBORE	ANTOINE	SFX	183	46	95	PROVENCHER	JOSEPH	85
RICHARD	FRANCOIS	SFX	86	89	46	RICHARD	FRANCO	84
RICHARD	FRANCOIS	SFX	87	193	89	RICHARD	LOUIS	84
RICHARD	LOUIS	ST LAURENT	105	73	193	RICHARD	PIERRE	1876
RICHARD	PIERRE	STE AGATHE	18	169	73	HUDSONS BAY	CO	1881
RICHARD	TREFFLEY	ST LAURENT	13	56	169	RICHARD	MARGARET	1878
RICHARD	WIDOW	ST CHARLES	19	90	56	RICHARDS	JAMES	1876
RICHARDS	JAMES	ST CHARLES	9	90	90	RICHARDS	JAMES	1876
RICHARDS	JAMES	ST CHARLES	10	90	90	RICHARDS	JAMES	1876
RICHARDS	JAMES	ST CHARLES	11	122	61	RICHARDSON	ETAL	1886
RICHARDS	WILLIAM	ST ANDREW	70	168	17	RICHARDSON	ALEX ETAL	1878
RICHARDSON	ALEX ETAL	PORTAGE	131	548	493	RICHARDSON	ALEXANDER	1878
RICHARDSON	ALEXANDER	PORTAGE	127	93	93	HAMELIN	SOLOMAN	1876
RICHOT	BAPTISTE	ST VITAL	29	201	201	RICHOT	REV	1885
RICHOT	REV	ST NORBERT	164	71	71	BEAUPIE	VJ	1884
RICHOT	REV	ST NORBERT	169	112	112	THELIERE	JEAN B	1886
RICHOT	REV	ST NORBERT	179	108	108	RICHOT	REV	1878
RICHOT	REV	ST NORBERT	188	108	108			

OCCUPANT NAMED BY SURVEYORS		PARISH	LOT	AREA	AREA CLAIMED	PATENTEE		YEAR OF PATENT
RICHOT	REV	ST NORBERT	201	137	137	RITCHOT	REV	1885
RICHOT	REV	ST NORBERT	204	176	176	RITCHOT	REV N J	1885
RICHOT	REV N J	ST NORBERT	225	130	130	RITCHOT	REV N J	1883
RIDSDALE	HARRIET	ST CHARLES	97	95	95	RIDSDALE	HARRIET	1877
RIDSDALE	HARRIET	ST CHARLES	101	223	223	ADSHEAD	MARY	1876
RIEL	LOUIS	ST BONIFACE	103	23	23	GUAY	ABRAHAM	1885
RIEL	LOUIS	ST VITAL	16	53	53	LALONDE	J B	1885
RIEL	LOUIS	STE AGATHE	533	261	261	DELORME	JOSEPH	1880
RITCHOT		ST NORBERT	36	136	136	CLOUTIER	GEORGE	83
RITCHOT	ANDRE	ST BONIFACE	36	24	24	CLARKE	F I	1883
RITCHOT	REV	ST NORBERT	38	48	48	RITCHOT	REV N J	1885
RITCHOT	REV	ST NORBERT	43	67	67	MORAND	HONORE	1878
RITCHOT	REV	STE AGATHE	549	151	151			
RITCHOT	REV N J	ST NORBERT	34	110	110	RICHOT	REVO	85
RITCHOT	REV N J	ST NORBERT	56	128	128	DUFORT	LOUIS	1885
RITCHOT	REV N J	ST NORBERT	57	121	121	DUFORT	LOUIS	1885
RITCHOT	REV N J	ST NORBERT	66	116	116	VOURIOT	CHARLES	1882
RITCHOT	REV N J	ST NORBERT	68	126	126	RITCHOT	REV N J	1885
RITCHOT	REV N J	ST NORBERT	71	182	182	RITCHOT	REV N J	1885
RITCHOT	REV N J	ST NORBERT	81	83	83	RITCHOT	REV N J	1885
RITCHOT	REV N J	ST NORBERT	83	98	2	LEMAY	JOSEPH	1877
RITCHOT	REV N J	ST NORBERT	88	31	31	RITCHOT	REV N J	1885
RITCHOTETAL	ANDRE	ST BONIFACE	36	48	24	MCTAVISH	J H	1886
RIVARD	BAPTISTE	ST NORBERT	18	100	100	CHARETTE	BAPTISTE	1877
ROBERTSON	FRANCOIS	SFX	212	101	101	ROBERTSON	PETER	1884
ROBINSON		PORTAGE	32	240	240	ROBERTSON	JOHN	79
ROBINSON	XAVIER	SFX	4	90	90	LODER	AUSTIN	1882
ROCHANS	OLIVER	STE AGATHE	118	91	91	ROBERT	OLIVER	1888
ROCHELEAU	BAPTISTE	ST NORBERT	133	77	77	ROCHELEAU	BAPTISTE	1877
ROFS	ALEXANDER	KILDONAN	53	100	100	THOMPSON	CATHERINE	1883
ROMAN CATHOL	IC	STE AGATHE	109	70	70	ROMAN CATHOL	IC	1881
ROMAN CATHOL	IC	STE AGATHE	111	64	64	ROMAN CATHOL	IC	1881
ROMAN CATHOL	IC MISSION	ST LAURENT	20	140	140	OBLATE	REV PERES	1878
ROSS	ALEXANDER	ST PAUL	1	59	59	BRUCE	GEORGE	1902
ROSS	CHARLES	SFX	134	98	98	ROSS	CHARLE	84
ROSS	DONALD	SFX	66	152		COWLARD	COPELAND	1877
ROSS	DONALD	ST ANDREW	121	43	43	HUNTER	JEAN	88
ROSS	GEORGE	ST ANDREW	79	125	125	ROSS	GEORGE	97
ROSS	GEORGE	ST ANDREW	188	82	14	MOWAT	THOMAS	1876
ROSS	GEORGE	ST ANDREW	189	40	13	MOWAT	THOMAS	1876
ROSS	JOHN	SFX	136	89	89	GIGOT	E F	1885
ROSS	RODERICK	SFX	135	93	93	ROSS	DONALD	1898
ROSS	WILLIAM	SFX	60	97	97	TAIT	ROBERT	1885
ROUSSIN	FRANCOIS	STE ANNE	31	187	187	COMPANY OF	ADVENTURERS	79
ROWAND	JOHN	ST CHARLES	31	100	100	PITGLADO	ISAAC	1902
ROWLAND	GEORGE	ST CLEMENT	13	49	49	DAVIS	GEORGE	83
ROY	AUGUST	STE AGATHE	535	245	245	VALENTINE	THOMAS B	83
ROY	JEAN BTE	ST NORBERT	76	101	66	CLOUTIER	GABRIEL	1915
ROY ETAL	FRANCIS	ST NORBERT	149	136	136	ROY	FRANCIS	1878
ROY ETAL	LOUIS	STE AGATHE	85	111	111	ROY	LOUIS	1882
ROY	JOSEPH	ST NORBERT	154	113	113	ROYAL	JOSEPH	1880

GOVERNMENT OF CANADA

OCCUPANT NAMED BY SURVEYORS	PARISH	LOT	AREA	AREA CLAIMED	PATENTEE	YEAR OF PATENT
RUPERTS LAND BISHOP OF	ST PAUL	90	62	62	RUPERTS LAND BISHOP OF	1881
RUTHEDGE CHRISTOPHER	PORTAGE	110	22	22	SCOTT JOHN	1877
SABINE H L	HEADINGLY	7	179	179	SABINE H L	1875
SABISTON ALEX	ST CLEMENT	114	51	51	GUNN ALEXAN	84
SALTER RICHARD	HEADINGLY	17	217	217	SALTER RICHARD	1875
SAMETH ETAL AMEDIE	STE AGATHE	117	94	94	RIVARD ANTOINE	1889
SANDERS JANE	ST PAUL	83	65	65	MUTTLEBURY GEORGE	92
SANDERSON A ETAL	PORTAGE	128	260	180	SANDERSON ALEX ETAL	1895
SANDERSON CATHERINE	POPLAR PT	87	214	214	SANDERSON JANE	1877
SANDERSON GEORGE	HIGH BLUFF	54	191	191	GERROND WILLIAM	1877
SANDERSON GEORGE	ST PAUL	72	73	73	CLARKE WILLIAM	1890
SANDERSON ROBERT	ST PAUL	47	94	94	CLARK WILLIAM	1877
SANDERSON WILLIAM	POPLAR PT	83	217	217	SANDERSON WILLIAM	1890
SANSREGRET BAPTISTE	SFX	175	88	88	SANSREGRET BAPTISTE	1877
SANSREGRET LOUIS	ST VITAL	5	83	83	SANSREGRET LOUIS	1875
SANSREGRET LOUIS	ST NORBERT	186	104	104	SANSREGRET LOUIS	1877
SAUNDERS RODERICK	ST ANDREW	92	41	41	SAUNDERS RODERI	85
SAUNDERS WILLIAM	ST ANDREW	97	68	68	SAUNDERS WILLIAM	76
SAVAGE FRANCOIS	ST CHARLES	34	97	97	MURRAY LETETIA	1882
SAYER CLEOPHAS	HEADINGLY	48	44	44	MORGAN JOSEPH	1891
SAYER GEORGE	BAIE S PAUL	113	121	121		
SAYER GEORGE	BAIE S PAUL	114	116	116		
SAYER HENRY	HEADINGLY	49	88	88	SAYER HENRY	1879
SAYER JOHN	BAIE S PAUL	110	127	127	BANNERMAN SAMUEL	1889
SAYER JOHN	BAIE S PAUL	111	125	125		
SAYER JOHN	BAIE S PAUL	172	123	123	INKSTER COLIN	1876
SAYES CLEOPHAS	ST CHARLES	102	114	114	SAYES CLEOPHAS	1882
SCHULTZ DR	STE AGATHE	151	147	147		
SCHULTZ DR	ST ANDREW	233	45	45	SCHULTZ JOHN	1883
SCHULTZ JOHN	ST ANDREW	281	99	99	FRASER H OO	85
SCISSON DANIEL	PORTAGE	33	160	160		
SCISSON THOMAS	PORTAGE	55	320	320	SISSONS THOMAS	81
SCISSONS THOMAS	STE AGATHE	103	149	149	SCOTT THOMAS	1879
SCOTT WILLIAM	ST ANDREW	46	56	56	SCOTT WILLIAM	1875
SCOTT WILLIAM	ST ANDREW	245	34	34	SCOTT WILLIAM	1876
SCOTT WILLIAM	ST ANDREW	246	33	33	SCOTT WILLIAM	1876
SELLWOOD JOHN	ST JAMES	55	73	73	GOOD ETAL JAMES	1887
SELMENT ANTOINE	ST CHARLES	100	109	109	WELCHE ANTOINE	1876
SERRES MRS	SFX	81	25	25	THORNE GEORGE	1876
SETTER CATHERINE	ST PAUL	59	137	137	SETTER CATHERINE	1875
SETTER GEORGE	ST PAUL	68	137	137	MCBETH ALEX	1885
SETTER JJ	PORTAGE	90	123	123	SETTER JOHN JAMES	78
SETTER JJ	PORTAGE	113	43	43	SETTER JOHN JAMES	78
SETTER JOHN	POPLAR PT	47	235	235	SETTER JOHN	1877
SETTER JOHN	ST ANDREW	9	144	144	SETTER JOHN	1885
SETTER JOHN	ST ANDREW	278	46	46	SETTER JOHN	1885
SETTER JOHN	ST CLEMENT	102	53	53	BANNATYNE A G B	79
SETTER THOMAS	ST PAUL	64	62	62	SETTER THOMAS	1879
SETTER WIDOW JAMES	ST ANDREW	229	48	48	NORQUAY JOHN	81
SETTER WILLIAM	ST ANDREW	30	72	72	SETTER ALEXANDER	75
SHORT	BAIE S PAUL	165	110	110	CHAFFEY BEN ELSWOOD	1897
SHORT	BAIE S PAUL	166	107	107	MCDERMOT ANDREW	1883

TABLE 5: RECOGNITION OF RIVERLOT OCCUPANTS BY THE GOVERNMENT OF CANADA

OCCUPANT NAMED BY SURVEYORS	PARISH	LOT	AREA	AREA CLAIMED	PATENTEE	YEAR OF PATENT
SILDEN ALEX	BAIE S PAUL	169	124	124	DAVIS ROBERT A	1882
SIMPSON JOHN	HEADINGLY	20	112	112	SIMPSON JOHN	1875
SINCLAIR BAKIE	ST ANDREW	91	59	59	SINCLAIR BAKIE	75
SINCLAIR BAKIE	ST ANDREW	180	43	43	CRAMER ANNIE	77
SINCLAIR DUNCAN	ST ANDREW	132	183	183	SCHULTZ JOHN	
SINCLAIR DUNCAN	ST ANDREW	133	139	139	SINCLAIR GEORGE	1882
SINCLAIR GEORGE	ST ANDREW	25	87	87	SCHULTZ JOHN	1884
SINCLAIR GEORGE	ST ANDREW	231	47	47	SINCLAIR JAMES	1878
SINCLAIR JAMES	ST CHARLES	49	61	61	SINCLAIR JAMES	1875
SINCLAIR JAMES	ST CHARLES	50	64	64	SINCLAIR JAMES	1875
SINCLAIR JAMES	ST CHARLES	51	68	68	SINCLAIR JAMES	1875
SINCLAIR JOHN	ST CLEMENT	43	128	128	HUNTER ETAL MATTHEW T	81
SINCLAIR PETER	ST ANDREW	14	83	83	SINCLAIR THOMAS	
SINCLAIR THOMAS	HIGH BLUFF	29	204	204	SARGENT CAROLI	1875
SINCLAIR THOMAS	ST ANDREW	59	96	96	SARGENT CAROLI	85
SINCLAIR THOMAS	ST ANDREW	218	103	103	YOUNG HELEN	85
SINCLAIR WILLIAM	ST CLEMENT	35	82	74	SISTERS OF C HARITY	1884
SISTERS OF C HARITY	SFX	128	104	104	SISTERS OF C HARITY CHARLOTTE	1880
SISTERS OF C HARITY	ST NORBERT	177	117	117	FIDLER ROBERT	1880
SLATER CHARLOTTE	BAIE S PAUL	174	104	104	TAIT JAMES	1878
SLATER GEORGE	BAIE S PAUL	173	98	98	SLATER JAMES	1885
SLATER GEORGE	ST PAUL	28	100	100	PEARCE WILLIAM	1881
SLATER JAMES	SFX	53	175	88	SLATER THOMAS	1884
SLATER JOHN	ST ANDREW	15	171	171	PERRAULT FRANCOIS X	1877
SLATER THOMAS	POPLAR PT	51	98	98	SLATER THOMAS	83
SLATER THOMAS	ST PAUL	31	135	135	SLATER THOMAS	1881
SLATER THOMAS	ST PAUL	94	118	118	SLATER WILLIAM	1875
SLATER WILLIAM	POPLAR PT	52	96	96	SLATER WILLIAM	75
SLATER WILLIAM	ST ANDREW	28	89	89	SETTER WILLIAM	1875
SMITH ANGUS	HIGH BLUFF	55	155	155	SMITH ANGUS	1877
SMITH BAPTISTE	ST NORBERT	16	267	107	BAIN JOHN	1963
SMITH BAPTISTE	STE AGATHE	626	199	199	DUFAULT LOUIS	1876
SMITH DONALD A	ST JAMES	18	123	123	SMITH DONALD A	1884
SMITH GILBERT	ST ANDREW	136	125	63	SMITH GILBERT	
SMITH J J S HEIRS	ST ANDREW	166	28	28	SMITH JACKSON	
SMITH JACKSON	POPLAR PT	69	146	146	NEWCOMB GEORGE	1877
SMITH JAMES	POPLAR PT	54	83	83	SMITH JOHN	1877
SMITH JAMES	ST ANDREW	103	46	46	SMITH JOHN	
SMITH JOHN	ST CHARLES	16	93	93	HALL WB	1877
SMITH JOHN	ST CHARLES	17	95	95	SMITH JAMES	1877
SMITH JOHN	ST CHARLES	36	97	97	SMITH JAMES	1882
SMITH JOHN	ST CHARLES	37	97	97	SMITH JOHN	1878
SMITH JOHN	POPLAR PT	38	98	98	SMITH JOHN	1878
SMITH JOHN	ST JAMES	39	259	230	SMITH JOHN	1878
SMITH JOHN	ST ANDREW	67	48	48	SMITH JOHN	1875
SMITH JOHN	ST CHARLES	114	55	55	SMITH JOHN	
SMITH PATRICK	ST CHARLES	18	97	97	SMITH PATRICK	1878
SMITH PATRICK	ST CHARLES	19	99	99	SMITH PATRICK	1878
SMITH RICHARD	ST ANDREW	101	66	66	SMITH RICHARD	76
SMITH RICHARD	ST ANDREW	142	62	62	FLETT GEORGE	78
SMITH THOMAS	KILDONAN	93	36	36	MUNROE ROBERT	1886

GOVERNMENT OF CANADA

OCCUPANT NAMED BY SURVEYORS		PARISH	LOT	AREA	AREA CLAIMED	PATENTEE		YEAR OF PATENT
SMITH ETAL	THOMAS	ST JOHN	52	33	117	SINCLAIR	JAMES	1875
SNOW ETAL	LEWIS	STE AGATHE	89	117	117	GRAVELINE	LOUIS	1882
SPENCE	ANDREW	HIGH BLUFF	71	263	263	SPENCE	ARCHIBALD	1877
SPENCE	ARCHIBALD	HIGH BLUFF	72	141	141	SPENCE	ARCHIBALD	77
SPENCE	DAVID	POPLAR PT	62	161	161	SPENCE	DAVID	1877
SPENCE	DONALD	ST ANDREW	11	123	98	SPENCE	ADAM	
SPENCE	JACOB	ST CLEMENT	6	51	51	SPENCE	JACOB	1877
SPENCE	JAMES	ST CHARLES	4	29	29	SPENCE	JAMES	1876
SPENCE	JAMES	ST ANDREW	10	39	39	SPENCE	JAMES	80
SPENCE	JAMES	ST ANDREW	276	40	40	GUNN	ALEXANDER	75
SPENCE	JOHN	ST CLEMENT		72	72	SPENCE	JOHN	1877
SPENCE	JOSEPH	POPLAR PT	65	123	123	SPENCE	JOSEPH	1887
SPENCE	PETER	STE ANNE	2	289	289	SPENCE	PETER	1878
SPENCE	PETER	ST CLEMENT	110	51	51	SPENCE	PETER	1881
SPENCE	SAMUEL	ST ANDREW	241	38	19	HYMAN ETAL	ANNA MARIA	1885
SPENCE	WILLIAM	ST CHARLES	3	88	88	MCGREGOR	JAMES	1875
SPENCE ETAL	JOHN	ST ANDREW	270	71	71	TRUSTEES		1887
ST ARNAUD	CHARLES	ST NORBERT	69	188	188	BONNEAU	NAPOLEON	1879
ST DENIS	PAUL	SFX	133	109	109	ST DENIS	JOSEPH	1886
ST DENNIS		SFX	125	111	111	HOUSE	CHARLES	1885
ST DENYS	BAPTISTE	BAIE S PAUL	241	148	148	STEPHEN	GEORGE	1877
ST DENYS	FRANCOIS	BAIE S PAUL	210	114	114	MALONEY	DANIEL	1878
ST DENYS	MOISE	BAIE S PAUL	212	151	66	MALONEY	DANIEL	1883
ST DENYS	PAUL	BAIE S PAUL	8	182	93	TAYLOR	JOHN	1886
ST GERMAIN	ANDRE	SFX	94	79	79	ST GERMAIN	ANDRE	1878
ST GERMAIN	ANDRE	SFX	99	45	45	STGERMAIN	ANDRE	4
ST GERMAIN	FRANCOIS	BAIE S PAUL	4	122	122	MORRISON	DONALD	
ST GERMAIN	HYACINTHE	SFX	102	182	182	STGERMAIN	HYACINTHE	1883
ST GERMAIN	JEAN BPTE	SFX	98	92	92	LYGAN	BAPTISTE	1877
ST GERMAIN	LEANDRE	SFX	101	118	118	STGERMAIN	JEAN	86
ST GERMAINE	ANGUSTIVE	ST NORBERT	151	100	100	ST GERMAINE	ANGUSTIVE	1875
ST GERMAINE	AUGUSTIVE	ST NORBERT	158	140	140	ST GERMAINE	AUGUSTIVE	1875
ST GERMAINE	JOSEPH	ST NORBERT	141	52	52	MONCHAMP	ONESIME	1884
ST GERMAINE	JOSEPH	ST NORBERT	163	140	140	ST GERMAINE	JOSEPH	1877
ST GERMAINE	JOSEPH	ST NORBERT	165	61	61	ST GERMAINE	JOSEPH	1876
ST GERMAINE	PIERRE	ST NORBERT	140	107	107	ST GERMAINE	PIERRE	1877
ST JOHN	MOLYNEAUX	ST JAMES	51	48	48	HALLETT	JAMES	79
ST PETERS	CHURCH	ST CLEMENT	20	99	99	BISHOP OF RU	PERTSLAND	1876
STALKER	ROBERT	HEADINGLY	35	90	90	HACKLAND	JAMES	1877
STANLY	JOSEPH	ST BONIFACE	44	14	14	MUNSON	JOHN H	1889
STEPHEN	PHILIP	HEADINGLY	26	49	49	STEVENSON	PHILIP	1877
STEPHENS	JAMES	SFX	6	86	86	HACKLAND	JAMES	1878
STEPHENS	JAMES	HEADINGLY	34	166	166	HACKLAND	JAMES	1875
STEPHENSON	WILLIAM	HEADINGLY	8	87	87	STEVENSON	WILLIAM	1875
STEVENS	GEORGE	ST CLEMENT	44	50	50	STEVENS	GEORGE	1882
STEVENS	WILLIAM	ST ANDREW	178	42	42	STEVENS	WILLIAM R	77
STEVENSON	WILLIAM	HEADINGLY	61	439	439	STEVENSON	WILLIAM	1875
STEWART	JAMES G	ST PAUL	32	411	411	STEWART	MARGARET	1881
STEWART	JAMES G	ST PAUL	39	80	80	STEWART	MARGARET	1881
STEWART	JAMES G	ST PAUL	40	35	35	STEWART	MARGARET	1881
STEWART	JAMES G	ST PAUL	96	34	34	STEWART	MARGARET	1881
STEWART	JAMES G	ST PAUL	99	68	68	STEWART	MARGARET	188

TABLE 5: RECOGNITION OF RIVERLOT OCCUPANTS BY THE GOVERNMENT OF CANADA

OCCUPANT NAMED BY SURVEYORS		PARISH	LOT	AREA	AREA CLAIMED	PATENTEE		YEAR OF PATENT
STGERMAIN	FRANCOIS	SFX	127	85	85	TAYLOR	JOHN	1878
STGERMAINE	JOSH SR	ST NORBERT	139	115	115	ST GERMAINE	JOSH	1877
STLUKE	FRANCOIS	STE ANNE	5	199	199	GIRARD	MARC	1881
STODGALL	CHARLES	ST JAMES	29	103	103	LANE	WILLIAM DOUG	1875
STOVIN	WILLIAM	STE AGATHE	128	91	91	STOVIN	WILLIAM	1883
SUTHERLAND	ALEX	PORTAGE	34	320	320	SUTHERLAND	ROBERT	1880
SUTHERLAND	GEORGE	KILDONAN	25	129	129	SUTHERLAND	GEORGE	1886
SUTHERLAND	GEORGE	KILDONAN	27	116	116	SUTHERLAND	DONALD	1885
SUTHERLAND	GEORGE	ST PAUL	79	60	60	MURRAY	FRANCIS	1885
SUTHERLAND	JAMES	POPLAR PT	36	144	144	SUTHERLAND	JAMES	1875
SUTHERLAND	JOHN	KILDONAN	24	161	161	SUTHERLAND	JOHN	1880
SUTHERLAND	JOHN	KILDONAN	35	165	83	SUTHERLAND	JOHN	1883
SUTHERLAND	JOHN	KILDONAN	86	194	194	SUTHERLAND	JOHN	1875
SUTHERLAND	JOHN	ST PAUL	22	207	207	SUTHERLAND	JOHN	1878
SUTHERLAND	JOHN	ST PAUL	93	124	124	SUTHERLAND	JOHN	1878
SUTHERLAND	JOHN SR	HEADINGLY	27	396	396	SUTHERLAND	JOHN SR	1875
SUTHERLAND	PIERRE	ST NORBERT	116	92	92	BEAUGRAND	JOSEPH	1884
SUTHERLAND	SAMUEL	PORTAGE	35	168	168	WATSON	ROBERT	1884
SUTHERLAND	SAMUEL	PORTAGE	36	160	160	WATSON	ROBERT	1877
SUTHERLAND	WILLIAM	HIGH BLUFF	39	144	144	FAWCETT	MICHAEL	1878
SUTHERLAND	WILLIAM	ST PAUL	20	117	117	SUTHERLAND	WILLIAM	1875
SUTHERLAND	WILLIAM	ST ANDREW	38	46	46	SUTHERLAND	WILLIAM	87
SUTHERLAND	WILLIAM	ST ANDREW	252	30	30	MORGAN	JOSEPH	1891
SWAIN	ALEXANDER	HEADINGLY	47	43	43	MORGAN	JOSEPH	1878
SWAIN	CHARLES	SFX	55	228	228	LUMSDEN	THOMAS	1884
SWAIN	CHARLES	ST ANDREW	141	62	62	BEDSON		1879
SWAIN	JOHN	ST CHARLES	75	96	96	GRANT	JOHN	1882
SWAIN	THOMAS	HEADINGLY	50	89	89	SCHULTZ	JOHN	1876
SYMESON	WILLIAM	HEADINGLY	5	203	203	BURD	JOHN	1875
SYMESON	WILLIAM	HEADINGLY	64	189	189	BURD	JOHN	1877
TAIT	ANDREW	POPLAR PT	74	137	137	TAIT	ANDREW	1875
TAIT	DAVID	POPLAR PT	79	178	178	TAIT	JANE	1886
TAIT	ISABELLA	ST JAMES	43	47	16	DREWER	WILLIAM	77
TAIT	JAMES	HIGH BLUFF	62	165	165	TAIT	JAMES	1875
TAIT	JAMES	HEADINGLY	16	421	421	TAIT	JAMES	75
TAIT	JAMES	ST ANDREW	34	88	88	MORRISON	JOHN	1877
TAIT	JOHN	POPLAR PT	73	190	190	TAIT	JOHN	1875
TAIT	JOHN	ST PAUL	62	132	66	TAIT	JOHN	1878
TAIT	JOHN	ST ANDREW	2	127	133	TAIT	JOHN	1882
TAIT	JOSEPH	ST ANDREW	172	104	104	SCHULTZ	JOHN	1881
TAIT	ROBERT	BAIE S PAUL	121	6	6	TAIT	ROBERT	1875
TAIT	ROBERT	ST CHARLES	11	68	68	TAIT	ROBERT	1875
TAIT	ROBERT	ST JAMES	22	93	93	TAIT	JAMES	1875
TAIT	ROBERT	ST JAMES	31	175	96	TAIT	ROBERT	1882
TAIT	ROBERT	KILDONAN	62	84	84	GUNN	ROBERT	81
TAIT	WILLIAM	ST CHARLES	114	40	40	TAIT	WILLIAM	1875
TAIT	WILLIAM	HIGH BLUFF	36	173	173	TAIT	WILLIAM	1879
TAIT	WILLIAM	HEADINGLY	14	551	551	TAIT	WILLIAM	1875
TAIT	WILLIAM	KILDONAN	14	82	82	TAIT	GEORGE	1876
TAIT	WILLIAM	KILDONAN	70	80	80	TAIT	GEORGE	1876

OCCUPANT NAMED BY SURVEYORS		PARISH	LOT	AREA	AREA CLAIMED	PATENTEE		YEAR OF PATENT
TAYLOR	E	ST ANDREW	118	30	30	YOUNG ETAL	PETER R	77
TAYLOR	JAMES	ST PAUL	27	126	126	TAYLOR	JAMES	1886
TAYLOR	JAMES	ST ANDREW	221	50	50	MCKAY	REV JOHN	1884
TAYLOR	JAMES JR	POPLAR PT	53	196	196	TAYLOR	JAMES	75
TAYLOR	JAMES SR	POPLAR PT	60	325	325	TAYLOR	JAMES	77
TAYLOR	JOHN	HEADINGLY	19	111	111	FARMER	WILLIAM A	1879
TAYLOR	JOHN	HEADINGLY	52	92	92	TAYLOR	JOHN	1882
TAYLOR	JOHN	ST ANDREW	56	50	50	MCKAY	REV JOHN	1884
TAYLOR	MARGARET	POPLAR PT	59	210	210	NONE		
TAYLOR	MATTHEW	BAIE S PAUL	106	316	316	TAYLOR	MATTHEW	1876
TAYLOR	PETER	POPLAR PT	49	180	180	TAYLOR	PETER	1877
TAYLOR	ROBERT	ST ANDREW	6	75	75			
TAYLOR	SAMUEL	ST CLEMENT	62	48	48	TAYLOR	SAMUEL	82
TAYLOR	WILLIAM	ST CLEMENT	65	63	31	TAYLOR	WILLIAM	1883
TELFORD	JOHN	STE AGATHE	27	119	119	TENNANT	HENRY	1881
TELU ETAL	LOUIS	STE AGATHE	133	267	267	LOUSDALE	ANNIE	1881
TEMPLETON	ALEXANDER	KILDONAN	19	183	183	TEMPLETON	ROBERT D	1891
TERROT	RICHARD	STE AGATHE	146	163	143	GODARD	JOSEPH	1893
THIBAULT	LOUIS	ST BONIFACE	104	24	24	DONALDSON	HUGH S	1884
THIBERT	ISIDORE	SFX	72	82	82	LUCIER	TOUSSAINT	1876
THIBERT	PIERRE	BAIE S PAUL	11	320	320	THIBERT	PIERRE	1877
THIBERT	PIERRE	BAIE S PAUL	238	118	118	MORIN DIT	JEAN	1884
THIBERT	PIERRE	SFX	146	197	197	THIBERT	PIERRE	1876
THIBERT	XAVIER	SFX	74	169	169	THIBERT	XAVIER	1881
THOMAS	CELESTIN	ST PAUL	13	34	34	SCHULTZ	JOHN	1878
THOMAS	CELESTIN	ST PAUL	15	101	101	MARKLEY	A S	1878
THOMAS	CHARLES	ST PAUL	11	89	45	THOMAS ETAL	WILLIAM	1884
THOMAS	HARRIET	ST PAUL	6	144	144	MURRAY	FRANCIS	1886
THOMAS	HARRIET	ST PAUL	119	97	97	GOOD	WILLIAM	1881
THOMAS	HENRY	ST ANDREW	99	29	29	ANDERSON	THOMAS	1881
THOMAS	HENRY	ST ANDREW	173	22	22	ANDERSON	THOMAS	1881
THOMAS	RICHARD	ST ANDREW	54	77	77	MOWAT	FRANCE	88
THOMAS	ROBERT	ST ANDREW	224	49	49	MOWAT	JOHN	88
THOMAS	THOMAS	ST CLEMENT	92	48	48	THOMAS	SIMON	82
THOMAS	WIDOW ALEX	ST ANDREW	171	39	39	THOMAS	VICTOR	86
THOMAS	WILLIAM	ST PAUL	9	151	76	HARROWER	JAMES	1882
THOMAS	WILLIAM	ST PAUL	10	71	36	THOMAS ETAL	WILLIAM	1884
THOMAS	WILLIAM	ST PAUL	113	582	327	THOMAS ETAL	WILLIAM	1884
THOMSON	JOHN	ST ANDREW	71	62	62	THOMPSON	JOHN	1875
THORNE	GEORGE	SFX	148	89	89	THORNE	GEORGE	1876
THORNE	JOHN	BAIE S PAUL	24	103	103	ZASTE	ISODORE	1910
TODD	ALBERT	ST CLEMENT	64	47	47	INKSTER	COLIN	1882
TODD	JOHN	ST JAMES	33	104	104	TODD	JOHN	1883
TOURON	JACQUE	ST NORBERT	159	133	133	TOURON	JACQUE	1875
TOURON	JOSEPH	ST NORBERT	77	99	99	TOURAND	JOSEPH	87
TOURON	JOSEPH	ST NORBERT	161	308	.	TOURAND	ROSALI	86
TOURON	JOSEPH	ST NORBERT	191	107	107	TOURON	JOSEPH	1877
TOURON SR	JOSEPH	ST NORBERT	156	37	37	TOUROND	ROSALIE ETAL	
TOUROND	J B	BAIE S PAUL	42	246	246	TOUROND	J B	1877
TOUROND	JOSEPH	BAIE S PAUL	223	96	96	TOURON	DAVID	1882
TOUROND	JOSEPH	SFX	150	83	83	TOURON	JOSEPH	1876
TRAKEE	JOSEPH	BAIE S PAUL	191	95	95	ASHDOWN	JAMES	1881

TABLE 5: RECOGNITION OF RIVERLOT OCCUPANTS BY THE GOVERNMENT OF CANADA

OCCUPANT NAMED BY SURVEYORS	PARISH	LOT	AREA	AREA CLAIMED	PATENTEE	YEAR OF PATENT
TRESTON JAMES	SFX	222	222	222	TRESTON JAMES	1877
TRESTON JAMES	SFX	224	393	393	TRESTON JAMES	1877
TROTTIER CHARLES	SFX	164	101	101	CRAWLEY CHARLES	1880
TRUTHWAITE THOMAS	ST CLEMENT	40	153	153	TRUTHWAITE THOMAS SR	82
TRUTHWAITE THOMAS	ST ANDREW	104	79	79	TRUTHWAITE THOMAS	1876
TRUTHWAITE THOMAS	ST ANDREW	105	152	152	TRUTHWAITE THOMAS	1876
TRUTHWAITE THOMAS	ST ANDREW	176	41	41	TRUTHWAITE THOMAS SR	78
TURCOTT JOSEPH	ST CHARLES	99	104	104	RICARD CESAIRE	1877
TURCOTTE JOSEPH	ST CHARLES	35	97	97	TURCOTTE JOSEPH	1880
TURNER JOHN	ST JAMES	57	60	60	TURNER JOHN	1886
TURNER ETAL DR J H	ST CHARLES	83	166	83	TURNER ALEX	1880
TURNER ETAL H	STE AGATHE	148	153	153	DUVAL JOSEPH	83
VACANT	ST LAURENT	3	357	357	DUCHARME BTE	1884
VACANT	ST LAURENT	4	287	179	LAVALLEE BAPTISTE	1878
VACANT	ST LAURENT	6	362	179	LAVALLEE ANTOINE	1885
VACANT	BAIE S PAUL	29	83	83	BREDIN LUCY	1903
VACANT	BAIE S PAUL	30	90	90		
VACANT	BAIE S PAUL	31	113	68	PERREAULT FR XAVIER	1883
VACANT	BAIE S PAUL	32	128	38	R C PARISH BAIE ST PAUL	1883
VACANT	BAIE S PAUL	33	113	113	R C PARISH BAIE ST PAUL	1883
VACANT	BAIE S PAUL	34	115	92	R C PARISH BAIE ST PAUL	1883
VACANT	BAIE S PAUL	35	127	26	LEUFESTY JOHN JAMES	1904
VACANT	BAIE S PAUL	36	140	140	MCKAY JAMES	1878
VACANT	BAIE S PAUL	37	122	49	TRUTHWAITE THOMAS	1883
VACANT	BAIE S PAUL	38	106	63	CHENIER FELIX	1883
VACANT	BAIE S PAUL	39	98	98	MORRISON DONALD	83
VACANT	BAIE S PAUL	40	96	96	MORRISON DONALD	1883
VACANT	BAIE S PAUL	41	997	3	CHISHOLM ALEXANDER	1877
VACANT	BAIE S PAUL	42	106	21	CHISHOLM ALEXANDER	1877
VACANT	BAIE S PAUL	43	121	97	ALLOWAY AND CHAMPION	1910
VACANT	BAIE S PAUL	44	71	71	CHENIER FELIX	1877
VACANT	BAIE S PAUL	45	113	57	CAMPBELL FRANK A	1916
VACANT	BAIE S PAUL	46	108	108	TAIT ROBERT	1883
VACANT	BAIE S PAUL	47	101	101	MURRAY LETITIA	1883
VACANT	BAIE S PAUL	48	95	95	BREMNER WILLIAM	1882
VACANT	BAIE S PAUL	49	92	92		
VACANT	BAIE S PAUL	50	93	37	SAYER HENRY	1877
VACANT	BAIE S PAUL	51	99	79	SAYER HENRY	1877
VACANT	BAIE S PAUL	52	264	264		
VACANT	BAIE S PAUL	53	91	91	BREMNER ALEXANDER	
VACANT	BAIE S PAUL	54	86	86		
VACANT	BAIE S PAUL	55	87	87		
VACANT	BAIE S PAUL	56	132	132	WILLIAMS JANE	1902
VACANT	BAIE S PAUL	57	125	125	NEFF ET AL JOSEPH	1913
VACANT	BAIE S PAUL	58	137	137	UNIVERSITY MANITOBA	1898
VACANT	BAIE S PAUL	59	155	155		
VACANT	BAIE S PAUL	60	164	164	HUDSON BAY C O	1883
VACANT	BAIE S PAUL	61	126	126	CAPLETTE DENIS	1882
VACANT	BAIE S PAUL	62	70	70		
VACANT	BAIE S PAUL	63	138	138	MACARTHUR DUNCAN EXTR	1883

OCCUPANT NAMED BY SURVEYORS	PARISH	LOT	AREA	AREA CLAIMED	PATENTEE		YEAR OF PATENT
VACANT	BAIE S PAUL	66	155	62	MCKENZIE	FREDERICK	1884
VACANT	BAIE S PAUL	67	128	128	UNIVERSITY	MANITOBA	1898
VACANT	BAIE S PAUL	68	102	102	ARCHIBALD	HEBER	1890
VACANT	BAIE S PAUL	69	99	99			
VACANT	BAIE S PAUL	70	121	121	LECUYER	AMBROISE	1912
VACANT	BAIE S PAUL	71	143	143			
VACANT	BAIE S PAUL	72	133	133	CAMERON	JOHN	1914
VACANT	BAIE S PAUL	73	121	121	GLADU	PASCAL	1899
VACANT	BAIE S PAUL	74	121	60			
VACANT	BAIE S PAUL	75	142	142	HUDSON	BAY CO	1880
VACANT	BAIE S PAUL	76	114	114			
VACANT	BAIE S PAUL	77	120	120			
VACANT	BAIE S PAUL	78	121	121	WHEELER	EDWIN J	1907
VACANT	BAIE S PAUL	79	120	120	WHEELER	EDWIN J	1907
VACANT	BAIE S PAUL	80	120	120	UNIVERSITY	MANITOBA	1898
VACANT	BAIE S PAUL	81	120	120	UNIVERSITY	MANITOBA	1898
VACANT	BAIE S PAUL	82	122	122			
VACANT	BAIE S PAUL	83	125	125			
VACANT	BAIE S PAUL	84	133	133	RIOULT	DAVID	1884
VACANT	BAIE S PAUL	85	141	141	RIOULT	DAVID	1884
VACANT	BAIE S PAUL	86	146	146			
VACANT	BAIE S PAUL	87	146	146	BANNATYNE	A G B	1882
VACANT	BAIE S PAUL	88	140	140	FAVEL	RICHARD	1901
VACANT	BAIE S PAUL	89	123	123			
VACANT	BAIE S PAUL	90	107	107	UNIVERSITY	MANITOBA	1898
VACANT	BAIE S PAUL	91	99	99	UNIVERSITY	MANITOBA	1898
VACANT	BAIE S PAUL	92	96	96	UNIVERSITY	MANITOBA	1898
VACANT	BAIE S PAUL	93	97	97	UNIVERSITY	MANITOBA	1898
VACANT	BAIE S PAUL	94	101	101	UNIVERSITY	MANITOBA	1898
VACANT	BAIE S PAUL	95	115	115	UNIVERSITY	MANITOBA	1898
VACANT	BAIE S PAUL	96	141	141	UNIVERSITY	MANITOBA	1880
VACANT	BAIE S PAUL	97	120	140	UNIVERSITY	MAINTOBA	1898
VACANT	BAIE S PAUL	98	120	120	UNIVERSITY	MANITOBA	1898
VACANT	BAIE S PAUL	99	112	112	UNIVERSITY	MANITOBA	1898
VACANT	BAIE S PAUL	100	185	185	UNIVERSITY	MANITOBA	1898
VACANT	BAIE S PAUL	101	176	176	UNIVERSITY	MANITOBA	1898
VACANT	BAIE S PAUL	102	165	165	UNIVERSITY	MANITOBA	1898
VACANT	BAIE S PAUL	124	280	280	CHENIER	FELIX	1883
VACANT	BAIE S PAUL	125	96		CHENIER	FELIX	1883
VACANT	BAIE S PAUL	131	95	95	BOURKE	EDWIN	1877
VACANT	BAIE S PAUL	171	113	113	TAIT	ROBERT	1881
VACANT	BAIE S PAUL	175	122	122	MCKAY	JAMES	1878
VACANT	BAIE S PAUL	176	123	123	MCKAY	JAMES	1878
VACANT	BAIE S PAUL	177	122	122	MCKAY	JAMES	1878
VACANT	BAIE S PAUL	180	101	101	MCKAY	JAMES	1878
VACANT	BAIE S PAUL	182	96	96	RICHARD	ANTOINE	1878
VACANT	BAIE S PAUL	184	95	95			
VACANT	BAIE S PAUL	185	97	97	GREEN	JAMES	1878
VACANT	BAIE S PAUL	186	101	101	GREEN	JAMES	1878
VACANT	BAIE S PAUL	190	168	168			
VACANT	BAIE S PAUL	192	97	97			
VACANT	BAIE S PAUL	193	99	99	TACHE EXRS	ALEX ETAL	1886

TABLE 5: RECOGNITION OF RIVERLOT OCCUPANTS BY THE GOVERNMENT OF CANADA

OCCUPANT NAMED BY SURVEYORS	PARISH	LOT	AREA	AREA CLAIMED	PATENTE		YEAR OF PATENT
VACANT	BAIE S PAUL	196	112	112	MCKAY	JAMES	1878
VACANT	BAIE S PAUL	198	114	114	CHENIER	FELIX	1882
VACANT	BAIE S PAUL	203	91	91	SENECAL	JOSEPH	1883
VACANT	BAIE S PAUL	204	96	96	SENECAL	JOSEPH	1883
VACANT	BAIE S PAUL	217	162	162	DESJARLAIS	ANDRE	1877
VACANT	BAIE S PAUL	220	101	101	DESJARLAIS	ALEXANDER	83
VACANT	BAIE S PAUL	233	91	91	CHENIER	LEON	1878
VACANT	BAIE S PAUL	240	103	103	SMITH	DONALD	1877
VACANT	SFX	33	83	83	LAVALLEE	PIERRE	85
VACANT	SFX	69	67	67	HOUSE	CHARLES	1885
VACANT	SFX	169	82	82	LUMSDEN	THOMAS	1884
VACANT	SFX	210	106	106	MORIN	CHARLES	1885
VACANT	SFX	219	230	230	DAUPHINAIS	WILLIAM	1885
VACANT	ST CHARLES	20	100	100	TAIT	R	1882
VACANT	ST CHARLES	21	101	101	MULLIGAN	JAMES	1876
VACANT	ST CHARLES	46	96	96	SINCLAIR	DUNCAN	1877
VACANT	ST CHARLES	47	62	62	SINCLAIR	DUNCAN	1877
VACANT	ST CHARLES	48	61	61	SINCLAIR	DUNCAN	1877
VACANT	ST CHARLES	58	79		GRANT	JOHN F	81
VACANT	ST CHARLES	123	19	19	CHAMPION	HENRY T	1902
VACANT	ST CHARLES	124			LOUGHEED	JAMES	1879
VACANT	ST BONIFACE	27	52	52	CLARKE	HENRY J	1882
VACANT	ST BONIFACE	38	4	4	MULLIGAN	JAMES	1887
VACANT	ST BONIFACE	39	4	4	SMITH	HON D A	1875
VACANT	ST BONIFACE	40	2	2	SMITH	HON D A	1894
VACANT	ST BONIFACE	46	193	193	MULLIGAN	JAMES	1876
VACANT	ST BONIFACE	47	99	99	STEWART	JAMES	1875
VACANT	ST BONIFACE	48	87	87	TAYLOR	GEORGE	1878
VACANT	ST BONIFACE	49	89	89	MULLIGAN	JAMES	1875
VACANT	ST BONIFACE	50	160	160	MCKAY	HON JAMES	1875
VACANT	ST BONIFACE	51	106	106	MULLIGAN	JAMES	1875
VACANT	ST BONIFACE	52	105	105	TACHE ET AL	REV A	1886
VACANT	ST BONIFACE	53	103	103	HARKNESS	SARAH	1882
VACANT	ST BONIFACE	54	103	103	MULHOLLAND	ROBERT	
VACANT	ST BONIFACE	55	98	98	MULHOLLAND	ROBERT	
VACANT	ST BONIFACE	56	102	102	HALETTE JR	JAMES	1875
VACANT	ST BONIFACE	57	103	103	OMAND	JOHN	1875
VACANT	ST BONIFACE	58	102	102	ALLARY	MARIE ANNE	1882
VACANT	ST BONIFACE	59	51	51	EATON	W C	1878
VACANT	ST BONIFACE	60	99	99	MULLIGAN	JAMES	1875
VACANT	ST BONIFACE	61	98	98	CORP ARCH	C R DE ST B	1878
VACANT	ST BONIFACE	62	49	49	CAPLETTE	JOSEPH	1898
VACANT	ST BONIFACE	63	98	98	TURCOTTE	VITAL	1875
VACANT	ST BONIFACE	64	62	62	LOGAN	ALEXANDER	1877
VACANT	ST BONIFACE	65	68	68	LOGAN	ALEXANDER	1877
VACANT	ST BONIFACE	66	60	60	YOUNG ET AL	GEORGE	
VACANT	ST BONIFACE	67	152	152	MCDOUGALL	COLIN	
VACANT	ST BONIFACE	68	108	108	GRANT	JOHN F	1878
VACANT	ST BONIFACE	69	25	25	GRANT	JOHN	1878
VACANT	ST BONIFACE	70	63	63	GRANT	JOHN	1878

OCCUPANT NAMED BY SURVEYORS	PARISH	LOT	AREA	AREA CLAIMED	PATENTEE	YEAR OF PATENT
VACANT	ST BONIFACE	73	58	58	COLLEGE DE S T BONIFACE	1878
VACANT	ST BONIFACE	74	57	57	LAGIMONIERE J BTE	1878
VACANT	ST BONIFACE	75	57	57	LAGIMONIERE E	1878
VACANT	ST BONIFACE	82	118	118	COMMON	
VACANT	ST BONIFACE	89	120	118	MARION ROGER	1879
VACANT	ST BONIFACE	90	1	1	MONCHAMP ONESIM	91
VACANT	ST BONIFACE	91	9	9	FREEMAN JOHN	1878
VACANT	ST BONIFACE	92	8	8	WILDER AMHERST H	1884
VACANT	ST VITAL	36	83	83	RICHOT ANDRE	85
VACANT	ST VITAL	37	54	54	MCMILLAN WILLIAM	1875
VACANT	ST VITAL	38	59	59	BEAUCHIMIN ANDRE	1875
VACANT	ST VITAL	39	53	53	BRUCE ROSALI	86
VACANT	ST VITAL	40	115	115	BEAUCHIMIN ANDRE	1875
VACANT	ST VITAL	41	103	103	NAULT ROMAIN	1881
VACANT	ST VITAL	42	134	134	NAULT BONIFACE	1876
VACANT	ST VITAL	43	162	162	DESCHAMBAULT PIERRE	1880
VACANT	ST VITAL	44	176	176	PLAUFFE J BTE	1876
VACANT	ST VITAL	45	134	45	LARENCE ELIZA	
VACANT	ST VITAL	46	228	228	LARENCE JOSEPHTE	1880
VACANT	ST VITAL	47	213	213	NAULT JOSEPH	1885
VACANT	ST VITAL	48	186	186	ST BONIFACE LA CORP ARCH	1880
VACANT	ST VITAL	49	105	105	SAUVE MARIE	1880
VACANT	ST VITAL	50	24	11	RIEL ALEXANDER	1892
VACANT	ST VITAL	51	232	232	RIEL JULIE	1884
VACANT	ST VITAL	52	87	87	NAULT CHARLES	1876
VACANT	ST VITAL	53	82	82	PROULX PAUL	1876
VACANT	ST VITAL	54	92	92	CHARITY SISTERS OF	1883
VACANT	ST VITAL	55	112	112	PLAUFFE JEAN BTE	1877
VACANT	ST VITAL	56	83	83	MARION FRANCOIS	1881
VACANT	ST VITAL	57	61	61	DESCHAMBAULT PIERRE	1903
VACANT	ST VITAL	58	55	55	DUBOIS FRANCOIS	1879
VACANT	ST VITAL	59	55	55	DEASE JOHN	1878
VACANT	ST VITAL	60	41	41	RANGEAU JOSEPH	1884
VACANT	ST VITAL	61	145	145	GLADU PIERRE	1877
VACANT	ST VITAL	62	81	81	NONE	
VACANT	ST NORBERT	1	107	107	JOHNSTON STEWART	1886
VACANT	ST NORBERT	4	178	178	HUTCHINGS ELISHA	1886
VACANT	ST NORBERT	5	166	166		
VACANT	ST NORBERT	6	159	159	RADFORD EBENEZER	1882
VACANT	ST NORBERT	13	156	156	BRUCE HERMANGILDE	1875
VACANT	ST NORBERT	32	61	61	LIZOTTE PIERRE	1878
VACANT	ST NORBERT	39	11	11	RITCHOT N J	1885
VACANT	ST NORBERT	51	106	106	BONNEAU NAPOLEON	1879
VACANT	ST NORBERT	104	95	63	PAYMENT LOUIS	1884
VACANT	ST NORBERT	105	98	98	HAMELIN JOSEPH	1883
VACANT	ST NORBERT	106	100	100	PAYMENT LOUIS	1885
VACANT	ST NORBERT	107	50	50	ALLARD OCTAVE	1878
VACANT	ST NORBERT	108	184	184	LACHANCE PIERRE	1882
VACANT	ST NORBERT	110	9	9	CHAMPAGNE HENRIETTE	1902
VACANT	ST NORBERT	111	9	9		
VACANT	ST NORBERT	112	8	8		
VACANT	ST NORBERT	113	8	8	CADOTTE BAPTIS	85

OCCUPANT NAMED BY SURVEYORS	PARISH	LOT	AREA	AREA CLAIMED	PATENTEE		YEAR OF PATENT
VACANT	ST NORBERT	114	8	8	VERMETTE	LOUIS	87
VACANT	ST NORBERT	148	47	47	TALIBUTE	MARGUERITE	1888
VACANT	ST NORBERT	171	104	104	SMITH	D A	.
VACANT	ST NORBERT	178	114	114	SMITH	DONALD A	1877
VACANT	ST NORBERT	187	106	106	SMITH	DA	1885
VACANT	ST NORBERT	193	106	106	VERY	CA	1877
VACANT	ST NORBERT	195	114	114	MULHOLLAND	ROBERT	1877
VACANT	ST NORBERT	196	108	108	BONNEAU	NAPOLEON	1877
VACANT	ST NORBERT	203	83	83	MULHOLLAND	ROBERT	1876
VACANT	ST NORBERT	205	326	209	FRONSECA	WILLIAM G	1877
VACANT	ST NORBERT	206	161	79	SCHULTZ	JOHN	1877
VACANT	ST NORBERT	207	69	69	FRONSECA	WILLIAM G	1876
VACANT	ST NORBERT	208	96	96	FREEMAN	JOHN	86
VACANT	ST NORBERT	209	89	89	ECCLES	JOHN	1876
VACANT	ST NORBERT	210	180	180	ECCLES	JOHN	1877
VACANT	ST NORBERT	211	132	132	CORNELL	HENRY	1877
VACANT	ST NORBERT	214	196	196	LARAMIE	PIERRE	1901
VACANT	ST NORBERT	215	184	184	PARISIEN	ROGER	.
VACANT	ST NORBERT	217	98	98	BANNATYNE	AGB	1881
VACANT	ST NORBERT	220	92	92	SCHULTZ	JOHN	1878
VACANT	ST NORBERT	221	93	93	BATHGATH	ROBERT D	82
VACANT	ST NORBERT	222	97	97	RICHOT	REV N J	1885
VACANT	ST NORBERT	223	104	104	RICHOT	REV N J	1883
VACANT	ST NORBERT	224	112	112	RICHOT	REV N J	1883
VACANT	ST NORBERT	226	163	163	RICHOT	REV N J	1883
VACANT	ST NORBERT	227	164	164	RICHOT	REV N J	1883
VACANT	ST NORBERT	228	161	161	LECOUST	JOSEPH	1882
VACANT	ST NORBERT	229	156	156	LECOUST	JOSEPH	1882
VACANT	ST NORBERT	230	154	154	GOVIN	WALTER	1882
VACANT	ST NORBERT	231	159	159	GOVIN	WALTER	1882
VACANT	ST NORBERT	232	169	169			.
VACANT	ST NORBERT	236	159	159	LAROCQUE	ANTOINE	1882
VACANT	ST NORBERT	237	162	162	NONE		.
VACANT	ST NORBERT	238	167	17	COTE	MAGLOIRE	.
VACANT	ST NORBERT	239	171	171	HANSEN	SKULI	1903
VACANT	ST NORBERT	240	175	175	H B CO		1880
VACANT	ST NORBERT	241	180	180			.
VACANT	ST NORBERT	242	185	185			.
VACANT	ST NORBERT	243	186	186	NONE		.
VACANT	ST NORBERT	244	183	183	CARRIER	ANDRE	1903
VACANT	ST NORBERT	248	125	125	LAND CO	CAN N W	1897
VACANT	ST NORBERT	249	153	153	SPENCER	G B	1877
VACANT	ST NORBERT	253	139	139	GRAHAM	JAMES	1900
VACANT	ST NORBERT	254	142	58	WILLIAMS	ROBERT A	1880
VACANT	STE AGATHE	3	122	122	NASH	WILLIAM	1877
VACANT	STE AGATHE	4	130	130	HUDSONS BAY	CO	1881
VACANT	STE AGATHE	4	112	112	CARNEY ETAL	THOMAS	1875
VACANT	STE AGATHE	6	106	106	CARNEY ETAL	THOMAS	1875
VACANT	STE AGATHE	8	99	99	CARNEY ETAL	THOMAS	1875
VACANT	STE AGATHE	10	91	91	CARNEY ETAL	THOMAS	1875
VACANT	STE AGATHE				CARNEY		

OCCUPANT NAMED BY SURVEYORS	PARISH	LOT	AREA	AREA CLAIMED	PATENTEE		YEAR OF PATENT
VACANT	STE AGATHE	14	73	73	CARNEY	THOMAS	1875
VACANT	STE AGATHE	15	180	180	HUDSONS BAY	CO	1881
VACANT	STE AGATHE	16	63	63	CARNEY ETAL	THOMAS	75
VACANT	STE AGATHE	18	135	135	DOUGLASS	PETER	1878
VACANT	STE AGATHE	19	112	112	FORRESTER	JAMES	1882
VACANT	STE AGATHE	21	113	113	MCMULLEN	MARTHA	1883
VACANT	STE AGATHE	22	130	130	BRADLEY	F	1877
VACANT	STE AGATHE	28	124	124	HUDSONS BAY	CO	1880
VACANT	STE AGATHE	29	124	124	TENNANT	HENRY	1881
VACANT	STE AGATHE	30	120	120	CLARK	HIRAM	1882
VACANT	STE AGATHE	31	121	104			
VACANT	STE AGATHE	31	121	17	FRASER ETAL	DONALD	1897
VACANT	STE AGATHE	32	115	115	CLARK	THOMAS	1882
VACANT	STE AGATHE	33	90	90			
VACANT	STE AGATHE	37	103	103	GOSSELIN	MARIE	1879
VACANT	STE AGATHE	39	164	164	CAMERON	DONALD R	75
VACANT	STE AGATHE	40	112	112	GRANT	WILLIAM	1883
VACANT	STE AGATHE	41	106	106	CAMERON	DONALD R	75
VACANT	STE AGATHE	43	99	99	BEDFORD	SALOMA	1879
VACANT	STE AGATHE	45	101	101	BEDFORD	JAMES	1889
VACANT	STE AGATHE	47	111	111	GOODHEW	GEORGE	1888
VACANT	STE AGATHE	48	129	129			
VACANT	STE AGATHE	49	124	124	FORRESTER	JAMES	1883
VACANT	STE AGATHE	52	110	110	ALLMON	COLTON	1877
VACANT	STE AGATHE	62	156	156	HUDSONS BAY	CO	1880
VACANT	STE AGATHE	64	153	153	HYLEACH	WILLIAM	1882
VACANT	STE AGATHE	65	131	131	NUGENT	ARNOLD I	82
VACANT	STE AGATHE	66	151	151	CLARK	HIRAM	1889
VACANT	STE AGATHE	68	150	150			
VACANT	STE AGATHE	70	156	156	MORTIMER	SIDNEY	1883
VACANT	STE AGATHE	74	174	174	MCDONALD	DUNCAN	1882
VACANT	STE AGATHE	75	109	109			
VACANT	STE AGATHE	76	171	171	MCDONALD	DUNCAN	1882
VACANT	STE AGATHE	77	114	114			
VACANT	STE AGATHE	79	111	111	LECUYER	HENRY	1882
VACANT	STE AGATHE	81	96	96	SARETTE	AMEDEE	1903
VACANT	STE AGATHE	82	134	134	MAJOR	JOHN	1900
VACANT	STE AGATHE	83	101	101	HUDSONS BAY	CO	1880
VACANT	STE AGATHE	84	137	137	MAJOR	JOHN	1879
VACANT	STE AGATHE	86	127	59	MERRICK	PALMERSTON	1909
VACANT	STE AGATHE	87	616	116	FAILLE	WILLIAM	1883
VACANT	STE AGATHE	91	116	116			
VACANT	STE AGATHE	93	114	114	EYRES	THOMAS	1887
VACANT	STE AGATHE	99	153	153	PELOQUIN	PAUL	1886
VACANT	STE AGATHE	102	89	89			
VACANT	STE AGATHE	104	91	91	HUDSONS BAY	CO	1880
VACANT	STE AGATHE	115	102	102	GRUNDBOIS	ISIDORE	1881
VACANT	STE AGATHE	116	99	99	LESPERANCE	JOSEPH	1882
VACANT	STE AGATHE	119	94	94	MARCHARD	BENJAMIN	1884
VACANT	STE AGATHE	120	106	106			
VACANT	STE AGATHE	129	132	132	TENNANT	JOSEPH F	81
VACANT	STE AGATHE	138	112	112	PAYETTE	PIERRE	1882

OCCUPANT NAMED BY SURVEYORS	PARISH	LOT	AREA	AREA CLAIMED	PATENTEE	YEAR OF PATENT
VACANT	STE AGATHE	141	99	99	GROVER HANNAH	1882
VACANT	STE AGATHE	147	158	20	MONDOR GASPARD	1884
VACANT	STE AGATHE	152	110	110	PINGLE WARREN HUME	82
VACANT	STE AGATHE	153	103	103	GODON JOSEPH	80
VACANT	STE AGATHE	154	132	132	PARENT JOSEPH	1886
VACANT	STE AGATHE	155	164	164		
VACANT	STE AGATHE	156	163	163	MARCHAND FLORA	1886
VACANT	STE AGATHE	157	197	197	PARENT JOSEPH	1882
VACANT	STE AGATHE	158	84	84	WRIGHT J HASSARD	1882
VACANT	STE AGATHE	159	87	87	WRIGHT J HASSARD	1882
VACANT	STE AGATHE	160	98	98		
VACANT	STE AGATHE	161	150	150	LEFORD JOSEPH	1882
VACANT	STE AGATHE	162	75	75	BUTCHER FRANCIS JOS	1905
VACANT	STE AGATHE	163	174	174		
VACANT	STE AGATHE	164	66	66	HENRY NARCISSE	1889
VACANT	STE AGATHE	165	175	175	DUPAS JOSEPH	1882
VACANT	STE AGATHE	166	66	66	L HALLIER VALENTINE	1890
VACANT	STE AGATHE	167	171	171	STVINCENT DIDIME	1882
VACANT	STE AGATHE	168	69	69	HBC	1883
VACANT	STE AGATHE	169	163	163	STVINCENT	1892
VACANT	STE AGATHE	170	76	76	MAGLOIRE	1883
VACANT	STE AGATHE	171	151	151	MCRAE TELESPHORE	1882
VACANT	STE AGATHE	172	87	87		1883
VACANT	STE AGATHE	173	140	140		
VACANT	STE AGATHE	174	98	98		
VACANT	STE AGATHE	175	135	67	LANDRY JOSEPH	1880
VACANT	STE AGATHE	176	105	105	HBC	1880
VACANT	STE AGATHE	177	133	133	HBC	1903
VACANT	STE AGATHE	178	106	106	GRAVELINE JOSEPHAT	1880
VACANT	STE AGATHE	179	132	132	HBC	
VACANT	STE AGATHE	180	108	108	HAMEL OVIDE	1891
VACANT	STE AGATHE	181	117	117	MCDONALD DONALD	1881
VACANT	STE AGATHE	182	112	112		
VACANT	STE AGATHE	183	93	93	MCDONALD DONALD	1889
VACANT	STE AGATHE	184	144	144	HBC	1883
VACANT	STE AGATHE	185	96	96		
VACANT	STE AGATHE	186	145	145	HBC	1883
VACANT	STE AGATHE	187	102	102		
VACANT	STE AGATHE	188	138	138	HBC	1883
VACANT	STE AGATHE	189	108	108	FILLION LOUIS	1907
VACANT	STE AGATHE	190	131	131	HBC	1883
VACANT	STE AGATHE	191	153	153	SCHULTZ HON JOHN	1884
VACANT	STE AGATHE	192	128	128	HBC	1883
VACANT	STE AGATHE	193	155	155	SCHULTZ HON JOHN	1884
VACANT	STE AGATHE	194	127	127	HBC	1883
VACANT	STE AGATHE	195	154	154		
VACANT	STE AGATHE	196	127	127	HBC	1883
VACANT	STE AGATHE	197	153	153		
VACANT	STE AGATHE	198	128	128		
VACANT	STE AGATHE	199	152	152		
VACANT	STE AGATHE	200	130	130	HERMIE J PATRICK	1911
VACANT	STE AGATHE	201	150	150		

TABLE 5: RECOGNITION OF RIVERLOT OCCUPANTS BY THE GOVERNMENT OF CANADA

OCCUPANT NAMED BY SURVEYORS	PARISH	LOT	AREA	AREA CLAIMED	PATENTEE		YEAR OF PATENT
VACANT	STE AGATHE	202	132	132	PAUL	LOUIS	1891
VACANT	STE AGATHE	203	151	151			
VACANT	STE AGATHE	204	131	131			.
VACANT	STE AGATHE	205	168	168			
VACANT	STE AGATHE	206	124	124	LAFONTAINE	PHILIAS	1920
VACANT	STE AGATHE	207	80	80	HBC		1881
VACANT	STE AGATHE	208	123	123			
VACANT	STE AGATHE	209	74	74	HBC		1881
VACANT	STE AGATHE	210	205	205	CHARETTE	DANIEL	1877
VACANT	STE AGATHE	211	79	79	HBC		1881
VACANT	STE AGATHE	212	147	147			
VACANT	STE AGATHE	213	134	134			
VACANT	STE AGATHE	214	96	96			.
VACANT	STE AGATHE	215	152	152	HUDSON BAY	COMPANY	1881
VACANT	STE AGATHE	216	91	91			
VACANT	STE AGATHE	217	136	70	LAVALLEE	JEAN BAPTIST	1886
VACANT	STE AGATHE	218	92	92			
VACANT	STE AGATHE	219	69	69	LAVALLEE	NARCISSE	1883
VACANT	STE AGATHE	220	146	29	MCCULLOCH	MARY	1883
VACANT	STE AGATHE	221	65	65			
VACANT	STE AGATHE	222	176	35	MCCULLOCH	MARY	1883
VACANT	STE AGATHE	223	63	63			
VACANT	STE AGATHE	224	178	354	MCMICKEN	ANNE THERESA	1878
VACANT	STE AGATHE	225	105	105	PELISSIER	JOSEPH	1882
VACANT	STE AGATHE	226	176	176	MCMICKEN	ANNE THERESA	1881
VACANT	STE AGATHE	227	112	112	BROWN	WM JOHN	1888
VACANT	STE AGATHE	228	169	169	LABRECQUE	LUDGER	1908
VACANT	STE AGATHE	229	119	119			
VACANT	STE AGATHE	230	161	161	CARRIERE	CHARLES	1890
VACANT	STE AGATHE	231	124	62	MARCILLES	LOUIS	1883
VACANT	STE AGATHE	232	156	156	CARRIERE	CELESTINE	1891
VACANT	STE AGATHE	233	124	124	MARION	MOISE	1883
VACANT	STE AGATHE	234	158	158	CARRIERE	JEAN BAPTIST	1891
VACANT	STE AGATHE	235	119	119	ROY	HILAIRE	1886
VACANT	STE AGATHE	236	162	162	CARRIERE	FRANCOIS	
VACANT	STE AGATHE	237	105	57	VANDAL	LOUIS	1882
VACANT	STE AGATHE	238	169	169	GUERTIN	ALFRED	1881
VACANT	STE AGATHE	239	67	67	LA CORP ACR	ST BONIFACE	1881
VACANT	STE AGATHE	240	206	206	LA CORP ACR	ST BONIFACE	1882
VACANT	STE AGATHE	241	109	54	PARENTEAU	PIERRE	
VACANT	STE AGATHE	242	132	132			
VACANT	STE AGATHE	243	117	59	DUCHARME	PROSPER	83
VACANT	STE AGATHE	244	124	124			
VACANT	STE AGATHE	245	128	128	GAUDRY	AMABLE	1883
VACANT	STE AGATHE	246	114	114			
VACANT	STE AGATHE	247	134	134	POULIN	THEODORE	1886
VACANT	STE AGATHE	248	108	108			
VACANT	STE AGATHE	249	138	138	DERY	CHARLES B	1883
VACANT	STE AGATHE	250	103	103			
VACANT	STE AGATHE	251	142	142			
VACANT	STE AGATHE	252	100	100			.
VACANT	STE AGATHE	253	145	145	DUBUC	JOSEPH	1879

OCCUPANT NAMED BY SURVEYORS	PARISH	LOT	AREA	AREA CLAIMED	PATENTEE		YEAR OF PATENT
VACANT	STE AGATHE	254	97	97	PARENTEAU	MICHAEL	1882
VACANT	STE AGATHE	255	149	149	VERMETTE	LOUIS	1882
VACANT	STE AGATHE	256	91	91			
VACANT	STE AGATHE	257	158	158	VERMETTE	LOUIS	1882
VACANT	STE AGATHE	258	80	80			
VACANT	STE AGATHE	259	170	34			
VACANT	STE AGATHE	260	70	70	VANDAL	JOSEPH	77
VACANT	STE AGATHE	261	108	32			
VACANT	STE AGATHE	262	72	72	VANDAL	ANTOINE	1877
VACANT	STE AGATHE	263	67	67			
VACANT	STE AGATHE	264	192	192	VANDAL	ANTOINE	1877
VACANT	STE AGATHE	265	68	68			
VACANT	STE AGATHE	266	173	173	BEGG	JAMES	82
VACANT	STE AGATHE	267	135	135			
VACANT	STE AGATHE	268	66	66	WALKER	JOHN A	82
VACANT	STE AGATHE	269	178	178			
VACANT	STE AGATHE	270	64	64			
VACANT	STE AGATHE	271	172	172			
VACANT	STE AGATHE	272	68	68	BRUNEAU	THEOPHILE	1886
VACANT	STE AGATHE	273	153	153	HUDSON BAY	CO	1881
VACANT	STE AGATHE	274	79	79	DOZOIS	ALFRED	83
VACANT	STE AGATHE	275	106	106	HUDSONS BAY	CO	81
VACANT	STE AGATHE	276	143	143	BORDELEAU	ONESIME	1890
VACANT	STE AGATHE	277	100	100	COMPANY OF	ADVENTURERS	79
VACANT	STE AGATHE	278	141	141	DOZAIS	GERMAINE	79
VACANT	STE AGATHE	279	99	99	COMPANY OF	ADVENTURERS	79
VACANT	STE AGATHE	280	142	142	GILL	EMILE	1883
VACANT	STE AGATHE	281	103	103	COMPANY OF	ADVENTURERS	79
VACANT	STE AGATHE	282	140	140	ROY	NAPOLEON H	82
VACANT	STE AGATHE	283	115	115	COMPANY OF	ADVENTURERS	79
VACANT	STE AGATHE	284	64	64	FERRAND	JEAN B	1882
VACANT	STE AGATHE	285	173	173	COMPANY OF	ADVENTURERS	79
VACANT	STE AGATHE	286	67	67	ROY	ROSARIO	82
VACANT	STE AGATHE	287	158	158	COMPANY OF	ADVENTURERS	79
VACANT	STE AGATHE	288	78	78			
VACANT	STE AGATHE	289	121	121	HOUGHTON	EDWIN J	83
VACANT	STE AGATHE	290	113	113	ROBERGE	RAPHAEL	82
VACANT	STE AGATHE	291	113	113	HOUGHTON	EDWIN J	83
VACANT	STE AGATHE	292	127	127	HUDSONS BAY	CO	1880
VACANT	STE AGATHE	293	112	112			
VACANT	STE AGATHE	294	129	129			
VACANT	STE AGATHE	295	110	110			
VACANT	STE AGATHE	296	121	121			
VACANT	STE AGATHE	297	132	132	GRANGER	DAVID	82
VACANT	STE AGATHE	298	80	80	GRENON	PIERRE	82
VACANT	STE AGATHE	299	182	182			
VACANT	STE AGATHE	300	54	27	GRENON	PIERRE	82
VACANT	STE AGATHE	301	180	180	DROUGHT	THOMAS	1882
VACANT	STE AGATHE	302	59	59	LANDRY	JOSEPH	1890
VACANT	STE AGATHE	303	165	165	ALBRIGHT	ALBERT	1886
VACANT	STE AGATHE	304	69	69	PROVEST	JOSEPH	1889
VACANT	STE AGATHE	305	143	143	RITCHIE	ALEXANDER	1882

TABLE 5: RECOGNITION OF RIVERLOT OCCUPANTS BY THE GOVERNMENT OF CANADA

OCCUPANT NAMED BY SURVEYORS	PARISH	LOT	AREA	AREA CLAIMED	PATENTE	YEAR OF PATENT
VACANT	STE AGATHE	306	91	91	BILADEAU HENRY	1884
VACANT	STE AGATHE	307	130	130	RITCHIE HENRY	83
VACANT	STE AGATHE	308	108	108	CLEMENT ZOTIQUE	1910
VACANT	STE AGATHE	309	125	125	NONE NONE	
VACANT	STE AGATHE	310	114	114	PROULX JOSEPH	1906
VACANT	STE AGATHE	311	120	120	NONE NONE	.
VACANT	STE AGATHE	312	119	119	PROULX JOSEPH	
VACANT	STE AGATHE	313	116	116	H B COMPANY	1880
VACANT	STE AGATHE	314	122	122	PROULX JOSEPH	
VACANT	STE AGATHE	315	114	114	MOODIE GEORGE	1883
VACANT	STE AGATHE	316	125	125	PROULX ESDRAS	1905
VACANT	STE AGATHE	317	112	112	COLLUM SIMON J	1888
VACANT	STE AGATHE	318	127	127	SAVOYARD NORBERT	1880
VACANT	STE AGATHE	319	110	110	COLLUM SIMON J	1888
VACANT	STE AGATHE	320	129	129	SAVOYARD ALEXIS	1879
VACANT	STE AGATHE	321	151	151	NONE NONE	
VACANT	STE AGATHE	322	88	88	GALLIE JANE	1898
VACANT	STE AGATHE	323	152	152	KENNEDY MARY ANN	
VACANT	STE AGATHE	324	87	87	GALLIE JANE	1898
VACANT	STE AGATHE	325	155	155	TURNER ADAM	1882
VACANT	STE AGATHE	326	84	84	ROBERT JOSEPH	1911
VACANT	STE AGATHE	327	159	159	TURNER CHARLES	1882
VACANT	STE AGATHE	328	79	79	NONE NONE	
VACANT	STE AGATHE	329	139	139	LANE JOHN	1881
VACANT	STE AGATHE	330	76	76	NONE NONE	
VACANT	STE AGATHE	331	116	116	LANE JOHN	
VACANT	STE AGATHE	332	125	125	SAVOYARD PIERRE	83
VACANT	STE AGATHE	333	111	111	GALLIE WILLIAM	1877
VACANT	STE AGATHE	334	127	127	MCMICHAEL CHARLES	82
VACANT	STE AGATHE	335	104	104	GALLIE WILLIAM	1877
VACANT	STE AGATHE	336	132	132	MCMICHAEL CHARLES	82
VACANT	STE AGATHE	337	131	131	KENNEDY W N	1877
VACANT	STE AGATHE	338	165	165	KENNEDY WILLIAM N	1883
VACANT	STE AGATHE	339	129	129	KENNEDY MARY ANN	1877
VACANT	STE AGATHE	340	168	168	KENNEDY WILLIAM N	1883
VACANT	STE AGATHE	341	138	138	KENNEDY W N	1877
VACANT	STE AGATHE	342	157	157		
VACANT	STE AGATHE	343	148	148	KENNEDY WILLIAM N	77
VACANT	STE AGATHE	344	149	149	BOWN WALTER RBT	83
VACANT	STE AGATHE	345	153	153	KENNEDY WILLIAM N	77
VACANT	STE AGATHE	346	163	163	BOWN WALTER	83
VACANT	STE AGATHE	347	156	156	MULVEY THOMAS	81
VACANT	STE AGATHE	348	163	163	H B CO	1880
VACANT	STE AGATHE	349	158	158	WALLIS CHARLES J	1882
VACANT	STE AGATHE	350	160	160	CATHOLIQUE LA CORP ARCH	1885
VACANT	STE AGATHE	351	182	182	CATHOLIQUE LA CORP ARCH	1881
VACANT	STE AGATHE	352	104	104	CATHOLIQUE LA CORP ARCH	1881
VACANT	STE AGATHE	353	161	161	NONE NONE	
VACANT	STE AGATHE	354	76	76	NONE NONE	
VACANT	STE AGATHE	355	167	167	NONE NONE	
VACANT	STE AGATHE	356	72	72	SMITH EUPLEMIA	1885
VACANT	STE AGATHE	357	168	168	MCLAKEN GEORGE GRANT	83

OCCUPANT NAMED BY SURVEYORS	PARISH	LOT	AREA	AREA CLAIMED	PATENTEE		YEAR OF PATENT
VACANT	STE AGATHE	358	71	71	GOW	GEORGE	1892
VACANT	STE AGATHE	359	168	168	GOW	NONE	1892
VACANT	STE AGATHE	360	70	70	GOW	GEORGE	·
VACANT	STE AGATHE	361	168	168	NONE	NONE	1903
VACANT	STE AGATHE	362	70	70	MODILL	WILLIAM J	
VACANT	STE AGATHE	363	173	173	NONE	NONE	1903
VACANT	STE AGATHE	364	67	67	MODILL	WILLIAM J	1887
VACANT	STE AGATHE	365	174	174	MALEY	JOHN A	1877
VACANT	STE AGATHE	366	63	13	REED	HAYTER	1882
VACANT	STE AGATHE	367	182	182	MALEY	JOHN A	1877
VACANT	STE AGATHE	368	52	52	REED	HAYTER	1883
VACANT	STE AGATHE	369	117	117	LEWIS	JAMES	1883
VACANT	STE AGATHE	370	219	219	KENNEDY	WILLIAM N	
VACANT	STE AGATHE	371	128	128	NONE	NONE	
VACANT	STE AGATHE	372	194	194	KENNEDY	WILLIAM N	1883
VACANT	STE AGATHE	373	165	33	REED	HAYTER	1877
VACANT	STE AGATHE	374	162	162	KENNEDY	MARY ANN	
VACANT	STE AGATHE	375	178	178	REED	HAYTER	1877
VACANT	STE AGATHE	376	161	161	NONE	NONE	·
VACANT	STE AGATHE	377	178	178	NONE	NONE	·
VACANT	STE AGATHE	378	160	160	NONE	NONE	
VACANT	STE AGATHE	379	180	180	BURWASH	EDWARD	1882
VACANT	STE AGATHE	380	158	158	CAMERON	JOHN	1899
VACANT	STE AGATHE	381	181	181	WANLESS	WILLIAM E	82
VACANT	STE AGATHE	382	157	157	LAND CO	CAN N W	1897
VACANT	STE AGATHE	383	183	183	WANLESS	GEORGE F	82
VACANT	STE AGATHE	384	155	155	LAND CO	CAN N W	1897
VACANT	STE AGATHE	385	102	102	NONE	NONE	
VACANT	STE AGATHE	386	155	155	LAND CO	CAN N W	1897
VACANT	STE AGATHE	387	101	101	HAYWARD	WILLIAM	1896
VACANT	STE AGATHE	388	156	156	LAND CO	CAN N W	1897
VACANT	STE AGATHE	389	101	101	SWAIN	ALFRED G	1911
VACANT	STE AGATHE	390	156	156	LAND CO	CAN N W	1897
VACANT	STE AGATHE	391	101	101	BEGGS	JOHN	1883
VACANT	STE AGATHE	392	155	155	LAND CO	CAN N W	1897
VACANT	STE AGATHE	393	104	104	H B CO	CAN N W	1880
VACANT	STE AGATHE	394	169	169	BURWASH	STEPHEN	1890
VACANT	STE AGATHE	395	110	110	NONE	NONE	
VACANT	STE AGATHE	396	167	167	SNARR	HENRY	1902
VACANT	STE AGATHE	397	118	118	NONE	NONE	
VACANT	STE AGATHE	398	158	158	HOPCRAFT	ARTHUR	1908
VACANT	STE AGATHE	399	127	127	EARL	JOHN	1902
VACANT	STE AGATHE	400	149	149	CLEMIS	ANNIE J	1921
VACANT	STE AGATHE	401	99	99	EARL	JOHN	1902
VACANT	STE AGATHE	402	178	178	NELSON	EDWIN J	1890
VACANT	STE AGATHE	403	108	108	EARL	HENRY	1899
VACANT	STE AGATHE	404	169	169	ANDERSON	HUGH	1904
VACANT	STE AGATHE	405	115	115	EARL	JOHN	1905
VACANT	STE AGATHE	406	163	163	NONE	NONE	
VACANT	STE AGATHE	407	119	119	PROCTOR	WILLIAM C	1889
VACANT	STE AGATHE	408	160	160	NONE	NONE	
VACANT	STE AGATHE	409	122	122	PROCTOR	ISAAC	1889

OCCUPANT NAMED BY SURVEYORS	PARISH	LOT	AREA	AREA CLAIMED	PATENTEE	YEAR OF PATENT
VACANT	STE AGATHE	410	157	157	NONE	
VACANT	STE AGATHE	411	126	126	PROCTOR ISAAC O	1884
VACANT	STE AGATHE	412	152	152	SHEWMAN WILLIAM	1901
VACANT	STE AGATHE	413	145	145	H B CO	1880
VACANT	STE AGATHE	414	123	123	HENRY WILLIAM	1889
VACANT	STE AGATHE	415	164	164	PROCTOR WILLIAM C	1889
VACANT	STE AGATHE	416	115	115	HENRY WILLIAM	1889
VACANT	STE AGATHE	417	131	2	C B MFG CO SILVERPLAINZ	
VACANT	STE AGATHE	418	149	149	HENRY WILLIAM	1889
VACANT	STE AGATHE	419	138	138	SNARR HENRY	1904
VACANT	STE AGATHE	420	140	107	CORNELL GEORGE A	1884
VACANT	STE AGATHE	421	141	141	SNARR EDWIN H	1912
VACANT	STE AGATHE	422	139	139	LAND CO CAN N W	1897
VACANT	STE AGATHE	423	139	139	SIMPSON RICHARD H	1882
VACANT	STE AGATHE	424	140	140	NONE	
VACANT	STE AGATHE	425	135	135	SIMPSON W D	1882
VACANT	STE AGATHE	426	144	144	CAN N W LAND CO	1897
VACANT	STE AGATHE	427	130	130	ELLISON THOMAS	1884
VACANT	STE AGATHE	428	148	148	ROBERTSON ORLAND	1906
VACANT	STE AGATHE	429	129	129	ELLISON THOMAS	1884
VACANT	STE AGATHE	430	148	148	CAN N W LAND CO	1897
VACANT	STE AGATHE	431	131	131		
VACANT	STE AGATHE	432	147	147		
VACANT	STE AGATHE	433	132	132	CAN N W LAND CO	1897
VACANT	STE AGATHE	434	166	166		
VACANT	STE AGATHE	435	132	132	HUDSONS BAY CO	1880
VACANT	STE AGATHE	436	165	165		
VACANT	STE AGATHE	437	133	133	HUDSONS BAY CO	1880
VACANT	STE AGATHE	438	165	165		
VACANT	STE AGATHE	439	135	135	HUDSONS BAY CO	1880
VACANT	STE AGATHE	440	163	163	VERRIER JOSEPH	1908
VACANT	STE AGATHE	441	140	140	HUDSONS BAY CO	1880
VACANT	STE AGATHE	442	157	157		
VACANT	STE AGATHE	443	151	76	BOUCHARD DAMASE	1889
VACANT	STE AGATHE	444	141	56	BANNATYNE ANDREW	1881
VACANT	STE AGATHE	445	170	85	HEBERT PIERRE	1920
VACANT	STE AGATHE	446	127	127	BERTHELETTE JOSEPH	1909
VACANT	STE AGATHE	447	160	160	HEBERT PIERRE	1920
VACANT	STE AGATHE	448	130	130	SCHULTZ JOHN	1877
VACANT	STE AGATHE	449	126	126		
VACANT	STE AGATHE	450	111	111	MERCHANT BAN K	1885
VACANT	STE AGATHE	451	123	123	ROY FRANCOIS	1884
VACANT	STE AGATHE	452	115	115	MORISSEAU HENRY	1910
VACANT	STE AGATHE	453	127	127	LA FERRIERE PHILLIP	1902
VACANT	STE AGATHE	454	110	110	LARIVIERE FRANCOIS	1927
VACANT	STE AGATHE	455	137	137	HUDSONS BAY CO	1880
VACANT	STE AGATHE	456	101	101		
VACANT	STE AGATHE	457	145	145	MORISSEAU HENRI	1902
VACANT	STE AGATHE	458	92	92	GRAVELINE JOSEPH	1906
VACANT	STE AGATHE	459	153	153	GRANT JOHN	1886
VACANT	STE AGATHE	460	85	85	PICHETTE GEORGE	1908
VACANT	STE AGATHE	461	161	161	ST ONGE JOSEPH	1927

OCCUPANT NAMED BY SURVEYORS	PARISH	LOT	AREA	AREA CLAIMED	PATENTEE		YEAR OF PATENT
VACANT	STE AGATHE	462	76	76	ROY	OCTAVE	1904
VACANT	STE AGATHE	463	165	165	ROY	VICTOR	83
VACANT	STE AGATHE	464	72	36	MCDOUGALL	MALCOLM	
VACANT	STE AGATHE	465	144	72	BRYDON	WILLIAM	1877
VACANT	STE AGATHE	466	132	66	MCDOUGALL	MALCOLM	
VACANT	STE AGATHE	467	139	139	BRYDON	WILLIAM	1877
VACANT	STE AGATHE	468	139	139			
VACANT	STE AGATHE	469	140	126	KLYNE	GEORGE	1882
VACANT	STE AGATHE	470	138	138	LALONDE	ARTHUR DE	83
VACANT	STE AGATHE	471	144	144	BERTHELET	JOSEPH	
VACANT	STE AGATHE	472	134	107	BERTHELET	JOSEPH	1883
VACANT	STE AGATHE	473	154	108	BERTHELET	JOSEPH	
VACANT	STE AGATHE	474	174	121	BERTHELET	JOSEPH	1883
VACANT	STE AGATHE	475	163	163			
VACANT	STE AGATHE	476	157	157	CLEMENT	JOSEPH	1921
VACANT	STE AGATHE	477	167	163	ROBERT	CELEVENE	
VACANT	STE AGATHE	478	150	150	KEATING	DANIEL	1893
VACANT	STE AGATHE	479	173	173	CLEMENT	ONESINE	1920
VACANT	STE AGATHE	480	145	145	CAN N W LAND	CO	1898
VACANT	STE AGATHE	481	141	141	GREEN	WILLIAM	1890
VACANT	STE AGATHE	482	196	196			
VACANT	STE AGATHE	483	152	152	FEEK	ASAHEL	82
VACANT	STE AGATHE	484	184	184			
VACANT	STE AGATHE	485	165	165			
VACANT	STE AGATHE	486	171	171	HUDSONS BAY	CO	1880
VACANT	STE AGATHE	487	176	176	MCDONALD	GEORGE	82
VACANT	STE AGATHE	488	162	162			
VACANT	STE AGATHE	489	177	177	TEEK	ASAHEL	1881
VACANT	STE AGATHE	490	163	163			
VACANT	STE AGATHE	491	169	169	TEEK	ASAHEL	1881
VACANT	STE AGATHE	492	168	168	JACKSON	ALEXANDER	1887
VACANT	STE AGATHE	493	163	163	FRASER	JOHN	1893
VACANT	STE AGATHE	494	174	174	MORRISSON	WILLIAM	1889
VACANT	STE AGATHE	495	162	162	SCHULTZ	JOHN	1883
VACANT	STE AGATHE	496	176	176	MCMILLAN	WILLIAM	1902
VACANT	STE AGATHE	497	152	152	ARCHIBALD	HEBER	1882
VACANT	STE AGATHE	498	176	176	MCMILLAN	HUGH	1902
VACANT	STE AGATHE	499	177	177	SAMOISETTE	C	1883
VACANT	STE AGATHE	500	156	156	CAUGHEY	ROLLAND	82
VACANT	STE AGATHE	501	186	93	TOUPIN	LOUIS	1892
VACANT	STE AGATHE	502	152	152	CAUGHEY	ROLLAND	82
VACANT	STE AGATHE	503	182	182	QUIMET	ALFRED	
VACANT	STE AGATHE	504	155	155			
VACANT	STE AGATHE	505	174	174			
VACANT	STE AGATHE	506	161	161	HUDSONS BAY	CO	1880
VACANT	STE AGATHE	507	166	166			
VACANT	STE AGATHE	508	170	170	FOX	ROBERT H	1892
VACANT	STE AGATHE	509	161	161	CLOUTIER	REV GABRIEL	1900
VACANT	STE AGATHE	510	176	176			
VACANT	STE AGATHE	511	158	158	MCLEAN	GEORGE	1895
VACANT	STE AGATHE	512	178	178	MCLEAN	DUNCAN	1890
VACANT	STE AGATHE	513	138	138			

OCCUPANT NAMED BY SURVEYORS	PARISH	LOT	AREA	AREA CLAIMED	PATENTEE	YEAR OF PATENT
VACANT	STE AGATHE	514	179	179	CAN N W LAND CO	1897
VACANT	STE AGATHE	515	139	139	TOWE SARAH	1884
VACANT	STE AGATHE	516	178	178	CAN N W LAND CO	1897
VACANT	STE AGATHE	517	144	144	LOWE DAVID	1876
VACANT	STE AGATHE	518	163	163	LOWE SARAH	1884
VACANT	STE AGATHE	519	165	165	LOWE DAVID	1883
VACANT	STE AGATHE	520	140	140	BRODEUR AUGUSTE	1895
VACANT	STE AGATHE	521	141	141	JENKINS GEORGE	1893
VACANT	STE AGATHE	522	157	157	BRODEUR FRANCOIS	1895
VACANT	STE AGATHE	523	142	142	JENKINS GEORGE	1893
VACANT	STE AGATHE	524	128	128	BRODEUR EPHREM	1895
VACANT	STE AGATHE	525	142	142	JENKINS EDMUND	1894
VACANT	STE AGATHE	526	92	92	HUDSONS BAY CO	1880
VACANT	STE AGATHE	527	144	144	TURNER WILLIAM	1900
VACANT	STE AGATHE	528	51	51	MCMILLAN DOUGAL	1909
VACANT	STE AGATHE	529	214	214	TIMLICK GEORGE	1909
VACANT	STE AGATHE	530				.
VACANT	STE AGATHE	532	240	240	LECOMTE JOSEPH	1884
VACANT	STE AGATHE	534	210	210	DUMAS CYRILL	1883
VACANT	STE AGATHE	536	184	184	BOURASSA NAPOLEON	1884
VACANT	STE AGATHE	546	208	208		.
VACANT	STE AGATHE	548	156	155		.
VACANT	STE AGATHE	550	138	138		.
VACANT	STE AGATHE	552	235	235	SCHULTZ JOHN	1883
VACANT	STE AGATHE	554	171	171	LECOMTE JOSEPH	1882
VACANT	STE AGATHE	556	177	177	MARSHALL ALBERT J	83
VACANT	STE AGATHE	558	172	172	MARSHALL ALBERT J	83
VACANT	STE AGATHE	560	169	169		.
VACANT	STE AGATHE	562	169	169		.
VACANT	STE AGATHE	564	176	176		.
VACANT	STE AGATHE	566	215	215	CATHOLIC PAR ISH	1881
VACANT	STE AGATHE	568	160	160	BOURRER ADOLPH	1896
VACANT	STE AGATHE	570	215	61	FILLION DAVID	1895
VACANT	STE AGATHE	572	167	167		.
VACANT	STE AGATHE	574	174	174	SUTHERLAND HUGH	1902
VACANT	STE AGATHE	576	168	168	LAVEILLE EDMUND	1886
VACANT	STE AGATHE	578	227	227	GAUTHIER AZAIRE	1884
VACANT	STE AGATHE	580	349	349	CORP CATHOLI C ROMAINE	1877
VACANT	STE AGATHE	581	327	327	STEPHEN GEORGE	1882
VACANT	STE AGATHE	582	216	216	CORP CATHOLI C ETC	1882
VACANT	STE AGATHE	584	212	212	CORP CATHOLI C ETC	1882
VACANT	STE AGATHE	586	161	161		.
VACANT	STE AGATHE	588	186	186	TACHE MGS ALEX	1882
VACANT	STE AGATHE	590	175	175		.
VACANT	STE AGATHE	592	132	132	WINZELL ETAL ALEXANDER	83
VACANT	STE AGATHE	594	148	148	PILON PIERRE	1878
VACANT	STE AGATHE	596	150	150		.
VACANT	STE AGATHE	597	161	161	ATCHISON THOMAS	1889
VACANT	STE AGATHE	598	154	154	HESPELER WILLIAM	1882
VACANT	STE AGATHE	599	123	123	ATCHISON THOMAS	1886
VACANT	STE AGATHE	600	157	157	PILON ANTOINE	1878
VACANT	STE AGATHE	601	155	155	GEOYERME JOHN W	1882

TABLE 5: RECOGNITION OF RIVERLOT OCCUPANTS BY THE GOVERNMENT OF CANADA

OCCUPANT NAMED BY SURVEYORS	PARISH	LOT	AREA	AREA CLAIMED	PATENTEE	YEAR OF PATENT
VACANT	STE AGATHE	602	157	157	LAMBERT MARGUERITE	1889
VACANT	STE AGATHE	603	166	166	BOLTON WM	1890
VACANT	STE AGATHE	604	153	153		
VACANT	STE AGATHE	605	171	171	BERNIER THOMAS A	1893
VACANT	STE AGATHE	606	147	147		
VACANT	STE AGATHE	607	175	175	LOCKHART GEO DAVIS	1882
VACANT	STE AGATHE	608	143	143		
VACANT	STE AGATHE	609	156	156	BESANT CALEB	1882
VACANT	STE AGATHE	611	157	157	BESANT CALEB	1882
VACANT	STE AGATHE	612	159	159		
VACANT	STE AGATHE	613	157	157	BESANT WM	1883
VACANT	STE AGATHE	615	155	155	BESANT RALPH	1893
VACANT	STE AGATHE	617	153	153		
VACANT	STE AGATHE	618	164	164		
VACANT	STE AGATHE	619	155	155	NONE	
VACANT	STE AGATHE	620	162	162	DUFAUIT SIMON	1908
VACANT	STE AGATHE	621	159	159	ANGELL ERASMUS	1900
VACANT	STE AGATHE	622	156	156		
VACANT	STE AGATHE	623	164	164	HARGRAVE JOHN	1899
VACANT	STE AGATHE	625	113	113	SCHULTZ JOHN	1878
VACANT	STE AGATHE	627	129	129	BROWN FRANCIS	1882
VACANT	STE AGATHE	629	145	145	BROWN FRANCIS	1882
VACANT	STE AGATHE	631	151	151	HAWKINS JOSEPH	1888
VACANT	STE AGATHE	632	164	164	COMPANY HB	1880
VACANT	STE AGATHE	633	157	157		
VACANT	STE AGATHE	634	160	160	GAUTHIER CONRAD	1919
VACANT	STE AGATHE	635	156	156	CHRISTIE JAMES JR	1891
VACANT	STE AGATHE	637	152	152	CHRISTIE WILLIAM	1891
VACANT	STE AGATHE	639	150	150	CHRISTIE JAMES JR	1883
VACANT	STE ANNE	32	98	98	ROUSSIN SR FRANCOIS	79
VACANT	STE ANNE	33	98	98		
VACANT	STE ANNE	34	101	101	MORIN MALVINA	1904
VACANT	STE ANNE	36	101	101	CAROW PIERRE	1886
VACANT	STE ANNE	42	210	210		
VACANT	STE ANNE	72	94	94	HAMELIN JOSEPH	1890
VACANT	STE ANNE	73	75	19	DESJARLAIS ANTOINE	1911
VACANT	STE ANNE	74	76	76	COMPANY HB	1880
VACANT	STE ANNE	75	16	16	NOLIN JOACHIM	1912
VACANT	STE ANNE	76	27	27	U OF M	1898
VACANT	STE ANNE	77	87	87	LAPOINTE JB	1885
VACANT	STE ANNE	78	110	110	DESAUTELS JBTE	1882
VACANT	STE ANNE	79	129	129	GIRARD MARC	1883
VACANT	STE ANNE	80	160	160		
VACANT	STE ANNE	81	174	174		
VACANT	STE ANNE	82	191	191	RAFOTTE LEON	1886
VACANT	STE ANNE	83	60	60	STLUKE FRANCOIS	1907
VACANT	PORTAGE	1	127	127		
VACANT	PORTAGE	2	119	119		
VACANT	PORTAGE	3	112	112		
VACANT	PORTAGE	4	107	107		
VACANT	PORTAGE	5	102	102		
VACANT	PORTAGE	6	92	92		

TABLE 5 : RECOGNITION OF RIVERLOT OCCUPANTS BY THE GOVERNMENT OF CANADA

OCCUPANT NAMED BY SURVEYORS	PARISH	LOT	AREA	AREA CLAIMED	PATENTEE		YEAR OF PATENT
VACANT	PORTAGE	7	80	80			.
VACANT	PORTAGE	8	70	70			.
VACANT	PORTAGE	9	142	142	COWAN	JAMES	1882
VACANT	PORTAGE	10	129	129	COWAN	JAMES	1882
VACANT	PORTAGE	11	120	120			.
VACANT	PORTAGE	12	114	114			.
VACANT	PORTAGE	13	112	112			.
VACANT	PORTAGE	14	109	109			
VACANT	PORTAGE	15	106	106			
VACANT	PORTAGE	16	103	103			
VACANT	PORTAGE	17	104	104			
VACANT	PORTAGE	18	104	104	HAY ETAL	CHARLES	1885
VACANT	PORTAGE	19	100	100	HOUSE	CHARLES	1882
VACANT	PORTAGE	20	94	94	HUDSONBAYCO		1880
VACANT	PORTAGE	21	106	106	HOUSE	CHARLES	1882
VACANT	PORTAGE	30	80	80	COWAN	JAMES	81
VACANT	PORTAGE	37	160	160	LEADER	THOMAS	82
VACANT	PORTAGE	39	160	160	GRAHAM	SAMUEL	1882
VACANT	PORTAGE	48	272	272	BANNATYNE	AGB	1881
VACANT	PORTAGE	71	46	46			
VACANT	PORTAGE	72	30	30	MCLEAN	ALEXANDER	79
VACANT	PORTAGE	73	34	34	MCLEAN	ALEXANDER	79
VACANT	PORTAGE	74	36	36	MCLEAN	ALEXANDER	79
VACANT	PORTAGE	75	38	38	HOUSE	CHARLES H	1882
VACANT	PORTAGE	76	38	38	HOUSE	CHARLES H	1882
VACANT	PORTAGE	77	38	38	HOUSE	CHARLES H	1882
VACANT	PORTAGE	78	72	72	HOUSE	CHARLES	1882
VACANT	PORTAGE	79	40	40	HOUSE	CHARLES	1882
VACANT	PORTAGE	80	41	41	HOUSE	CHARLES	1882
VACANT	PORTAGE	81	55	55	HOUSE	CHARLES	1882
VACANT	PORTAGE	82	33	33	GRANT	JOHN ROBERT	82
VACANT	PORTAGE	83	49	49	HOUSE	CHARLES	1882
VACANT	PORTAGE	84	40	40	HOUSE	CHARLES	1882
VACANT	PORTAGE	85	26	26	TRAUT	JOHN ROBERT	1882
VACANT	PORTAGE	86	22	22	MCLEAN	ALEXANDER	79
VACANT	PORTAGE	87	22	22	MCLEAN	ALEXANDER	79
VACANT	PORTAGE	88	22	22	BODDY	FRANCIS	82
VACANT	PORTAGE	89	40	40	SCOTT	THOMAS	1882
VACANT	PORTAGE	91	33	33	SMART	JANE	1893
VACANT	PORTAGE	95	12	12	UNIVERSITY	MAN	1898
VACANT	PORTAGE	96	28	- 28	UNIVERSITY	MAN	1898
VACANT	PORTAGE	97	41	41	UNIVERSITY	MAN	1898
VACANT	PORTAGE	98	39	39	UNIVERSITY	MAN	1898
VACANT	PORTAGE	99	25	25	CLEMENTS	GEORGE	82
VACANT	PORTAGE	100	16	16	MARTIN ETALJ	OSEPH	1898
VACANT	PORTAGE	101	49	49	UNIVERSITY	MAN	1898
VACANT	PORTAGE	102	29	29	UNIVERSITY	MAN	1898
VACANT	PORTAGE	103	25	25	UNIVERSITY	MAN	1898
VACANT	PORTAGE	104	27	27	UNIVERSITY	MAN	1898
VACANT	PORTAGE	105	28	28	UNIVERSITY	MAN	1898
VACANT	PORTAGE	106	32	32	GARRIOCH	JOHN	1889
VACANT	PORTAGE	117	7	7			

TABLE 5: RECOGNITION OF RIVERLOT OCCUPANTS BY THE GOVERNMENT OF CANADA

OCCUPANT NAMED BY SURVEYORS	PARISH	LOT	AREA	AREA CLAIMED	PATENTEE		YEAR OF PATENT
VACANT	PORTAGE	118	10	5	CORRIGAL	JOHN	1883
VACANT	HIGH BLUFF	1	100	100	CADMAN	GEORGE	1894
VACANT	HIGH BLUFF	2	163	163	MUNROE	HUGH	1878
VACANT	HIGH BLUFF	3	164	82	MUNROE	HUGH	1878
VACANT	HIGH BLUFF	4	160	80	U OF M		1898
VACANT	HIGH BLUFF	5	137	137	MCDONALD	ARCHIBALD	1878
VACANT	HIGH BLUFF	13	142	71	CAMPBELL	ALEX	1878
VACANT	HIGH BLUFF	14	98	98	CAMPBELL	ALEX	1878
VACANT	HIGH BLUFF	15	100	34	HARVEY	CHARLES G	1878
VACANT	HIGH BLUFF	16	109	109	HARVEY	CHARLES	1878
VACANT	HIGH BLUFF	17	106	106	BARTLETT	OKEE	1902
VACANT	HIGH BLUFF	18	103	103	ADAMS	GEORGE	1901
VACANT	HIGH BLUFF	19	100	100	ADAMS	GEORGE	1901
VACANT	POPLAR PT	1	148	148	HUNT	FRANK	1879
VACANT	POPLAR PT	2	129	129	HUNT	HARRIET	1882
VACANT	POPLAR PT	3	121	121	HUNT	HARRIET	1882
VACANT	POPLAR PT	4	121	121	COMPANY	HB	1880
VACANT	POPLAR PT	5	124	124	UNIVERSITY	MANITOBA	1898
VACANT	POPLAR PT	6	129	129	UNIVERSITY	MANITOBA	1898
VACANT	POPLAR PT	7	133	133	UNIVERSITY	MANITOBA	1898
VACANT	POPLAR PT	8	135	135			
VACANT	POPLAR PT	9	135	135	COMPANY	HB	1883
VACANT	POPLAR PT	10	130	130			
VACANT	POPLAR PT	11	123	123			
VACANT	POPLAR PT	12	131	131	UNIVERSITY	MANITOBA	1898
VACANT	POPLAR PT	13	101	101			
VACANT	POPLAR PT	14	129	129	UNIVERSITY	MANITOBA	1898
VACANT	POPLAR PT	15	118	118	UNIVERSITY	MANITOBA	1898
VACANT	POPLAR PT	16	110	110	UNIVERSITY	MANITOBA	1898
VACANT	POPLAR PT	17	108	108	UNIVERSITY	MANITOBA	1898
VACANT	POPLAR PT	18	112	112			
VACANT	POPLAR PT	19	125	125	ARCHIBALD	HEBER	1882
VACANT	POPLAR PT	20	138	138			
VACANT	POPLAR PT	21	144	144	FOULDS	ROBERT	81
VACANT	POPLAR PT	22	146	146	FOULDS	ABRAHAM	1881
VACANT	POPLAR PT	23	143	143	FIDLER	JAMES	1888
VACANT	POPLAR PT	24	135	135	LAND	JAMES	1888
VACANT	POPLAR PT	25	130	130	RYAN	JOSEPH	1882
VACANT	POPLAR PT	26	128	128	RYAN	JOSEPH	1882
VACANT	POPLAR PT	27	129	129	SABISTON	JOHN	81
VACANT	POPLAR PT	28	133	133	MCPHAIL	DUNCAN	1881
VACANT	POPLAR PT	29	140	140	RYAN	MARY	1884
VACANT	POPLAR PT	30	148	148	ARCHIBALD	HEBER	1884
VACANT	POPLAR PT	31	154	154	RYAN	JOSEPH	1882
VACANT	POPLAR PT	32	188	188	DRAIN	EDWARD	1882
VACANT	POPLAR PT	33	95	38	HARRIOCH	WALTER	1901
VACANT	POPLAR PT	34	95	57	SCHULTZ	JOHN	1878
VACANT	HEADINGLY	2	208	208	SMITH	DONALD A	1875
VACANT	HEADINGLY	3	103	103	LONSDALE	RICHARD	1885
VACANT	HEADINGLY	38	98	98	BROWN	JOHN	1876
VACANT	HEADINGLY	51	91	91	TAYLOR	JOHN	1879
VACANT	HEADINGLY	53	284	284	TAYLOR	JOHN	1885

OCCUPANT NAMED BY SURVEYORS	PARISH	LOT	AREA	AREA CLAIMED	PATENTEE		YEAR OF PATENT
VACANT	HEADINGLY	57	108	108	CAMERON	DONALD	1876
VACANT	HEADINGLY	59	104	104	CAMERON	DONALD	1876
VACANT	HEADINGLY	65	94	94	BEWELL	EDWARD	1877
VACANT	HEADINGLY	67	369		BISHOPRUPERT	OO	89
VACANT	ST JAMES	72	65	23	MULLIGAN	JAMES	1890
VACANT	ST JAMES	73	19	19	LAND	CHARLES	1883
VACANT	ST JAMES	74	21	4	TRESTON	JAMES	1878
VACANT	ST JAMES	75	11	11	MULLIGAN	JAMES	1872
VACANT	ST JAMES	76	11	11	YOUNG	REV GEORGE	1876
VACANT	ST JAMES	77	13	8	MCKENZIE	F	1877
VACANT	ST JAMES	78	31	31	SPENCE	JAMES	1877
VACANT	ST JAMES	79	48	48	MULLIGAN	JAMES	1875
VACANT	ST JAMES	80	17	17	CHUBBOCK	HARRIETT J	1876
VACANT	ST JAMES	81	19	19	TRESTON	JAMES	1876
VACANT	ST JAMES	82	11	11	MULLIGAN	JAMES	1876
VACANT	ST JAMES	83	10	10	MULLIGAN	JAMES	1876
VACANT	ST JAMES	84	50	50	SPENCE	JAMES	1877
VACANT	ST JAMES	85	30	30	SPENCE	JAMES	1883
VACANT	ST JAMES	86	53	53	HILL	J F	1882
VACANT	ST JOHN	1			HUDSONS BAY	CO	1873
VACANT	ST JOHN	2	5	5	SCHULTZ	JOHN	1875
VACANT	ST JOHN	3	7	7	LA CORP DE	ST BONIFACE	1880
VACANT	ST JOHN	4	2	2	DREVER SR	WILLIAM	1885
VACANT	ST JOHN	5	39	15	MORRIS	A	1874
VACANT	ST JOHN	6	160	160	MCDERMOT	A	1875
VACANT	ST JOHN	7	76	76	BANNATYNE	AGB	1875
VACANT	ST JOHN	8	91	91	ROSS ETAL	WR	1878
VACANT	ST JOHN	9	138	138	CALDWELLETAL	WILLIAM	1883
VACANT	ST JOHN	10	47	47	HEATON ETAL		1880
VACANT	ST JOHN	11	200	200	LOGAN	ALEX	1874
VACANT	ST JOHN	12	29	29	MCDONALDETAL	ROBERT	1877
VACANT	ST JOHN	13	6	6	HIGGINS	JOHN	1875
VACANT	ST JOHN	14	18	5	LOGAN	ALEX	1882
VACANT	ST JOHN	15	5	5	MCTAVISH	JH	1881
VACANT	ST JOHN	16	5	5	STOBART	DN	1883
VACANT	ST JOHN	17	13	13	STOBART	WILLIAM	1883
VACANT	ST JOHN	18	4	4	SCHULTZ ETAL	JOHN	1876
VACANT	ST JOHN	19	3	3	SCHULTZ ETAL	JOHN	1876
VACANT	ST JOHN	20	2	2	SCHULTZ ETAL	JOHN	1876
VACANT	ST JOHN	21	2	2	SCHULTZ ETAL	JOHN	1876
VACANT	ST JOHN	22	4	4	SCHULTZ ETAL	JOHN	1876
VACANT	ST JOHN	23	4	4	SCHULTZ ETAL	JOHN	1876
VACANT	ST JOHN	24	5	5	SCHULTZ ETAL	JOHN	1882
VACANT	ST JOHN	25	5	5	SUTHERLAND	JOHN	1875
VACANT	ST JOHN	26	6	6	SUTHERLAND	JOHN	1875
VACANT	ST JOHN	27	14	14	GROAT	GEORGE	1875
VACANT	ST JOHN	28	28	28	FONSECA	WG	1878
VACANT	ST JOHN	29	23	14	FONSECA	WG	1881
VACANT	ST JOHN	30	10	6	SCHULTZ	JOHN	1881
VACANT	ST JOHN	31	12	12	SUTHERLAND	JOHN	1876
VACANT	ST JOHN	32	10	10	MCDONALD	JAMES	1882
VACANT	ST JOHN	33	4	4	LUSTED	THOMAS	1875

OCCUPANT NAMED BY SURVEYORS	PARISH	LOT	AREA	AREA CLAIMED	PATENTEE		YEAR OF PATENT
VACANT	ST JOHN	34	6	6	SCHULTZ	JOHN	1877
VACANT	ST JOHN	35	667	50	SCHULTZ	JOHN	1879
VACANT	ST JOHN	36	94	94	PRITCHARD	REV S	1878
VACANT	ST JOHN	37	87	87	SCHULTZ	JOHN	1876
VACANT	ST JOHN	38	43	43	SCHULTZ	JOHN	1876
VACANT	ST JOHN	39	193	193	BURROWS	HJ	1875
VACANT	ST JOHN	40	49	49	GROAT	GEORGE	75
VACANT	ST JOHN	41	82	82	BOYD	ALFRED	1879
VACANT	ST JOHN	42	81	81	BOYD	ALFRED	1879
VACANT	ST JOHN	43	331	331	BP OF R LAND		1876
VACANT	ST JOHN	44	176	176	BP OF R LAND		1876
VACANT	ST JOHN	45	93	93	MATHESON	DONALD	1879
VACANT	ST JOHN	54	1	1	MCNAUGHTON	CHARLES	
VACANT	ST JOHN	55	1	1	BROWN	MAGNUS	1876
VACANT	ST JOHN	56	4	4	SCHULTZ	JOHN	1876
VACANT	ST JOHN	57	12	12	PRITCHARD	REV SAM	1878
VACANT	ST JOHN	58	8	8	SCHULTZ	JOHN	1877
VACANT	ST ANDREW	151	57	57	MCCORRISTER	WILLIAM	81
VACANT	ST ANDREW	152	56	56	SMITH	RODERICK	1888
VACANT	ST ANDREW	153	55	55	FALSTER	JOHN	87
VACANT	ST ANDREW	154	54	54	CLOUSTON SR	JOHN	78
VACANT	ST ANDREW	186	43	43	CORRIGAL	JOHN	76
VACANT	ST ANDREW	208	39	39	ANDERSON	NANCY	85
VACANT	ST ANDREW	274	37	37	SETTER	JOHN	1885
VACANT	ST ANDREW	277	43	43	SCHULTZ	JOHN	1882
VACANT	ST CLEMENT	71	202	202	BANNATYNE	A G B	82
VACANT	ST CLEMENT	72	165	165	DENNIS JR	JOHN A	1882
VACANT	ST CLEMENT	73	167	33	HUNT	FRANK	1882
VACANT	ST CLEMENT	74	168	34	HUNT	FL	1882
VACANT	ST CLEMENT	116	185	110	GUNN	JAMES	1877
VACANT	ST CLEMENT	117	195	117	BEDSON	SL	1884
VACANT	ST CLEMENT	118	206	206	HUDSONS BAY	CO	1884
VACANT	ST CLEMENT	119	213	213	HUDSONS BAY	CO	1884
VACANT	ST CLEMENT	120	215	215	HUDSONS BAY	CO	1884
VACANT	ST PETER	1	61	30	HEAP	JAMES	1909
VACANT	ST PETER	2	38	38	COOK	HENRY	1908
VACANT	ST PETER	3	36	36	EVANS	ROBERT	1884
VACANT	ST PETER	4	74	74	CHRISTIANSON	CHRISTINA	1887
VACANT	ST PETER	5	49	34	SETTER	ALBERT	1888
VACANT	ST PETER	6	37	37	STEVENSON	GEORGE	1908
VACANT	ST PETER	7	36	36	NORQUAY	JOHN	1883
VACANT	ST PETER	8	34	17	BEAR	THOMAS	1908
VACANT	ST PETER	9	35	35	SINCLAIR	ALFRED	1908
VACANT	ST PETER	10	35	35	WESLEY	FLORA	1908
VACANT	ST PETER	11	24	24	STEVENSON	RODERICK	1908
VACANT	ST PETER	12	35	35			
VACANT	ST PETER	13	36	36			
VACANT	ST PETER	14	55	34	SCHULTZ	JOHN	1883
VACANT	ST PETER	15	79	48	STEVENSON	RODERICK JR	1908
VACANT	ST PETER	16	45	18	COOK	KITTY	1908
VACANT	ST PETER	17	48	48	JOHNSTON	JEREMIAH	1897
VACANT	ST PETER	18	58	58	SUTHERLAND	THOMAS	1909

TABLE 5: RECOGNITION OF RIVERLOT OCCUPANTS BY THE GOVERNMENT OF CANADA

OCCUPANT NAMED BY SURVEYORS	PARISH	LOT	AREA	AREA CLAIMED	PATENTEE	YEAR OF PATENT
VACANT	ST PETER	19	36	36	FLETT JOHN	1908
VACANT	ST PETER	20	39	39	SINCLAIR ARTHUR	1908
VACANT	ST PETER	21	65	33	HARPER JH	1909
VACANT	ST PETER	22	37	37		
VACANT	ST PETER	23	28	28	SCHULTZ JOHN	1883
VACANT	ST PETER	24	71	36	BEAR PETER	1908
VACANT	ST PETER	25	50	30	THOMAS MARY	1883
VACANT	ST PETER	26	39	39	SCHULTZ JOHN	1883
VACANT	ST PETER	27	38	38	FIELDING ALEX	1908
VACANT	ST PETER	28	50	50	SINCLAIR WILLIAM	1909
VACANT	ST PETER	29	39	39	ASHAM WILLIAM	1908
VACANT	ST PETER	30	26	26	ASHAM WILLIAM	1908
VACANT	ST PETER	31	48	48	THOMAS JOHN	1908
VACANT	ST PETER	32	49	39	PAROO JOHN	1909
VACANT	ST PETER	33	68	68	SINCLAIR ROBERT	1908
VACANT	ST PETER	34	131	131	THOMAS EDWARD	1912
VACANT	ST PETER	35	85	20	STEVENSON ELIZABETH	78
VACANT	ST PETER	36	51	51		
VACANT	ST PETER	37	50	50	MCCORRISTER WILLIAM	1908
VACANT	ST PETER	38	33	33		
VACANT	ST PETER	39	60	60	ROSS CHRISTINA	1908
VACANT	ST PETER	40	53	53	THOMAS JACOB	1908
VACANT	ST PETER	41	349	349	FIN COMM CMS	1878
VACANT	ST PETER	42	94	78	SPENCE HENRY	1908
VACANT	ST PETER	43	51	51	BIRD JAMES	1887
VACANT	ST PETER	44	64	64	WATT ALEXANDER	1908
VACANT	ST PETER	45	64	16	ASHAM FRED	1908
VACANT	ST PETER	46	48	48	CAMERON FRED	1908
VACANT	ST PETER	47	52	51	CAMERON FRED	1908
VACANT	ST PETER	48	51	17	SMITH THOMAS	1908
VACANT	ST PETER	48	51	34	THOMAS JOHN	1908
VACANT	ST PETER	49	68	68	BRUCE CHIEF WM	1908
VACANT	ST PETER	50	149	149		
VACANT	ST PETER	51	68	68		
VACANT	ST PETER	52	47	47	ROBIN ELLEN	1908
VACANT	ST PETER	53	71	71		
VACANT	ST PETER	54	72	72	THOMAS JOSEPH	1909
VACANT	ST PETER	55	186	57	CLEMENS MARGARET	1908
VACANT	ST PETER	56	69	52	STEVENSON PETER	1908
VACANT	ST PETER	57	125	32	SMITH FREDERICK	1908
VACANT	ST PETER	58	104	17	WEST MARIA	1908
VACANT	ST PETER	59	100	100		
VACANT	ST PETER	60	100	61		
VACANT	ST PETER	61	103	87	SMITH BEN SR	1908
VACANT	ST PETER	62	206	206		
VACANT	ST PETER	63	146	20		
VACANT	ST PETER	64	65	49	RAMSAY JULIA	1908
VACANT	ST PETER	65	83	83	SPENCE ALEXANDER	1908
VACANT	ST PETER	66	57	57	PEEBLES THOMAS	
VACANT	ST PETER	67	40	40	HEAP FREDERICK	1909
VACANT	ST PETER	68	55	55	PASSAGE JOHN	1908
VACANT	ST PETER	69	49	49	LACLAIR GEORGE	1908

TABLE 5: RECOGNITION OF RIVERLOT OCCUPANTS BY THE GOVERNMENT OF CANADA

OCCUPANT NAMED BY SURVEYORS	PARISH	LOT	AREA	AREA CLAIMED	PATENTEE	YEAR OF PATENT
VACANT	ST PETER	70	81	65	STEVENSON WILLIAM	1908
VACANT	ST PETER	71	47	47	BALLENDINE JOHN	1891
VACANT	ST PETER	72	56	48	SMITH COLIN	1908
VACANT	ST PETER	73	49	49	.	1908
VACANT	ST PETER	74	60	60	STEVENSON GEORGE	1908
VACANT	ST PETER	75	57	57	BEAR WILLIAM	1908
VACANT	ST PETER	76	57	19	THOMAS BENJAMIN	1908
VACANT	ST PETER	77	75	75	THOMAS HENRY	1909
VACANT	ST PETER	78	89	32	PAROD HENRY	1908
VACANT	ST PETER	79	72	72	PEEBLES THOMAS	1887
VACANT	ST PETER	80	66	33	STEVENSON CHARLES	1909
VACANT	ST PETER	81	76	38	HARPER JOHN	1909
VACANT	ST PETER	82	142	53	MISS SOC FIN COMM	1878
VACANT	ST PETER	83	179	179	HARPER ROBERT	1879
VACANT	ST PETER	84	98	98	SINCLAIR JANE	1882
VACANT	ST PETER	85	119	119	MONKMAN PHILLIP	1882
VACANT	ST PETER	86	113	113	HARPER WILLIAM	1908
VACANT	ST PETER	87	57	57	PRINCE WILLIAM	1908
VACANT	ST PETER	88	74	60	MCIVER DUNCAN	1909
VACANT	ST PETER	89	75	55	KING JOSEPH	1908
VACANT	ST PETER	90	146	38	THOMAS HENRY	1888
VACANT	ST PETER	91	38	3	TRUTHWAITE THOMAS	1887
VACANT	ST PETER	92	88	88		
VACANT	ST PETER	93	86	86	MACLAND OLIVER	1909
VACANT	ST PETER	94	88	24	LECLAIR FREDERICK	1908
VACANT	ST PETER	95	220	220	MONKMAN JOSEPH	1882
VACANT	ST PETER	96	54	54	MONKMAN JOSEPH	1887
VACANT	ST PETER	97	300	300	MONKMAN JOSEPH	1882
VACANT	ST PETER	98	61	61	PARISIAN CHARLES	1908
VACANT	ST PETER	99	48	16	MOWATT MARYANN	1908
VACANT	ST PETER	100	87	87	LEASK WILLIAM	1879
VACANT	ST PETER	101	70	70	BIRD JAMES	1880
VACANT	ST PETER	102	142	142	MONKMAN JOSEPH	1887
VACANT	ST PETER	103	62	46	HUDSON MARY	1908
VACANT	ST PETER	104	92	92	COCHRANE HENRY	1888
VACANT	ST PETER	105	57	57	BALLENDINE GEORGE	1887
VACANT	ST PETER	106	12	12		
VACANT	ST PETER	107	41	20	CUMMINGS FANNY	1908
VACANT	ST PETER	108	40	40	KING JAMES	1908
VACANT	ST PETER	109	57	57	BIRD ANNIE	1897
VACANT	ST PETER	110	109	109	HESPELER WILLIAM	1883
VACANT	ST PETER	111	89	89	MCLENNAN MURDOCH	1880
VACANT	ST PETER	112	71	20	FAVEL ANGELIQUE	1908
VACANT	ST PETER	113	42	42	SMITH JOHN	1908
VACANT	ST PETER	114			.	.
VACANT	ST PETER	115	65	65	SINCLAIR WILLIAM JR	1909
VACANT	ST PETER	116	53	32	RAIN ALBERT	1941
VACANT	ST PETER	117	196	65	MANAQUAY ROBERT	1908
VACANT	ST PETER	119	49	10	HEAP MARGARET	1911
VACANT	ST PETER	120	132	132	CESSFORD JAMES	1926
VACANT	ST PETER	121	120	60	LEFTERUH ALEX	1946
VACANT	ST PETER	122	59	59		

OCCUPANT NAMED BY SURVEYORS	PARISH	LOT	AREA	AREA CLAIMED	PATENTEE		YEAR OF PATENT
VACANT	ST PETER	123	35	17	MORRISSEAU	JOHN	1909
VACANT	ST PETER	124	35	35	BECK	MARTHA	1946
VACANT	ST PETER	125	54	54	BECK	MARTHA	1946
VACANT	ST PETER	126	32	32			.
VACANT	ST PETER	127	31	31			.
VACANT	ST PETER	128	42	42			
VACANT	ST PETER	129	31	31	TRUDEL	CHARLES	1909
VACANT	ST PETER	130	66	33	LIGHT	GUSTAV	1947
VACANT	ST PETER	131	53	53	KOSACK	MICHAEL	1946
VACANT	ST PETER	132	52	36	GREYEYES	EDWARD	1908
VACANT	ST PETER	133	62	4	KOSACK	M	1945
VACANT	ST PETER	134	30	30	KOSACK	M	1945
VACANT	ST PETER	135	35	35	KOSACK	M	1943
VACANT	ST PETER	136	44	44	FLETT	WILLIAM	1908
VACANT	ST PETER	137	44	16	HENDERSON	WILLIAM	1909
VACANT	ST PETER	138	29	4	SMITH	GEORGE	1908
VACANT	ST PETER	139	16	16	JONES	GEORGINA	1908
VACANT	ST PETER	140	44	18	STEVENSON	THOMAS	1908
VACANT	ST PETER	141	32	32	STEVENSON	EDITH	1942
VACANT	ST PETER	142	30	30	KIPPLING	GEORGE	1943
VACANT	ST PETER	143	30	30	KINGSBERRY	GEORGE	1908
VACANT	ST PETER	144	68	68			1908
VACANT	ST PETER	145	78	78			
VACANT	ST PETER	146	120	43	SMITH	GILBERT	1908
VACANT	ST PETER	147	49	49	CHIEF	THOMAS	1908
VACANT	ST PETER	148	94	94			
VACANT	ST PETER	149	35	17	FAVEL	WILLIAM	1908
VACANT	ST PETER	150	56	56	FAVEL	JAMES	1918
VACANT	ST PETER	151	90	62	MONKMAN	JOSEPH	1883
VACANT	ST PETER	152	119	119	MONKMAN	JOSEPH	1908
VACANT	ST PETER	153	76	4	WILLIAMS	ALEXANDER	1908
VACANT	ST PETER	154	91	86	CHIEF	RICHARD	1908
VACANT	ST PETER	155	70	30	WILLIAMS	CHARLES	1908
VACANT	ST PETER	156	35	35	MCIVOR	COLIN	1908
VACANT	ST PETER	157	58	40	SMITH	DAVID	1908
VACANT	ST PETER	158	34	34	MACDOUGALL	JOHN	1924
VACANT	ST PETER	159	25	5	HOPE	HENRY	1947
VACANT	ST PETER	160	25	25	SINCLAIR	JOHN	1909
VACANT	ST PETER	161	19	19	SINCLAIR	ANDREW	1908
VACANT	ST PETER	162	7	4	SINCLAIR	DAVID	1908
VACANT	ST PETER	163	69	68	SINCLAIR	DAVID	1908
VACANT	ST PETER	164	70	35	PRINCE	JOHN	1908
VACANT	ST PETER	165	36	18	GREYEYES	WILLIAM	1908
VACANT	ST PETER	166	49	7	HENDERSON	WILLIAM	1908
VACANT	ST PETER	167	86	43	STRANGER	DAVID	1908
VACANT	ST PETER	168	84	42	CMS	FIN COMM OF	1878
VACANT	ST PETER	169	45	45	BECK	ERNEST	1949
VACANT	ST PETER	170	42	9	COOK	JACOB	1909
VACANT	ST PETER	171	43	43	STEVENSON	ALEXANDER	1909
VACANT	ST PETER	172	28	28	PRINCE	CAROLINE	1908
VACANT	ST PETER	173	50	50	SUTHERLAND	MURDOCH	1908
VACANT	ST PETER	174	30	30	STAR	WILLIAM	1908

TABLE 5: RECOGNITION OF RIVERLOT OCCUPANTS BY THE GOVERNMENT OF CANADA

OCCUPANT NAMED BY SURVEYORS	PARISH	LOT	AREA	AREA CLAIMED	PATENTEE		YEAR OF PATENT
VACANT	ST PETER	175	30	30	FLETT	JOHN	1908
VACANT	ST PETER	176	20	20	FLETT	WILLIAM	1908
VACANT	ST PETER	177	20	20	FLETT	JAMES	1908
VACANT	ST PETER	178	30	30	KWEWESACE	CATHERINE	1918
VACANT	ST PETER	179	32	32	HARPER	PETER	1908
VACANT	ST PETER	180	22	16	RAMSAY	JULIA	1908
VACANT	ST PETER	181	26	16	PARISEAU	JOHN	1908
VACANT	ST PETER	182	7	7	PARISEAU	JOHN	1958
VACANT	ST PETER	183	40	40	SMITH	GEORGE	1908
VACANT	ST PETER	184	24	9	NIXON	ELIZABETH	1908
VACANT	ST PETER	185	24	12	SMITH	GEORGE	1908
VACANT	ST PETER	186	22	15	HEAP	FRED	1909
VACANT	ST PETER	187	23	23	WILLIAMS	JAMES	1908
VACANT	ST PETER	188	22	22	WILLIAMS	JAMES	1908
VACANT	ST PETER	189	23	8	COOK	WILLIAM	1908
VACANT	ST PETER	190	17	17	KUWEWESACE	JAMES	1925
VACANT	ST PETER	191	26	26	LAND CO	SELKIRK	1883
VACANT	ST PETER	192	75	42	MCLEAN	DUNCAN	1908
VACANT	ST PETER	193	118	53	SPENCE	ALFRED	1909
VACANT	ST PETER	194	55	15	FIDLER	MRS JAMES	1909
VACANT	ST PETER	195	139	25	COCHRANE	ADAM	1909
VACANT	ST PETER	196	36	10	COCHRANE	ADAM	1908
VACANT	ST PETER	197	37	9	COCHRANE	JOHN	1908
VACANT	ST PETER	198	68	20	SPENCE	WILLIAM	1908
VACANT	ST PETER	199	47	24	STEVENSON	JOHN	1930
VACANT	ST PETER	200	38	38	ROURKE	CATHERINE	1908
VACANT	ST PETER	201	60	34	THOMAS	JOHN	1908
VACANT	ST PETER	202	76	19			
VACANT	ST PETER	203	55	55	THOMAS	JOSEPH	1909
VACANT	ST PETER	204	72	40	OLSEN	RUDOLPH	1908
VACANT	ST PETER	205	39	39	JOHNSTON	MRS JAMES	1908
VACANT	ST PETER	206	89	19	THOMAS	RODERICK	1909
VACANT	ST PETER	207	26	26	OLSEN	JOHN	1909
VACANT	ST PETER	208	14	14	SCHULTZ	JOHN	1883
VACANT	ST PETER	209	27	27	SHEVRISON	JOHN	1908
VACANT	ST PETER	210	41	41	SERUSH	GEORGE	1908
VACANT	ST PETER	211	59	32	THOMAS	JACOB	1908
VACANT	ST PETER	212	242	59	PRINCE	SARAH	1908
VACANT	ST PETER	213	32	32	SETTER	ALBERT	1908
VACANT	ST PETER	214	46	46	THOMAS	HERBERT	1908
VACANT	ST PETER	215	29	29			
VACANT	ST PETER	216	51	51			
VACANT	ST PETER	217	38	38	STRANGER	ANNIE	1908
VACANT	ST PETER	218	56	17	STRANGER	DAVID	1908
VACANT	ST PETER	219	25	25			
VACANT	ST PETER	220	25	25	SETTER	REV JAMES SR	1895
VACANT	ST PETER	221	56	56	SUTHERLAND	FREDERICK	1908
VACANT	ST PETER	222	33	33	SUTHERLAND	FRED	1908
VACANT	ST PETER	223	33	33			
VACANT	ST PETER	224	66	66	SAUNDERSON	JOHN	1908
VACANT	ST PETER	225	44	44			

OCCUPANT NAMED BY SURVEYORS		PARISH	LOT	AREA	AREA CLAIMED	PATENTEE		YEAR OF PATENT
VACANT		ST PETER	227	36	18	DANIELS	HECTOR	1908
VACANT		ST PETER	228	42	42	SPENCE	THOMAS	1908
VACANT		ST PETER	229	34	34	STEVENSON	THOMAS	1908
VACANT		ST PETER	230	59	48	PEUAIS	ANGE	1908
VACANT		ST PETER	231	105	62	SAUNDERSON	GEORGE	1908
VACANT		ST PETER	232	140	32	HUDSON	RODERICK	1908
VACANT		ST PETER	233	39	32	MORRISSEAU	JOSEPH	1908
VACANT		ST PETER	234	132	96	SURISH	ROBERT	1908
VACANT		ST PETER	235	116	96	WILLIAMS	JOSEPH JR	1909
VACANT		ST PETER	236	76	76			.
VACANT		ST PETER	237	125	125			.
VACANT		ST PETER	238	76	76			.
VACANT		ST PETER	239	35	35			.
VACANT		ST PETER	240	34	34			.
VACANT		ST PETER	241	119	119			
VACANT		ST PETER	242	135	124	LECLAIR	MARY	1909
VACANT		ST PETER	243	83	83			.
VACANT		ST PETER	244	48	48			
VACANT		ST PETER	245	117	117	TRUST CO	NORTHERN	1907
VACANT		ST PETER	246	125	125	MCLENNAN	RR	1882
VALLEE ETUX	LOUIS	SFX	83	107	107	SMITH	DONALD A	1877
VALLER	JAMES	ST ANDREW	88	62	62	VALLER	JAMES	1876
VALLER	JAMES	ST ANDREW	184	43	43	VALLER	JAMES	75
VANDAL	A	STE ANNE	18	153	153	VANDALE	ANTOINE	79
VANDAL	ANTOINE	ST NORBERT	118	109	109	SMITH	HON DA	1877
VANDAL	ANTOINE	ST NORBERT	123	231	46	BANNATYNE	AGB	1877
VANDAL	ANTOINE	ST NORBERT	138	75	75	VANDAL	ANTOINE	1877
VANDAL	BAPTISTE	ST NORBERT	120	104	104	BOYD	ALFRED	77
VANDAL	JOHN	ST ANDREW	253	30	30	VANDALL	JOHN	76
VANDAL	JOHN	ST ANDREW	284	41	41	SMITH	DONALD A	11
VANDAL	JOSEPH	ST ANDREW	287	76	76	VANDAL	ALEXAN	1876
VANDAL	LOUIS	ST ANDREW	285	41	41	MCGILL	JOHN	1875
VANDAL	DAVID	ST NORBERT	70	130	130	VENNE	SOLOMON	1877
VENNE	SOLOMON	ST NORBERT	86	67	67	VENNE	SOLOMON	1876
VENNE	SOLOMON	STE AGATHE	541	201	201	LECOMTE	JOSEPH	1883
VENNE	LOUIS	ST NORBERT	119	111	111	LAMBERT	GENEVIEVE	1885
VERMET	NORBERT	ST NORBERT	101	89	89	BOYER	WILLIAM	1877
VERMET	PETITE	SFX	78	43	43	BANNATYNE	AGB	1876
VERMET	PIERRE	STE AGATHE	537	210	210	VERMET SR	JOSEPH	1875
VERMET SR	JOSEPH	ST NORBERT	150	101	101	VERMETE	ANTOINE	1882
VERMETE	ANTOINE	ST NORBERT	157	219	219	CHARITY	SISTERS OF	94
VILLEBRUN	HEIRS OF L	ST BONIFACE	83	13	13	TACHE	ALEXAN	1899
VILLEBRUN	HEIRS OF L	ST BONIFACE	85	11	11	VILLEBRUN	LOUIS	1879
VILLEBRUN	HEIRS OF L	ST BONIFACE	105	20	20	VILLEBRUN	LOUISE	90
VILLEBRUN	LOUIS	ST NORBERT	182	107	107	VILLENEUVE	WIDOW	1878
VILLEBRUN	LOUISE	ST NORBERT	155	75	75	IREDALE	MARY	1885
VILLENEUVE	WIDOW	ST NORBERT	29	57	57	SCHULTZ	JOHN	
VILLIERS	JAMES	ST JAMES	17	124	124	JAMES	SAMUEL H	
VINCENT	JOHN	ST PAUL	14	84	17	VINCENT	GEORGE	1884
VINCENT	JOHN	ST PAUL	21	110	110	VINCENT	GEORGE	1884
VINCENT	THOMAS	ST PAUL	16	30	30			
VINCENT	WILLIAM	ST PAUL	17	152	152			

TABLE 5: RECOGNITION OF RIVERLOT OCCUPANTS BY THE GOVERNMENT OF CANADA

OCCUPANT NAMED BY SURVEYORS		PARISH	LOT	AREA	AREA CLAIMED	PATENTEE		YEAR OF PATENT
VIVIEN	ALEXIS	ST CHARLES	68	109	109	MURRAY	LETITIA	1887
VIVIER	ALEXIS	BAIE S PAUL	128	94	94	PELLY	FRANCES ANNA	1887
VIVIER	ALEXIS	BAIE S PAUL	129	95	95	COWIE	ISAAC	1883
VIVIER	MICHEL	SFX	58	104	104	LUMSDEN	THOMAS	1884
VIVIER	MICHEL	SFX	59	100	100	KAVANAGH	REV FRS X	1878
WAGNER	MICH	ST ANDREW	138	62	62	MCLEOD	JOHN	1881
WALSH	EDWARD	BAIE S PAUL	23	120	120	UNIVERSITY	MANITOBA	1898
WALSH	FRANCIS	ST CHARLES	14	89	89	WALSH	FRANCIS	1876
WARD	JAMES	STE ANNE	3	299	299	WARD	JAMES	1878
WATTS	ELIZABETH	ST CLEMENT	99	98	98	DANIEL	CAROLI	84
WATTS	F	ST CLEMENT	21	50	50	WATTS	FREDER	5
WELLS	XAVIER	ST CHARLES	2	47		WRIGHT	ARCHIB	83
WHITE	JAMES	ST NORBERT	256	167	100	WHITE	JAMES	1877
WHITE	THOMAS	ST JOHN	46	162	162	WHITE	THOMAS	1875
WHITEFORD	ALESER	PORTAGE	119	130	130	SCHULTZ	JOHN	1877
WHITEFORD	JAMES	BAIE S PAUL	236	219	219	WHITEFORD	JAMES	1879
WHITEWAY	JAMES	ST ANDREW	269	70	70	WHITEWAY	JAMES	1875
WHITEWAY	JOSEPH	ST CLEMENT	45	57	57	WHITEWAY	JOSEPH	1878
WHITEWAY	SAMUEL	ST ANDREW	3	125	63	WHITEWAY	WILLIAM	1875
WHITFORD	GEORGE	ST CLEMENT	46	97	97	COLELEUGH	JAMES ETAL	1878
WHITFORD	JAMES	ST ANDREW	240	39	20	HYMAN ETAL	ANNA MARIA	1885
WHITFORDETAL	JOHN	ST CLEMENT	75	169	169			
WILD	CHARLES	POPLAR PT	84	115	115	WILD	CHARLES	1875
WILSON	DANIEL	POPLAR PT	56	139	139	WILSON	DANIEL	1875
WISHART	JAMES	POPLAR PT	48	199	199	WISHART	JAMES	1877
WOLSEY	BENJAMIN	BAIE S PAUL	208	149	149	CHENIER	LEON	1877
WORK	WILLIAM	ST PAUL	36	148	148	WORK	WILLIAM	1878
WORK	WILLIAM	ST PAUL	88	125	63	WORK	WILLIAM	1878
YOUNG	A	ST ANDREW	172	40	40	SNIDER	ALPHEUS	83
ZASTE	ALEX	SFX	107	79	79	MORRISON	JOHN	1885
ZASTE	ANDRE	SFX	110	97	97	TROTTIER	PASCAL	84
ZASTE	BAPTISTE	ST NORBERT	48	147	147	ZASTE	BAPTISTE	1878
ZASTE	GONZAGUE	ST NORBERT	50	158	158	ZASTE	GONZAGUE	1884
ZASTE	GONZALVE	SFX	77	97	97	ZASTE	GONZALVE	1883

Table 6:

Dispersal and Relocation of the Mantoba Metis

TABLE 6:   DISPERSAL AND RELOCATION OF THE MANITOBA METIS

NAME	YEAR BORN	NAMES OF PARENTS		ID OF PARENTS	NEW LOCATION	YEAR LOCATED
ADAMS DAVID J	1883	ADAMS JAMES	BRUCE ELIZA	21	LINDSAY	1900
ADAMS FRANCES	1885	ADAMS JAMES	BRUCE ELIZ	21	LINDSAY	1900
ADAMS HORACE L	1885	ADAMS ROBERT	POCHA ANN	26	LINDSAY	·
ADAMS JOE ALEX	1883	ADAMS ROBERT	POCHA ANN	26	LINDSAY	1900
ADAMS THOMAS H	1880	ADAMS JAMES	BRUCE ELIZ	21	LINDSAY	1901
ALARY ALEX	1875	ALARY LOUIS	CYR MARG	40	WINNIPEG	1901
ALARY ALEX	1875	ALARY LOUIS	CYR MARG	40	WINNIPEG	1901
ALARY ANTOINE	1879	ALARY ANTOINE	LAROCQUE JULIE	33	FT ELLICE	1901
ALARY ELISE	1873	ZACE ALEXIS	ROSS ANGEL	5278	MOOSOMIN	1901
ALARY JOE	1883	ALARY ANTOINE	LAROCQUE JULIE	33	FT ELLICE	1901
ALARY JOHN	1875	ALARY ANTOINE	LAROCQUE JULIE	33	MOOSOMIN	1901
ALARY MARIE R	1872	DUCHARME ROGER	LUCIER MARG	1364	KILLARNEY	1901
ALARY PIERRE	1872	ALARY ANTOINE	LAROCQUE JULIE	33	FT ELLICE	1901
ALLARD AMBROISE	1884	ALLARD MICHEL	ROSS BETSY	52	OAK LAKE	1901
ANDERSON ALFRED G	1878	ANDERSON CHARLES	COOK MARIA	71	ST CATHERINES	1900
ANDERSON CAROL	1884	ANDERSON ED	WHITFORD ANN	84	VICTORIA	
ANDERSON CAROLINE	1884	ANDERSON JOHN	HALCRO MARY	83	ST CATHERINES	
ANDERSON CHARLES	1882	ANDERSON JOHN ED	COOK MARIA	85	KINOSOTA	1901
ANDERSON ED	1878	ANDERSON PETER	MCKAY LETITIA	90	PRINCE ALBERT	
ANDERSON ELIZA	1881	ANDERSON ROBERT	KIPP ELIZA	91	PRINCE ALBERT	1900
ANDERSON HENRY	1879	ANDERSON MICHAEL	HALRAW HANNAH	83	MACLEOD	
ANDERSON JEMINA	1874	ANDERSON JOHN H	HALCRO MARY	83	ST CATHERINES	1900
ANDERSON JEREMIAH	1877	ANDERSON ROBERT	KIPP ELIZA	91	PRINCE ALBERT	1900
ANDERSON JOHN G	1879	ANDERSON JAMES F	GILLIS FANNY	80	WINGARD	1900
ANDERSON JULIA	1870	ANDERSON PETER	MCKAY LELITA	90	KINOSOTA	1887
ANDERSON MARGRET	1881	ANDERSON JOHN	HALCRO MARY	83	ST CATHERINES	1900
ANDERSON MARYJANE	1876	ANDERSON ROBERT	KIPP ELIZ	91	PRINCE ALBERT	1900
ANDERSON RACHEL	1876	ANDERSON JOHN	WHITFORD CHRISTINA	84	DUCK LK	1900
ANDERSON SARAH J	1880	ANDERSON CHARLES	COOK MARIA	71	WINGARD	1900
ANDERSON WALTER	1874	ANDERSON JAMES F	GILLIS FANNY	80	WINGARD	1900
ARCAND ELISE	1873	ARCAND JOE	MCKAY JOSEPHTE	104	DUCK LAKE	
ARCAND FRANCOIS	1873	ARCAND FRANCOIS	BERARD PHILOMENE	102	DUCK LAKE	
ARCAND FRANCOIS	1885	ARCAND JOE	BERARD PHILOMENE	102	DUCK LAKE	
ARCAND HYACINTHE	1874	ARCAND FRANCOIS	BERARD PHILOMENE	102	DUCK LAKE	
ARCAND JONAS	1878	ARCAND FRANCOIS	BERARD PHILOMENE	102	DUCK LAKE	
ARCAND MARIA R	1870	ARCAND BTE	MCKAY NANCY	103	ALDINA	
ARCAND MARIE C	1870	ARCAND BTE	MCKAY NANCY	103	CARLTON	
ARCAND NANCY	1883	ARCAND FRANCOIS	BERARD PHILOMENE	102	DUCK LAKE	1900
ARCAND PIERRE	1881	ARCAND JOE	MCKAY JOSEPHTE	104	CARLTON	
ARCAND ST PIERRE	1876	ARCAND FRANCOIS	BERARD PHILOMENE	102	DUCK LAKE	
ARCAND VICTOIRE	1874	ARCAND FRANCOIS	BERARD PHILOMENE	102	DUCK LK	1900
ARCAND VIRGINIE	1884	ARCAND JOE	MCKAY JOSEPHTE	104	CARLTON	
ARMIT CHRISTINA	1874	ARMIT DAVID	TAYLOR MARY	117	WINNIPEG	1901
ARMIT DAVID ED	1884	ARMIT DAVID	TAYLOR MARY	117	WINNIPEG	1901
ARMIT JOHN R	1877	ARMIT DAVID	TAYLOR MARY	117	KINOSOTA	1901
ARMIT MARY L	1883	ARMIT DAVID	TAYLOR MARY	117	WINNIPEG	1901
ARMIT NELLIE	1879	ARMIT DAVID	TAYLOR MARY	117	WINNIPEG	1900
ARMIT ROBERT	1876	ARMIT DAVID	TAYLOR MARY	117	TWH	1900
ASMUS FLORA	1881	BEGG DUNCAN	BALTON JANE	267	WINNIPEG	1901
BALLENDINE ALEX	1879	BALLENDINE GEORGE	BALLENDINE JANE	168	COXBY	
BALLENDINE ANDREW	1873	BALLENDINE GEORGE	BALLENDINE JANE	168	COXBY	1900
MARTIN ALPHONSE		MARTIN ALPHONSE	PAGETF ISARFLLE	3062	QU APPELLE	

NAME	YEAR BORN	NAMES OF PARENTS		ID OF PARENTS	NEW LOCATION	YEAR LOCATED
BARON JOSEPH	1880	BARON CHARLES	COMTOISOMARIE	211	WINNIPEG	1900
BEADS MAGGIE	1871	BEADS JACOB	ADIMER CHARLOTTE	238	COLLISTON	1900
BEAUCHENE JOE	1870	BEAUCHENE JOE	FLETT JOSE	186	PRINCE ALBERT	
BEAUCHENE JOE	1870	BEAUCHENE JOE	FLETT JOSPHTE	186	PRINCE ALBERT	1886
BEAUDRY MARIE P	1872	MCGILLIS ANGUS	FAYANT ISABELLE	3354	SWIFT CURRENT	
BEAUDRY PATRICE	1873	BEAUDRY NARCISSE	BRELAND LOUISE J	253	FT QU APPELLE	
BEGG DUNCAN	1872	BEGG DUNCAN	BOLTON JANE	267	WINNIPEG	1900
BEGG DUNCAN	1879	BEGG DUNCAN	BOLTON JANE	267	WINNIPEG	1900
BEGG JESSIE	1883	BEGG DUNCAN	BALTON JANE	267	WINNIPEG	1900
BEGG JOHN	1876	BEGG DUNCAN	BOLTON JANE	267	WINNIPEG	1900
BELANGER ABE	1883	BELANGER ABE	DELORME PHILOMENE	210	JACK FISH LAKE	1900
BELANGER ALEXIS	1884	BELANGER ABE	DELORME PHILOMENE	210	JACK FISH LAKE	1900
BELANGER NORBERT	1881	BELANGER ABE	DELORME PHILOMENE	210	JACK FISH LAKE	1900
BELHUMEUR THERESE	1880	FLEURY MICHEL	PICHE MARIE	1610		1900
BELLEGARDE ADELAID	1877	LANDRY MOISE	LAFRAMBOISE PHILO	2684	LETHBRIDGE	1900
BELLEGARDE ATHELA	1881	FAYANT FRSX	BRUNEAU MARIE	1476	LETHBRIDGE	1900
BERCIER PIERRE	1872	BERCIER ANTOINE	BAYER JUSTINE	286	RASSER	
BESANT MATHILDA	1874	CHAMPAGNE MAX	COMTOIS MARIE	738	KILLARNEY	1900
BIRD ALFRED	1878	BIRD CHARLES G	HALCRO ANN	367	BIRCH HILLS	1900
BIRD FRED	1883	BIRD WM G	CUMMINGS HARRIET	397	PRINCE ALBERT	1900
BIRD MARIA A	1884	BIRD WM	SUTHERLAND MARY J	398	BIRCH HILLS	1900
BIRD PHILIP	1882	BIRD PHILIP	KIPPLING MARY	391	CARLTON	1900
BLAYONNE JOE	1972	BLAYONNE JOE	DESMARAIS VIRG	348	FILE HILLS	
BONNEAU PHILIPPE	1871	BONNEAU CHARLES	POITRAS ROSALIE	416	FILE HILLS	
BONNEAU PHILIPPE	1872	BONNEAU CHARLES	POITRAS ROSALIE	416	FILE HILLS	
BONNEAU PHILIPPE	1874	BONNEAU CHARLES	POITRAS ROSALIE	416	FILE HILLS	
BONNEAU PHILIPPE	1876	BONNEAU CHARLES	POITRAS ROSALIE	416	FILE HILLS	
BONNEAU PHILLIPPE	1881	BONNEAU CHARLES	POITRAS ROSALIE	416	FILE HILLS	
BOUCHER DELINA	1882	BOUCHER JEAN	LESPERANCE CAROL	437	DUCK LK	
BOUCHER PIERRE	1885	BOUCHER JEAN	LESPERANCE CAROL	437	ST LOUIS	1900
BOUSQUET ISABELLE	1884	BOUSQUET LOUIS	ST DENIS ELISE	470	BATTLEFORD	1900
BOUSQUET JEAN BTE	1881	BOUSQUET LOUIS	ST DENIS ELISE	470	BATTLEFORD	1900
BOUSQUET MARIE	1879	BOUSQUET LOUIS	ST DENIS ELISE	470	BATTLEFORD	1900
BOYER ALFRED	1884	BOYER BTE	BOUSQUET ELIZ	9	BATOCHE	1900
BOYER AMBROISE	1880	BOYER WM	BOUSQUET JULIENNE	11	ST LAURENT	1900
BOYER BETSY	1874	BOYER BTE	BOUSQUET ELIZA	9	ST LAURENT	1900
BOYER BTE	1872	BOYER BTE	BOUSQUET ELIZA	9	BATTLEFORD	1900
BOYER CHRYSOSTOME	1881	BOYER WM	BOUSQUET JULIENNE	11	ST LAURENT	1900
BOYER JOHN	1870	VIRIER MICHEL	DUCHAMPS ELISE	5033	FT ELLICE	1901
BOYER JULIENNE	1875	BOYER WM	BOUSQUET JULIE	11	FISH CREEK	1900
BOYER JULIENNE	1875	BOYER WM	BOUSQUET JULIENNE	11	FISH CREEK	1900
BOYER JULIENNE	1875	BOYER WM	BOUSQUET JULIENNE	11	FISH CREEK	1900
BOYER MARIE	1882	BOYER WM	BOUSQUET JULIENNE	11	ST LAURENT	1900
BOYER TOBIE	1878	BOYER BTE	BOUSQUET ELIZA	9	ST LAURENT	1900
BRABANT ERNESTINE	1873	CHARETTE JOE	COLLIN ROSALIE	744	FILE HILLS	1900
BRANCONNIER JOE	1877	BRANCONNIER SARA	1900	488	PRINCE ALBERT	
BRANCONNIER JULIE	1872	BRANCONNIER DAN	DUCHARME SARAH	488	BATOCHE	1900
BRANCONNIER JULIEN	1872	BRANCONNIER DAN	DUCHARME SARAH	488	BATOCHE	
BRANCONNIER WM	1882	BRANCONNIER DAN	DUCHARME SARA	488	PRINCE ALBERT	1900
BRELAND ALFRED	1875	BRELAND PATRICE	DESS HELENE	511	SKILL CREEK	
BRELAND ANTOINE	1878	BRELAND GIL	BOYER FELICITE	512	ALDINA	
BRELAND CECILE	1870	BRELAND GILBERT	BOYER FELICITE	512	ST LAURENT	1886
BRELAND EMILE	1873	BRELAND GIL	BOYER FELICITE	512	ALDINA	

TABLE 6: DISPERSAL AND RELOCATION OF THE MANITOBA METIS

NAME	YEAR BORN	NAMES OF PARENTS	ID OF PARENTS	NEW LOCATION	YEAR LOCATED
BRELAND JEAN BTE	1882	BRELAND GIL / BOYER FELICITE	512	ALDINA	1901
BRELAND JOE A	1877	BRELAND MOISE / PAGE PHILOMENE	510	ST FRS XAVIER	1900
BRELAND LOUIS	1884	BRELAND ZACHARIE / TRATHIER MARIE	13350	ST PAUL	
BRELAND MARIE R	1880	BRELAND GIL / BOYER FELICITE	512	ALDINA	
BRELAND MOISE	1874	BRELAND MOISE / PAGE PHILO	510	ST FRS XAVIER	1900
BREMNU ALICE	1882	BREMNU CHARLES / WELLS EMELIE	500	STURGEONRIVER	1900
BREMNU MABLE	1885	BREMNU CHARLES / WELLS EMELIE	500	STURGEONRIVER	1900
BROWN GEORGE	1883	BROWN MAGNUS / NORN ANN	543	ATHABASCA LDG	1900
BROWN HENRY	1880	BROWN MAGNUS / NORN ANN	543	ATHABASCA LDG	1900
BROWN MARG	1885	BROWN MAGNUS / NORN ANN	543	ATHABASCA LDG	1900
BROWN MARY	1888	BROWN MAGNUS / NORN ANN	543	ATHABASCA LDG	1900
BROWN ROSE	1890	BROWN MAGNUS / NORN ANN	543	ATHABASCA LDG	1900
CADOTTE PIERRE	1870	CADOTTE PIERRE / BLONDION JULIE	620	CUMBERLAND	1887
CADOTTE PIERRE	1872	CADOTTE POIERRE / BLONDION JULIE	620	CUMBERLAND	
CAMPBELL MARY	1877	DESMARAIS HENRY / WHITFORD MARY ANN	1148	PRINCE ALBERT	1900
CAMPBELL MARY S	1877	DESMARAIS HENRY C / WHITFORD MARYANN	1148	PRINCE ALBERT	1900
CAPELLETTE MARIE N	1875	TROTTIER JEAN B / MCGILLIS LA ROSE	4971	WILLOW BUNCH	
CARDINAL FRANCOIS	1874	CARDINAL CHARLES / DESMARAIS JOSEPHTE	695	FILE HILLS	
CARON CHRISTINE	1873	CARON JEAN / DUMAS MARG	697	DUCK LAKE	
CARON JEAN	1874	CARON JEAN / DUMAS MARG	697	BATOCHE	
CARON JEAN	1877	CARON JEAN / DUMAS ANGEL	697	BATOCHE	
CARON JEAN	1880	CARON JEAN / DUMAS MARG	697	BATOCHE	
CARON JEAN	1883	CARON JEAN / DUMAS MARG	697	BATOCHE	
CARON JEAN	1885	CARON JEAN / DUMAS MARG	697	BATOCHE	
CARON PIERRE	1875	CARON JEAN / DUMAS MARG	697	BATOCHE	
CARRIERE MARIE	1882	CARRIERE CHARLES / BEAUCHEMIN CECILE	710	FISH CREEK	1900
CARRIERE VIRG	1874	CARRIERE CHARLES / BEAUCHEMIN CECILE	710	BATOCHE	1901
CHAMPAGNE DOLPHIS	1879	CHAMPAGNE MAX / COMTOIS MARIE	738	KILLARNEY	1901
CHAMPAGNE GEORGINA	1885	CHAMPAGNE MAX / COMTOIS MARIE	738	KILLARNEY	1901
CHAMPAGNE JOSE	1885	CHAMPAGNE MAX / COMTOIS MARIE	738	KILLARNEY	1901
CHAMPAGNE RAYMOND	1872	CHAMPAGNE MAX / COMTOIS MARIE	738	KILLARNEY	1901
CHARETTE DAN	1875	CHARETTE JOE / COLLIN ROSALIE	744	FILE HILLS	
CHARTIER ANTOINE	1874	CHARTIER ANTOINE / DORION JOSE	783	GRAND RAPIDS	
CHARTIER ANTOINE	1876	CHARTIER ANTOINE / DORION JOSE	783	GRAND RAPIDS	
CHARTIER MARIE	1870	CHARTIER ANTOINE / DORION JOSEPHTE	783	GRAND RAPIDS	1887
CHARTIER MARY	1871	CHARTIER ANTOINE / DORION JOSEPHITE	783		
CHARTIER ROSALIE	1885	CHARTIER ANTOINE / DORION JOSEPHITE	783	GRANDXCRAPIDS	
CHARTRAND JEAN	1884	CHARTRAND PIERRE / PANGMAN ROSE	764	PINE CREEK	1901
CHARTRAND LOUISON	1879	CHARTRAND LOUISON / DELORME MONIQUE	755	PINE CREEK	
CHARTRAND PHILOMEN	1883	CHARTRAND PIERRE / PANGMAN ROSE	764	PINE CREEK	1901
CHARTRAND PIERRE	1881	CHARTRAND PIERRE / PANGMAN ROSE	764	PINE CREEK	1901
CHASTELAIN MARYJAN	1878	CHASTELLAIN NARCIS / HOURIE FRANCIS	787	WINNIPEG	1900
CHISHOLM ELIZA	1884	CHISHOLM ALEX R / TAYLOR ANNIE	792	BRESAYLOR	1900
CLEMENTS LUKE	1878	CLEMENTS JOHN / BEAR MARG	803	WINNIPEG	1901
CLEMENTS MARY	1875	BEGG DUNCAN / BALTON JANE	267	WINNIPEG	1901
COLLIN ANTOINE	1878	COLLIN MAX / OUELLETTE MARG	818	SASKATOON	1900
COLLIN FLORESTINE	1873	COLLIN MAX / OUELLETTE MARG	818	SASKATOON	1900
COLLIN MARIA	1881	COLLIN MAX / OUELLETTE MARG	818	SASKATOON	
COLLIN MAXIME	1876	COLLIN MAX / OUELLETTE MARG	818	SASKATOON	1900
COLLIN PAULINE	1884	COLLIN MAX / OUELLETTE MARG	818	SASKATOON	
COOK ELISE	1881	LAFONTAINE FRAN / HUGHER LIZA	1900	QU APPELLE	
COOK HERBERT B	1882	COOK GILBERT / BRUCE CATHY	935	TWH	1900

NAME	YEAR BORN	NAMES OF PARENTS	ID OF PARENTS	NEW LOCATION	YEAR LOCATED
CORRIGAL KATE	1884	CORRIGAL THOMAS / HODGSON ANN	850	PRINCE ALBERT	1900
CORRIGAL ROD	1879	CORRIGAL TOM / HODGSON ANN	850	PRINCE ALBERT	1900
CROMARTIE ANDREW	1884	CROMARTIE WM / HOURIE MARY ANN	978	BIRCH HILLS	1900
CROMARTIE CAROLINE	1879	CROMARTIE WM / HOURIE MARY	978	REDDEERHILL	1900
CYR ELIZA	1872	LEVEILLE GABRIEL / POITRAS ELIZA	2829	DUHAMEL	1900
CYR ELIZA	1874	LEVEILLE GABRIEL / POITRAS ELIZA	2829	DUHAMEL	1900
CYR ELIZA	1875	LEVEILLE GABRIEL / POITRAS ELIZA	2829	DUHAMEL	1900
DANIEL GEORGE	1879	DANIEL WM / MITCHELL ISABELLE	1020	FILE HILLS	
DELARONDE SARA	1872	DELARONDE PAUL / SINCLAIR MARG	2658	SNAKE PLAION	1900
DELARONDE WM	1874	DELARONDE PAUL / SINCLAIR MARG	2658	MEADOW LAKE	1900
DELORME MARIE	1881	DELORME NORBERT / GERVAIS CHARLOTTE	1116	FT ELLICE	
DESJARLAIS CLEM	1875	FISHER ALEX / RACETTE MARG	1571	LEBRET	1900
DESJARLAIS JOE	1879	DESJARLAIS JOE / LAFRENIERE ISABELLE	1285	TWH	
DESJARLAIS JOE	1880	DESJARLAIS JOE / LAFRENIERE ISABELLE	1285	TWH	
DESJARLAIS MARG	1879	DESMARAIS HENRY / WHITFORD MARYANN	1148	PRINCE ALBERT	1900
DESJARLAIS MARIE R	1879	CARDINAL CHARLES / DESMARAIS JOSEPHTE	695	FILE HILLS	1900
DESMARAIS CLEM	1884	DESMARAIS JOHN / GOSSELIN ELLEN	1137	PINCHER CREEK	1900
DESMARAIS ELZEAR	1882	DESMARAIS JOHN / GOSSELIN ELLEN	1137	PINCHER CREEK	1900
DESMARAIS HARRIET	1870	DESMARAIS MICHEL / SINCLAIR BELLA	1237	TOTAGUN	
DESMARAIS HARRIET	1871	DESMARAIS MICHEL / SINCLAIR BELLA	1237	TOTAGUN	1887
DESMARAIS JOE	1881	DESMARAIS MICHEL / SINCLA$R ISABELLE	1237	KILLARNEY	1901
DESMARAIS JOHN	1871	DESMARAIS JOHN / GOSSELIN ELLEN	1137	PINCHER CREEK	1900
DESMARAIS JOHN	1876	DESMARAIS JOHN / GOSSELIN ELLEN	1137	PINCHER CREEK	1900
DESMARAIS JOHN	1877	DESMARAIS JOHN / GOSSELIN ELLEN	1137	BATOCHE	1900
DESMARAIS JOHN	1879	DESMARAIS JOHN / GOSSELIN ELLEN	1137	PINCHER CREEK	1900
DESMARAIS MARIE	1877	DESMARAIS JOHN / GOSSELIN ELLEN	1137	PINCHER CREEK	1900
DESMARAIS MARY	1875	DESMARAIS HENRY / WHITFORD MARY	1148	PINCHER CREEK	1900
DESMARAIS ROSINA	1881	DESMARAIS HARNRY / WHITFORD MARYANN	1148	PRINCE ALBERT	1900
DESMARAIS WM R	1882	DESMARAIS HARNRY / WHITFORD MARYANN	1148	PRINCE ALBERT	1900
DUBOIS ALFRED	1874	DUBOIS JEAN BTE / LARENCE JOSETTE	1319	WINNIPEG	1901
DUBOIS BTE	1875	DUBOIS JEAN / LARENCE JOSETTE	1319	OAK LAKE	1901
DUBOIS CELINA	1873	OUELLETTE FRANCOIS / DUBOIS MARG	3708	WINNIPEG	1901
DUBOIS JEAN BTE	1872	DUBOIS EUGENE / GEORGE ELIZ	1325	WINNIPEG	1901
DUBOIS JEAN BTE	1873	DUBOIS JEAN BTE / LARENCE JOSETTE	1319	OAK LAKE	1901
DUBOIS JOE	1885	LILLY JAMES / MORIN MARIE	2958	WINNIPEG	1901
DUCHARME MARIE J	1875	DUCHARME ROGER / LUCIER MARG	1364	KILLARNEY	1901
DUCHARME TOUSSAINT	1884	DUCHARME ROGER / LUCIER MARG	1364	KILLARNEY	1901
DUCHARTIE PIERRE	1877	PICHE LOUIS / DESMARAIS CECILE	3929	WILLOW BUNCH	1901
DUMAIS VITALINE	1880			CLARKLEIGH	
ESJARLAIS LOUISE	1870	DESJARLAIS JOE / SLATER MARY	1283	BATOCHE	1901
FAGNANT ALFRED	1875	FAGNANT CUTHBERT / MCGILLIS ISABELLE	1467	QU APPELLE	1900
FAVEL WM P	1875	FAVEL WM / GADDIE ANN	1501	KILLARNEY	1901
FAYANT ADELINE	1881	DELORME URBAIN / BELANGER ELISE	1118	KILLARNEY	1901
FAYANT FRANCOIS	1873	FAYANT JEAN BTE / WARD ANGELIQUE	1466	WILLOW BUNCH	
FAYANT JEAN BTE	1878	FAYANT JEAN BTE / WARD ANGEL	1466	WILLOW BUNCH	
FAYANT JEAN BTE	1880	FAYANT J B / WARD ANGEL	1466	WILLOW BUNCH	
FAYANT JEAN BTE	1871	FAYANT J B / WARD ANGEL	1466	WILLOW BUNCH	
FAYANT JOE	1873	FAYANT ANTOINE / LEDOUX MOISE	1470	QU APPELLE	
FAYANT PATRICE	1879	FAYANT ANTOINE / LEDOUX MARIE	1470	LEBRET	
FAYANT THEODORE	1880	FAYANT ANTOINE / LEDOUX MARIE	1470	LEBRET	
FIDDLER EUGENE	1882	FIDDLER GEORGE / LAPLANTE MARIE	1543	SPY HILL	1901
FIDDLER JOHN	1884	FIDDLER THOMAS / LAMBERT MARG	1536	KILLARNEY	1901
FIDDLER FRED	1884	FIDDLER FRANCOIS / LAPLANTE JOSE	1542	JACK FISH LAKE	1900

TABLE 6: DISPERSAL AND RELOCATION OF THE MANITOBA METIS

NAME	YEAR BORN	NAMES OF PARENTS	ID OF PARENTS	NEW LOCATION	YEAR LOCATED
FIDLER JOE	1874	FIDLER FRANK / LAPLANTE JOSE	1542	BATTLEFORD	1901
FIDLER MARIE D	1882	FIDLER FRANCOIS / LAPLANTE JOSE	1542	JACK FISH LAKE	1900
FIDLER MOISE	1879	FIDLER FRAN / LAPLANTE JOSEPHINE	1542	BATTLEFORD	.
FIDLER MOISE	1879	FIDLER FRANCOIS / LAPLANTE JOSE	1542	BATTLEFORD	.
FISHER ADELINE	1883	FISHER AMBROISE / CHALIFOUX ROSE	1529	DUCK LAKE	.
FISHER ALEX	1871	FISHER ALEX / RACETTE MARG	1571	KATEPWA	.
FISHER ALEX	1873	FISHER ALEX / RACETTE MARG	1571	KATEPWA	.
FISHER AMBROISE F	1877	FISHER AMBROISE / CHALIFOUX ROSE	1529	DUCK LAKE	1900
FISHER ED	1874	FISHER AMBROISE / CHALIFOUX ROSE	1529	DUCK LK	.
FISHER JULES	1885	FISHER AMBROISE / CHALIFOUX ROSE	1529	DUCK LAKE	.
FISHER MADELINE	1873	FISHER AMBROISE / CHALIFOUX ROSE	1529	DUCK LAKE	.
FISHER MARIE M	1875	FISHER GEORGE / BOYER EMELINE	1567	FT QU APPELLE	.
FISHER MARIE M	1875	FISHER GEORGE / BOYER EMELINE	1567	FT QU APPELLE	.
FLAMAND CHARLES	1883	FLAMAND LOUIS / BRUCE MARG	1857	BATTLEFORD	1900
FLAMAND JOE R	1881	FLAMAND LOUIS / BRUCE MARG	1857	BATTLEFORD	1900
FLEURY AGATHE	1870	FLEURY ED / MORAND MELANIE	1589	FT ELLICE	1886
FLEURY AGATHE	1870	FLEURY ED / MORAND MELANIE	1589	FT ELLICE	1886
FLEURY DOMITILDE	1870	FLEURY MICHEL / PICHE MARIE A	1610	FT ELLICE	1901
FLEURY ED	1883	FLEURY ED / MORAN MELANIE	1589	MOOSOMIN	1901
FLEURY JOHN	1878	FLEURY ED / MORAN MELANIE	1589	MOOSE JAW	1901
FLEURY MAX	1877	FLEURY MICHEL / PICHE MARIEANN	1610	FT QU APPELLE	1901
FONTAINE MARIE	1878	MORRISETTE PHILO	1976	WINNIPEG	1901
FORBISTER ELLEN	1872	MCBETH MARY	4507	WINNIPEG	1886
FOURNIER NORBERT	1870	LACOUTURE MADELEINE	1555	FT QU APPELLE	1886
FRASER ALBERT	1875	VINCENT SARAH J	1664	ONION LK	1900
FRASER GEORGE	1873	VINCENT SARA	1664	ATHABASCA L	1900
FRAZER JUSTINE	1871	LAFONTAINE BTE / GARUFRY MATHILDE	2477	CRANBROOK	1900
GALE MARIA	1872	MCKAY JOE / POITRAS FLAVIE	3404	MAPLE CREEK	.
GARIEPY GABRIEL	1880	GARIEPY PHIL / PARENTEAU ROSALIE	1894	BELLEVUE	.
GARIEPY VICTOR	1872	GARIEPY PHILIPPE / PARENTEAU ROSALIE	1894	BELLEVUE	1900
GARRIEPY ISIDORE	1876	GARRIEPY PHIL / PARENTEAU ROSALIE	1894	BELLEVUE	.
GARRIEPY ROSALIE	1877	GARRIEPY PHIL / PARENTEAU ROSALIE	1894	BELLEVUE	.
GARRIEPY ROSALIE	1881	GARRIEPY PHIL / PARENTEAU ROSALIE	1894	BELLEVUE	.
GARRIEPY ROSALIE	1884	GARRIEPY PHIL / PARENTEAU ROSALIE	1894	BELLEVUE	.
GARRIOCH CHARLES	1874	GARRIOCH WM / BROWN MARY	1907	KINOSOTA	1901
GARRIOCH EMMA C	1870	GARRIOCH WM / BROWN MARY	1907	KINOSOTA	1887
GARRIOCH JESSIE L	1880	GARRIOCH WM / BROWN MARY	1907	KINOSOTA	1901
GARRIOCH MELVILLE	1878	GARRIOCH WM / BROWN MARY	1907	KINOSOTA	1901
GARRIOCH WM C	1876	GARRIOCH WM / BROWN MARY	1907	MINITONAS	1901
GAUDRY PAUL	1874	GAUDRY FRANCOIS / GUIBAUCHE MELANIE	1916	WINNIPEG	1901
GERVAIS MARIE	1871	DELORME URBAIN / DESMARAIS MARIE	1118	PINCHERCREEK	1900
GOSSELIN ANTOINE	1874	GOSSELIN ANTOINE / DELORME FRAN	2000	WILLOW BUNCH	.
GOSSELIN MARIE R	1876	FAYANT JEAN BTE / WARD ANGEL	1466	WILLOW BUNCH	.
GOSSELIN PHILOMENE	1885	GOSSELIN ANTOINE / DELORME FRANCOISE	2000	WILLOW BUNCH	.
GRENON ELIZA	1874	MARION JOE / MCDERMOTT ANN	3030	KILLARNEY	1901
GUNVILLE LOUIS	1872	VIVIER MICHEL / DESCHAMPS ELISE	5033	QU APPELLE	.
HAMELIN ALBERT	1879	HAMELIN ANTOINE / PERRAULT MATHILDE	1776	FILE HILLS	.
HAMELIN ANTOINE	1875	HAMELIN ANTOINE / PERRAULT PHILOMENE	1776	FILE HILLS	.
HAMELIN ANTOINE	1877	HAMELIN ANTOINE / PERRAULT PHILOMENE	1776	FILE HILLS	.
HANSON FLORA	1872	GARIEPY BONAV / LAROCQUE MAD	1893	MAPLE CREEK	.
		TYOMS JANEMARY /	1795	PUCKHAM	1900

NAME	YEAR BORN	NAMES OF PARENTS	ID OF PARENTS	NEW LOCATION	YEAR LOCATED
HASTERS HARRIET	1870	HARPER JAMES	TURNER CHARLOTTE	2133	OAK LAKE	1901
HASTERS HARRIET	1870	HARPER JAMES	TURNER CHARLOTTE	2133	OAK LAKE	1901
HAYDEN AGATHE	1873	FLEURY ED	MORIN MELANIE	1589	MOOSOMIN	1901
HAYDEN JOSETTE	1879	FLEURY ED	MORAN MELANIE	1589	MOOSOMIN	1901
HAYDEN NOEMIE	1883	HAYDEN FELIX	PLANT BETSY	2195	SPY HILL	1901
HAYDEN ROSE	1877	HOULE CHARLES	FLEURY ELISE	2223	SPY HILL	1901
HAYDEN THERESE	1879	HAYDEN FELIX	PLANTE BETSY	2195	SPY HILL	1901
HENRY MARIE A	1885	HENRY PIERRE	BEAUCHEMIN CAROLINE	2187	FISH CREEK	
HOULE CHARLES	1881	HOULE CHARLES	FLEURY ELISE	2223	FT ELLICE	1901
HOULE ELISE	1884	HOULE CHARLES	FLEURY ELISE	2223	FT ELLICE	
HOULE ELIZ	1874	HOGG AMABLE	MORRISETTE BETSY	2209	MOOSOMIN	1901
HOULE ELIZ	1874	HOGG AMABLE	MORRISETTE BETSY	2209	MOOSOMIN	1901
HOULE JOHN	1875	HOULE CHARLES	FLEURY ELISE	2223	FT ELLICE	1901
HOURIE CHARLES	1877	HOURIE THOMAS	BIRD AGNES	2249	BIRCH HILLS	1900
HOURIE FLORA	1870	HOURI PETER	WHITFORD SARAH	2236	PRINCE ALBERT	1886
HOURIE HENRY	1881	HOURIE PETER	WHITFORD SARAH	2236	REGINA	1900
HOURIE MARY	1879	HOURIE THOMAS	BIRD AGNES	2249	BUTTLERS	1900
HOUSE ROSALIE	1873	DESJARLAIS JOE	LAFRENIERE ISAB	1285	TWH	
HUNT MARY J	1871	SMITH ANGUS	INKSTER MARY	4811	POPLAR PT	1901
INKSTER ANDREW	1879	INKSTER ROBERT	ANDERSON HARRIET	2401	EAGLE HILLS	1900
INKSTER SARAH	1883	INKSTER GEORGE	FRANKS KEZIAH	2407	ST CATHERINES	1900
INKSTER WM	1875	INKSTER GEORGE	FRANKS KEZIAH	2407	PRINCE ALBERT	1900
JEANNOTTE ALEX	1871	JEANNOTTE ALEX	PAGE MARG	2354	KILLARNEY	1901
JOHNSTON ALEX	1877	JOHNSTON JOE	BRUYERE SARAH	2339	FT ALEXANDER	1901
JOHNSTON MAGLOIRE	1879	JOHNSTON JOE	BRUYERE SARAH	2339	FT ALEXANDER	1901
KNOTT ANNIE	1874	KNOTT ALEX	LINKLATER BARBARA	2273	WINNIPEG	1901
KNOTT JESSIE	1881	KNOTT ALEX	LINKLATER BARBARA	2273	FT ALEXANDER	1901
KNOTT THOMAS	1876	KNOTT ALEX	LINKLATER BARBARA	2273	FT ALEXANDER	1901
LACERTE FLORESTINE	1881	MCGILLIS ANGUS	FAYANT ISABELLE	3354	WILLOW BUNCH	
LAFOND CYRILLE	1875	LAFOND CYRILLE	PEPIN AGATHE	2509	CARLTON	
LAFOND CYRILLE	1881	LAFOND CYRILLE	PEPIN AGATHE	2509	CARLTON	
LAFOND CYRILLE	1882	LAFOND CYRILLE	PEPIN AGATHE	2509	CARLTON	
LAFOND ELIZA	1870	LAFOND CYRILLE	PEPIN AGATHE	2509	CARLTON	1886
LAFOND PAULINE	1884	LAFOND CYRILLE	PAPIN AGATHE	2509	CARLTON	1900
LAFONTAINE AGENOR	1872	LAFONTAINE LOUIS	PELLETIER MAD	2485	FT QU APPELLE	
LAFONTAINE ANTOINE	1874	LAFONTAINE ANTOINE	JEANNOT PHILO	2514	GRD CLAIRIERE	1901
LAFONTAINE JOE	1882	LAFONTAINE ANTOINE	JEANNOTTE PHILM	2514	OAK LAKE	
LAFONTAINE LOUIS	1885	LAFONTAINE LOUIS	PELLETIER MAD	2485	FT QU APPELLE	
LAFONTAINE MARIE E	1877	LAFONTAINE ANTOINE	JEANNOTTE PHILM	2514	FT QU APPELLE	
LAFONTAINE MARY M	1875	LAFONTAINE ANTOINE	JEANNOTTE PHILO	2514	HARTNEY	
LAFOURNAISE MICHEL	1882	LAFOURNAISE GAB	LANDRY ELIZA	2523	DAHAMEL	1900
LAFRAMBOISE ELISE	1870	LAFRAMBOISE FRAN	CHABOYER LOUISE	2680	SWIFT CURRENT	1886
LAFRAMBOISE PHILO	1880	LAFRAMBOISE AUG	LEDOUX LOUISE	2528	DUCK LAKE	
LAPIERRE AZILDA	1877	PELLETIER ALPHONSE	DESJARLAIS MAD	3892	TWH	
LAPLANTE CAROLINE	1870	LAPLANTE ANTOINE	ROY JOSE	2622	FT QU APPELLE	1886
LAPLANTE CAROLINE	1870	LAPLANTE ANTOINE	ROY JOSEPHTE	2622	FT QU APPELLE	
LAPLANTE LOUISE	1877	LEVEILLE LOUIS	GERVAIS MARG	2811	MOOSE JAW	1901
LAROCQUE ALFRED	1875	LAROCQUE OLIVIER	SWAN MARG	2694	KILLARNEY	1901
LAROCQUE ALFRED	1875	LAROCQUE OLIVIER	SWAN MARG	2694	KILLARNEY	1901
LAROCQUE BETSY	1882	LAROCQUE JEAN BTE	CHARTRAND LOUISE	2782	ALDINA	
LAROCQUE FRANCOIS	1874	LAROCQUE BTE	CHARTRAND LOUISE	2782	CARLTON	1900
LAROCQUE JEROME	1872	LAROCQUE ANTOINE	LAPLANTE ROSALIE	2663	MASCOWPETINGS	
LAROCQUE JOE	1881	LAROCQUE ANTOINE	LAPLANTE ROSALIE	2663	LEBRET	

NAME	YEAR BORN	NAMES OF PARENTS	ID OF PARENTS	NEW LOCATION	YEAR LOCATED
LAROCQUE JOHN	1870	LAROCQUE ANTOINE	LAPLANTE ROSALIE	2663	FT QU APPELLE	.
LAROCQUE LEO	1874	LAROCQUE ANTOINE	LAPLANTE ROSALIE	2663	SASK LANDING	.
LAROCQUE LOUIS	1884	LAROCQUE JEAN BTE	CHARTRAND LOUISE	2782	ALDINA	.
LAROCQUE MARG	1875	LAROCQUE JEAN BTE	CHARTRAND LOUISE	2782	CARLTON	1900
LAROCQUE MARYJANE	1871	DUBOIS JEAN BTE	LARENCE JOSETTE	1319	KILLARNEY	1901
LAROCQUE PATRICE	1871	LAROCQUE LOUIS	BARTHELETTE MARY	2789	KILLARNEY	1901
LAROCQUE PATRICE	1871	LAROCQUE LOUIS	BARTHELETTE MARY	2789	KILLARNEY	1901
LAROQUE MARIE R	1879	LAROQUE JEAN BTE	CHARTRAND LOUISE	2782	ALDINA	.
LECLAIRE JEAN	1879	LECLAIRE JOE	BOUSQUET LOUISE	2858	FT ELLICE	.
LECLAIRE JOE	1874	LECLAIRE JOE	BOUSQUET LOUISE	2858	FT ELLICE	.
LEDOUX ALEX	1874	LEDOUX JOE	CREOL MARG	2833	CARLTON	.
LEDOUX FELIX	1880	LEDOUX GREGOIRE	FISHER CAROLINE	2876	FT ELLICE	.
LEDOUX FLAVIE	1871	LEDOUX JEROME	MORAND ANGEL	2880	DUCK LAKE	.
LEDOUX GREG	1871	LEDOUX GREG	FISHER CAROLINE	2876	DUCK LAKE	.
LEDOUX MARIE D	1880	LEDOUX JEROME	MORAND ANGEL	2880	DUCK LAKE	1900
LEDOUX NAP	1875	LEDOUX JEROME	MORRAND ANGEL	2880	PRINCE ALBERT	.
LEGARE JUSTINE	1879	PICHE LOUISON	DESMARAIS CECILE	3929	WILLOW BUNCH	.
LEPINE ELIE	1883	LEPINE ATHANASE	BELANGER MARIE	2925	BATTLEFORD	1900
LEPINE NORBERT	1879	LEPINE ATHANASE	BELANGER MARIE	2925	WINNIPEG	1901
LEPINE ZEPHIRIN	1873	LEPINE ATHANASE	BELANGER MARIE	2925	WINNIPEG	1901
LETENDRE EMMANUEL	1884	LETENDRE XAVIER	PARENTEAU MARG	2942	BATOCHE	.
LETENDRE FLOR	1877	LETENDRE XAVIER	PARENTEAU MARG	2942	BATOCHE	1900
LETENDRE JOE A	1885	LETENDRE XAVIER	PARENTEAU MARG	2942	BATOCHE	.
LETENDRE JOHN	1876	LETENDRE XAVIER	PARENTEAU MARG	2942	FISH CREEK	1900
LETENDRE JOSEPHTE	1880	LETENDRE XAVIER	PARENTEAU MARG	2942	FISH CREEK	.
LETENDRE MARIE L	1882	LETENDRE XAVIER	PARENTEAU MARG	2942	BATOCHE	.
LETENDRE XAVIER	1871	LETENDRE XAVIER	PARENTEAU MARG	2942	BATOCHE	.
LUCIER PAULINE	1879	LUSSIER TOUSSAINT	BRAZEAU LOUISE	2999	CARLTON	1900
LUSSIER CHRYSOST	1870	LUSSIER LOUISSAINT	BRAZEAU LOUISE	2999	PRINCE ALBERT	.
LUSSIER CHRYSOSTOM	1870	LUSSIER LOUISST	BRAZEAU LOUISE	2999	PRINCE ALBERT	1887
MAHONEY MARY	1872	SHANNON WM	HOURIE CATHY	4797	STE ROSE DU LK	.
MARION AGNES	1876	MARION LOUIS	ROSS MARIE A	3042	BATOCHE	1900
MARION ART J	1884	MARION LOUIS	ROSS MARIE A	3042	BATOCHE	.
MARION ELISE	1874	MARION LOUIS	ROSS MARIE A	3042	BATOCHE	.
MARION JOE G	1882	MARION LOUIS	ROSS MARIE A	3042	DAWSON CITY	1900
MARION LOUIS N	1879	MARION LOUIS	ROSS MARIE A	3042	DAWSON CITY	1900
MARION THOMAS	1879	MARION ADOLPHE	LARENCE SARA	2722	OAK LAKE	.
MCBEATH ALEX	1900	MCBEATH WM	HERON ELLEN	3287	SANDY LK	1900
MCBEATH ANN	1877	MCBEATH WM	HERON HELON	3287	SANDY LK	1900
MCBEATH ED V	1872	MCBEATH WM	HERON ELLEN	3287	DAWSON CITY	1900
MCBEATH MORRISSON	1875	MCBEATH WM	HERON ELLEN	3287	SANDY LK	1900
MCBEATH WM R	1882	MCBEATH WM	HERON ELLEN	3287	SANDY LK	1900
MCBETH CATHY	1877	MCBETH ALEX	HARPER CATHY	3271	PRINCE ALBERT	1900
MCBETH JOHN	1873	MCBETH ALEX	HARPER CATHY	3271	PRINCE ALBERT	1900
MCBETH JOHN H	1873	MCBETH ALEX	HARPER CATHY	3271	PRINCE ALBERT	.
MCBETH MARY M	1879	MCBETH ALEX	HARPER CATHY	3271	PRINCE ALBERT	.
MCBETH ROBERT	1875	MCBETH ALEX	HARPER CATHY	3271	LUMSDEN	1900
MCBETH ROD G	1884	MCBETH ALEX	HARPER CATHY	3271	PRINCE ALBERT	1900
MCDONALD ANGUS J	1883	MCDONALD WM	MCKAY CATHY	3266	MELFORT	1900
MCDONALD JOE	1877	MCDONALD JOHN	TURNER NANCY	3336	PRINCE ALBERT	1900
MCDONALD JOHN	1884	MCDONALD JOHN	TURNER NANCY	3336	PRINCE ALBERT	1900
MCDONALD JOHN	1973	MCDONALD JOHN	TURNER NANCY	3336	PRINCE ALBERT	1900

NAME	YEAR BORN	NAMES OF PARENTS	ID OF PARENTS	NEW LOCATION	YEAR LOCATED
MCDONALD KATY	1885	MCDONALD WM	MCKAY CATHY	3266	MELFORT	1900
MCDONALD MARY M	1874	MCDONALD JOHN A	TURNER NANCY	3336	PRINCE ALBERT	1900
MCDONALD NANCY I	1879	MCDONALD JOHN A	TURNER NANCY	3336	PRINCE ALBERT	1900
MCDONALD SARAH	1871	MCDONALD JOHN A	TURNER NANCY	3336	PRINCE ALBERT	1900
MCDONALD WM	1881	MCDONALD WM	MCKAY CATHY	3266	MELFORT	1900
MCGILLIS ALEX	1872	JEANNOTTE MARIE	MCGILLIS ALEX	3594	WILLOW BUNCH	
MCGILLIS ALEX	1873	MCGILLIS ALEX	JEANNOTTE MARIE	3594	WILLOW BUNCH	
MCGILLIS ALEX	1874	MCGILLIS ALEX	JEANNOTTE MARIE	3594	WILLOW BUNCH	
MCGILLIS ALEX	1882	MCGILLIS ALEX	JEANNOTTE MARIE	3594	WILLOW BUNCH	
MCGILLIS GREGOIRE	1878	MCGILLIS ALEX	JEANNOTHE MARIR	3594	WILLOW BUNCH	
MCGILLIS JEAN M	1876	MCGILLIS ALEX	JEANNOTHE MARIR	3594	WILLOW BUNCH	
MCGILLIS JOSETTE	1873	GOSSELIN ANTOINE	DELORME FRAN	2000	WILLOW BUNCH	
MCGILLIS LOVIS	1874	MCGILLIS MODESTE	POITRAS ISABELLE	3596	WILLOW BUNCH	
MCGILLIS MARG	1883	MCGILLIS MODESTE	POITRAS ISABELLE	3596	WILLOW BUNCH	
MCGILLIS MATHILDE	1879	MCGILLIS MODESTE	POITRAS ISABELLE	3596	WILLOW BUNCH	
MCGILLIS NORBERT	1881	MCGILLIS MODESTE	POITRAS ISABELLE	3596	WILLOW BUNCH	
MCKAY ANGUS	1874	MCKAY JOHN	MCBETH CHRISTINA	3396	SNAKE PLAIN	
MCKAY ANGUS T	1883	MCKAY ANGUS	ROLLETTE VIRGINIE	3400	FT ALEXANDER	1901
MCKAY ANNIE	1879	MCKAY JOHN	MCBETH CHRISTINA	3396	SNAKE PLAIN	
MCKAY CATHERINE	1877	MCKAY JOHN	MCBETH CHRISTINA	3396	SNAKE PLAIN	
MCKAY ELIZA	1884	MCKAY ALEX	LAROCQUE VIRGINIE	3376	CYPRESS HILLS	
MCKAY ELLEN	1871	MCKAY WM H	DENNETT SOPHIE	3652	PRINCE ALBERT	1900
MCKAY FRED J	1870	MCKAY JOHN	MCCORRISTER MARY	3650	PRINCE ALBERT	1885
MCKAY IDA	1879	MCKAY GEORGE	TAIT SARAH	3395	PRINCE ALBERT	1900
MCKAY JAMES	1872	MCKAY GEORGE	TAIT SARAH	3395	PRINCE ALBERT	1900
MCKAY LEO	1885	MCKAY ANGUS	ROLLETTE VIRGINIE	3400	FT ALEXANDER	1901
MCKAY PHILIP	1874	MCKAY ALEX	LAROCQUE VIRGINIE	3376	CYPRESS HILLS	
MCKAY SARAH	1874	MCKAY GEORGE	TAIT SARAH	3395	PRINCE ALBERT	
MCKAY THOMAS	1872	MCKAY JOHN M	MCCORRISTER MARY	3650	WYNYARD	1900
MCKAY VIRGINIA	1877	MCKAY GEORGE	TAIT SARAH	3395	PRINCE ALBERT	1900
MCKAY WM ED	1871	MCKAY JOE	POITRAS FLAVIE	3404	PRINCE ALBERT	1900
MCKAY WM H	1884	MCKAY WM H	DENNETT SOPHIA	3652	WYNYARD	
MCLEOD PIERRE	1873	MCLEOD JOE	DELORME ISABELLE	3444	KILLARNEY	1901
MCLEOD PIERRE	1873	MCLEOD JOE	DELORME ISABELLE	3444	KILLARNEY	1901
MCLEOD ROBERT	1885	MCLEOD KEN	JOHNSTON MATILDA	3546	PRINCE ALBERT	
MCNABB LOUISE	1875	PELLETIER ALPH	DESJARLAIS MAD	3892	TWH	
MCNABB JOHN	1870	MCNABB JOHN	WISHART MARY	3460	WINNIPEG	1901
MERCREDI MARIE	1875	MERCREDI FRANCOIS	LAMIRANDE GENEVIEVE	3050	SELKIRK ISLE	
MERCREDI NORBERT	1870	MERCREDI FRANCOIS	LARNIRANDE GENEV	3050	GRAND RAPIDS	
MERCREDI NORBERT	1870	MERCREDI FRANCOIS	LARNIRANDE GENEV	3050	GRAND RAPIDS	1887
MERCREDI NORBERT	1871	MERCREDI FRANCOIS	LAMIRANDE GENEVIEVE	3050	GRAND RAPIDS	
MOREAU CHARLES	1878	MOREAU JONAS	DESJARLAIS CECILE	3176	PRINCE ALBERT	1900
MOREAU FRANCOISE	1878	MOREAU JONAS	DESJARLAIS CECILE	3176	PRINCE ALBERT	1900
MOREAU MARIE A	1883	MOREAU JONAS	DESJARLAIS CECILE	3176	PRINCE ALBERT	1900
MORIN CHRISTINE	1882	MORIN CHARLES	DAUPHINAIS MARIE	3196	WINNIPEG	1901
MORIN FRED	1880	MORIN JOE	PELLETIER ELLEN	3102		1901
MORIN JOE	1882	MORIN JOE	PELLETIER ELLEN	3102		1901
MORIN JOE	1885	MORIN JOE	PELLETIER ELLEN	3102		1901
MUGGABERG CATHY	1874	DESMARAIS MICHEL	SINCLAIR ISABELLE	1237	KILLARNEY	1901
NABES ELIZ	1880	NABES JAMES	HALLETT JOSEPHTE	3693	WINNIPEG	1901
NABES JOE	1875	NABES JAMES	HALLET JOSETTE	3693	FORTELLICE	1901
NABESS PHILOM	1877	ST DENIS CUTHBERT	LAVIOLETTE CECILE	4846	MOOSE JAW	1901
OUELLETTE ADELAIDE	1872	OUELLETTE BTE	COURCHENE CECILE	3712	BATTLEFORD	1900

TABLE 6: DISPERSAL AND RELOCATION OF THE MANITOBA METIS

NAME	YEAR BORN	NAMES OF PARENTS	ID OF PARENTS	NEW LOCATION	YEAR LOCATED
OUELLETTE ANGILE	1873	OUELLETTE MOISE	DUMONT ELIZA	3718	DUCK LAKE	.
OUELLETTE ELEONORE	1879	OUELLETTE BTE	COURCHENE CECILE	3712	BATTLEFORD	.
OUELLETTE JEAN	1879	OUELLETTE MOISE	DUMONT ELIZA	3718	ST LAURENT	1900
OUELLETTE JOE T	1881	OUELLETTE BTE	COURCHENE CECILE	3712	BATTLEFORD	1900
OUELLETTE MARIE F	1878	OUELLETTE MOISE	DUMONT ELIZA	3718	ST LAURENT	.
OUELLETTE MARIE L	1872	OUELLETTE PIERRE	GINGRAS MARG	3564	PRINCE ALBERT	.
OUELLETTE MARIE R	1873	OUELLETTE JOE	PAUL MAG	3707	DUCK LAKE	.
OUELLETTE MARIE R	1875	OUELLETTE BTE	COURCHENE CECILE	3712	JACK FISH LAKE	1900
OUELLETTE MOISE	1875	OUELLETTE MOISE	DUMONT ELIZA	3718	ST LAURENT	.
OUELLETTE MOISE	1877	OUELLETTE MOISE	DUMONT ELIZ	3718	ST LAURENT	1900
OUELLETTE VIRGINIE	1883	OUELLETTE MOISE	DUMONT ELIZA	3718	ST LAURENT	.
OUELLETTE WM	1877	OUELLETTE BTE	COURCHENE CECILE	3712	EAGLE HILLS	1900
PAGE ELZEAR	1883	PAGE ELZEAR	BRELAND MARG	3779	ST ALBERT	1900
PAGE LUCIE	1885	PAGE ELZEAR	BRELAND MARG	3779	ST ALBERT	1900
PANGMAN ISABELLE	1876	LEDOUX GREGOIRE	FISHER CAROLINE	2876	PINE CREEK	1900
PARENTEAU AMANDA	1880	PARENTEAU MOISE	ST GERMAINE VER	3815	CROOKED LAKE	1900
PARENTEAU DAMASE	1877	PARENTEAU JOE	HOULE JULIE	3810	DUCK LAKE	1900
PARENTEAU ELEONORE	1883	PARENTEAU MOISE	ST GERMAINE VER	3815	BATOCHE	1900
PARENTEAU FRANCOIS	1874	PARENTEAU PIERRE	CARON MARIE	3813	PRINCE ALBERT	1901
PARENTEAU FRANCOIS	1874	PARENTEAU PIERRE	CARON MARIE	3813	PRINCE ALBERT	1901
PARENTEAU JOACHIM	1878	PARENTEAU MOISE	STGERMAINE VERONIQU	3815	PRINCE ALBERT	1901
PARENTEAU JOE	1873	PARENTEAU MOISE	HOULE JULIE	3810	ENGLISH RIVER	1900
PARENTEAU JULIENNE	1872	PARENTEAU PIERRE	NORMAND HELENE	3809	BATOCHE	1900
PARENTEAU MARG	1884	PARENTEAU PIERRE	HORMAND HELENE	3809	BATOCHE	1900
PARENTEAU MARIE L	1871	PARENTEAU JOE	HOULE JULIE	3810	DUCK LAKE	1900
PARENTEAU MODESTE	1871	PARENTEAU MOISE	ST GERMAINE VERN	3815	BATOCHE	1900
PAUL ISABELLE	1870	PAUL DANIEL	DESCHAMPS MARG	3867	PRINCE A_BERT	1886
PAUL PATRICE	1874	PAUL WM	LEPAGE FLAVIE	3864	WINNIPEG	1901
PELLETIER ALPHONSE	1885	PELLETIER ALPH	DESJARLAIS MAD	3892	TWH	.
PELLETIER GREGOIRE	1870	PELLETIER ALPHONSE	DESJARLAIS MADELEIN	3892	FT QU APPELLE	1886
PELLETIER MADELEIN	1870	PELLETIER BTE	DESCHAMPS MADELEINE	3858	QU APPELLE	1886
PELLETIER PIERRE	1873	PELLETIER ALPHONSE	DESJARLAIS MAD	3892	TWH	.
PELLEY MARIE	1882	LAFONTAINE FRANCOI	HUGHES LIZA	1900	FT QU APPELLE	.
PETER MARIA	1879	MCKAY ALEX	LAROCQUE VIRGINIE	3376	CYPRESS HILLS	.
PICHE ALEX	1881	PICHE FRANCOIS	ROSS NANCY	4042	DUCK LAKE	1900
PICHE ANNE E	1883	PICHE FRANCOIS	ROSS NANCY	4042	DUCK LAKE	1900
PICHE NATHALIE	1876	PICHE FRANCOIS	ROSS NANCY	404	BEAR LAKE	1900
PICHE NATHALIE	1876	PICHE FRAN	ROSS NANCY	4042	BEAR LAKE	.
PICHE PATRICE	1874	PICHE FRAN	ROSS NANCY	4042	BATTLEFORD	.
PICHE PATRICE	1874	PICHE FRANCOIS	ROSS NANCY	4042	BATTLEFORD	.
PICHE XAVIER	1878	PICHE FRANCOIS	ROSS NANCY	4042	DUCK LAKE	1900
PICHE ZACHARIE	1875	PICHE LOUISON	DESMARAIS CECILE	3929	WILLOW BUNCH	1900
PILON ADELAIDE	1883	PILON JOE	MORMAND ANGEL	3934	BATOCHE	1900
PILON PATRICE	1878	PILON JOE	NORMAND ANGEL	3934	BATOCHE	1900
PILON PATRICE	1878	PILON JOE	NORMAND ANGELIQUE	3934	BATOCHE	.
POITRAS FLORA	1870	POITRAS DAVID	ST DENIS MAD	3957	BATTLEFORD	1886
POITRAS FLORA	1870	POITRAS DAVID	STDENIS MAD	3957	BATTLEFORD	.
POITRAS FLORA	1872	POITRAS DAVID	ST DENIS MAG	3957	BATTLEFORD	1900
POITRAS FRANCOIS	1880	POITRAS JOE	BRELAND ELISE	3955	QU APPELLE	.
POITRAS HENOCHG	1875	POITRAS JOE	BRELAND ELISE	3955	LEBRET	.
POITRAS HENRI	1877	POITRAS IGNACE	MCGILLIS HELENE	3939	BATOCHE	1900
POITRAS IGNACE	1873	POITRAS PIERRE	BREMNER ISABELLE	1694	FT QU APPELLE	.

NAME	YEAR BORN	NAMES OF PARENTS	ID OF PARENTS	NEW LOCATION	YEAR LOCATED
POITRAS JOE	1874	POITRAS JOE	BRELAND ELISE	3955	LEBRET	
POITRAS JOE	1878	POITRAS JOE	BRELAND ELISE	3955	LEBRET	
POITRAS LOUIS	1877	POITRAS PIERRE	BREMNER ISABELLE	1694	FT QU APPELLE	
POITRAS MAD	1877	POITRAS DAVID	ST DENIS MAG	3957	BRESAYLOR	1900
POITRAS MAGDELEINE	1876	POITRAS DAVID	ST DENIS MAG	3957	BRESAYLOR	1900
POITRAS MARIE M	1883	POITRAS DAVID	ST DENIS MAD	3957	BRESAYLOR	1900
POITRAS PIERRE	1878	POITRAS DAVID	ST DENIS MAD	3957	BRESAYLOR	1900
POITRAS WM	1875	POITRAS PIERRE	BREMNER ISABELLE	1694	FT QU APPELLE	
PRIMEAU ELIZA	1875	PRIMEAU AUGUSTIN	LAMBERT ELIZA	3982	EAGLE HILLS	1900
PRIMEAU ELIZA	1875	PRIMEAU AUGUSTIN	LAMBERT ELIZA	3982	EAGLE HILLS	
PRIMEAU FRED	1886	PRIMEAU AUGUST	LAMBERT ELIZA	3982	WILLOUGHBY	
PRIMEAU FRED	1886	PRIMEAU AUGUSTINE	LAMBERT ELIZA	3982	WILLOUGHBY	1900
PRIMEAU JEAN BTE	1878	PRIMEAU AUGUST	LAMBERT LOUISA	3982	WILLOUGHBY	1900
PRIMEAU JUSTINE	1881	PRIMEAU AUGUST	LAMBERT ELIZA	3982	WILLOUGHBY	1900
PRIMEAU LOUIS	1883	PRIMEAU AUGUST	LAMBERT ELIZA	3982	WILLOUGHBY	1900
PRIMEAU ROSALIE	1872	PRIMEAU AUGUTIN	LAMBERT ELIZA	3982	WILLOUGHBY	1900
PRIMEAU VIRGINIE	1884	PRIMEAU AUGUST	LAMBERT ELIZA	3982	CARLTON	1900
PRITCHARD ADELE	1877	PRITCHARD JOHN	DELORME ROSE	4007	WILLOUGHBY	1900
PRITCHARD ALFRED	1881	PRITCHARD JOHN	DELORME ROSE	4007	BATTLEFORD	1900
PRITCHARD AMELIA	1875	PRITCHARD JOHN	DELORME ROSE	4007	BATTLEFORD	1900
PRITCHARD EHTEL	1883	PRITCHARD RICHARD	MATHESON CATHY	3997	BATTLEFORD	1900
PRITCHARD FRED M	1885	PRITCHARD RICHARD	MATHESON CATHY	3997	HALCRO	1900
PRITCHARD HINA	1881	PRITCHARD RICHARD	MATHESON CATHY	3997	SOUTH BRANCH	1900
PRITCHARD JOHN	1871	PRITCHARD JOHN	DELORME ROSE	4007	SOUTH BRANCH	1900
PRITCHARD MAGGIE	1884	PRITCHARD JOHN	DELORME ROSE	4007	BATTLEFORD	1900
PRITCHARD MARIE R	1874	PRITCHARD JOHN	DELORME ROSE	4007	BATTLEFORD	1900
PRITCHARD RAPHAEL	1879	PRITCHARD JOHN	DELORME ROSE	4007	BRESAYLOR	1900
PRITCHARD SOLOMAN	1870	PRITCHARD JOHN	DELORME ROSA	4007	BATTLEFORD	1885
PRITCHARD SOLOMON	1870	PRITCHARD JOHN	DELORME ROSA	4007	BATTLEFORD	1885
RACETTE ADELINE	1879	RACETTE JOE	FISHER SARA	4003	FT QU APPELLE	
RACETTE CHARLES	1880	RACETTE CHARLES	DENOMME CATHERINE	4148	LEBRET	1900
RACETTE CHARLES	1882	RACETTE CHARLES	DENOMME CATHERINE	4148	LEBRET	1900
RACETTE ELLEN	1875	RACETTE CHARLES	BOYER HELEN	4025	PRINCE ALBERT	1900
RACETTE ELLEN	1875	RACETTE CHARLES	BOYER HELEN	4025	PRINCE ALBERT	1900
RACETTE FRED J	1877	RACETTE JOE	FISHER SARA	4003	WOLSELEY	
RACETTE MADELEINE	1875	RACETTE CHAS	DENOMME CATHERINE	4148	FT QU APPELLE	
RACETTE MONIQUE	1870	RACETTE CHARLES	DENOMME CATHERINE	4148	FT QU APPELLE	
RACETTE PIERRE	1872	RACETTE JOE	FISHER SARA	4003	WOLSELEY	
RACETTE PIERRE	1877	RACETTE CHARLES	DENOMME CATHERINE	4148	LEBRET	
ROBILLARD SARA	1878	HAMELIN ANTOINE	PERREAULT PHILOM	1776	FILE HILLS	
ROBINSON ANN	1874	SHANNON WM	HAURIE CATHY	4797	STE ROSE DU LK	
RONDEAU OLIVE	1877	DUBOIS JEAN BTE	LARENCE JOSETTE	1319	KILLARNEY	1901
ROSS JOE	1876	ROSS WM	LEFORT MARIE	4247	FISH CREEK	1900
ROSS VITAL	1878	ROSS WM	LEFORT MARIE	4247	FISH CREEK	1900
ROURKE MICHEL	1882	MCLEOD KEN	JOHNSTON MATILDA	3546	PRINCE ALBERT	1900
SALOIS JOSE	1873	GARIEPY BTE	GARIEPY JUDITH	1808	LETHBRIDGE	1901
SAUNDERS BARBARA	1875	MCNABB JOHN	WISHART MARY	3460	WINNIPEG	1901
SAYER MARY J	1874	BEAUCHENE JOS	FLETT JOSETTE	186	OAK LAKE	1901
SCHOONOVER FLORENC	1880	DESMARAIS MICHEL	SINCLAIR ISABELLE	1237	KILLARNEY	1901
SETTEE FLORA A	1873	SETTEE JOHN	MOORE LOUISA	4872	THE PAS MT	1900
SETTEE JOHN R	1875	SETTEE JOHN R	MOORE LOUISA	4872	CUMBERLAND	1900
SETTEE JOHN R	1879	SETTEE JOHN R	MOORE LOUISA	4872	CUMBERLAND	1900

TABLE 6: DISPERSAL AND RELOCATION OF THE MANITOBA METIS

NAME	YEAR BORN	NAMES OF PARENTS	ID OF PARENTS	NEW LOCATION	YEAR LOCATED
SETTEE MIRIAM	1885	SETTEE JOHN R	4872	CUMBERLAND	1900
SETTEE NATHAN	1881	SETTEE JOHN	4872	CUMBERLAND	1900
SETTEE THOMAS A	1877	SETTEE JOHN	4872	CUMBERLAND	1900
SHANNON JOHN	1878	SHANNON WM	4797	STE ROSE DU LK	.
SHORT DOLPHIS	1872	SHORT JOE	4369	WILLOW BUNCH	1901
SIMPSON MARY	1883	SIMPSON JOHN	4373	KILLARNEY	1900
SINCLAIR ALFRED	1881	SINCLAIR JOHN	4787	GRAND RAPIDS	1900
SINCLAIR FRANCIS	1879	SINCLAIR JOHN	4787	GRAND RAPIDS	1900
SINCLAIR JOE	1876	SINCLAIR JOHN	4787	GRAND RAPIDS	1900
SINCLAIR MARY	1873	SINCLAIR JOHN	4787	GRAND RAPIDS	1900
SINCLAIR SARAH	1871	SINCLAIR JOHN	4787	GRAND RAPIDS	1900
SLADE ISABELLE	1874	INSTER ISABELLE	3551	WINNIPEG	1901
SMITH FLORA	1876	COOK ELIZA	4412	LINDSAY	1900
SMITH SUSAN	1882	COOK ELIZA	4412	LINDSAY	1900
SMOKE MARG	1880	JOHNSON MATILDA	3546	WINNIPEG	1901
SPENCE ARCHIBALD	1870	PEEBLER SOPHIA	4459	KINOSOTA	1901
ST CYR HYAC	1873	MCKAY JUSTINE	4848	CARLTON	1900
ST CYR HYAC	1875	LEDOUX LOUISE	2528	CARLTON	1900
ST DENIS JOE	1880	LAVALLEE CECILE	4846	LEBRET	.
ST DENIS JONAS	1878	LAVALLEE CECILE	4846	LEBRET	.
STEVENS JOHN C	1870	FOULDS MARY	4474	PAKAN	1887
SUTHERLAND ANNIE	1874	MATHESON MARG	4491	PRINCE ALBERT	.
SUTHERLAND ANNIE M	1874	MATHESON MARG	4491	PRINCE ALBERT	1886
SUTHERLAND ALEX	1881	MCBEATH MARY	4507	WINNIPEG	1901
SUTHERLAND PLACIDE	1871	PAGE PHILOMENE	514	STE ROSE DU LA	.
SUTHERLAND WM R	1874	MCBEATH MARY	4507	WINNIPEG	.
SWAIN SARAH E	1870	BREMNER ELLEN	4915	LILY PLAIN	1901
SWAN FRANCOIS	1883	THEBERT CATHERINE	4563	CROWN LAKE	1900
SWAN JEAN	1874	BRUYERE ANGEL	4563	BINSCARTH	.
TAIT CLARA	1881	ANDERSON ELIZA	4631	LINDSAY	1900
TAIT CLARA	1881	ANDERSON ELIZA	4631	LINDSAY	1900
TAYLOR ANN M	1884	MCDONALD MARY	4635	BRESAYLOR	1900
TAYLOR COLIN	1882	MCDONALD MARY	4635	BRESAYLOR	1900
TAYLOR JAMES	1881	COOPER ADELAIDE	4636	EDMONTON	1900
TAYLOR GEORGE	1878	NANCY CHARLOTTE	4678	WINNIPEG	1901
THOMAS BELLA	1876	PARISIERS CHAROLETT	4678	WINNIPEG	1901
THOMAS HENRY G	1872	THOMAS MARY	4677	WINNIPEG	1901
THOMAS JAMES H	1905	BALLENDINE SARAH	4532	REINDEER LK	1908
THOMAS PETER	1885	THOMAS MARY	4677	WINNIPEG	1901
THOMAS PHILIP	1882	PARISIERS CHARLOTTE	4678	WINNIPEG	1901
THOMAS ROBERT	1880	PARISIERS CHARLOTTE	4678	WINNIPEG	1901
THOMAS WM R	1882	THOMAS MARY	4677	WINNIPEG	1901
THORN JOSEPHINE	1881	BERLAND ADELAIDE	3859	KILLARNEY	1901
TODD WM	1881	MCKAY MARY	4957	ST FRS XAVIER	1901
TRAVERS ROSINE	1874	BERLAND ADELAIDE	3859	KILLARNEY	1901
TROTTIER JEAN BTE	1884	VERSAILLES EUPHR	4001	FT ASSINIBOINE	1906
VANDAL ALEX	1870	BEAUCHEMIN ISABELLE	5054	BATOCHE	1887
VANDAL ALEX	1870	BEAUCHEMIN ISABELLE	5054	BATOCHE	1887
VANDAL BTE	1873	BRANCONNIER HENRIE	5060	FISH CREEK	1900
VANDAL EULALIE	1878	PRIMEAU MARIE	5059	FISH CREEK	1900
VANDAL EULALIE	1878	PRIMEAU MARIE	5059	FISH CREEK	1900
VENNE ELMOS	1873	ST ARNAUD JOSE	5091	BATOCHE	1900

TABLE 6: DISPERSAL AND RELOCATION OF THE MANITOBA METIS

NAME	YEAR BORN	NAMES OF PARENTS	ID OF PARENTS	NEW LOCATION	YEAR LOCATED
VIVIER PATRICE	1877	VIVIER ALEXIS BOUSQUET ELISE	5136	FT ELLICE	1901
WHITFORD EDWIN	1877	WHITFORD ALEX COOK ELIZ	5179	WHITFORD LAKE	1900
WHITFORD JOHN	1874	WHITFORD JAMES FAYANT MARG	5175	WILLOW BUNCH	
WHITFORD JOHN J	1880	WHITFORD ALEX COOK ELIZA	5179	WHITFORD LAKE	1900
WHITFORD MARG	1870	WHITFORD JAMES ROBILLARD MARY	5170	TOTAGUN	1887
WHITFORD MARGRET	1870	WHITFORD JAMES ROBILLARD MARY	5170	TOTAGUN	